W9-BRI-386

3 1135 01993 7033

Fodor's 2018

MAP IN
BACK POCKET

LONDON

WELCOME TO LONDON

History and tradition greet you at every turn in London; it's also one of the coolest, most modern cities in the world. If London contained only landmarks such as Westminster Abbey and Buckingham Palace, it would still rank as one of the world's great destinations, but Britain's capital is much more. People come to glimpse the royals and stop by hot galleries; to take in theater and trendy shops; to sample tea and scones or cutting-edge cuisine. When you need a break from the action, pop into a pub, relax in a park—or take a walk and make London your own.

TOP REASONS TO GO

★ **Architectural Icons:** The Tower of London and Big Ben are quintessential London.

★ **Art Museums:** From the National Gallery to the Tate Modern, a visual feast awaits.

★ **Top Theater:** Whether it's Shakespeare or avant-garde drama, the play's the thing.

★ **City of Villages:** Unique neighborhoods from Mayfair to the East End invite discovery.

★ **Shopping:** Fun markets, famous flagship department stores, chic boutiques.

★ **Parks and Squares:** Distinctive green spaces large and small are civilized retreats.

20 ULTIMATE EXPERIENCES

London offers terrific experiences that should be on every traveler's list. Here are Fodor's top picks for a memorable trip.

1 Big Ben and Houses of Parliament

The neo-gothic Palace of Westminster contains the Houses of Parliament (made up of the Houses of Commons and Lords, the legislative bodies of the United Kingdom's government) as well as the giant clock tower that houses Big Ben, one of London's most beloved icons. *(Ch. 2)*

2 Drinking in Historic Pubs

The history of London's taverns and pubs is the history of the city itself. Grab a pint or a gin cocktail, and get to know how the locals live. *(Ch. 16)*

3 British Museum

It would take a lifetime to do justice to the extraordinary collection (spanning 8 million artifacts from over 2 million years) here at Britain's most visited tourist attraction. *(Ch. 5)*

4 Hampton Court Palace

One of Britain's grandest royal palaces, Hampton Court contains some of the finest Tudor architecture in the world and is imbued with an overwhelming sense of history. *(Ch. 5)*

5 Gallery Hopping in East London

With one of the highest concentrations of artists in Europe, East London is fertile ground for some serious contemporary art gallery hopping, from Whitechapel to Hackney. *(Ch. 7)*

6 Hyde Park & Kensington Gardens

London is famous for its awesome Royal Parks, and the contiguous Hyde Park and Kensington Gardens are perfect for escaping the hustle and bustle of the city. *(Ch. 10)*

7 The Markets

From gourmet food to antiques, you can find nearly everything at London's most famous street markets, Portobello Market in Notting Hill and Borough Market on Southbank. *(Ch. 18)*

8 London Eye

For an unrivalled bird's-eye view of the metropolis and beyond, take a ride on one of the world's tallest observation wheels. *(Ch. 8)*

9 Afternoon Tea

For a quintessential English ritual, enjoy a pot of tea served in bone china alongside finger sandwiches, fruit scones, and cakes at one of the city's fanciest hotels. *(Ch. 1)*

10 Shakespeare's Globe

A replica of the original Globe Theatre just yards from where Shakespeare's Elizabethan playhouse stood, the modern-day Globe still hosts performances of the Bard's plays. *(Ch. 8)*

11 Indian food in Brick Lane

Thanks to waves of immigrants, Whitechapel's Brick Lane is famous for London's highest concentration of curry houses and some of the best Indian food outside India. *(Ch. 14)*

12 Victoria and Albert Museum

With a vast collection of 2.3 million objects, the V&A is one of the world's greatest museums of decorative arts and design. *(Ch. 9)*

13 Tate Modern

A must-visit for global art lovers, the Tate Modern wows with its extensive collection of modern and contemporary art. *(Ch. 8)*

14 St. Paul's Cathedral

With the second largest cathedral dome in the world, St. Paul's is a towering masterpiece of English Baroque design, both inside and out. *(Ch. 6)*

15 Covent Garden

Covent Garden is considered the very heart of London, thanks to its markets, pubs, restaurants, museums, theaters, open-air cafés , boutique shops, street entertainers, and more. *(Ch. 14)*

16 Buckingham Palace

The official residence of the British monarch is opulently filled with priceless tapestries, artwork, and marble and gilt galore. *(Ch. 2)*

17 Theater in the West End

Thanks to some of the world's best actors and directors (and the most historic theaters), London's contributions to the theater world give Broadway a run for its money. *(Ch. 17)*

18 National Gallery

With more than 2,300 of the world's masterpieces, this museum is considered Britain's greatest art collection. *(Ch. 2)*

19 Tower of London

With a gory 950-year history of beheadings, imprisonments, and torture, myths and legends shroud England's most perfect medieval fortress and home of the Crown Jewels. *(Ch. 6)*

20 Westminster Abbey

The site of all but two royal coronations since 1066, the Abbey is steeped in English history—from tombs of monarchs to monuments for great nobles, statesmen, and poets. *(Ch. 2)*

Fodor's LONDON 2018

Editorial: Douglas Stallings, *Editorial Director*; Margaret Kelly, *Senior Editor*; Alexis Kelly, Jacinta O'Halloran, and Amanda Sadlowski, *Editors*; Teddy Minford, *Content Editor*; Rachael Roth, *Content Manager*

Design: Tina Malaney, *Design and Production Director*; Jessica Gonzalez, *Production Designer*

Photography: Jennifer Arnow, *Senior Photo Editor*

Maps: Rebecca Baer, *Senior Map Editor*; David Lindroth, Mark Stroud (Moon Street Cartography), *Cartographers*

Production: Jennifer DePrima, *Editorial Production Manager*; Carrie Parker, *Senior Production Editor*; Elyse Rozelle, *Production Editor*; David Satz, *Director of Content Production*

Business & Operations: Chuck Hoover, *Chief Marketing Officer*; Joy Lai, *Vice President and General Manager*; Stephen Horowitz, *Director of Business Development and Revenue Operations;* Tara McCrillis, *Director of Publishing Operations;* Eliza D. Aceves, *Content Operations Manager and Srategist*

Public Relations and Marketing: Joe Ewaskiw, *Manager;* Esther Su, *Marketing Manager*

Writers: Jo Caird, Kate Hughes, James O'Neill, Toby Orton, Ellin Stein, Alex Wijeratna

Editors: Amanda Sadlowski (lead editor), Debbie Harmsen

Production Editor: Jennifer DePrima

Production Design: Liliana Guia

ISBN 978-1-64097-004-5

ISSN 0149–631X

PRINTED IN THE UNITED STATES OF AMERICA

10 9 8 7 6 5 4 3 2 1

CONTENTS

Fodor's Features

CONTENTS

ABOUT
THIS GUIDE

Fodor's Ratings
Everything in this guide is worth doing—we don't cover what isn't—but exceptional sights, hotels, and restaurants are recognized with additional accolades. **Fodor'sChoice★** indicates our top recommendations. Care to nominate a new place? Visit Fodors.com/contact-us.

Trip Costs
We list prices wherever possible to help you budget well. Hotel and restaurant price categories from $ to $$$$ are noted alongside each recommendation. For hotels, we include the lowest cost of a standard double room in high season. For restaurants, we cite the average price of a main course at dinner or, if dinner isn't served, at lunch. For attractions, we always list adult admission fees; discounts are usually available for children, students, and senior citizens.

Hotels
Our local writers vet every hotel to recommend the best overnights in each price category, from budget to expensive. Unless otherwise specified, you can expect private bath, phone, and TV in your room. For expanded hotel reviews, visit Fodors.com.

Top Picks	Hotels &
★ **Fodor's**Choice	**Restaurants**
	⬚ Hotel
Listings	⤵ Number of
✉ Address	rooms
✉ Branch address	⦿ Meal plans
☎ Telephone	✗ Restaurant
📠 Fax	⬚ Reservations
⊕ Website	⬚ Dress code
✉ E-mail	⬚ No credit cards
⬚ Admission fee	$ Price
☉ Open/closed	
times	**Other**
Ⓜ Subway	⇨ See also
⊹ Directions or	☞ Take note
Map coordinates	⅄ Golf facilities

Restaurants
Unless we state otherwise, restaurants are open for lunch and dinner daily. We mention dress code only when there's a specific requirement and reservations only when they're essential or not accepted.

Credit Cards
The hotels and restaurants in this guide typically accept credit cards. If not, we'll say so.

EUGENE FODOR

Hungarian-born Eugene Fodor (1905–91) began his travel career as an interpreter on a French cruise ship. The experience inspired him to write *On the Continent* (1936), the first guidebook to receive annual updates and discuss a country's way of life as well as its sights. Fodor later joined the U.S. Army and worked for the OSS in World War II. After the war, he kept up his intelligence work while expanding his guidebook series. During the Cold War, many guides were written by fellow agents who understood the value of insider information. Today's guides continue Fodor's legacy by providing travelers with timely coverage, insider tips, and cultural context.

EXPERIENCE
LONDON

LONDON TODAY

Welcome to London—variously described by poets and statesmen as "modern Babylon," "Unreal City," "enormous Babel," and "the City of the free." Indeed, majestic London has always been a great city in flux, and these days it's hard to turn a corner without stumbling into some work-in-progress crater so vast you can only imagine what was there before. New neighborhoods continually bubble up and burst to the fore—for example, a visit to Shoreditch at the eastern edge of The City should provide you with your quotient of London hipness. The anything-goes creative fervor that swirls through London like a fog shows up in DIY art galleries, cutting-edge boutiques, pop-up restaurants, nighttime street-food markets, and slick hipster hotels.

Discovery can take a bit of work, however. Modern London still largely reflects its medieval layout, a difficult tangle of streets and alleys. Even Londoners get lost in their own city. But London's bewildering street pattern will be a plus for the visitor who wants to experience its indefinable historic atmosphere. London is a walker's city and will repay every moment you spend exploring on foot.

Although many images are seared on your consciousness before you arrive— the guards at Buckingham Palace, the big red double-decker buses, Big Ben, and the River Thames—time never stands still in this ancient and yet gloriously modern city. Instead, "London, the buskin'd stage. ... The heart, the centre of the living world!" is in permanent revolution, and evolves, organically, mysteriously, historically through time.

Architecture

With the exceptions of Canary Wharf, the former Swiss Re HQ ("the Gherkin"), the Lloyd's of London building, and the London Eye, London's skyline has traditionally been low-key, with little of the sky-scraping swagger of, say, Manhattan, Hong Kong, or Shanghai. But a spectacular crop of soaring new office towers with wonderful monikers—the Quill, the Shard, the Pinnacle, the Cheese Grater, and the Walkie-Talkie—is taking over the city skyline. With an astonishing 254 new skyscrapers being built or planned, opinions are split. Not everyone loves Renzo Piano's pointy Shard and its 95-floor cloud-piercing "Vertical City" at London Bridge, which has stunning viewing galleries on the 68th, 69th, and 72nd floors. However, once you whiz up and enjoy the view, your take on the vast immensity of London is transformed forever.

Immigration

There's no doubt that London was built on immigration and is now one of the most diverse cities on Earth, with 300 languages spoken on the streets and nearly every world religion practiced at its places of worship. Immigrants make up over a third of the population and "white Britons" are in the minority for the first time, representing 45% of London's population of 8.2 million. The largest first-generation immigrant communities are from India, Poland, Ireland, Nigeria, Pakistan, Bangladesh, and Jamaica. To Londoners, this is no big deal, as this has always been a city of immigrants—from invaders like the Romans, Anglo-Saxons, Vikings, and Normans to those seeking sanctuary like the French Huguenots and east European Jews, along with those seeking their postwar fortunes from Caribbean islands and the Indian subcontinent. Despite the populist tendencies sprouting up in other parts of the United Kingdom and Europe, London remains proud of its immigrant heritage, and welcoming to any who wish to call themselves a Londoner.

Arts and Culture

Have you swiped a free copy of the daily London *Evening Standard* newspaper lately? They're full of world-class shows, plays, jazz performances, readings, recitals, concerts, fashion follies, lectures, talks, tastings, cabarets, auctions, and blockbuster art exhibitions. Whether it's modern art and rare Old Master paintings at Frieze London art fair in Regents Park or a Dinerama nighttime food truck feast in Hoxton, London is one of the most happening places on the planet.

Public Transportation

You'll notice that the public transport's more frequent and more reliable. Although London's traffic often seems more chaotic than New York City's, the Congestion Charge, a £12-per-day fee imposed on vehicles entering central London during the day, has reduced traffic and pollution. Also, the Underground now runs 24 hours a day on weekends on five key "Night Tube" lines, and massive excitement rests on London's £15 billion flagship, high-speed east–west Cross Rail underground railway line, which includes new interchanges at Paddington, Bond Street, Tottenham Court Road, and Farringdon stations. Meanwhile, don't miss London's bike-sharing program, Santander Cycles. With 11,145 bikes available at 729 docking stations, you'll find (after paying £2 for a 24-hour pass) that the first half hour's free, and each additional 30 minutes is £2.

Politics

With its heady mix of modernity, migrants, and money, London is historically a pretty liberal city. It elected its first Muslim mayor in 2016, Sadiq Khan, a former London MP, human rights lawyer, and son of a London bus driver, but the city is increasingly braced for the fallout from the 2016 Brexit vote. The majority of Londoners voted to remain in the European Union, and many of the city's hundreds of thousands of E.U.-origin residents, students, and workers are nervous about what leaving the E.U. will mean for them, and if they will continue to have a legal right to live, study, or work in the United Kingdom. Nothing is known for sure until the terms of the withdrawal are decided; currently, the date for withdrawal is set for spring 2019. Until then, London carries on as ever—vibrant, vital, and open for business.

New Upgrades and Exhibits

Some of London's top cultural attractions seem to be caught in an upgrade arms race and are investing heavily in new galleries, exhibits, extensions, and assorted shiny new bells and whistles. Look for the major £50 million revamp of the National Theatre, which includes a series of scrubbed-up Brutalist public spaces, or enjoy the recently sprung-to-life Granary Square at King's Cross, where 1,080 choreographed water jets are the buzzy area's answer to an Italian piazza. Tate Modern has added a £50 million modern brick extension, but look for the city's quirkier historic openings such as the 670-year-old Charterhouse in Smithfield, which you can now tour with residents of this Wolf Hall–like former Carthusian monastery, mansion, boys' school, and latter-day almshouse.

WHAT'S WHERE

The following numbers refer to chapters.

2 Westminster, St. James's, and Royal London. This is the place to embrace your inner tourist. Snap pictures of the mounted Horse Guards, watch kids clambering onto the monumental bronze lions in Trafalgar Square, and visit stacks of world-class art in the fantastic national galleries. Brave the crowds to peruse historic Westminster Abbey and its ancient narrative in stone.

3 Mayfair and Marylebone. You may not have the wallet for London's most prestigious shops, but remember window-shopping in Mayfair is free. Meanwhile, chic boutiques in Marylebone are a refreshing change from gaudy Oxford Street a few blocks south.

4 Soho and Covent Garden. More sophisticated than seedy these days, the heart of London puts Theatreland, strip joints, Chinatown, burger boîtes, and the trendiest of film studios side by side. Hold tight through the hectic hordes in Leicester Square. Covent Garden's historic paved piazza is one of the most raffishly enjoyable parts of the city.

5 Bloomsbury and Holborn. Once the bluestocking and intellectual center of London, elegant 17th- and 18th-century Bloomsbury is now also a mixed business district. The British Museum has enough amazing objets d'art and artifacts to keep you busy for a month; the Law Courts, the University of London, and quaint Lamb's Conduit Street are worth a gander. Clerkenwell, meanwhile, is a hotbed of history and culinary invention.

6 The City. London's Wall Street might be the oldest part of the capital, but thanks to new skyscrapers and a sleek Millennium Bridge, it also looks like the newest. History fans won't be short-changed, however: head for St. Paul's Cathedral, Tower Bridge, and the Tower of London.

7 East London. Once famed for the noxious 19th-century slums immortalized by Charles Dickens and Jack the Ripper, today the area is a fulcrum of London's contemporary art scene and a youthful party zone. For spit-and-sawdust sensations of market London on the weekend, dive headfirst into the eclectic wares at Spitalfields, Brick Lane (popular for Bangladeshi curry houses and 24-hour Jewish bagel bakeries), and Columbia Road's much-loved early-morning flower market.

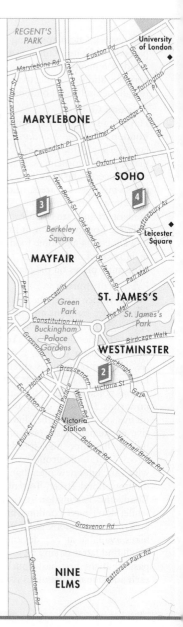

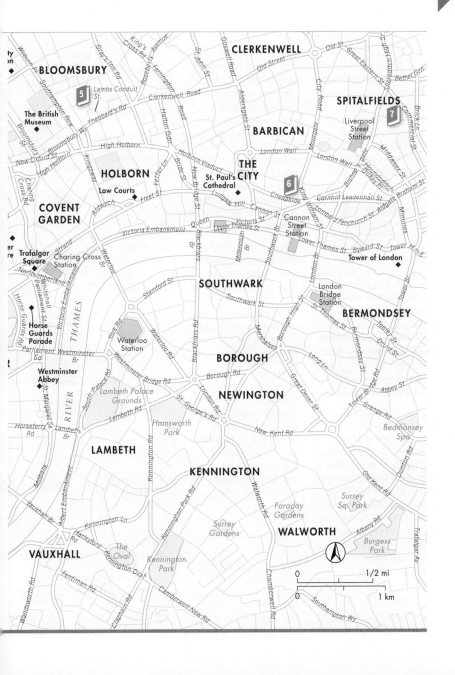

WHAT'S WHERE

8 South of the Thames.
The Southbank Centre—including the National Theatre and Royal Festival Hall, the Haywood Gallery, Purcell Room, and Queen Elizabeth Hall, plus nearby Shakespeare's Globe and Tate Modern—showcases the capital's crowning artistic glories. Or put it all in aerial perspective from the 72nd floor of the Shard.

9 Kensington, Chelsea, Knightsbridge, and Belgravia. Although the many boutiques of King's Road have lost much of their heady '60s swagger, the free museums are as awe-inspiring as ever. Kensington High Street is slightly more affordable than King's Road; otherwise, flash your cash at London's snazziest department stores, Harrods and Harvey Nichols.

10 Notting Hill and Bayswater. North of Kensington, around Portobello Road, Notting Hill Gate is a trendsetting couple of square miles of multiethnic finds, photographers' galleries, bookshops, fashionable boutiques, and hip restaurants. Nearby, Bayswater mixes eclectic ethnic fashions, organic fresh food shops, and gaudy Middle Eastern and Chinese restaurants.

11 Regent's Park and Hampstead. Surrounded by elegant, stucco-fronted "terraces"—in truth, mansions as big as palaces—designed by 19th-century architect John Nash, Regent's Park is a Regency extravaganza. The nearby ancient hilltop villages of Hampstead and Primrose Hill attract starry residents like Kate Moss and Jude Law.

12 Greenwich. The Royal Observatory, Sir Christopher Wren's architecture, the Old Royal Naval College, *Cutty Sark*, and the Prime Meridian all add up to one of the best Thames-side excursions beyond the cut-and-thrust of central London.

13 The Thames Upstream. As an idyllic retreat from the city, stroll around London's historic gardens and enjoy the stately homes of Kew, Richmond, and Putney. Better yet, take a gentle river cruise and end up at the famous Hampton Court Palace.

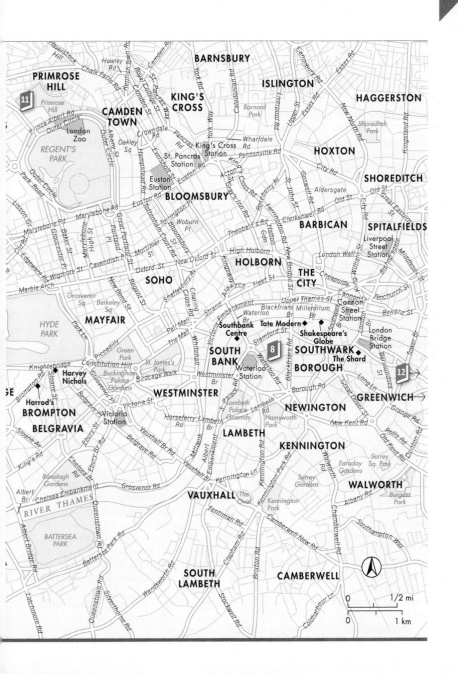

LONDON PLANNER

When to Go

The heaviest tourist season runs April through September, with another peak around Christmas. Late spring is the time to see the Royal Parks and gardens at their freshest; fall brings autumnal beauty and fewer people. Summer gives the best chance of good weather, although the crowds are intense. Winter can be dismal—it's dark by 5—but all the theaters, concerts, and exhibitions go full-speed ahead, and Christmas lights bring a major touch of festive magic. Weather-wise, winter is cold and wet with occasional light snow and spring is colorful and fair. June through August can range from a total washout to a long hot summer and anything in between. Autumn ranges from warm to cool to mild. It's impossible to forecast London weather, but you can be certain that it will not be what you expect.

When Not to Go

The October "half-term," when schools in the capital take a break for a week or two, results in most attractions being overrun by children. The start of August can be a very busy time, and hot weather makes Tube travel a sweltering and sweaty nightmare. Air-conditioning is far from the norm in London, even in hotels; although it rarely tops 90°F, it can feel much hotter. And festive shopping in central London just before Christmas borders on the insane.

Getting Around

London is, above all, a walker's city, and will repay every moment you spend exploring on foot. But if you're in a rush, there are other options. By far the easiest and most practical way to get around is on the Underground, known as the Tube. Trains run daily from early morning to past midnight during the week, with

five key lines now operating 24 hours a day on weekends. Frequent cash-free red buses crisscross London and often have their own lanes, which only buses and black taxis can use. They are a great way to see London, but navigation can be more complicated than the Tube's; scan the route posted at the bus stop and check the number and destination on the front of the bus, and ask the bus conductor if in doubt.

Put a deposit on an Oyster card for £5, which will allow you to use London's transport—including bus, Tube, tram, Dockland Light Railway (DLR), London Overground, and most National Rail services in London—at a lower cost than using paper tickets. The plastic card can be topped up as often as you want, and your £5 deposit is reimbursed when you hand the card back.

Alternatively, buy a Travelcard pass (from £13 per day in the central Zones 1 and 2), which offers unlimited use of the Tube, buses, and the commuter rail. Check ⊕ *www.tfl.gov.uk* for details on ongoing Tube renovations and schedules.

Addresses

Central London and its surrounding districts are divided into 32 boroughs (33, counting The City of London). More useful for navigating, however, are the subdivisions of London into postal districts. Throughout the guide we've given the abbreviated postal code for most listings. The first one or two letters give the location: N means north, NW means northwest, and so on. Don't expect the numbering to be logical, however. (You won't, for example, find W2 next to W3.) The general rule is that the lower numbers, such as W1 or SW1, are closest to the city center.

WHAT IT COSTS

	IN LONDON	IN NEW YORK
Pair of theater tickets	£40–£120	$75–$260
Museum admission	Usually free; sometimes £4–£16	Usually $8–$35; rarely free
Fast-food value meal	£9	$10
Tall latte	£4	$4
Pint of beer in a pub	£5 and up	$7 and up
1-mile taxi ride before tip	£9	$8
Subway ride within city center	Up to £9 without Oyster or Travelcard	$3

London Hours

The usual shop hours are Monday to Saturday 9–6 and Sunday 11–5. Around Oxford Street, Kensington High Street, and Knightsbridge, hours are 9:30–6, with late-night hours (until 7:30 or 8) on Wednesday or Thursday.

Many businesses are closed on Sunday and national ("bank") holidays, except in the center, where most are open 10–4. Banks are open weekdays 9:30–4:30; offices are generally open 9–6.

The major national museums and galleries are open daily, mainly 10–6, and often they're open late one night a week.

Street Smarts

On long-term high-alert against terrorist attacks, London is generally a safe and surprisingly friendly place, but like any large city it's wise to take a few precautions. Make sure your possessions are properly insured before you travel, and don't carry all your valuables around with you. Carry as much cash as you'll need that day, and leave the rest in your hotel safe. Don't use ATMs after dark, avoid isolated or poorly lighted spots, and try not to travel around on your own late at night. Keep bags zipped up and close to you in the Tube, on buses, and at pubs and other crowded places. Never leave bags unattended in any public place—they may be stolen or seen as a security threat. Finally, use black cabs and don't get into a minicab on your own.

Saving Money

There's no getting around it: London can be as expensive as—or even more expensive than—New York, Paris, or any other large global city. So it's best to accept this fact in advance and factor it into your vacation planning, tailoring outings and trips to your interests—and your budget.

Often, booking in advance, harnessing cut-price and low-season deals, and taking advantage of Internet specials for flights and hotel rooms can cut down on costs. London is also great at offering things for free (particularly the museums), and the quality of the culture, entertainment, relaxation, and general fun to be had in the city means that if you target your spending wisely, you'll go home penny-pinched but deeply satisfied.

LONDON'S ROYAL LEGACY

The Rocky Monarchy
From medieval castles and keeps, to Royal Parks, palaces, pageants, ceremonies and processions, London has had a tumultuous and sometimes bloody royal history, which can still be encountered at practically every turn. London has been the royal capital of England since 1066, when the Norman king William the Conqueror began the tradition of royal coronations at Westminster Abbey. All but two reigning monarchs since then—from Richard I (the "Coeur de Lion") in 1189 to the current Queen Elizabeth II in 1953—have been crowned at the Abbey. Many of England's illustrious—and sometimes downright notorious—kings and queens have left a legacy or their majestic mark on the city. You'll find many of the finest places have royal associations: William I subjugated London with the imposing Tower of London; Henry VIII hunted deer at Hampton Court; Elizabeth I enjoyed bear baiting in Southwark; and Charles I was publicly executed on Whitehall. Tyrannical but weak monarchs like King John (1199–1216) granted the City of London extra power under the Magna Carta, while the first "Parliament" sat at the royal Palace of Westminster in 1265 under Henry III. The Tudors, however, rarely brooked dissent: Elizabeth I's half-sister, "Bloody" Mary I (1553–58), burned heretic Protestant bishops at the stake, and traitors were hung, drawn, and quartered, with their heads stuck on pikes on London Bridge.

A Cultural Renaissance
From 1558 to 1601, peace under Elizabeth I ("the Virgin Queen") led to a cultural renaissance and the great flowering of English theater, poetry, letters, and drama, centered on Shakespeare's Globe and the open-air playhouses of Southwark. Charles I was later captured by the formidable Puritan Oliver Cromwell during the English Civil War, and beheaded on a freezing day outside Banqueting House in Westminster in 1649. Although the Interregnum lasted only 16 years (outlawing simple pleasures, such as dancing and theater), the Restoration of Charles II in 1660 and subsequent monarchs including the Dutch Protestant William III and Mary II—who moved into Kensington Palace, now the current home of the Duke and Duchess of Cambridge—and the House of Hanover's four Georgian kings and later Queen Victoria saw London grow and transform into a teeming metropolis.

The Down-to-Earth Duke and Duchess
These days you might spot the glamorous Duke and Duchess of Cambridge walking with the young Prince George and Princess Charlotte in Kensington Gardens, or elegantly stepping out onto the red carpet at a royal gala performance in the West End. Besides the color, pageantry, and marching bands of the Changing the Guard ceremony at Buckingham Palace, there's also a rich calendar of royal ceremonies. The Ceremony of the Keys to lock up the Tower of London has taken place at 9:53 pm each night for more than 700 years, and you can see the Monarch take the Royal Salute from the Household Division at the annual Trooping the Colour march from Horse Guards Parade to St. James's Park. The Queen is also drawn by four horses in the dazzling Irish State Coach from Buckingham Palace to the Palace of Westminster in a huge royal procession for the State Opening of Parliament each autumn, and you can see her pay homage to the war dead at the Cenotaph on Remembrance Sunday.

SPORTS IN LONDON

Sports in the capital are probably best watched rather than participated in. If you're lucky enough to score a ticket for a Premier League football match, you'll experience a seething mass of mockery, jeering, and tribal chanting. Rugby, tennis, horse-racing, and cricket also impinge on Londoners' horizons at crucial times of the year, but you're unlikely to see grown men crying at the outcome of the Wimbledon Men's Final.

Cricket

At its best, cricket can be a slow build of smoldering tension and unexpected high-wire excitement. At its worst, it can be too slow and uneventful for the casual observer, as five-day games crawl toward a draw or as rain stops play. But try to visit Lord's—known as the home of cricket—on match days, just to hear the *thwack* of leather on willow and to see the English aristocracy and upper middle classes on full display.

Lord's. Lord's Cricket Ground, home of the venerable 1787 Marylebone Cricket Club (MCC), has been hallowed cricketing turf since 1814, and MCC rules codified the game. Tickets for major Test matches are hard to come by: obtain an application form online and enter the ballot (lottery) to purchase them. ✉ *Marylebone Cricket Club, Lord's Cricket Ground, St. John's Wood Rd., St. John's Wood* ☎ *020/7432–1000* ⊕ *www.lords.org* Ⓜ *St. John's Wood.*

Football

London's top soccer teams—Chelsea, Tottenham Hotspur, Arsenal, and West Ham—are top-class outfits and the first three often progress in the Europe-wide Champions League. It's unlikely you'll get tickets for anything except the least popular Premier League games during the August–May season, despite the high ticket prices—£30 for a walk-up match-day seat at Chelsea, and £97 for the most expensive tickets at Arsenal.

Rowing

The Boat Race. Join more than a quarter of a million merry devotees along the banks of the River Thames between Putney and Mortlake for a glimpse of the annual Oxford and Cambridge University Boat Race, held on the last Saturday of March or the first Saturday of April. Sink a few pints and soak up the tweed-cap-and-Barbour-clad atmosphere as these heavyweight eight-man university crews clash oars and tussle head-to-head for supremacy. First raced in 1829, the 4-mile route is a picturesque stretch between Putney and Chiswick Bridges. The equally exciting women's eight Boat Race is also held the same day. ✉ *Putney Bridge, Putney* ⊕ *www.theboatraces.org.*

Tennis

Wimbledon Lawn Tennis Championships. The All England Club's Wimbledon Lawn Tennis Championships are famous for Centre Court, strawberries and cream, a gentle spot of rain, and a nostalgic old-school insistence on players wearing white. Thankfully, the rain has been banished on Centre Court by the nifty retractable roof, but whether you can get tickets for Centre Court all comes down to the luck of the draw—there's a ballot system for advance purchase (see website for more details). ✉ *The All England Lawn Tennis Club, Church Rd.* ☎ *020/8944–1066 for general inquiries* ⊕ *www.wimbledon.com.*

FREE AND CHEAP

The exchange rate may vary, but there is one conversion that will never change: £0 = $0. Here are our picks for the top free (and cheap) things to do in London.

Concerts

St. Martin-in-the-Fields, St. Stephen Walbrook, St. Olaves in the City, and St. James's Church Piccadilly all host free lunchtime concerts and recitals, as do St. Giles-in-the-Fields on Friday and St. George, Bloomsbury, on Sunday afternoon. There are also regular organ recitals at Westminster Abbey.

Of the elite music colleges, the Royal Academy of Music, the Royal College of Music, the Guildhall, Trinity College, and the Royal Opera House offer free recitals. For contemporary ears, there's free jazz and classical music on an exquisite 1897 Bechstein on the first Sunday of the month at the Dysart Petersham restaurant (☎ 0208/940–8005) in Richmond and live jazz at the Lamb & Flag (✉ 33 Rose St. ☎ 0207/497–9504) in Covent Garden, from 8 pm one Sunday a month. For free blues Sunday–Thursday or before 8:30 pm on Friday and Saturday, head to the Ain't Nothin But … honky-tonk blues bar in Soho (✉ 20 Kingly St. ☎ 020/7287–0514).

Film, Theater, and Opera

If all seats have been sold, the National Theatre sells unobstructed-view £5 standing-room tickets on the day of performances at their Olivier, Lyttleton, and Dorfman theaters. Standing-room tickets run £3–£15 at the Royal Opera House, with 49 cheap tickets available each Friday at 1 pm for sold-out performances. If you're under 30 or a student, becoming an "Access all Arias" member of the English National Opera is free, and allows you to buy £10–£30 tickets. There are 700 £5 standing-room tickets available for every performance at the replica Shakespeare's Globe theater, as well as £10 standing-room tickets for magical candle-lit plays and concerts at the adjacent indoor Sam Wanamaker Playhouse. At Sloane Square, the Royal Court Theatre has a limited number of standing-room tickets for 10 pence each at the Jerwood Theatre Downstairs, available an hour before performances.

Sightseeing

Prop yourself on the top deck of a red double-decker bus for a fantastic sightseeing tour through the most scenic parts of the city. Routes 9 and 15 also operate Heritage routes on the traditional 1930s Routemaster buses. With all buses now cashless, you can instead use your Oyster card or buy tickets from machines at bus stops for the following routes:

Bus 11: King's Road, Sloane Square, Victoria Station, Westminster Abbey, Houses of Parliament and Big Ben, Whitehall, Trafalgar Square, the Strand, Royal Courts of Justice, Fleet Street, and St. Paul's Cathedral.

Bus 19: Sloane Square, Knightsbridge, Hyde Park Corner, Green Park, Piccadilly Circus, Shaftsbury Avenue, Bloomsbury, Angel, and Islington.

Bus 88: Oxford Circus, Conduit Street, Piccadilly Circus, Haymarket, Trafalgar Square, Whitehall, Horse Guards Parade, Westminster Station, Westminster Abbey, Horseferry Road, and Tate Britain.

LONDON WITH KIDS

Activities

Ride the London Eye. Europe's largest observation wheel looks like a giant fairground ride, and you can see across what seems like half of London from the top.

Pose with a Queen's Horse Guard. There's always an erect soldier in uniform standing watch by the entrance to Horse Guards on the Trafalgar Square end of Whitehall. They don't mind posing for pictures, but they're not allowed to smile.

Ice-skating at Somerset House. Send your kids whizzing, arms whirling, across ice mid-November–January at this spotlighted open-air ice rink in a former Renaissance royal palace.

Night at the Natural History Museum. Find out what the dinosaurs really do when the lights go out at the monthly Dino Snores sleepover (minimum of one adult and five kids per group).

Pedalo on the Serpentine. Pack a picnic and take a blue pedalo out into the middle of Hyde Park's famed Serpentine lake; settle back and tuck in to lunch.

Lose the kids at Hampton Court Maze. The topiary might be more than 300 years old, but the quest to reach the middle of Hampton Court's world-famous trapezoid-shape yew hedge maze remains as challenging as ever.

West End musicals. Foot-stompingly good West End musicals and shows like *Les Misérables, Billy Elliot, Matilda, Mamma Mia!, The Lion King, Oliver!, Grease,* and *The Phantom of the Opera* will mesmerize the over-seven crowd.

Education Without Yawns

Kew Gardens. Kew Gardens is great for young ones, with activities, the "climbers and creepers" play zone, a 60-foot high treetops Sky Walk, zip wires, scramble slides, and children's trails; it's free for kids under four.

The London Dungeon. It's guts and gore galore at this top South Bank attraction that plunges you into the blood-soaked depths of London history, with tales from a gruesome Jack the Ripper pub, Sweeney Todd barbers, and Mrs. Lovett's pie shop.

London Zoo. Disappear into the animal kingdom among the enclosures, complete with sessions for kids about all kinds of bugs and spiders in this popular animal retreat in Regent's Park.

Natural History Museum. It doesn't get more awe-inspiring than bloodsucking bats, a cabinet of hummingbirds, simulated Kobe earthquakes, and a life-size blue whale. Just make sure you know your dodo from your *diplodocus.*

Science Museum. Special effects, virtual space voyages, 800 interactive exhibits, puzzles, and mysteries from the world of science can keep kids effortlessly amused all day.

Tower of London. Perfect for playing prince and princess in front of the Crown Jewels, but not so perfect for imagining what becomes of the fairy tale—watch your royal necks.

Performances

Covent Garden street performers. You can't beat the open-air gaggle of jugglers, fire-eaters, unicyclists, mime artists, and human statues tantalizing crowds at Covent Garden piazza.

Regent's Park Open-Air Theatre. Welcome to the land of fairy dust and magic. Don't miss an evening performance under the stars of *A Midsummer Night's Dream* in high summer.

GREAT ITINERARIES

The sheer diversity of what London offers, along with its constantly evolving culture, means you can easily live a lifetime here and still not see it all. But if you're like most visitors and only visiting for a short time, you can still get a taste of London life. In one day, you can get to the heart of the city's history and feel the force of its river setting. With five days, you can tick off many of the main attractions, and have a deeper sense of the seen and unseen majesty of this global metropolis.

LONDON IN 1 DAY

Do a giant best-of loop of the city by open top boat and bus through six key districts, with a stop at the 950-year-old Tower of London and fun in Soho at the end. Start early, with the first ride of the London Eye at 10 am; you'll have the rest of the day to explore at whatever pace you wish, but be sure to get to Buckingham Palace before the sun sets or you'll miss out on some great photo opportunities.

On your morning ride on the **London Eye,** you'll be able to get an unrivaled bird's-eye view of the city. Then launch from the Eye's namesake pier for a swivel-eyed Thames cruise past four famous bridges and Traitors' Gate before landing in front of the iconic **Tower of London.**

Once inside the Tower, take in the Crown Jewels and gory history on a Yeoman Warder's tour, before jumping on a double-decker bus over **Tower Bridge,** past Monument, the Embankment, Park Lane, Oxford, and Piccadilly Circus and stopping at **Trafalgar Square,** where you can glimpse Big Ben and the Houses of Parliament, before stopping for lunch at a historic pub. Then take a walk over to **Westminster Abbey,** where a self-guided tour will take you through centuries of

British history within one awe-inspiring building (note that the Abbey closes early on Saturday). Then take another short walk through **St. James's Park** to **Buckingham Palace;** you'll have missed the daily Changing the Guard, but that means the palace grounds will be less crowded, with more photo ops. End the day by meandering over to the hip Soho neighborhood, where foodies will find endless eclectic restaurants for dinner, and party-goers will find the city's best nightlife.

LONDON IN 5 DAYS

In five days you can check off most of London's cultural and sightseeing highlights, and weave in enough time for some world-class shopping and people-watching. Iconic photo ops abound with stops at places like Big Ben, Buckingham Palace, and the London Eye. For a shorter stay, mix and match from this list.

Day 1: Buckingham Palace, Trafalgar Square, and the National Portrait Gallery

Start day one with coffee in a Dickensian alleyway just north of **St. James's Palace,** before being first into the 19 impossibly grand State Rooms at **Buckingham Palace.** Afterward, join the crowds outside the palace to watch a sea of bearskin Foot Guards perform the **Changing the Guard** ceremony, held 11:30 am most days. Some Palace tickets include tours of the **Queen's Gallery,** which showcases top Old Masters art from the Royal Collection. Then take a stroll through **St. James's Park** before lunch at a historic Pall Mall pub. It's a short stroll to the **National Gallery** at **Trafalgar Square.** Hit its quieter Sainsbury Wing, pick up an audio guide, and hunt down a few choice Renaissance masterpieces. Enjoy portraits of Tudor monarchs at the

National Portrait Gallery next door, before browsing the antiquarian booksellers on Charring Cross Road or Cecil Court and enjoying fresh dim sum in **Chinatown.**

Day 2: Westminster Abbey, Houses of Parliament, and the East End

Devote the early morning of day two to a 90-minute tour of **Westminster Abbey.** Then investigate the **Houses of Parliament.** If in session, you can attend debate in the Public Galleries or take a 75-minute tour of both houses. The **Members' Dining Room** in the House of Commons is now open to the public twice a week for lunch; otherwise have a ploughman's lunch at a historic pub. Take pics of **Big Ben** and walk up Whitehall to the gates of **No 10. Downing Street,** the Prime Minister's residence. For a complete change of tune, take the Tube over to the gritty yet hip East End and Indian-influenced Brick Lane, where you can stroll along the art galleries and have a classic Indian curry for dinner.

Day 3: The South Bank

Day three is all about the South Bank and its unique culture. Start with a ride on the **London Eye** for eye-popping city panoramas. Take a long walk along the Thames, popping into any galleries, cinemas, or shops that catch your eye, like the excellent **Hayward Gallery.** Eventually meander along to **Tate Modern** for a modern art fix, stopping for lunch nearby. Then enjoy a Shakespeare hit with tours of the replica Elizabethan **Shakespeare's Globe.** Wiggle along for venison burgers and foodie stall heaven at **Borough Market** before backtracking over the pedestrian **Millennium Bridge** for a stunning approach to **St. Paul's Cathedral.** Hopefully you'll catch Choral Evensong there at 5 pm, then head east towards Bow Lane alleyway for a customary City pub fish-and-chips dinner.

Day 4: The British Museum and Soho

On day four, start early at the **British Museum** in Bloomsbury and leave a few hours to explore hits like the Egyptian mummies, Rosetta Stone, and 7th-century Anglo-Saxon Sutton Hoo treasures. Afterward, Tube it to restaurant-mad **Soho** where you can stop for Sri Lankan curry at Hoppers, before browsing **Carnaby Street** and the surrounding indie fashion boutiques. Cut across Regent Street via the dapper gentlemen's tailors of **Savile Row** and head south for **Fortnum & Mason** and the old world outfitters on Jermyn Street. Work back through the twinkly Regency red-carpet **Burlington Arcade** and pop into the **Royal Academy** gallery before taking Afternoon Tea at a cozy wood-paneled and open-fire Mayfair hotel.

Day 5: Kensington's Museums, Piccadilly, and the West End

Finally on day five, start with a one-hour tour of the **V&A Museum** of decorative arts and design, whose collection ranges from Persian rugs to Tudor chalices. Once out, refuel with a crepe on pedestrianized Exhibition Road near the South Kensington Tube, then choose either all things science at the **Science Museum,** or the *T. rex* dinosaur trail at the **Natural History Museum.** Then stroll up Knightsbridge to **Harrod's** Food Hall, where you can drool over salamis and people-watch to your heart's content. Either duck in for the ace fashion at **Harvey Nichols** or sip early cocktails at **The Ritz** at Green Park. Enjoy the lights at **Piccadilly Circus** and **Leicester Square** before having a pre-theater dinner in **Covent Garden** and then seeing a West End play.

BEST TOURS IN LONDON

With its crooked medieval streets, layers of history, and atmospheric buildings, London is a true walking city often best explored on a guided tour. Tours are a great way to investigate out-of-the-way, hidden, historic, and secret districts; to get an insider's eye on where locals like to eat, drink, and be merry; and to learn all the juicy and infamous aspects of London's history, architecture, and inhabitants.

Boat Tours

City Cruises. In nice weather, an open top-deck ride from Westminster, the London Eye, or Tower Piers to the ancient royal romping ground of Greenwich along the Thames River is one of the best ways to get acquainted with the city. You'll pass sights like Tower Bridge, the Tower of London, and St. Paul's Cathedral, all with a chirpy Cockney boatman running commentary. Lunch, Afternoon Tea, and nighttime cruises are also available. ⊠ *Cherry Garden Pier, Cherry Garden St.* ☎ *020/7740–0400* ⊕ *www.citycruises.com* ⊠ *From £10.*

London Duck Tours. Hop aboard one of the garish yellow, vintage amphibious trucks (originally used during World War II), and get ready to sputter past a stack of sights including 10 Downing Street and Westminster Abbey. Once at the MI6 building, you'll take like a duck to water and gently amble up the Thames to the Houses of Parliament. Other tours focus on James Bond and the D-Day Landings. ⊠ *55 York Rd.* ☎ *020/7928–3132* ⊕ *www.londonducktours.co.uk* ⊠ *From £27.*

Thames RIB Experience. Make like James Bond in an exhilarating special forces–style inflatable speedboat as you whiz past the MI6 building, Shakespeare's Globe, and Tower Bridge on a high-speed 50-minute round-trip to Canary Wharf.

There are also 20-minute roller-coaster blasts to the O2 Arena in Greenwich and 75-minute round-trips from Tower Pier to the Thames Barrier. ⊠ *Embankment Pier* ☎ *020/3613–2354* ⊕ *www.thames-ribexperience.com* ⊠ *From £25.*

Bus Tours

Golden Tours. Various hop-on, hop-off open-top double-decker tours with this company take in the main sites on three key loops. With 60 drop-off points and 48-hour passes, they also offer discount tickets to attractions like the Tower of London and the London Dungeon, as well as nighttime tours and free walking tours and boat rides on the Thames. ⊠ *London* ☎ *020/7630–2028* ⊕ *www.goldentours.com* ⊠ *From £35.*

The Original London Sightseeing Tour. Like its double-decker competitors, the Original London Sightseeing Tour offers various hop-on, hop-off open-top tours of the city, but its most popular feature is its 48-hour pass that includes loops of the main historic sites, the City, Westminster, and the museum districts. They also throw in free tickets for a Thames boat cruise, plus Jack the Ripper, Changing of the Guard, and Rock 'n' Roll walking tours. ⊠ *London* ☎ *020/8877–1722* ⊕ *www.theoriginaltour.com* ⊠ *From £26.*

Free Tours

City Tours. The City of London City Guides offer a small program of top-quality daily walks, including an insider tour of Guildhall, Mansion House, the Bank of England, and Royal Exchange, plus others focusing on topics like the city's gardens, Charles Dickens, and famed architect Sir Christopher Wren's churches. ⊕ *www.cityoflondonguides.com* ⊠ *£7.*

Sandemans New Europe London. It seems almost too good to be true: Sandemans offers an excellent free, two-and-a-half-hour Royal London walking tour daily, which winds from Buckingham Palace to Big Ben. Led by wisecracking actors, poets, and art historians, other paid walks include a boozy five-stop pub crawl and spooky East End's Dark Secrets tours. ☎ *30/5105–0030* ⊕ *www. neweuropetours.eu/london* ✉ *Free.*

Specialty Tours

Brit Movie Tours. See the exterior of Grantham House and the spot where Branson first confesses his love for Lady Sybil on this insiders' central London tour of Downton Abbey filming locations. Other tours focusing on James Bond, *Sherlock, The Da Vinci Code,* and Harry Potter filming locations, among many others, are also available. ☎ *0844/247–1007* ⊕ *www.britmovietours.com* ✉ *From £90.*

Walking Tours

Context Travel. This company takes a high-brow approach to its intellectually curious small-group walks program, providing PhD- and MA-level scholars, authors, architects, and historians to lead walks of no more than six people. Lasting up to three hours, walks include the evolution of London theater to Charles Dickens and Victorian London. ☎ *800/691–6036* ⊕ *www.contexttravel. com* ✉ *From £75.*

London Food Lovers. Combine walking, talking, and eating (but not at the same time) on these fabulous multistop trails, featuring restaurants and London cultural history. There are four half-day Soho-focused food tours complete with 10 stops, as well as two shorter three-hour evening options that include five stops, like the Jack the Ripper Happy Hour tasting tour, which focuses on gin, bagels, and locally brewed craft ales. ☎ *07404/802–703* ⊕ *www.londonfood-lovers.com* ✉ *From £55.*

London Walks. With London's oldest established walking tours, there's no need to book ahead; instead, just turn up at the meeting point at the allotted hour and pay £10 for a first-rate, guided two-hour walk with themes like Secret London, Literary London, Harry Potter film locations, Haunted London, and much more. Top crime historian and leading Ripper authority Donald Rumbelow often leads the 7:30 pm Jack the Ripper walk in Whitechapel. ☎ *020/7624–3978* ⊕ *www.walks.com* ✉ *From £10.*

Sophie Campbell. Travel journalist and former BBC *Travel Show* broadcaster Sophie Campbell specializes in superlong London walks. Full-day walks include Old Church Chelsea (by the river) to St. Michael's Highgate (high on a north London hill); or Hampton Court Palace to Richmond Palace via the noble palazzi of the nontidal Thames. Half-day hikes include a forensic examination of Fleet Street journalism and James Bond's London. ☎ ⊕ *www.sophiecampbell.london* ✉ *From £200.*

AFTERNOON TEA

An Age-Old Tradition

So what is Afternoon Tea, *exactly*? Well, it is real loose-leaf tea—Earl Grey, English Breakfast, Ceylon, Darjeeling, or Assam—brewed in a silver or porcelain pot and served with fine bone china cups and saucers, milk or lemon, and silver spoons, taken between noon and 6 pm. For the full experience, there should be elegant finger foods on a three-tier silver cake stand: finely cut crustless finger sandwiches on the bottom; scones with Devonshire clotted cream and strawberry jam in the middle; and rich English fruitcake, shortbread, patisseries, macarons, and dainty *petits gateaux* on top.

Teagoers dress smartly, and conversation by tradition should naturally avoid politics and religion.

Classic Choices

The Savoy on the Strand offers one of the most beautiful settings for Afternoon Tea. The Thames Foyer, a symphony of grays and golds centered on a winter garden wrought-iron gazebo and great glass cupola, is just the place for the house pianist to accompany you as you enjoy 72 rare house teas along with finger sandwiches, homemade scones, and pastries.

Setting the standard in its English Tea Room for some of London's best-known traditional teas, **Brown's Hotel** in Mayfair offers Afternoon Tea for £55 in an Agatha Christie-esque wood-paneled salon or, if you wish to splurge, Champagne Afternoon Tea for £65.

If you seek timeless chic, the art deco dining room at the **The Delaunay** grand café at the Aldwych remains a deeply fashionable hangout. The silver service teas here— light Cream Tea is £10, Viennese Tea is £20, and Champagne Tea, £30—come

with wheat-free poppyseed *gugelhupf* cakes and are among the best in town.

Something Different

Add spice to your tea time by trying a popular Moroccan-style Afternoon Tea (£22 or £32) at the souk-chic tearoom at **Momo** off Regent Street, where you'll enjoy sweet mint tea plus scones with fig jam, Maghrebian pastries, Moroccan chicken wraps, and honey-and-nut-rich Berber-style crepes.

Alternatively, you can munch Coronation chicken wraps and look out onto the immaculate lawns amid mini potted orange trees at **The Orangery** at Prince William and Kate's London pad, Kensington Palace, inside resplendent Kensington Gardens. Afternoon Tea is £28, and a suitably Royal Afternoon Tea (with a glass of Laurent-Perrier Brut NV) is £38.

Covent Garden's grand French brasserie **Balthazar** has a fabulous fashion-focused English Afternoon Tea, curated by feted cosmetics guru Bobbi Brown. From Coronation chicken and apricot sandwiches to coco-citrus cheesecake and pecan macarons, everything has a creative twist.

An Edwardian Escape

For some gilt-edged grandeur, few can compete with Afternoon Tea at **The Ritz** on Piccadilly. It's served in the stunning Palm Court, replete with linen-draped tables, Louis XIV chaise longues, chandeliers, resplendent bouquets, and musical accompaniment; it's a true taste of Edwardian London in the 21st century. Afternoon Tea is £54, and Celebration Champagne Tea is £81. There are five sittings from 11:30 am; be sure to book three months ahead and men should wear a jacket and tie.

WESTMINSTER, ST. JAMES'S, AND ROYAL LONDON

Getting Oriented

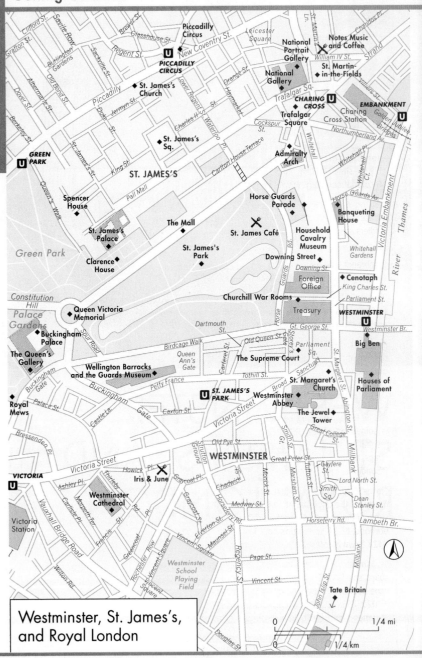

Piccadilly Circus
Leicester Square
Notes Music and Coffee
National Portrait Gallery
William IV St.
St. Martin-in-the-Fields
Strand
PICCADILLY CIRCUS
New Coventry St.
National Gallery
St. James's Church
Trafalgar Sq.
CHARING CROSS
EMBANKMENT
Charing Cross Station
Golden Jubilee Bridges
Trafalgar Square
Cockspur St.
Northumberland Av.
St. James's Sq.
GREEN PARK
Admiralty Arch
ST. JAMES'S
Horse Guards Parade
Banqueting House
Spencer House
The Mall
St. James Café
Household Cavalry Museum
Whitehall Gardens
St. James's Palace
St. James's Park
Green Park
Downing Street
Clarence House
Downing St.
Cenotaph
King Charles St.
Foreign Office
Parliament St.
Constitution Hill
Churchill War Rooms
WESTMINSTER
Palace Gardens
Queen Victoria Memorial
Treasury
Westminster Br.
Buckingham Palace
Dartmouth St.
Big Ben
The Queen's Gallery
Birdcage Walk
Queen Ann's Gate
Parliament Sq.
Gt. George St.
Wellington Barracks and the Guards Museum
Petty France
The Supreme Court
St. Margaret's Church
Houses of Parliament
Royal Mews
Castle La.
Caxton St.
ST. JAMES'S PARK
Tothill St.
Westminster Abbey
The Jewel Tower
Bressenden Pl.
Victoria Street
Old Pye St.
Great College St.
VICTORIA
Victoria Street
Howick Pl.
Iris & June
WESTMINSTER
Great Peter St.
Gayfere St.
Lord North St.
Westminster Cathedral
Chadwick
Medway St.
Smith Sq.
Dean Stanley St.
Victoria Station
Horseferry Rd.
Lambeth Br.
Page St.
Westminster School Playing Field
Vincent St.
Tate Britain

0   1/4 mi
0   1/4 km

Westminster, St. James's, and Royal London

TOP REASONS TO GO

Glorious Westminster Abbey: This Gothic church was not only the site of William and Kate's marriage but also has seen 38 coronations, starting with William the Conqueror in 1066.

Calling on Buckingham Palace: Even if you miss the palace's summer opening, keep pace with the marching soldiers as they enact the time-honored Changing the Guard.

Masterpieces Theater: Leonardo, Raphael, Van Eyck, Rembrandt, and many other artistic greats are shown off in the gorgeous rooms at the National Gallery.

Discover the preserved Churchill War Rooms: Listen to Churchill's radio addresses to the British people as you explore this cavernous underground wartime hideout.

Pose with Big Ben: As the Eiffel Tower is to Paris, so is Big Ben to London—walk from Trafalgar Square to catch sight of the 320-foot-high clock tower.

FEELING PECKISH?

Iris & June. The area between Victoria and Westminster is something of a wasteland in terms of quick bite eateries, but this minimalist café serves excellent coffee, salads, wraps, and more. ⊠ *1 Howick Pl.* ☎ *020/7828–3130* ⊕ *www.irisandjune.com* Ⓜ *Victoria.*

Notes Music and Coffee. Next door to the London Coliseum (home of the English National Opera), this hip café serves some of the best sandwiches, salads, and coffee in the neighborhood. ⊠ *31 St. Martin's La., Westminster* ☎ *020/7240–0424* ⊕ *www.notes-uk.co.uk* Ⓜ *Charing Cross.*

St. James's Café. Come here at lunch for delicious homemade soups, salads, and light mains, or for an early evening glass of wine before it closes at 6 pm. ⊠ *St. James's Park, St. James's* ☎ *020/7839–1149* ⊕ *www.benugo.com/public-spaces/st-james-s-park* Ⓜ *St. James's Park.*

GETTING THERE

Trafalgar Square is in the center of the action. Take the Tube to Embankment (Northern, Bakerloo, District, and Circle lines) and walk north until you cross the Strand, or exit to Northumberland Avenue at Charing Cross (Bakerloo and Northern lines). Buses are another great option, as almost all roads lead to Trafalgar Square.

Two Tube stations are right in the heart of St. James's: Piccadilly Circus (Piccadilly and Bakerloo lines) and Green Park (Piccadilly, Victoria, and Jubilee lines).

MAKING THE MOST OF YOUR TIME

For royal pageantry, begin with Buckingham Palace, Westminster Abbey, and the Guards Museum, followed by the Houses of Parliament and Big Ben. For art, the National Gallery, Tate Britain, and the Queen's Gallery top anyone's list.

NEAREST PUBLIC RESTROOMS

Paid restrooms (50 p) are across the street from Westminster Abbey at the bottom of Victoria Street. Banqueting House and the Queen's Gallery have elegant restrooms.

Sightseeing
★★★★★
Nightlife
★★
Dining
★★★
Lodging
★
Shopping
★★

This is postcard London at its best. Crammed with historic churches, grand state buildings, and some of the world's best art collections, Royal London and Westminster unite politics and high culture. (Oh, and the Queen lives here, too.) The places you'll want to explore are grouped into four distinct areas—Trafalgar Square, Whitehall, St. James's, and Buckingham Palace—each nudging a corner of triangular St. James's Park. There is as much history in these few acres as in many whole cities, so pace your-self—this is concentrated sightseeing.

WESTMINSTER

Updated by
Jo Caird

Home to London's most photogenic pigeons, **Trafalgar Square** is not only the official center of the district known as **Westminster,** nominally a separate city but in fact the official center of London. What will bring you here are the two magnificent museums on the northern edge of the square, the **National Gallery** and the **National Portrait Gallery.** From the square, two boulevards lead to the seats of different areas of governance. The avenue called **Whitehall** drops south to the neo-Gothic **Houses of Parliament,** where members of both (Commons and Lords) hold debates and vote on pending legislation. Just opposite, **Westminster Abbey** is a monument to the nation's history and for centuries the scene of daily worship, coronations, and royal weddings. Poets, political leaders, and 17 monarchs are buried in this world-famous, 13th-century Gothic building. Sandwiched between the two is the **Jewel Tower,** the only surviving part of the medieval Palace of Westminster (a name still given to Parliament and its environs). Halfway down Whitehall, **10 Downing Street** is both the residence and the office of the prime minister. One of the most celebrated occupants, Winston Churchill, is commemorated in the **Churchill War Rooms,** his

A BRIEF HISTORY OF WESTMINSTER

The Romans may have shaped The City, but England's royals created Westminster. Indeed, it's still technically a separate city—notice it reads "City of Westminster" on street signs, not "City of London"—although any formal divide between the two vanished centuries ago, along with the open countryside that once lay between them. Edward the Confessor started the first Palace of Westminster in the 11th century; in the 1040s, he also founded Westminster Abbey, where every British coronation has taken place. The district became the focus of political power in England after the construction of Whitehall Palace in the 16th century; a vast and opulent building, it was the official residence of the monarch until it burned down in 1698. It survives both as the name of Westminster's most important road, and as a term still used in Britain to refer to the seat of government in general. The first Parliament building was part of the same complex; it, too, was nearly destroyed by the Gunpowder Plot of 1605 (still commemorated annually on November 5, Guy Fawkes Day) and eventually succumbed to fire in 1834. The Westminster we see today took shape during the Georgian and Victorian periods, as Britain reached the zenith of its imperial power. Grand architecture sprang up, and Buckingham Palace became the principal royal residence in 1837, when Victoria acceded to the throne. Trafalgar Square and Nelson's Column were built in 1843, to commemorate Britain's most famous naval victory, and the Houses of Parliament were rebuilt in the 1840s in the trendy neo-Gothic style of the time. The illustrious Clarence House, built in 1825 for the Duke of Clarence (later William IV), is now the home of Prince Charles and Camilla, Duchess of Cornwall.

underground wartime headquarters off Whitehall. Just down the road is the **Cenotaph,** built for the dead of World War I and since then a focal point for the annual remembrance of others lost in war.

The Mall, a wide, elegant avenue beyond the stone curtain of **Admiralty Arch,** heads southwest from Trafalgar Square toward the **Queen Victoria Memorial** and **Buckingham Palace,** the sovereign's official residence. The building is open to the public only in summer (and for tours on select dates throughout the year), but you can see much of the royal art collection in the **Queen's Gallery** and spectacular ceremonial coaches in the **Royal Mews,** both open all year. Farther south toward Pimlico, **Tate Britain** focuses on prominent British artists from 1500 to today.

The main drawback to sightseeing here is that half the world is doing it at the same time. So, for a large part of the year a lot of Royal London is floodlit at night (when there's more elbow room), adding to the theatricality of the experience.

TOP ATTRACTIONS

FAMILY

Fodor's Choice

★

Churchill War Rooms. It was from this small warren of underground rooms—beneath the vast government buildings of the Treasury—that Winston Churchill and his team directed troops in World War II. Designed to be bombproof, the whole complex has been preserved almost exactly as it was when the last light was turned off at the end of the war. Every clock shows almost 5 pm, and the furniture, fittings, and paraphernalia of a busy, round-the-clock war office are in situ, down to the colored map pins.

During air raids, the leading government ministers met here, and the Cabinet Room is still arranged as if a meeting were about to convene. In the Map Room, the Allied campaign is charted on wall-to-wall maps with a rash of pinholes showing the movements of convoys. In the hub of the room, a bank of differently colored phones known as the "Beauty Chorus" linked the War Rooms to control rooms around the nation. The Prime Minister's Room holds the desk from which Churchill made his morale-boosting broadcasts; the Telephone Room (a converted broom cupboard) has his hotline to FDR. You can also see the restored rooms that the PM used for dining and sleeping. Telephonists (switchboard operators) and clerks who worked 16-hour shifts slept in lesser quarters in unenviable conditions.

A great addition to the War Rooms is the Churchill Museum, a tribute to the great wartime leader himself. ⊠ *Clive Steps, King Charles St., Westminster* 📞 *020/7416–5000* ⊕ *www.iwm.org.uk/visits/churchill-war-rooms* 💷 *£18* Ⓜ *Westminster.*

Downing Street. Were it not for the wrought-iron gates and armed guards that block the entrance, you'd probably miss this otherwise unassuming Georgian side street off Whitehall—but this is the location of the famous **No. 10,** London's modest equivalent of the White House. The Georgian entrance to the mid-17th century mansion is deceptive; it's actually a huge complex of discreetly linked buildings. Since 1732 it has been the official home and office of the prime minister—the last private resident was the magnificently named Mr. Chicken (the current prime minister actually lives in the private apartments above No. 11, traditionally the residence of the Chancellor of the Exchequer, the head of the Treasury). There are no public tours, but the famous black front door to No. 10 is clearly visible from Whitehall. Keep your eyes peeled for Larry the cat, whose official title is Chief Mouser to the Cabinet Office. Just south of Downing Street, in the middle of Whitehall, is the **Cenotaph,** a stark white monolith built to commemorate the 1918 armistice. On Remembrance Day (the Sunday nearest November 11), it's strewn with red poppy wreaths to honor the dead of both world wars and all British and Commonwealth soldiers killed in action since; the first wreath is always laid by the Queen. A hundred yards farther, toward Parliament, is the **Monument to the Women of World War II.** The prominent black marble sculpture uses a string of empty uniforms to symbolize the vital service of women in then-traditionally male jobs during the war, as well as in frontline roles, such as medics and auxiliary officers. ⊠ *Whitehall* ⊕ *www.number10.gov.uk* Ⓜ *Westminster.*

2

FAMILY **Horse Guards Parade.** Once the tiltyard for jousting tournaments, Horse Guards Parade is best known for the annual Trooping the Colour ceremony, in which the Queen takes the salute on her official birthday, on the second Saturday in June. (Though it's called a birthday it's actually the anniversary of her coronation—her real birthday is April 21.) It's a must-see if you're around, with marching bands and throngs of onlookers. Throughout the rest of the year, the changing of two mounted sentries known as the **Queen's Life Guard** at the Whitehall facade of Horse Guards provides what may be London's most popular photo opportunity. The ceremony takes place daily from April to July, and on alternate days from August to March (usually odd numbered days, but check the monthly schedule at ⊕ *www. householddivision.org.uk/changing-the-guard-calendar*). It starts at 10:30 am at St. James's Palace, where the guard begins its march to Buckingham Palace, and the new guards take up their posts in a ceremony at 11. (It's sometimes cancelled in bad weather). At 4 pm daily is the dismounting ceremony, aka the 4 O'Clock Parade, during which sentries are posted and horses are returned to their stables. It began in 1894, when Queen Victoria discovered the guards on duty drinking and gambling. As a punishment she decreed that the regiment should be inspected every day at 4 pm for the next 100 years—by the time 1994 swung around they decided to continue the tradition indefinitely. ⊠ *Whitehall* ☎ *020/7930–4832* ⊕ *www.royalcollection. org.uk* ⊠ *Free* Ⓜ *Westminster.*

Fodor's Choice **Houses of Parliament.** The Palace of Westminster, as the complex is called,
★ was first established on this site by Edward the Confessor in the 11th century. William II built a new palace in 1097, and this became the seat of English power. A fire destroyed most of the palace in 1834, and the current complex dates largely from the mid-19th century. The best view is from the opposite (south) bank of the Thames, across Lambeth Bridge. It is most dramatic at night when lighted green and gold.

The **Visitors' Galleries** of the House of Commons provide a view of democracy in action when the benches are filled by opposing MPs (members of Parliament). Debates are formal but raucous, especially during the **Prime Minister's Questions** (PMQs), when any MP can put a question to the nation's leader. Tickets to PMQs are free but highly sought after, so the only way for non-U.K. citizens to gain access is by lining up on the day and hoping for returns or no-shows. The action starts at noon every Wednesday when Parliament is sitting, and the whole shebang is broadcast live on television. For non-PMQ debates, Embassies and High Commissions have a quota of tickets available to their citizens, which can help you avoid long lines. The easiest time to get into the Commons is during an evening session—Parliament is still sitting if the top of the Clock Tower is illuminated. There are also Visitors Galleries for the House of Lords. The Clock Tower—renamed **Elizabeth Tower** in 2012, in honor of the Queen's Diamond Jubilee—was completed in 1858, and contains the 13-ton bell known as **Big Ben.** At the southwest end of the main Parliament building is the 323-foot-high Victoria Tower.

Engaging guided and audio tours of Parliament are available daily for most of the year, but sell out six months in advance. Other tours, including afternoon tea on the Pavillion Terrace, overlooking the Thames, are also available. ⊠ *St. Stephen's Entrance, St. Margaret St., Westminster* ☎ *0207/219–4114 for public tours* ⊕ *www.parliament.uk/visiting* 🖾 *Free; tours £26 (must be booked ahead)* ⊘ *Closed Sun.* Ⓜ *Westminster.*

The Jewel Tower. Overshadowed by the big-ticket attractions of Parliament to one side and Westminster Abbey to the other, this is the only significant portion of the Palace of Westminster complex to have survived intact from medieval times. Built in the 1360s to contain treasures belonging to Edward III, it once formed part of the palace's defensive walls—hence the fortresslike appearance. Check out the original ribbed stone ceiling on the ground floor; look up to see the carved stone images of men and beasts. The Jewel Tower was later used as a records office for the House of Lords, but hasn't served any official function since the rest of the old palace was destroyed by fire in 1834 and the ancient documents were moved to the greater safety of the Tower of London. Today it contains an exhibition on the history of Parliament. ⊠ *Abingdon St., Westminster* ☎ *020/7222–2219* ⊕ *www.english-heritage.org.uk/visit/places/jewel-tower* 🖾 *£6* Ⓜ *Westminster.*

FAMILY
Fodor's Choice
★

National Gallery. Anyone with even a passing interest in art will want to put this near the top of their to-do lists while visiting London, for it is truly one of the world's great art museums. More than 2,300 masterpieces are on show here, including works by Michelangelo, Leonardo, Turner, Monet, Van Gogh, Picasso, and more. Enter through the grand portico overlooking the north side of Trafalgar Square to delve headlong into the highlights of the collection, although the Sainsbury Wing (the modern building immediately to the left), which focuses mainly on medieval art, is invariably less crowded. You could easily spend all day discovering what the National Gallery has to offer, but among the best-known highlights are: in Room 4, *The Ambassadors* by Hans Holbein (1497–1543), a portrait of two wealthy visitors from France, surrounded by objects laden with enough symbolism to fill a book—including, most beguilingly, a giant skull at the base, which only takes shape when viewed from an angle; in Room 56, the *Arnolfini Portrait* by Van Eyck (1390–1441), in which a solemn couple holds hands, the fish-eye mirror behind them mysteriously illuminating what can't be seen from the front view; in Room 66, *The Virgin of the Rocks* by Leonardo da Vinci (1452–1519), a magnificent sculpted altarpiece commissioned in 1480; in Room 34, *Rain, Steam and Speed–The Great Western Railway* by J.M.W. Turner (1775–1851), which seems, in its mad whirl of rain, steam, and mist, to embody the mystical dynamism of the steam age (spot the fleeing hare); and, perhaps more famous than any of them, the *Sunflowers* by Van Gogh (1853–90), in Room 43. Special exhibitions, of which there are several every year, tend to be major events. Generally they're ticketed, so booking is advisable if it's a big name. The permanent collection, however, is always free. Also free are weekday lunchtime lectures and Ten Minute Talks, which illuminate the story behind a key work of art. Daily hour-long free guided tours start at the Sainsbury Wing at 11:30 and 2:30. ⊠ *Trafalgar Sq., Westminster* ☎ *020/7747–2885* ⊕ *www.nationalgallery.org.uk* 🖾 *Free; special exhibitions £7–£16; audio guide £4* Ⓜ *Charing Cross, Embankment, Leicester Sq.*

FAMILY
Fodor'sChoice
★

National Portrait Gallery. The National Portrait Gallery was founded in 1856 with a single aim: to gather together portraits of famous (and infamous) Britons throughout history. More than 150 years and 200,000 portraits later, it is an essential stop for all history and literature buffs. If you visit with kids, ask at the desk about the excellent Family Trails, which make exploring the galleries with children much more fun. Galleries are arranged clearly and chronologically, from Tudor times to contemporary Britain. A Holbein miniature of Henry VIII is among the most famous images in the Tudor Gallery, although the enormous portrait of Elizabeth I—bejeweled and literally astride the world in a powerful display of imperial intent—may be the most impressive. The huge permanent collections include portraits of Shakespeare, the Brontë sisters, and Jane Austen. Look for the four Andy Warhol *Queen Elizabeth II* silkscreens from 1985 and Maggi Hambling's surreal self-portrait. Contemporary portraits range from the iconic (*Julian with T-shirt*—an LCD screen on a continuous loop—by Julian Opie) to the extreme (Marc Quinn's *Self*, a realization of the artist's head done in frozen blood). Temporary exhibitions can be explored on the first three floors, particularly in the Wolfson and Porter galleries on the ground floor. ■ TIP➜ On the top floor, the Portrait Restaurant has one of the best views in London—a panoramic vista of Nelson's Column and the backdrop along Whitehall to the Houses of Parliament. ⊠ *St. Martin's Pl., Westminster* ☎ *020/7306–0055* ⊕ *www.npg.org.uk* 🖾 *Free; special exhibitions £6–£18; audiovisual guide £3; family audio guides £5 for 5 people* Ⓜ *Charing Cross, Leicester Sq.*

FAMILY
St. Martin-in-the-Fields. One of London's best-loved and most welcoming of churches is more than just a place of worship. Named after St. Martin of Tours, known for the help he gave to beggars, this parish has long been a welcome sight for the homeless, who have been given soup and shelter at the church since 1914. The church is also a haven for music lovers; the internationally known Academy of St. Martin-in-the-Fields Chamber Ensemble was founded here, and a popular program of concerts continues today. (Although the interior is a wonderful setting for a recital, beware the hard wooden benches!) The crypt is a hive of activity, with a popular café and shop. Here you can also make your own life-size souvenir knight, lady, or monarch from replica tomb brasses, with metallic waxes, paper, and instructions. ⊠ *Trafalgar Sq., Westminster* ☎ *020/7766–1100* ⊕ *www.smitf. org* 🖾 *Free; concerts free–£33* Ⓜ *Charing Cross, Leicester Sq.*

FAMILY
Fodor'sChoice
★

Tate Britain. First opened in 1897, and funded by the sugar magnate Sir Henry Tate, this stately neoclassical institution may not be as ambitious as its South Bank sibling, Tate Modern, but its bright galleries lure only a fraction of the Modern's overwhelming crowds and are a great place to explore British art from 1500 to the present. The museum includes the Linbury Galleries on the lower floors, which stage temporary exhibitions, and a permanent collection on the upper

The Tate Britain showcases British art from the last 500 years, including contemporary works.

floors. And what a collection it is—with classic works by John Constable, Thomas Gainsborough, Rachel Whiteread, Francis Bacon, Duncan Grant, Barbara Hepworth, and Vanessa Bell, and an outstanding display from J.M.W. Turner in the Clore Gallery, including many later vaporous and light-infused works such as *Sunrise with Sea Monsters*. Sumptuous Pre-Raphaelite pieces are a major draw, while the Contemporary British Art galleries bring you face to face with Damien Hirst's *Away from the Flock* and other recent conceptions. The Tate Britain also hosts the annual Turner Prize exhibition, with its accompanying furor over the state of contemporary art, from about October to January each year. There's a good little café, and the excellent Rex Whistler Restaurant has been something of an institution since it first opened in 1927. It's open daily for lunch, and for dinner on semiregular Late at Tate Friday evening events, when the gallery is open late for talks or performances; check the website for details.

■**TIP→ Craving more art? Head down the river on the Tate Boat (£9 one-way) to the Tate Modern; it runs between the two museums every 40 minutes. A Family River Roamer ticket (£37 for two adults and three children) permits a day's travel, with stops including the London Eye and the Tower of London. You get a discount of roughly a third if you have a Travelcard.** ⊠ *Millbank, Westminster* ☎ *020/7887–8888* ⊕ *www.tate. org.uk/britain* ☞ *Free; special exhibitions £11–£17* Ⓜ *Pimlico.*

Fodor's Choice **Trafalgar Square.** This is officially the center of London: a plaque on
★ the corner of the Strand and Charing Cross Road marks the spot from which distances on U.K. signposts are measured. (London's *actual* geographic center is a rather dull bench on the Victoria Embankment.)

Medieval kings once kept their aviaries of hawks and falcons here; today the humbler gray pigeons flock en masse to the open spaces around the ornate fountains (feeding them is banned). The square was designed in 1830 by John Nash, who envisaged a new public space with striking views of the Thames, the Houses of Parliament, and Buckingham Palace. Of those, only Parliament is still clearly visible from the square, but it remains an important spot for open-air concerts, political demonstrations, and national celebrations, such as New Year's Eve. Dominating the square is 168-foot **Nelson's Column,** erected as a monument to the great admiral in 1843. Note that the lampposts on the south side, heading down Whitehall, are topped with ships—they all face Portsmouth, home of the British navy. The column is flanked on either side by enormous bronze lions. Climbing them is a very popular photo op, but be extremely careful, as there are no guardrails and it's a long fall onto concrete if you slip. Four plinths border the square; three contain militaristic statues, but one was left empty—it's now used for contemporary art installations, often with a wry and controversial edge. Surprisingly enough, given that this was a square built to honor British military victories, the lawn at the north side, by the National Gallery, contains a statue of George Washington—a gift from the state of Virginia in 1921. At the southern point of the square is the **equestrian statue of Charles I.** After the Civil War and the king's execution, Oliver Cromwell, the antiroyalist leader, commissioned a brazier, John Rivett, to melt the statue down. The story goes that Rivett instead merely buried it in his garden. He made a fortune peddling knickknacks wrought, he claimed, from its metal, only to produce the statue miraculously unscathed after the restoration of the monarchy—and then made another fortune reselling it. In 1675 Charles II had it placed where it stands today, near the spot where his father was executed in 1649. Each year, on January 30, the day of the king's death, the Royal Stuart Society lays a wreath at the foot of the statue. ✉ *Westminster* Ⓜ *Charing Cross.*

Fodor's Choice
★
Westminster Abbey. Steeped in hundreds of years of rich and occasionally bloody history, Westminster Abbey is one of England's most iconic buildings. An abbey has stood here since the 10th century, although the current building mostly dates to the 1240s. It has hosted 38 coronations—beginning in 1066 with William the Conqueror—and no fewer than 16 royal weddings, the latest being that of Prince William and Kate Middleton in 2011. But be warned: there's only one way around the abbey, and it gets very crowded, so you'll need to be alert to catch the highlights. The **Coronation Chair,** which you'll find in St. George's Chapel by the east door, has been used for nearly every coronation since Edward II's in 1308, right up to Queen Elizabeth II's in 1953. Farther along, the exquisite confection of the Henry VII's **Lady Chapel** is topped by a magnificent fan-vaulted ceiling. The tomb of Henry VII lies behind the altar. Elizabeth I is buried above her sister "Bloody" Mary I in the tomb in a chapel on the north side, while her arch enemy, Mary Queen of Scots, rests in the tomb to the south. The **Chapel of St. Edward the Confessor** contains the shrine of the pre-Norman king, who reigned from 1042 to 1066. Because of its great age, you must join the vergers' tours to be admitted to the chapel (£3; book at the admission desk).

One of London's most iconic sites, Westminster Abbey contains more than 600 monuments and memorials, and serves as the final resting place of some of England's most famous citizens.

To the left, you'll find **Poets' Corner.** Geoffrey Chaucer was the first poet to be buried here, and other statues and memorials include those to William Shakespeare, D. H. Lawrence, T. S. Eliot, and Oscar Wilde. The medieval **Chapter House** is adorned with 14th-century frescoes and a magnificent 13th-century tiled floor, one of the finest in the country. Near the entrance is Britain's oldest door, dating from the 1050s. If you walk toward the West Entrance, you'll see a plaque to Franklin D. Roosevelt—one of the Abbey's very few tributes to a foreigner. The poppy-wreathed **Grave of the Unknown Warrior** commemorates soldiers who lost their lives in both world wars. Exact hours for the various parts of the abbey are frustratingly long and complicated, and can change daily, so it's important to check before setting out, particularly if you're visiting early or late in the day, or off-season. The full schedule is posted online daily (or you can call). Certain areas of the abbey are completely inaccessible to wheelchair users; however, you will get free entry for yourself and one other. ✉ *Broad Sanctuary, Westminster* ☎ *020/7222–5152* ⊕ *www.westminster-abbey.org* 💷 *£20; audio tour free* ⊗ *Closed Sun., except for worship* Ⓜ *Westminster, St. James's Park*.

WORTH NOTING

Banqueting House. James I commissioned Inigo Jones, one of England's great architects, to undertake a grand building on the site of the original Tudor Palace of Whitehall, which was (according to one foreign visitor) "ill-built, and nothing but a heap of houses." Jones's Banqueting House, finished in 1622 and the first building in England to be completed in the neoclassical style, bears all the hallmarks of the Palladian sophistication and purity that so influenced Jones during his time in Italy. James's son, Charles I, enhanced the interior by employing the Flemish painter Peter Paul Rubens to glorify his father and himself (naturally) in a series of vibrant painted ceiling panels called *The Apotheosis of James I.* As it turned out, these allegorical paintings, depicting a wise monarch being received into heaven, were the last thing Charles saw before he stepped through the open first-floor window onto the scaffold, which had been erected directly outside for his execution by Cromwell's Parliamentarians in 1649. Twenty years later, his son, Charles II, would celebrate the restoration of the monarchy in the exact same place. ⌧ *Whitehall, Westminster* ☎ *084/4482–7777* ⊕ *www.hrp.org.uk/BanquetingHouse* 🎫 *£7* Ⓜ *Charing Cross, Embankment, Westminster.*

FAMILY **Household Cavalry Museum.** Hang around Horse Guards for even a short time and you'll see a member of the Household Cavalry on guard, or trotting past on horseback, resplendent in a bright crimson uniform with polished brass armor. Made up of soldiers from the British Army's most senior regiments, the Life Guards and the Blues and Royals, membership is considered a great honor; they act as the Queen's official bodyguards and play a key role in state occasions. (It is they who perform the daily Changing the Guard ceremony at 11 am, 10 am on Sunday.) Housed in the cavalry's original 17th-century stables, the museum has displays of uniforms and weapons going back to 1661 as well as interactive exhibits on the regiments' current operational roles. In the tack room you can handle saddles and bridles, and try on a trooper's uniform, including a distinctive brass helmet with horsehair plume. You can also observe the working horses being tended to in their stable block behind a glass wall. ⌧ *Horse Guards Parade, Whitehall* ☎ *020/7930–3070* ⊕ *www.house-holdcavalrymuseum.co.uk* 🎫 *£7* Ⓜ *Charing Cross, Westminster.*

St. Margaret's Church. Dwarfed by its neighbor, Westminster Abbey, St. Margaret's was probably founded in the 11th century and rebuilt between 1482 and 1523. It's the unofficial parish church of the House of Commons—Winston Churchill tied the knot here in 1908, and since 1681, a pew off the south aisle has been set aside for the Speaker of the House (look for the carved portcullis). Samuel Pepys and John Milton also worshipped here. The stained glass in the north windows is classically Victorian, facing abstract glass from John Piper in the south, while the east windows date from the early 16th century. These were to replace the originals, which were ruined in World War II. ⌧ *St. Margaret's St., Parliament Sq., Westminster* ☎ *020/7654–4840* ⊕ *www. westminster-abbey.org/st-margarets-church* 🎫 *Free* Ⓜ *Westminster.*

The Supreme Court. The highest court of appeal in the United Kingdom is a surprisingly young institution, only having heard its first cases in 2009. Visitors are welcome to drop by and look at the three courtrooms, housed in the carefully restored Middlesex Guildhall, including the impressive Court Room 1, with its magnificent carved wood ceiling. The Court's art collection, on permanent display, includes portraits by Thomas Gainsborough and Joshua Reynolds. Guided tours are available on Friday (book ahead). There is a café downstairs. ⌧ *Parliament Sq., Westminster* ☎ *020/7960–1500* ⊕ *www.supremecourt.uk* 🎫 *Free; guided tour £7, audio guide £1* Ⓜ *Westminster.*

FAMILY **Wellington Barracks and the Guards Museum.** These are the headquarters of the Guards Division, the Queen's five regiments of elite foot guards (Grenadier, Coldstream, Scots, Irish, and Welsh), who protect the sovereign and, dressed in tunics of gold-purled scarlet and tall bearskin caps, patrol her palaces. Guardsmen alternate these ceremonial postings with serving in current conflicts, for which they wear more practical uniforms. If you want to learn more about the guards, visit the **Guards Museum,** which has displays on all aspects of a guardsman's life in conflicts dating back to 1642; the entrance is next to the Guards Chapel. Next door is the **Guards Toy Soldier Centre,** a great place for a souvenir. ⊠ *Birdcage Walk, Westminster* ☏ *020/7414–3428* ⊕ *www.theguardsmuseum.com* ▨ *£6* Ⓜ *St. James's Park, Green Park.*

Westminster Cathedral. Tucked away on traffic-clogged Victoria Street lies this remarkable neo-Byzantine gem, seat of the Archbishop of Westminster, head of the Roman Catholic Church in England and Wales. Faced with building a church with Westminster Abbey as a neighbor, architect John Francis Bentley looked to the east for inspiration, to the basilicas of St. Mark's in Venice and the Hagia Sofia in Istanbul. The asymmetrical redbrick edifice, dating to 1903, is banded with stripes of Portland stone and abutted by a 272-foot bell tower at the northwest corner, ascendable by elevator for sterling views. The interior remains incomplete, but the unfinished overhead brickwork of the ceiling lends the church a dark, brooding intensity. Several side chapels, such as the Chapel of the Blessed Sacrament and the Holy Souls Chapel, are beautifully finished in glittering mosaics. The Lady Chapel—dedicated to the Virgin Mary—is also sumptuously decorated. Look out for the Stations of the Cross, done here by Eric Gill, and the striking baldachin—the enormous stone canopy standing over the altar with a giant cross suspended in front of it. The nave, the widest in the country, is constructed in green marble, which also has a Byzantine connection—it was cut from the same place as the marble used in the Hagia Sofia, and was almost confiscated by warring Turks as it traveled west. All told, more than 100 different types of marble can be found within the cathedral's interior. There's a café in the crypt. ⊠ *Ashley Pl., off Victoria St., Westminster* ☏ *020/7798–9055* ⊕ *www.westminstercathedral.org.uk* ▨ *Bell Tower and viewing gallery £6, Treasures of the Cathedral exhibition £5; combination ticket £9* Ⓜ *Victoria.*

ST. JAMES'S

As a fitting coda to all of Westminster's pomp and circumstance, St. James's—packed with old-money galleries, restaurants, and gentlemen's clubs that embody the history and privilege of traditional London—is found to the south of Piccadilly and north of the Mall.

When Whitehall Palace burned down in 1698, all of London turned its attention to St. James's Palace, the new royal residence. In the 18th and 19th centuries, the area around the palace became the place to live, and many of the estates surrounding the palace disappeared in

ROYALTY WATCHING

2

You've seen Big Ben, the Tower, and Westminster Abbey. But somehow you feel something is missing: a close encounter with Britain's most famous attraction—Her Royal Majesty, Elizabeth II. The Queen and the Royal Family attend hundreds of functions a year, and if you want to know what they are doing on any given date, turn to the Court Circular, printed in the major London dailies, or check out the Royal Family website (⊕ www.royal.uk) for the latest events on the Royal Diary. Trooping the Colour is usually held on the second Saturday in June, to celebrate the Queen's official birthday. This spectacular parade begins when she leaves Buckingham Palace in her carriage and rides down the Mall to arrive at Horse Guards Parade at 11 exactly. To watch, just line up along the Mall with your binoculars.

Another time you can catch the Queen in all her regalia is when she and the Duke of Edinburgh ride in state to open the Houses of Parliament. The famous black and gilt-trimmed Irish State Coach travels from Buckingham Palace—on a clear day, it's to be hoped, for this ceremony takes place in late October or early November. The Gold State Coach, an icon of fairy-tale glamour, is used for coronations and jubilees only.

But perhaps the most relaxed, least formal time to see the Queen is during Royal Ascot, held at the racetrack near Windsor Castle—a short train ride out of London—usually during the third week of June (Tuesday–Saturday). The Queen and members of the Royal Family are driven down the track to the Royal Box in an open carriage, giving spectators a chance to see them. After several races, the famously horse-loving Queen invariably walks down to the paddock, greeting racegoers as she proceeds. If you meet her, the official etiquette is to first make a short bow or curtsy, and then to address her first as "Your Majesty," and then "Ma'am" thereafter.

a building frenzy, as mansions were built and streets laid out. Most of the homes here are privately owned and therefore closed to visitors, but there are some treasure houses that you can explore (such as Spencer House), as well as many fancy shops that have catered to the great and good for centuries.

Today, St. James's remains a rather masculine enclave, containing most of the capital's celebrated gentlemen's clubs (especially the classic Athenaeum), long-established men's outfitters and clothiers, and some interesting art galleries and antiques shops. In one corner is St. James's Park, framed on its western side by the biggest monument in the area: Buckingham Palace, the official London residence of the Queen. The smaller St. James's Palace is where much of the office work for the House of Windsor gets done; nearby is Clarence House, London home of Prince Charles and his wife, Camilla.

A classic photo op: cavalry from the Queen's Life Guard at Buckingham Palace

TOP ATTRACTIONS

Fodor's Choice ★ **Buckingham Palace.** If Buckingham Palace were open year-round, it would be by far the most visited tourist attraction in Britain; as it is, the Queen's main residence, home to every British monarch since Victoria in 1837, opens its doors to the public only in the summertime, with a handful of other dates throughout the year. The Queen is almost never there at the time—traditionally she heads off to Scotland for a couple of months every summer, where she takes up residence at Balmoral Castle. (Here's a quick way to tell if the Queen's at home: if she's in residence, the Royal Standard flies above the palace; if not, it's the more famous red, white, and blue Union Jack.) The tour covers the palace's 19 State Rooms, with their fabulous gilt moldings and walls adorned with old masters. The **Grand Hall,** followed by the **Grand Staircase** and **Guard Room,** are visions in marble and gold leaf, filled with massive, twinkling chandeliers. Don't miss the theatrical **Throne Room,** with the original 1953 coronation throne, or the sword in the Ballroom, used by the Queen to bestow knighthoods and other honors with a touch on the recipient's shoulders. Royal portraits line the **State Dining Room,** and the **Blue Drawing Room** is dazzling in its splendor. The bow-shape **Music Room** features lapis lazuli columns between arched floor-to-ceiling windows, and the alabaster-and-gold plasterwork of the **White Drawing Room** is a dramatic statement of wealth and power. Admission is by timed-entry ticket every 15 minutes throughout the day. Allow up to two hours for your visit. Those with impaired mobility should contact the Palace in advance, as they may have to enter a different way (it's no bad thing, as you are sometimes taken via the front instead;

practice your wave to the crowds on the Mall). Changing the Guard remains one of London's best free shows and culminates in front of the palace. Marching to live military bands, the old guard proceed up the Mall from St. James's Palace to Buckingham Palace. Shortly afterward, the new guard approach from Wellington Barracks. Then within the forecourt, the captains of the old and new guards symbolically transfer the keys to the palace. Get there early for the best view. ⊠ *Buckingham Palace Rd., St. James's* ☎ *020/7766–7300* ⊕ *www.royalcollection. uk/visit* ⌨ *£23 (£33 including garden highlights tour); joint ticket with Queen's Gallery and Royal Mews £40* ⊗ *Closed Oct.–July except on selected dates* Ⓜ *Victoria, St. James's Park, Green Park.*

The Mall. This stately, 115-foot-wide processional route sweeping towards Trafalgar Square from the Queen Victoria Memorial at Buckingham Palace is an updated 1911 version of a promenade laid out around 1660 for the game of *paille-maille* (a type of croquet crossed with golf), which also gave the parallel road Pall Mall its name. (That's why Mall is pronounced to rhyme with "pal," not "ball.") The tarmac is colored red to represent a ceremonial red carpet. During state visits, several times a year, the Mall is traditionally bedecked with the flag of the visiting nation, alongside the Union Jack. The **Duke of York Memorial** up the steps toward Carlton House Terrace is a towering column dedicated to George III's second son, who was further immortalized in the English nursery rhyme "The Grand Old Duke of York." Be sure to stroll along the Mall on Sunday when the road is closed to traffic, or catch the bands and troops of the Household Division on their way from St. James's Palace to Buckingham Palace for the Changing the Guard. At the northernmost end of the Mall is Admiralty Arch, a stately gateway named after the adjacent Royal Navy headquarters. It was designed by Sir Aston Webb and built in 1910 as a memorial to Queen Victoria. Actually comprising five arches—two for pedestrians, two for traffic, and the central arch, which is only opened for state occasions—it was a government building until 2012, and has even served as an alternative residence for the Prime Minister while Downing Street was under renovation. It is now expected to become a luxury hotel. Look out for the bronze nose grafted onto the inside wall of the right-hand traffic arch (when facing the Mall); it was placed there in secret by a mischievous artist in 1997 and has been allowed to remain. ⊠ *St. James's* Ⓜ *Charing Cross, Green Park.*

Piccadilly Circus. The origins of the name "Piccadilly" relate to a humble 17th-century tailor from the Strand named Robert Baker who sold piccadills—stiff ruffled collars all the rage in courtly circles—and built a house with the proceeds. Snobs dubbed his new-money mansion Piccadilly Hall, and the name stuck. Pride of place in the circus—a circular junction until the construction of Shaftesbury Avenue in 1886—belongs to the statue universally referred to as Eros, dating to 1893 (although even most Londoners don't know that it is, in reality, a representation of Eros's brother Anteros, the Greek God of requited love). The other instantly recognizable feature of Piccadilly Circus is the enormous bank of lit-up billboards on the north side; if you're passing at night, frame them behind the Tube entrance sign on the corner of Regent Street for an unforgettable photograph. ⊠ *St. James's* Ⓜ *Piccadilly Circus.*

The Queen's Gallery. Technically speaking, the sovereign doesn't "own" the rare and exquisite works of art in the Royal Collection: she merely holds them in trust for the nation—and what a collection it is. Only a selection is on view at any one time, presented in themed exhibitions. Let the excellent (and free) audio guide take you through the elegant galleries filled with some of the world's greatest artworks.

A rough time line of the major royal collectors starts with Charles I (who also commissioned Rubens to paint the Banqueting House ceiling). An avid art enthusiast, Charles established the basis of the Royal Collection, purchasing works by Raphael, Titian, Caravaggio, and Dürer. During the Civil War and in the aftermath of Charles's execution, many masterpieces were sold abroad and subsequently repatriated by Charles II. George III, who bought Buckingham House and converted it into a palace, scooped up a notable collection of Venetian (including Canaletto), Renaissance (Bellini and Raphael), and Dutch (Vermeer) art, and a large number of baroque drawings, in addition to patronizing English contemporary artists such as Gainsborough and Beechey. The Prince Regent, later George IV, had a particularly good eye for Rembrandt, equestrian works by Stubbs, and lavish portraits by Lawrence. Queen Victoria had a penchant for Landseer animals and landscapes, and Frith's contemporary scenes. Later, Edward VII indulged Queen Alexandra's love of Fabergé, and many royal tours around the empire produced gifts of gorgeous caliber, such as the Cullinan diamond from South Africa and an emerald-studded belt from India. ✉ *Buckingham Palace, Buckingham Palace Rd., St. James's* ☎ *030/3123–7334* ⊕ *www.royalcollection.org.uk* ✉*£11; joint ticket with Royal Mews and Buckingham Palace £40* Ⓜ *Victoria, St. James's Park, Green Park.*

FAMILY **Royal Mews.** Fairy-tale gold-and-glass coaches and sleek Rolls-Royce state cars emanate from the Royal Mews, next door to the Queen's Gallery. Designed by John Nash, the Mews serves as the headquarters for Her Majesty's travel department (so beware of closures for state visits), complete with the Queen's own special breed of horses, ridden by wigged postilions decked in red-and-gold regalia. Between the stables and the riding school arena are exhibits of polished saddlery and riding tack. The highlight of the Mews is the splendid Gold State Coach, a piece of art on wheels, with its sculpted tritons and sea gods. There are activities for children, and free guided tours are available April through October (daily at 10:15, then hourly 11–4). ✉ *Buckingham Palace, Buckingham Palace Rd., St. James's* ☎ *030/3123–7302* ⊕ *www. royalcollection.org.uk* ✉ *£10; joint ticket with Queen's Gallery and Buckingham Palace £40* ⊘ *Closed Sun. in Feb., Mar., and Nov.* Ⓜ *Victoria, St. James's Park.*

St. James's Palace. Commissioned by Henry VIII, this Tudor brick palace was the residence of kings and queens for more than 300 years; indeed, while all monarchs have actually lived at Buckingham Palace since Queen Victoria's day, it is still one of the official residences of the Royal Family. (This is why foreign ambassadors are received by the "Court of St. James.") Today it contains various royal apartments and offices, including the working office of Prince Charles. The palace is not open to the public, but the surprisingly low-key Tudor exterior is well worth the short detour from the Mall. Friary Court out front is a splendid setting for Trooping the Colour, part of the Queen's official birthday celebrations. Everyone loves to take a snapshot of the scarlet-coated guardsman standing sentry outside the imposing Tudor gateway. Note that the Changing the Guard ceremony at St. James's Palace occurs only on days when the guard at Buckingham Palace is changed. If you're approaching from St. James Street, take a quick peek at the delightfully old-looking **Berry Bros. & Rudd** wine store at No. 3, near the back entrance to the palace; it's been trading here continuously since 1698. ⊠ *Friary Ct., St. James's* ⊕ *www.royal. uk* Ⓜ *Green Park.*

FAMILY

Fodor's Choice

★

St. James's Park. There is a story that, many years ago, a royal once inquired of a courtier how much it would cost to close St. James's Park to the public. "Only your crown, ma'am" came the reply. Bordered by three palaces—Buckingham, St. James', and the governmental complex of the Palace of Westminster—this is one of London's loveliest public parks. It's also the oldest; the former marshland was acquired by Henry VIII in 1532 as a nursery for his deer. Later, James I drained the land and installed an aviary, which gave Birdcage Walk its name, and a zoo (complete with crocodiles, camels, and an elephant). When Charles II returned from exile in France, where he had been hugely impressed by the splendor of the gardens at the Palace of Versailles, he transformed the park into formal gardens, with avenues, fruit orchards, and a canal. Lawns were grazed by goats, sheep, and deer, and in the 18th century the park became a different kind of hunting ground, for wealthy lotharios looking to pick up nighttime escorts. A century later, John Nash redesigned the landscape in a more naturalistic, romantic style, and if you gaze down the lake toward Buckingham Palace, you could easily believe yourself to be on a country estate.

A large population of waterfowl—including pelicans, geese, ducks, and swans (which belong to the Queen)—breed on and around Duck Island at the east end of the lake. The pelicans are fed at 2:30 daily. From April to September, the deck chairs (charge levied) come out, crammed with office workers at midday, eating lunch while being serenaded by music from the bandstands. One of the best times to stroll the leafy walkways is after dark, with Westminster Abbey and the Houses of Parliament rising above the floodlit lake. ⊠ *The Mall or Horse Guards approach or Birdcage Walk, St. James's* ⊕ *www. royalparks.org.uk* Ⓜ *St. James's Park, Westminster.*

WORTH NOTING

Spencer House. Ancestral abode of the Spencers—Princess Diana's family—this is perhaps the finest extant example of an elegant 18th-century London townhouse. Reflecting his passion for the Grand Tour and classical antiquities, the first Earl Spencer commissioned architect John Vardy to adapt designs from ancient Rome for a magnificent private palace. Vardy was responsible for the exteriors, including the gorgeous west-facing Palladian facade, its pediment adorned with classical statues, and the ground-floor interiors, notably the lavish Palm Room, with its spectacular screen of columns covered in gilded carvings that resemble gold palm trees. The lavish style was meant not only to attest to Spencer's power and wealth but also to celebrate his marriage, a love match then rare in aristocratic circles (the palms are a symbol of marital fertility). Midway through construction—the house was built between 1756 and 1766—Spencer changed architects and hired James "Athenian" Stuart, whose designs were based on a classical Greek aesthetic, to decorate the gilded State Rooms on the first floor. These include the Painted Room, the first completely neoclassical room in Europe. Since the 1940s, the house has been leased by the Spencers to a succession of wealthy residents. Entry is by tour only, which occur on Sundays only. ■TIP➔ Note that children under ten are not allowed inside. ⊠ *27 St. James's Pl., St. James's* ☎ *020/7514–1958* ⊕ *www.spencerhouse.co.uk* ⊠ *£12* ☉ *Closed Mon.–Sat.* Ⓜ *Green Park.*

St. James's Church. Bombed by the German Luftwaffe in 1940 and not restored until 1954, this was one of the last of Sir Christopher Wren's London churches—and his favorite. Completed in 1684, it contains one of the finest works by the master carver Grinling Gibbons (1648–1721): an ornate limewood *reredos* (the screen behind the altar). The church is a lively place, with all manner of lectures and concerts (some are free). A café occupies a fine location right alongside the church, while a small, sedate garden is tucked away at the rear. The market out front is full of surprises; come Monday and Tuesday for food stalls, and Wednesday through Saturday for arts and crafts. ⊠ *197 Piccadilly, St. James's* ☎ *020/7734–4511, 020/7381–0441 for concert program and tickets* ⊕ *www.sjp.org.uk* ⊠ *Free* Ⓜ *Piccadilly Circus, Green Park.*

St. James's Square. One of London's oldest squares, St. James's was first laid out in the 1660s. It soon became the capital's most fashionable address; by 1720, it was home to 14 dukes and earls. These days you're more likely to find it populated with office workers eating their lunches under the shade of its leafy old trees on a warm summer's day, but it still has some prestigious residents. Most famous among them is the **London Library** at No. 14, one of the several 18th-century residences spared by World War II bombs. Founded by Thomas Carlyle, it contains a million or so volumes, making it the world's largest independent lending library, and is also considered the best private humanities library in the land. Nonmembers can take an evening tour of the library, although reservations must be made in advance. ⊠ *St. James's* Ⓜ *Piccadilly Circus.*

MAYFAIR AND MARYLEBONE

Getting Oriented

Mayfair and Marylebone

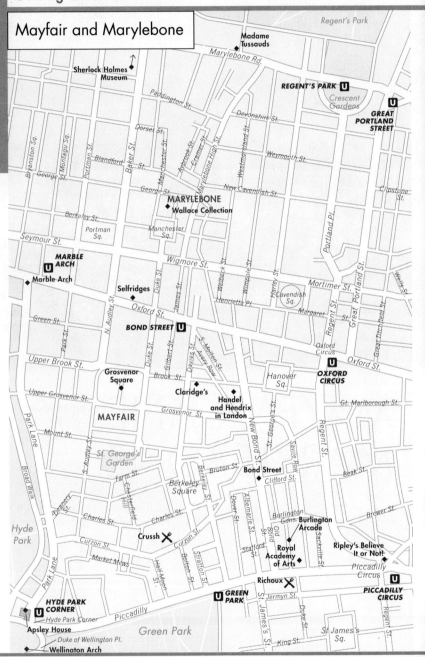

TOP REASONS TO GO

At home with the Duke of Wellington: The Iron Duke's Apsley House is filled with splendid salons lined with grand old master paintings.

Get a passion for fashion: There's great shopping aplenty on Bond and Mount streets, where the likes of McQueen and McCartney will keep your credit card occupied, but don't forget stylish, gigantic Selfridges.

London's most charming shopping arcade: Built for Lord Cavendish in 1819, the beautiful Burlington Arcade is right out of a Victorian daguerreotype.

The Wallace Collection: Savor room after room of magnificent furniture, porcelain, silver, and top old master paintings, in the former residence of the marquesses of Hertford.

Dress to impress at Claridge's: Afternoon tea at this sumptuous art deco gem is the perfect end to a shopping spree in Mayfair.

FEELING PECKISH?

Crussh. This successful chain serves up delicious juices and smoothies, as well as sandwiches, soups, and wraps. Decamp to nearby Green Park, where—if you're lucky—you can grab one of the deck chairs. ⊠ *1 Curzon St., Mayfair* ☎ *020/7629–2554* ⊕ *www.crussh.com* ☉ *Closed weekends* Ⓜ *Green Park.*

Richoux. This has been an affordable refuge from busy Piccadilly for more than a century. Simple but well-executed French bistro food is served all day, as well as scrumptious afternoon tea. ⊠ *172 Piccadilly, Mayfair* ☎ *020/7493–2204* ⊕ *www.richoux.co.uk* Ⓜ *Green Park, Piccadilly Circus.*

GETTING THERE

Three Tube stations on the Central line are handy for reaching these neighborhoods: Marble Arch, Bond Street (also on the Jubilee line), and Oxford Circus (also on the Victoria and Bakerloo lines).

You can also take the Piccadilly or Bakerloo line to the Piccadilly Circus Tube station, the Piccadilly line to the Hyde Park Corner station, or the Piccadilly, Victoria, or Jubilee line to the Green Park station.

The best buses are the C2, which takes in Green Park, Berkeley Square, and New Bond Street, and the 9—London's oldest existing bus route—which runs along Piccadilly.

MAKING THE MOST OF YOUR TIME

Set aside at least a day to experience Mayfair and Marylebone. Leave enough time for shopping and also to wander casually through the streets and squares.

The only areas to avoid are the Tube stations at rush hour, and Oxford Street if you don't like crowds. At all costs, stay away from Oxford Circus around 5 pm, when the commuter rush can, at times, resemble an East African wildebeest migration—but without the charm.

The area becomes quiet at night, so plan to party elsewhere.

3

Sightseeing
★★★★
Nightlife
★
Dining
★★★★
Lodging
★★★★
Shopping
★★★★

Mayfair forms the core of London's West End, the city's most stylish central area. This neighborhood oozes class and old-school style. The sense of being in one of the world's most wealthy and powerful cities is palpable as you wander along its grand and graceful streets. Scoot across the district's one exception to all this elegance—Oxford Street—and you'll discover the pleasant thoroughfares of Marylebone, the most central of London's many "villages."

MAYFAIR

Updated by
James O'Neill

Ultraritzy Mayfair, lined with beautiful 18th-century mansions (along with Edwardian apartment buildings made of deep-red brick), is the address of choice for many of London's wealthiest residents—note the number of Rolls-Royces, Bentleys, and Jaguars on the streets. Even the delivery vans all seem to bear some royal coat of arms, advertising that they've been purveyors of fine goodies for as long as anyone can remember.

The district can't claim to be stuffed with must-sees, but that is part of its appeal. There is no shortage of history and gorgeous architecture; the streets here are custom-built for window-shopping, expansive strolling, and getting a peek into the lifestyles of London's rich and famous, past and present. Mayfair is primarily residential, so its homes are off-limits except for one satisfyingly grand example: **Apsley House,** the Duke of Wellington's home, built by Robert Adam in 1771, and once known as No. 1, London; the nearby **Wellington Arch** also commemorates the great hero.

Despite being bordered by four of the busiest streets in London—the busy budget-shopping mecca Oxford Street (to the north), the major traffic artery Park Lane (to the west), and the bustling Regent Street and Piccadilly (to the east and south, respectively)—Mayfair itself is remarkably traffic-free and a delight to explore. Starting at **Selfridges,**

Each June for the past 240 years, the iconic Royal Academy of Arts has put on its Summer Exhibition, a huge draw for art-loving visitors and Londoners alike.

on Oxford Street, a southward stroll will take you through quiet streets lined with Georgian townhouses (the area was largely developed in the 17th and 18th centuries). From there, with a bit of artful navigating, you can reach four pleasant patches of green: **Grosvenor Square, Berkeley Square, Hanover Square,** with its splendid **St. George's Church** where Handel worshipped, and the quiet **St. George's Gardens,** bounded by a maze of streets and mews. Some of London's most exclusive shopping destinations are here, including **Mount Street, Bruton Street, Savile Row,** and the **Burlington Arcade.** The **Royal Academy of Arts** is at the southern fringe of Mayfair on Piccadilly, beyond which begins more sedate St. James's.

TOP ATTRACTIONS

Fodor'sChoice
★
Apsley House. Apsley House was built by Robert Adam in the 1770s and was bought by the Duke of Wellington two years after his famous victory over Napoléon at the Battle of Waterloo in 1815. Long known simply as No. 1, London, on account of its being the first mansion at the old tollgate from Knightsbridge village, the Duke's old regency abode is looking hale and hearty after a major refurbishment. Victory over the French made Wellington the greatest soldier and statesman in the land. The so-called Iron Duke lived here from 1817 until his death in 1852, and, although the 7th Duke of Wellington gave the house to the nation, the family retained some residential rights. Opposite the house, and now marooned in a roundabout in the middle of the constant Hyde Park traffic, is the **Wellington Arch,** designed by Decimus Burton and unveiled in 1828, although Burton's original plan to

Marble Arch was originally a gateway to Buckingham Palace before it was moved to the corner of Hyde Park.

have a sculpture of the Angel of Peace descending upon a chariot of war at the arch's pinnacle wasn't realized until 1912. As you'd expect, the mansion has many uniforms and weapons on display, but it also houses a celebrated art collection, the bulk of which was once owned by Joseph Bonaparte, onetime King of Spain and younger brother of Napoléon. With works by Brueghel, Van Dyck, and Rubens, as well as the Spanish masters Velázquez and Murillo (note the former's famous portrait of Pope Innocent X), the collection also includes a Goya portrait of the duke himself on horseback. An 11-foot-tall statue of a nude (fig-leafed) Napoléon looms over you as you approach the grand central staircase. The statue was taken from the Louvre and given as a gift to Wellington from the grateful British government in 1816. ⊠ *149 Piccadilly, Hyde Park Corner, Mayfair* ☎ *0370/333–1181* ⊕ *www.english-heritage.org.uk* ✉ *£10; joint ticket with Wellington Arch £12* ☉ *Closed Mon. and Tues. in Apr.–Oct. and weekdays in Nov.–Feb.* Ⓜ *Hyde Park Corner.*

Bond Street. This world-class shopping haunt is divided into northern "New" (1710) and southern "Old" (1690) halves. You can spot the juncture by a bronzed bench on which Franklin D. Roosevelt sits companionably next to Winston Churchill. At No. 35, on New Bond Street, you'll find **Sotheby's,** the world-famous auction house, as well as upscale retailers like Asprey's, Burberry, Louis Vuitton, Georg Jensen, and Church's. You'll find even more opportunities to flirt with financial ruin on Old Bond Street, with flagship boutiques of top-end designers like Chanel, Gucci, and Yves Saint Laurent; an array of fine jewelers including Tiffany; and art dealers Colnaghi, Spink Leger, and

Agnew's. **Cork Street,** which parallels the top half of Old Bond Street, is where many top dealers in contemporary art have their galleries. ✉ *Mayfair* ⊕ *www.bondstreet.co.uk* Ⓜ *Bond St., Green Park.*

Fodor's Choice
★
Burlington Arcade. With ceilings and lights now restored to how they would have looked when it was built in 1819, Burlington Arcade is the finest of Mayfair's enchanting covered shopping alleys. Originally built for Lord Cavendish, it was meant to stop the hoi polloi from flinging garbage into his garden at next-door Burlington House. Top-hatted watchmen called beadles—the world's smallest private police force—still patrol, preserving decorum by preventing you from singing, running, or carrying an open umbrella. The arcade is also the main link between the Royal Academy of Arts and its extended galleries at 6 Burlington Gardens. ✉ *Piccadilly, Mayfair* ☏ *020/7493–1764* ⊕ *www.burlington-arcade.co.uk* Ⓜ *Green Park, Piccadilly Circus.*

Marble Arch. John Nash's 1827 arch, moved here from Buckingham Palace in 1851, stands amid the traffic whirlpool where Bayswater Road segues into Oxford Street, at the top of Park Lane. The arch actually contains three small chambers, which served as a police station until the mid-20th century. Search the sidewalk on the traffic island opposite the movie theater for the stone plaque recalling the Tyburn Tree, an elaborately designed gallows that stood here for 400 years, until 1783. The condemned would be conveyed here in their finest clothes from Newgate Prison in The City, and were expected to affect a casual indifference or face a merciless heckling from the crowds. Towering across the grass from the arch toward Tyburn Way is *Horse at Water,* a vast patina-green statue of a horse's head by sculptor Nic Fiddian. Cross over (or under) to the northeastern corner of Hyde Park for Speakers' Corner, a parcel of land long-dedicated to the principle of free speech. On Sunday, people of all views—or none at all—come to pontificate, listen, and debate about everything under the sun. ✉ *Park La., Mayfair* Ⓜ *Marble Arch.*

Fodor's Choice
★
Royal Academy of Arts. Burlington House was built in 1664, with later Palladian additions for the 3rd Earl of Burlington in 1720. The piazza in front dates from 1873, when the Renaissance-style buildings around the courtyard were designed by Banks and Barry to house a gaggle of noble scientific societies, including the Royal Society of Chemistry and the Royal Astronomical Society.

The house itself is home to the Royal Academy of Arts. An ambitious redevelopment of the Royal Academy for its 250th anniversary in 2018 has meant that even more of its 46,000 treasures can now be put on display. The statue of the academy's first president, Sir Joshua Reynolds, palette in hand, stands prominently in the piazza. Free tours show off part of the collection and the excellent temporary exhibitions. Every June to August, the RA puts on its Summer Exhibition, a huge and eclectic collection of art by living Royal Academicians and many other contemporary artists. ✉ *Burlington House, Piccadilly, Mayfair* ☏ *020/7300–8000* ⊕ *www.royalacademy.org.uk* 🎟 *£10–£18* Ⓜ *Piccadilly Circus, Green Park.*

At 221B Baker Street, you can immerse yourself in the world of one Mr. Sherlock Holmes.

Wellington Arch. Opposite the Duke of Wellington's mansion, Apsley House, this majestic stone arch surveys the traffic rushing around Hyde Park Corner. Designed by Decimus Burton and completed in 1828, it was created as a grand entrance to the west side of London and echoes the design of that other landmark gate, Marble Arch. Both were triumphal arches commemorating Britain's victory against France in the Napoleonic Wars. Atop the building, the Angel of Peace descends on the *quadriga,* or four-horse chariot of war. Inside the arch, three floors of permanent and temporary exhibits reveal the monument's history. From the balconies at the top of the arch you can peek into the Queen's back garden at across-the-road Buckingham Palace. ⊠ *Hyde Park Corner, Mayfair* ☎ *020/7930–2726* ⊕ *www.english-heritage.org.uk* 🎫 *£5* Ⓜ *Hyde Park Corner.*

WORTH NOTING

Grosvenor Square. Pronounced "*Grove*-na," this leafy square was laid out in 1725–31 and is as desirable an address today as it was then. Americans have certainly always thought so—from John Adams, the second president, who as ambassador lived at No. 38, to Dwight D. Eisenhower, whose wartime headquarters was at No. 20. The entire west side of the square was home to the U.S. Embassy for over 50 years until its relocation south of the river. In the square itself stand memorials to Franklin D. Roosevelt and those who died on September 11, 2001. Grosvenor Chapel, completed in 1730 and used by Eisenhower's men during World War II, stands a couple of blocks south of the square on South Audley Street, with the entrance to pretty **St. George's Gardens** to its left. ⊠ *Mayfair* Ⓜ *Bond St.*

Handel and Hendrix in London. This newly renamed museum celebrates the lives of not one, but two, musical geniuses: classical composer George Frederick Handel and rock guitar legend Jimi Hendrix. Comprising two adjoining buildings, the bulk of the museum centers on the life and works of Handel who lived at No. 25 for more than 30 years until his death in 1759. In rooms decorated in fine Georgian style, you can linger over original manuscripts and gaze at portraits. Some of the composer's most famous pieces were created here, including the *Messiah* and *Music for the Royal Fireworks*. Fast-forward 200 years or so, and the apartment on the upper floors of No. 23 housed one of rock's great innovators, Jimi Hendrix, for a short but creative period in the late 1960s. Formerly the museum's administrative offices, Hendrix's apartment has now been lovingly restored to its late 1960s heyday and is open to the public. ✉ *23–25 Brook St., entrance in Lancashire Court, Mayfair* ☎ *020/7495–1685* ⊕ *www.handelhendrix.org* ✉ *£10 combined ticket for both* ☉ *Closed Sun.* Ⓜ *Bond St.*

3

MARYLEBONE

A favorite of newspaper style sections everywhere, Marylebone High Street forms the heart of Marylebone Village (pronounced "Marr-le-bone"), a vibrant, upscale neighborhood that encompasses the squares and streets around High Street and nearby Marylebone Lane. The district took its name from a church dedicated to St. Mary and the bourne (another word for "stream") that ran through the original village. Nowadays, it's hard to believe you're just a few blocks north of gaudy Oxford Street as you wander in and out of Marylebone's small shops and boutiques, the best of which include Cadenheads Whisky Shop and Tasting Room (26 Chiltern Street); La Fromagerie (2–6 Moxon Street), an excellent cheese shop; Daunt Books (Nos. 83–84 Marylebone High Street), a superlative travel bookshop; the "Cabbages and Frocks" market (Saturday 11–5) on the grounds of the St. Marylebone Parish Church, purveying specialty foods and vintage clothing; and a large farmers' and artisanal-food market (Sunday 10–2) in a parking lot on Cramer Street, just behind High Street. But some memorable sights await, too, including the best remnant of ancien régime France in London, the fabled Wallace Collection. The best Tube stop for the area is Bond Street.

TOP ATTRACTIONS

Sherlock Holmes Museum. Outside Baker Street station, by the Marylebone Road exit, is a nine-foot-high bronze statue of Arthur Conan Doyle's celebrated detective, who "lived" around the corner at number 221B Baker Street—now a museum to all things Sherlock. Inside, Mrs. Hudson, Holmes's housekeeper, guides you into a series of Victorian rooms where the great man lived, worked, and played the violin. It's all carried off with such genuine enthusiasm and attention to detail that you could be forgiven for thinking that Mr. Holmes actually *did* exist. ✉ *221B Baker St., Regent's Park* ☎ *020/7224–3688* ⊕ *www.sherlock-holmes.co.uk* ✉ *£15* Ⓜ *Baker St.*

FAMILY
Fodor's Choice
★

Wallace Collection. With its Great Gallery stunningly refurbished, there's even more reason to visit this exquisite gem of an art gallery—although housing one of the world's finest collections of old master paintings is reason enough. This glorious collection and the 18th-century mansion in which it's located were bequeathed to the nation by the widow of Sir Richard Wallace (1818–90). Wallace's father, the 4th Marquess of Hertford, took a house in Paris after the French Revolution and set about snapping up paintings by what were then dangerously unpopular artists, for a song. Frans Hals's *Laughing Cavalier* is probably the most famous painting here, or perhaps Jean-Honoré Fragonard's *The Swing*. The full list of painters in the collection reads like a "who's who" of classical European art—from Rubens, Rembrandt, and Van Dyck to Canaletto, Titian, and Velázquez. English works include paintings by Gainsborough and Turner. There are also fine collections of furniture, porcelain, Renaissance gold, and *majolica* (15th- and 16th-century Italian tin-glazed pottery). With craft activities, hands-on sessions, the "Little Draw" drawing workshops, as well as the chance to try on a suit of armor in the "Arms and Armour" collection, there's plenty to keep kids occupied, too. The conditions of the bequest mean that no part of the collection can leave the building; this is the only place in the world you'll ever be able to see these works. ✉ *Hertford House, Manchester Sq., Marylebone* ☎ *020/7563–9500* ⊕ *www.wallacecollection.org* 🎫 *Free* Ⓜ *Bond St.*

WORTH NOTING

FAMILY
Madame Tussauds. One of London's busiest tourist attractions, this is nothing less than the world's most famous exhibition of lifelike wax-work models of celebrities. Madame T. learned her craft while making death masks of French Revolution victims, and in 1835 she set up her first show of the famous ones near this spot. Top billing still goes to the murderers in the Chamber of Horrors, who stare glassy-eyed at visitors—one from an electric chair, one sitting next to the tin bath where he dissolved several wives in quicklime. ■ **TIP→ Beat the crowds by booking timed-entry tickets in advance. You can also buy nondated, "priority access" tickets via the website (at a premium).** ✉ *Marylebone Rd., Regent's Park* ☎ *0844/248–2624 for timed-entry tickets* ⊕ *www.madametussauds.com* 🎫 *£29–£70* Ⓜ *Baker St.*

FAMILY
Ripley's Believe It Or Not! Inspired by the legendary American traveler/cartoonist/curator Robert Ripley, this museum has six floors of the weird, the wacky, and the downright bizarre (life-size knitted Ferrari, anyone?) to delight even the most tired and jaded among us. Nothing is too unusual or outlandish to take its place among the 700-plus authentic artifacts. From dinosaur eggs to a sculpture of the Beatles made from chewing gum (yes, chewing gum!), there is so much to see, with interactive exhibits aplenty. ✉ *The London Pavilion, 1 Piccadilly Circus, Mayfair* ☎ *020/3238–0022* ⊕ *www.ripleyslondon.com* 🎫 *£24–£28* Ⓜ *Piccadilly Circus (Exit 4 to Coventry St.).*

4

SOHO AND
COVENT GARDEN

Getting Oriented

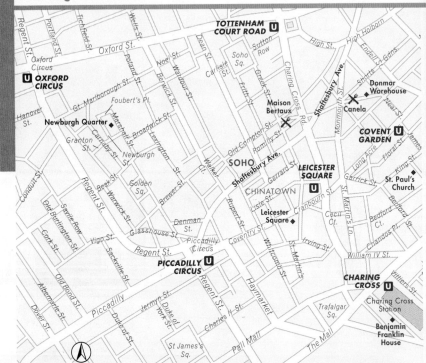

GETTING THERE	TOP REASONS TO GO

<table>
<tr><td>

Almost all Tube lines cross the Covent Garden and Soho areas, so it's easy to hop off for dinner or a show in one of the hippest parts of London. For Soho, take any train to Piccadilly Circus, Leicester Square, Oxford Circus, or Tottenham Court Road. For Covent Garden, get off at Covent Garden station on the Piccadilly line. (It may be easier to exit the Tube at Leicester Square or Holborn and walk.) Thirty buses connect to the Covent Garden area from all over London; check out the area's website (⊕ *www. coventgarden.london*).

</td><td>

Find tomorrow's look in the Newburgh Quarter: Head to this adorable warren of cobblestone streets for stylish boutiques, edgy stores, and young indie upstarts.

Indulge yourself in gourmet country: London has fallen in love with its chefs, and Soho is home to many of the most talked-about restaurants in town.

Covent Garden Piazza: Eliza Doolittle's former backyard has been taken over by boutiques and street performers who play to the crowds at night.

Royal Opera House: Even if you're not going to the opera or ballet, take in the beautiful architecture and sense of history.

See a West End hit in Theatreland: Shaftesbury Avenue is the heart of London's theater district, where more than 40 West End theaters pull in the crowds with a mix of extravagant musicals, Shakespeare, and new plays.

</td></tr>
</table>

Soho and Covent Garden

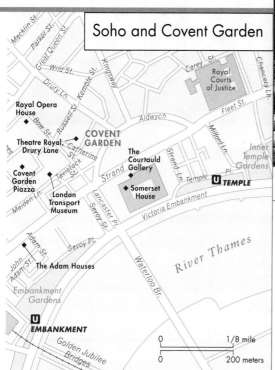

MAKING THE MOST OF YOUR TIME

You can comfortably tour all the sights around Soho and Covent Garden in a day. Visit the small but perfect Courtauld Gallery in the morning, leaving plenty of time to watch street entertainment or shop at the stalls around Covent Garden Piazza or in the fashion boutiques of Soho in the afternoon. Save some energy for a night on the town in Soho.

FEELING PECKISH?

The coffee shops on Covent Garden Piazza can be overpriced and mediocre. Head north for Seven Dials or west for Soho when the munchies strike.

Canela. Bright and casual by day, intimate and atmospheric by night, this is a great spot for refueling mid–shopping trip, grabbing a bite before a show (think filling dishes like pork stew or salted cod, plus charcuterie and sandwiches), or lingering over a glass of reasonably priced Portuguese wine. ✉ *33 Earlham St., Covent Garden* ☎ *020/7240–6926* ⊕ *www.canelacafe.com* Ⓜ *Covent Garden, Leicester Sq.*

Maison Bertaux. This eccentric little place has been around since the end of the 19th century. Not the finest coffee around, but a wide range of teas, plus fab French cakes, tarts, and savory quiches more than make up for that. ✉ *28 Greek St., Soho* ☎ *020/7437–6007* ⊕ *www.maisonbertaux.com* Ⓜ *Leicester Sq.*

GAY LONDON

Old Compton Street in Soho is the epicenter of London's affluent, stylish gay scene. There are some fun nightclubs in the area, with crowds forming in Soho Square, south of Oxford Street. Some of the more well-known clubs and bars in the area include Friendly Society, Ku Bar, the Yard, and She.

Sightseeing
★★★
Nightlife
★★★★★
Dining
★★★★
Lodging
★★
Shopping
★★★

A red-light district no more, today's Soho is more stylish than seedy and offers some of London's best bars, live music venues, restaurants, and theaters. By day, this hotbed of media production reverts to the business side of its late-night scene. If Soho is all about showbiz, neighboring Covent Garden is devoted to culture. Both districts offer an abundance of narrow streets packed with one-of-a-kind shops and lots of antique character.

SOHO

Updated by
Jo Caird

Soho, which, along with Covent Garden, is loosely known as "the West End," has long been known as the entertainment and arts quarter of London's center. Bordered to the north by Oxford Street, Regent Street to the west, and Chinatown and Leicester Square to the south, the narrow streets of Soho are unabashedly devoted to pleasure. Wardour Street bisects the neighborhood, with lots of interesting boutiques and some of London's best-value restaurants to the west (especially around Foubert's Place and on Brewer and Lexington streets). Most nightlife lies to the east—including the gay clubs of Old Compton Street—and beyond that is the city's densest collection of theaters, on Shaftesbury Avenue. London's compact Chinatown is wedged between Soho and Leicester Square. A bit of erudition surfaces to the east of the square on Charing Cross Road, famous for its secondhand bookshops, and on tiny Cecil Court, a pedestrianized passage lined with small antiquarian booksellers.

TOP ATTRACTIONS

Fodor's Choice
★

Newburgh Quarter. Want to see the hip style of today's London? Find it one block east of Carnaby Street—where the look of the '60s "Swinging London" was born—in an adorable warren of cobblestone streets now lined with specialty boutiques, edgy stores, and young indie upstarts. A

A BRIEF HISTORY OF SOHO

Almost as soon as a 17th-century housing development covered what had been a royal park and hunting ground, Soho earned a reputation for entertainment, bohemianism, and cosmopolitan liberality. When the authorities adopted a zero-tolerance policy towards soliciting in 1991 (the most recent of several attempts to end Soho's sex trade), they cracked down on an old neighborhood tradition that still resurfaces from time to time.

Successive waves of refugees— French Huguenots in the 1680s, followed by Germans, Russians, Poles, Greeks, Italians, and Chinese— settled and brought their national cuisines with them. So when dining out became fashionable after World War I, Soho was the natural place for restaurants to flourish (as they continue to do today).

Among the luminaries who have made their home here are landscape painter John Constable; Casanova; Canaletto, the great painter of Venice; the poet William Blake; and Karl Marx. In the 1950s and '60s, Soho was London's artists' quarter and the place to find the top jazz clubs and art galleries.

The outlines of present-day Covent Garden took shape in the 1630s, when Inigo Jones turned what had been agricultural land into Britain's first planned public square. After the Great Fire of 1666, it became the site of England's largest fruit-and-vegetable market (the flower market arrived in the 19th century). The district's many theaters and taverns gave the area a somewhat dubious reputation, and after the produce market relocated in 1973, the surviving buildings were scheduled for demolition. A local campaign saved them, and the restored market opened in 1980.

check of the ingredients reveals one part '60s London, one part futuristic fetishism, one part steampunk, and one part British street swagger. The new-bohemian look best flourishes in shops like Peckham Rye, a tiny boutique crowded with rockers and fashionistas who adore its grunge– meets– *Brideshead Revisited* vibe. Quality independent coffee shops abound—take a break at Department of Coffee and Social Affairs, where you can also browse for home coffee-making equipment. ⊠ *Newburgh St., Foubert's Pl., Ganton St., and Carnaby St., Soho* ⊕ *www.carnaby.co.uk.*

COVENT GARDEN

To the east of Charing Cross Road lies Covent Garden, the famous marketplace turned shopping mall. Although boutiques and haute fashion shops line the surrounding streets, many Londoners come to Covent Garden for its two outposts of culture: the **Royal Opera House** and the **Donmar Warehouse,** one of London's best and most innovative theaters. The area becomes more sedate just to the north, at the end of Wellington Street, where semicircular Aldwych is lined with grand buildings, and from there the Strand leads to the huge, stately piazza of **Somerset House,** a vibrant center of contemporary arts and home to the many masterpieces on view at the **Courtauld Gallery.** You'll get a sense of old-fashioned London just behind the Strand, where small lanes are little changed since the 18th century. On the way to the verdant **Embankment Gardens** bordering the Thames, you may pass the **Adam Houses,** the remnants of a grand 18th-century riverside housing development, and the **Benjamin Franklin House,** where the noted statesman lived in the years leading up to the American Revolution.

Covent Garden joins Soho as an arts-and-entertainment center in the city, popularly referred to as "the West End." The neighborhood centers on the Piazza, site of the original Covent Garden market. High Holborn to the north, Kingsway to the east, and the Strand to the south form its other boundaries.

ICE-SKATING

It's hard to beat the skating experience at Somerset House, where November to January a rink is set up in the grand courtyard of this central London palace. Check the website for current prices; its popularity is enormous, and if you can't get a ticket, other atmospheric venues such as Hampton Court, the Tower of London, the London Eye, and the Natural History Museum are following Somerset House's lead in having temporary winter rinks. ☎ 0844/847–1520 ⊕ www. somersethouse.org.uk/ice-rink.

TOP ATTRACTIONS

Fodor'sChoice ★ **The Courtauld Gallery.** One of London's most beloved art collections, the Courtauld is to your right as you pass through the archway into the grounds of the beautifully restored, grand 18th-century neoclassical **Somerset House.** Founded in 1931 by the textile magnate Samuel Courtauld to house his remarkable private collection, this is one of the world's finest Impressionist and post-Impressionist galleries, with artists ranging from Bonnard to Van Gogh. A déjà-vu moment with Cézanne, Degas, Seurat, or Monet awaits on every wall (Manet's *Bar at the Folies-Bergère* and a study for *Le Déjeuner sur L'Herbe* are two of the stars). Botticelli, Bruegel, Tiepolo, and Rubens are also represented, thanks to the exquisite bequest of Count Antoine Seilern's Princes Gate collection. German Renaissance paintings, bequeathed in 1947, include the colorful and sensual *Adam and Eve* by Lucas Cranach the Elder. The second floor has a more provocative, experimental feel, with masterpieces such as Modigliani's iconic *Female Nude.* Don't miss the little café downstairs, a perfect place for a spot of tea. ✉ *Somerset House, Strand, Covent Garden* ☎ *020/7848–2526* ⊕ *www.courtauld.ac.uk* ✆ *£7; additional charge for special exhibits* Ⓜ *Temple, Covent Garden.*

Covent Garden Piazza. Once home to London's main flower market, where *My Fair Lady's* Eliza Doolittle peddled her blooms, the square around which Covent Garden pivots is known as the Piazza. In the center, the fine old market building now houses stalls and shops selling expensive clothing, plus several restaurants and cafés, and knickknack stores that are good for gifts. One particular gem is Benjamin Pollock's Toyshop at No. 44 in the market. Established in the 1880s,

DID YOU KNOW?

Somerset House was lapped by the River Thames before the Victoria Embankment was built in the 19th century. The neoclassical building's grand courtyard is home to ice-skating in winter and dancing fountains in summer.

it sells delightful toy theaters. The superior **Apple Market** has good crafts stalls on most days, too. On the south side of the Piazza, the indoor **Jubilee Market,** with its stalls of clothing, army-surplus gear, and more crafts and knickknacks, feels a bit like a flea market. In summer it may seem that everyone in the huge crowds around you in the Piazza is a fellow tourist, but there's still plenty of office life in the area. Londoners who shop here tend to head for Neal Street and the area to the north of Covent Garden Tube station, rather than the market itself. In the Piazza, street performers—from global musicians to jugglers and mimes—play to the crowds, as they have done since the first English Punch and Judy Show, staged here in the 17th century. ⊠ *Covent Garden* ⊕ *www.coventgarden.london* Ⓜ *Covent Garden.*

FAMILY
Fodor's Choice
★
London Transport Museum. Housed in the old flower market at the southeast corner of Covent Garden, this stimulating museum is filled with impressive vehicle, poster, and photograph collections. As you watch the crowds drive a Tube-train simulation and gawk at the steam locomotives and horse-drawn trams (and the piles of detritus that remained behind), it's unclear who's enjoying it more: children or adults. Best of all, the kid-friendly museum (under 18 admitted free) has a multilevel approach to education, including information for the youngest visitor and the most advanced transit aficionado alike. Food and drink are available at the Upper Deck café, and the shop has lots of good options for gift-buying. ■**TIP→ Tickets are valid for unlimited entry for 12 months.** ⊠ *Covent Garden Piazza, Covent Garden* ☏ *020/7379–6344* ⊕ *www.ltmuseum.co.uk* ⊠ *£18* Ⓜ *Covent Garden, Leicester Sq.*

FAMILY
Fodor's Choice
★
Somerset House. In recent years this huge complex—the work of Sir William Chambers (1723–96), and built during the reign of George III to house offices of the Navy—has been transformed from dusty government offices to one of the capital's most buzzing centers of culture and the arts, often hosting several interesting exhibitions at one time. The cobblestone Italianate courtyard, where Admiral Nelson used to walk, makes a great setting for 55 playful fountains and is transformed into a romantic ice rink in winter; the grand space is the venue for music and outdoor movie screenings in summer. The **Courtauld Gallery** occupies most of the north building, facing the busy Strand. Across the courtyard are the Embankment Galleries, with a vibrant calendar of design, fashion, architecture, and photography exhibitions. The East Wing has another fine exhibition space, and events are sometimes also held in the atmospherically gloomy cellars below the Fountain Court. Tom's Kitchen offers gourmet dining, and Fernandez & Wells is a great spot for a more informal meal or snack. In summer eating and drinking spills out onto the large terrace next to the Thames. ⊠ *Strand, Covent Garden* ☏ *020/7845–4600* ⊕ *www.somersethouse.org.uk* ⊠ *Embankment Galleries price varies, Courtauld Gallery £7, other areas free* Ⓜ *Charing Cross, Waterloo, Blackfriars.*

Leicester Square is home to many movie theaters and a half-price theater ticket booth.

WORTH NOTING

The Adam Houses. Only a few structures remain of what was once a regal riverfront row of houses on a 3-acre site, but such is their quality that they are worth a detour from the Strand. The work of 18th-century Scottish architects and interior designers (John, Robert, James, and William Adam, known collectively as the Adam brothers), the original development was damaged in the 19th century during the building of the Embankment, and mostly demolished in 1936 to be replaced by an art deco tower. The original houses still standing are protected, and give a glimpse of their former grandeur. Numbers 1–4 Robert Street and 7 and 10 Adam Street are the best. ⊠ *Robert St. and Adam St., off The Strand, Covent Garden* Ⓜ *Charing Cross, Embankment.*

Benjamin Franklin House. This architecturally significant 1730 house is the only surviving residence of American statesman, scientist, writer, and inventor Benjamin Franklin, who lived and worked here for 16 years preceding the American Revolution. The restored Georgian townhouse has been left unfurnished, the better to show off the original features: 18th-century paneling, stoves, beams, bricks, and windows. Visitors are led around the house by the costumed character of Polly Hewson, the daughter of Franklin's landlady, who interacts with engaging video projections and recorded voices (Wednesday–Sunday). On Monday you can take a guided tour focusing on the architectural details of the building, and a walking tour of the surrounding area lasting up to 90 minutes sets off from the house every morning at 10:30. ⊠ *36 Craven St., Covent Garden* ☎ *020/7839–2006* ⊕ *www.benjaminfranklinhouse.org* ✉ *Historical Experience £8; architectural* *tour £6; walking tour £5 (reservations recommended)* ☉ *Closed Tues.* Ⓜ *Charing Cross, Embankment.*

Leicester Square. Looking at the neon of the major movie houses, the fast-food outlets, and the disco entrances, you'd never guess that this square (pronounced "Lester") was a model of formality and refinement when it was first laid out around 1630. By the 19th century, the square was already bustling and disreputable, and although it's not a threatening place, you should still be on your guard, especially at night—any space so full of people is bound to attract pickpockets, and Leicester Square certainly does. Although there's a bit of residual glamour (red-carpet film premiers) Londoners generally tend to avoid the place, though it's worth a visit for its hustle and bustle, its mime artists, and the pleasant modern fountain at its center. Also in the middle is a statue of a sulking Shakespeare, perhaps remembering the days when the movie houses were live theaters—burlesque houses, but live all the same. On the northeast corner, in Leicester Place, stands the church of **Notre Dame de France,** with a wonderful mural by Jean Cocteau in one of its side chapels. For more in the way of atmosphere, head north and west from here, through Chinatown and the narrow streets of Soho. ✉ *Covent Garden* Ⓜ *Leicester Sq.*

St. Paul's Church. If you want to commune with the spirits of Vivien Leigh, Noël Coward, Edith Evans, and Charlie Chaplin, this might be just the place. Memorials to them and many other theater greats are found in this 1633 work of the renowned Inigo Jones, who, as the King's Surveyor of Works, designed the whole of Covent Garden Piazza. St. Paul's Church has been known as "the actors' church" since the Restoration, thanks to the neighboring theater district and St. Paul's prominent parishioners. (Well-known actors often read the lessons at services, and the church still hosts concerts and small-scale productions.) Fittingly, the opening scene of Shaw's *Pygmalion* takes place under its Tuscan portico. The western end of the Piazza is a prime pitch for street entertainers, but if they're not to your liking, you can repair to the serenity of the garden entered from King or Bedford street. Charming open-air theater performances of Shakespeare plays and other works are staged there in the summertime. ✉ *Bedford St., Covent Garden* ☎ *020/7836–5221* ⊕ *www.actorschurch.org* Ⓜ *Covent Garden.*

Theatre Royal, Drury Lane. This is London's best-known auditorium—popularly known simply as Drury Lane—and almost its largest. Since World War II, its forte has been musicals (from *My Fair Lady* and *South Pacific* to *Miss Saigon* and *Shrek*), although David Garrick, who managed the theater from 1747 to 1776, made its name by reviving the works of the by-then-obscure William Shakespeare. Drury Lane enjoys all the romantic accessories of a London theater: a history of fires (it burned down three times), riots (in 1737, when a posse of footmen demanded free admission), attempted regicides (George II in 1716 and his grandson George III in 1800), and even sightings of the most famous phantom of Theaterland, the Man in Grey (in the Circle during matinees). Seventy-five-minute dramatized tours, led by actors, take place daily. ✉ *Catherine St., Covent Garden* ☎ *0844/412–4660* ⊕ *www.reallyusefultheatres.co.uk* 🎫 *Tickets from £25, tours £11* Ⓜ *Covent Garden.*

BLOOMSBURY
AND HOLBORN

Getting Oriented

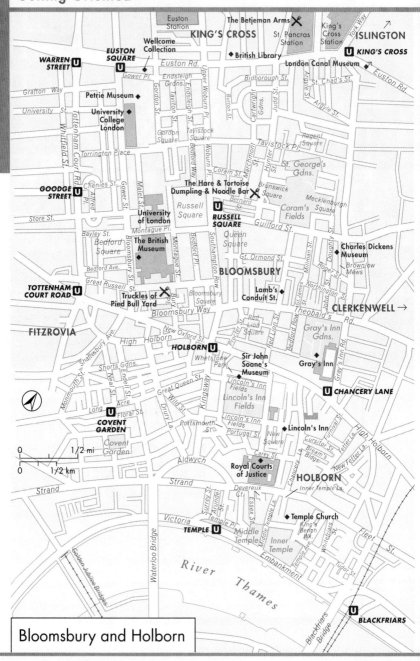

Euston
Station
KING'S CROSS
The Betjeman Arms ✕
St. Pancras
Station
King's
Cross
Station
ISLISTON
York Way
↗

WARREN
STREET U
EUSTON
SQUARE U
Wellcome
Collection
British Library
London Canal Museum ◆
King's Cross U
KING'S CROSS
Euston Rd.

Grafton Way
Gower Pl.
Euston Rd.
Endsleigh
Gdns.
Bidborough St.
St. Chad's St.
Argyle St.
Argyle St.
Judd St.

Petrie Museum ◆
Gordon St.
Endsleigh St.
Upper Woburn Pl.
Burton St.
Cartwright Gdns.

University St.
University
College
London
Gordon
Square
Tavistock
Square
Regent
Square

Whitfield St.
Tottenham Court Rd.
Torrington Place
Woburn Pl.
Bedford Way
Tavistock Pl.
St. George's
Gdns.

GOODGE
STREET U
Chenies St.
Alfred Pl.
Gower St.
Malet St.
Coram St.
Marchmont St.
Hunter St.
Brunswick
Square
Mecklenburgh Square

The Hare & Tortoise
Dumpling & Noodle Bar ✕
Russell
Square
University
of London
RUSSELL
SQUARE U
Bernard
St.
Coram's
Fields

Store St.
Bayley St.
Bedford
Square
Montague Pl.
Queen
Square
Guilford St.
Doughty St.

The British
Museum
Southampton Row
Gt. Ormond St.
Charles Dickens
Museum ◆
Brownlow
Mews

Bedford Ave.
Great Russell St.
Montague St.
BLOOMSBURY
Milman St.
Roger St.

TOTTENHAM
COURT ROAD U
Truckles of ✕
Pied Bull Yard
Bloomsbury
Square
Lamb's
Conduit St. ◆
Gt. James St.
Northington St.
CLERKENWELL →

FITZROVIA
Bloomsbury Way
High Holborn
New Oxford St.
Red
Lion
Square
Theobald's Rd.
Gray's Inn
Gdns.
Bedford Row
Gray's Inn Rd.

Shaftesbury Ave.
Shorts Gdns.
Endell St.
Whetstone
Park
HOLBORN U
Kingsway
Sir John
Soane's
Museum ◆
Gray's Inn ◆
CHANCERY LANE U

Monmouth St.
Neal St.
Great Queen St.
Wild St.
Lincoln's Inn
Fields

COVENT
GARDEN
Long Acre
Floral St.
Drury La.
Lincoln's Inn
Fields
Lincoln's Inn ◆
Furnival St.
Fetter La.
High Holborn

0   1/2 mi
0   1/2 km
Covent
Garden
Portsmouth St.
Portugal St.
New
Square
Cursitor St.
Bream's Bldgs.
Chancery La.
New Fetter La.

Aldwych
Carey St.
Royal Courts
of Justice
HOLBORN

Strand
Strand
Devereux
Ct.
Inner Temple La.
King's
Bench
Wk.

Victoria
Arundel St.
Temple Pl.
Essex St.
Temple Church ◆
Temple Ave.
Fleet St.

Waterloo Bridge
TEMPLE U
Middle
Temple
Inner
Temple
Whitefriars St.
Tudor St.

Golden Jubilee Bridges
River Thames
Blackfriars
Bridge
BLACKFRIARS U

Bloomsbury and Holborn

TOP REASONS TO GO

Take a tour of "Mankind's Attic": From the Rosetta Stone to the Elgin Marbles, the British Museum is the golden hoard of booty amassed over centuries by the British Empire.

Stroll through the Inns of Court: The quiet courts, leafy gardens, and magnificent halls that make up the heart of Holborn are the closest thing to the spirit of Oxford in London.

Time travel at Sir John Soane's Museum: Quirky and fascinating, the former home of the celebrated 19th-century architect is a treasure trove of antiquities and oddities.

View rare treasures at the British Library: In keeping with Bloomsbury's literary traditions, this repository holds the Magna Carta, a Gutenberg Bible, and Shakespeare's First Folio.

Pay your respects to Charles Dickens: The former residence of the *Oliver Twist* author is now a fascinating museum.

FEELING PECKISH?

The Betjeman Arms. Inside St. Pancras International's renovated Victorian station, this pub is the perfect place to grab a pint and some pub fare. ⊠ *Pancras Rd., Unit 53, King's Cross* ☎ *020/7923–5440* ⊕ *www.thebetjemanarms. co.uk* Ⓜ *King's Cross St. Pancras.*

The Hare and Tortoise Dumpling & Noodle Bar. This informal eatery serves scrumptious Asian fast food in huge portions at reasonable prices. ⊠ *11–13 Brunswick Shopping Centre, Brunswick Sq., Bloomsbury* ☎ *020/7278–9799* ⊕ *www.hareandtortoise.co.uk/bloomsbury* Ⓜ *Russell Sq.*

Truckles of Pied Bull Yard. The main attraction of this wine bar and café is the Georgian courtyard, where you can relax within a stone's throw of the British Museum. ⊠ *Off Bury Pl., Bloomsbury* ☎ *020/7404–5338* ⊕ *www.davy.co.uk/truckles* ۞ *Closed weekends.*

GETTING THERE

The Russell Square Tube stop on the Piccadilly line leaves you right at the corner of Russell Square.

The best Tube stops for the Inns of Court are Holborn on the Central and Piccadilly lines or Chancery Lane on the Central line.

Tottenham Court Road on the Northern and Central lines is best for the British Museum.

Once you're in Bloomsbury, you can easily get around on foot.

MAKING THE MOST OF YOUR TIME

If you plan to visit the Inns of Court as well as the British Museum, and you'd like to get a feel for the neighborhood, devote an entire day to this literary and legal enclave.

An alternative scenario is to set aside a separate day for a visit to the British Museum, which can easily consume as many hours as you have to spare.

It's a pleasure to wander through the leafy squares at your leisure, examining historic Blue Plaques or relaxing at a streetside café. The students in the neighborhood add a bit of street life.

5

Sightseeing
★★★
Nightlife
★★
Dining
★★
Lodging
★★★★
Shopping
★★

With the British Library, the British Museum, and countless colleges of the University of London among its residents, Bloomsbury might appear all bookish and cerebral—but fear not, it's much more than that. There's a youthfulness about its buzzing thoroughfares, and this vitality extends from down-by-the-Thames Holborn—once Dickens territory, now the heartbeat of legal London—way up to revamped King's Cross and classy Islington to the north, and cool Clerkenwell out east.

BLOOMSBURY

Updated by
James O'Neill

Fundamental to the region's spirit of open expression and scholarly debate is the legacy of the Bloomsbury Group, an elite corps of artists and writers who lived in this neighborhood during the first part of the 20th century. **Gordon Square** was at one point home to Virginia Woolf, John Maynard Keynes (both at No. 46), and Lytton Strachey (at No. 51). But perhaps the best-known square in Bloomsbury is the large, centrally located **Russell Square,** with its handsome gardens. Scattered around the **University of London** campus are Woburn Square, Torrington Square, and Tavistock Square. The **British Library,** with its vast treasures, is a few blocks north, across busy Euston Road.

Bloomsbury is bordered by Tottenham Court Road on the west, Euston Road on the north, Woburn Place (which becomes Southampton Row) on the east, and New Oxford Street on the south.

The area from Somerset House on the Strand, all the way up to Kingsway to the Euston Road, is known as London's **Museum Mile** for the myriad historic houses and museums that dot the area. The **Charles Dickens Museum,** in the house where the author wrote *Oliver Twist,* pays homage to the master, and artists' studios and design shops share space near the majestic **British Museum.** And guaranteed to raise a smile from the most blasé and footsore tourist is **Sir John Soane's Museum**, where the colorful collection reflects the eclectic interests of the namesake founder.

Bloomsbury's liveliness extends north to the exciting redevelopment of King's Cross, now fast becoming a cultural and culinary destination in its own right. Newly polished King's Cross merges seamlessly into upscale Islington, with its bustling streets and elegant squares. Due south of Islington, and east of Bloomsbury, don't miss out on the charms of easygoing, fashionable Clerkenwell.

TOP ATTRACTIONS

FAMILY **British Library.** With a collection totaling more than 150 million items, plus 3 million new additions every year, the British Library is a world-class repository of knowledge. Its greatest treasures are on view to the general public: the Magna Carta, the Codex Sinaiticus (an ancient bible containing the oldest complete copy of the New Testament), Jane Austen's writings, and Shakespeare's First Folio. Musical manuscripts by G.F. Handel as well as the Beatles are on display in the Sir John Ritblat Gallery. ⊠ *96 Euston Rd., Bloomsbury* ☎ *0330/333–1144* ⊕ *www.bl.uk* ✉ *Free, donations appreciated; charge for special exhibitions* Ⓜ *Euston, Euston Sq., King's Cross St. Pancras.*

KING'S CROSS STATION

Sick of living in the shadow of its sumptuously renovated next-door neighbor, St. Pancras station, King's Cross—and the area behind it—has undergone a major makeover of its own, with bars, restaurants, shops, cultural venues, and a stunning fountain display for all to enjoy. It's also a place dear to Harry Potter fans everywhere, because it was from the imaginary platform 9¾ that our hero boarded the *Hogwarts Express* (the station has helpfully put up a sign for platform 9¾ if you want to take a picture there).

Fodor's Choice ★ **The British Museum.** *See the highlighted feature in this chapter for more information.* ⊠ *Great Russell St.* ☎ *020/7323–8299* ⊕ *www.britishmuseum.org* ✉ *Free; donations encouraged.*

Charles Dickens Museum. This is one of the few London houses Charles Dickens (1812–70) inhabited that is still standing, and it's the place where the master wrote *Oliver Twist* and *Nicholas Nickleby* and finished *The Pickwick Papers.* The house looks exactly as it would have in Dickens's day, complete with first editions, letters, and a tall clerk's desk (Dickens wrote standing up). The museum also houses a shop and a garden café. ⊠ *48 Doughty St., Bloomsbury* ☎ *020/7405–2127* ⊕ *www.dickensmuseum.com* ✉ *£9* ⊘ *Closed Mon.* Ⓜ *Chancery La., Russell Sq.*

Lamb's Conduit Street. If you think Bloomsbury is about all things intellectual, then think again. Lamb's Conduit Street, a pedestrian-only street of gorgeous Georgian townhouses nestled to the east of Russell Square, is building a reputation as one of the capital's most charming—and fashionable—shopping thoroughfares. Avail yourself of what the boutiques

Continued on page 90

THE BRITISH MUSEUM

Anybody writing about the British Museum had better have a large stack of superlatives close at hand: most, biggest, earliest, finest. This is the golden hoard of nearly three centuries of the Empire, the booty brought from Britain's far-flung colonies.

The first major pieces, among them the Rosetta Stone and the Parthenon Sculptures (Elgin Marbles), were "acquired" from the French, who "found" them in Egypt and Greece. The museum has since collected countless goodies of worldwide historical significance: the Black Obelisk, some of the Dead Sea Scrolls, the Lindow Man. And that only begins the list.

The British Museum is a vast space split into 94 galleries, generally divided by continent or period of history, with some areas spanning more than one level. There are marvels wherever you go, and—while we don't like to be pessimistic—it is, yes, impossible to fully appreciate everything in a day. So make the most of the tours, activity trails, and visitors guides that are available.

The following is a highly edited overview of the museum's greatest hits, organized by area. Pick one or two that whet your appetite, then branch out from there, or spend two straight hours indulging in the company of a single favorite sculpture. There's no wrong way to experience the British Museum, just make sure you do!

✉ Great Russell St., Bloomsbury WC1

☎ 020/7323-8299

⊕ www.britishmuseum.org

🎟 Free; donations encouraged. Tickets for special exhibits vary in price.

🕐 Galleries (and Reading Room exhibition space): Sat.–Thurs. 10–5:30, Fri. 10–8:30. Great Court: Sat.–Thurs. 9–6, Fri. 9–8:30.

Ⓤ Russell Square, Holborn, Tottenham Court Rd.

(left) The Great Court
(top) *Cradle to Grave* by Pharmacopoeia

MUSEUM HIGHLIGHTS

Ancient Civilizations

The Rosetta Stone. Found in 1799 and carved in 196 BC by decree of Ptolemy V in Egyptian hieroglyphics, demotic, and Greek, it was this multilingual inscription that provided French Egyptologist Jean-François Champollion with the key to deciphering hieroglyphics. *Room 4.*

Colossal statue of Ramesses II. A member of the 19th dynasty (ca. 1270 BC), Ramesses II commissioned innumerable statues of himself—more than any other preceding or succeeding king. This one, a 7-ton likeness of his perfectly posed upper half, comes from his mortuary temple, the Ramesseum, in western Thebes. *Room 4.*

(top) Portland vase
(bottom) Colossal statue of
Ramesses II

The Parthenon Sculptures. Perhaps these marvelous treasures of Greece shouldn't be here—but while the debate rages on, you can steal your own moment with the Elgin Marbles. Carved in about 440 BC, these graceful decorations are displayed along with an in-depth, high-tech exhibit of the Acropolis; the **handless, footless Dionysus** who used to recline along its east pediment is especially well known. *Room 18.*

Mausoleum of Halikarnassos. All that remains of this, one of the Seven Wonders of the Ancient World, is a fragmented form of the original "mausoleum," the 4th-century tomb of Maussollos, King of Karia. The highlight of this gallery is the marble forepart of the **colossal chariot horse from the** *quadriga. Room 21.*

The Egyptian mummies. Another short flight of stairs takes you to the museum's most popular galleries, especially beloved by children: the Roxie Walker Galleries of Egyptian Funerary Archaeology have a fascinating collection of relics from the Egyptian realm of the dead. In addition to real corpses, wrapped mummies, and mummy cases, there's a menagerie of animal companions and curious items that were buried alongside them. *Rooms 62–63.*

Portland Vase. Made in Italy from cameo glass at the turn of the first century, it is named after the Dukes of Portland, who owned it from 1785 to 1945. It is considered a technical masterpiece—opaque white mythological figures cut by a gem-cutter are set on cobalt-blue background. *Room 70.*

The **Enlightenment Gallery** should be visited purely for the fact that its antiquarian cases hold the contents of the British Museum's first collections—Sir Hans Sloane's natural-history loot, as well as that of Sir Joseph Banks, who acquired specimens of everything from giant shells to fossils to rare plants to exotic beasts during his voyage to the Pacific aboard Captain Cook's *Endeavour.* *Room 1.*

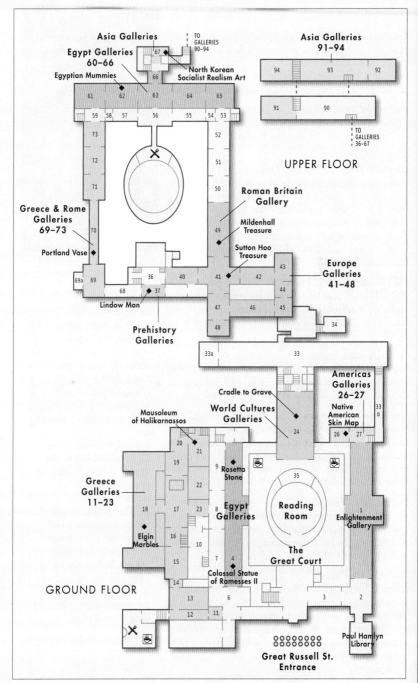

Asia Galleries

Egypt Galleries
60–66

Egyptian Mummies

TO GALLERIES 90–94

67

66

North Korean
Socialist Realism Art

Asia Galleries
91–94

94 93 92

91 90

TO GALLERIES 36–67

61 62 63 64 65

59 58 57 56 55 54 53

73

52

72

51

71

50

UPPER FLOOR

Greece & Rome
Galleries
69–73

70

Portland Vase

Roman Britain
Gallery

49

Mildenhall
Treasure

Sutton Hoo
Treasure

43

Europe
Galleries
41–48

69a 69

36 40 41 42

44

68 37

47 46 45

Lindow Man

48

34

Prehistory
Galleries

33a 33

Americas
Galleries
26–27

Cradle to Grave

World Cultures
Galleries

Native
American
Skin Map

33b

24

26 27

Mausoleum
of Halikarnassos

20

21

19

9 Rosetta
Stone

35

Greece
Galleries
11–23

22

18 17 23

Egypt
Galleries

Reading
Room

1

Enlightenment
Gallery

16

10

Elgin
Marbles

15

The
Great Court

4

14

Colossal Statue
of Ramesses II

13 6

3 2

GROUND FLOOR

12 11

Paul Hamlyn
Library

Great Russell St.
Entrance

Asia
The Korea Foundation Gallery. Delve into striking examples of **North Korean Socialist Realism art** from the 1950s to the present and a reconstruction of a **sarangbang**, a traditional scholar's study, complete with hanji paper walls and tea-making equipment. *Room 67.*

The Percival David Collection. More than 1400 pieces of Chinese ceramics (the most comprehensive collection outside China) are on display. *Room 95.*

World Cultures
The North American Gallery. This is one of the largest collections of native culture outside North America, going back to the earliest hunters 10,000 years ago. Here a 1775 **native American skin map** serves as an example of the importance of such documents in the exploration and cartography of North America. Look for the beautifully displayed **native American costumes.** *Room 26.*

The Mexican Gallery. The most alluring pieces sit in this collection side by side: a 15th-century **turquoise mask of Xiuhtecuhtli,** the Mexican Fire God and Turquoise Lord, and a **double-headed serpent** from the same period. *Room 27.*

Britain and Europe
The Mildenhall Treasure. This glittering haul of 4th-century Roman silver tableware was found beneath the sod of a Suffolk field in 1942. *Room 49.*

The Sutton Hoo Treasure. Next door to the loot from Mildenhall—and equally splendid, including brooches, swords, and jewel-encrusted helmets—the treasure was buried at sea with (it is thought) Redwald, one of the first English kings, in the 7th century, and excavated from a Suffolk field in 1938–39. *Room 41.*

Lindow Man. "Pete Marsh"—so named by the archaeologists who unearthed the body from a Cheshire peat marsh—was ritually slain, probably as a human sacrifice, in the 1st century and lay perfectly pickled in his bog until 1984. *Room 50.*

Theme Galleries
Living & Dying. The "Cradle to Grave" installation pays homage to the British nation's wellbeing—or ill-being, as it were. More than 14,000 drugs (the number estimated to be prescribed to every person in the U.K. in his lifetime) are displayed in a colorful tapestry of pills and tablets. *Room 24.*

Colossal chariot horse from the *quadriga* of the Mausoleum at Halikarnassos

LOWER GALLERY
The three rooms that comprise the **Sainsbury African Galleries** are of the main interest here: together they present a staggering 200,000 objects, featuring intricate pieces of old ivory, gold, and wooden masks and carvings—highlighting such ancient kingdoms as the Benin and Asante. The displays include a collection of **55 throwing knives**; ceremonial garments including a dazzling pink and green **woman's coif** (*qufiya*) from Tunisia made of silk, metal, and cotton; and the *Oxford Man*, a 1992 woodcarving by Owen Ndou, depicting a man of ambiguous race clutching his Book of Knowledge.

DID YOU KNOW?

Galleries help divide this
sprawling space into
manageable sizes for visitors.
The Sainsbury African
Galleries are just some of
the 94 galleries; the British
Museum's collection totals
more than 7 million objects.

THE NATION'S ATTIC: A HISTORY OF THE MUSEUM

The collection began when Sir Hans Sloane, physician to Queen Anne and George II, bequeathed his personal collection of curiosities and antiquities to the nation. The collection quickly grew, thanks to enthusiastic kleptomaniacs after the Napoleonic Wars—most notoriously the seventh Earl of Elgin, who obtained the marbles from the Parthenon and Erechtheion on the Acropolis in Athens during his term as British ambassador in Constantinople.

Soon thereafter, it seemed everyone had something to donate—George II gave the old Royal Library, Sir William Hamilton gave antique vases, Charles Townley gave sculptures, the Bank of England gave coins. When the first exhibition galleries opened to visitors in 1759, the trustees agreed to admit only small groups guided by curators. The British Museum quickly became one of the most fashionable places to be seen in the capital, and tickets, which had to be booked in advance, were treated like gold dust.

The museum's holdings quickly outgrew their original space in Montague House. After the addition of such major pieces as the Rosetta Stone and other Egyptian antiquities (spoils of the Napoleonic War) and the Parthenon sculptures, Robert Smirke was commissioned to build an appropriately large and monumental building on the same site. It's still a hot ticket: the British Museum now receives more than 6 million visitors every year.

THE GREAT COURT & THE READING ROOM

The museum's classical Greek-style facade features figures representing the progress of civilization, and the focal point is the awesome Great Court, a massive glass-roofed space. Here is the museum's inner courtyard (now the largest covered square in Europe) that, for more than 150 years, had been used for storage.

The 19th-century Reading Room, an impressive 106-foot-high blue-and-gold-domed library, forms the centerpiece of the Great Court. H.G. Wells, Thomas Hardy, Lord Tennyson, Oscar Wilde, George Orwell, T.S. Elliot, and Beatrix Potter are just a few writers who have used this space as a literary and academic sanctuary over the past 150 years or so.

(above) Reading Room

PLANNING YOUR VISIT

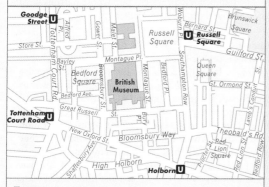

Tours

The **30–40 minute eyeOpener tour (free)** by Museum Guides does just what it says; ask for details at the information desk. After this tour, you can then dip back into the collections that most captured your imagination at your leisure.

An excellent **multimedia guide** is a good way to explore the galleries at your own pace, via a series of differently-themed tours.

Alternatively, the **Visitor's Guide** gives a brief but informative overview of the museum's history and is, again, divided into self-guided themed tours.

Before you go, take a look at the online **COMPASS tour** using the museum's navigation tool (www.thebritishmuseum.org/compass), which allows users to browse past and present exhibits as well as search for specific objects. A children's version can also be found here. Computer stations in the Reading Room offer onsite access to COMPASS.

■ **TIP→** The closest underground station to the British Museum is Russell Square on the Piccadilly line. However, since you will be entering via the back entrance on Montague Place, you will not experience the full impact of the museum's grand facade. To do so, alight at Holborn on the Central and Piccadilly lines or Tottenham Court Road on the Central and Northern lines. The walk from these stations is about 10 minutes.

WITH KIDS

■ Take a look at the "Family Visits" page online for the top 12 objects to see with children.

■ The Families Desk in the Great Court has trails for kids ages 3 to 5 and 6 to 11. The Ford Centre for Young Visitors has free activity backpacks.

■ Art materials are available for free from information points, where you can also find out about workshops, performances, storytelling sessions, and other free events.

■ Around the museum, there are Hands On desks open daily 11–4, which let visitors handle objects from the collections.

WHERE TO REFUEL

The British Museum's self-service **Gallery Café** gets very crowded but serves an acceptable menu beneath a plaster cast of a part of the Parthenon frieze that Lord Elgin didn't remove. It's open daily, but isn't particularly family friendly.

The **café in the Great Court** keeps longer hours and is a great place to people-watch and admire the spectacular glass roof while you eat your salad and sandwich.

If the weather is nice, exit the museum via the back entrance on Montague Place and amble over to **Russell Square,** which has grassy lawns, water fountains, and a glass-fronted café for post-sandwich coffee and ice cream.

have to offer, from fashion to ceramics, books to jewelry, fine art to flowers; there's even an excellent run-by-locals food cooperative called the People's Supermarket. Alternatively, you could just window-shop your way down to **The Lamb,** a Victorian-era pub whose patrons have included Ted Hughes, Sylvia Plath, and Mr. Dickens himself. ⊠ *Bloomsbury* Ⓜ *Russell Sq.*

Fodor's Choice **Sir John Soane's Museum.** Sir John (1753–1837), architect of the Bank of
★ England, bequeathed his eccentric house to the nation on one condition: that nothing be changed. It's a house full of surprises. In the Picture Room, two of Hogarth's famous *Rake's Progress* paintings swing away to reveal secret gallery recesses where you can find works by Canaletto and Turner. Everywhere, mirrors play tricks with light and space, and split-level floors worthy of a fairground funhouse disorient you. Restoration work has opened up Soane's private apartments to the public, but they can be viewed only as part of a first-come, first-served tour at 1 and 2 pm, daily. ⊠ *13 Lincoln's Inn Fields, Bloomsbury* ☎ *020/7405–2107* ⊕ *www. soane.org* ✉ *Free; guided tours £10* ⊗ *Closed Sun. and Mon.* Ⓜ *Holborn.*

WORTH NOTING

OFF THE BEATEN PATH **London Canal Museum.** This quirky museum, dedicated to the rise and fall of London's once-extensive canal network, is based in the former warehouse of ice-cream maker Carlo Gatti (hence it also partly features the ice-cream trade as well as London's canals). Children enjoy the activity zone and learning about Henrietta, the museum's horse. Outside, on the Battlebridge Basin, you'll find the painted narrowboats of modern canal dwellers—a stone's throw from the hustle and bustle of the King's Cross redevelopment. You can walk to the museum along the towpath from Camden Lock; download a free audio tour from the museum's website to accompany the route. ⊠ *12–13 New Wharf Rd., King's Cross* ☎ *020/7713–0836* ⊕ *www.canalmuseum.org.uk* ✉ *£5* ⊗ *Closed Mon.* Ⓜ *King's Cross.*

Petrie Museum. If you don't get your fill of Egyptian artifacts at the British Museum, you can see more in the neighboring Petrie Museum, located on the first floor of the DMS Watson library. The museum houses an outstanding collection of Egyptian and Sudanese archaeological objects, including jewelry, toys, and some of the world's oldest garments. ⊠ *Malet Pl., Bloomsbury* ☎ *020/7679–2884* ⊕ *www.ucl. ac.uk/museums/petrie* ✉ *Free, donations appreciated* ⊗ *Closed Sun. and Mon.* Ⓜ *Euston Sq., Goodge St.*

University College London. Founded in 1826 the college is set in a classical edifice designed by the architect of the National Gallery, William Wilkins. Committed to providing higher education without religious exclusion, in 1878 it also became the first British University to accept women on an equal footing with men. The college has within its portals the **Slade School of Fine Art,** which did for many of Britain's artists what the nearby Royal Academy of Dramatic Art (on Gower Street) did for actors. The South Cloisters contain one of London's weirder treasures: the skeleton of one of the university's founders, Jeremy Bentham, who bequeathed himself to the college. ⊠ *Malet Pl., Bloomsbury* Ⓜ *Euston Sq., Goodge St.*

Wellcome Collection. If you fancy something quirky, sample this collection by U.S. pharmaceutical millionaire and philanthropist Henry Wellcome (1853–1936). Styled as "the free destination for the incurably curious," this museum explores the connections between medicine, life, and art (some exhibits may not be suitable for younger children). Comprising an estimated 1 million items, the collection includes Napoléon's toothbrush, Horatio Nelson's razor, and Charles Darwin's walking stick. There are also anatomical models, Peruvian mummies, and Japanese sex aids as well as two permanent exhibitions to inspire debate, Medicine Man and Medicine Now. Watch out for original art works in the lobby by Picasso (just above the entrance when you come in) and Anthony Gormley. ⊠ *183 Euston Rd., Bloomsbury* ☎ *020/7611–2222* ⊕ *www.wellcomecollection.org* 🗺 *Free* ☉ *Closed Mon.* Ⓜ *Euston Sq., Euston.*

HOLBORN

5

Southeast of Bloomsbury and west of The City, Holborn may appear to be little more than a buffer zone between the two—but although it may lack the panache of its neighbors, don't underestimate this varied slice of the capital. Home to legal London and the impressive Inns of Court, this is also Charles Dickens territory, with the Old Curiosity Shop snug within its borders and the Dickens museum close by. Add to that its fair share of churches and quirky places of interest, and you'll soon discover that Holborn can be a rewarding place to while away an hour or three. Holborn's massive Gothic-style **Royal Courts of Justice** ramble all the way to the Strand, and the **Inns of Court**—Gray's Inn, Lincoln's Inn, Middle Temple, and Inner Temple—are where most British trial lawyers have offices to this day. Geographically, Holborn's borders are probably best defined as: west, Kingsway; north, Theobald's Road; east, Gray's Inn Road; south, where the Strand becomes Fleet Street.

WORTH NOTING

Gray's Inn. Although the least architecturally interesting of the four Inns of Court and the one most heavily damaged by German bombs in the 1940s, Gray's still has romantic associations. In 1594 Shakespeare's *Comedy of Errors* was performed for the first time in the hall, which was restored after World War II and has a fine Elizabethan screen of carved oak. You must make advance arrangements to view the hall, but the secluded and spacious gardens, first planted by Francis Bacon in 1597, are open to the public. The four Inns of the Court—Gray's Inn, Lincoln's Inn, Middle Temple, and Inner Temple—are where most British trial lawyers have offices to this day. In the 14th century, the inns were lodging houses where barristers lived so that people would know how to easily find them (hence, the label "inn"). ⊠ *Gray's Inn Rd., Holborn* ☎ *020/7458–7800* ⊕ *www.graysinn.org.uk* 🗺 *Free* ☉ *Closed weekends* Ⓜ *Holborn, Chancery La.*

Lincoln's Inn. There's plenty to see at one of the oldest, best preserved, and most attractive of the Inns of Court—from the Chancery Lane Tudor brick gatehouse to the wide-open, tree-lined, atmospheric Lincoln's Inn Fields and the 15th-century chapel remodeled by Inigo Jones in 1620. The chapel and the gardens are open to the public, but to see more you must reserve a place on one of the official tours. But be warned: they tend to prefer group bookings of 15 or more, so it's best to check the website or call for details. ⊠ *Chancery La., Holborn* ☎ *020/7405–1393* ⊕ *www.lincolnsinn.org.uk* ⊠ *Free* ☉ *Closed weekends and Aug.* Ⓜ *Chancery La.*

Royal Courts of Justice. Here is the vast Victorian Gothic pile of 35 million bricks containing the nation's principal law courts, with 1,000-odd rooms running off 3½ miles of corridors. This is where the most important civil law cases—that's everything from divorce to fraud, with libel in between—are heard. You can sit in the viewing gallery to watch any trial you like, for a live version of Court TV; the more dramatic criminal cases are heard at the Old Bailey. Other sights are the 238-foot-long main hall and the compact exhibition of judges' robes. Guided tours must be booked in advance. ⊠ *The Strand, Holborn* ☎ *020/7947–6000* ⊕ *www.theroyalcourtsofjustice.com* ⊠ *Free, tours £13* ☉ *Closed weekends* Ⓜ *Temple, Holborn, Chancery La.*

Temple Church. As featured in *The Da Vinci Code*, this church was built by the Knights Templar in the late 12th century. The Red Knights held their secret initiation rites in the crypt here. Having started poor, holy, and dedicated to the protection of pilgrims, they grew rich from showers of royal gifts until, in the 14th century, they were stripped of their wealth, charged with blasphemy and sodomy, and thrown into the Tower. ⊠ *King's Bench Walk, The Temple, Holborn* ☎ *020/7353–3470* ⊕ *www.templechurch.com* ⊠ *£5* ☉ *Closed weekends* Ⓜ *Temple.*

ISLINGTON

Islington is one of the most fashionable of London's villagelike neighborhoods. Upper Street, with its high-street stores, independent boutiques, and myriad restaurants and bars, is where most of the action takes place. But wander off the main drag and you'll discover elegant residential streets and squares, as well as bustling charming markets. You'll also find a handful of top-flight Off West End theaters and music venues in the area, including the Almeida, the hugely atmospheric Union Chapel, and—down on Islington's border with Clerkenwell—the renowned contemporary dance venue, Sadler's Wells.

Camden Passage. A pretty pedestrian thoroughfare just off Upper Street, Camden Passage is famous for its many antiques shops selling everything from vintage furniture to period jewelry to timeless timepieces. In recent years, a sprinkling of independent boutiques, delis, and cafés has given the passage an eclectic, vibrant feel. Check out the antiques market held on Wednesday and Saturday. ⊠ *Islington* ⊕ *www.camdenpassageislington.co.uk* Ⓜ *The Angel.*

Chapel Market. Chapel Market is what Islington used to be: an unpretentious, working-class enclave. There's a lively food market that runs for half the length of the street every day except Monday—just listening to the stallholders advertising their wares can be entertainment enough. Although trendy eateries are beginning to pop up here and there, it is still home to London's oldest eel, pie, and mash shop, Manze's, with its marble tables and tiled interior largely untouched since it was established in 1902. ⊠ *Chapel Market, Islington* Ⓜ *The Angel.*

KING'S CROSS

What a difference a decade makes; until recently, King's Cross was a byword for sleaze and street crime, but after a multibillion-pound redevelopment—actually, make that transformation—it's become a lively urban quarter. On what was once postindustrial wasteland and railroad yards, the 67-acre site is now home to bars, restaurants, street-food vendors, and shops. What's more, with the capital's premier art college, the University of the Arts in London, having relocated to Granary Square, alongside a raft of cultural venues, this spot now has a certain air of artistic credibility about it, too. If all that weren't enough, by courtesy of the Regent's Canal, this bustling quarter even has the occasional peaceful oasis of calm as well.

FAMILY **Camley Street Natural Park.** These 2 acres of splendid calm are bang in the middle of the King's Cross hustle and bustle. This urban nature reserve, just across the road from the concrete and glass of the Eurostar terminal, provides a habitat for birds, butterflies, bats, and a wide variety of plant and pond life. It's a delightful gem that's popular with schoolchildren and office workers on lunch break, but chances are you could have the whole place pretty much to yourself. ⊠ *12 Camley St., King's Cross* ☏ *020/3897–6150* ⊕ *www.wildlondon.org.uk/reserves/camley-street-natural-park* ⊡ *Free* Ⓜ *King's Cross St. Pancras.*

Granary Square. The heart of the new King's Cross, Granary Square is one of London's liveliest open spaces. Pride of place is given to the ever-changing 1,000-strong fountain display, which is even more spectacular by night when lights accompany the choreography. The immense, six-story granary building—designed in 1852 to store wheat for London's bakers—has been renovated to house the University of the Arts in London, as well as a selection of excellent eateries. The square's south-facing steps double as an amphitheater for site-specific arts events; at times, the steps themselves become the installation—such as when they're covered with carved pumpkins at Halloween or a blanket of flowers in spring. ⊠ *King's Cross* Ⓜ *King's Cross St. Pancras.*

CLERKENWELL

Once home to medieval religious orders such as the Knights of the Hospitallers of St. John of Jerusalem, Clerkenwell later became an epicenter of the industrial revolution in the capital and, subsequently, of political radicalism (a young Joseph Stalin is said to have met a young Vladimir

Lenin at the Crown Tavern pub in Clerkenwell Green). The monks are long gone—so, too, the communists—and the neighborhood's warehouses and factory floors are now home to cutting-edge design agencies, new media start-ups, and ubertrendy apartments. With its fashionable boutiques, bars, and restaurants, Clerkenwell can be a pleasant place to spend a few hours. Like its neighbor immediately to the east, the City of London, this area can be quite deserted on weekends.

Exmouth Market. At this charming pedestrianized thoroughfare, trendy clothing stores, bookshops, jewelers, gift shops, and even a tattoo parlor all jostle for space with Exmouth Market's excellent cafés and restaurants, many of which offer outdoor seating. At its southern end is the 19th-century Church of Our Most Holy Redeemer, the only Italian basilica–style church in London. There's a vibrant food market on weekdays serving gourmet street food. ⊠ *Exmouth St., Clerkenwell* ⊕ *www.exmouth.london* Ⓜ *Farringdon, The Angel.*

Museum of the Order of St. John. This fascinating museum tells the story of the Knights Hospitallers of St. John, from the Order's 11th-century Crusader origins in Jerusalem to its present-day incarnation as the St. John Ambulance service. The museum is spread across two adjacent sites: the arched St. John's Gatehouse, which dates back to 1504, and the Priory Church with its atmospheric Norman crypt. An excellent interactive display explores the Order's past, both as a military force and a religious institution that cared for sick pilgrims, and the eclectic variety of objects on display reflects that colorful history: from antique medicinal jars and medical equipment to pieces of armor worn by the Knights when they defended Malta from the Ottomans in the 16th century, as well as a bronze cannon given by Henry VIII before he dissolved the Order altogether a few years later. ⊠ *St. John's Gate, St. John's La., Clerkenwell* ☎ *020/7324–4005* ⊕ *www.museumstjohn. org.uk* ⊠ *Free, guided tours £5 (suggested donation)* ⊘ *Closed Sun. Oct.–June* Ⓜ *Farringdon.*

FITZROVIA

To the north of Soho, on the other side of Oxford Street, is Fitzrovia, famed for its dining and drinking. It is known affectionately by some as "Noho." Like its brasher southern sibling, it has some excellent bars and restaurants (especially on Charlotte Street) but more breathing space and fewer crowds. Its name most likely derives from nearby Fitzroy Square. Originally designed by the Adam brothers, the square and its environs quickly became fashionable for haute bohemia; George Bernard Shaw and James McNeil Whistler lived here. To the west, Great Portland Street separates it from Marylebone, while Tottenham Court Road marks its eastern border, beyond which is Bloomsbury. Busy Euston Road (and the Circle Line beneath it) is its northern extent.

THE CITY

Getting Oriented

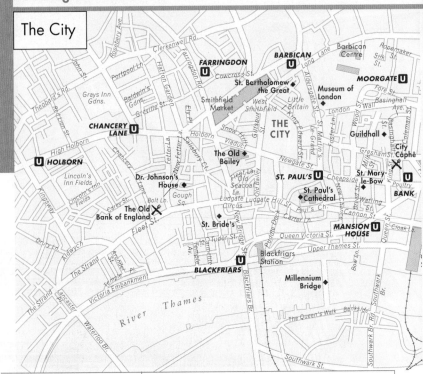

The City

GETTING THERE	TOP REASONS TO GO
The City is well served by a concentration of Tube stations—St. Paul's and Bank on the Central line, and Mansion House, Cannon Street, and Monument on the District and Circle lines. Liverpool Street and Aldgate border The City's eastern edge, while Chancery Lane and Farringdon lie to the west. Barbican and Moorgate provide easy access to the theaters and galleries of the Barbican, and Blackfriars, to the south, leads to Ludgate Circus and Fleet Street.	**St. Paul's Cathedral, the "Symbolic Heart of London":** Although the Cathedral is increasingly surrounded by skyscrapers, the beauty of Sir Christopher Wren's 17th-century masterpiece nevertheless remains undiminished.

Linger on the Millennium Bridge: Travel from past to present on this promenade between St. Paul's and Tate Modern—and get a great river view, too.

Treachery and treasures at the Tower: This complex filled with atmospheric towers is bursting at the seams with history, pageantry, and the stunning Crown Jewels.

Channel history at the Museum of London: From skimpy leather briefs dating to Roman times and Queen Victoria's crinolines to Selfridges's art deco elevators and a diorama of the Great Fire (including sound effects and flickering flames), this gem of a museum has got it all. |

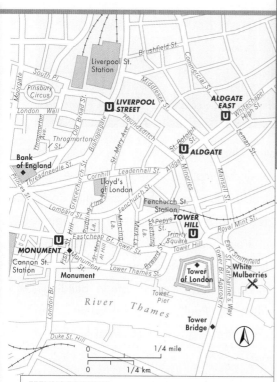

MAKING THE MOST OF YOUR TIME

The City is also known as the "Square Mile," which hints at how compact it is with little distance between points of interest. This means you can pack a lot of sightseeing into one afternoon. For full immersion in the Tower of London, however, set aside half a day, especially if seeing the Crown Jewels is a priority. Allow an hour minimum each for the Museum of London, St. Paul's Cathedral, and Tower Bridge. On weekends, without the workers who make up 90% of the daytime population, The City is nearly deserted and many affordable lunch places are closed—and yet this is when the major attractions are at their busiest.

A GOOD WALK

Crossing the Millennium Bridge from Tate Modern to St. Paul's is one of the finest walks in London—with the river to either side and Christopher Wren's iconic dome gleaming at one end.

FEELING PECKISH?

City Càphê. This unpretentious but charming Vietnamese street-food café offers delicious quick bites and take-out dishes for lunch. Try the pho, banh mi, or spring rolls. ⊠ *17 Ironmonger La., City of London* ⊕ *www.citycaphe.com* ⊘ *Closed weekends* Ⓜ *Mansion House, Bank.*

The Old Bank of England. The appeal of this former bank-turned-pub next to the Royal Courts of Justice on Fleet Street is in the grand setting rather than the food, although the homemade pies are well worth trying. Don't be put off by the plaque connecting the site to Sweeney Todd's barber-shop—he actually operated in a different part of Fleet Street. ⊠ *194 Fleet St., City of London* ☎ *020/7430–2255* ⊕ *www.oldbankofengland.co.uk* Ⓜ *Temple.*

White Mulberries. This friendly coffee shop at St. Katharine Docks serves outstanding coffee, along with fresh juices, tasty cakes, and light bites. ⊠ *D3 Ivory House, St. Katharine Docks, City of London* ☎ *07507/572–600* ⊕ *www.whitemulberries.com* Ⓜ *Tower Hill, Tower Gateway (DLR).*

Sightseeing
★★★★★
Nightlife
★
Dining
★★★
Lodging
★
Shopping
★★★

The capital's fast-beating financial heart, The City is associated with power and pomp, embodied in the three institutions at its epicenter: the Bank of England, the Royal Exchange, and Mansion House. The site of the original Roman settlement from which all of London grew, the "Square Mile" has statement skyscrapers cheek-by-jowl with some of London's most iconic historic buildings, from Wren's uplifting St. Paul's Cathedral to the Tower of London, a royal fortress, prison, and jewel house surrounded by a moat.

Updated by
Ellin Stein

Home to both the latest financial high-tech and the descendants of medieval guilds, The City is where the historic past and fast-moving present collide. Begin your explorations on **Fleet Street,** the site of England's first printing press and the undisputed seat of British journalism until the 1980s. Nestled behind Fleet Street is **Dr. Johnson's House,** where the noted lexicographer, famous for asserting "when a man is tired of London, he is tired of life," compiled the original *Dictionary of the English Language.* Nearby **St. Bride's,** a Wren gem recognizable by its tiered-wedding-cake steeple, is still known as "the journalists' church" while to the east is Wren's masterpiece of the English Baroque, **St. Paul's Cathedral.** Legacies of London's past are everywhere: at the **Central Criminal Court,** better known as The Old Bailey (and in its various incarnations, the venue for many of London's most notorious criminal trials); the soaring Victorian **Smithfield Market,** built on a site where livestock has been sold since the 14th century and where a dusk-to-dawn wholesale meat market—the largest in Britain—still operates; the Romanesque church **St. Bartholomew the Great** and next to it **St. Bartholomew Hospital,** both begun in 1123 at the eastern end of Smithfield; the **Guildhall,** from whose Gothic Great Hall The City was governed and where you can see recently excavated remains of the only Roman amphitheater in London; the church of **St. Mary-le-Bow,** home of the "Bow Bells," of which true Cockneys are supposedly born within earshot of; and the maze of charmingly old-fashioned, narrow streets around **Bow Lane.**

To the south, is the **Monument,** another Wren edifice begun in 1671 to commemorate the Great Fire of London five years earlier, while farther east is the historically rich **Tower of London,** that clocks in at over a thousand years old. Looking towards the river, you'll immediately spot the Victorian Gothic **Tower Bridge,** one of London's most recognizable landmarks. You can put all this history into context at the **Museum of London,** where the archaeological displays include a segment of the **Roman Wall** that ringed the city when it was known to Romans as "Londinium."

The City is also home to some of London's most distinctive contemporary architecture. To the north of Smithfield is the **Barbican Centre,** a Brutalist concrete complex of arts venues and apartments that was controversial when it was built between 1965 and 1976, but has since become an indispensable part of the London streetscape. A plethora of distinctive new structures now tower over The City, not all of which are popular; bold designs such as **20 Fenchurch Street** (aka The Walkie Talkie) and the **Swiss Re Tower** (The Gherkin) are almost as contentious today as the Barbican was 40 years ago (but several have top-floor restaurants, where you can take in superb views). They all add to the mix in this constantly evolving area, and whenever you return—whether in months or years—The City is guaranteed not to be the same as when you saw it last.

TOP ATTRACTIONS

Monument. Designed by Sir Christopher Wren and Dr. Robert Hooke to commemorate 1666's "dreadful visitation" of the Great Fire of London (note the gilded orb of flame at the column's pinnacle), the world's tallest isolated stone column offers spectacular views of the city from the viewing platform at the top. The two architects were asked to erect the monument as close as possible to where the fire began, and so it's located exactly 202 feet from the alleged point of origin, Farrier's baking house on Pudding Lane. The monument also stands 202 feet tall, so if climbing the 311 steps of the beautiful spiral staircase to the top seems too arduous, you can watch a live view from the platform played on a screen at the entrance. ✉ *Monument St., City of London* ☎ *020/7403–3761* ⊕ *www.themonument.info* ⛁ *£5, combined ticket with Tower Bridge £11* Ⓜ *Monument.*

FAMILY
Fodor's Choice
★

Museum of London. This fascinating museum reveals London in its many incarnations, from its first days as a Roman settlement around 50 AD (and even before, with finds going back to 450,000 BC) up to the present. The more than 7,000 objects encompass everything from Queen Victoria's crinolines and Selfridges's original art deco elevators to grim Georgian iron doors from the city's infamous Newgate Prison and Thomas Heatherwick's cauldron from the 2012 London Olympics. Permanent galleries are devoted to nearly every era of English history, including the current globalized megalopolis period. The Roman London collection contains some extraordinary gems, including an

A BRIEF HISTORY

Although there is evidence of scattered Celtic rural settlements on the north bank of the Thames, London truly begins with the Romans, who established an outpost of the empire called Londinium (which was about the size of Hyde Park) in 47 AD. In 60 AD, the warrior queen Boudicca led an uprising of the native Iceni, burning the city to the ground, but the Romans soon regained control, adding a defensive wall. Not much is known of what happened to the city after the Romans left in the 5th century (while England as a whole suffered successive invasions by the Angles, Saxons, Jutes, and Vikings), beyond the establishment of a 7th-century cathedral dedicated to Saint Paul (the famous one now stands on the same site). After the Norman invasion of 1066 and William the Conqueror's building of the fortress-cum-castle that became known as the Tower of London, the city started to prosper again within those old Roman walls. By the early 13th century, King John acknowledged the city's importance by granting it the right to elect a Lord Mayor. During the Middle Ages, powerful guilds took root that helped nurture commerce, and in the Tudor era, London became the center of both government and trade, reaching a population of some 200,000 people.

Dockyards were built to service the British ships that plied lucrative new trade routes, both to the New World and India, laying the foundations for London's role as the world's premier city for the next three centuries.

After the Restoration of 1660, London immediately faced two disasters: the Great Plague of 1665, which killed almost a quarter of the city's population, and then, in 1666, the Great Fire, which destroyed most of its old medieval wood structures. However, the reconstruction gave rise to buildings created by one of Britain's greatest architects, Sir Christopher Wren. He, along with John Nash in the 18th century, gave shape to much of the city we see today. Subequent Regency and Victorian expansion created the characteristic look of new neighbor-hoods to the west and north like Kensington, Notting Hill, Camden, and Hampstead. Another disaster befell London, particularly in the East End and The City, when Luftwaffe bombs rained down relentlessly during World War II (a destruc-tion equalled by, some argue, the unimaginative urban planners of the 1960s and 1970s). However, as the plethora of shiny new skyscrapers attest, the capacity for reinvention that has enabled this city to thrive for 2,000 years remains undimmed.

astonishingly well-preserved floor mosaic uncovered just a few streets away; don't miss the extraordinary Bronze Age and Roman artifacts unearthed during construction of the new Crossrail underground railway. There are also themed temporary exhibitions, often future-oriented with an interactive element. Visit the website to download the fascinating Street Museum app, which allows you to use your phone to see how any street you're on would have looked in the past. ⊠ *London Wall, City of London* ☎ *020/7001–9844* ⊕ *www.museumoflondon.org.uk* ☜ *Free* Ⓜ *Barbican, St. Paul's.*

Walking over the Millennium Bridge takes you to St. Paul's Cathedral, the Sir Christopher Wren–designed masterpiece that is one of the most beautiful cathedrals in England.

Fodor's Choice
★

St. Paul's Cathedral. For centuries this iconic structure has represented London's spirit of survival and renewal, and it remains a breathtaking structure, inside and out. Sir Christopher Wren started planning the current cathedral in 1666, immediately after the previous medieval building was destroyed in the Great Fire, hence the word "resurgam" ("I shall rise again") inscribed on the pediment of the south door. St. Paul's again became a symbol of the city's resilience during the Blitz, when local volunteers risked death to put out a blaze on the dome. It has often been the scene of great State occasions, such as Winston Churchill's funeral and the wedding of Prince Charles and Princess Diana.

Construction started in 1675 and took 35 years to finish. It was actually Wren's third design: the first was rejected for being too modern; the second for being too modern *and* too Italian, that is, Catholic (you can see the 20-foot "Great Model" of this design in the Crypt). Despite mollifying the Anglican clergy with the promise of a traditional English spire, Wren installed a neoclassical triple-layered dome, the second largest cathedral dome in the world after St. Peter's in Rome.

The interior is a superb example of the English Baroque. Climb 257 steps up the Geometric Staircase, a perfectly engineered stone spiral, to the Whispering Gallery, so named because a whisper against one wall can be heard on the wall 112 feet opposite. Another 119 steps up is the Stone Gallery, which encircles the exterior of the dome and provides panoramic views over London. If you have a head for heights, tackle another 152 steps to the small Golden Gallery, an observation platform at the dome's highest point. At 280 feet above the Cathedral floor, it offers even more spectacular vistas. Back on the ground, in the south choir aisle, you'll find the grave of John Donne, the poet who was Dean of St. Paul's from 1621 until his death in 1631. His marble effigy is the oldest memorial in the cathedral and one of the few to survive the Great Fire. The intricate, lively figures on the choir-stall nearby are the work of master carver Grinling Gibbons, who also embellished the Wren-designed great organ. Behind the high altar is the American Memorial Chapel, dedicated to the 28,000 American GIs stationed in the United Kingdom during World War II. Among the notables buried in the Crypt are the Duke of Wellington, Admiral Lord Nelson, Sir Joshua Reynolds, Henry Moore, and Wren himself. The Latin epitaph above his tomb fittingly reads, "Reader, if you seek his monument, look around you."

Free, introductory 20-minute talks are offered regularly throughout the day. Free 90-minute guided tours take place Monday through Saturday at 10, 11, 1, and 2; reserve a place at the welcome desk when you arrive. An hour-long tour of the Triforium (the three upper galleries) is available on some Mondays, Tuesdays, and Fridays at 11:30 or 2, but booking at least two working days in advance is required; call or see website for details. ■ TIP→ Save £2 per ticket and get fast-track entry by booking online. ⊠ *St. Paul's Churchyard, City of London* ☎ *020/7246–8350, 020/7246–8357 for Triforium tours* ⊕ *www.stpauls.co.uk* ⊠ *£18; Triforium tours £8* ⊙ *Closed Sun. except for services* Ⓜ *St. Paul's.*

Tower Bridge. Despite its medieval appearance, London's most iconic bridge was actually built at the tail end of the Victorian era in the then-popular neo-Gothic style, first opening to traffic in 1894. With a latticed steel construction clad in Portland stone, the bridge is famous for its enormous bascules—the 1,000-ton "arms" that open to allow ships taller than its normal 28-foot clearance to glide beneath. The steam-powered bascules were a marvel of Victorian engineering when they were created (you can still visit the Engine Room, now with explanatory films and interactive displays), and required 80 people to raise and lower. Initially, heavy river traffic meant this happened 20 to 30 times a day, but it's now reduced to just a few times per month (see the bridge's website for a schedule).

The family-friendly **Tower Bridge Exhibition** includes the ground-level Engine Room, displays in the North Tower documenting the bridge's history, access to the east and west walkways that run alongside the road between the turrets and provide views over the river and city, and for those untroubled by vertigo, a transparent walkway 138 feet up between the towers that lets you look down on the traffic or, if the bascules are raised, the ships below. ⊠ *Tower Bridge Rd., City of London* ☎ *020/7403–3761* ⊕ *www.towerbridge.org.uk* ⊠ *£10; joint admission with Monument £12* Ⓜ *Tower Hill.*

Fodor's Choice   **Tower of London.** *See the highlighted feature in this chapter for more infor-*
★   *mation.* ⊠ *Tower Hill* ☎ *020/3166–6000* ⊕ *www.hrp.org.uk* ⊠ *£24.80*

Continued on page 112

THE TOWER OF LONDON

The Tower is a microcosm of the city itself—a sprawling, organic hodgepodge of buildings that inspires reverence and terror in equal measure. See the block on which Anne Boleyn was beheaded, marvel at the Crown Jewels, and pay homage to the ravens who keep the monarchy safe.

An architectural patchwork of time, the oldest building of the complex is the fairytale White Tower, conceived by William the Conqueror in 1078 as both a royal residence and a show of power to the troublesome Anglo-Saxons he had subdued at the Battle of Hastings. Today's Tower has seen everything, as a palace, barracks, a mint for producing coins, an armoury, and the Royal menagerie (home of the country's first elephant). The big draw is the stunning opulence of the Crown Jewels, kept on-site in the heavily fortified Jewel House. Most of all, though, the Tower is known for death: it's been a place of imprisonment, torture, and execution for the realm's most notorious traitors as well as its martyrs. These days, unless you count the killer admission fees, there are far less morbid activities taking place in the Tower, but it still breathes London's history and pageantry from its every brick and offers hours of exploration.

TOURING THE TOWER

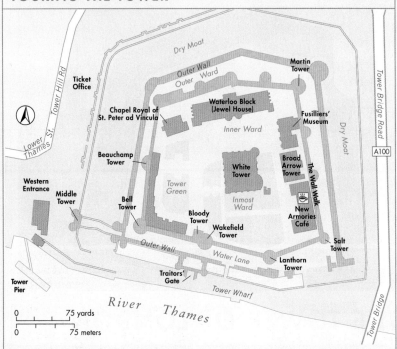

Entry to the Tower is via the **Western Entrance** and the **Middle Tower,** which feed into the outermost ring of the Tower's defenses.

Water Lane leads past the dread-inducing **Traitors' Gate,** the final point of entry for many Tower prisoners.

Toward the end of Water Lane, the **Lanthorn Tower** houses by night the ravens rumored to keep the kingdom safe, and by day a timely high-tech reconstruction of the Catholic Guy Fawkes's plot to blow up the Houses of Parliament in 1605.

The **Bloody Tower** earned its name as the apocryphal site

of the murder of two young princes, Edward and Richard, who disappeared from the Tower after being put there in 1483 by their uncle, Richard III. Two little skeletons (now in Westminster Abbey) were found buried close to the White Tower in 1674 and are thought to be theirs.

The **Beauchamp Tower** housed upper-class miscreants: Latin graffiti about Lady Jane Grey can be glimpsed today on its walls.

Like a prize gem set at the head of a royal crown, the **White Tower** is the centerpiece of the complex. Its four towers dominate the Inner

GOLD DIGGER?

Keep your eyes peeled as you tour the Tower: according to one story, Sir John Barkstead, goldsmith and Lieutenant of the Tower under Cromwell, hid £20,000 in gold coins here before his arrest and execution at the Restoration of Charles II.

Ward, a fitting and forbidding reminder of Norman strength at the time of the conquest of England.

Once inside the White Tower, head upstairs for the **Armouries,** where the biggest attraction, quite literally,

Jewel House, Waterloo Barracks

ROYAL BLING

The Crown of Queen Elizabeth, the Queen Mother, from 1937, contains the exotic 105-carat Koh-i-Noor (mountain of light) diamond.

TIME KILLERS

Some prisoners managed to keep themselves plenty amused: Sir Walter Raleigh grew tobacco on Tower Green, and in 1561 suspected sorcerer Hugh Draper carved an intricate astronomical clock on the walls of his Salt Tower cell.

is the suit of armor worn by a well-endowed Henry VIII. There is a matching outfit for his horse.

Other fascinating exhibits include the set of Samurai armor presented to James I in 1613 by the emperor of Japan, and the tiny set of armor worn by Henry VIII's young son Edward.

The **Jewel House** in **Waterloo Block** is the Tower's biggest draw, perfect for playing pick-your-favorite-crown from the wrong side of bul-

letproof glass. Not only are these crowns, staffs, and orbs encrusted with heavy-duty gems, they are invested with the authority of monarchical power in England, dating back to the 1300s.

Outside, pause at **Tower Green,** permanent departure point for those of noble birth. The hoi polloi were dispatched at nearby Tower Hill. The Tower's most famous female victims—Anne Boleyn, Margaret Countess of Salisbury, Catherine Howard, and Lady Jane Grey—all went this "priviledged" way.

Behind a well-kept square of grass stands the **Chapel Royal of St. Peter ad Vincula,** a delightful Tudor church and final resting place of six beheaded Tudor bodies. ■ TIP→ **Visitors are welcome for services and can also enter after 4:30 pm daily.**

The **Salt Tower,** reputedly the most haunted corner of the complex, marks the start of the **Wall Walk,** a bracing promenade along the stone spiral steps and battlements of the Tower that looks down on the trucks, taxis, and shimmering high-rises of modern London.

The Wall Walk ends at the **Martin Tower,** former home of the Crown Jewels and now host to the crowns and diamonds exhibition that explains the art of fashioning royal headwear and tells the story of some of the most famous stones.

On leaving the Tower, browse the **gift shop,** and wander the wharf that overlooks the Thames, leading to a picture-postcard view of Tower Bridge.

WHO ARE THE BEEFEATERS?

First of all, they're Yeoman Warders, but probably got the nickname "beefeater" from their position as Royal Bodyguards which entitled them to eat as much beef as they liked. Part of the "Yeoman of the Guard," started in the reign of Edmund IV, the warders have formed the Royal Bodyguard as far back as 1509 when Henry VIII left a dozen of the Yeoman of the Guard at the Tower to protect it.

Originally, the Yeoman Warders also served as jailers of the Tower, doubling as torturers when necessary. (So it would have been a Beefeater tightening the thumb screws, or ratchetting the rack another notch on some unfortunate prisoner. Smile nicely.) Today 36 Yeoman Warders (men and women since 2007), along with the Chief Yeoman Warder and the Yeoman Gaoler, live within the walls of the Tower with their families, in accommodations in the Outer Ward. They stand guard over the Tower, conduct tours, and lock up at 9:53 pm every night with the Ceremony of the Keys.

■ TIP➔ Free tickets to the Ceremony of the Keys are available by writing several months in advance; check the Tower Web site for details.

HARK THE RAVENS!

Legend has it that should the hulking black ravens ever leave, the White Tower will crumble and the kingdom fall. Charles II, no doubt jumpy after his father's execution and the monarchy's short-term fall from grace, made a royal decree in 1662 that there should be at least six of the carrion-eating nasties present at all times. There have been some close calls. During World War II, numbers dropped to one, echoing the precarious fate of the war-wracked country. In 2005, two (of eight) died over Christmas when Thor—the most intelligent but also the largest bully of the bunch—killed new recruit Gundolf, named after the Tower's 1070 designer. Pneumonia put an end to Bran, leaving lifelong partner Branwen without her mate.

■ DID YOU KNOW? In 1981 a raven named Grog, perhaps seduced by his alcoholic moniker, escaped after 21 years at the Tower. Others have been banished for "conduct unbecoming."

The six that remain, each one identified by a colored band around a claw, are much loved for their fidelity (they mate for life) and their cheek (capable of 440 noises, they are witty and scolding mimics). It's not only the diet of blood-soaked biscuits, rabbit, and scraps from the mess kitchen that keeps them coming back. Their lifting feathers on one wing are trimmed, meaning they can manage the equivalent of a lop-sided air-bound hobble but not much more. For the first half of 2006 the ravens were moved indoors full-time as a preventive measure against avian flu but have since been allowed out and about again. In situ they are a territorial lot, sticking to Tower Green and the White Tower, and lodging nightly by Wakefield Tower. They've had free front-row seats at all the most grisly moments in Tower history—Anne Boleyn's execution included.

■ TIP➔ Don't get too close to the ravens: they are prone to pecking and not particularly fond of humans, unless you are the Tower's Raven Master.

And *WHAT* are they wearing?

A **pike** (or halberd), also known as a partisan, is the Yeoman Warder's weapon of choice. The Chief Warder carries a staff topped with a miniature silver model of the White Tower.

Anyone who refers to this as a costume will be lucky to leave the Tower with head still attached to body: this is the ceremonial uniform of the Yeoman Warders, and it comes at a cool £13,000 a throw.

The black Tudor **bonnet** is made of velvet; the blue undress consists of a felt top hat, with a single Tudor rose in the middle.

This **Tudor-style ruff** helps date the ceremonial uniform, which was first worn in 1552.

Insignia on a Yeoman Warder's upper right arm denote the rank he carried in the military.

The **medals** on a Yeoman Warder's chest are more than mere show: all of the men and women have served for at least 22 years in the armed forces.

This version of the **royal livery** bears the insignia of the current Queen ("E" for Elizabeth) but originally dates from Tudor times. The first letter changes according to the reigning monarch's Christian name; the second letter is always an "R" for *rex* (king) or *regina* (queen).

Slits in the **tunic** date from the times when Beefeaters were expected to ride a horse.

Red socks and **black patent shoes** are worn on special occasions. Visitors are more likely to see the regular blue undress, introduced in 1858 as the regular working dress of the Yeoman Warders.

The **red lines down the trousers** are a sign of the blood from the swords of the Yeoman Warders in their defense of the realm.

(IN)FAMOUS PRISONERS OF THE TOWER

Anne Boleyn   Lady Jane Grey   Sir Walter Raleigh

Sir Thomas More. A Catholic and Henry VIII's friend and chancellor, Sir Thomas refused to attend the coronation of Anne Boleyn (Henry VIII's second wife) or to recognize the multi-marrying king as head of the Church. Sent to the Tower for treason, in 1535 More was beheaded.

Anne Boleyn. The first of Henry VIII's wives to be beheaded, Anne, who failed to provide the king with a son, was accused of sleeping with five men, including her own brother. All six got the chop in 1536. Her severed head was held up to the crowd, and her lips were said to be mouthing prayer.

Margaret, Countess of Salisbury. Not the best-known prisoner in her lifetime, she has a reputation today for haunting the Tower. And no wonder: the elderly 70-year-old was condemned by Henry VIII in 1541 for a potentially treacherous bloodline (she was the last Plantagenet princess) and hacked to death by the executioner after she refused to put her head on the block like a common traitor and attempted to run away.

Queen Catherine Howard. Henry VIII's fifth wife was locked up for high treason and infidelity and beheaded in 1542 at age 20. Ever eager to please, she spent her final night practicing how to lay her head on the block.

Lady Jane Grey. The nine-days-queen lost her head in 1554 at age 16. Her death was the result of sibling rivalry gone seriously wrong, when Protestant Edward VI slighted his Catholic sister Mary in favor of Lady Jane as heir, and Mary decided to have none of it.

Guy Fawkes. The Roman Catholic soldier who tried to blow up the Houses of Parliament and kill the king in the 1605 Gunpowder plot was first incarcerated in the chambers of the Tower, where King James I requested he be tortured in ever-worsening ways. Perhaps unsurprisingly, he confessed. He met his seriously grisly end in the Old Palace Yard at Westminster, where he was hung, drawn, and quartered in 1607.

Sir Walter Raleigh. Once a favorite of Elizabeth I, he offended her by secretly marrying her Maid of Honor and was chucked in the Tower. Later, as a conspirator against James I, he paid with his life. A frequent visitor to the Tower (he spent 13 years there in three stints), he managed to get the Bloody Tower enlarged on account of his wife and growing family. He was finally executed in 1618 in Old Palace Yard, Westminster.

Josef Jakobs. The last man to be executed in the Tower was caught as a spy when parachuting in from Germany and executed by firing squad in 1941. The chair he sat in when he was shot is preserved in the Royal Armouries' artifacts store.

FOR FURTHER EVIDENCE . . .

A trio of buildings in the Inner Ward, the **Bloody Tower, Beauchamp Tower,** and **Queen's House,** all with excellent views of the execution scaffold in Tower Green, are the heart of the Tower's prison accommodations and home to a permanent exhibition about notable inmates.

TACKLING THE TOWER (without losing your head)

MAKING THE MOST OF YOUR TIME:
Without doubt, the Tower is worth two to three hours. A full hour of that would be well spent by joining one of the Yeoman Warders' tours (included in admission). It's hard to better their insight, vitality, and humor—they are knights of the realm living their very own fairytale castle existence.

The Crown Jewels are worth the wait, the White Tower is essential, and the Medieval Palace and Bloody Tower should at least be breezed through.

■ TIP➔ It's best to visit on weekdays, when the crowds are smaller.

WITH KIDS: The Tower's centuries-old cobblestones are not exactly stroller-friendly, but strollers are permitted inside most of the buildings. If you do bring one, be prepared to leave it temporarily unsupervised (the stroller, that is—not your child) outside the White Tower, which has no access. There are baby-changing facilities in the Brick Tower restrooms behind the Jewel House. Look for regular free children's events such as the Knight's school where children can have a go at jousting, sword-fighting, and archery.

■ TIP➔ Tell your child to find one of the Yeoman Warders if he or she should get lost; they will in turn lead him or her to the Byward Tower, which is where you should meet.

IN A HURRY? If you have less than an hour, head down Wall Walk, through a succession of towers, which eventually spit you out at the Martin Tower. The view over modern London is quite a contrast.

TOURS: Tours given by a Yeoman Warder leave from the main entrance near Middle Tower every half-hour from 10–4, and last about an hour. Beefeaters give occasional 30-minute talks in the Lanthorn Tower about their daily lives. Both tours are free. Check website for talks and workshops

6

IN FOCUS THE TOWER OF LONDON

WORTH NOTING

Bank of England. Since its establishment in 1694 as England's central bank, the role of the "Old Lady of Threadneedle Street" (a caption of a political cartoon that stuck) has grown to include managing foreign exchanges, issuing currency, storing the nation's gold reserves, and regulating the United Kingdom's banking system. Since 1997, it has had operational responsibility for Britain's monetary policy, most visibly setting interest rates (similar to the Federal Reserve in the United States). The three-acre site is enclosed in a massive, neoclassical curtain wall designed by Sir John Soane and erected in 1828. This windowless outer wall is all that survives of Soane's original Bank building, which was demolished in 1925. You can discover more about the bank's history in the surprisingly varied Bank of England Museum (the entrance is around the corner on Bartholomew Lane). In addition to the bank's original Royal Charter, there's a lively program of special exhibitions, plus interactive displays (you can even try your hand at controlling inflation). The most popular exhibit remains the solid-gold bar in the central trading hall that you can actually hold—but before you get any ideas, there's security everywhere. ⊠ *Threadneedle St., City of London* ☎ *020/3461–4878* ⊕ *www.bankofengland.co.uk* ⊡ *Free* ⊙ *Closed weekends and bank holidays* Ⓜ *Bank, Monument.*

Dr. Johnson's House. Built in 1700, this elegant Georgian residence, with its restored interiors, paneled rooms, and period furniture, is where Samuel Johnson lived between 1748 and 1759, compiling his landmark *A Dictionary of the English Language* in the garret as his health deteriorated. There's a research library with two early editions on view, along with other mementos of Johnson and his friend and biographer, James Boswell, one of literature's greatest diarists. After your visit, enjoy more 17th-century atmosphere around the corner in Wine Office Court at the venerable pub **Ye Olde Cheshire Cheese,** once Johnson and Boswell's favorite watering hole. ⊠ *17 Gough Sq., City of London* ☎ *020/7353–3745* ⊕ *www.drjohnsonshouse. org* ⊡ *£6* ⊙ *Closed Sun. and bank holidays* Ⓜ *Holborn, Chancery La., Temple.*

Guildhall. For centuries, this building has been the administrative and ceremonial base of the Corporation of London, the world's oldest continuously elected municipal governing authority (the Corporation still oversees The City's civic administration but now in a more modern building). Built between 1411 and 1440, it is The City's only surviving secular medieval building, and although it lost roofs to both the Great Fire of 1666 and the Blitz of 1940, its Gothic Great Hall has remained intact. Adding to the Hall's period atmosphere are the colorful coats of arms and banners of the 110 City Livery Companies, descendants of medieval trade guilds, which still officially elect the Lord Mayor of London. These range from older companies originally formed by trades of yesteryear to new ones representing up-to-the minute activities like information technology, along with several that remain eternally relevant (e.g., carpenters, upholsterers, and fishmongers).

The Hall has been the site of several historic trials, including that of "the Nine Day Queen" Lady Jane Grey in 1553 and the landmark *Zong* case (1783), which helped end Britain's involvement in the slave trade. Even more ancient is the 11th Century East Crypt, a survivor of the original Saxon Hall. To the right of Guildhall Yard is the **Guildhall Art Gallery,** which includes portraits of notables, cityscapes, and a slightly cloying pre-Raphaelite section. The construction of the gallery in the 1980s led to the exciting discovery of London's only **Roman Amphitheater,** which had lain undisturbed for more than 1,800 years. Visitors can walk through the excavation, although most of the artifacts are now at the Museum of London. There are 75-minute guided tours on City Council meeting days at 10:45 am (advance booking required); check the website for dates. ⊠ *Aldermanbury, City of London* ☎ *020/7332–3803* ⊕ *www.cityoflondon.gov.uk* ✉ *Roman Amphitheatre and Art Gallery free; Guildhall tours £7* ☽ *Closed Aug.* Ⓜ *St. Paul's, Moorgate, Bank, Mansion House.*

The Old Bailey. Visitors are allowed into the public galleries of the 16 courtrooms at London's **Central Criminal Court** (universally known as "the Old Bailey," a reference to the street where it's located, which follows the line of the original fortified city wall, or "bailey" in Middle English). Historically it has been the venue for many of Britain's most famous criminal trials. It was here that Oscar Wilde was condemned for "gross indecency" in 1895, where notorious murderers like the Kray twins in the 1960s and the Yorkshire Ripper in the 1980s were convicted, and, more recently, where high-profile terrorism cases have been tried. Originally the site of a medieval courthouse destroyed in the Great Fire, a courthouse was built here next to the grim Newgate Prison, the poor man's version of the Tower, in 1673. The building went through two more incarnations before the present Edwardian Baroque building opened in 1907 (it was rebuilt again after the Blitz). Until 1868, executions were held on the street outside (a great public attraction) and you can still see the "Dead Man's Walk" along which condemned prisoners were taken from their cells to the gallows under a series of ever-narrowing arches. Note the 12-foot gold leaf statue of Lady Justice at the top of the dome, not wearing a blindfold like she is usually portrayed. Trials take place from 10 am to 1 pm and 2 pm to 4:30 pm. There are security restrictions, and children under 14 and overly casual dress are not allowed. ⊠ *The Old Bailey, City of London* ☎ *020/7248–3277* ⊕ *www.cityoflondon.gov.uk* ✉ *Free* ☽ *Closed bank holidays* ☞ *Line forms at Newgate St. entrance or in Warwick St. Passage* Ⓜ *St. Paul's.*

St. Bartholomew the Great. Originally founded in 1123 as part of an Augustinian monastery, this is one of the oldest churches in London and one of the city's few surviving Norman buildings. Although much of the church has been destroyed or demolished over the centuries, with restoration only beginning in the mid-19th century (it even saw use as a stable and a factory in the interim), it nevertheless remains perhaps the best preserved example of Romanesque architecture in London. Most notable are the 13th-century arch with a half-timbered gatehouse at the entrance and the fine Romanesque chancel, apse, and triforum at the east end of the interior. The artist William Hogarth was baptized in the font, which dates back to 1404. The redolent atmosphere has made it a favorite filming location, and you can see it in *The Other Boleyn Girl*, *Four Weddings and a Funeral*, and *Shakespeare in Love*, to name just a few. ✉ *Cloth Fair, West Smithfield, City of London* ☎ *020/7600–0440* ⊕ *www.greatstbarts.com* 💷 *£5 (free for prayer in the chapel), photography £1* Ⓜ *Barbican, Farringdon.*

St. Bride's. Located just off Fleet Street, traditionally a hotbed of British printers and newspaper offices, St. Bride's is known as "the journalists' church," and indeed a small altar in the north aisle marks a memorial dedicated to the sadly ever-growing list of reporters, photographers, and crew who have lost their lives covering 21st-century conflicts. St. Bride's is another of Sir Christopher Wren's English baroque gems, built nine years after the Great Fire of 1666. Allegedly, the distinctively tiered steeple, Wren's highest, inspired a baker parishioner to create a similarly shaped tiered cake for his own wedding, thus creating the modern wedding cake design. This is thought to be the seventh church on the site, with the first one built during the 7th century. Evidence for this, along with a section of a Roman mosaic sidewalk, was discovered in the crypt, where you can now see the many archaeological finds unearthed from the thousands of coffins there. Ninety-minute guided tours are held on Tuesday afternoon. ✉ *Fleet St., City of London* ☎ *020/7427–0133* ⊕ *www.stbrides.com* 💷 *Free, guided tours £6* Ⓜ *St. Paul's, Blackfriars.*

St. Mary-le-Bow. Founded around 1080 as the Archbishop of Canterbury's London seat, this church is a survivor; it collapsed and was rebuilt three times before being completely destroyed in the Great Fire of 1666. Once again, Sir Christopher Wren was called in, creating a new building that was completed in 1673, but sadly this, too, was destroyed during the Blitz. The version you see today is a re-creation of Wren's design that was reconsecrated in 1965. According to tradition, only Londoners born within earshot of the church's famous "Bow Bells" (which used to echo more widely than they do now) can be considered true Cockneys, a concept that may date back to the 9 pm curfew bells rung during the 14th century. The Norman crypt is the oldest parochial building in London still in use, and you can see the bow-shape arches from which the church takes its name. The garden contains a statue of former parishioner Captain John Smith, the founder of the Virginia Colony. Opening times on weekends and holidays are irregular, so calling ahead is advised. Classical music concerts are held here regularly; check the website for listings. ✉ *Cheapside, City of London* ☎ *020/7248–5139* ⊕ *www.stmarylebow.co.uk* 💷 *Free* Ⓜ *Mansion House, St. Paul's.*

EAST LONDON

Getting Oriented

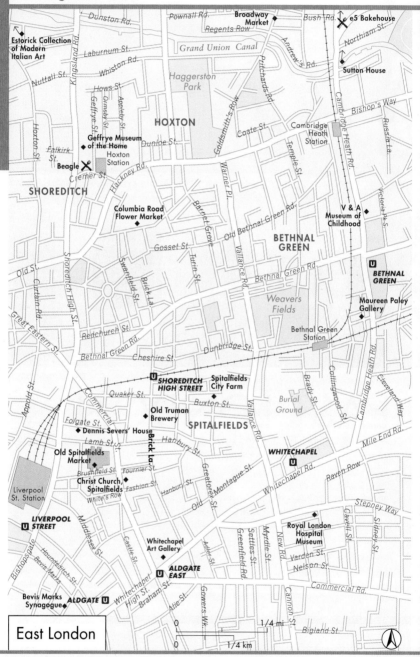

Estorick Collection of Modern Italian Art
Dunston Rd.
Pownall Rd.
Broadway Market
Bush Rd.
e5 Bakehouse
Regents Row
Laburnum St.
Grand Union Canal
Northiam St.
Kingsland Rd.
Whiston Rd.
Sutton House
Nuttall St.
Hows St.
Haggerston Park
Cambridge Heath Rd.
Bishop's Way
Falkirk St.
Ormsby St.
Appleby St.
Geffrye St.
HOXTON
Coate St.
Cambridge Heath Station
Russia La.
Hoxton St.
Geffrye Museum of the Home
Dunloe St.
Temple St.
Beagle
Hoxton Station
Hackney Rd.
Goldsmith's Row
SHOREDITCH
Cremer St.
Warner Pl.
V & A Museum of Childhood
Victoria Pk. S.
Columbia Road Flower Market
Barnet Grove
Old Bethnal Green Rd.
BETHNAL GREEN
Gosset St.
Turin St.
Vallance Rd.
Old St.
Swanfield St.
Bethnal Green Rd.
BETHNAL GREEN
Curtain Rd.
Shoreditch High St.
Brick La.
Weavers Fields
Maureen Paley Gallery
Great Eastern St.
Redchurch St.
Bethnal Green Station
Cottingwood St.
Cambridge Heath Rd.
Cleveland Way
Bethnal Green Rd.
Cheshire St.
Dunbridge St.
SHOREDITCH HIGH STREET
Spitalfields City Farm
Brady St.
Quaker St.
Buxton St.
Burial Ground
Commercial St.
Folgate St.
Old Truman Brewery
SPITALFIELDS
Vallance Rd.
Mile End Rd.
Dennis Severs' House
Lamb St.
Hanbury St.
Brick La.
Greatorex St.
Old Montague St.
WHITECHAPEL
Old Spitalfields Market
Brushfield St.
Fournier St.
Raven Row
Liverpool St. Station
Christ Church, Spitalfields
Fashion St.
Hanbury St.
Whitechapel Rd.
Stepney Way
White's Row
Old Montague St.
Cavell St.
Sidney St.
LIVERPOOL STREET
Middlesex St.
Royal London Hospital Museum
New Rd.
Bishopsgate
Houndsditch
Castle St.
Whitechapel Art Gallery
Adler St.
Settles St.
Greenfield Rd.
Myrtle St.
Varden St.
Bevis Marks
Bevis Marks Synagogue
ALDGATE
Whitechapel High St.
Braham St.
ALDGATE EAST
Gowers Wk.
Nelson St.
Commercial Rd.
Cannon St.
Aldie St.
Bigland St.

East London

0   1/4 mi
0   1/4 km

TOP REASONS TO GO

Dennis Severs' House by candlelight: The atmospheric set-pieces in this Georgian townhouse use visuals, sounds, and aromas to evoke the lives of its fictional previous inhabitants.

Eat artisanal at Broadway Market: Check out more than 100 food stalls here on Saturday, offering everything from cheeses to oysters.

Immerse yourself in London's hottest art scene: Edgy galleries mix with large collections.

Trace the footsteps of Jack the Ripper: Track Britain's most infamous serial killer through streets that were part of a major slum area in Victorian times.

Peek into the lives of Londoners at the Geffrye Museum of the Home: This former almshouse showcases middle-class domestic interiors over the centuries.

SAFETY

Around Shoreditch, Spitalfields, and Brick Lane, streets are largely safe during daylight hours. Be cautious on the rougher streets of Whitechapel, Bethnal Green, and Hackney at night.

FEELING PECKISH?

Beagle. A great spot (with terrace) for weekend brunch after a morning's shopping. Beagle also serves lunch and dinner, including venison, oysters, and house-smoked salmon. ✉ 397–400 Geffrye St., Hoxton ☎ 020/7613–2967 ⊕ www.beaglelondon.co.uk Ⓜ Overground: Hoxton.

E5 Bakehouse. This bakery, which supplies bread to many of East London's top eateries, has a friendly café on-site, where you can sample some of the tastiest toasted sandwiches in London. ✉ Mentmore Terr., Arch 395, Dalston ☎ 020/8986–9600 ⊕ www.e5bakehouse.com ⊘ No dinner Ⓜ Overground: London Fields.

GETTING THERE

The London Overground, with stops at Shoreditch High Street, Hoxton, Whitechapel, Dalston Junction, Dalston Kingsland, London Fields, Hackney Central, and Hackney Wick is the easiest way to reach East London. Alternatively, the best Tube stations to use are Old Street on the Northern line, Bethnal Green on the Central line, and Liverpool Street on the Metropolitan and Circle lines.

MAKING THE MOST OF YOUR TIME

To experience East London at its most lively, visit on the weekend. Spitalfields Market bustles all weekend, while Brick Lane and Columbia Road are best on a Sunday morning and Broadway Market on Saturday. If you're planning to explore East London's art galleries, pick up a free map at the Whitechapel Art Gallery. As for the area's booming nightlife scene, there's no time limit: you'll find people partying Wednesday through Sunday.

GUIDED TOURS

The two-hour **Jack the Ripper Walk** (⊕ www.walks.com) departs from Tower Hill Tube station daily at 7:30 pm, plus Saturday at 3. **Street Art London** (⊕ www.streetart-london.co.uk) offers two- and four-hour walking tours of East London's street art on Tuesday and Thursday at 10 am and weekends at 11 am.

7

Sightseeing
★★★
Nightlife
★★★★★
Dining
★★★★
Lodging
★★★
Shopping
★★★★

Made famous by Dickens and infamous by Jack the Ripper, East London is one of London's most enduringly evocative neighborhoods, rich in popular history, architectural gems, and artists' studios. Since the early 1990s, hip gallerists, designers, and new-media entrepreneurs have colonized its handsome Georgian buildings and converted industrial lofts. Today, this collection of neighborhoods lays claim to being the city's most trendsetting area.

Updated by
Jo Caird

The British equivalent of parts of Brooklyn, East London is a patchwork of districts encompassing struggling artists, multicultural enclaves, and upscale professionals occasionally teetering, like its New York equivalent, on the edge of self-parody. The vast area ranges from gentrified districts like Spitalfields, where bankers and successful artists live in desirable renovated townhouses, to parts of Hackney, where seemingly derelict, graffiti-covered industrial buildings are hives of exciting creative activity. It remains a little rough around the edges, so stick to busier streets at night.

At the start of the new millennium, Hoxton, an enclave of Shoreditch, became the glossy hub of London's buzzing contemporary art scene, which accelerated the gentrification process. Some artists, such as Tracey Emin and Gilbert & George, long-term residents of Spitalfields' handsome Georgian terraces—and successful enough to still afford the area—have remained.

One such residence, **Dennis Severs' House,** was transformed two decades ago by the eponymous American artist into a unique "living house museum" that evokes how past generations of a fictional Huguenot family might have lived there. Not far away, **Spitalfields Market** offers an ever-changing selection of crafts and funky clothes stalls under a glass roof in what was once a Victorian produce market. Across from the market, **Christ Church, Spitalfields,** Nicholas Hawksmoor's masterpiece, soars above Fournier Street.

GUIDE TO THE STREETS IN LONDON'S EAST END

Brick Lane and the narrow streets running off it offer a paradigm of East London's development. Its population has moved in waves: communities seeking refuge, others moving out in an upwardly mobile direction.

Brick Lane has seen the manufacture of bricks (during the 16th century), beer, and bagels, but nowadays it's primarily known as the heart of Banglatown—Bangladeshis make up one-third of the population in this London borough, and you'll see that the names of the surrounding streets are written in Bengali—where you find many kebab and curry houses along with shops selling DVDs, colorful saris, and stacks of sticky sweets. On Sunday morning, cars aren't allowed on the upper section of the street. Shops and cafés are open, and several stalls are set up, creating a companion market to the one on nearby **Petticoat Lane.**

Fournier Street contains fine examples of the neighborhood's characteristic Georgian terraced houses, many of them built by the richest of the early-18th-century Huguenot silk weavers (note the enlarged windows on the upper floors to maximize light for the intricate work). Most of those along the north side of Fournier Street have been restored, but some still contain textile sweatshops—only now the workers are Bengali.

Wilkes Street, with more 1720s Huguenot houses, is north of Christ Church, Spitalfields; and neighboring **Princelet Street** was once important to East London's Jewish community. Where No. 6 stands now, the first of several thriving Yiddish theaters opened in 1886. **Elder Street,** just off Folgate, is another gem of original 18th-century houses. On the south and east side of Spitalfields Market are yet more time-warp streets that are worth a wander, such as **Gun Street,** where artist Mark Gertler (1891–1939) was born, at No. 16.

In the last decade, streets around the Old Street roundabout (as well as converted warehouses in Hackney and Dalston) have flourished with start-ups, with attendant stylish boutiques (especially on Redchurch Street), destination restaurants, and hipster bars as part of a government initiative to attract IT-oriented businesses to the neighborhood. Old and new Shoreditch meet on **Brick Lane,** the heart of the Bangladeshi community, lined with innumerable curry houses and glittering sari shops, plus vintage-clothing emporia. Here you'll also find the **Old Truman Brewery,** an East London landmark converted into a warren of street fashion and pop-up galleries. On Sunday, the Columbia Road Flower Market to the north of Brick Lane becomes a colorful, fragrant oasis of greenery.

As property prices have climbed, up-and-coming artists have sought more affordable studio spaces in former industrial buildings eastward toward Whitechapel and Bethnal Green, where there are also some notable galleries. Here you'll find the **V&A Museum of Childhood,** a delight for children of all ages, and—a design connoisseur's favorite—the **Geffrye Museum,** a collection of domestic interiors through the ages that occupies a row of early-18th-century almshouses.

Probably the best start to an East London tour is via the London Overground, getting off at Shoreditch High Street Station. Immediately northwest of the station, on the west side of Shoreditch High Street, is the heart of the neighborhood that aspires to be the U.K. equivalent to Silicon Valley. To the northeast is Shoreditch's boutique, gallery, and restaurant zone. The subneighborhood of Hoxton is located just above Shoreditch, north of the Old Street roundabout. To the southeast of the station are the handsome Georgian streets of Spitalfields. Bethnal Green is due east, past busy Brick Lane. Whitechapel, formerly Jack the Ripper's patch, is to the south of Spitalfields. All of these neighborhoods are within what is traditionally referred to as the "East End," although East London extends farther to the north and east.

TOP ATTRACTIONS

Fodor'sChoice **Christ Church, Spitalfields.** This is the 1729 masterpiece of Sir Chris-
★ topher Wren's associate Nicholas Hawksmoor, one of his six London churches and an example of English baroque at its finest. It was commissioned as part of Parliament's 1711 "Fifty New Churches" Act, passed in response to the influx of immigrants with the idea of providing for the religious needs of the "godless thousands"—and to help ensure they joined the Church of England, as opposed to such nonconformist denominations as the Protestant Huguenots. (It must have worked; you can still see gravestones with epitaphs in French in the crypt.) As the local silk industry declined, the church fell into disrepair, and by 1958 the structure was crumbling, with the looming prospect of demolition. But after 25 years—longer than it took to build the church—and a huge local fund-raising effort, the structure was meticulously restored and is a joy to behold, from the colonnaded Doric portico and tall spire to its soaring, heavily ornamented plaster ceiling. Its excellent acoustics make it a superb concert venue. Tours that take you "backstage" to the many hidden rooms and passages, from the tower to the vaults, are offered by appointment. There's also a café in the crypt. ✉ *Commercial St., Spitalfields* ☎ *020/7377–2440* ⊕ *www.ccspitalfields.org* ✆ *Free, tours £6* ⊗ *Closed Sat.* Ⓜ *Overground: Shoreditch High St.*

Fodor'sChoice **Dennis Severs' House.** The remarkable interiors of this extraordinary
★ time machine of a house are the creation of Dennis Severs (1948–99), a performer-designer-scholar from Escondido, California, who dedicated his life to restoring this Georgian terraced house. More than that, he created "still-life dramas" using sight, sound, and smell to evoke the world of a fictitious family of Huguenot silk weavers, the Jervises, who might have inhabited the house between 1728 and 1914. Each of the 10 rooms has a distinctive, compelling atmosphere that encourages visitors to become lost in another time, deploying evocative design details like rose-laden Victorian wallpaper, Jacobean paneling, Georgian wing-back chairs, baroque carved ornaments, rich "Catholic" wall colors downstairs, and more sedate "Protestant" shades upstairs. The Silent Night candlelight tour offered Monday, Wednesday, and Friday evenings, a stroll through the rooms with no

The East End Art Scene

Banksy, the Bristol-based artist and provocateur who has maintained his anonymity despite works that now command six figures, is widely credited with making Londoners see street art as more than mere vandalism. He first came to public attention in the East End in the late '80s, and the area continues to attract new talent from around the globe today. Unfortunately, much of Banksy's early work has been lost, either from being covered over by local councils and building owners, defaced by other graffiti artists, or removed by profiteers. Currently murals remain at Rivington Street near Old Street (in the garden of Cargo bar and nightclub), and Stoke Newington Church Street. **Street Art London** (⊕ www.streetartlondon.co.uk) offers a knowledgeable, insider view on the ever-changing scene, taking you through the history of street art and graffiti in this area and highlighting the best of Banksy's successors. Take the Saturday tour to avoid the noise of weekday traffic.

Today, East London is a global hotbed of contemporary art, but its avant-garde roots go way back. **Shoreditch's** cheap industrial units and Georgian–Victorian terraced streets have attracted artists since the 1960s, when op-art pioneer Bridget Riley established a service to find affordable studio space for her contemporaries. In the early '90s it gained new notoriety when Young British Artists Sarah Lucas and Tracey Emin began selling their own and their friends' work in The Shop, joining Maureen Paley's influential Bethnal Green gallery, and the long-established Whitechapel Art Gallery, where many leading abstract expressionists and pop artists had their first U.K. shows. **Hoxton** truly became a destination for well-heeled collectors when Jay Jopling, the most important modern-art dealer in town, set up his White Cube gallery in 2000 (it's now in Bermondsey, with a second location at Mason's Yard in Westminster), followed by Kate MacGarry's gallery in 2002.

Priced out by the area's fashionability, the emerging artists themselves have relocated farther off the beaten path to edgier neighborhoods such as **Hackney,** with several trendsetting galleries found clustered around **Cambridge Heath Road** and **Vyner Street.**

talking allowed, is the most theatrical and memorable way to experience the house. The Exclusive Silent Night visits, which conclude with champagne or mulled wine by the fire and a chat with the curators, are available one night per month (more frequently near the Christmas holiday), and private group visits can also be arranged. ⊠ *18 Folgate St., Shoreditch* ☎ *020/7247–4013* ⊕ *www.dennissevershouse.co.uk* ⊠ *£10 Sun. and Mon., £15 Mon. and Wed. evenings* ☉ *Closed Tues., Thurs., and Sat.* Ⓜ *Overground: Shoreditch High St.*

FodorśChoice ★ **Geffrye Museum of the Home.** In contrast to the West End's grand aristocratic townhouses, this charming museum is devoted to the life of the city's middle class over the years. Originally a row of almshouses built in 1714 by Sir Robert Geffrye, a former Lord Mayor of London, it

On Sunday, additional clothing and craft stalls surround Spitalfields covered market.

contains a series of 11 period rooms that re-create everyday domestic interiors from the Elizabethan period through the 1950s to the present day. One of the almshouses has been restored to its original condition, offering a glimpse into how the poor and the dependent elderly lived in previous centuries (to visit the almshouse you must go as part of a tour). Outside, a series of period gardens charts the evolution of the town garden over the past 400 years, and next to them is a walled herb garden. The museum's extension wing houses the 20th-century galleries, a lovely café overlooking the gardens, and a shop. ✉ *136 Kingsland Rd., Hoxton* ☎ *020/7739–9893* ⊕ *www.geffrye-museum. org.uk* ✉ *Free (charge for special exhibitions), almshouse £4* ⊘ *Closed Mon.* Ⓜ *Overground: Hoxton.*

FAMILY **Old Spitalfields Market.** An impressive piece of architecture in itself, this large restored Victorian market hall (covered by a glass canopy) is part bazaar and part food court. The main market days are Thursday through Sunday, with a notable antiques market on Thursday and a fashion and art market on Friday. On every first and third Friday and every second Saturday, there's a record fair, and a vintage fair sets up here every third Saturday of the month. Markets on other days sell goods that include handmade clothes, toys, hats, and jewelry. While some of the quality is pedestrian, you can also find interesting clothes, accessories, and leather goods by new designers. Late-night shopping, dining, and nightlife events take place every first Thursday. ✉ *16 Horner Sq., Spitalfields* ☎ *020/7375–2963* ⊕ *www.oldspital-fieldsmarket.com* ✉ *Free* Ⓜ *Liverpool St.*

FAMILY **V&A Museum of Childhood.** A treat for children of all ages, this East
Fodor's Choice London outpost of the Victoria & Albert Museum—in an iron, glass,
★ and brown-brick building transported here from South Kensington
in 1868—houses one of the world's biggest toy collections. One highlight (among many) is the large Dolls' Houses collection—a bit like a
miniature Geffrye Museum, with interiors from 1673 up to the present. You'll find everything from board games and puzzles to teddy
bears and train sets. The collection is organized into galleries: Moving Toys, which includes everything from rocking horses to Xboxes;
Creativity, which encompasses dolls, puppets, chemistry sets, play
kitchens, construction toys, and musical instruments; and Childhood,
with areas devoted to babies, an exhibit of children's clothes from the
mid-1600s to the present, and toys inspired by adult pursuits, such as
toy soldiers, toy guns, and toy hospitals. Don't miss the magnificent
18th-century commedia dell'arte puppet theater, thought to have been
made in Venice. There are special activities for the under-fives. The
shop has replica toys that make great presents. ⌂ *Cambridge Heath
Rd., Bethnal Green* ☎ *020/8983–5200* ⊕ *www.museumofchildhood.
org.uk* ⌷ *Free* Ⓜ *Bethnal Green.*

Fodor's Choice **Whitechapel Art Gallery.** Founded in 1901, this internationally renowned
★ gallery mounts exhibitions that rediscover overlooked masters and
showcase tomorrow's legends. Painter and leading exponent of
abstract expressionism Jackson Pollock was exhibited here in the
1950s as was pop artist Robert Rauschenberg in the 1960s; the 1970s
saw a young David Hockney's first solo show. The exhibitions continue to be on the cutting edge of contemporary art. The gallery also
hosts talks, film screenings, workshops, and other events; tours of
local galleries take place on the first Thursday of every month. Pick
up a free East London art map to help you plan your visit to the
area. ⌂ *77–82 Whitechapel High St., Whitechapel* ☎ *020/7522–7888*
⊕ *www.whitechapelgallery.org* ⌷ *Free (charge for some special exhibits)* ⊗ *Closed Mon.* Ⓜ *Aldgate East.*

WORTH NOTING

Bevis Marks Synagogue. This is Britain's oldest synagogue still in use
and is certainly its most splendid. It was built in 1701, after the Jews,
having been expelled from England in 1290, were allowed to return
under Cromwell in 1656. Inspired by the Spanish and Portuguese
Great Synagogue of Amsterdam, the interior is embellished with rich
woodwork, seven hanging brass candelabra (representing the seven
days of the week), and 12 trompe l'oeil wood columns painted to look
like marble. The magnificent Ark, which contains the sacred scrolls of
the five books of Moses, is modeled on contemporary Wren neoclassical altar pieces, with oak doors and Corinthian columns. In 1992
and 1993 the synagogue was seriously damaged by IRA bombs, but
was subsequently completely restored. ⌂ *4 Heneage La., Whitechapel* ☎ *020/7626–1274* ⊕ *www.bevismarks.org.uk* ⌷ *£5* ⊗ *Closed Sat.*
Ⓜ *Aldgate, Liverpool St.*

Columbia Road Flower Market. On Sunday morning this largely built-up area is transformed into a riot of color and scent with the arrival of the flower sellers. There's everything from bedding plants to banana trees, including herbs, cut flowers, and bouquets at very reasonable prices. The vendors' patter is part of the fun. Columbia Road itself is lined with some 60 independent shops, so you can pick up some art, antiques, handcrafted jewelry, or, of course, garden accessories to go with your greenery. To avoid the crowds, get here the earlier the better. ⊠ *Columbia Rd., Hackney* ⊕ *www.columbiaroad.info* Ⓜ *Old St., Northern Line.*

Estorick Collection of Modern Italian Art. West of Hoxton, toward the eastern end of Islington, is this small, restored Georgian mansion with an extraordinary collection of early-20th-century Italian art. The works were acquired by Eric Estorick, an American collector and sociologist, who was particularly keen on Italian Futurists; there are works by Balla, Boccioni, and Severini, among others. The downstairs Estorick Caffè is a good place to grab a bite, especially in summer when you can sit outdoors. ⊠ *39A Canonbury Sq., off Canonbury Rd., Islington* ☎ *020/7704–9522* ⊕ *www.estorickcollection.com* 🖃 *£7* ⊘ *Closed Mon. and Tues.* Ⓜ *Highbury & Islington.*

Maureen Paley Gallery. Inspired by the DIY punk aesthetic and the funky galleries of New York's Lower East Side, Maureen Paley started putting on exhibitions in her East End home back in 1984, when it was virtually the only gallery in the area. Since then, this American artist and gallerist has shown such respected contemporary artists as Gillian Wearing, Helen Chadwick, Jenny Holzer, Peter Fischli, and Wolfgang Tillmans and, today, is considered the doyenne of East End gallerists. The gallery has been in its current home, a converted warehouse in Bethnal Green, since 1999. ⊠ *21 Herald St., Bethnal Green* ☎ *020/7729–4112* ⊕ *www.maureenpaley.com* ⊘ *Closed Mon. and Tues.* Ⓜ *Bethnal Green.*

FAMILY **Old Truman Brewery.** The last East End brewery still standing—a handsome example of Georgian and 19th-century industrial architecture, and in late Victorian times the largest brewery in the world—has been transformed into a cavernous hipster mall housing galleries, record shops, fashion-forward boutiques, bars, clubs, and restaurants, along with an array of international street-food vendors. The retailers are at street level with offices and studios on the upper floors. Events include fashion shows for both new and established designers, excellent sample sales, art installations, and, on weekends, a food hall and a vintage clothes fair. The brewery itself shut down in 1989. ⊠ *91 Brick La., Spitalfields* ☎ *0207/770–6000* ⊕ *www.trumanbrewery.com* Ⓜ *Overground: Shoreditch High St.*

Royal London Hospital Museum. Located in the crypt of a Victorian church, the Royal London Hospital Museum uses exhibits of historic medical equipment, surgical instruments, and archives to document the history of this East London institution from its foundation in 1740 to the present day. Highlights include a forensic medicine section with documentation and original materials connected to the Jack the

Ripper murders and the RLH surgeon who helped investigate them. There are also artifacts and documents relating to Joseph Merrick (aka the Elephant Man) who spent his final years in the hospital, and a set of dentures worn by George Washington. Opening hours are subject to change on short notice, so call ahead. ⊠ *St. Augustine with St. Philip's Church, Newark St., Whitechapel* ☎ *020/7377–7608* ⊕ *www. bartshealth.nhs.uk/the-royal-london-hospital-museum-and-archives* ☜ *Free* ⊙ *Closed Sat.–Mon.*

FAMILY **Spitalfields City Farm.** An oasis of rural calm in an urban landscape, this little community farm raises a variety of animals, including some rare breeds, to help educate city kids about life in the country. A tiny farm shop sells freshly laid eggs, along with organic seasonal produce. ⊠ *Buxton St., Spitalfields* ☎ *020/7247–8762* ⊕ *www.spitalfieldscity-farm.org* ☜ *Free* ⊙ *Closed Mon.* Ⓜ *Overground: Shoreditch High St.*

FAMILY **Sutton House.** Built by a courtier to King Henry VIII, this Tudor mansion has since been home to merchants, Huguenot silk weavers, and, in the 1980s, a group of arty squatters. The house dates back to 1535, when Hackney was a village on the outskirts of London surrounded by fields. Later, in 1751, it was split into two self-contained houses. Its oak-paneled rooms, tranquil courtyard, and adorable café are an unexpected treat in an area that's yet to entirely shake off its grit. Guided tours are available by appointment. ⊠ *2–4 Homerton High St., Hackney* ☎ *020/8986–2264* ⊕ *www.nationaltrust.org.uk/sutton-house* ☜ *£6, tours £20* ⊙ *Closed Mon. and Tues.* Ⓜ *Overground: Hackney Central.*

8

Sightseeing
★★★
Nightlife
★★★
Dining
★★★
Lodging
★
Shopping
★★

This area is one of London's leading destinations, with attractions including the IWM London, the Southbank Centre (Europe's largest arts center), and the heavenly Borough Market. Most are clustered around the Southbank and in Bankside and Southwark, but the surrounding neighborhoods of Bermondsey and Lambeth are rising rapidly, with galleries, shops, and restaurants proliferating. And the formerly drab Nine Elms area (near Vauxhall) is in the process of being totally transformed, with luxury high-rises and shops proliferating in the wake of the huge new U.S. embassy in the area.

ated by
Stein

A borough of the City of London since 1327, Southwark first became well known for its inns (the pilgrims in Chaucer's *A Canterbury Tale* set off from one), theaters, prisons, tanneries, and brothels, as well as entertainments such as cockfighting. For four centuries, this was a sort of border town outside the city walls (and jurisdiction) where Londoners went to let their hair down and behave badly. Originally, you were just as likely to see a few bouts of bearbaiting at the Globe as you were Shakespeare's most recent work. But now that south London encompasses a world-class museum, high-caliber art, music, film, and theater venues, as well as an aquarium, a historic warship, two popular food markets, and greatly improved transportation links, this neighborhood has become one of London's leading destinations.

Today, you can walk the **Thames Path** along the river from the London Eye all the way to Greenwich. The segment beside the South Bank is alive with skateboarders, secondhand-book stalls, and street entertainers. At one end the **London Eye**, a 21st-century landmark that became an instant favorite with both Londoners and out-of-towners, rises next to the **London Aquarium** and the **Southbank Centre**, home to the **Royal Festival Hall**, the **Hayward Gallery**, the **BFI Southbank**, and the **National Theatre.**

SOUTH OF THE THAMES

Getting Oriented

South of the Thames

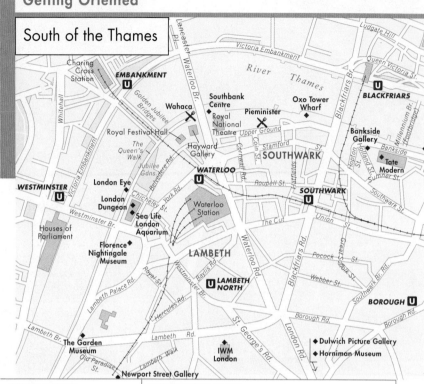

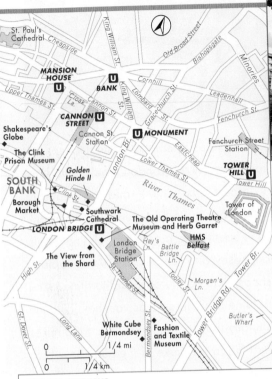

GETTING THERE

For the South Bank, use Embankment on the District, Circle, Northern, and Bakerloo lines and walk across the Golden Jubilee Bridges; or Waterloo on the Northern, Jubilee, and Bakerloo lines, from where it's a 10-minute walk.

London Bridge on the Northern and Jubilee lines is five minutes from Borough Market and Southwark Cathedral. The station also serves Bermondsey Street, although, confusingly, the next stop on the Jubilee line is called Bermondsey. Brixton has its own stop on the Victoria line.

TOP REASONS TO GO

Join the "groundlings" at Shakespeare's Globe: See one of Shakespeare's plays in this historically accurate replica of the Elizabethan theater where they were first performed.

View a new master at Tate Modern: One of the world's great collections of post-1900 modern art, the centerpiece of this Tate branch is the huge renovated electric turbine hall, now an exhibition space used for large installations.

Take in a Waterloo sunset on Waterloo Bridge: This is one of London's most romantic views, with St. Paul's to the east and the Houses of Parliament to the west.

Take a spin on the London Eye: One of the city's tallest structures, this observation wheel gives you a bird's-eye view of some of the city's most iconic sights.

FEELING PECKISH?

Pieminister. In the shopping enclave of Gabriel's Wharf, you'll find this branch of Pieminister, which began life in Borough Market. Have a meat pie made with ethically farmed ingredients like chicken and tarragon. ⊠ *Gabriel's Wharf, 56 Upper Ground, South Bank* ☎ *020/7928–5755* ⊕ *www. pieminister.co.uk* ⊙ *No dinner* Ⓜ *Waterloo.*

Wahaca. This canteen-style outpost of the eco-conscious chain serves mildly spiced Mexican food like marinated grilled chicken or tostadas with Devon crab, plus the usual burritos, quesadillas, tacos, and salads. ⊠ *119 Waterloo Rd., South Bank* ☎ *020/3697–4140* ⊕ *www.wahaca.co.uk* Ⓜ *Waterloo.*

MAKING THE MO[...]
TIME

Don't attempt to [...] south of the Thar [...] Tate Modern alo[...] whole afternoon [...] you want to do j[...] the temporary ex[...] the permanent c[...] Globe requires ab[...] for the exhibition [...] and two to three [...] performance. Finis[...] at the Oxo Tower [...] Shard's restaurant [...] spectacular view[...] return across the ri[...] London via South[...] Jubilee line from 1[...] although it's a go[...] the station. Crossin[...] nium Bridge for S[...] the Central line or [...] Jubilee Bridge to E[...] station offers longe[...] scenic alternatives.[...]

Up[...]
Elli[...]

The restaurant at Tate Modern has some of the best views in London. Here you can see St. Paul's Cathedral in the distance.

Farther east you'll come to a reconstruction of Sir Francis Drake's 16th-century ship the *Golden Hinde*; **Butler's Wharf**, where some notable restaurants occupy what were once shadowy Dickensian docklands; **The Shard**, the tallest building in the EU, which offers spectacular views over the city; and, next to **Tower Bridge**, the massive headlight-shape **City Hall.** Nearby Bermondsey Street (from "Beormund's Eye," as it was known in Saxon times) is home to the bright yellow Fashion Museum, the White Cube Gallery, and lots of trendy shops, restaurants, and cafés. Meanwhile, younger visitors will enjoy the **London Dungeon** and **HMS *Belfast,*** a decommissioned Royal Navy cruiser, while food lovers should make a straight line to London's oldest food market, **Borough Market,** where the independent stallholders sell farm-fresh produce, artisanal bread and cheese, and specialty fish and meat.

Even from the Shard's lofty viewing platform 1,016 feet up, the area south of the Thames still isn't one of London's most beautiful, but you'll be able to see how this patchwork of neighborhoods fits together. The heart is the South Bank, which extends east from the London Eye to Blackfriars Bridge, with the river to the north and Waterloo station to the south. From Blackfriars Bridge east to London Bridge is Bankside, where you'll find the Globe and Tate Modern. Moving east from London Bridge is Borough, with its cobbled streets and former factories now turned into expensive lofts. Next, southeast of Borough, is buzzy, urban Bermondsey, while leafy Dulwich, with its renowned gallery and charming period streets, is quite a distance to the south. Returning up the river to the west of the South Bank is Lambeth and then Vauxhall, with the imposing IWM London (formerly the Imperial

War Museum), a thriving gay scene, and scary through-traffic routes. It's a rapidly changing district, thanks to a regeneration spearheaded by the opening of the U.S. Embassy in adjacent Nine Elms and a slew of upscale riverside residential developments. South of here is Brixton, long the heartland of London's Afro-Caribbean community—with a lively club scene—and now attracting young families priced out of nearby Clapham.

TOP ATTRACTIONS

FAMILY

Fodor's Choice

★

Dulwich Picture Gallery. Famed for its regal old master painting collection, the Dulwich (pronounced "Dull-ich") Picture Gallery, designed by Sir John Soane, was the world's first purpose-built art museum when it opened in 1811 (the recent extension was designed by Rick Mather). The permanent collection includes landmark works by Rembrandt, Van Dyck, Rubens, Poussin, and Gainsborough, and the museum also hosts three or so major temporary exhibitions each year. Check the website for its schedule of family activities; there's a lovely café here, too. While you're in the area, take a short wander and you'll find a handful of cute clothing and crafts stores and the well-manicured Dulwich Park, which has lakeside walks and a fine display of rhododendrons in late May. Development in Dulwich Village is tightly controlled, so it feels a bit like a time capsule, with old-fashioned street signs and handsome 18th-century houses on the main street. ⌂ *Gallery Rd., Dulwich* ☎ *020/8693–5254* ⊕ *www.dulwichpicturegallery.org.uk* ⌐ *£7 (temporary exhibitions may be extra)* ⊗ *Closed Mon.* Ⓜ *Brixton station, then Bus P4. National Rail: West Dulwich from Victoria or North Dulwich from London Bridge.*

Fashion and Textile Museum. The bright yellow and pink museum (it's hard to miss) designed by Mexican architect Ricardo Legorreta features changing exhibitions devoted to developments in fashion design, textiles, and jewelry from the end of World War II to the present. Founded by designer Zandra Rhodes, and now owned by Newham College, the FTM is a favorite with fashion lovers. There are weekday fashion-based workshops and lectures on design and aspects of fashion history; the excellent gift shop sells books on fashion and one-of-a-kind pieces by local designers. After your visit, check out the many trendy restaurants, cafés, and boutiques that have bloomed on Bermondsey Street. ⌂ *83 Bermondsey St., Bermondsey* ☎ *020/7407–8664* ⊕ *www.ftmlondon. org* ⌐ *£10* ⊗ *Closed Mon.* Ⓜ *London Bridge.*

FAMILY **London Dungeon.** Saved by a keen sense of its own borderline ridiculousness, this gory attraction is more funny than frightening, with tableaux depicting the bloody demise of famous figures alongside the torture, murder, and ritual slaughter of lesser-known victims, all to a sound track of screaming, wailing, and agonized moaning. There are lively dramatizations about the Great Plague, Henry VIII, (the fictional) Sweeney Todd, and (the real) Jack the Ripper, to name a few, with costumed characters leaping out of the gloom to bring the information to life and add to the fear and fun. Perhaps most shocking are the crowds of children baying to get in: most kids absolutely love this

Built at the site of the original theater where Shakespeare's plays were performed, the modern-day Globe is a painstaking reconstruction of an open-air theater.

place, although those with more a sensitive disposition may find it too frightening (that goes for adults as well). Expect long lines on weekends and during school holidays. There are also adults-only evening tours that include drinks. ⊠ *Riverside Bldg., County Hall, Westminster Bridge Rd., South Bank* ☎ *0870/423–2240* ⊕ *www.thedungeons.com* 🖃 *From £21* Ⓜ *Waterloo.*

FAMILY

Fodor's Choice

★

London Eye. To mark the start of the new millennium, architects David Marks and Julia Barfield devised an instant icon that allows Londoners and visitors alike to see the city from a completely new perspective. The giant Ferris wheel was the largest cantilevered observation wheel ever built at the time, and remains one of the city's tallest structures. The 25-minute slow-motion ride inside one of the enclosed passenger capsules is so smooth you'd hardly know you were suspended over the Thames. On a clear day you can see up to 25 miles, with a bird's-eye view of London's most famous landmarks as you circle 360 degrees. If you're looking for a special place to celebrate, champagne and canapés can be arranged ahead of time. ■TIP→ **Buy your ticket online to avoid the long lines and get a 10% discount. For an extra £9, you can save even more time with a Fast Track flight (check in 15 minutes before your "departure."** You can also buy a combination ticket for the Eye and other London attractions (check online for details) or combine with a River Cruise for a 40-minute sightseeing voyage on the Thames. In December, there's a scenic ice rink just below the wheel. ⊠ *Jubilee Gardens, South Bank* ☎ *0871/781–3000* ⊕ *www.londoneye.com* 🖃 *From £24; cruise package from £31 (bookable online only)* Ⓜ *Waterloo.*

FAMILY **Shakespeare's Globe.** This spectacular theater is a replica of Shake-
Fodor's Choice speare's open-roof, wood-and-thatch Globe Playhouse (built in 1599
★ and burned down in 1613), where most of the Bard's greatest works
premiered. American actor and director Sam Wanamaker worked
ceaselessly for several decades to raise funds for the theater's reconstruction 200 yards from its original site, using authentic materials
and techniques, a dream that was finally realized in 1997. "Groundlings" (patrons with £5 standing-only tickets) are not allowed to sit
during the performance, but you get the best view of the stage and the
most authentic viewing experience. Fortunately, you can reserve an
actual seat on any one of the theater's three levels, but you will want
to rent a cushion for £1 (or bring your own) to soften the backless
wooden benches. The show must go on, rain or shine, warm or chilly,
so come prepared for anything. Umbrellas are banned, but you can
bring a raincoat or buy a cheap Globe rain poncho, which doubles
as a great souvenir. In the winter months, the Sam Wanamaker Playhouse, a 350-seat re-creation of an indoor Jacobean theater lighted
by candles, offers plays and concerts in a less exposed though still
atmospheric setting.

Shakespeare's Globe Exhibition, a museum under the theater (the entry
is adjacent), provides background material on Shakespeare's life, the
London in which he lived, the original Elizabethan Globe, and the
construction of the modern version. Admission to the museum also
includes a 30-minute tour of the theater (tours leave every half hour
9:30–5, but may be unavailable due to performances, rehearsals, or
events). You can also book a tour of the surrounding Bankside area,
emphasizing places Shakespeare would have frequented, including the
archaeological remains of the nearby Rose Theatre, the oldest theater
in Bankside. Or take a tour of the Wanamaker, offered every half-
hour between 1:30 and 5 on limited dates due to the performance
schedule. On days when no tours are available, the Exhibition has
reduced price admission (check the website). ⊠ *21 New Globe Walk,
Bankside* ☎ *020/7902–1500 general info, 020/7401–9919 box office*
⊕ *www.shakespearesglobe.com* ✉ *Exhibition and Globe Theatre tour
£16; Bankside tour £12.50; Wanamaker Playhouse tour £12.50 (all £2
off with valid performance ticket); Globe performances £5 (standing),
£20–£45 (seated); Wanamaker performances £10 (standing), £15–£62
(seated)* ⊘ *No Globe performances mid-Oct.–mid-Apr.; no Wanamaker
Playhouse performances mid-Apr.–mid.-Oct.* Ⓜ *London Bridge; Mansion House, then cross Southwark Bridge.*

Southbank Centre. *Please see listing in the Performing Arts chapter.*

Fodor's Choice **Tate Modern.** This spectacular renovation of a mid-20th-century power
★ station is one of the most-visited museums of modern art in the world.
Its great permanent collection, which starts in 1900 and ranges from
modernist masters like Matisse to the most cutting-edge contemporary artists, is arranged in eight areas by theme ("Media Networks"
about artists' responses to mass media) rather than by chronology. Its
blockbuster temporary exhibitions showcase the work of individual
artists like Gaugin, Rauschenberg, Modigliani, Picasso, and O'Keefe,
among others. Other major temporary exhibitions have a conceptual

focus, like works created in response to the American Black Power movement or by Soviet and Russian artists between the Revolution and the death of Stalin.

The vast **Turbine Hall** is a dramatic entrance point used to showcase big, audacious installations that tend to generate a lot of publicity. Past highlights include Olafur Eliasson's massive glowing sun, Ai Weiwei's porcelain "sunflower seeds," and Carsten Holler's huge metal slides.

On the ground floor of a 10-story addition, you'll find a gallery devoted to various types of new art, including moving image, performance, soundscapes, and interactive works, while at the top is a roof terrace offering spectacular views of the London skyline. In between are three exhibition floors offering more room for large-scale installations, for art from outside Europe and North America, and for digital and interactive projects. The Start display provides an introduction to the collection, highlighting art from various countries, cultures, and periods, all linked by color. Not to be missed in the original building is the collection of Rothko murals, originally created for the Four Seasons restaurant in New York, and displays devoted to Gerhard Richter (both on Level 2) and works by the video pioneer Nam June Paik (Level 4).

Head to the café on Level 1 or the Espresso Bar on Level 3 for stunning vistas of the Thames. The view of St. Paul's from the Espresso Bar's balcony is one of the best in London. Near the café you'll find the Drawing Bar, which lets you create work on one of several digital sketch pads and then project your result on the gallery wall.

You can join free 45-minute guided tours, each covering a different gallery: The Artist and Society at 11, In the Studio at noon, Materials and Objects at 2, and Media Networks at 3. If you plan to visit Tate Britain too, take advantage of the Tate to Tate Boat, which takes visitors back and forth between the two Tates every 40 minutes. ⊠ *Bankside* ☎ *020/7887–8888* ⊕ *www.tate.org.uk/modern* ⊠ *Free (charge for special exhibitions)* Ⓜ *Southwark, Blackfriars, St. Paul's.*

WORTH NOTING

Bankside Gallery. Two artistic societies—the Royal Society of Painter–Printmakers and the Royal Watercolour Society—have their headquarters in this gallery next to Tate Modern. Together they mount exhibitions of current members' work, which is usually for sale, along with art books, making this a great place for finding that unique, not too expensive gift. There are also regular themed exhibitions. ⊠ *48 Hopton St., Southwark* ☎ *020/7928–7521* ⊕ *www.banksidegallery.com* ⊠ *Free* ⊙ *Call ahead for hrs* Ⓜ *Mansion House, Southwark, St. Paul's.*

FAMILY **The Clink Prison Museum.** This attraction devoted to re-creating life in a medieval prison is built on the site of the original "Clink," the oldest of Southwark's five prisons and the reason why the "clink" is now slang for jail. Owned by the Bishops of Winchester from 1144 to 1780 and the oldest of Southwark's five prisons, it was the first to detain women, many for prostitution. Because of the bishops' relaxed attitude toward the endemic trade—they decided to license prostitution rather than ban it—the area within their jurisdiction was known as "the Liberty of the Clink." Inside, you'll discover how grisly a Tudor prison could be, operating on a code of cruelty, deprivation, and corruption. The prison was only a small part of Winchester Palace, a huge complex that was the bishops' London residence. You can still see the remains of the early 13th-century Great Hall, with its famous rose window, next to Southwark Cathedral. ⊠ *1 Clink St., Borough* ☎ *020/7403–0900* ⊕ *www.clink.co.uk* ✆ *£7.50* Ⓜ *London Bridge.*

Florence Nightingale Museum. Compact, highly visual, and engaging, this museum on the grounds of St. Thomas's hospital is dedicated to Florence Nightingale, who founded the first school of nursing and played a major role in establishing modern standards of health care. Exhibits are divided into three areas: one is devoted to Nightingale's Victorian childhood, the others to her work tending soldiers during the Crimean War (1854–56) and her subsequent health-care reforms. The museum incorporates Nightingale's own books and famous lamp as well as interactive displays of medical instruments and medicinal herbs. There are free half-hour tours on Wednesday at 3:30, evening lectures, temporary exhibitions, and a shop with unexpectedly amusing gifts like syringe highlighters. ⊠ *2 Lambeth Palace Rd., Lambeth* ☎ *020/7620–0374* ⊕ *www.florence-nightingale.co.uk* ✆ *£8* Ⓜ *Waterloo.*

The Garden Museum. This celebration of one of England's favorite hobbies was created in the mid-1970s after two gardening enthusiasts came upon a medieval church, which, they were horrified to discover, was about to be bulldozed. The churchyard contained the tombs of two adventurous 17th-century plant collectors, a father and son both called John Tradescant, who introduced many new species to England. Inspired to action, the gardeners rescued the church and created the museum. It has subsequently acquired one of the largest collections of historic garden tools, artifacts, and curiosities in Britain—virtually all donated by individuals—in addition to creating beautiful walled gardens that are maintained year-round by dedicated volunteers. There are also temporary exhibitions on subjects ranging from noted garden designers like Charles Jencks to the contemporary Guerilla Gardening movement (cultivating neglected land that doesn't belong to you). There's also a café and a green-thumb gift shop. It's worth visiting the church itself, which contains the tombs of William Bligh, captain of the *Bounty*, several members of the Boleyn family, and quite a few Archbishops of Canterbury. ⊠ *5 Lambeth Palace Rd., Lambeth* ☎ *020/7401–8865* ⊕ *www.gardenmuseum.org.uk* ✆ *£8* ☉ *Closed Sun.* Ⓜ *Lambeth North, Vauxhall.*

FAMILY **HMS *Belfast*.** At 613½ feet, this large light cruiser is one of the last remaining big-gun armored warships from World War II, in which it played an important role in protecting the Arctic convoys and supporting the D-Day landings in Normandy; the ship later saw action during the Korean War. This floating museum has been moored in the Thames as a maritime branch of **IWM London** since 1971. A tour of all nine decks—including the admiral's quarters, mess decks, bakery, punishment cells, operations room, engine room, and more—gives a vivid picture of life on board the ship, while the riveting interactive gun-turret experience puts you in the middle of a World War II naval battle. ☒ *The Queen's Walk, Borough* ☎ *020/7940–6300* ⊕ *www.iwm. org.uk* ☞ *£16* Ⓜ *London Bridge.*

OFF THE BEATEN PATH

Horniman Museum. Set amid 16 acres of gardens, this eclectic museum is considered something of a well-kept secret by the residents of south London—perhaps because of its out-of-the-way location. You can explore world cultures, natural history, and a fine collection of some 1,300 musical instruments (including a giant tuba) here. The emphasis is on fun and a wide range of activities, including London's oldest nature trail that features domesticated creatures such as sheep, chickens, and alpacas, and an aquarium stocked with endangered species. There's also a café and shop. It's a 15-minute bus ride from here to the Dulwich Picture Gallery; Bus P4, heading toward Brixton, takes you from door to door. ☒ *100 London Rd., Forest Hill, London* ☎ *020/8699–1872* ⊕ *www.horniman.ac.uk* ☞ *Free (small charge for temporary exhibitions and aquarium)* Ⓜ *Overground: Forest Hill.*

FAMILY
Fodor's Choice
★

IWM London. Despite its name, the cultural venue formerly known as the Imperial War Museum (one of five IWM branches around the country) does not glorify either Empire or bloodshed but emphasizes understanding through conveying the impact of 20th- and 21st-century warfare on citizens and soldiers alike. A dramatic six-story atrium at the main entrance encloses an impressive amount of hardware—including a Battle of Britain Spitfire, a German V2 rocket, tanks, guns, and submarines—along with accompanying interactive material and a café. The First World War galleries explore the wartime experience on both the home and fighting fronts, with the most comprehensive collection on the subject in the world—some 1,300 objects ranging from uniforms, equipment, and weapons to letters and diaries. Three permanent exhibitions in the Second World War galleries shed light on that conflict: an extensive and haunting Holocaust exhibition; *A Family In Wartime,* which documents the story of one London family living through the Blitz; and *Turning Points 1934–1945,* which relates key moments in the conflict to objects on display. *Peace and Security 1945–2015* looks at more contemporary hostilities, including the Cold War, Iraq, Afghanistan, and Kosovo. Other galleries are devoted to works relating to conflicts from World War I to the present day by painters, poets, documentary filmmakers, and photographers. James Bond fans won't want to miss the intriguing Secret War Gallery, which charts the work of secret agents. ☒ *Lambeth Rd., South Bank* ☎ *020/7416–5000* ⊕ *www.iwm.org.uk* ☞ *Free (charge for special exhibitions)* Ⓜ *Lambeth North.*

Newport Street Gallery. Putting the seal on Vauxhall's status as an up-and-coming neighborhood, business-savvy artist Damien Hirst opened this gallery in a cavernous space that was a former Victorian scenery-painting workshop. It currently houses a rotating selection from his large private collection of contemporary art that includes works by Francis Bacon, Banksy, Picasso, Jeff Koons, Richard Hamilton, and Tracey Emin, to name just a few, along with solo and group shows devoted to emerging artists. There's also a shop selling artists' books, limited edition prints, and sculptures, as well as a restaurant, Pharmacy 2, a reincarnation of

8

Designed by renowned architect Renzo Piano, The Shard punctures the London skyline with its record-breaking height and spectacular modernity.

Hirst's fashionable millennium-era Notting Hill watering hole. ⊠ *Newport St., London* ☎ *020/3141–9320* ⊕ *www.newportstreetgallery.com* ☒ *Free* ⊘ *Closed Mon.* Ⓜ *Vauxhall, Lambeth North.*

The Old Operating Theatre Museum and Herb Garret. This rare example of a 19th-century operating theater, the oldest in Europe, dates back to 1822, when part of the large herb garret in the roof of the 17th-century St. Thomas's church was converted for surgical use. The English baroque church was part of St. Thomas's Hospital, which was founded in the 12th century as a monastery that looked after the sick. In 1862, the hospital moved to its present Lambeth location and the operating theater was closed. It remained abandoned until 1956, when it was restored and turned into a medical museum. Today you can see the artifacts of early-19th-century medical practice: the wooden operating table under a skylight; the box of sawdust underneath used for absorbing blood; and the surrounding banks of seats where students crowded in to observe operations. Every Saturday at 2 there are demonstrations of pre-anesthetic surgical practices incorporating the knives, pliers, and handsaws that were the surgeons' tools back in the day (not for the faint-hearted or small children). Next door is a re-creation of the 17th century **Herb Garret,** with displays of the medicinal herbs St. Thomas's apothecary would have used, and there are Sunday afternoon talks on herbal medicine at 2, as well as museum tours at 12. There are also guided themed local walks like one that explores the haunts of the "bodysnatchers" who supplied corpses for Victorian medical research. ⊠ *9A St. Thomas St., Lambeth* ☎ *020/7188–2679* ⊕ *www.oldoperatingtheatre.com* ☒ *£7* ⊘ *Closed mid-Dec.–early Jan.* Ⓜ *London Bridge.*

FAMILY **Sea Life London Aquarium.** The curved, colonnaded, neoclassical former County Hall that once housed London's municipal government is now home to a superb three-level aquarium where you can walk above sharks and stingrays and view more than 600 other aquatic species, both common and rare. There are also hands-on displays. It's not the biggest aquarium you've ever seen, but the educational exhibits are particularly well arranged, with 14 zones for different oceans, water environments, and climates, ranging from a stunning coral reef to the Antarctic to a rain forest. Regular feeding times and free talks are offered throughout the day. There are also special experiences that include behind-the-scenes tours and feeding (or, for the brave, snorkeling with) sharks at an extra charge. ■TIP➔ Admission is by time slot, but for an additional £4.50 you can purchase flexible priority-entry tickets that also avoid the long lines. ⊠ *County Hall, Westminster Bridge Rd., South Bank* ☎ *0871/663–1678* ⊕ *www.visitsealife.com* ⊠ *From £26* Ⓜ *Westminster, Waterloo.*

Southwark Cathedral. Pronounced "Suth-uck," this is the oldest Gothic church in London, parts of it dating back to the 12th century. It remains off-the-beaten track, despite being the site of some remarkable memorials and a concert program that offers frequent organ recitals at lunchtime on Monday (except in August and December) and classical music at 3:15 on Tuesday (except in December), with occasional choir concerts on Thursday and Saturday evening. Originally the priory church of St. Mary Overie (as in "over the water," on the South Bank), it became a palace church under Henry VIII (when it became known as St Saviour's) until some merchant parishioners bought it from James I in 1611. It was only promoted to cathedral status in 1905. Look for the vivid 15th-century roof bosses (small ornamental wood carvings), the gaudily renovated 1408 tomb of John Gower, Richard II's poet laureate and a friend of Chaucer's, and for the Harvard Chapel, where John Harvard, a local butcher's son who went on to found the American university, was baptized. Another notable buried here (between the choir stalls) is Edmond Shakespeare, brother of William. Tours are offered on Friday at 11 am and 1 pm and on Sunday at 1 pm (£3). ⊠ *London Bridge, Bankside* ☎ *020/7367–6700* ⊕ *cathedral.southwark.anglican.org* ⊠ *Free (suggested donation £4)* Ⓜ *London Bridge.*

The View from the Shard. At 800 feet, this addition to the London skyline currently offers the highest vantage point in Western Europe. Designed by the noted architect Renzo Piano, it has attracted both admiration and disdain. While the building itself is generally highly regarded, many felt it would have been better sited in Canary Wharf (or perhaps Dubai), as it spoils views of St. Paul's Cathedral from traditional vantage points such as Hampstead's Parliament Hill. No matter how you feel about the building, there's no denying that it offers a spectacular 360-degree view over London (extending 40 miles on a clear day) from viewing platforms on levels 68 and 69, and the open-air skydeck on level 72—almost twice as high as any other viewpoint in the city. Digital telescopes provide information about 200 points of interest. There's a weather guarantee that lets you return on a more clement day if visibility is seriously impeded, and various themed events like silent discos or early morning yoga classes are offered at an extra charge. If you find the price as eye-wateringly high as the viewing platforms, there's a less dramatic but still very impressive (and free) view from the lobby of the Shangri-La hotel on the 35th floor, or, in the evenings, the hotel's chic Gong bar on the 52nd floor (over-18s only). ✉ *Railway Approach, Borough* ☎ *0344/499–7222* ⊕ *www.theviewfromtheshard.com* ✉ *From £31* Ⓜ *London Bridge.*

White Cube Bermondsey. When the United Kingdom's highest-profile commercial gallery moved to this huge converted 1970s-era warehouse on Bermondsey Street, it sealed the area's reputation as a rising art-scene hot spot. This is the home gallery of some of today's top contemporary artists, including Jake and Dinos Chapman, Gilbert and George, Gary Hume, Anthony Gormley, Sam Taylor-Wood, Chuck Close, Anselm Kiefer, and several other artists with international reputations. An antiseptic central cuboid gallery, the "white cube"—also called 9 x 9 x 9 (meters, that is)—rests between two other spaces that host smaller exhibitions. There is also a bookshop and auditorium. ✉ *144–152 Bermondsey St., Bermondsey* ☎ *0207/930–5373* ⊕ *whitecube.com* ☯ *Closed Mon.* Ⓜ *London Bridge.*

KENSINGTON, CHELSEA, KNIGHTSBRIDGE, AND BELGRAVIA

Getting Oriented

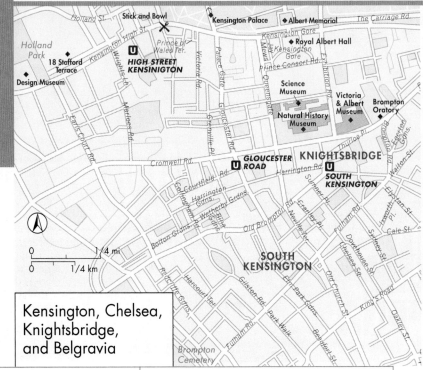

Kensington, Chelsea, Knightsbridge, and Belgravia

GETTING THERE	TOP REASONS TO GO
Several Tube stations are nearby: Sloane Square and High Street Kensington on the District and Circle lines; Knightsbridge and Hyde Park Corner on the Piccadilly line; Earl's Court, South Kensington, and Gloucester Road on the District, Circle, and Piccadilly lines; Holland Park on the Central line; Ladbroke Grove on the Hammersmith and City line; and Victoria on the District, Circle, and Victoria lines.	**Hunt for treasure at the V&A Museum:** The Victoria & Albert is the world's best decorative arts museum, with millions of objects to dazzle you. **Attract a dinosaur's attention at the Natural History Museum:** Your face may turn from delight to fright as you realize that the museum's animatronic *T. rex* has noticed you—and is licking its rather large chops! **Glimpse royal domestic life at Kensington Palace:** The public areas and gardens of this royal family home show off some of the beauty enjoyed by its past and present residents, including Queen Victoria, Princess Diana, and the Duke and Duchess of Cambridge (William and Kate).

SAFETY	
This is one of London's safest districts, but beware of pickpockets in shopping areas.	

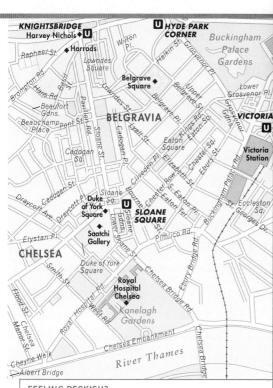

MAKING THE MOST OF YOUR TIME

You could fill three or four days in this borough, especially if you enjoy museums. Give yourself at least a half-day for the Victoria & Albert Museum, a half-day for Kensington Palace, and a half-day for either the Natural History Museum or the Science Museum.

A GRAZER'S PARADISE

Duke of York Square Farmers' Market. West London's answer to Borough Market, this Saturday open-air market is in a pedestrian-only plaza off Duke of York Square, a chic shopping precinct. It hosts 40 stalls purveying artisanal and locally produced products from more than 150 small producers. Like Borough Market, this is a grazer's paradise, giving you the chance to sample fresh oysters and cooked sausages as well as yummy hot snacks from countries ranging from Brazil to Thailand. ⊠ *Duke of York Sq., Chelsea* ☎ *020/7823-5577* ⊕ *www.dukeofyorksquare.com* ⊘ *Closed Sun.–Fri.* Ⓜ *Sloane Sq.*

FEELING PECKISH?

Stick and Bowl. This hole-in-the-wall restaurant, a neighborhood favorite for more than 20 years, is an amazing bargain for this pricey part of town, serving good basic Chinese food at reasonable prices. Standouts on the extensive menu include roast duck, BBQ pork, and crispy pork in noodle soup. ⊠ *31 Kensington High St., Kensington* ☎ *020/7937-2778* ▤ *No credit cards* Ⓜ *High St. Kensington.*

NEAREST PUBLIC RESTROOMS

Most public restrooms have been replaced by futuristic "autoloos": booths on street corners that cost £1. If you're not brave enough to try them, head to the restrooms at department store Peter Jones or Harvey Nichols. Or ask for the "loo" in a pub, but be prepared for "sorry" if you're not a customer.

9

Sightseeing
★★★★
Nightlife
★★
Dining
★★★★
Lodging
★★★★
Shopping
★★★★★

The Royal Borough of Kensington & Chelsea (or K&C, as the locals call it) is where you'll find London at its richest, and not just in the moneyed sense. South Kensington offers a concentration of great museums near Cromwell Road, with historic Kensington Palace nearby in Kensington Gardens. Once-raffish Chelsea, where the Pre-Raphaelites painted and Mick Jagger partied, is now a thoroughly respectable home for the discreetly wealthy, while flashier Knightsbridge has become a haven for international plutocrats, with shopping to match their tastes.

KENSINGTON

Updated by
Ellin Stein

Kensington comprises the area along the southern edge of Hyde Park from Exhibition Road (where the big museum complex is) and the area to the west of the park bordered by leafy Holland Park Avenue on the north and traffic-heavy Cromwell Road on the south. This more westerly zone includes the satellite neighborhood of Holland Park, with its serenely grand villas and charming park, as well as local shopping mecca Kensington High Street and the antiques shops on Kensington Church Street.

Kensington's first royal connection was created when King William III became fed up with the dampness arising from the Thames, so he bought a country place there in 1689 and converted it into **Kensington Palace.** Queen Victoria's consort, Prince Albert, added the jewel in the borough's crown when he turned the profits of the Great Exhibition of 1851 into South Kensington's metropolis of museums: the **Victoria & Albert Museum (V&A),** the **Science Museum,** and the **Natural History Museum.** Posthumous tributes to the prince in the area include the **Royal Albert Hall,** with bas-reliefs that make it resemble a giant, redbrick Wedgwood teapot, and the lavish **Albert Memorial.**

Turn into Derry Street or Young Street and enter **Kensington Square,** one of the most complete 17th-century residential squares in London. **18 Stafford Terrace,** the perfectly preserved family home of a well-to-do, aesthetically inclined Victorian household, is nearby.

TOP ATTRACTIONS

Design Museum. Opened in late 2016 in its new home in the former Commonwealth Institute, this museum was the first in the United Kingdom to place everyday contemporary objects in a social and cultural context and to consider their role in the history of design. A free, permanent exhibition displays some 1,000 examples of 20th- and 21st-century design—from furniture, fashion, and domestic products to digital technology, architecture, and engineering. The temporary exhibitions may be focused on leading individual designers, such as Charles and Ray Eames, Isamu Noguchi, Terence Conran, or Christian Louboutin, or on themes such as the global influence of Californian design. There's also a design library and archive, two shops, a café, and a restaurant. ■ **TIP➔** Young designers ages 5–11 may enjoy the free, drop-in "Create and Make" workshops held the last Sunday of every month. ✉ *224–238 Kensington High St., Kensington* ☎ *020/3862–5900* ⊕ *www.design-museum.org* 🖾 *Free (charge for temporary exhibitions)* 🕤 *Closed Dec. 25-26* Ⓜ *High St. Kensington.*

18 Stafford Terrace. The home of *Punch* cartoonist Edward Linley Sambourne in the 1870s, this charming house is a rare example of the "Aesthetic interior" style; it displays delightful Victorian and Edwardian antiques, fabrics, and paintings, as well as several samples of Linley Sambourne's work for *Punch.* The Italianate house was the scene for society parties when Anne Messel was in residence in the 1940s. This being Kensington, there's inevitably a royal connection: Messel's son, Antony Armstrong-Jones, was married to the late Princess Margaret, and their son has preserved the connection by taking the title Viscount Linley. Admission in the morning is by reservation on a 75-minute guided tour only (Saturday morning tours are given by costumed actors), but in the afternoon you are free to wander at will. There's also an evening tour the third Wednesday of every month. ✉ *18 Stafford Terr., Kensington* ☎ *0207/602–3316* ⊕ *www.rbkc.gov.uk/linleysambournehouse* 🖾 *£7 (£10 with guided tour, £12 evening tour)* 🕤 *Closed Mon., Tues., Thurs., and Fri.* Ⓜ *High St. Kensington.*

FAMILY **Kensington Palace.** This is a rare chance to get a glimpse into the more domestic and personal side of royal life. Neither as imposing as Buckingham Palace nor as charming as Hampton Court, Kensington Palace is something of a Royal Family commune, with various close relatives of the Queen occupying large apartments in the private part of the palace. Bought in 1689 by Queen Mary and King William III, it was converted into a palace by Sir Christopher Wren and Nicholas Hawksmoor, and royals have been in residence ever since. Princess Diana lived here with her sons after her divorce, and this is where Prince William now lives with his wife, Catherine, Duchess of Cambridge, their young son, George, and daughter, Charlotte, while Prince Harry has a cottage on the grounds.

The State Apartments are open to the public. The Queen's State Apartments are the private quarters of Queen Mary II, who ruled jointly with her husband, William II. By contrast, the lavish King's State Apartments, originally built for George I, are a stage set, a circuit of sumptuous rooms where Georgian monarchs received and entertained courtiers, politicians, and foreign dignitaries. Look for the King's Staircase, with its panoramic trompe-l'oeil painting, and the King's Gallery, with royal artworks surrounded by rich red damask walls, intricate gilding, and a beautiful painted ceiling. One permanent exhibition, *Victoria Revealed,* is devoted to the private life of Queen Victoria, who was born and grew up here. There are also temporary exhibitions, such as *Diana: Her Fashion Story,* a display of some of the late princess's most iconic outfits, running through February 2019.

Outside, the grounds are almost as lovely as the palace itself, and are a fine location for a picnic on one of the benches—or head for the delightful café (busy during peak hours) in the Orangery, near the Sunken Garden. A new extension adjoining the Orangery is planned to house the Royal Ceremonial Dress Collection. Also at the Orangery you can indulge in a formal afternoon tea.

■ **TIP**→ If you plan to also visit the Tower of London, Hampton Court Palace, Banqueting House, and Kew Palace, become a member of Historic Royal Palaces. It costs $80 per person, or $105 for a family, and gives you free entry to all five sites for a year. ⊠ *The Broad Walk, Kensington Gardens, Kensington* ☎ *0207/482–7799 for advance booking in U.K., 0203/166–6000* ⊕ *www.hrp.org.uk* ✆ *£19 (£18 online)* ☉ *Closed Dec. 24–26* ⌨ *The palace has a wheelchair-accessible elevator, and Kensington Gardens has electric buggies for mobility-impaired visitors* Ⓜ *Queensway, High St. Kensington.*

FAMILY
Fodor's Choice
★
Natural History Museum. Originally built to house the British Museum's natural history collection and bolstered by samples provided by Britain's great 19th-century explorers and scientists—notably Charles Darwin—this is one of the world's preeminent museums of natural history and earth sciences. The terra-cotta facade of this enormous Victorian cathedral of science (which was featured prominently in the movie *Paddington*) is embellished with relief panels depicting living creatures to the left of the entrance and extinct ones to the right (although some species have subsequently changed categories). Most are represented inside the museum, which contains more than 70 million different specimens. Only a small percentage is on public display, but you could still spend a day here and not come close to seeing everything.

The skeleton of a giant blue whale dominates the vaulted, cathedral-like entrance hall. Meanwhile, similarly huge dino bones can be found in the **Dinosaur Gallery** (Blue Zone), along with fossils and some extremely long Iguanodon teeth. You'll also come face-to-face with a virtual Jurassic sea dragon and a giant animatronic *T. rex* that's programmed to sense when human prey is near and "respond" in character. When he does, you can hear the shrieks of fear and delight all the way across the room. Kids love it.

Ice-skaters outside the Natural History Museum in South Kensington

An escalator takes you into a giant globe in the **Earth Galleries,** where there's a choice of levels to explore. Don't leave without checking out the earthquake simulation in the **Volcanoes and Earthquake Gallery.** The **Darwin Centre** houses some of the millions of items the museum itself doesn't have room to display, including "Archie," a 28-foot giant squid. If you want to see Archie and some of the other thousands of animal specimens preserved in spirit, you'll need to book one of the low-cost behind-the-scenes Spirit Collection tours (around £10). These 45-minute tours take place at 11:30, 12:30, and 1:30, plus 3:30 on weekends, and can be booked on the same day (space is limited, so come early). The center's interactive **Cocoon Experience** is a free 45-minute tour that reveals how the museum stores, preserves, and uses specimens from its plant and insect collections. In the David Attenborough Studio, there are free, half-hour drop-in talks (usually on Friday and Saturday afternoon) given by scientists and curators, covering a wildly eclectic range of subjects. Night owls might prefer one of the evening talks or spending an entire night in the museum at one of the "Dino Snores" events.

The museum has an outdoor ice-skating rink October through January, and a popular Christmas fair. ✉ *Cromwell Rd., South Kensington* ☎ *0207/942–5000* ⊕ *www.nhm.ac.uk* 🎟 *Free (some fees for special exhibitions)* 🕙 *Closed Dec. 24–26* Ⓜ *S. Kensington.*

FAMILY
Fodor'sChoice
★
Science Museum. With attractions ranging from entertainingly educational exhibits—like the Wonderlab interactive gallery, where kids can perform their own scientific experiments, to a sublime exhibition on science in the 18th century—the Science Museum brings the subject alive for visitors of all ages. Highlights include *Puffing Billy,* the oldest

9

steam locomotive in the world; Watson and Crick's original DNA model; and the actual Apollo 10 capsule. The six floors are devoted to subjects as diverse as space exploration, jet fighter flight simulators, the large Hadron collider, 3-D printing, historical ship models, and the history of robots over the last 400 years. The **Information Age** gallery, devoted to communication networks from the telegraph to the Internet, was opened in 2014 by Queen Elizabeth, who marked the occasion by sending her first tweet. Overshadowed by a three-story blue-glass wall, the **Wellcome Wing** is an annex to the rear of the museum, devoted to contemporary science and technology. It contains a 450-seat IMAX theater and the Legend of Apollo—an advanced motion simulator that combines seat vibration with other technical gizmos to re-create the experience of a moon landing. If you're a group of at least five, you might be able to get a place on one of the popular monthly Science Night sleepovers by booking well in advance. Aimed at kids 7 to 11 years old, these overnight experiences include hands-on science workshops and an IMAX show the next morning; check the website for details. One of the three great South Kensington museums, it stands next to the Natural History Museum in a more modern, plainer building. ✉ *Exhibition Rd., South Kensington* ☎ *0870/870–4868* ⊕ *www.sciencemuseum.org.uk* 🎫 *Free (charge for special exhibitions, IMAX, and simulator rides)* Ⓜ *South Kensington.*

Fodors Choice **Victoria & Albert Museum.** Known to all as the V&A, this huge museum
★   with more than 2 million items on display in 145 galleries is devoted to the applied arts of all disciplines, all periods, and all nationalities. First opened as the South Kensington Museum in 1857, it was renamed in 1899 in honor of Queen Victoria's late husband and has since grown to become one of the country's best-loved cultural institutions, with high-profile temporary exhibitions alongside an impressive permanent collection. Many collections at the V&A are presented not by period but by category—textiles, sculpture, jewelry, and so on. ■TIP➜ It's a tricky building to navigate, so use the free map.

Nowhere is the benefit of the categorization more apparent than in the **Fashion Gallery** (Room 40), where formal 18th-century court dresses are displayed alongside the haute couture styles of contemporary designers. The museum has become known for high-profile temporary exhibitions exploring fashion icons such as Alexander McQueen and Balenciaga and pop legends including David Bowie and Pink Floyd.

The **British Galleries** (Rooms 52–58 and 118–125) survey British art and design from 1500 to 1900 and are full of rare and beautiful artifacts such as the Tudor Great Bed of Ware (immortalized in Shakespeare's *Twelfth Night*). Among the series of actual rooms that have been painstakingly reconstructed piece by piece are the glamorous rococo Norfolk House Music Room and the serenely elegant Henrietta St. drawing room, originally designed in 1722.

The **Asian Galleries** (Rooms 44–47) are full of treasures, but among the most striking items on display is a remarkable collection of ornate samurai armor in the **Japanese Gallery** (Room 44). Works from China, Korea, and the Islamic Middle East have their own displays. Also of note is a new gallery thematically grouped around Buddhist art from different regions and periods. The Europe Gallery (Rooms 1–7) brings together more than 1,100 objects created between 1600 and 1815, while the Medieval and Renaissance galleries, which document European art and culture from 300 to 1600, have the largest collection of works from the period outside of Italy. A recently enhanced entrance off Exhibition Road offers access through the U.K.'s first porcelain-tiled public courtyard that also serves as a venue for contemporary installations and a new glass-fronted café. From late 2018, a new photography center will house books, equipment, and more than 270,000 prints formerly held by the Royal Photographic Society, joining the more than 500,000 photos already in the museum's collection.

As a whirlwind introduction, you could take a free one-hour Introductory tour (daily at 10:30, 11:30, 12:30, 1:30, and 3:30, plus Friday night at 7). There are also free weekend tours of the British, Medieval and Renaissance, and Europe Galleries, each one hour, and a one-hour tour of the Theatre and Performance collections (including costumes from *The Lion King* plus posters, costumes, and sets from other shows) at 2 daily. Occasional public lectures during the week are delivered by bigwigs from the art and fashion worlds in addition to free lectures throughout the week given by museum staff. ■ TIP→ Whatever time you visit, the spectacular sculpture hall will be filled with artists, both amateur and professional, sketching the myriad artworks on display there. Don't be shy; bring a pad and join in. ✉ *Cromwell Rd., South Kensington* ☎ *020/7942–2000* ⊕ *www.vam.ac.uk* ✑ *Free (charge for some special exhibitions, from £5)* ⊙ *Closed Dec. 24–26* Ⓜ *South Kensington.*

CHELSEA

Chelsea was settled before the Domesday Book was compiled and already fashionable when two of Henry VIII's wives lived there. On the banks of the Thames are the vast grounds of the **Royal Hospital**, designed by Christopher Wren. A walk along the riverside embankment will take you to **Cheyne Walk,** a lovely street dating back to the 18th century. Several of its more notable residents—from J. M. W. Turner and Henry James to Laurence Olivier and Keith Richards—are commemorated by blue plaques on their former houses.

The **Albert Bridge,** a sherbet-color Victorian confection of a suspension bridge, provides one of London's great romantic views, especially at night. Leave time to explore the tiny Georgian lanes of pastel-color houses that veer off King's Road to the north—especially **Jubilee Place** and **Burnsall Street,** leading to the hidden "village square" of **Chelsea Green.** On Saturday there's an excellent farmers' market up from the Saatchi Gallery in Duke of York's Square selling artisanal cheese and chocolates, local oysters, and organic meats, plus stalls serving international food.

Residential Chelsea extends along the river from the Chelsea Bridge west to the Battersea Bridge and north as far as the Old Brompton Road.

TOP ATTRACTIONS

RHS Chelsea Flower Show. Run by the Royal Horticultural Society, the Chelsea Flower Show, the year's highlight for thousands of garden-obsessed Brits, is held every May (usually the third week). The huge showcase for garden design and horticultural innovation takes up all of the Royal Hospital's large grounds. You can buy all manner of gardening supplies and accessories from the many exhibitors, and the end of the last day sees a scrimmage for discount plants from the displays. ✉ *Chelsea* ☎ *0844/995–9664 for tickets, 0203/176–5800 from outside U.K.* ⊕ *www.rhs.org.uk* ✎ *From £41 (discounts for RHS members)* ⊘ *Closed Sun. and Mon.*

Royal Hospital Chelsea. Charles II founded this residence for elderly and infirm soldiers in 1682 to reward the troops who had fought for him in the civil wars of 1642–46 and 1648. No sick people are treated here today; it's more of a historic retirement home. A creation of three of England's greatest architects—Wren, Vanbrugh, and Hawksmoor—this small enclave of brick and Portland stone set in expansive manicured grounds (which you can visit) surrounds the Figure Court (the figure being a 1682 gilded bronze statue of Charles II dressed as a Roman general). The beautiful Wren-designed chapel, a working church, and the Great Hall (dining room), where you can see Antonio Verrio's vast oil painting of Charles on horseback, are open to the public at certain times during the day. There is a small museum devoted to the history of the resident "Chelsea Pensioners," but the real attraction, along with the building, is the approximately 300 pensioners themselves. Recognizable by their traditional scarlet frock coats with gold buttons, medals, and tricorne hats, they are all actual veterans, who wear the uniform, and the history it represents, with a great deal of pride. Individuals can visit the grounds, chapel, Great Hall, and museum for free, or you can go on a 90-minute guided tour for groups of 10 or more (from £180 per group; must be booked a month in advance) led by one of the pensioners. ✉ *Royal Hospital Rd., Chelsea* ☎ *020/7881–5298* ⊕ *www.chelsea-pensioners.co.uk* ✎ *Free* ⊘ *Closed Sun., holidays, and for special events. Museum closed on weekends. Great Hall closed noon–2* Ⓜ *Sloane Sq.*

Saatchi Gallery. Charles Saatchi, who made his fortune in advertising, is one of Britain's canniest collectors of contemporary art, credited with popularizing the Young British Artists movement through his championing of early works by the likes of Damien Hirst and Tracey Emin. The museum's home is at the former Duke of York's HQ, just off King's Road. Built in 1803, its grand period exterior belies its imaginatively restored modern interior, which was transformed into 15 exhibition spaces of varying size and shape. Unlike Tate Modern, there is no permanent collection other than ongoing site-specific installations: at any one time, galleries are devoted to between one and three exhibitions that normally run for up to six months, some quite pop culture oriented, like the Rolling Stones' "Exhibitionism" retrospective. There's also an excellent café, which is open late. ✉ *Duke of York's HQ Bldg., King's Rd., Chelsea* ☎ *020/7811–3070* ⊕ *www.saatchigallery.com* ✎ *Free* Ⓜ *Sloane Sq.*

World-famous Harrods has been luring shoppers with its classic wares since 1834.

KNIGHTSBRIDGE

There's no getting away from it. With two world-famous department stores, **Harrods** and **Harvey Nichols**, a few hundred yards apart; numerous boutiques selling the biggest names in international luxury and expensive jewelry; and people-watching including viewing street racers in Maseratis—London's wealthiest enclave will appeal most to those who enjoy conspicuous consumption.

Posh Sloane Street is lined with top-end designer boutiques such as Prada, Dior, and Tods. If it all starts to become a bit generic (expensive generic), **Beauchamp Place** (pronounced "Beecham") is lined with equally luxe one-off boutiques, which tend to be more distinctive and less global.

Knightsbridge is located to the east of Kensington, bordered by Hyde Park on the north and Pont Street just past Harrods on the south.

WORTH NOTING

Brompton Oratory (*London Oratory*). This is a late product of the mid-19th-century English Roman Catholic revival led by John Henry Cardinal Newman (1801–90), who established the oratory in the 1840s and whose statue you see outside. Architect Herbert Gribble was an unknown 29-year-old when he won a competition to design the church, bringing a baroque exuberance to his concept for the vast, incredibly ornate interior. It's punctuated by treasures far older than the church itself, like the giant Carrara marble *Twelve Apostles* in the nave, sculpted by Giuseppe Mazzuoli in the 1680s for Siena's cathedral. The Oratory is known for the quality of its organs and choir, with exceptional music being an integral part of services here. ✉ *Brompton Rd., Knightsbridge* ☎ *0207/808–0900* ⊕ *www.bromptonoratory.com* ✉ *Free* Ⓜ *South Kensington.*

BELGRAVIA

Steps away from the roaring traffic of Hyde Park Corner, lying just to the east of Kensington and Chelsea, is quiet, fashionable Belgravia, one of the most impressive set pieces of 19th-century urban planning. Street after street is lined with grand, cream-color stucco terraces, once aristocrats' townhouses and most still part of the Grosvenor estate owned by the Duke of Westminster. Many buildings are leased to embassies or organizations, but a remarkable number around **Lowndes Square, Eaton Place,** and **Eaton Square** remain in the hands of private owners, whether old money or new oligarchs who put their security guards in the attached mews houses. Some people consider the area near **Elizabeth Street** to be southern Belgravia; others call it Pimlico-Victoria. Whatever its name, here small, unique stores specialize in baked goods, wine, gifts, and stationery.

TOP ATTRACTIONS

Belgrave Square. This is the heart of Belgravia, once the preferred address for the gentry's London townhouses, though now mostly occupied by organizations, embassies, and the international rich. The Square and the streets leading off it share a remarkably consistent elegant architectural style thanks to all being part of a Regency redevelopment scheme commissioned by the Duke of Westminster and designed by Thomas Cubitt with George Basevi. The grand, cream-color stucco terraced houses were snapped up by aristocrats and politicians due to their proximity to Buckingham Palace just around the corner, and still command record prices on the rare occasions when they come onto the market. The private garden in the center is open to the public once a year (⊕ *www.opensquares.org*). Walk down Belgrave Place toward Eaton Place and you pass two of Belgravia's most beautiful mews: Eaton Mews North and Eccleston Mews, both fronted by grand rusticated entrances right out of a 19th-century engraving. ■TIP➔ Traffic can really whip around Belgrave Square, so be careful. ✉ *Belgravia* Ⓜ *Hyde Park Corner.*

NOTTING HILL
AND BAYSWATER

Getting Oriented

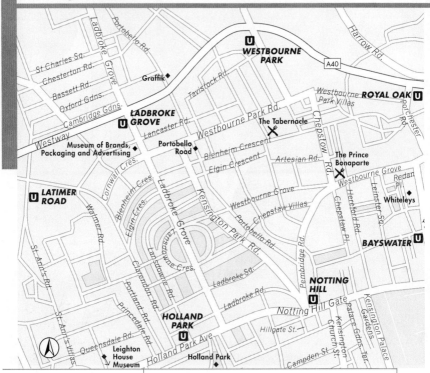

GETTING THERE	TOP REASONS TO GO
For Portobello Market and environs, the best Tube stops are Ladbroke Grove and Westbourne Park (Hammersmith and City line); ask for directions when you emerge. The Notting Hill Gate stop on the District, Circle, and Central lines enables you to walk the length of Portobello Road while going slightly downhill.	**Unearth a bargain on Portobello Road:** The early bird can catch considerably more than the worm; go before 10 am on Saturday to hook the good stuff at London's world-famous antiques market, or come during the week for a leisurely browse.

A GOOD WALK	**Refresh in Hyde Park:** Explore one of London's largest green spaces by walking, cycling ("Boris bikes" are available at several sites), skating with the Friday Night Skate, or rowing on the Serpentine, the tranquil lake that snakes through the park.
To spot Notting Hill's grandest houses, stroll over to Lansdowne Road, Lansdowne Crescent, and Lansdowne Square—two blocks west of Kensington Park Road.	**Take in contemporary art at the Serpentine Galleries:** Expand your cultural horizons at one of London's foremost showcases for modern art, or just have a bite at the café in the extension to the Serpentine Sackler Gallery, designed by famed architect Zaha Hadid and a work of art in itself.

Notting Hill and Bayswater

Westway

Bishop's Bridge Rd.

Leinster Gdns.

Queensborough Ter.

Porchester Ter.

Inverness Ter.

Queensway

Westbourne Ter.

Gloucester Ter.

Eastbourne Ter.

Praed St.

Paddington Station

PADDINGTON Ⓤ

Sussex Gardens

Sussex Place

Craven Hill

Lancaster Gate

LANCASTER GATE Ⓤ

Bayswater Rd.

Bayswater Rd.

Ⓤ **QUEENSWAY**

The Broad Walk

Kensington Gardens ◆

Serpentine Galleries ↘

Hyde Park ◆ ↘

E. Carriage Dr.

0 _____ 1/4 mi
0 _____ 1/4 km

MAKING THE MOST OF YOUR TIME

Saturday is the most exciting day for shopping, eating, and drinking here.

The market gets crowded by noon in summer, so come early if you are serious about shopping.

Head south from the north end of Portobello Road, using the parks to take a break on the way.

On Sunday, the Hyde Park and Kensington Gardens railings along Bayswater Road are lined with artists displaying their work, which may slow your progress.

Well-heeled locals are often out on Sunday with friends in the pubs or with kids in the parks.

SAFETY

At night, avoid straying from the main streets north of Westbourne Park Road toward Ladbroke Grove's high-rise estates (projects) and the surrounding areas.

10

FEELING PECKISH?

The Prince Bonaparte. It's had an art deco makeover, but one thing hasn't changed: the high standard of its modern British food and a fine selection of artisanal ales and carefully chosen wines. A stone's throw from Portobello Market, it's the perfect place for a drink or a bite to eat. ✉ *80 Chepstow Rd., Bayswater* ☎ *020/7313–9491* ⊕ *www.theprincebonapartew2.co.uk* Ⓜ *Notting Hill Gate, Royal Oak.*

The Tabernacle. The Victorian Gothic interior of this bar, café, and arts center combo hosts intimate music gigs, literary events with the likes of Tales of The City's Armistead Maupin, and 15-minute talks with speakers such as historian Niall Ferguson. The food is Caribbean-influenced, and the atmosphere, especially in the outdoor courtyard, is relaxed. ✉ *34–35 Powis Sq., Notting Hill* ☎ *020/7221–9700* ⊕ *www.tabernaclew11.com* ☺ *Closed Sun.* Ⓜ *Notting Hill Gate.*

Sightseeing
★★
Nightlife
★★★
Dining
★★★
Lodging
★★★
Shopping
★★★★

The center of London's West Indian community from the 1950s through the '70s, Notting Hill these days is the address of choice for the well-heeled, be they bankers, rock stars, media and advertising types, or rich hippies. Teeming with trendy restaurants, cool bars, and buzzing street markets, the area is also studded with some of London's most handsome historic residences, crescents, and terraces. Every weekend, the hordes descend on Portobello Road to go bargain-hunting at one of the world's great antiques markets. Holland Park, to the west, has even grander villas, while Bayswater (to the east) has excellent world-cuisine restaurants.

NOTTING HILL

Updated by
James O'Neill

Notting Hill as we know it emerged in the 1840s when the wealthy Ladbroke family developed a small suburb to the west of London. Before then, the area had the far less glamorous name of "the Potteries and the Piggeries," after the two industries it was best known for: ceramics and pig farming.

During the 1980s, Notting Hill transformed from a lively but down-at-heel and sometimes dangerous West Indian enclave to a supertrendy fashionable neighborhood. The area's Caribbean legacy persists, however, not least in the form of the annual Notting Hill Carnival in late August. The new millennium saw Notting Hill's fame go global thanks to the hit romcom of the same name, though the movie itself was criticized by locals for downplaying the area's cultural diversity. For the Notting Hill of the silver screen, head for fashionable **Westbourne Grove** and **Ledbury Road,** lined with eclectic independent boutiques offering highly desirable designer goods for the home and family, as well as contemporary art—prices and taste levels are high.

The Wellington Arch Monument proudly welcomes visitors to Hyde Park, one of London's largest royal parks.

For less rarefied shopping, try **Portobello Road**; the famous Saturday antiques market and shops are at the southern end. A little farther southwest lies the elegant splendor of **Holland Park**, at the end of which you'll find the exotic delights of the **Leighton House Museum.**

TOP ATTRACTIONS

FAMILY **Holland Park.** Formerly the grounds of an aristocrat's house and open to the public only since 1952, Holland Park is an often-overlooked gem and possibly London's most romantic park. The northern "Wilderness" end offers woodland walks among native and exotic trees first planted in the early 18th century. Foxes, rabbits, and hedgehogs are among the residents. The central part of the park is given over to the manicured lawns—still stalked by raucous peacocks—one would expect at a stately home, although Holland House itself, originally built by James I's chancellor and later the site of a 19th-century salon frequented by Byron, Dickens, and Disraeli, was largely destroyed by German incendiary bombs in 1940. The east wing was reconstructed and has been incorporated into a youth hostel, while the remains of the front terrace provide an atmospheric backdrop for the open-air performances of the April–September **Holland Park Opera Festival** (☎ *0300/999–1000 box office* ⊕ *www.operahollandpark.com*). The glass-walled Garden Ballroom is now the **Orangery,** which hosts art exhibitions and other public events, as does the **Ice House,** while an adjoining former granary has become the upscale Belvedere restaurant. In spring and summer the air is fragrant with aromas from a rose garden, great banks of rhododendrons, and an azalea walk. Garden

10

enthusiasts will also not want to miss the tranquil, traditional **Kyoto Garden,** a legacy of London's 1991 Japan Festival. The southern part of the park is given over to sport and play: cricket and football (soccer) pitches; a golf practice area; tennis courts; a well-supervised children's Adventure Playground; and a giant outdoor chess set. ⊠ *Ilchester Pl., West Holland Park* ⊕ *www.rbkc.gov.uk/leisure-and-culture/parks/ holland-park* Ⓜ *Holland Park, High Street Kensington.*

FAMILY
Fodor'sChoice
★
Hyde Park. Along with the smaller St. James's and Green parks to the east, the 350-acre Hyde Park started as Henry VIII's hunting grounds. Along its south side runs Rotten Row, once Henry's royal path to the hunt—the name is a corruption of *Route du Roi* (Route of the King). It's still used by the Household Cavalry, who live at the Hyde Park Barracks—a high-rise and a low, ugly red block, now up for sale—to the left. You can see the Guardsmen in full regalia leaving on horseback for guard duty at Buckingham Palace at about 10:30 (or come at noon when they return). Hyde Park is wonderful for strolling, cycling, or just relaxing by the Serpentine, the long body of water near its southern border. On the south side, by the 1930s **Serpentine Lido**, is the site of the **Diana Princess of Wales Memorial Fountain**, which opened in 2003 and is a good spot to refuel at a café. On Sunday, close to Marble Arch you'll find the uniquely British tribute to free speech, Speakers' Corner. Though not what it was in the days before people could use the Internet to vent their spleen, it still offers a unique assortment of passionate, if occasionally irrational, advocates literally getting up on soapboxes. ⊠ *Hyde Park* ☎ *030/0061–2114* ⊕ *www.royalparks.org.uk* ✉ *Free* Ⓜ *Hyde Park Corner, Knightsbridge, Lancaster Gate, Marble Arch.*

FAMILY
Fodor'sChoice
★
Kensington Gardens. Laid out in 1689 by William III, who commissioned Sir Christopher Wren to build Kensington Palace, the gardens are a formal counterpart to neighboring Hyde Park. Just to the north of the palace itself is the Dutch-style **Sunken Garden**. Nearby, the 1912 bronze statue *Peter Pan* commemorates the boy in J. M. Barrie's story who lived on an island in the Serpentine and who never grew up. Kids will enjoy the magical **Diana Princess of Wales Memorial Playground**, whose design was also inspired by Barrie's book. The **Elfin Oak** is a 900-year-old tree trunk that was carved with scores of tiny elves, fairies, and other fanciful creations in the 1920s. The **Italian Gardens** (1860) comprise several ornamental ponds and fountains, while the **Round Pond** attracts model-boat enthusiasts. ⊠ *Kensington* ☎ *030/0061–2000* ⊕ *www.royalparks.org.uk* ✉ *Free* Ⓜ *High Street Kensington, Lancaster Gate, Queensway, South Kensington.*

Fodor'sChoice
★
Leighton House Museum. Leading Victorian artist Frederic (Lord) Leighton lived and worked in this building on the edge of Holland Park, spending 30 years (and quite a bit of money) transforming it into an opulent "private palace of art" infused with an orientalist aesthetic sensibility. The interior is a sumptuous Arabian Nights fantasy, with walls lined in peacock blue tiles designed by Leighton's friend, the ceramic artist William de Morgan, and beautiful mosaic wall panels and floors, marble pillars, and gilded ceilings. The centerpiece is the Arab Hall, its marble walls adorned with even more intricate murals made from 16th- and 17th-century ceramic tiles imported from Syria, Turkey, and

Iran, surmounted by a domed ceiling covered in gold leaf with a gold mosaic frieze running underneath. You can also visit Leighton's studio, with its huge north window and dome; the house is filled with paintings, several of his own along with works by other Pre-Raphaelites. ✉ *12 Holland Park Rd., West Holland Park* ☎ *020/7602–3316 weekdays, 020/7471–9160 weekends* ⊕ *www.leightonhouse.co.uk* ✉ *£9* ⊘ *Closed Tues.* Ⓜ *Holland Park, South Kensington.*

Portobello Road. Looking for a 19th-century snuff spoon? Perhaps a Georgian salt cellar? What about a 1960s-era minidress? Then head to Portobello Road's famous Saturday market—and arrive at about 9 am to avoid the giant crowds. Stretching almost 2 miles from Notting Hill, the market is made up of four sections, each with a different emphasis: antiques, fresh produce, household goods, and a flea market. The antiques stalls are packed in between Chepstow Villas and Westbourne Grove, where you'll also find almost 100 antiques shops plus indoor markets, which are open on weekdays, when shopping is much less hectic. Where the road levels off, around Elgin Crescent, youth culture and a vibrant neighborhood life kicks in, with a variety of interesting small stores and food stalls interspersed with a fruit-and-vegetable market. On Friday and Saturday the section between Talbot Road and the Westway elevated highway becomes one of London's best flea markets, specializing in discounted new household goods, while north of the Westway you'll find secondhand household goods and bric-a-brac. Scattered throughout, but especially under the Westway, are vendors selling a mishmash of designer, vintage, and secondhand clothing, together with jewelry, custom T-shirts, and assorted junk. There's a Trinidad-style Carnival centered on Portobello Road on the late August bank-holiday weekend, a tribute to the area's past as a center of the West Indian community. ✉ *Notting Hill* ⊕ *www.portobelloroad.co.uk* Ⓜ *Notting Hill Gate, Ladbroke Grove.*

Serpentine Galleries. Taking its name from the lake that curves its way through Hyde Park, the Serpentine Gallery, housed in a modest red-brick building in Kensington Gardens, is one of London's foremost showcases for contemporary art. Just about everyone who's anyone has exhibited here: Louise Bourgeois, Jeff Koons, Marina Abramovic, and Gerhard Richter, to name a few. A permanent work on the gallery's grounds, consisting of eight benches and a carved stone circle, commemorates its former patron, Princess Diana. The Serpentine Sackler Gallery, a second exhibition space that's in a small Georgian gunpowder storeroom just over the water, has a dramatic extension designed by Zaha Hadid as well as a stylish restaurant. If you're in town between May and September, check out the annual Serpentine Pavilion, where each year a leading architect is given free rein to create a temporary pavilion of their choosing—always with imaginative results. Past designers have included Frank Gehry, Daniel Liebeskind, and Jean Nouvel. ✉ *Kensington Gardens, Kensington* ☎ *0207/402–6075* ⊕ *www.serpentinegalleries.org* ✉ *Free* ⊘ *Closed Mon.* Ⓜ *Lancaster Gate, Knightsbridge, South Kensington.*

10

WORTH NOTING

Graffik. Not everyone thinks graffiti can be a bonus to the urban landscape, but those who do should head for this leading gallery of contemporary street art. The big name here is Banksy, but there are works for sale by several other artists in the same vein such as Trust. iCON and CODE FC, who are more concerned with social commentary than tagging. This is one gallery experience that really appeals to young people, especially if the visit coincides with one of Graffik's two-hour weekend workshops. ✉ *284 Portobello Rd., Notting Hill* ☎ *020/8354–3592* ⊕ *www.graffikgallery.com* ⬛ *Free* Ⓜ *Notting Hill Gate, Ladbroke Grove.*

Museum of Brands, Packaging and Advertising. This fascinating museum specializes in branded toys, clothes, games, and domestic goods, and explores how advertising has come to infiltrate our lives. Curios from the 1800s to the present day include World War II–era toilet paper (brand name: Nasti toilet roll) that has Adolf Hitler's face on every sheet. ✉ *111–117 Lancaster Rd., Notting Hill* ☎ *020/7243–9611* ⊕ *www. museumofbrands.com* ⬛ *£9* ⊘ *Closed Mon.* Ⓜ *Ladbroke Grove.*

BAYSWATER

East of Notting Hill Gate Tube station, Notting Hill turns into Bayswater, characterized by wide streets lined with imposing white stucco terraced houses. Traditionally given over to cheap B&Bs, many are being converted back to private homes as the area continues to gentrify. The eastern end of Westbourne Grove and the streets around it are known for their excellent restaurants, particularly Chinese, Lebanese, and Greek. On **Queensway**, Bayswater's main street, **Whiteleys**, originally a huge department store built in 1912, has been converted into a shopping center containing a luxury movie theater, restaurants (try Le Café Anglais for a swanky evening out), a bowling alley, and, of course, shops.

Nearby **Paddington station** is as well known for its association with the world's most famous marmalade fan, Paddington Bear, as it is for being one of London's most handsome rail terminals.

REGENT'S PARK
AND HAMPSTEAD

Getting Oriented

Regent's Park and Hampstead

◆ Kenwood House

Waterlow Park

Highgate Hill

Highgate Cemetery

Fitzroy Park

Millfield Ln.

Highgate West Hill

Highgate Rd.

Hampstead Heath ◆

Oakeshott Ave.

Makepeace Ave.

Langbourne Ave.

Chester Rd.

St. Albans Rd.

Swains Ln.

Ladies Bathing Pond

N. End Way

Spaniards Rd.

West Heath Rd.

Heath St.

Christchurch Hill

East Heath Rd.

2 Willow Rd.

Mixed Bathing Pond

Dartmouth Park Hill

Croftdown Rd.

Parliament Hill

Dartmouth Pk. Rd.

Junction Rd.

Burgh House and Hampstead Museum

Fenton House ◆

Redington Rd.

Oak Hill

Flask Wk.

Willow Rd.

HAMPSTEAD Ⓤ

Heath St.

HAMPSTEAD

Hampstead Heath Rail

Gospel Oak Rail

Savernake Rd.

Mansfield Rd.

Fortess Rd.

Highgate Rd.

Church Row

High St.

Frognal

Frognal Ln.

Ginger and White

Keats Gr.

Constantine Rd.

Agincourt Rd.

The Parish Church of St. John's-at-Hampstead

Keats House

Downshire Hill

Fleet Rd.

Well Wk.

Willoughby Rd.

Rosslyn Hill

S. End Rd.

Finchley Rd.

Arkwright Rd.

Lyndhurst Rd.

Wedderburn Rd.

Ornan Rd.

Tanza Rd.

Parliament Hill

Nassington Rd.

Savernake Rd.

Gilles Rd.

Finchley Road & Frognal Rail

Nethercott Gdns.

Maresfield Gdns.

Fitzjohn's Ave.

Daleham Gdns.

Akenside Rd.

Belsize Ave.

Glenilla Rd.

Glenloch Rd.

Haverstock Hill

Upper Park Rd.

Parkhill Rd.

Mansfield Rd.

Malden Rd.

Grafton Rd.

Prince of Wales Rd.

Wales Rd.

Kentish Town Rd.

Freud Museum London

Broadhurst Gdns.

Compayne Gdns.

Clive R. Canfield

Greencroft Gdns.

Aberdare Gdns.

Goldhurst Ter.

Fairfax Rd.

Belsize Square

Lancaster Grove

Belsize Park Gdns.

Antrim Rd.

Primrose Gdns.

England's Ln.

Steele's Rd.

Marsden St.

Prince of Wales Rd.

Queen's Cres.

Camden Rd.

Kentish Town Rail

Everholt

SWISS COTTAGE Ⓤ

Hilgrove Rd.

Eton Ave.

Fellows Rd.

Adelaide Rd.

Henry's Rd.

PRIMROSE HILL

CHALK FARM

Marine Ices

Gloucester Ave.

Chalk Farm Rd.

CAMDEN TOWN Ⓤ

Boundary Rd.

Elsworthy Rd.

Primrose Hill Rd.

Queen's Grove

Primrose Hill

Chalcot Rd.

Fitzroy Rd.

Gloucester Ave.

Jamestown Rd.

Canal

Union St.

Boundary Rd.

Loudoun Rd.

Marlborough Hill

Finchley Rd.

Queen's Grove

Ordnance Hill

Norfolk Rd.

Marazzano Rd.

Cecil Sharp House ◆

CAMDEN TOWN

Prince Albert Rd.

Parkway

Delaney St.

Jewish Museum

Camden High Street

Abbey Road

Carlton Hill

ST. JOHNS WOOD Ⓤ

Acacia Rd.

St. John's Wood Ter.

Allitsen Rd.

Albany St.

Park Village East

Prince Albert Rd.

Marlborough Pl.

ST. JOHN'S WOOD

Wellington Rd.

St. John's Wood High St.

Prince Albert Rd.

ZSL London Zoo ◆

Broad Walk

Outer Circle

Regent's Park

Outer Circle

Cumberland Terrace

Outer Circle

Maida Vale

Abercorn Pl.

Grove End Rd.

Circus Rd.

Lord's Cricket Ground & Museum

St. John's Wood Rd.

Park Rd.

Inner Circle

Chester Rd.

Lamont Rd.

Randolph Av.

Lodge Rd.

Lisson Grove

York Bridge

Clifton Gdns.

Clifton Rd.

Rossmore Rd.

Gloucester Pl.

Baker St.

Outer Circle

REGENT'S PARK Ⓤ

Marylebone Rd.

GREAT PORTLAND STREET Ⓤ

Edgware Rd.

Church St.

MARYLEBONE Ⓤ

Broadley St.

Marylebone Rd.

BAKER STREET Ⓤ

Marylebone High St.

0   1/4 mi

0   1/4 km

TOP REASONS TO GO

Ramble across Hampstead Heath: Londoners adore the Heath for bringing a bit of countryside to the city.

Go romantic at Keats House: Visit the rooms where one of England's greatest poets wrote some of his greatest works inspired by his love for the girl-next-door, Fanny Brawne.

Get sporty in Regent's Park: Cycle past Nash's grand neoclassical stucco terraces or walk up Primrose Hill for a great view over the city.

Gracious living at Kenwood: See one of Britain's best art collections at this 18th-century gentleman's estate largely designed by Robert Adam.

Meet the penguins at the London Zoo: A VIP ticket will let you get up close and personal with the penguins.

SAFETY

Avoid Hampstead Heath, Primrose Hill, and Regent's Park at night unless there's an event; all are perfectly safe during the day. Also to be avoided after dark: the canal towpath in Primrose Hill and Camden.

FEELING PECKISH?

Ginger and White. Family-friendly and thoroughly modern, Ginger and White is a delightful fusion of continental-style café and traditional British "caff"—all bound up with a sophisticated Hampstead vibe. ⊠ *4A–5A Perrins Ct., Hampstead* ☎ *020/7431–9098* ⊕ *www.gingerandwhite.com* ⊗ *No dinner* Ⓜ *Hampstead.*

Marine Ices. Near the Camden Lock market, this family-owned gelato and sorbet parlor is one of London's best. ⊠ *Old Dairy Mews, 61 Chalk Farm Rd., Camden Town* ☎ *020/7428–9990* ⊕ *www.marineices.co.uk* Ⓜ *Chalk Farm.*

GETTING THERE

To get to Hampstead by Tube, take the Northern line (the Edgware branch) to Hampstead or Golders Green station, or take the London Overground to Hampstead Heath station. The south side of Hampstead Heath can also be reached by the London Overground Gospel Oak station. To get to Regent's Park, take the Bakerloo line to Regent's Park Tube station or, for Primrose Hill, the Chalk Farm stop on the Northern line. Little Venice is reachable by the Warwick Avenue stop on the Bakerloo line and St. John's Wood has its own stop on the Jubilee Line.

MAKING THE MOST OF YOUR TIME .

Regent's Park, Primrose Hill, and Hampstead can be covered in a day. Spend the morning in Hampstead, with a brief foray onto the Heath, then head south to Regent's Park in the afternoon so that you're closer to central London come nightfall, if that is where your hotel is located. (You'll also be heading downhill instead of up.) You can always return to Hampstead another day for a long walk across the Heath or to head west to Little Venice's canals.

Sightseeing
★★★★
Nightlife
★★★
Dining
★★
Lodging
★★
Shopping
★★★

Regent's Park, Primrose Hill, Belsize Park, and Hampstead are four of London's prettiest and most civilized neighborhoods. The city becomes noticeably calmer and greener as you head uphill from Marylebone Road through Regent's Park to the refreshing greenery of Primrose Hill and the handsome Georgian houses and Regency villas of Hampstead. To the west, the less bucolic but equally elegant St. John's Wood and Little Venice also provide a taste of moneyed London.

Updated by
Ellin Stein

Leaving the park at the London Zoo, walk up adjoining **Primrose Hill** for one of the most picturesque views of London. Long a magnet for the creative (though these days within reach of only the most well-heeled creatives), this is the kind of neighborhood where the local library's screening of *The Madness of King George* is introduced by its writer, longtime resident Alan Bennett. Peel off from the Hill to explore Regent's Park Road and its attractive independent shops and cafés, as well as the surrounding streets with their pastel Victorian villas.

Alternatively, continue hugging the Hill heading north along Primrose Hill Road. This will take you to Belsize Park, itself a celebrity hot spot (Tim Burton and Hugh Laurie have houses here) with a mixture of Victorian, Arts and Crafts, and art deco buildings. Turn right onto England's Lane, another street full of independent shops and nice cafés, then left onto Haverstock Hill and head farther uphill. At the corner of Pond Street you will see two enormous Victorian Gothic buildings: one, St. Stephen's Church, is now a community arts center. The other, AIR Studios, founded by the Beatles' producer, Sir George Martin, is where scores for movies, including *Iron Man 3*, *Les Misérables*, and *Brave*, have been recorded.

Turn right onto Pond Street and go downhill past the unlovely Royal Free hospital to South End Green and the entrance to **Hampstead Heath.** Or go straight to stay on Rosslyn Hill and then Hampstead High Street, the neighborhood's main drag. Turn left onto Church Row, with its unspoiled early Georgian terraced houses leading to **St.**

John's-at-Hampstead, where the painter John Constable is buried. To the north of Hampstead Heath is Highgate, another upscale north London "village" with a large concentration of Georgian and early Victorian buildings, particularly around The Grove (home to Kate Moss [who lives in Samuel Taylor Coleridge's former residence] and Jude Law).

To reach **Little Venice,** go to the west entrance of Regent's Park by the gold-domed London Central Mosque and then north past **Lord's Cricket Ground** to the St. John's Wood Tube stop. Turn left onto Grove End Road, which will bring you to the famous Abbey Road crosswalk featured on the Beatles' album of the same name. Head southwest for Little Venice, known as the Belgravia of north London due to its stucco terraces (found on streets such as Randolph Avenue, Clifton Avenue, and Randolph Road) that are very similar to the other neighborhood's. The "Venice" comes from its proximity to a picturesque stretch of the Grand Union Canal along Blomfield Road, where highly decorative houseboats are moored. If you happen to be here on the second Sunday in May, you'll be able to see houseboats from all over London's canals gather here in Paddington Basin for the Blessing of the Boats.

REGENT'S PARK

Commissioned by his patron the Prince Regent (later George IV) to create a master plan for this part of London, formerly a royal hunting ground, London's great urban planner and architect John Nash laid out the plans for the 410-acre Regent's Park in 1812. Bordered by grand neoclassical terraces, the park holds many attractions, including the London Zoo and the summer display of more than 400 varieties of rose in Queen Mary's Gardens.

TOP ATTRACTIONS

FAMILY **Primrose Hill.** More conventionally parklike than Hampstead Heath,
Fodor'sChoice the rolling lawns of Primrose Hill, the northerly extension of Regent's
★ Park, which rises to 256 feet, provide outstanding views over the city to the southeast, encompassing Canary Wharf and the London Eye. Filled with families and picnickers in nice weather, it has featured in books—it was here that Pongo engaged in "twilight barking" in *The Hundred and One Dalmatians* and the Martians set up an encampment in H.G. Wells's *The War of The Worlds*. It's also been mentioned in songs by Blur, Madness, and Paul McCartney, among others, and served as a location for films including *Bridget Jones: The Edge of Reason* and *Paddington.* ⊠ *Regent's Park Rd., Regent's Park* ☎ *0300/061–2300* ⊕ *www.royalparks.org.uk* ⊠ *Free* Ⓜ *Chalk Farm.*

FAMILY **Regent's Park.** One of London's principal charms is to find the formal,
Fodor'sChoice cultivated serenity of Regent's Park—more country-house grounds than
★ municipal amenity—just on the edge of the intensely urban West End, a world away from the traffic-clogged surrounding roads. The 395-acre park, with the largest grass area for sports in central London, draws the athletically inclined from around the city.

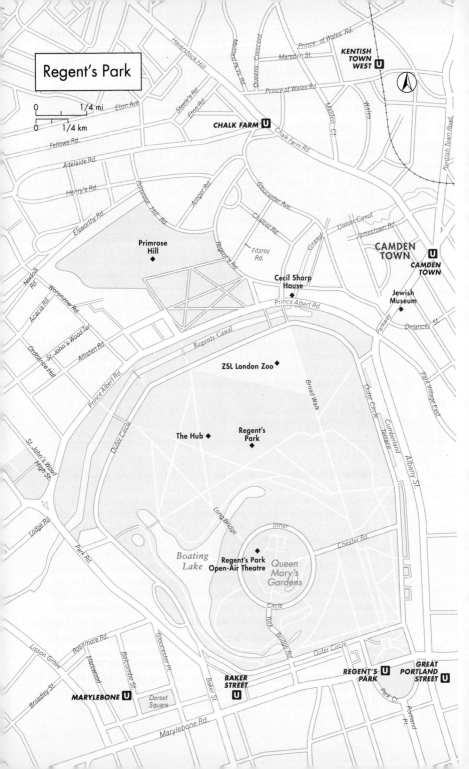

Regent's Park

0   1/4 mi
0   1/4 km

Haverstock Hill
Eton Ave.
Steele's Rd.
Eton Rd.
Maitland Pk. Vs. Rd.
Queens Crescent
Prince of Wales Rd.
Marsden St.
KENTISH TOWN WEST
Prince of Wales Rd.

Fellows Rd.
CHALK FARM U
Chalk Farm Rd.
Maiden Ct.
Wales
Kentish Town Road

Adelaide Rd.
Henry's Rd.
Elsworthy Rd.
Primrose Hill Rd.
Regent's Rd.
Gloucester Ave.
Chalcot Rd.
Fitzroy Rd.
Grand
Union Canal
Jamestown Rd.

Norfolk Rd.
Acacia Rd.
Woronzow Rd.
St. John's Wood Ter.
Ordnance Hill
Allitsen Rd.
Prince Albert Rd.
Primrose Hill ◆
Cecil Sharp House
CAMDEN TOWN
CAMDEN TOWN U
Jewish Museum ◆
Parkway
Delancey St.

St. John's Wood High St.
Prince Albert Rd.
Regents Canal
ZSL London Zoo ◆
Broad Walk
Outer Circle
Cumberland Terrace
Park Village East

Lodge Rd.
Park Rd.
Outer Circle
The Hub ◆
Regent's Park ◆
Albany St.

Boating Lake
Long Bridge
Inner
Chester Rd.
Queen Mary's Gardens
Regent's Park Open-Air Theatre ◆

Lisson Grove
Rossmore Rd.
Hartwood
Gloucester Pl.
Balcombe St.
Broadway St.
Baker St.
MARYLEBONE U
Dorset Square
BAKER STREET U
Circle
York Bridge Rd.
Outer Circle
Park Cr.
REGENT'S PARK U
GREAT PORTLAND STREET U
Portland Pl.

Marylebone Rd.

At the center of the park, **Queen Mary's Gardens,** created in the 1930s, are a fragrant 17-acre circle containing some 30,000 individual specimens and more than 400 varieties of roses. Unsurprisingly, it's a favorite spot for weddings. Just to the east of the Gardens is the **Regent's Park Open-Air Theatre** and the **Boating Lake,** which you can explore by renting a pedalo (paddleboat) or rowboat. Heading east from the rose gardens along Chester Road past the **Broad Walk** will bring you to Nash's iconic white stucco **Cumberland Terrace,** with its central Ionic columns surmounted by a triangular Wedgwood-blue pediment (home to artist Damien Hirst). At the north end of the Broad Walk you'll find the **London Zoo,** while to the northwest of the central circle is **The Hub** (☎ 0300/061–2323), a state-of-the-art community sports center that has changing rooms, exercise classes, and a café with 360-degree views of the surrounding sports fields, used for soccer, rugby, cricket, field hockey, and softball contests. There are also tennis courts toward the park's southeast (Baker Street) entrance, and the park is a favorite north–south route for cyclists.

If watching all this activity works up an appetite, in addition to the Hub's own café there's the Regent's Bar & Kitchen outside the rose garden that serves salads, sandwiches, and wood-fired pizzas, the Smokehouse near the zoo that specializes in BBQ, burgers, and summer salads, the Boatyard Cafe by the boating lake, the Tennis Centre Cafe by the courts, an espresso bar with wraps and cakes, and a kiosk by the children's playground that serves sandwiches and snacks. ■ TIP→ Regent's Park also hosts two annual events: the prestigious Frieze Art Fair, and the Taste of London, a foodie-oriented extravaganza. ⊠ *Chester Rd., Regent's Park* ☎ *0300/061–2300* ⊕ *www.royalparks.org.uk* ⊠ *Free* Ⓜ *Baker St., Regent's Park, Great Portland St.*

FAMILY
Fodor'sChoice
★

ZSL London Zoo. With an emphasis on education, wildlife conservation, and the breeding of endangered species, London Zoo offers visitors the chance to see tigers, gorillas, meerkats, and more in something resembling a natural environment rather than a cage. Operated by the nonprofit Zoological Society of London, the zoo was begun with the royal animals collection, moved here from the Tower of London in 1828; the zoo itself did not open to the public until 1847. A recent modernization program has seen the introduction of several big attractions. Land of the Lions is a walk-through recreation of an Indian forest where you can see three resident Asiatic lions relaxing at close range, while Gorilla Kingdom provides a similar recreated habitat (in this case an African rain forest) for its colony of six Western Lowland Gorillas. Another recent innovation offers the chance to get up close and personal with 15 ringtailed lemurs. The huge B.U.G.S. pavilion (Biodiversity Underpinning Global Survival) is a self-sustaining, contained ecosystem for 140 less-cuddly species, including invertebrates such as spiders and millipedes, plus some reptiles and fish. Rainforest Life is an indoor tropical rain forest (complete with humidity) inhabited by the likes of armadillos, monkeys, and sloths. A special nighttime section offers glimpses of nocturnal creatures like slow lorises and bats. The Animal Adventures Children's Zoo allows kids to get up close to animals including coatis and llamas, as well as to feed and groom sheep and goats. Two of the most popular attractions are Penguin Beach, especially at feeding time (1:30 and 4:30), and Meerkat Manor, where you can see the sociable animals keeping watch over their own sandy territory.

If you're feeling flush, try to nab one of the six daily "Meet the Penguins" VIP tickets (1:45 pm) that offer a 20-minute guided close encounter with the locals (£54); there are similar VIP encounters with giraffes, meerkats, kangaroos, and rain forest monkeys. Other zoo highlights include Butterfly Paradise and Tiger Territory, an enclosure for five beautiful endangered Sumatran tigers (including three cubs born at the zoo). Adults-only Zoo Nights held Friday nights in June offer street food, alcoholic drinks, and entertainment. You can also experience the zoo after-hours by booking an overnight stay in one of the cozy cabins near (not *in*) the lion enclosure. Check the website or the information board out front for free events, including creature close encounters and "ask the keeper" sessions. ⊠ *Outer Circle, Regent's Park* ☎ *0844/225–1826* ⊕ *www.zsl.org* 🎫 *From £25* Ⓜ *Camden Town, then Bus 274.*

WORTH NOTING

Cecil Sharp House. The home of the English Folk Dance and Song Society, this soaring building from 1930 hosts concerts by artists ranging from Mumford & Sons and Laura Marling to the Ukulele Orchestra of Great Britain, as well as family barn dances and *céilidhs* (Irish barn dances). Meet the locals at one of the drop-in dance classes offering everything from baroque and English and Irish folk dancing to zydeco and tango. There are also temporary exhibitions on British folk arts, a café and bar, and an outstanding specialist library with an extensive collection of recordings, manuscripts, sheet music, and images relating to British folk song, dances, and regional cultures in general. ⊠ *2 Regent's Park Rd., Primrose Hill* ☎ *020/7485–2206* ⊕ *www.cecilsharphouse.org* 🎫 *Free, classes from £4* Ⓜ *Chalk Farm, Camden Town.*

Jewish Museum. This fascinating museum tells the story of the Jewish people in Britain from 1066 to today, including the period between the 13th and 17th century when Judaism was outlawed in England. Using a combination of art, religious artifacts, photographs, manuscripts, and interactive displays, its permanent galleries include one on the Holocaust told through the story of a Britain-based survivor. There's also one that explores Jewish history in Britain, which features a re-creation of a Jewish East End street from the Victorian era and an exhibit documenting the 10,000 Jewish refugee children who came to Britain as World War II loomed. There's also a free overview of the collection on the ground floor that includes a medieval *mikveh* (ritual bath) excavated a few miles from here in 2001. ⊠ *Raymond Burton House, 129–131 Albert St., Camden Town* ☎ *020/7284–7384* ⊕ *www.jewishmuseum. org.uk* 🎫 *£8* ⊙ *Closed on major Jewish holidays* Ⓜ *Camden Town.*

Lord's Cricket Ground & Museum. The spiritual home of this most English of games—and the headquarters of the MCC (Marylebone Cricket Club)—opens its "behind the scenes" areas to visitors during a 100-minute tour. Highlights include the beautiful Long Room, a VIP viewing area where portraits of cricketing greats are on display (you can also book a traditional Afternoon Tea here); the players' dressing rooms; and the world's oldest sporting museum, where cricket's 400-year progress from gentlemanly village-green game to worldwide sport is charted via memorabilia, equipment, trophies, and footage of memorable performances. Don't miss the prize exhibit: the urn known as the Ashes—allegedly the remains of a cricket bail (part of the wicket assembly) presented to the English captain in 1883 by a group of Australian women, a jokey allusion to a newspaper's satirical obituary for the death of English cricket published after a resounding defeat. It's been a symbol of the two nations' long-running rivalry ever since. They still play for possession of the Ashes—an official (as opposed to joke) trophy only since 1998—every two years. A Waterford crystal version changes hands these days, although the winners still hold a replica of the original urn aloft. There is no separate nontour admittance to the museum, except for match ticket holders. Tours are not available during major matches but are offered during smaller "county" matches. All tours must be booked in advance. ⊠ *St. John's Wood Rd., St. John's Wood* ☎ *020/7616–8500* ⊕ *www.lords. org* ▱ *Tour £20; museum £3 with county match ticket, free with major match ticket* ☉ *No tours Apr.–Sept. on match days, preparation days, and event days* Ⓜ *St. John's Wood.*

HAMPSTEAD

Back in 1818, even impoverished Romantic poet John Keats could afford to live in **Hampstead.** His former residence, now known as **Keats House,** is a pretty Regency villa where he spent two years and wrote several of his most famous works. These days Hampstead's bohemian past is long gone, although several distinguished writers, actors, and musicians still live here. Artisanal food shops and boutiques for the skinny of frame and fat of wallet cluster along Hampstead High Street, where upscale high-street chains proliferate the closer you get to Hampstead Tube station. Be sure to leave the beaten path to explore the numerous narrow charming roads, like Flask Walk, Well Walk, and New End Road. Also hidden among Hampstead's winding streets are **Fenton House,** a Georgian townhouse with a lovely walled garden, and Burgh House, the oldest (1704) house in the village and a repository of local history.

Hampstead's biggest claim to fame, however, is **Hampstead Heath** (known locally as "The Heath"), 791 acres of verdant open space, woods, spring-fed swimming ponds, and some of Europe's oldest oaks. It's also home to one of London's highest vantage points (321 feet), Parliament Hill. On the Highgate end of Hampstead Heath, you'll find **Kenwood House,** an 18th-century mansion that was designed by Robert Adam and is noted for its remarkable art collection and grounds.

TOP ATTRACTIONS

FAMILY

Fodor's Choice

★

Hampstead Heath. For generations, Londoners have headed to Hampstead Heath to escape the dirt and noise of the city, and this unique 791-acre expanse of *rus in urbe* ("country in the city") is home to a variety of wildlife and habitat: grassy meadows, woodland, scrub, wetlands, and some of Europe's most venerable oaks. Be aware that, aside from the Parliament Hill area to the south and Golders Hill Park in the west, it is more like countryside than a park, with signs and amenities in short supply. Pick up a map at Kenwood House or at the "Enquiries" window of the Staff Yard near the tennis courts off Highgate Road, where you can also find details about the history of the Heath and its flora and fauna. An excellent café near the Athletics Field serves Italian food.

Coming onto the Heath from the South End Green entrance, walk east past a well-equipped children's adventure **Playground** and **Paddling Pool,** turn left, and head to the top of **Parliament Hill.** At 321 feet above sea level, it's one of the highest points in London, providing a stunning panorama over the city. On clear days you can see all the way to the Surrey Hills beyond the city's southern limits.

If you keep heading east from the playground instead, you'll come to the **Lido,** an Olympic-size outdoor unheated swimming pool that gets packed on all-too-rare hot summer days. More swimming options are available at the Hampstead ponds, which have been refreshing Londoners for generations. You'll find the "Mens" and "Ladies" ponds to the northeast of Parliament Hill, with a "Mixed" pond closer to South End Green. A £2 donation is requested.

■ TIP➔ Golders Hill Park, on the Heath Extension to the northwest, offers a good café, tennis courts, a duck pond, a croquet lawn, and a walled flower garden, plus a Butterfly House (May–September) and a small zoo with native species including Muntjac deer, rare red squirrels, and a Scottish wildcat. ⊠ *Hampstead* ☎ *020/7482–7073 for Super* ⊕ *www.cityoflondon.gov.uk/hampstead* 🎫 *Free* Ⓜ *Overground: Hampstead Heath for south of Heath or Gospel Oak for Lido; Hampstead for east of Heath; Golders Green, then Bus 210 or 268 to Whitestone Pond for north and west of Heath.*

Highgate Cemetery. Highgate is not the oldest cemetery in London, but it is probably the best known, both for its roster of famous "inhabitants" and the quality of its funerary architecture. After it was consecrated in 1839, Victorians came from miles around to appreciate the ornate headstones, the impressive tombs, and the view. Such was its popularity that 19 acres on the other side of the road were acquired in 1850, and this additional East Cemetery is the final resting place of numerous notables, including the most visited, Karl Marx (1818–83), as well as George Eliot and, a more recent internment, George Michael. At the summit is the **Circle of Lebanon,** a ring of vaults built around an ancient cypress tree, a legacy of the 17th-century gardens that formerly occupied the site. Leading from the circle is the **Egyptian Avenue,** a subterranean stone tunnel lined with catacombs, itself approached by a dramatic colonnade that screens the main cemetery from the road. Both sides are impressive, with a grand (locked) iron gate leading to a sweeping courtyard built for the approach of horses and carriages. By the 1970s the cemetery had become unkempt and neglected until a group of volunteers, the Friends of Highgate Cemetery, undertook the huge upkeep. Tours are conducted by the Friends, who will show you the most interesting graves among the numerous statues and memorials once hidden by overgrowth. The West side can only be seen during a one-hour tour, which you must prebook for weekdays but not weekends; tours of the East side on Saturday are first come, first served. You're expected to dress respectfully, so skip the shorts and the baseball cap; children under eight are not admitted and neither are dogs, tripods, or video cameras. ✉ *Swains La., Highgate* ☎ *020/8340–1834* ⊕ *www.highgatecemetery. org* ✉ *East Cemetery £4, tours £8; West Cemetery tours £12, includes admission to East Cemetery. No credit cards* Ⓜ *Archway, then Bus 210, 271, or 143 to Waterlow Park; Belsize Park, then Bus C11 to Brookfield Park.*

Keats House. It was while living in this house between 1818 and 1820 that the major Romantic poet John Keats (1795–1821) fell in love with girl-next-door Fanny Brawne and wrote some of his best-loved poems. (Soon after, ill health forced him to move to Rome, where he died the following year.) After a major refurbishment to make the rooms more consistent with their original Regency style, the house now displays all sorts of Keats-related material, including portraits, letters, many of the poet's original manuscripts and books, the engagement ring he gave to Fanny, and items of her clothing. A pretty garden contains the plum tree under which Keats supposedly composed *Ode to a Nightingale.* There are frequent guided tours and special events featuring local literary luminaries. The ticket gives you entry for a full year, so you can come back as often as you like. Picnics can be taken onto the grounds during the summer. ✉ *10 Keats Grove, Hampstead* ☎ *020/7332–3868* ⊕ *www.cityoflondon.gov.uk/things-to-do/keats-house* ✉ *£7* ☉ *Closed Mon. and Tues. in Mar.–Oct. and Mon.–Thurs. in Nov.–Feb.* Ⓜ *Overground: Hampstead Heath.*

Fodor's Choice
★

Kenwood House. This largely Palladian villa offers an escape to a gracious country house with a magnificent collection of Old Masters and beautiful grounds, all within a short Tube ride from Central London. Originally built in 1616, Kenwood was expanded by Robert Adam starting in 1767 and later by George Saunders in 1795. Adam refaced most of the exterior and added the splendid library, which, with its vaulted ceiling and Corinthian columns, is the highlight of the house's design. A major renovation restored four rooms to reflect Adam's intentions as closely as possible, incorporating the furniture he designed for them and his original color schemes. Kenwood is also home to the **Iveagh Bequest,** a world-class collection of some 60 paintings that includes masterworks like Rembrandt's *Portrait of the Artist* and Vermeer's *The Guitar Player,* along with major works by Reynolds, Van Dyck, Hals, Gainsborough, Turner, and more. The grounds, designed by Humphrey Repton and bordered by Hampstead Heath, are equally elegant and serene, with lawns sloping down to a little lake crossed by a trompe-l'oeil bridge. All in all, it's the perfect home for an 18th-century gentleman. In summer, the grounds host a series

The fabled cover of the Beatles' album *Abbey Road,* with the world's most famous traffic crossing

of popular and classical concerts, culminating in fireworks on the last night. The Brew House café, occupying part of the old coach house, has outdoor tables in the courtyard and a terraced garden. ✉ *Hampstead La., Highgate* ☎ *0870/333–1181* ⊕ *www.english-heritage.org.uk/visit/places/kenwood* ✉ *Free, house and estate tour £16* Ⓜ *Golders Green or Archway, then Bus 210. Overground: Gospel Oak.*

WORTH NOTING

Burgh House and Hampstead Museum. One of Hampstead's oldest buildings, Burgh House was built in 1704 to take advantage of the natural spa waters of the then-fashionable Hampstead Wells. A private house until World War II, it was saved from dereliction in the 1970s by local residents, who have maintained it ever since. The building is a fine example of the genteel elegance common to the Queen Anne period, with redbrick box frontage, oak-paneled rooms, and a terraced garden that was originally designed by Gertrude Jekyll. Today the house contains a small but diverting museum on the history of the area, and also hosts regular talks, concerts, and recitals. The secluded garden courtyard of the café is a lovely spot for lunch, tea, or a glass of wine on a summer's afternoon. ✉ *New End Sq., Hampstead* ☎ *020/7431–0144* ⊕ *www.burghhouse.org.uk* ✉ *Free* ⊗ *Closed Mon., Tues., and Sat.* Ⓜ *Hampstead.*

Fenton House. This handsome 17th-century merchant's home, Hampstead's oldest surviving house, has fine collections of porcelain, Georgian furniture, and 17th-century needlework. The 2-acre walled garden, with its rose plantings and apple orchard, has remained virtually unchanged

A TRIP TO ABBEY ROAD

11

The black-and-white crosswalk (known as a "zebra crossing") near the Abbey Road Studios at No. 3, where the Beatles recorded their entire output, from "Love Me Do" onward, is a place of pilgrimage for Beatles' fans from around the world, many of them teenagers born long after the band split up. They converge here to re-create the cover of the Beatles' 1969 *Abbey Road* album, posing on the crossing despite the onrushing traffic. ■TIP➜ Be careful if you're going to attempt this; traffic on Abbey Road is busy. One of the best ways to explore landmarks in the Beatles' story is to take one of the excellent walking tours offered by **Original London Walks** (☎ 020/7624–3978 ⊕ www.walks.com). Try **The Beatles In-My-Life Walk** (Saturday and Tuesday at 11:20 am outside Marylebone Underground) or **The Beatles Magical Mystery Tour** (Wednesday at 2 pm and Thursday and Sunday at 11 am, at Underground Exit 1, Tottenham Court Road).

for 300 years. International musicians give recitals on the important collection of early keyboard instruments throughout the week; check the website for details. ✉ *Hampstead Grove, Hampstead* ☎ *020/7435–3471* ⊕ *www.nationaltrust.org.uk* 🎫 *£8; £11 combination ticket, includes 2 Willow Rd.* ⊗ *Closed Mon. and Tues.* Ⓜ *Hampstead.*

Freud Museum London. The father of psychoanalysis lived here with his family for a year, between his escape from Nazi persecution in his native Vienna in 1938 and his death in 1939. His daughter Anna (herself a pioneer of child psychoanalysis) remained in the house until her own death in 1982, bequeathing it as a museum to honor her father. The centerpiece is Freud's unchanged study, containing his remarkable collection of antiquities and his library. Also on display is the family's Biedermeier furniture—and, of course, the couch. As well, there are lectures, study groups, and themed exhibitions, in addition to a psychoanalysis-related archive and research library. Looking for a unique souvenir for the person who has everything? The gift shop here sells "Freudian Slippers." ✉ *20 Maresfield Gardens, Swiss Cottage* ☎ *020/7435–2002* ⊕ *www.freud.org. uk* 🎫 *£8* ⊗ *Closed Mon. and Tues.* Ⓜ *Swiss Cottage, Finchley Rd.*

The Parish Church of St. John-at-Hampstead. There has been a church here since 1312, but the current building—consecrated in 1747 and later extended in 1877—is a fine example of neoclassical serenity, enhanced by Ionic columns and vaulting arches. The church stands at the end of Church Row, a narrow street lined with flat-fronted brick Georgian houses that gives you a sense of what Hampstead was like when it truly was a rural village as opposed to a traffic-clogged North London neighborhood. Many local notables are buried in the picturesque churchyard, including painter John Constable (some of whose most famous works depict the Heath), John Harrison (the inventor of the marine chronometer at the heart of the book *Longitude*), members of the artistic Du Maurier family, Jane Austen's aunt, and comedy god Peter Cook. ✉ *Church Row, Hampstead* ☎ *020/7794–5808* ⊕ *www. hampsteadparishchurch.org.uk* 🎫 *Free* Ⓜ *Hampstead.*

2 Willow Road. Among the many artists and intellectuals fleeing Nazi persecution who settled in the area was noted architect Erno Goldfinger, who built this outstanding modernist home opposite Hampstead Heath in 1939 as his family residence. (His plans drew the ire of several local residents, including novelist Ian Fleming, who supposedly got his revenge by naming a Bond villain after his neighbor.) As well as design touches and building techniques that were groundbreaking at the time, the unique house, a place of pilgrimage for 20th-century architecture enthusiasts, also contains Goldfinger's impressive collection of modern art and self-designed innovative furniture. Before 2 pm, admission is by first-come, first-served hourly tour only, but you can visit independently after 3. ✉ *2 Willow Rd., Hampstead* 🕾 *020/7435–6166* ⊕ *www.nationaltrust.org.uk* 💷 *£7; £11 combination ticket with Fenton House* ⊘ *Closed Mon. and Tues.* Ⓜ *Overground: Hampstead Heath.*

GREENWICH

Getting Oriented

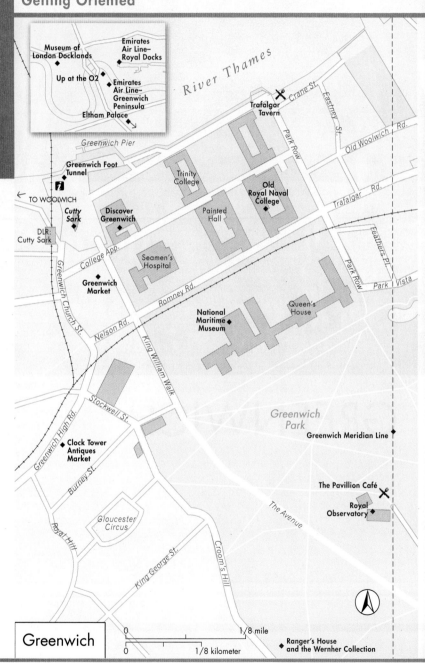

River Thames

Museum of London Docklands

Emirates Air Line– Royal Docks

Up at the O2

Emirates Air Line– Greenwich Peninsula

Eltham Palace

Greenwich Pier

Crane St.

Eastney St.

Trafalgar Tavern

Old Woolwich Rd.

Park Row

Greenwich Foot Tunnel

TO WOOLWICH

Cutty Sark

DLR: Cutty Sark

Greenwich Church St.

College App.

Discover Greenwich

Trinity College

Painted Hall

Old Royal Naval College

Trafalgar Rd.

Feathers Pl.

Park Row

Park Vista

Greenwich Market

Seamen's Hospital

Romney Rd.

National Maritime Museum

Queen's House

Nelson Rd.

King William Walk

Stockwell St.

Greenwich Park

Greenwich Meridian Line

Clock Tower Antiques Market

Greenwich High Rd.

Burney St.

Gloucester Circus

Royal Hill

The Pavillion Café

Royal Observatory

The Avenue

King George St.

Croom's Hill

| Greenwich | 0 | 1/8 mile |
| | 0 | 1/8 kilometer |

Ranger's House and the Wernher Collection

TOP REASONS TO GO

Stand astride the Greenwich Meridian Line: At the Royal Observatory—where the world's time is set—you can be in the eastern and western hemispheres simultaneously.

See the Queen's House, an architectural masterwork: Sir Inigo Jones's 17th-century building was the first in England to embrace the styles of the Italian Renaissance.

Discover Britain's seafaring past at the National Maritime Museum: See how Britannia ruled the waves and helped shape the modern world.

Step aboard the *Cutty Sark*: Take a stroll along the deck of the last surviving 19th-century tea clipper, now shipshape after years of renovation.

FEELING PECKISH?

The Pavilion Café. Healthy snacks and lunches are served at this excellent café next to the Royal Observatory. Homemade soups and sandwiches are good for a quick refuel, or try one of the delicious stone-baked pizzas for something more substantial. ⊠ *Charlton Way, Greenwich* ☎ *020/8853–4777* ⊕ *www.royalparks.org.uk.*

Trafalgar Tavern. With its excellent vista of the Thames, there is no more handsomely situated pub in Greenwich than the Trafalgar Tavern. The model for the Six Jolly Fellowship Porters pub in Charles Dickens's *Our Mutual Friend*, it's still as grand a place as it ever was to have a pint and a quick, tasty meal. ⊠ *Park Row, Greenwich* ☎ *020/8858–2909* ⊕ *www.trafalgartavern.co.uk.*

12

GETTING THERE

The Docklands Light Railway (DLR) is a zippy way to get to Cutty Sark station from Canary Wharf or Bank Tube station in The City. Or take the DLR to Island Gardens and walk the old Victorian Foot Tunnel under the river. (Sitting at the front of a train can be disconcerting, as you watch the controls in the fully automated driver's cab move about as if a ghost were at the helm.) The best way to arrive, however—time and weather permitting—is like a sea captain of old: by water (although it takes an hour from central London).

MAKING THE MOST OF YOUR TIME

Set apart from the rest of London, Greenwich is worth a day to itself—those who love maritime history will want to spend two—in order to make the most of walks in the rolling parklands and to immerse yourself in the richness of Greenwich's history, science, and architecture. The boat trip takes about an hour from Westminster Pier (next to Big Ben) or 25 minutes from the Tower of London, so factor in enough time for the round-trip.

NEAREST PUBLIC RESTROOMS

Duck into Discover Greenwich, where the loo is free.

Sightseeing
★★★★
Nightlife
★
Dining
★★
Lodging
★
Shopping
★★★

About 8 miles downstream (meaning seaward, to the east) from central London, Greenwich is a small borough that looms large across the world. Once the seat of British naval power, it is not only home to the Old Royal Observatory, which measures time for our entire planet, but also the Greenwich Meridian, which divides the world into two—you can stand astride it with one foot in either hemisphere.

Updated by
Jo Caird

Bear in mind that the journey to Greenwich is an event in itself. In a rush, you can take the driverless DLR train, but many opt for arriving by boat along the Thames. This way, you glide past famous sights on the London skyline—there's a guaranteed spine chill on passing the Tower—and ever-changing docklands, and there's usually a chirpy Cock-er-ney navigator enlivening the journey with fun commentary.

A visit to Greenwich feels like a trip to a rather elegant seaside town—albeit one with more than its fair share of historic sites. The grandiose **Old Royal Naval Hospital,** designed by Sir Christopher Wren, was originally a home for veteran sailors. Today it's a popular visitor attraction, with a more glamorous second life as one of the most widely used movie locations in Britain.

Greenwich was originally home to one of England's finest Tudor palaces, and the birthplace of Henry VIII, Elizabeth I, and Mary I. Inigo Jones began what is considered the first "classical" building in England in 1616: the **Queen's House,** which now houses a collection of fine art. Britain was the world's preeminent naval power for more than 500 years, and the excellent **National Maritime Museum** details that history in an engaging way. Its prize exhibits include the coat worn by Admiral Lord Nelson (1758–1805) in his final battle—bullet hole and all. The 19th-century tea clipper *Cutty Sark* was nearly destroyed by fire in 2007 but reopened in 2012 after a painstaking restoration. Now it's more pristine than ever and has an impressive visitor center.

Greenwich Park, London's oldest royal park, is still home to fallow red deer, just as it has been since they were first introduced here for hunting by Henry VIII. The **Ranger's House** now houses a private art collection, next door to a beautifully manicured rose garden. Above it all is the **Royal Observatory,** where you can be in two hemispheres at once by standing along the **Greenwich Meridian Line,** before seeing a high-tech planetarium show.

Toward north Greenwich, the hopelessly ambitious Millennium Dome has been successfully reborn as the O2 and now hosts major concerts and stand-up comedy gigs. More adventurous visitors can also go **Up at the O2** on a climbing expedition across the massive domed surface. Meanwhile, those who prefer excursions of a gentler kind may prefer to journey a couple of miles south of the borough, farther out into London's southern suburbs, to the shamefully underappreciated **Eltham Palace,** once a favorite of Henry VIII. Parts of the mansion were transformed into an art deco masterpiece in the 1930s.

TOP ATTRACTIONS

Fodor'sChoice ★   *Cutty Sark.* This sleek, romantic clipper was built in 1869, one among a vast fleet of tall-masted wooden ships that plied the oceanic highways of the 19th century, trading in exotic commodities—in this case, tea. *Cutty Sark* (named after a racy witch in a Robert Burns poem) was the fastest in the fleet, sailing the London–China route in 1871 in only 107 days. The clipper has been preserved in dry dock as a museum ship since the 1950s, but was severely damaged in a devastating fire in 2007. Yet up from the ashes, as the song goes, grow the roses of success: after a major restoration project, the visitor facilities are now better than ever. Not only can you tour the ship in its entirety, but the glittering visitor center (which the ship now rests directly above) allows you to view the hull from below. There's plenty to see here, and the cramped quarters form a fantastic time capsule to walk around in—this boat was never too comfortable for the 28-strong crew (as you'll see). Don't forget to take in the amusing collection of figureheads. ⊠ *King William Walk, Greenwich* ☎ *020/8858–4422* ⊕ *www.rmg.co.uk/cuttysark* ⊠ *£14; £19 combination ticket, includes Royal Observatory attractions* Ⓜ *DLR: Cutty Sark.*

Discover Greenwich. Intended as a kind of anchor point for Greenwich's big three attractions—the Old Royal Naval College, *Cutty Sark,* and the National Maritime Museum—this excellent, state-of-the-art visitor center includes interactive exhibitions on the history of Greenwich, plus an assortment of local treasures and artifacts. Most intriguing among them is a 17th-century "witch bottle," once used to ward off evil spirits. High-tech scans have revealed it to contain a mixture of human hair, fingernails, and urine. ⊠ *Pepys Bldg., King William Walk, Greenwich* ☎ *020/8269–4799* ⊕ *www.ornc.org/visitor-centre* ⊠ *Free* Ⓜ *DLR: Greenwich.*

Fodor'sChoice ★   **Eltham Palace.** Once a favorite getaway for Henry VIII (who liked to spend Christmas here), Eltham Palace has been drastically remodeled twice in its lifetime: once during the 15th and 16th centuries, and again during the 1930s, when a grand mansion was annexed onto the Tudor

12

DID YOU KNOW?

Once sailors could deter-
mine their distance from the
Greenwich meridian (longitude), maritime navigation
was greatly improved. Look
for the brass line marking the
two hemispheres throughout
the cobblestone streets.

great hall by the superwealthy Courtauld family. Today it's an extraordinary combination of late medieval grandeur and art deco masterpiece, laced with an eccentric whimsy—the Courtaulds even built an entire room to be the personal quarters of their beloved pet lemur. The house and its extensive gardens were fully restored when the palace finally entered public ownership in the late 1990s. Be sure to get a glimpse of the Map Room, where the Courtaulds planned their round-the-world adventures, and the reconstruction of a lavish 1930s walk-in wardrobe, complete with genuine dresses from the time period. ✉ *Court Rd., Eltham* ☎ *020/8294–2548* ⊕ *www.english-heritage.org.uk/elthampalace* ⊠ *£15* ⊘ *Closed Sat.* Ⓜ *Eltham.*

Greenwich Market. Established as a fruit-and-vegetable market in 1700, the covered market now offers around 120 mixed stalls of art and crafts on Monday, Wednesday, Friday, Saturday, and Sunday, and vintage antiques on Tuesday, Thursday, and Friday. You can buy food on each day, although the offerings are usually best on weekends. Shopping for handicrafts is a pleasure here, as in most cases you're buying directly from the artist. ✉ *College Approach, Greenwich* ☎ *020/8269–5096* ⊕ *www.greenwichmarketlondon.com* Ⓜ *DLR: Cutty Sark.*

Museum of London Docklands. This wonderful old warehouse building, on a quaint cobbled quayside near the tower of Canary Wharf, is worth a visit in its own right. With uneven wood floors, beams, and pillars, the museum used to be a storehouse for coffee, tea, sugar, and rum from the West Indies, hence the name: West India Quay. The fascinating story of the old port and the river is told using films, together with interactive displays and reconstructions. Excellent permanent exhibitions include *City and River,* which chronicles the explosion of trade and industry that, by the mid-19th century, had transformed this district into the world's most important port. *Sailortown* is an effective reconstruction of the Wapping district in Victorian times, complete with period shops, a pub, spooky alleys, and costumed guides. Young kids can hunt for treasure and let off some steam in the soft play area in the Mudlarks Gallery. Special events happen year-round; check the museum's website for details. ✉ *No. 1 Warehouse, West India Quay, Canary Wharf* ☎ *020/7001–9844* ⊕ *www.museumoflondon.org.uk/docklands* ⊠ *Free, special exhibitions sometimes extra* Ⓜ *Canary Wharf. DLR: West India Quay.*

Fodor's Choice ★ **National Maritime Museum.** From the time of Henry VIII until the 1940s, Britain was the world's preeminent naval power, and the collections here trace half a millennia of that seafaring history. The story is as much about trade as it is warfare: *Atlantic: Slavery, Trade, Empire* gallery explores how trade in goods (and people) irrevocably changed the world, while *Traders: The East India Company and Asia* focuses on how the epoque-defining company shaped trade with Asia for 250 years. One gallery is devoted to Admiral Lord Nelson, Britain's most famous naval commander, and among the exhibits is the uniform he was wearing, complete with bloodstains, when he died at the Battle of Trafalgar in 1805. Temporary exhibitions here are usually fascinating—those in recent years have included personal accounts of the First World War at sea. Borrow a tablet computer from the front desk and take it to the giant map of the world in the courtyard at the

DID YOU KNOW?

The Docklands Light Railway (DLR) connects former warehouses that have been converted to museums and malls, such as Hay's and Butler's wharves, and the gleaming office buildings of Canary Wharf shown here.

center of the museum; here, a high-tech, interactive app opens up hidden stories and games as you walk between continents. The adjacent **Queen's House** is home to the museum's art collection, the largest collection of maritime art in the world, including works by William Hogarth, Canaletto, and Joshua Reynolds. Permission for its construction was granted by Queen Anne only on condition that the river vista from the house be preserved, and there are few more majestic views in London than Inigo Jones's awe-inspiring symmetry. ⊠ *Romney Rd., Greenwich* ☎ *020/8312–6608* ⊕ *www.rmg.co.uk/national-maritime-museum* 🖃 *Free* Ⓜ *DLR: Greenwich.*

Fodor's Choice
★ **Old Royal Naval College.** Begun by Sir Christopher Wren in 1694 as a rest home for ancient mariners, the college became a school in 1873. It's still used for classes by the University of Greenwich and the Trinity College of Music, although you're more likely to recognize it as a film location—recent blockbusters to have made use of its elegant interiors include *Skyfall*, *Les Misérables*, and *The King's Speech*. Architecturally, you'll notice how the structures part to reveal the **Queen's House** across the central lawns. Behind the college are two more buildings you can visit. The **Painted Hall,** the college's dining hall, derives its name from the baroque murals of William and Mary (reigned jointly 1689–94; William alone 1695–1702) and assorted allegorical figures. James Thornhill's frescoes, depicting scenes of naval grandeur with a suitably pro-British note, were painstakingly completed 1707–12 and 1718–26, and were good enough to earn him a knighthood. Hour-long ceiling tours take place daily. In the opposite building stands the **College Chapel,** which was rebuilt after a fire in 1779 in an altogether more restrained, neo-Grecian style. Free guided tours of the grounds are also offered daily; they depart from the Discover Greenwich Visitor Center. Check the website for an outstanding program of special events, including talks, tours, and concerts—many of them free. ⊠ *King William Walk, Greenwich* ☎ *020/8269–4747* ⊕ *www.ornc.org* 🖃 *Free, Painted Hall tours £10* Ⓜ *DLR: Greenwich.*

FAMILY
Fodor's Choice
★ **Royal Observatory.** Greenwich is on the prime meridian at 0° longitude, and the ultimate standard for time around the world has been set here at the Royal Observatory since 1884, when Britain was the world's maritime superpower. The observatory is actually split into two sites, a short walk apart: one devoted to astronomy, the other to the study of time. The enchanting **Peter Harrison Planetarium** is London's only planetarium, its bronze-clad turret glinting in the sun. Shows on black holes

---

GREENWICH FOOT TUNNEL

In a brilliant piece of foresight in 1849, Greenwich Hospital bought Island Gardens, on the other side of the Thames, to guard against industrial sprawl and to preserve one of the most beautiful views in London. Take the stone spiral steps down into Greenwich Foot Tunnel and head under the Thames (enjoying the magnificently creepy echo) to Island Gardens, at the southern tip of the Isle of Dogs. Then look back over the river for a magnificent vista: the Old Royal Naval College and Queen's House in all their glory, framed by the verdant green borders of the park.

12

Without a central support, the Tulip Stairs spiral up to the Great Hall of Queen's House.

and how to interpret the night sky are enthralling and enlightening. Even better for kids are the high-technology rooms of the **Astronomy Centre,** where space exploration is brought to life through cutting-edge interactive programs and fascinating exhibits—including the chance to touch a 4½-billion-year-old meteorite.

Across the way is **Flamsteed House,** designed by Sir Christopher Wren in 1675 for John Flamsteed, the first Royal Astronomer. The Time Ball atop Flamsteed House is one of the world's earliest public time signals. Each day at 12:55, it rises halfway up its mast. At 12:58 it rises all the way to the top, and at 1 exactly, the ball falls. A climb to the top of the house also reveals a **28-inch telescope,** built in 1893 and now housed inside an onion-shape fiberglass dome. It doesn't compare with the range of modern optical telescopes, but it's still the largest in the United Kingdom. Regular viewing evenings reveal startlingly detailed views of the lunar surface. In the **Time Galleries,** linger over the superb workmanship of John Harrison (1693–1776), whose famous **maritime clocks** won him the Longitude Prize for solving the problem of accurate timekeeping at sea, paving the way for modern navigation. Outside, a brass line laid among the cobblestones marks the meridian. As darkness falls, a green laser shoots out, following exactly the path of the meridian line. The hill that is home to the observatory gives fantastic views across London, topped off with £1-a-slot telescopes to scour the skyline. ⊠ *Romney Rd., Greenwich* ☎ *020/8858–4422* ⊕ *www.rmg.co.uk/royal-observatory* ✆ *Astronomy Centre free, Flamsteed House and Meridian Line courtyard £10, planetarium shows £8; combined "Astro Ticket" £13; combined ticket with Cutty Sark £19* Ⓜ *DLR: Greenwich.*

WORTH NOTING

Clock Tower Antiques Market. The weekend Clock Tower Antiques Market on Greenwich High Road has vintage shopping, and browsing among the "small collectibles" makes for a good half-hour diversion. ⊠ *166 Greenwich High Rd., Greenwich* ☎ *020/7237–2001* ⊕ *www.clocktowermarket.co.uk* ⊙ *Closed weekdays* Ⓜ *Greenwich Rail.*

12

FAMILY **Emirates Air Line.** It may not have become the essential commuter route its makers envisioned, but this cable car, which connects Greenwich Peninsula with the Docklands across the Thames, offers spectacular views from nearly 300 feet up. The journey takes about 10 minutes each way and cable cars arrive every 30 seconds. Entrance to the Emirates Aviation Experience, a small exhibition about commercial air travel that includes life-size models of aircraft and flight simulators, is included with "Discovery Experience" round-trip tickets. ⊠ *Edmund Halley Way* ☎ *0203/440–7021* ⊕ *www.emiratesairline.co.uk* 🎫 *One-way ticket £5, Discovery Experience £11, Aviation Experience £5* Ⓜ *North Greenwich, Royal Victoria.*

Fan Museum. This quirky little museum is as fascinating and varied as the uniquely prized object whose artistry it seeks to chronicle. The simple fan is more than a mere fashion accessory; historically, fans can tell as much about craftsmanship and social mores as they can about fashion. There are 5,000 of them in the collection, dating from the 17th century onward, often exquisitely crafted from ivory, mother-of-pearl, and tortoiseshell. It was the personal vision of Helene Alexander that brought this enchanting museum into being, and the workshop and conservation–study center that she has also set up ensure that this art form continues to have a future. Afternoon tea is served in the café on Tuesday and Friday through Sunday at 2:45 and 3:45 pm. ⊠ *12 Crooms Hill, Greenwich* ☎ *020/8305–1441* ⊕ *www.thefanmuseum.org.uk* 🎫 *£4* ⊙ *Closed Mon.* Ⓜ *DLR: Cutty Sark.*

Ranger's House and the Wernher Collection. This handsome, early-18th-century villa, which was the Greenwich Park ranger's official residence during the 19th century, is hung with Stuart and Jacobean portraits, but the most interesting diversion is the Wernher Collection, which contains nearly 700 art works that were amassed by the diamond millionaire Sir Julius Wernher (1850–1912) and were once housed in his fabulous stately house, Luton Hoo, in Bedfordshire. The collection ranges from Old Master paintings to Renaissance jewelry and assorted pieces of decorative art and curios from the medieval period onward. Entry is by guided tour only and space is limited, so it's a good idea to book ahead on Sunday. The Ranger's House is just under a mile's walk from the DLR station at Greenwich, or you can catch a bus there from Greenwich or Deptford DLR. ⊠ *Blackheath, Chesterfield Walk, Greenwich Park, Greenwich* ☎ *020/8853–0035* ⊕ *www. english-heritage.org.uk* 🎫 *£9* ⊙ *Closed Thurs.–Sat.* Ⓜ *DLR: Deptford Bridge, then Bus 53; or Greenwich, then Bus 386.*

Fodor's Choice ★ **Up at the O2.** Certainly one of the most original ways to see London, this thrilling urban expedition takes you on a 90-minute journey across the giant dome of the O2 arena. After a short briefing, you're dressed in safety gear and taken in small groups across a steep walkway, running all the way to the summit and down the other side. The high point (literally) is a viewing platform, 171 feet above ground, with magnificent views of the city. On a clear day you can see for 15 miles (that's as far as Waltham Abbey to the north and Sevenoaks to the south). Climbs at sunset and twilight are also available. It's quite an experience, but unsurprisingly there are restrictions: you have to be at least 10 years old, taller than 4 feet, have a waist measurement that's less than 49 inches, weigh less than 286 pounds, and pregnant women can't make the climb at all. Wheelchairs can be accommodated on a few tours. Advance booking is essential. ⊠ *Peninsula Sq., London* ☎ *020/8463–2680* ⊕ *www.theo2.co.uk/do-more-at-the-o2/up-at-the-o2* ⊠ *From £29* Ⓜ *North Greenwich.*

THE THAMES
UPSTREAM

Getting Oriented

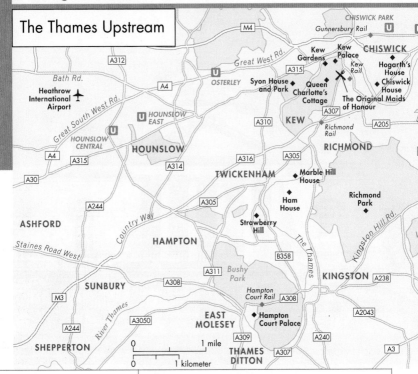

The Thames Upstream

A GOOD WALK	MAKING THE MOST OF YOUR TIME
From Chiswick House, follow Burlington Lane and take a left onto Hogarth Lane—which, in reality, is anything but a lane—to reach Hogarth's House. Chiswick's Church Street (reached by a rather unappealing underpass from Hogarth's House) is the nearest thing to a sleepy country village street you're likely to find in London. Follow it down to the Thames and turn left at the bottom to reach the 18th-century riverfront houses of Chiswick Mall, referred to by locals as "Millionaire's Row." There are several pretty riverside pubs near Hammersmith Bridge.	Hampton Court Palace requires half a day to experience its magic, although you could make do with a few hours for the other attractions. Because of the distance between sights, it's best to focus on one sight, add in some others within the area, then a riverside walk and a pint at a pub.

FEELING PECKISH?

The Original Maids of Honour. This most traditional of old English tearooms is named for a kind of cheese tart invented near here in Tudor times. Legend has it that Henry VIII loved them so much he had the recipe kept under armed guard. ✉ *288 Kew Rd., Kew* ☎ *020/8940–2752* ⊕ *www.theoriginal-maidsofhonour.co.uk.*

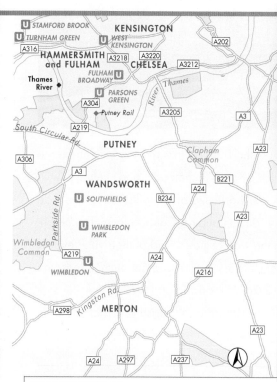

13

GETTING THERE

The District line is your best Tube option, stopping at Turnham Green (in the heart of Chiswick but a walk from the houses), Gunnersbury (for Syon Park), Kew Gardens, and Richmond. For Hampton Court, overland train is quickest: South West trains run from Waterloo four times an hour, with roughly half requiring a change at Surbiton. There are also regular, direct trains from Waterloo to Chiswick station (best for Chiswick House), Kew Bridge, Richmond (for Ham House), and St. Margaret's (best for Marble Hill House). London Overground trains also stop at Gunnersbury, Kew Gardens, and Richmond.

A pleasant way to go is by river. Boats depart from Westminster Pier, by Big Ben, for Kew (1½ hours), Richmond (2 hours), and Hampton Court (3 hours). The trip is worth taking if you make it an integral part of your day, and know that it gets breezy. Round-trip tickets run £20–£25. For more details contact **Thames River Boats** (☎ 020/7930–2062 ⊕ www. wpsa.co.uk).

TOP REASONS TO GO

Explore Hampton Court Palace: Go ghost hunting or just admire the beautiful Tudor architecture at Henry VIII's beloved home, then lose yourself in the maze as night begins to fall.

Go "Goth" at Strawberry Hill: The 19th-century birthplace of connoisseur Horace Walpole's Gothic style, this mock-castle is a joyous riot of color and invention.

Escape to magical Kew Gardens: See the earth from above by visiting Kew's treetop walkway at the famous Royal Botanic Gardens.

Pay your respects to Father Thames: Enjoy a pint from the creaking balcony of a centuries-old riverside pub as you watch the boats row by on the loveliest stretch of England's greatest river.

NEAREST PUBLIC RESTROOMS

Richmond Park, Kew Gardens, and all the stately homes have public restrooms.

Sightseeing
★★★★
Nightlife
★★
Dining
★★★
Lodging
★★
Shopping
★★

The upper stretch of the Thames links a string of fashionable districts—Chiswick, Kew, Richmond, and Putney—with winding old streets, horticultural delights, cozy riverside pubs, and Henry VIII's Hampton Court Palace. The neighborhoods along the way are as proud of their villagey feel as of their stately history, witnessed by such handsome estates as Strawberry Hill and Syon House. After the sensory overload of the West End, it's easy to forget you're in a capital city.

CHISWICK

Updated by Jo
Caird

On the banks of the Thames just west of central London, far enough out to escape the crush and crowds you're just getting used to, Chiswick is a low-key, upscale district, content with its run of restaurants, stylish shops, and film-star residents. No doubt its most famous son wouldn't approve of all the conspicuous wealth, though; Chiswick was home to one of Britain's best-loved painters, William Hogarth, who tore the fabric of the 18th-century nation to shreds with his slew of satirical engravings. **Hogarth's House** has been restored to its former glory. Incongruously stranded among Chiswick's row houses are a number of fine 18th-century buildings, which are now some of the most desirable suburban houses in London. By far the grandest of all is **Chiswick House,** a unique Palladian-style mansion born from the 3rd Earl of Burlington's love of classical and Renaissance architecture—a radical style at the time.

TOP ATTRACTIONS

Fodor's Choice
★

Chiswick House. Completed in 1729 by the 3rd Earl of Burlington (also known for Burlington House—home of the Royal Academy—and Burlington Arcade on Piccadilly), this extraordinary Palladian mansion was envisaged as a kind of temple to the arts. Burlington was fascinated by the architecture he saw in Italy while on the Grand Tour as a young man and loosely modeled this building on the Villa Capra near Vicenza and the Pantheon in Rome (note the colonnaded frontage and the domed roof, which is visible from the inside in the Upper Tribunal).

The sumptuous interiors were the work of William Kent (1685–1748), and it's easy to see how they made such a profound impact at the time; the astonishing Blue Velvet Room, with its gilded decoration and intricate painted ceiling, is an extraordinary achievement, as are the gilded domed apses that punctuate the Gallery (an homage to the Temple of Venus and Roma from the Fora Romana in Rome). Such ideas were so radical in England at the time that wealthy patrons clamored to have Kent design everything from gardens to party frocks.

The rambling grounds are one of the hidden gems of West London. Italianate in style (of course), they are filled with classical temples, statues, and obelisks. Also on the grounds are a café and a children's play area. ⊠ *Burlington La., Chiswick* ☎ *020/8995–0508* ⊕ *www.chgt.org. uk* 🖾 *£8, grounds free* ⊗ *House closed Tues.–Sat.* Ⓜ *Turnham Green, Chiswick. National Rail: Chiswick.*

Hogarth's House. The satirist and painter William Hogarth (1697–1764), little-known in the rest of the world, is hugely famous in Britain. His witty, acerbic engravings, which railed against the harsh injustices of the time, may be called the visual equivalent of the satires of Jonathan Swift and were no less influential in their time. Unfortunately his beloved house has had an appalling streak of bad luck; as if the decision, in the 1960s, to route one of the nation's busiest highways outside the front gates wasn't ignoble enough, it was closed after a fire in 2009. Now fully restored, the rooms contain absorbing exhibitions, featuring many of Hogarth's 18th-century prints, together with replica furniture of the period. Look out for the 300-year-old mulberry tree in the garden; Hogarth and his wife used its fruit to bake pies for destitute children. The original copies of some of Hogarth's most famous works can be seen elsewhere in the city: *A Rake's Progress* at Sir John Soane's Museum; *Marriage A-la-Mode* at the National Gallery; and *Gin Lane* at the British Museum. His tomb is in the cemetery of St. Nicholas's church on nearby Chiswick Mall. ⊠ *Hogarth La., Great West Rd. (A4), Chiswick* ☎ *020/8994–6757* ⊕ *www.hounslow. info/arts/hogarthshouse* 🖾 *Free* ⊗ *Closed Mon.* Ⓜ *Turnham Green. National Rail: Chiswick.*

KEW

A mile or so beyond Chiswick is Kew, a leafy suburb with little to see other than its two big attractions: the lovely **Kew Palace** and the **Royal Botanic Gardens**—anchored in the landscape for several miles around by a towering, mock-Chinese pagoda.

TOP ATTRACTIONS

13

FAMILY

Fodor's Choice

★

Kew Gardens. Enter the Royal Botanic Gardens, as Kew Gardens are officially known, and you are enveloped by blazes of color, extraordinary blooms, hidden trails, and lovely old follies. Beautiful though it all is, Kew's charms are secondary to its true purpose as a major center for serious research; over 200 academics are consistently hard at work here on projects spanning 110 countries. First opened to the public in 1840, this 326-acre site has been supported by royalty and nurtured by landscapers, botanists, and architects since the 1720s. Today the gardens, now a UNESCO World Heritage Site, hold more than 30,000 species of plants, from every corner of the globe.

Architect Sir William Chambers built a series of temples and follies, of which the crazy 10-story **Pagoda**, visible for miles around, is the star. The Princess of Wales conservatory houses 10 climate zones, and the Xstrata Treetop Walkway takes you 59 feet up into the air. Two great 19th-century greenhouses—the **Palm House** and the **Temperate House**—are filled with exotic blooms, and many of the plants have been there since the final glass panel was fixed into place. Unfortunately the enormous Temperate House is closed for maintenance until spring 2018, so until then you won't be able to gawk at the largest greenhouse plant in the world, a Chilean wine palm planted in 1846 (and so big that you have to climb the spiral staircase to the roof to get a proper view of it).

To get around the gardens, the Kew Explorer bus runs on a 40-minute, hop-on, hop-off route, starting at the Victoria Gate, every 30 minutes 11–4:30. Free guided tours, run by volunteers, are given daily at 11 and 1:30, plus special seasonally themed tours at noon. Discovery Tours, fully accessible for visitors in wheelchairs, are also available daily with advance booking. ⊠ *Kew Rd. at Lichfield Rd., for Victoria Gate entrance, Kew* ☎ *020/8332–5655* ⊕ *www.kew.org* ☜ *£15, Explorer bus £5, Discovery tour £5* Ⓜ *Kew Gardens. National Rail: Kew Gardens, Kew Bridge.*

Fodor's Choice

★

Kew Palace and Queen Charlotte's Cottage. The elegant redbrick exterior of the smallest of Britain's royal palaces seems almost humble when compared with the grandeur of, say, Buckingham or Kensington palace. Yet inside is a fascinating glimpse into life at the uppermost end of society from the 17th to 19th century. This is actually the third of several palaces that stood here; once known as Dutch House, it was one of the havens to which George III retired when insanity forced him to withdraw from public life. Queen Charlotte had an *orné* (a rustic-style cottage retreat) added in the late 18th century. In a marvelously regal flight of fancy, she kept kangaroos in the paddock outside. The main house and gardens are maintained in the 18th-century style. Entry to the palace itself is free, but it lies within the grounds of Kew Gardens, and you must buy a ticket to that to get here. ⊠ *Kew Gardens, Kew Rd. at Lichfield Rd., Kew* ☎ *020/3166–6000* ⊕ *www.hrp.org.uk* ✉ *Free with entry to Kew Gardens* ◷ *Closed Oct.–Apr.* Ⓜ *Kew Gardens.*

RICHMOND

Named after the (long-vanished) palace Henry VII started here in 1500, Richmond is still a welcoming suburb with a small-town feel, marred only by choking levels of traffic. Duck away from the main streets to find many handsome Georgian and Victorian houses, antiques shops, a Victorian theater, a grand stately home—and, best of all, the largest of London's royal parks.

TOP ATTRACTIONS

Ham House. To the west of Richmond Park, overlooking the Thames and nearly opposite the memorably named Eel Pie Island, Ham House was built in 1610 and remodeled 60 years later. It's one of the most complete examples in Europe of a lavish 17th-century house, and as such you can get a clear sense of how the English aristocracy really lived during that period (in short: comfortably). The beautiful formal gardens, with their distinctive spherical and conical topiary, have become an influential source for other palaces and grand villas seeking to restore their gardens to how they were in their heyday. The original decorations in the Great Hall, Round Gallery, and Great Staircase have been replicated, and most of the furniture and fittings are on permanent loan from the Victoria & Albert Museum. Note that from January to March, visits are by guided tour only, lasting around 30 minutes (no need to book). A tranquil and scenic way to reach the house is on foot, which takes about 30 minutes, along the eastern riverbank south from Richmond Bridge. ⊠ *Ham St., Richmond* ☎ *020/8940–1950* ⊕ *www.nationaltrust.org.uk/hamhouse* ✉ *£11* Ⓜ *Richmond, then Bus 65 or 371.*

FAMILY

Fodor's Choice ★

Hampton Court Palace. The beloved seat of Henry VIII's court, sprawled elegantly beside the languid waters of the Thames, Hampton Court is steeped in more history than virtually any other royal building in England. The Tudor mansion, begun in 1515 by Cardinal Wolsey to curry favor with the young Henry, actually conceals a larger 17th-century baroque building, which was partly designed by Sir Christopher Wren. The earliest dwellings on this site belonged to a religious order founded in the 11th century and were expanded over the years by its many subsequent residents, until George II moved the royal household closer to London in the early 18th century. After entering through the magnificent Tudor courtyard, start with a look through the **State Apartments,** decorated in the Tudor style, and on to the wood-beamed magnificence of Henry's Great Hall, before taking in the strikingly azure ceiling of the **Chapel Royal.** Watch out for the ghost of Henry VIII's doomed fifth wife, Catherine Howard, who lost her head yet is

Hampton Court Palace, the seat of Henry VIII's court, is a prime example of a Tudor mansion, and features the oldest hedge maze in the world.

said to scream her way along the **Haunted Gallery**. (Believe it or not, what is certainly true is that the corridor is prone to sudden drops in temperature—and no one quite knows why.) Latter-day masters of the palace, the joint rulers William and Mary (reigned 1689–1702), were responsible for the beautiful **King's and Queen's Apartments** and the elaborate baroque of the **Georgian Rooms**.

Well-handled reconstructions of Tudor life take place all year, from live appearances by "Henry VIII" to cook-historians preparing authentic feasts in the **Tudor Kitchens**. (Dishes on offer in the adjacent café include a few of these traditional recipes.) The highlight of the formal grounds is undoubtedly the famous maze (the oldest hedge maze in the world), its half-mile of pathways among clipped hedgerows still fiendish to negotiate. There's a trick, but we won't give it away here; it's much more fun just to go and lose yourself. Meanwhile, the **Lower Orangery Garden** shows off thousands of exotic species that William and Mary, avid plant collectors, gathered from around the globe. Family ghost tours are given on evenings from October to February. Not only are they entertainingly spooky, but they're a great opportunity to see the older parts of the palace without the crowds. Scarier, adults-only versions last two hours. Note that tours can sell out several weeks in advance. ⊠ *Hampton Court Rd., East Molesey* ☎ *020/3166–6000* ⊕ *www.hrp.org.uk/hamptoncourtpalace* 🎫 *£21 palace, maze, and gardens; £5 maze only; £6 gardens only* Ⓜ *Richmond, then Bus R68. National Rail: Hampton Court, 35 mins from Waterloo (most trains require change at Surbiton).*

Marble Hill House. This handsome Palladian mansion is set on 66 acres of parkland on the northern bank of the Thames, almost opposite Ham House. It was built in the 1720s by George II for his mistress, the "exceedingly respectable and respected" Henrietta Howard. Later the house was occupied by Mrs. Fitzherbert, who was secretly (and illegally) married to the Prince Regent (later George IV) in 1785. The house was restored and opened to the public in 1903, looking very much like it did in Georgian times, with extravagant gilded rooms in which Mrs. Howard entertained the literary superstars of the age, including Alexander Pope and Jonathan Swift. A ferry service from Ham House operates during the summer; access on foot is a half-hour walk south along the west bank of the Thames from Richmond Bridge. Note that entry is by guided tour only, run by English Heritage and volunteers from a local history group. ⊠ *Richmond Rd., Twickenham* ☎ *037/0333–1181* ⊕ *www.english-heritage.org.uk/marblehillhouse* ⊡ *£7* ☉ *Closed Nov.– Apr. and weekdays* Ⓜ *Richmond. National Rail: St. Margaret's.*

FAMILY **Richmond Park.** This enormous park was enclosed in 1637 for use as a royal hunting ground—like practically all other London parks. Unlike the others, however, Richmond Park still has wild red and fallow deer roaming its 2,500 acres (three times the size of New York's Central Park) of grassland and heath. Its ancient oaks are among the last remnants of the vast, wild forests that once encroached on London in medieval times. The Isabella Plantation (near the Ham Gate entrance) is an enchanting and colorful woodland garden, first laid out in 1831. There's a splendid, protected view of St. Paul's Cathedral from King Henry VIII's Mound, the highest point in the park; find it, and you have a piece of magic in your sights. The park is also home to White Lodge, a 1727 hunting lodge that now houses the Royal Ballet School. ⊠ *Richmond* ☎ *030/0061–2000* ⊕ *www.royalparks.org.uk* ⊡ *Free* Ⓜ *Richmond, then Bus 371 or 65.*

Fodor's Choice ★ **Strawberry Hill.** From the outside, this rococo mishmash of towers, crenellations, and white stucco is dazzling in its faux-medieval splendor. Its architect and owner, Sir Horace Walpole (1717–97), knew a thing or two about imaginative flights of fancy; the flamboyant son of the first British prime minister, Robert Walpole, he all but single-handedly invented the Gothic novel with *The Castle of Otranto* (1764). Once you pass through Strawberry Hill's forbidding exterior, you'll experience explosion of color and light, for Walpole boldly decided to take elements from the exteriors of Gothic cathedrals and move them inside. The detail is extraordinary, from the cavernous entrance hall with its vast Gothic trompe-l'oeil decorations, to the Great Parlour with its Renaissance stained glass, to the Gallery, where extraordinary fan vaulting is a replica of the vaults found in Henry VII's chapel at Westminster Abbey. Neglected for years, Strawberry Hill reopened in 2010 after a stunningly successful £9 million restoration. The gardens have also been meticulously returned to their original 18th-century design, right down to a white marble loveseat sculpted into the shape of a shell. Opening days can vary, so call ahead to check times. ⊠ *268 Waldegrave Rd., Twickenham* ☎ *020/8744–1241* ⊕ *www.strawberryhillhouse.org.uk* ⊡ *£13* ☉ *House closed Thurs.–Sat.* Ⓜ *Richmond, then Bus 33 or R68. National Rail: Strawberry Hill.*

FAMILY

Fodor's Choice

★

Syon House and Park. The residence of the Duke and Duchess of Northumberland, this is one of England's most lavish stately homes. Set in a 200-acre park landscaped by the great gardener "Capability" Brown (1716–83), the core of the house is Tudor—it was one of the last stopping places for Henry VIII's fifth wife, Catherine Howard, and the extremely short-lived monarch Lady Jane Grey before they were sent to the Tower. It was remodeled in the Georgian style in 1762 by famed decorator Robert Adam. He had just returned from studying the sights of classical antiquity in Italy and created two rooms sumptuous enough to wow any Grand Tourist: the entryway is an amazing study in black and white, pairing neoclassical marbles with antique bronzes, and the Ante Room contains 12 enormous verd-antique columns surmounted by statues of gold—and this was just a waiting room for the duke's servants and retainers. The Red Drawing Room is covered with crimson Spitalfields silk, and the Long Gallery is one of Adam's noblest creations. ⊠ *Syon Park, Brentford* ☎ *020/8560–0882* ⊕ *www.syonpark.co.uk* ☞ *£13, £8 gardens and conservatory only* ⊘ *Property closed Dec.–mid-Mar. and weekdays Nov.; house closed Mon., Tues., Fri., and Sat. mid-Mar.–Oct.* Ⓜ *Gunnersbury, then Bus 237 or 267 to Brentlea.*

Thames River. The twists and turns of the Thames through the heart of the capital make it London's best thoroughfare and most compelling viewing point. Every palace, church, theater, wharf, museum, and pub along the bank has a tale to tell, and traveling on or alongside the river is one of the best ways to soak up views of the city. Frequent daily tourist-boat services are at their height April through October. In most cases you can turn up at a pier, and the next departure won't be far away; however, it never hurts to book ahead if you can. The trip between Westminster Pier and the Tower of London takes about 40 minutes, while that between the Tower and Greenwich takes around half an hour. A full round-trip can take several hours. Ask about flexible fares and hop-on, hop-off options at the various piers. ⊠ *London.*

WHERE TO EAT

EAT LIKE A LOCAL

A handful of foods are forever associated with London: think fish-and-chips, full English breakfasts, and Indian curry. All these and other innovations are permanently on locals' lips, not to mention their Twitter and Instagram accounts.

CHINESE

Endless waves of Londoners and tourists alike throng the lantern-strewn grid of Georgian streets centered on Chinatown's pulsating Gerrard Street. Breaking out from Hong Kong Cantonese to embrace a wider spread of Sichuan, Hunan, Taiwanese, and Malaysian offerings, Londoners tend to hit old favorites like the Wardour Street Four Seasons for roast Peking duck, the Joy Luck Restaurant for Lanzhou noodles, Beijing Dumpling for hand-made dim sum, Ba Shan for Hunan steamed fish and chilies, and Rasa Sayang for spicy Malay chicken curries.

CURRY

As a one-time global port and seat of the British Empire, London has enjoyed Indian cuisine for over four hundred years and opened its first dedicated Indian curry house for Colonial returnees (the Hindostanee Coffee House in Marylebone) in 1809. Originally linked to Sylheti Bengali "lascar" seamen and ship boiler stokers, and later an exotic cuisine championed by Queen Victoria, London's love affair with spicy curry has only gotten stronger since the Edwardian era. Nowadays, the capital's curry hounds can be found along the gaudy Bengali-focused Brick Lane in the East End, but look to the newbies of Kricket, Gunpowder, Jamavar, and

Darjeeling Express in Soho for the best of the new-wave Indian menus.

ENGLISH BREAKFAST

A full English breakfast at one of the city's many workmen's cafés is every Londoner's favorite guilty pleasure. While there are endless varieties, a typical English breakfast consists of fried, poached, or scrambled eggs, streaky bacon, sausages, baked beans, white toast, fried mushrooms, grilled tomatoes, black pudding, chips, fried bread, brown sauce, and scorching mugs of tea.

14

FISH-AND-CHIPS

With a focus on crisp batter, juicy cod or haddock, and thick crispy chips, locals seek out low-key traditional fish-and-chip shops and old-school Formica-topped "chippies" for their insatiable fix. Old stagers like The Golden Hind in Marylebone, The Fryer's Delight in Holborn, and The Rock & Sole Plaice in Covent Garden have their nostalgic charms, while a fresh batch of new-comers like the Golden Union in Soho, Poppies Fish & Chips in Spitalfields, and Kurbisher & Malt in Clerkenwell tweak around with beer batters, double-cooked chips, homemade tartar sauce, and sustainably sourced fish.

GASTROPUBS

Londoners still love heading to their local gastropub for a rowdy combo of unpretentious Brit-focused dishes and draught beer, cask ales, and cheap wines served in soaring Victorian pubs or ornate gin palaces. Ever since exotic food started being served in The Eagle pub in Farringdon in 1991, the home-grown, foodie-led gastropub revolution has swept London asunder. From still-going-remarkably-strong The Eagle in Farringdon to game-centric The Harwood Arms in Fulham to the crab-heavy menu at The Marksman in Hackney, ducking into a bristling gastropub is a surefire way of dining out like a true-grit Londoner.

NIGHT MARKETS

A welcome development to the London food scene, Street Feast's night street-food markets and "food arenas" have begun popping up in hipster zones like Shoreditch and Dalston. Housed in edgy DIY indoor/outdoor venues, thousands of London's young foodie fanatics blitz their way through the mini-festivals to try some of the best experimental food trucks, stalls, and stands around. With kooky tunes, ample brews, and communal raw bench seating, it's impossible not to have a blast flipping from cheap Korean burritos to Folkestone crab buns to a pimped-up Devil Burger with green chili sauce and double jalapeños.

Updated
by Alex
Wijeratna

British food hasn't always had the best reputation, but nowhere in the country is that reputation being completely stomped on more than in London. The city has zoomed up the global gastro charts, and can now seriously mix it with the world's top culinary heavyweights. No other city—barring New York—has the immense range of global cuisines that London has to offer. Standards have rocketed at all price points and it seems like the London restaurant scene might be in the most robust health ever.

A bottom-up local foodie revolution and a top-down cascade of the city's wealth has juiced things up fabulously. Feel like eating the most-tender Kagoshima wagyu beef on planet Earth? It can be yours for £140 at CUT at 45 Park Lane. Want to try old English gastronomy from the time of Henry VIII with an ultramodern twist? Ashley Palmer-Watts is your man at Dinner by Heston Blumenthal. Do you only eat Sri Lankan *hoppers*? No worries, we've got just the thing: try Hoppers in Soho to get a taste of the south Indian pancake, for £3.50 a pop. Can't stand any more snobby culinary nonsense? The low-key British wild game is so good at The Harwood Arms in Fulham that they've earned London's first gastropub-based Michelin star.

To appreciate how far London has risen in the culinary game, just look back to the days of Somerset Maugham, who was once justified in warning, "To eat well in England you should have breakfast three times a day." Change was slow after World War II, when it was understood that the British ate to live, while the French lived to eat. When people thought of British cuisine, fish-and-chips—a greasy grab-and-gulp dish that tasted best wrapped in yesterday's newspaper—first came to mind. Then there was always shepherd's pie, ubiquitously found in smoke-filled pubs, though not made, according to *Sweeney Todd,* "with real shepherd in it."

These days, standards are miles higher and shepherd's pie has been largely replaced by the city's unofficial dish, Indian curry. London's restaurant revolution is built on its extraordinary ethnic diversity, and you'll find the quality of other global cuisines has grown immeasurably in recent years, with London becoming known for its Chinese, Japanese, Indian, Thai, Spanish, Italian, French, Peruvian, and North African restaurants. Thankfully, pride in the best of British food—local, seasonal, wild, and foraged—is enjoying a renaissance. And you, too, will be smitten: you'll be spending an average 24% of your travel budget on eating out, but it'll be worth every penny.

PLANNING

14

EATING OUT STRATEGY

Where should you eat? With thousands of London eateries competing for your attention, it may seem like a daunting question. But fret not: our expert writers and editors have done most of the legwork. The selections here represent the best this city has to offer—from haute cuisine to humble pub food. *Search "Best Bets" for top recommendations by price, cuisine, and experience. Or find a review quickly in the neighborhood listings.*

RESERVATIONS

Plan ahead if you're determined to snag a sought-after reservation. Some renowned restaurants like Chiltern Firehouse, Palomar, or Duck & Waffle are booked weeks or even months in advance. It's always a good idea to book as far ahead as you can and reconfirm when you arrive in London. Note that some top restaurants also now take credit card details and charge a penalty fee if you're a no-show. *In the reviews, we mention reservations only when they're essential or not accepted.*

DINING TOURS

FAMILY

Fodor's Choice

★

London Food Lovers Food Tours. London's a top global foodie city now, and the London Food Lovers walking tour of Soho is a fascinating way to explore the capital's gastro delights. The four-hour walk kicks off with Hawaiian blueberry pancakes at burger bar Kua'Aina off Carnaby Street and takes in offbeat stops for truffle pumpkin ravioli at Soho's vintage Italian delicatessen Lina Stores, a hot chocolate tasting at SAID artisanal Roman chocolatiers, and a sit-down lunch of cod and chips and Indian pale ale in quaint Soho boozer The Dog and Duck. Well-led and synchronized throughout, you'll stop in Chinatown to sample steamed prawn dim sum at Beijing Dumpling, and spot celebrities amid the clink of china for Afternoon Tea at the Maison Bertaux French patisserie and tearoom. The tour ends with a dessert and wine pairing in the Dickensian underground cellar vaults of the 1890 Gordon's Wine Bar. ⊠ *Islington* ☎ *07404/802–703* ⊕ *www.londonfoodlovers.com* 🖾 *£55.*

WHAT TO WEAR

When in England's style capital, do as the natives do: dress up to eat out. Whatever your style, dial it up a notch and have some fun while you're at it. Pull out the clothes you've been saving for a special occasion and get a little glamorous. As unfair as it seems, the way you look can influence how you're treated—and where you're seated. Generally speaking, jeans and a button-down shirt will suffice at most table-service restaurants in the budget to moderate range. Moving up from there, many pricier restaurants require jackets, and some (like the Ritz) insist on ties. Shorts, sweatpants, baseball caps, and sports jerseys are rarely appropriate. *Note that in reviews we mention dress only when men are required to wear a jacket, or a jacket and tie.*

TIPPING AND TAXES

Do not tip bar staff in pubs and bars, although you can always offer to buy them a drink. In restaurants, tip 12.5% of the check for full meals if service is not already included; tip a small token if you're just having coffee or tea. If paying by credit card, double-check that a tip has not already been included in the bill.

CHILDREN

Unless your children behave impeccably, it's best to avoid the haute-cuisine establishments, although increasingly many top places like the Wolseley and Fischer's are surprisingly child-friendly. London's many burger and rib joints, pizzerias, and Italian restaurants are popular with kids. Other family-friendly establishments include chains like Bill's, Côte, Byron, and Wagamama.

HOURS

In London you can find breakfast all day, but it's generally served 7 am–noon. Lunch is noon–3, and brunch 11–4. Afternoon tea, often a meal in itself, is taken 1–6, and dinner is typically eaten 7–11, although it can be taken earlier. Many ethnic restaurants, especially Indian, serve food until midnight. Sunday is a proper lunch day, and some restaurants are open for lunch only. Over the Christmas period, London has a reputation for shutting down, but a growing number of hotels and other brave bastions are prepared to feed all visitors.

PRICES

London is a very pricey city by global standards. A modest meal for two can easily cost £40, and the £100-a-head meal is not unknown. Damage-control strategies include making lunch your main meal (the top places have bargain midday menus), going for early- or late-evening deals, or sharing an à la carte entrée and ordering a second appetizer instead. Seek out fixed-price menus, and watch for hidden extras on the check, that is, bread, vegetables, or a cover charged separately.

WHAT IT COSTS				
	$	**$$**	**$$$**	**$$$$**
Restaurants	Under £16	£16–£23	£24–£31	Over £31

Prices in the reviews are the average cost of a main course at dinner or, if dinner is not served, at lunch. Note: If a restaurant offers only prix-fixe (set-price) meals, it has been given the price category that reflects the full prix-fixe price.

RESTAURANT REVIEWS

Listed alphabetically within neighborhoods. Use the coordinate (✢ 1:B2) at the end of each listing to locate a property on the Where to Eat and Stay in London atlas at the end of this chapter. Restaurant reviews have been shortened. For full information, visit Fodors.com.

14

WESTMINSTER, ST. JAMES'S, AND ROYAL LONDON

ST. JAMES'S

St. James's—home to Buckingham Palace and Clarence House, where Prince Charles and Camilla live—has a magnificent olde-world, royal feel. Appropriately, most of the restaurants here are fit for a future king. This is where you'll find London's top-end restaurants—dining experiences that are geared toward a well-heeled, deep-pocketed clientele. Mere mortals should make reservations well in advance to dine at any of these restaurants for dinner (or reserve a table for the earlier or later parts of the evening, when demand is lower). Keep in mind that no-shows mean last-minute tables often crop up, and lunch here can be a great money-saving strategy.

$$$
BRASSERIE
FAMILY
✕ **45 Jermyn St.** A sophisticated crowd enjoys the clubhouse vibe and huge burnt-orange booths at this classic all-day brasserie at the back of the Queen's grocer Fortnum & Mason. An old-school trolley trundles up tableside to serve Siberian Sturgeon cavier with scrambled eggs, baked new potatoes, and blinis, while creamy beef Stroganoff and whole duck with elderberry sauce gets the full tableside *flambé* treatment. **Known for:** unique caviar trolley; glamorous decor; collection of boozy ice cream floats. ⑤ *Average main: £26* ✉ *45 Jermyn St., St. James's* ☎ *020/7205-4545* ⊕ *www.45jermynst.com* Ⓜ *Green Park* ✢ *5:A1.*

$$$
MODERN
EUROPEAN
FAMILY
✕ **Le Caprice.** Celebville Le Caprice commands the deepest loyalty of any restaurant in London. It must be the 36-odd-year celebrity history (think Liz Taylor, Joan Collins, Lady Di, and Victoria Beckham), the sparkling monochrome decor, the giddy David Bailey '60s black-and-white pics, the pitch-perfect service, and the long-standing menu that sits somewhere between Euro peasant and trendy fashion plate. Sit at the raised counter or at a coveted corner table and enjoy calves' liver with crispy pancetta, slip soles with Amalfi lemon butter, and the signature Scandinavian iced berries with a swirl of hot white chocolate sauce. **Known for:** celebrity sightings galore; classic fish-and-chips with minted pea puree; live jazz on Sunday night. ⑤ *Average main:*

£26 ✉ *Arlington House, 20 Arlington St., St. James's* ☎ *020/7629–2239* ⊕ *www.le-caprice.co.uk* Ⓜ *Green Park* ⬦ *5:A1.*

$$$$ ✕**The Ritz Restaurant.** London's most opulent dining salon here at the
BRITISH Ritz would moisten the eye of even Marie Antoinette with its sumptu-
FAMILY ous Gilded Age Rocco Revival *trompe-l'oeil*frescoes, tasseled silk drap-
ery, and towering marble columns. Sit at the late Baroness Thatcher's
favorite seat overlooking Green Park (Table 1) and luxuriate in unre-
constructed British haute cuisine such as Bresse chicken with black
Périgord truffles or beef Wellington carved tableside. **Known for:** luxurious dining made for the British elite; possibly London's best beef
Wellington; legendary Afternoon Tea. ⑤ *Average main: £42* ✉ *The Ritz
London, 150 Piccadilly, St. James's* ☎ *020/7300–2370 for reservations
only* ⊕ *www.theritzlondon.com* 🔺*Jacket and tie* Ⓜ *Green Park* ⬦ *5:A1.*

$$$$ ✕**Wiltons.** Lords, Ladies, aristocrats, and European princes-in-exile
BRITISH blow the family bank at this Edwardian bastion of traditional English
fine dining on Jermyn Street (the place first opened on the Haymarket
as a shellfish stall in 1742). Posh patrons tend to order half a dozen
Beau Brummell oysters, followed by grilled Dover sole, honey-glazed
gammon from the carving trolley, or fabulous native game, such as roast
partridge, teal, or grouse. **Known for:** traditional English dining focused
on shellfish and game; waiter service that would put Jeeves to shame;
Bordeaux-heavy wine menu. ⑤ *Average main: £36* ✉ *55 Jermyn St., St.
James's* ☎ *020/7629–9955* ⊕ *www.wiltons.co.uk* ⊘ *Closed Sun. and
bank holidays. No lunch Sat.* 🔺*Jacket required* Ⓜ *Green Park* ⬦ *5:A1.*

$$ ✕**The Wolseley.** A glitzy procession of famous faces, media moguls,
AUSTRIAN and hedge-funders comes for the spectacle, swish service, and soaring
FAMILY elegance at this bustling Viennese-style grand café on Piccadilly. Framed
with 1920s black lacquerware in a former Wolseley Motors luxury-car
showroom, this all-day brasserie begins its long decadent days with
breakfast at 7 am and serves Dual Monarchy delights until midnight.
Known for: old-country Austrian and Hungarian delights; Afternoon
Tea with a Vienesse twist; classic grand café ambience. ⑤ *Average main:
£21* ✉ *160 Piccadilly, St. James's* ☎ *020/7499–6996* ⊕ *www.thewolse-
ley.com* Ⓜ *Green Park* ⬦ *5:A1.*

MAYFAIR AND MARYLEBONE

If you're looking for something more wallet-friendly, head north to
Marylebone, formerly dowdy but now prized for its überchic, villagelike
feel. Here you'll find an array of low-key little cafés, boîtes, and tapas
bars, Champagne-and-hot-dog joints, and the odd world-class sizzler,
offering everything from Moroccan and Spanish to Thai and Japanese.

MAYFAIR

$$$$ ✕**Alain Ducasse at the Dorchester.** One of only two three-Michelin-starred
FRENCH restaurants in the city, Alain Ducasse at the Dorchester achieves the
FAMILY pinnacle of classical French haute cuisine in a surprisingly fun, lively,
Fodor's Choice and unstuffy salon. Diners feast on a blizzard of beautifully choreo-
★ graphed dishes ranging from sensational sauté lobster with truffled
chicken quenelles to rum baba with Chantilly cream, sliced open
and served in a silver domed tureen. **Known for:** impeccable five-star

service; surprisingly unstarchy vibe; signature sauté lobster with chicken quenelles. ⑤ *Average main: £45* ✉ *The Dorchester, Park Lane, Mayfair* ☎ *020/7629–8866 for reservations only* ⊕ *www.alainducasse-dorchester.com* Ⓜ *Marble Arch, Green Park* ✛ *1:H6.*

$$$ ╳ **Cecconi's.** Join the A-list and wallow in the glamorous buzz at this
MODERN ITALIAN upscale Italian brasserie wedged strategically between Cork Street, Savile Row, and the Royal Academy of Arts. Perfect for a pit stop during a West End shopping spree or after browsing the nearby Mayfair galleries and auction houses, the fine art world connoisseurs spill out onto pavement tables for breakfast, brunch, and *cicchetti* (Italian tapas), and return later in the day for something more substantial. **Known for:** favorite of nearby Sotheby's and Vogue House staff; popular veal Milanese; all-day jetsetter hangout. ⑤ *Average main: £28* ✉ *5A Burlington Gardens, Mayfair* ☎ *020/7434–1500* ⊕ *www.cecconis.co.uk* Ⓜ *Green Park, Piccadilly Circus* ✛ *3:A6.*

14

$$$ ╳ **The Colony Grill Room.** Glide past the parked royal blue Armstrong
AMERICAN Siddeley, through the foyer of the five-star Beaumont hotel, and into the
FAMILY swank art deco–inspired dining salon of the Colony Grill Room. Fans of 1920s New York cool will admire the burnished wood, blood-red leather banquettes, and endless stack of vintage caricatures (from Clark Gable to Dorothy Parker), before digging into throwbacks like the mock turtle soup, clam chowder, and the *flambé* Bananas Foster. **Known for:** evocative American 1920s panache and glamour; bespoke sundae menu; classic buttermilk fried chicken. ⑤ *Average main: £26* ✉ *The Beaumont, 8 Balderton St., Brown Hart Gardens, Mayfair* ☎ *020 /7499–9499* ⊕ *www.colonygrillroom.com* Ⓜ *Marble Arch* ✛ *1:G4.*

$$$ ╳ **Corrigan's Mayfair.** There's a stylish hunting, shooting, and fishing
BRITISH theme going on at burly Irish chef-patron Richard Corrigan's luxuri-
FAMILY ous, clublike Mayfair salon. Part plush brasserie and part game and chophouse, the ever-obliging waitstaff welcomes you to sit among the starched napery and deep blue leather seats, where you can choose from a menu of outstanding game and Irish soda bread. **Known for:** traditional seasonal game dishes and game pies; boned Dover sole from the carvery trolley; affordable Sunday roast set menu. ⑤ *Average main: £33* ✉ *29 Upper Grosvenor St., Mayfair* ☎ *020/7499–9943* ⊕ *www. corrigansmayfair.co.uk* Ⓜ *Marble Arch* ✛ *1:G5.*

$$$$ ╳ **CUT at 45 Park Lane.** Austrian-born star chef Wolfgang Puck amps
STEAKHOUSE up the stakes at this ultraexpensive steak specialist on Park Lane. Set
FAMILY against a luxe backdrop of Damien Hirst artwork and globe lights, carnivores go crazy for the pricey prime cuts from England, Australia, Japan, and the United States, including impeccable 35-day Creekstone filet mignon, Black Angus New York sirloins, and an 8-ounce rib eye of Kagoshima wagyu beef from Kyusyu in Japan. **Known for:** rare Kagoshima Wagyu beef steaks; celebrity chef hotspot; art gallerylike interior. ⑤ *Average main: £48* ✉ *45 Park La., Mayfair* ☎ *020/7439– 4554 for reservations only* ⊕ *www.dorchestercollection.com* Ⓜ *Marble Arch, Hyde Park Corner* ✛ *1:H6.*

$$$$ ╳ **Goodman.** This Manhattan-themed, Russian-owned, Mayfair-based
STEAKHOUSE swanky steak house, named after Chicago jazz legend Benny Good-
FAMILY man, has everyone in agreement: these truly are some of the best steaks

in town. USDA-certified, 150-day corn-fed, and on-site dry-aged Black Angus T-bones, rib eye, porterhouse, and New York sirloins compete for taste and tenderness with heavily marbled grass-fed prime cuts from Scotland and the Lake District. **Known for:** awesome grass-fed and corn-fed steaks; whole king crab available on request; long list of classy Cornovan-extracted red wines by the glass. $ *Average main: £35* ✉ *24–26 Maddox St., Mayfair* ☎ *020/7499–3776* ⊕ *www.goodmanrestaurants.com* ⊗ *Closed Sun.* Ⓜ *Oxford Circus, Piccadilly Circus* ✛ *3:A5.*

$$$
MODERN INDIAN
FAMILY
Fodor'sChoice
★

✕ **Gymkhana.** The last days of the Raj are invoked here at London's finest top-end curry emporium, where top choices include dosas with fennel-rich Chettinad duck, wild Muntjac deer biryani, or famed suckling pig vindaloo. Inspired by the Colonial-era gymkhana sporting clubs of yesteryear, diners admire the whirring ceiling fans, rattan chairs, and dark chocolate leather banquettes and chuckle at the vintage Punch sketches and hunting trophies from the Maharajah of Jodhpur. **Known for:** unusual game curries; unique cocktails in the basement private dining booths; signature kid goat methi keema. $ *Average main: £28* ✉ *42 Albemarle St., Mayfair* ☎ *020/3011–5900* ⊕ *www.gymkhanalondon.com* ⊗ *Closed Sun.* Ⓜ *Green Park* ✛ *1:H5.*

$$$$
FRENCH
FAMILY

✕ **Hélène Darroze at the Connaught.** The crème de la crème of the city flock to French virtuoso Hélène Darroze's restaurant at the Connaught for her dazzling regional French haute cuisine, served up in a stylish Edwardian wood-paneled dining salon tricked out with geometric carpets, India Mahdavi tableware, and comfy high-back chairs. Taking inspiration from Les Landes in southwestern France, Darroze sallies forth with a procession of magnificent dishes, like Robert Dupérier foie gras with fig and port or Limousin sweetbreads with Jerusalem artichokes. **Known for:** sumptuous oak-panelled dining salon; classy French haute dishes; nifty three-course set lunch. $ *Average main: £38* ✉ *The Connaught, Carlos Pl., Mayfair* ☎ *020/3147–7200 for reservations only* ⊕ *www.the-connaught.co.uk* 🏛 *Jacket required* Ⓜ *Green Park* ✛ *1:H5.*

$$
INDIAN
FAMILY
Fodor'sChoice
★

✕ **Jamavar.** There is no finer fish dish in town than the stone bass *tikka* at this upmarket Indian restaurant; it's a charred vision of tandoor-blasted and mace-marinated stone bass with chili-spiked avocado chutney. Sumptuously kitted with gilded wall coverings and Indian artwork, the food and spices here are so authentic that it regularly buzzes with Bollywood stars, wealthy Mayfair moguls, and the entire well-heeled Indian diaspora. **Known for:** stunning dark wood, marble, and Indian artwork interior; unmissable stone bass tikka; glossy, luxurious crowd. $ *Average main: £24* ✉ *8 Mount St., Mayfair* ☎ *020/7499–1800* ⊕ *www.jamavarrestaurants.com* Ⓜ *Bond St., Green Park* ✛ *1:H5.*

$$$
MODERN BRITISH
Fodor'sChoice
★

✕ **Kitty Fisher's.** Named after an infamous 18th-century courtesan, Kitty Fisher's is situated in a tiny, creaky 40-seat Georgian townhouse in Mayfair's Shepherd Market. Crammed with antique prints, portraits, and silver candelabras, come and let it seduce you with some of the finest woodgrill and smokehouse fare around, including a singed and seared yet pink and oozing carved column of 12-year-old Galician dairy cow sirloin, accompanied by a heap of grilled onions, pickled walnuts, and barbecued Pink Fir potatoes with soft white Tunworth cheese. **Known for:** cozy and candle-lit Georgian-era townhouse setting; signature wood-grilled Galician beef with scorched onions; high-end media, arts, and politico diners. $ *Average main: £27* ⊠ *10 Shepherd Market, Mayfair* ☏ *020/3302–1661* ⊕ *www.kittyfishers.com* ☙ *Closed Sun.* Ⓜ *Green Park* ✛ *1:H6.*

$$$$ ✕ **La Petite Maison.** With the legend "*Tous Célèbres Ici*" ("All Famous
FRENCH   Here") boldly etched on the frosted glass front doors, the light-filled
FAMILY   and delightful Petite Maison boasts an impressively well-sourced and balanced French Mediterranean, Ligurian, and Provençal menu. Based on the relaxed Riviera style of the original La Petite Maison in Nice, try the figure-friendly broad bean and Pecorino salad, soft burrata cheese with sweet Datterini-tomato-and-basil spread, or aromatic baked turbot with artichokes, chorizo, five spices, and gloppy white wine sauce. **Known for:** French Riviera-inspired dining; excellent selection of rosé wines; whole roast black leg chicken. $ *Average main: £35* ⊠ *53–54 Brook's Mews, Mayfair* ☏ *020/7495–4774* ⊕ *www.lpmlondon.co.uk* Ⓜ *Bond St., Oxford Circus* ✛ *1:H4.*

$$$$ ✕ **Le Gavroche.** Masterchef Michel Roux Jr. works the floor in the
FRENCH   old-fashioned proprietorial way at this old-school Mayfair basement
FAMILY   institution—established by his father and uncle in 1967—which many
Fodor's Choice still rate as the best formal dining in London. Resplendent with mag-
★   nificent silver domes, unpriced ladies' menus, and a collection of fine Chagall and Picasso prints, Roux's mastery of classical French haute cuisine hypnotizes with signature dishes like foie gras with cinnamon-scented crispy duck pancake, roast venison with red wine jus, or saddle of rabbit with Parmesan cheese. **Known for:** swank old money Mayfair basement setting; relatively affordable three-course set lunch menus; tasty soufflé Suissesse. $ *Average main: £44* ⊠ *43 Upper Brook St., Mayfair* ☏ *020/7408–0881* ⊕ *www.le-gavroche. co.uk* ☙ *Closed Sun. and Mon. No lunch Tues. and Sat.* 🎩 *Jacket required* Ⓜ *Bond St., Marble Arch* ✛ *1:G5.*

$$$ ✕ **Little Social.** A neon sign may caution "*Silence, Logique, Securité,*
MODERN FRENCH *Prudence,*" but there's always a warm glow and hubbub here at this below-the-radar French bistro hidden away in a cute alley in Mayfair. Ease into a Burgundy banquette booth and admire the elm tables, art deco lamps, and Michelin road maps in the narrow dining salon before diving into the Cornish crab salad appetizer on a round of tomato with miso dressing or the braised Irish ox cheeks with roast bone marrow, carrots, and horseradish mash. **Known for:** refined classic-with-a-twist French dishes; fabulous set lunches; aged Scottish beef cheeseburgers. $ *Average main: £27* ⊠ *5 Pollen St., Mayfair* ☏ *020/7870–3730* ⊕ *www.littlesocial.co.uk* Ⓜ *Oxford Circus, Piccadilly Circus* ✛ *3:A4.*

$$$ ✕ **Ormer Mayfair.** Hidden away in the depths of a Mayfair hotel is famed
BRITISH   Shaun Rankin's triumphant ode to all things Jersey (in the Channel Islands, that is). In the art deco–inspired basement haven, indulge on world-class Jersey seashore caught, reared, and foraged dishes—from sweet Jersey lobster ravioli with crab bisque and Thai-inspired shallot salad to Jersey turbot with cockles and sea vegetables. **Known for:** stand

out Jersey crab and lobster ravioli; top English wine selection; treacle tart with Jersey clotted cream for dessert. $ *Average main: £32* ✉ *Flemings Hotel, 7–12 Half Moon St., Mayfair* ☎ *020/7499–0000* ⊕ *www. flemings-mayfair.co.uk/fine-dining-london/ormer-mayfair-restaurant* Ⓜ *Green Park* ✛ *5:A1.*

$$$$
MODERN
EUROPEAN

✗ **Pollen Street Social.** Gastro god Jason Atherton may not man the stoves here anymore, but his smash-hit flagship in a cute Dickensian alleyway off Regent Street still knocks the London dining scene for a loop. Fans enjoy refined small and large dishes ranging from a full English breakfast appetizer (a miniature poached egg on tomato compote with parsley-flecked bacon, morels, and croutons) to sublime Scottish ox cheek with 50-day Black Angus rib eye. **Known for:** Michelin-star riffs on classic British dishes; dedicated dessert bar; Lake District roast lamb with shallots and mint sauce. $ *Average main: £36* ✉ *8–10 Pollen St., Mayfair* ☎ *020/7290–7600* ⊕ *www.pollenstreetsocial.com* ☾ *Closed Sun.* Ⓜ *Oxford Circus, Piccadilly Circus* ✛ *3:A5.*

$$$
MODERN ITALIAN
FAMILY

✗ **Sartoria.** Italian maestro Francesco Mazzei bestrides this plush and patterned Savile Row salon and warmly welcomes diners like the proud chef-patron that he is. Inhale a whiff of Alba truffle as it's delicately sliced tableside over an extravagantly egg yolk-rich spaghetti carbonara. **Known for:** Mayfair hedge fund clientele; the chef-patron's big smile and warm welcome; wonderfully silky handmade pastas. $ *Average main: £32* ✉ *20 Savile Row, Mayfair* ☎ *020/7534–7000* ⊕ *www. sartoria-restaurant.co.uk* ☾ *No dinner Sun.* Ⓜ *Oxford Circus* ✛ *3:A5.*

$$$$
SEAFOOD
FAMILY

✗ **Scott's.** Imposing doormen in bowler hats greet visitors with a wee nod at this ever-fashionable seafood haven on Mount Street in Mayfair. Originally founded in 1851 in the Haymarket, and a former haunt of James Bond author Ian Fleming (he apparently enjoyed the potted shrimps), Scott's draws the wealthiest of London, who enjoy day-boat fresh Lindisfarne oysters, Dover sole off the bone, platters of fruits de mer, and tasty shrimp burgers. **Known for:** possibly London's most magnificent crustacea bar; huge platters of fresh fruits de mer; extravagant prices. $ *Average main: £36* ✉ *20 Mount St., Mayfair* ☎ *020/7495–7309 for reservations only* ⊕ *www.scotts-restaurant.com* Ⓜ *Green Park, Bond St.* ✛ *1:H5.*

$$$
INTERNATIONAL
FAMILY

✗ **34.** A-listers head straight for 34, off Grosvenor Square in Mayfair, simply because all the other celebrities seem to hang out here, too. It must be the plush Edwardian- and neo art deco dining salon, the neat fish, game, and steak-focused menu, and the achingly smooth Upper Manhattan–style service. **Known for:** an endless procession of top Hollywood stars; nightly live jazz and classy British art adorning the walls; impressive global meats off an Argentine-inspired grill. $ *Average main: £28* ✉ *34 Grosvenor Sq., entrance on S. Audley St., Mayfair* ☎ *020/3350–3434* ⊕ *www.34-restaurant.co.uk* Ⓜ *Marble Arch* ✛ *1:G5.*

MARYLEBONE

$$
AUSTRIAN
FAMILY
Fodor's Choice
★

✗ **Fischer's.** It almost feels like Gustav Klimt or Sigmund Freud might doff their Homburg hats and shuffle into a dark leather banquette at this evocative, early century–style Viennese neighborhood café on Marylebone High Street. Savor the antique light fittings, distressed wallpaper, and gilt-edged paintings before diving into *brötchen* chopped chicken livers with dill on rye bread or the Emmental and bacon-wrapped *Berner Würstel* sausages piled high with sauerkraut and mustard-swooshed potatoes. **Known for:** evocative turn-of-the-century Old Vienna café decor; some of London's best breaded Wiener schnitzel; decadent ice cream desserts. ⑤ *Average main: £21* ✉ *50 Marylebone High St., Marylebone* ☎ *020/7466–5501* ⊕ *www.fischers.co.uk* Ⓜ *Baker St., Bond St.* ✛ *1:H3.*

$$ ✕**Galvin Bistrot de Luxe.** The godlike Galvin brothers, Chris and Jeff,
BRASSERIE blaze a trail for the time-tested French modern bistro formula on this
FAMILY fast-moving stretch of Baker Street. Loyalists return time and again for the impeccable food, smart service, and Parisian-style dining salon. **Known for:** unashamed French bistro de luxe classics; proper French-style service; top value three-course lunches and set dinners. ⑤ *Average main: £24* ✉ *66 Baker St., Marylebone* ☎ *020/7935–4007* ⊕ *www. galvinrestaurants.com* Ⓜ *Baker St.* ✛ *1:G3.*

$ ✕**The Golden Hind.** You'll land some of the best fish-and-chips in town
SEAFOOD at this great British chippy in a cheery retro 1914 art deco café. Gag-
FAMILY gles of Marylebone locals, office workers, and satisfied tourists hunker down for the neatly prepared and decidedly nongreasy deep-fried or steamed battered cod, haddock, and plaice, the classic hand-cut Maris Piper chips, and the traditional mushy peas and homemade tartare sauce. **Known for:** some of the city's best deep-fried battered cod and chips; hard-to-find traditional mushy peas; BYO alcohol policy. ⑤ *Average main: £9* ✉ *73 Marylebone La., Marylebone* ☎ *020/7486–3644* ⊘ *Closed Sun. No lunch Sat.* Ⓜ *Bond St.* ✛ *1:H3.*

$$ ✕**Les 110 de Taillevent.** Dazzling dishes mark out Les 110 de Taillevent
FRENCH as the city's top French *brasserie de luxe*. Housed in a chic former bank on Cavendish Square, diners delight in the exquisite cuisine (like the lobster knuckle ravioli in a fragrant consommé) and accompanying master list of 110 fine wines by the glass. **Known for:** soaring classic dining salon; brilliant list of paired fine wines by the glass; haunt for wine merchants and experts. ⑤ *Average main: £24* ✉ *16 Cavendish Sq., Marylebone* ☎ *020/3141–6016* ⊕ *www.les-110-taillevent-london.com* ⊘ *Closed Sun.* Ⓜ *Bond St., Oxford Circus* ✛ *1:H3.*

SOHO AND COVENT GARDEN

Soho and Covent Garden are the city's historic playground and pleasure zone, an all-day, all-night jostling neon wonderland of glitz, glamour, grime, and greasepaint. This area is London's cultural heart, with old and new media companies, late-night dive bars, cabaret, street performers, West End musicals, and world-class theater, ballet, and opera houses. Rising rents have recently forced out many of Soho's seedier red-light businesses and ushered in more edgy, top-notch restaurants. Just follow your nose in Covent Garden and Theatreland to find copious options for pretheater dining.

SOHO

$ ✕**Andrew Edmunds.** Candlelit at night, with a haunting Hogarthian
MEDITERRANEAN moody vibe, Andrew Edmunds is a permanently packed, old-school dining institution. Tucked away behind Carnaby Street in an atmospheric

18th-century Soho townhouse, it's a cozy favorite whose unpretentious and keenly priced dishes draw on the tastes of Ireland, the Mediterranean, and Middle East, from harissa-spiced mackerel to seafood paella and woodcock on toast. **Known for:** deeply romantic, Georgian-era townhouse setting; daily changing handwritten menus; bargains galore on the acclaimed wine list. $ *Average main: £17* ⌂ *46 Lexington St., Soho* ☎ *020/7437–5708* ⊕ *www.andrewedmunds.com* Ⓜ *Oxford Circus, Piccadilly Circus* ✛ *3:C5.*

$$$
SCANDINAVIAN

✕ **Aquavit.** There's a hygge-style warmth at this ritzy New Nordic emporium off Piccadilly Circus. Swedish designer Martin Brudnizki pulls out all the best Scandinavian design stops, while a hip, upscale crowd dish over the pickled Matjes herrings from the small-jars *smörgåsbord* and pair Swedish meatballs with mash and lingonberries. **Known for:** nifty Nordic smorgasbord starters; soaring Scandinavian design showcase; knock-out sea bass with Sandefjord sauce. $ *Average main: £26* ⌂ *St. James's Market, 1 Carlton St., Piccadilly Circus* ☎ *020/7024–9848* ⊕ *www.aquavitrestaurants.com/london* Ⓜ *Piccadilly Circus.* ✛ *3:C6.*

$
TAIWANESE

✕ **BAO.** Lines form daily to secure a prized seat, perch, or stool at this diminutive, no-reservations 32-seater from a crack team of Taiwanese steamed bao bun specialists. The gloriously soft and plump milk-based, rice-flour bao buns—skillfully stuffed with organic Cornish braised pork, peanut powder, and fermented greens—are the undisputed stars of the zenlike show. **Known for:** long lines for the stuffed steamed bao buns; highly Instagramable pig blood cake; Horlicks ice cream for dessert. $ *Average main: £5* ⌂ *53 Lexington St., Soho* ⊕ *www.baolondon. com* ⊘ *Closed Sun.* Ⓜ *Oxford Circus, Tottenham Court Rd.* ✛ *3:B5.*

$
CAFÉ

✕ **Bar Italia.** This legendary Italian coffee bar on Frith Street is Soho's unofficial beating heart and a 22-hours-a-day classic institution. Established in 1949 during the postwar Italian coffee bar craze and still run by the founding Polledri family, today most regulars grab an espresso or frothy cappuccino made from the vintage Gaggia coffee machine, and wolf down a slice of pizza, hot bacon sandwich, or chocolate cake at one of the mirrored bar counters. **Known for:** tiny hole-in-the-wall plastered with pics of 1950s boxers and Italian movie stars; old-school Italian espresso; sturdy sausage or bacon sandwiches. $ *Average main: £6* ⌂ *22 Frith St., Soho* ☎ *020/7437–4520* ⊕ *www.baritaliasoho.co.uk* Ⓜ *Leicester Sq.* ✛ *3:D5.*

$
STEAKHOUSE
FAMILY
Fodor's Choice
★

✕ **Blacklock.** Set in a former basement brothel, this Soho meatopia cranks out £20 platters of delectable char-grilled grass-fed lamb, beef, and pork skinny chops and juice-soaked flatbread, all served on retro antique pearlware. Supplied by organic butchers Philip Warren from Launceston in Cornwall, Blacklock's killer chops are beautifully seasoned and seared on an open charcoal grill under heavy vintage Blacklock irons from the Deep South. **Known for:** young and bubbly service with top '80s tunes; huge platters of skinny chops and flat bread; affordable Sunday roasts with all the trimmings. $ *Average main: £10* ⌂ *The Basement, 24 Great Windmill St., Soho* ☎ *020/3441–6996* ⊕ *www. theblacklock.com* Ⓜ *Piccadilly Circus, Oxford Circus* ✛ *3:C5.*

$$
FRENCH

✕ **Blanchette.** French tapas may sound sacrilegious, but Blanchette hits the nail on the head at this rustic chic, hipster headquarters where a dreamy jazzy soundtrack complements the charming candlelit, art nouveau–tiled interior. Visually feast on the Paris flea market bric-a-brac and order a few small plates to share, like the crispy frogs' legs and truffle saucisson or baked scallops with a spunky Café de Paris sauce. **Known for:** unusual French tapas-style dishes and shared plates; cool crowd with jazzy soundtrack; crunchy French frogs' legs. $ *Average main: £18* ⊠ *9 D'Arblay St., Soho* ☎ *020/7439–8100* ⊕ *www.blanchettesoho.co.uk* Ⓜ *Tottenham Court Rd.* ✛ *3:C4.*

$$$

ITALIAN

FAMILY

✕ **Bocca di Lupo.** This redbrick-fronted, upscale Italian restaurant is always crammed and the tables jammed too close together, but everyone still comes for *la dolce vita* and chef Jacob Kenedy's wicked spread of rustic regional Italian small plates. Located off Theatreland's Shaftesbury Avenue, the family-run open-counter trattoria offers a magnificent menu featuring peasant-based pastas, stews, roasts, and crudité from Piedmont to Bologna. **Known for:** open kitchen counter serving a medley of small plates; enticing all-Italian wine list; crowd-pleasing lobster spaghettini. $ *Average main: £25* ⊠ *12 Archer St., Soho* ☎ *020/7734–2223* ⊕ *www.boccadilupo.com* Ⓜ *Piccadilly Circus* ✛ *3:C5.*

$

FRENCH

FAMILY

Fodor's Choice

★

✕ **Brasserie Zédal.** Enjoy great value, prix-fixe menus of classic French dishes at Piccadilly's spectacular 220-seat subterranean morning-'til-midnight Parisian grand brasserie. Dripping with beaux arts gilt sconces, brass rails, and monumental marble pillars, you can enjoy French standards like steak haché, choucroute, and crème brûleé. **Known for:** London's largest and most spectacular beaux arts all-day brasserie; fantastically cheap set meal deals; nightly live music. $ *Average main: £14* ⊠ *20 Sherwood St., Piccadilly Circus* ☎ *020/7734–4888* ⊕ *www.brasseriezedel.com* Ⓜ *Piccadilly Circus.* ✛ *3:C6.*

$$

BURGER

FAMILY

✕ **Burger & Lobster.** Don plastic bibs at this mobbed, limited-choice burger and lobster shack, where there are no reservations (apart from larger groups), no starters, and no printed menu—the blackboard says it all: "Burger or lobster or lobster roll. All with chips & salad. £22." Of the three choices available, the Nova Scotia lobster is the best value; it comes in a butter-soaked brioche bun, with truffle and tarragon mayo and a sturdy pot of fries. **Known for:** wonderfully simple menu of lobster, burgers and chips; one-and-a-half pound jumbo Canadian lobster with salad; lively, fun-loving crowd. $ *Average main: £23* ⊠ *36 Dean St., Soho* ☎ *020/7432–4800* ⊕ *www.burgerandlobster.com* Ⓜ *Piccadilly Circus, Tottenham Court Rd.* ✛ *3:D5.*

$$

BRITISH

FAMILY

✕ **Dean Street Townhouse.** Everyone feels 10 billion times more glamorous just stepping inside at this candlelit restaurant attached to the swanky 39-room Georgian-era hotel of the same name; *simpatico* lighting, dark oak floors, red leather banquettes, raised bar seats, and crack service create a hip hangout for media London's finest. No frills, no fuss retro-British favorites include ham-and-pea soup, old-school mince and potatoes, smoked haddock soufflé, and yummy sherry trifle. **Known for:** classy candle-lit dining salon with British art on the walls; super professional service; cheery High Tea and Afternoon Tea. $ *Average main: £24* ⊠ *69–71 Dean St., Soho* ☎ *020/7434–1775* ⊕ *www.deanstreet-townhouse.com* Ⓜ *Oxford Circus, Tottenham Court Rd.* ✛ *3:D5.*

14

$ ✗ **Flat Iron.** Premium £10 Dexter featherblade steaks are the only mains
STEAKHOUSE on the printed menu at this three-story no-reservations hipster canteen
FAMILY on Beak Street, decked out in regulation exposed brick walls, enamel
lights, and shared wooden tables. The char-grilled shoulder cuts of
grass-fed British beef arrive sliced on wooden blocks with watercress
and mini meat cleavers; sides include beef-dripping chips, creamed
spinach, and roasted eggplant with Parmesan. **Known for:** ridiculously
cheap and well-marbled featherblade steaks served on wooden slabs;
bench seating and fast-paced vibe; house burgers with creamed spinach.
⑤ *Average main: £10* ✉ *17 Beak St., Soho* ⊕ *www.flatironsteak.co.uk*
Ⓜ *Oxford Circus, Piccadilly Circus* ✛ *3:B5.*

$ ✗ **Hoppers.** Sri Lankan curry fiends have gone mad for the cheap egg
SRI LANKAN hopper pancakes (a Sri Lankan specialty) and paper-thin griddled hoppers
FAMILY at this highly spiced, no-reservations Frith Street snuggery. Diners gorge
Fodor's Choice on chili mutton rolls, curried duck hearts, and piles of steamed string
★ hoppers dipped in spicy broth, coconut chutney, or onion and Maldives
fish flakes relish. **Known for:** crispy egg hoppers with coconut sambol;
authentic Colombo-style curry cabin atmosphere; signature black pork
kari curry. ⑤ *Average main: £7* ✉ *49 Frith St., Soho* ⊕ *www.hopperslon-
don.com* Ⓜ *Tottenham Court Rd., Oxford Circus* ✛ *3:D4.*

$ ✗ **Kiln.** Earthy northern Thai cuisine bursts out of the charcoal-fired
THAI claypot, iron wok, and kiln at this BBQ-focused wonderland in Soho.
Fodor's Choice Take a peek at the open kitchen and you'll see sizzling cumin-dusted
★ hogget skewers and charcoal-grilled chicken thigh bites, along with other
village-style dishes that show influences from Laos, Myanmar, and the
Yunnan province of China. **Known for:** open kitchen counter setup with
charcoal grill and hot clay pots; awesome array of specially grown Thai,
Burmese, and other Asian herbs and spices; popular cumin-dusted fatty
hogget skewers. ⑤ *Average main: £8* ✉ *58 Brewer St., Soho* ☎ *No phone*
⊕ *www.kilnsoho.com* Ⓜ *Oxford Circus, Piccadilly Circus.* ✛ *3:C5.*

$ ✗ **Kricket.** Upsized dishes of zingy Indian street food fly from the open
INDIAN kitchen at this Piccadilly party spot. Sit at the L-shaped, lava-topped
FAMILY counter and watch the chefs haul out bone marrow-smeared *kulcha*
breads from the blazing clay tandoor and conjure up funky dishes like
yolk-topped kedgeree, garlic butter crab, and puffed rice *bhel puri*
starters, pepped up with mango, Greek yogurt, and tamarind sauce.
Known for: pepped-up Indian street food faves; colonial cocktails in
the raucous downstairs dining den; young crowds. ⑤ *Average main:
£10* ✉ *12 Denman St., Piccadilly Circus* ☎ *No phone* ⊕ *www.kricket.
co.uk* Ⓜ *Piccadilly Circus.* ✛ *3:C6.*

$ ✗ **Maison Bertaux.** Romantics and Francophiles cherish this quirky, two-
CAFÉ story 1871 French patisserie, vintage tea parlor, and occasional pop-
FAMILY up art space, where nothing seems to have changed since the 1940s.
Colorful pastries, tarts, croissants, and sweet cakes are still well loved
and baked on-site; you can choose from the chocolate and fruit éclairs,
Saint-Honoré and Black Forest gâteaux, marzipan figs, and flaky almond
croissants. **Known for:** mesmerizing vintage French interiors; glamorous
and eccentric owner; old-fashioned collection of creamy patisseries.
⑤ *Average main: £8* ✉ *28 Greek St., Soho* ☎ *020/7437–6007* ⊕ *www.
maisonbertaux.com* ▭ *No credit cards* Ⓜ *Leicester Sq.* ✛ *3:D5.*

$ ✕ **The Palomar.** It's Jerusalem meets Palestine meets Beirut meets a bon-
MIDDLE EASTERN   kers scenester vibe at this Arab-Israeli funky spot off Chinatown. Sit at
the open-kitchen zinc counter and down shots of *arak* while "*L'chaim-ing!*" and trading quips over the booming soundtrack with the Middle
Eastern chefs, who offer a medley of Levantine delights, including
Yemeni-Jewish *kubaneh* bread, Palestinian steak tartare, Jerusalem
truffled mushroom polenta, and tangy paprika-rich pork belly tagine
with Israeli couscous. **Known for:** fun, Middle Eastern party atmosphere and free arak shots; lively pork pie-hatted chefs brigade in the
open kitchen; popular Persian oxtail stew. ⑤ *Average main: £14* ✉ *34
Rupert St., Soho* ☎ *020/7439–8777* ⊕ *www.thepalomar.co.uk* Ⓜ *Piccadilly Circus, Leicester Sq.* ✛ *3:D6.*

$$$ ✕ **Social Eating House.** At Jason Atherton's underrated but brilliant
FRENCH   French bistronomie Soho hangout, witty and pretty dishes like smoked
FAMILY   duck's ham (made from cured duck's breast), boil-in-a-bag wild mush-
rooms, and Scotch egg-and-chips are served alongside classics like the
"CLT," consisting of white crabmeat, lettuce, and roast heritage tomato.
The moodily lit bare-brick ground-floor salon is tricked out with dark
parquet floors, antique mirrored ceilings, and red leather banquettes.
Known for: vintage cocktails in the speakeasy lounge; affordable set
lunches and extravagant tasting menus at the chef's table; signature
boil-in-the-bag British wild mushrooms on toast. ⑤ *Average main: £26*
✉ *58 Poland St., Soho* ☎ *020/7993–3251* ⊕ *www.socialeatinghouse.
com* ☽ *Closed Sun.* Ⓜ *Oxford Circus, Tottenham Court Rd.* ✛ *3:B4.*

$ ✕ **Spuntino.** Moody Edison bulbs, bluegrass tunes, a popcorn machine,
DINER   and only 27 raised counter stools at this pewter-top speakeasy make for
one of the coolest spots in town. Once seated, settle in with a Brooklyn
Manhattan cocktail and then dive into truffled egg toast before mov-
ing on to deep-fried grits, softshell crab, buttermilk fried chicken, or
mini-Yankee sliders (try the salt beef with dill). **Known for:** cult collec-
tion of ground beef and pulled pork sliders; hipster speakeasy scene;
homebrewed hooch and killer rare whiskies. ⑤ *Average main: £13* ✉ *61
Rupert St., Soho* ⊕ *www.spuntino.co.uk* Ⓜ *Piccadilly Circus* ✛ *3:C5.*

$ ✕ **temper.** Smokehouse maven Neil Rankin smashes the live fire meat
BARBECUE   scene at this Soho speakeasy-like basement joint. Sit at the central open
kitchen counter and feel the heat from a Heath Robinson-esque com-
plex of white-hot charcoal smoke pits, clay ovens, and English log-
fired roasting spits before wolfing down nine-hour-smoked Cabrito goat
tacos or Daphne Tilley Welsh lamb chunks on baked flat breads. **Known
for:** tough-looking tattooed chef's brigade; hand-rolled tacos and low-
and-slow smoked rare breed beef, lamb, and goat; plenty of natural
and low intervention wines. ⑤ *Average main: £9* ✉ *25 Broadwick St.,
Soho* ☎ *020/3879–3834* ⊕ *www.temperrestaurant.com* Ⓜ *Oxford Cir-
cus, Piccadilly Circus.* ✛ *3:C4.*

$$ ✕ **10 Greek Street.** There may only be 28 table seats and 9 counter
MODERN   stools overlooking the open kitchen at this stripped-down Modern
EUROPEAN   European humdinger, but the consistently great food, cheap wine,
affable prices, and excellent service more than make up for it. Once
seated, expect simple starters and mains like butternut ravioli with
sage or gutsy Brecon lamb shank with couscous, broccoli, and olives.

14

Known for: buzzed up foodie atmosphere in a pared back dining space; gutsy seasonal Modern European mains; generous platters of house-cured charcuterie. ⑤ *Average main: £21* ✉ *10 Greek St., Soho* ☎ *020/7734–4677* ⊕ *www.10greekstreet.com* ⊘ *Closed Sun.* Ⓜ *Tottenham Court Rd.* ✛ *3:D4.*

COVENT GARDEN

$$ ✗ **Balthazar.** British restaurateur Keith McNally re-creates his famed
BRASSERIE New York Parisian brasserie at this monumental all-day corner spot
FAMILY off Covent Garden. The decor—all distressed vintage mirrors, illuminated columns, and mosaic floors—creates an enchanting backdrop to enjoy a classic French brasserie menu of few surprises, including flavor-packed dishes like macaroni and Gruyère cheese, duck Shepherd's pie, or ox cheek bourguignonne. **Known for:** Parisian-style all-day grand café; handy prix-fixe, brunch, and Afternoon Tea menus; classic French plats du jour. ⑤ *Average main: £23* ✉ *4–7 Russell St., Covent Garden* ☎ *020/3301–1155* ⊕ *www.balthazarlondon.com* Ⓜ *Covent Garden, Charing Cross* ✛ *3:F5.*

$$$ ✗ **Clos Maggiore.** Insist on a seat in the dreamy, white blossom–filled
FRENCH conservatory at this warm, cozy, and seriously romantic Provençal
FAMILY country inn–style escape in the heart of Covent Garden. Once inside, you'll be wooed by unapologetically old-fashioned and refined French cuisine, such as Loire Valley rabbit ballotine, poached wild turbot, and Charolais beef cheeks with fine French beans. **Known for:** one of London's most romantic restaurants; a warren of blossom-filled conservatories and open wood-fired hideaways; plenty of lunch and pre- and posttheater meal deals. ⑤ *Average main: £26* ✉ *33 King St., Covent Garden* ☎ *020/7379–9696* ⊕ *www.closmaggiore.com* Ⓜ *Covent Garden* ✛ *3:F5.*

$ ✗ **Côte.** Where else can you find an amazing three-course French meal
BISTRO in Covent Garden for £14? The Côte brasserie chain—softly lit and
FAMILY decked out in gray-and-white striped awnings and Parisian-style café tables—does the trick, and offers a menu loaded with classic French brasserie favorites: crepes with mushrooms and Gruyère cheese, boeuf bourguignonne, *moules marinières* (mussels with white wine), and iced berries and white chocolate sauce. **Known for:** part of a dependable chain of French brasseries; very reasonable pre- and posttheater deals; reliable French classics like moules marinere. ⑤ *Average main: £14* ✉ *17–21 Tavistock St., Covent Garden* ☎ *020/7379–9991* ⊕ *www.cote-restaurants.co.uk* Ⓜ *Covent Garden* ✛ *3:G5.*

$$ ✗ **Great Queen Street.** Expect a boisterous West End foodie crowd here
MODERN BRITISH at one of Covent Garden's leading gastropubs, which serves hearty
FAMILY retro-British dishes in a bare cream walls and oak tables setting. Wine-fueled diners dive into yesteryear offerings like pressed tongue, pickled herrings, pigs' cheeks, or smoked mackerel with rhubarb. **Known for:** bare and rustic oak table gastropub vibe; hearty carve-your-own roasts for the table; no-nonsense, old English dishes. ⑤ *Average main: £20* ✉ *32 Great Queen St., Covent Garden* ☎ *020/7242–0622* ⊕ *www.greatqueenstreetrestaurant.co.uk* ⊘ *No dinner Sun.* Ⓜ *Covent Garden, Holborn* ✛ *3:G4.*

$$ ✕ **The Ivy.** London's one-time most famous celebrity haunt and West
BRITISH End landmark is still so popular it receives over a thousand calls a day.
FAMILY Established in 1917 by Abele Giandolini, nowadays a mesmerizing mix
of celebrities and London's wealthiest dine on haddock and chips, bang
bang chicken and Thai-baked sea bass, and good ole English classics like
shepherd's pie and sticky toffee pudding. **Known for:** celebrity-filled his-
tory; famed house staples like shepherd's pie or grilled calf's liver; great
people-watching. $ *Average main: £24 ⊠ 1–5 West St., Covent Garden
☎ 020/7836–4751 ⊕ www.the-ivy.co.uk Ⓜ Covent Garden ✛ 3:E5.*

$$$ ✕ **J Sheekey.** This timelessly chic 1896 side-alley seafood haven is a dis-
SEAFOOD creet alternative to the more overtly celeb-central Scott's, 34, or The Ivy.
Sheekey charms with warm wood paneling, vintage black-and-white
showbiz portraits, and an accessible menu of snappingly fresh Atlantic
prawns, pickled Arctic herrings, scallop, shrimp, and salmon burgers,
or the famous Sheekey fish pie. **Known for:** low-key celebrity haunt;
old-school seafood menu; glamorous art deco oyster bar. $ *Average
main: £26 ⊠ 28–35 St. Martin's Ct., Covent Garden ☎ 020/7240–2565
⊕ www.j-sheekey.co.uk Ⓜ Leicester Sq. ✛ 3:E6.*

$$ ✕ **Opera Tavern.** Ibérico pig's head terrine or moreish foie gras and Man-
TAPAS chego minicheeseburgers are a few of the outstanding hybrid Spanish
FAMILY and Italian tapa delights found at the overflowing Opera Tavern in
Covent Garden. After enjoying a snack of crispy pigs' ears or guin-
dilla peppers, opt for a gentle flow of rich venison empanadas, Italian
Scotch eggs, or char-grilled Venetian-style sardines. **Known for:** winning
fusion of Italian and Spanish tapas; informal waitstaff and boister-
ous atmosphere; signature Ibérico pork miniburgers. $ *Average main:
£18 ⊠ 23 Catherine St., Covent Garden ☎ 020/7836–3680 ⊕ www.
saltyardgroup.co.uk/opera-tavern Ⓜ Covent Garden, Holborn ✛ 3:G5.*

$$$ ✕ **Rules.** Opened by Thomas Rule in 1798, London's oldest restaurant is
BRITISH still arguably its most beautiful. Resembling a High Victorian bordello
FAMILY with scarlet velvet banquettes, lacquered yellow walls, and alabaster
Fodor's Choice busts, here you can dig into classic traditional British fare like jugged
★ hare, steak and kidney pie, or roast beef and Yorkshire pudding. **Known
for:** being the oldest restaurant in London; fancy, high-class game menu;
famous diners from Charles Dickens to the Prince of Wales. $ *Aver-
age main: £29 ⊠ 35 Maiden La., Covent Garden ☎ 020/7836–5314
⊕ www.rules.co.uk ⓐ Jacket required Ⓜ Covent Garden ✛ 3:F6.*

$$$ ✕ **Savoy Grill.** You can feel the history in the room at this 1889 art deco
BRITISH hotel-dining powerhouse, which has wined and dined everyone from
FAMILY Oscar Wilde and Winston Churchill to Liz Taylor and Marilyn Monroe.
Nowadays it caters to business barons, nostalgia lovers, and wealthy
West End tourists who come for the Grill's famed tableside trolley,
which might trundle up laden with hulking great roasts like beef Wel-
lington, Suffolk rack of pork, or saddle of lamb. **Known for:** ravishing
old-school dining salon; beef Wellington from the daily carvery trolley
service; excellent glazed omelet Arnold Bennett. $ *Average main: £31
⊠ The Savoy, 100 The Strand, Covent Garden ☎ 020/7592–1600 for
reservations only ⊕ www.gordonramsay.com/savoy-grill Ⓜ Charing
Cross, Covent Garden ✛ 3:G6.*

14

$$$
ITALIAN
FAMILY
Fodor's Choice
★

✗ Spring. Australian chef Skye Gyngell worships the four seasons at her high-ceilinged and wild flower-filled 120-seat dining salon in majestic Somerset House off the Strand. Housed in the former Inland Revenue's neoclassical 1856 New Wing, former *Vogue* editor and purist Gyngell offers her high-powered crowd healthy root-to-stem produce-driven Italian dishes, from a tousled heap of biodynamic Fern Verrow salad leaves to egg yolk-rich crab tagliolini. **Known for:** homemade bread, butter, and ice cream; highly seasonal and ingredient-driven dishes; biodynamic Fern Verrow salads. ⑤ *Average main: £30* ✉ *Somerset House, New Wing, Lancaster Pl., Covent Garden* ✛ *Turn right on entering courtyard at Somerset House from the Strand* ☎ *020/3011–0115* ⊕ *www.springrestaurant.co.uk* ☽ *No dinner Sun.* Ⓜ *Holborn, Charing Cross* ✛ *3:G6.*

$
MEXICAN
FAMILY

✗ Wahaca. Crowds come for the fab-value Mexican street food at this brightly colored Covent Garden subterranean foodie spot. Concrete walls, shared wooden bench seating, and colorful Mexican murals make for a brisk and breezy basement setting, but it's the inexpensive, sustainable, and ethically sourced Mexican market-style tacos, enchiladas, quesadillas, taquitos, and burritos that pull in the budget-conscious crowds. **Known for:** loud music and colorful basement setting; menu of relatively authentic Mexican tacos, quesadillas, and taquitos; cheap cocktails. ⑤ *Average main: £9* ✉ *66 Chandos Pl., Covent Garden* ☎ *020/7240–1883* ⊕ *www.wahaca.co.uk* Ⓜ *Covent Garden* ✛ *3:F6.*

BLOOMSBURY, HOLBORN, AND FITZROVIA

The literary giants of the Bloomsbury set—from Virginia Woolf to E.M. Forster and Vanessa Bell—may be long gone but this bluestocking enclave (centered on the British Library and University of London) still excels at a cultured and pleasure-loving dining scene. Holborn, bordering Covent Garden, has some of those big, old-establishment hotel dining rooms, as well as a big, bright elegant shining star in The Delaunay on the Aldwych.

BLOOMSBURY

$
MODERN INDIAN
FAMILY

✗ Dishoom. Whirring ceiling fans, old family portraits, and vintage Indian cola bottles create an evocative Bombay backdrop for this vast all-day Indian café and former industrial goods depot at Granary Square in King's Cross. Modeled after the Persian-run Irani cafés of Victorian-era Bombay, try the hot naan bread with keema minced lamb and peas, or classic chili-jam spiked and spicy-charred chicken tikka roomali roti rolls. **Known for:** faded Indian train terminal vibe; famous Ginger Pig-sourced bacon naan rolls and chicken biryani; no reservations except for groups larger than six people. ⑤ *Average main: £9* ✉ *5 Stable St., King's Cross* ☎ *020/7420–9321* ⊕ *www.dishoom. com* Ⓜ *King's Cross* ✛ *2:C1.*

HOLBORN

$$
AUSTRIAN
FAMILY

✗ The Delaunay. It's all *fin de siècle* Vienna at this evocative art deco–style grand café on the Aldwych near Covent Garden. Dishes on the majestic 60-item all-day menu would do the Austro-Hungarian Empire proud—think Wiener schnitzel, Hungarian goulash, beef

Stroganoff, and wonderful *würstchen* (frankfurters and hot dogs), served with sauerkraut and onions. **Known for:** elegant old-world Austro-Hungarian haunt; proper Holstein schnitzel and frankfurters; affordable and light lunches. $ *Average main: £24* ⊠ *55 Aldwych, Holborn* ☎ *020/7499–8558* ⊕ *www.thedelaunay.com* Ⓜ *Covent Garden, Holborn* ✛ *3:G4.*

FITZROVIA

$$$ ✕**Berners Tavern.** All the cool cats swing by this grand brasserie at
MODERN BRITISH Ian Schrager's insanely trendy London Edition hotel near Tottenham Court Road. Enter the monumental Edwardian dining salon, where you might swoon over a light lunch of ironbark pumpkin risotto or an evening dinner of Creedy caver duck or Cornish cod. **Known for:** knockout dining salon crammed with the beautiful people; cool back-lit cocktail bar; slow-roast Herdwick lamb with Wye Valley asparagus. $ *Average main: £26* ⊠ *The London Edition, 10 Berners St., Fitzrovia* ☎ *020/7908–7979* ⊕ *www.bernerstavern.com* Ⓜ *Oxford Circus, Tottenham Court Rd.* ✛ *3:C3.*

$$ ✕**Bonnie Gull Seafood Shack.** It almost feels like you're seaside here at
SEAFOOD London's top seafood shack in Fitzrovia, where awesome fresh seafood (from Brixham brill to Shetland mussels) takes diners on a tour of the British Isles. Everything's bleached-out and weather-beaten at this tiny 42-seater, where you can start with Isle of Man queen scallops and move on to line-caught sea bass or Selsey cod with Wye Valley asparagus. **Known for:** fresh day-boat fish from around the British Isles; passionate service; popular Looe plaice with samphire and clams. $ *Average main: £21* ⊠ *21A Foley St., Fitzrovia* ☎ *020/7436–0921* ⊕ *www.bonniegull. com* Ⓜ *Oxford Circus, Goodge St.* ✛ *3:B2.*

$$ ✕**Clipstone.** Exceptionally inventive dishes (such as calves' brains with
FRENCH capers on toast) elevate this hipster casual Fitzrovia neighborhood joint
Fodor's Choice to the top rank of London's midrange gastro titans. With a focus on in-
★ house curing, pickling, smoked meats, and heritage vegetables, expect a cavalcade of crudos, unlikely combinations, and classic *Larousse Gastronomique* barnstormers in a classic school-chair-and-white-wall setting. **Known for:** classic French dishes in a minimalist setting; lots of house-made, pickled, or cured extras; soothing blanquette de veau (veal ragout) and sweetbreads. $ *Average main: £19* ⊠ *5 Clipstone St., Fitzrovia* ☎ *020/7637–9871* ⊕ *www.clipstonerestaurant.co.uk* ⊙ *Closed Sun.* Ⓜ *Great Portland St.* ✛ *3:A1.*

$$ ✕**Portland.** Consistently brilliant modern European fare in a low-key
MODERN setting characterizes this restaurant on a one-way street just north
EUROPEAN of Oxford Circus. Marvel at the chef's brigade in the open kitchen before turning to a highly inventive seasonal produce–driven menu that might feature luscious Denham Estate deer with glazed heritage carrot and pickled elderberry sauce or a rustic game pithivier heavy with mallard breasts, *duxelles* mushrooms, black truffles, and game sauce. **Known for:** gloriously edgy and inventive slew of veg-centric delights; a masterpiece game pithivier (pastry pie); artfully presented house-pickled heritage carrots. $ *Average main: £24* ⊠ *113 Great Portland St., Fitzrovia* ☎ *020/7436–3261* ⊕ *www.portlandrestaurant. co.uk* Ⓜ *Oxford Circus* ✛ *3:A2.*

14

$ ✕ **The Riding House Café.** London diners flock to this relaxed NYC-style
BURGER   small plates and luxe burger brasserie behind the BBC's Broadcast-
FAMILY   ing House in Fitzrovia. Dotted with salvaged, reclaimed, or bespoke
boho-chic furnishings, opt for bargain small plates of spicy crayfish
tails and the famed lobster lasagna, or dive into the English breakfasts,
brunches, milkshakes, sundaes, and cocktails. **Known for:** NYC-esque
style and buzz; popular all-day weekend brunches; one of the best
burgers in town. ⑤ *Average main: £14* ⊠ *43–51 Great Titchfield St.,
Fitzrovia* ☎ *020/7927–0840* ⊕ *www.ridinghousecafe.co.uk* Ⓜ *Oxford
Circus* ✥ *3:A2.*

CLERKENWELL AND THE CITY

Historic and just beyond The City limits, chef-centric Clerkenwell is
one of the most trendy and interesting quarters for London gastro-
dining, which sets it in marked contrast to the adjacent City, which
caters overwhelmingly to business-focused dining. In Clerkenwell, the
starchiness of The City fades into relaxed artiness: a fertile ground for
avant-garde chefs and restaurants.

$$ ✕ **Anglo.** Modern British bistronomy takes a giant leap forward at
MODERN BRITISH   chef-patron Mark Jarvis's tasting menu mecca in the Hatton Garden
Fodor's Choice   jewelery quarter in Farringdon. Feast on the Brit-sourced seasonal
★   foodie creations here, which are offered as seven-course tasting menus
at dinner; pretty dishes include Cornish plaice with sea beet or art-
on-a-plate skate, salsify, and lemon verbena. **Known for:** fantasti-
cally well-priced tasting menus for lunch and dinner; signature grated
cheese and onion on malt toast; wacky desserts like lemon curd and
horseradish. ⑤ *Average main: £19* ⊠ *30 St Cross St., Clerkenwell*
☎ *020/7430–1503* ⊕ *www.anglorestaurant.com* ☾ *Closed Sun. No
lunch Mon.* Ⓜ *Farringdon* ✥ *2:E4.*

$ ✕ **Berber & Q - Shawarma Bar.** Every night feels as crushed and crowded
ISRAELI   as downtown Tel Aviv at Exmouth Market's superb 40-seat Jerusalem
charcoal grill and spit-roasted lamb shawarma bar. Overflowing with
trailing plants, distressed metro tiles, and battered Middle Eastern street
signs, dip *chollah* toast into tahini-rich mezze and hummus spreads
before delving into slow-cooked sumac and harissa-heavy lamb sha-
warmas. **Known for:** Tel Aviv–style hip hangout; wondrous lamb and
beef shawarmas; unmissable BBQ-ed cauliflower shawarma. ⑤ *Aver-
age main: £13* ⊠ *45 Exmouth Market, Clerkenwell* ☎ *020/7837–1726*
⊕ *www.shawarmabar.co.uk* ☾ *Closed Sun.* Ⓜ *Farringdon* ✥ *2:E3.*

$ ✕ **Blixen.** Within a magnificent Kew Gardens–style tropical garden and
BRASSERIE   plant conservatory, you'll find this devilishly stylish all-day brasserie
FAMILY   backing out onto Old Spitalfields Market. Housed in a converted former
Victorian bank, Blixen offers evergreen European comfort food like
squid, saffron, and chorizo or mushroom papardelle with semi-soft
Taleggio cheese and hearty greens on its short but sweet (and inexpen-
sive) menu. **Known for:** captivating, palm-filled tropical conservatory;
great cocktails in the basement bar; popular weekend brunches. ⑤ *Aver-
age main: £15* ⊠ *65A Brushfield St., City of London* ☎ *020/7101–0093*
⊕ *www.blixen.co.uk* Ⓜ *Liverpool St.* ✥ *2:G2.*

$$$ ✕ **City Social.** A largely corporate crowd comes here for the Manhat-
MODERN BRITISH tan-esque views of The City and chef Jason Atherton's masterful or
straightforward cuisine. Impressed diners look out from level 24 of
Tower 42 on a majestic view that takes in iconic buildings like the
Gherkin and the Walkie Talkie while enjoying the Highland veni-
son with braised red cabbage and smoked chestnuts or a generous
chunk of Isle of Gigha halibut with pancetta and sea kale. **Known
for:** majestic panoramas of the city; gutsy steak and fish standards;
suited financiers and corporate deal-maker crowd. Ⓢ *Average main:
£26* ✉ *Tower 42, 25 Old Broad St., City of London* ☎ *020/7877–7703*
⊕ *www.citysociallondon.com* ◔ *Closed Sun. No lunch Sat.* Ⓜ *Liver-
pool St.* ✛ *2:G2.*

$$ ✕ **Duck & Waffle.** Zoom up to the 40th floor of the Heron Tower and
MODERN BRITISH head straight for the cult signature dish of confit duck leg, Belgium
FAMILY waffle, fried duck egg, and grainy mustard maple syrup for a taste of
Fodor's Choice foodie bliss. Open 24/7, with spectacular panoramas of the City, you
★ might satisfy the munchies with a foie gras breakfast, served all day,
alongside streaky bacon and homemade Nutella or an Elvis PB&J
waffle with banana brûlée. **Known for:** rare-to-London 24-hour service; awe-inspiring panoramas of London's skyline; eponymous duck
and waffle dish. Ⓢ *Average main: £18* ✉ *Heron Tower, 110 Bishopsgate, City of London* ☎ *020/3640–7310* ⊕ *www.duckandwaffle.com*
Ⓜ *Liverpool St.* ✛ *2:G2.*

$$$ ✕ **HKK.** World-class Peking duck—arguably the best in London—is
CHINESE the big thing at this Chinese trendsetter near Liverpool Street in The
FAMILY City. The Irish-sourced glazed Peking duck is marinated in five Chinese
spices, cherrywood-roasted in a Beech oven, and carved ceremoniously
by a duck specialist in the middle of a sleek modernist dining room,
full of knowing Chinese and City corporate account diners. **Known for:**
wonderful glazed Peking duck carved tableside; sleek and minimalist
grey interior; epic 15-course tasting menu available. Ⓢ *Average main:
£26* ✉ *88 Worship St., City of London* ☎ *020/3535–1888* ⊕ *www.
hkklondon.com* ◔ *Closed Sun.* Ⓜ *Liverpool St.* ✛ *2:G2.*

$$ ✕ **The Modern Pantry.** It's around the world in 80 ways at this ever popu-
ECLECTIC lar Georgian townhouse, fusion food emporium on St. John's Square
FAMILY in Clerkenwell. Approach via the historic Jerusalem Passage, and kick
off with a famed sugar-cured New Caledonia prawn omelet with green
chilies, coriander, and Sri Lankan chilli sambol, before moving on to
slow-roasted Paddock Farm pork belly with Persian-spiced sweet pota-
toes, sour cherries, and *hijiki* relish. **Known for:** wildly eclectic global
fusion menu; sugar-cured New Caledonian prawn omelet; serene, light-
filled space. Ⓢ *Average main: £19* ✉ *47–48 St. John's Sq., Clerkenwell*
☎ *020/7553–9210* ⊕ *www.themodernpantry.co.uk* ◔ *Closed Mon. No
dinner Sun.* Ⓜ *Farringdon* ✛ *2:F3.*

$$ ✕ **Moro.** Up from The City, you'll find Exmouth Market, a cluster of
MEDITERRANEAN cute indie boutiques, bookstores, vinyl shops, hardware stores, artisan
FAMILY bakeries, and more fine indie-spirited restaurants like this one. Lovingly
nurtured for over a decade by husband-and-wife chefs Sam and Sam
Clark, the menu includes a mélange of Spanish, Moroccan, and Moor-
ish North African flavors. **Known for:** loud and buzzy dining room

14

with booming acoustics; expressive Moorish delights; house yogurt cake. $\boxed{\$}$ *Average main: £22* ✉ *34–36 Exmouth Market, Clerkenwell* ☎ *020/7833–8336* ⊕ *www.moro.co.uk* ☾ *No dinner Sun.* Ⓜ *Farringdon, Angel* ✛ *2:E3.*

$
BARBECUE

✗ **Pitt Cue Co.** Everyone's gone bonkers for the American BBQ rare-breed Mangalitza pork-loin chops and bone marrow mash at this Broadgate trendsetter in the City. Charred and flavor-packed oak- and ash-smoked offerings emerge from a Michigan-imported, custom-built wood grill, including delicately sliced lambs' hearts in a pool of viridian rosemary oil and Cornish-reared Mangalitza pork chops, rack, or rib caps. **Known for:** vast custom-made wood-burning grill; smoked Mangalitza pork belly with malt bread and dripping; house-churned ice cream for dessert. $\boxed{\$}$ *Average main: £15* ✉ *1 The Ave., Devonshire Sq., City of London* ☎ *020/7324–7770* ⊕ *www.pittcue.co.uk* ☾ *Closed Sun. No lunch Sat.* Ⓜ *Liverpool St.* ✛ *2:G2.*

$
BRITISH
FAMILY

✗ **Simpson's Tavern.** The City of London's oldest tavern and chop house was founded in 1757 and is every bit as raucous now as the day it opened. Approached via a cobbled Dickensian alleyway off Cornhill near the Bank of England, it draws diners who revel in the old boarding school surroundings and are eager to down oodles of claret and English tavern-style grub. **Known for:** lots of history, with past diners from Samuel Pepys to Charles Dickens; signature stewed cheese on toast; charming but old-fashioned service. $\boxed{\$}$ *Average main: £9* ✉ *Ball Court, 38½ Cornhill, City of London* ☎ *020/7626–9985* ⊕ *www.simpsonstavern.co.uk* ☾ *Closed weekends. No dinner* Ⓜ *Bank* ✛ *2:G2.*

$$
MODERN BRITISH
FAMILY

✗ **St. John.** Global foodie fanatics join Clerkenwell locals for the pioneering nose-to-tail cuisine at this Puritan-esque converted smokehouse near Smithfield Market. Here the chef uses all scraps of a carcass—from tongue and cheeks to tail and trotters—so brace for radically stark signatures like bone marrow and parsley salad, chitterlings with dandelion, or pheasant and pig's trotter pie. **Known for:** ground zero of influential Modern British nose-to-tail dining; great wine list; bone marrow with parsley salad. $\boxed{\$}$ *Average main: £22* ✉ *26 St. John St., Clerkenwell* ☎ *020/7251–0848* ⊕ *www.stjohngroup.uk.com* ☾ *No dinner Sun.* Ⓜ *Farringdon, Barbican* ✛ *2:F4.*

$$$
SEAFOOD

✗ **Sweetings.** Established in 1889 not far from St. Paul's Cathedral, little seems to have changed since the height of the British Empire at this City time warp. Although there are some things Sweetings doesn't do (dinner, reservations, coffee, or weekends), it does, mercifully, do decent seafood. **Known for:** fresh Billingsgate fish served at raised linen-covered counters; tankards of "Black Velvet" Guinness and Champagne; popular potted shrimp and Dover sole. $\boxed{\$}$ *Average main: £30* ✉ *39 Queen Victoria St., City of London* ☎ *020/7248–3062* ⊕ *www. sweetingsrestaurant.co.uk* ☾ *Closed weekends. No dinner* Ⓜ *Mansion House* ✛ *2:H6.*

EAST LONDON

An invasion of hipsters and foodies has transformed the once-bleak East End food scene into the city's most daring dining zone. Seek out new British breakout stars like Lyle's in Shoreditch or the Typing Room in Bethnal Green, or hunt down a nighttime food truck for a blast of the foodie underground.

$$$
MODERN
EUROPEAN
FAMILY

✕ **Bistrotheque.** You'll need some help finding this East End fashionista headquarters located down a side alley in hipster Bethnal Green. Once inside, check out the striking loft dining space and the Manchichi bar in its postindustrial chic setting, before polishing off fine figure-friendly French and English dishes. **Known for:** classic choices like steak tartare and croque madame; weekend brunch with pancakes and maple syrup; resident pianist at brunch. $ *Average main: £25* ⊠ *23–27 Wadeson St., Bethnal Green* ☎ *020/8983–7900* ⊕ *www.bistrotheque.com* ⊘ *No dinner Sun.* Ⓜ *Bethnal Green* ⊹ *2:H1.*

$
CAFÉ
FAMILY

✕ **E Pellicci.** It's all Cockney banter and full English breakfasts at this tiny 1900 family-run greasy spoon café and one-time gangsters' lair near the East End's Brick Lane and Columbia Road markets. It's a rowdy hole-in-the-wall for the greasy fry-ups Londoners still adore: copious eggs, bacon, sausages, baked beans, toast, tomatoes, fried mushrooms, black pudding, cabbage 'n' mash, and scorching hot tea. **Known for:** full cast of East End chirpy Cockney characters; copious full English breakfasts and builders' brew tea; cash-only cheap dishes. $ *Average main: £8* ⊠ *332 Bethnal Green Rd., Bethnal Green* ☎ *020/7739–4873* ⊕ *www.epellicci.com* ▭ *No credit cards* ⊘ *Closed Sun.* Ⓜ *Bethnal Green* ⊹ *2:H1.*

$$
MODERN BRITISH
Fodor's Choice
★

✕ **Lyle's.** Globally acclaimed young Brit chef and co-owner James Lowe forsakes sauces and sorcery at this stripped-back, informal British neobistronomy dining mecca in Shoreditch. Uberstark but highly inventive locally sourced dishes may include house-cured cod with radiant nasturtium flowers or 24-hour Cornish Helford Estuary monkfish with wood sorrel and pick-your-own East Sussex greengages. **Known for:** modern and airy dining space; serious new wave British neobistronomy; excellent cheese plates and wines by the glass. $ *Average main: £19* ⊠ *Tea Building, 56 Shoreditch High St., East End* ⊹ *Entrance on Bethnal Green Rd.* ☎ *020/3011–5911* ⊕ *www. lyleslondon.com* ⊘ *Closed Sun. and bank holidays* Ⓜ *Shoreditch High St.* ⊹ *2:G1.*

$$
FRENCH FUSION
FAMILY

✕ **Merchants Tavern.** The legend on the front of this Hoxton sleeper reads "Merchants of Good Fortune," and that neatly sums up the exceptional smart-casual gastro dining experience you'll encounter within. Seasonal, veg-focused left-field hits from France, Italy, and Britain emerge from the open counter kitchen inside the spacious dining salon and craft-beer bar, housed in a former Victorian warehouse and onetime apothecary. **Known for:** unique Modern European cuisine; swish 1960s interior and open kitchen; rare-pink venison with Alsace bacon. $ *Average main: £22* ⊠ *38 Charlotte St., Hoxton* ☎ *020/7060–5335* ⊕ *www.merchantstavern.co.uk* Ⓜ *Old St.* ⊹ *2:G1.*

14

$$ ✕ **Typing Room.** British chef Lee Westcott attracts all of London's dining
MODERN BRITISH underground elite and Instagram foodie stars with his baroque pure/
Fodor'sChoice natural/seasonal dishes at this dark, elegant, and downright stupendous
★ dining salon within the Town Hall Hotel in Bethnal Green. Watch West-
cott in the open kitchen plate up fizzy dishes like raw, roasted, and deep-
fried yeasted cauliflower with capers, raisins, and mint sauce and crinkly
cod skins with smoked cod-roe cream on the two- to seven-course tast-
ing menus. **Known for:** some of the finest Modern British dining in
town; great natural wine list; two- to five-course tasting menus. $ *Aver-*
age main: £22 ✉ *Town Hall Hotel, Patriot Sq., entrance on Cambridge*
Heath Rd., Bethnal Green ☎ *020/7871–0461* ⊕ *www.typingroom.com*
Ⓜ *Bethnal Green* ✛ *2:H1.*

SOUTH OF THE THAMES

First mentioned in 1276 and believed to have existed as far back as
Roman times, Borough Market in Southwark on the South Bank is a
firm favorite with tourists, chefs, and foodies alike. Open Wednesday
and Thursday 10–5, Friday 10–6, and Saturday 8–5, this Dickensian
location under moody Victorian wrought-iron railway arches at Lon-
don Bridge is packed with food lovers eager to pick up the finest and
freshest fruit, vegetables, and grub in town. There are more than 130
stalls, plus a bunch of nearby pubs, bars, restaurants, and specialty
shops. Ever more groovy new eateries are springing up in nearby Ber-
mondsey Street, just south of The Shard.

$$ ✕ **Casse-Croûte.** French tunes play in the background and a chubby
BISTRO Michelin Man perches benignly over the bar at this jaunty, Gallic bear-
FAMILY hug of a French bistro on Bermondsey Street near the Shard. The daily
Fodor'sChoice changing blackboard offers a limited three-options per course menu
★ of exceptional Gallic bistro classics and riffs—from *côte de boeuf* to
glazed stuffed pig's trotters with mash. **Known for:** authentic Parisian-
style neighborhood bistro; stuffed pig's trotters and côte de boeuf with
French beans; delicious pastries with Chantilly cream. $ *Average main:*
£18 ✉ *109 Bermondsey St., Bermondsey* ☎ *020/7407–2140* ⊕ *www.*
cassecroute.co.uk ⊗ *No dinner Sun.* Ⓜ *London Bridge* ✛ *5:H2.*

$$$ ✕ **Chez Bruce.** Top-notch French and Mediterranean cuisine, faultless
MODERN FRENCH service, a winning wine list, and a straight-off-the-pistes glossy south-of-
FAMILY the-river Wandsworth neighborhood vibe make for one of London's all-
star favorite restaurants. At this cozy, gimmick-free haunt overlooking
Wandsworth Common, prepare for unfussy grown-up gastro wonders
ranging from homemade charcuterie or offal to lighter, simply grilled
fish dishes. **Known for:** elegant neighborhood salon; luxe classics like
lobster and scallop ravioli; impressive sommelier. $ *Average main: £27*
✉ *2 Bellevue Rd., Wandsworth Common, Battersea* ☎ *020/8672–0114*
⊕ *www.chezbruce.co.uk* Ⓜ *Overland: Wandsworth Common* ✛ *4:E6.*

$$ ✕ **José.** Revered Spanish chef José Pizarro packs in diners at this tapas-
TAPAS and-sherry treasure trove on red hot gastro-trail Bermondsey Street,
just south of the Shard. With just 30 seats and no reservations, you'll
be hard-pressed to find a spot after 6 pm, but it's worth the wait: the
Spanish tapas dishes here are superb. **Known for:** notoriously long waits

and big crowds; wondrous green padron peppers and Ibérico pork fillet; creative sherry menu. $ *Average main: £18* ⊠ *104 Bermondsey St., Southwark* ☎ *020/7403–4902* ⊕ *www.josepizarro.com/jose-tapas-bar* ⊙ *No dinner Sun.* Ⓜ *Borough, London Bridge* ✛ *5:H2.*

$$$
FRENCH
FAMILY

✕ **Le Pont de la Tour.** You'll find the winning combo of top-end French cuisine and smashing views of the River Thames, Tower Bridge, and the Tower of London at the storied Le Pont de la Tour in scrubbed-up Butler's Wharf. Enjoy favorites like seared duck foie gras with caramelized black fig and a touch of Madeira, or *recherché* roast Challans duck and herb-crusted rack of lamb with Provençal vegetables. **Known for:** stunning views of the city; lavish art deco main dining room; destination and celebration meals. $ *Average main: £28* ⊠ *36D Shad Thames, Bermondsey* ☎ *020/7403–8403* ⊕ *www.lepontdelatour.co.uk* Ⓜ *London Bridge, Tower Hill* ✛ *2:H6.*

$
ITALIAN
FAMILY
Fodor's Choice
★

✕ **Padella.** Pitch up at the galley kitchen counter at London's top pasta bar in Borough Market, and watch as the chefs toss and serve endless hot pans of authentic handmade Italian pasta. Seriously epic and amazingly cheap pasta dishes include egg-free Parmesan and black pepper-rich *pici cacao e pepe* from Tuscany, or devilishly addictive ricotta ravioli with a slick of sage butter. **Known for:** supercheap handmade pasta; papardelle with eight-hour beef shin ragù; fast-moving lines and no reservations. $ *Average main: £7* ⊠ *6 Southwark St., Borough* ☎ *No phone* ⊕ *www.padella.co* Ⓜ *Borough, London Bridge* ✛ *5:H1.*

$$$$
MODERN BRITISH

✕ **Restaurant Story.** Talented British chef-patron Tom Sellers storms the ramparts at this set-menu gastro mecca, with his conceptual take on intensively flavored ingredient-led New British and New Nordic cuisine. Housed in a modish Scandinavian-inspired dining space, expect clever touches like edible nasturtium flowers or eel-mousse Oreos to kick things off before the real fun begins with a surprise beef-dripping candle that melts into a silver candle holder, which you mop up with heritage grain sourdough throughout the meal. **Known for:** intricate and unhurried set lunch and dinner extravaganzas; global foodie destination; signature beef dripping candle. $ *Average main: £34* ⊠ *199 Tooley St., Bermondsey* ☎ *020/7183–2117* ⊕ *www.restaurantstory.co.uk* ⊙ *Closed Sun. No lunch Mon.* Ⓜ *London Bridge* ✛ *2:H6.*

KENSINGTON, CHELSEA, KNIGHTSBRIDGE, AND BELGRAVIA

If you're fab, famous, wealthy, or preferably all three, chances are you'll be living—and dining—in one of these neighborhoods among London's world-class museums, royal parks, shops, hotels, monuments, fashion boutiques, and top restaurants. (Does the name of superchef Heston Blumenthal ring a bell?) In Chelsea, made famous in the swingin' '60s, restaurants range from bijou boîtes to exclusive little froufrou places ideal for gossip, an Aperol, and a no-carb bite on the go. Over in upscale Knightsbridge, you'll find Harrods and the high-end fashion boutiques of Sloane Street, plus a heap of platinum-class hotel-based restaurants. Come here for an amazing celebratory dining experience, but don't expect bargains (except at lunch). Nearby Kensington is a Victorian residential neighborhood with a wider range of restaurants, from French bistros to funky Persian hideaways.

14

KENSINGTON

$$$

JAPANESE

✕ **Yashin.** At this top London sushi bar off Kensington High Street, you can watch Japanese head chef and co-founder Yasuhiro Mineno tease, slice, tweak, and blowtorch his way to the most awesome, fresh, funky, spunky, colorful, and exquisite sushi, sashimi, salads, and carpaccio that you're likely to find this side of the East China Sea. Tofu-topped miso cappuccino comes in a Victorian cup and saucer, while delectable sushi spreads might mesmerize with ponzu-spiked salmon or Japanese sea bream with rice cracker dust. **Known for:** exquisite sushi and sashimi with the odd twist; five- to 15-piece chef-decides omakase sets; super-affordable five-piece salmon sushi lunch. $ *Average main: £28* ✉ *1A Argyll Rd., Kensington* ☎ *020/7938–1536* ⊕ *www.yashinsushi.com* Ⓜ *High St. Kensington* ✛ *4:B1.*

CHELSEA

$$

FRENCH

Fodor's Choice

★

✕ **Elystan Street.** Former Michelin-starred chef and co-patron Phil Howard ditches the West End's typical starched linen and cuts loose at this more relaxed high-end Chelsea *boîte.* Head for immaculately burnished dishes such as duck breast with caramelized endive in the lively salon tricked out with café curtains and Air Force blue chairs. **Known for:** Michelin-level cuisine in a relaxed salon; flawless lemon tart; smart wine list. $ *Average main: £24* ✉ *43 Elystan St., Chelsea* ☎ *020/7628–5005* ⊕ *www.elystanstreet.com* Ⓜ *S. Kensington.* ✛ *4:E3.*

$$$

MODERN BRITISH

FAMILY

Fodor's Choice

★

✕ **The Harwood Arms.** British game doesn't get much finer than at this forest-floor and game-lover's paradise (and London's only Michelin-star gastropub off Fulham Broadway). Alongside bare wooden tables and Sloaney leather Chesterfields, sample a catalog of awesome roasts or game like haunch of Berkshire roe deer with pickled mushrooms or the popular carve-your-own whole roast lamb, pork, or beef joints with all the trimmings. **Known for:** stand-out Michelin-star grub in a gastropub setting; seasonal game from the pub's own hunting estate; Berkshire fallow deer. $ *Average main: £26* ✉ *27 Walham Grove, Chelsea* ☎ *020/7386–1847* ⊕ *www.harwoodarms.com* ☾ *No lunch Mon.* Ⓜ *Fulham Broadway* ✛ *4:A5.*

$$

HUNAN

FAMILY

✕ **Hunan.** There's no menu at this quirky family-run Taiwanese stalwart situated a few blocks south of Sloane Square in Pimlico. Instead, diners simply state how spicy they like it, and sit back, relax, and chopstick their way through a succession of tasty tapas-size Hunan, Hakka, Cantonese, and Japanese-inspired dishes to share. **Known for:** unique menu-free dining experience; generous portions; tour de force procession of Taiwanese tapas-size delights. $ *Average main: £23* ✉ *51 Pimlico Rd., Pimlico, Chelsea* ☎ *020/7730–5712* ⊕ *www.hunanlondon. com* ☾ *Closed Sun.* Ⓜ *Sloane Sq.* ✛ *4:G3.*

KNIGHTSBRIDGE

$$$

SPANISH

FAMILY

✕ **Ametsa with Arzak Instruction.** At this modernist romp at the Halkin, trendsetters and lovers of all things Spain can bask in a fantasia of New Basque cuisine. Oscar-winning movie stars and Premier League managers enjoy the passionate service and marvel at high-spec riffs on traditional Basque dishes, like slow-cooked hen's eggs flecked with paprika-rich chistorra sausage, wild ceps, and chorizo, or lobster updated with a white cassava powder. **Known for:** modernist New Basque molecular gastronomy; stunning wavelike ceiling feature, with 7,000 spice-filled glass vials; jaw-dropping Fractal mead dessert. $ *Average main: £28* ✉ *Halkin Hotel, 5 Halkin St., Knightsbridge* ☎ *020/7333–1234* ⊕ *www. comohotels.com/thehalkin/dining/ametsa* ☉ *Closed Sun. No lunch Mon.* Ⓜ *Hyde Park Corner, Knightsbridge* ✛ *4:G1.*

$$ ✗ **Bar Boulud.** United States–based French superchef Daniel Boulud com-

BRASSERIE bines the best of French high-end brasserie fare with a dash of supe-

FAMILY rior Yankee gourmet burgers and fries at this popular hangout in the Mandarin Oriental. Lilliputian-size platters of the most delicate Gilles Verot charcuterie, heartier *coq au vin,* or white pork sausages with truffle mash compete with palm-size Yankee, Frenchie, Piggie, or signature BB foie gras–beef burgers and fries in black onion or sesame-seed buns. **Known for:** awesome beef, BBQ pork, and foie gras burgers; very affordable set meals from noon until 6:30; global 5-star hotel crowd. $ *Average main: £23* ✉ *Mandarin Oriental Hyde Park, 66 Knightsbridge, Knightsbridge* ☎ *020/7201–3899 for reservations only* ⊕ *www. barboulud.com/london* Ⓜ *Knightsbridge* ✛ *4:F1.*

$$$$ ✗ **Dinner by Heston Blumenthal.** Splendidly revived old English gastronomy

BRITISH dishes executed with ultramodern precision is the *schtick* here at Ashley

FAMILY Palmer-Watts's wildly popular celebration destination at the Mandarin Oriental. As you take in views of Hyde Park, slice into options like the Meat Fruit appetizer (circa 1500), a ball of ultrasmooth chicken liver parfait in a mandarin jelly. **Known for:** one of London's top destination dining spots overlooking Hyde Park; Meat Fruit chicken liver parfait; Sauternes-soaked brioche and pineapple tipsy cake for dessert. $ *Average main: £34* ✉ *Mandarin Oriental Hyde Park, 66 Knightsbridge, Knightsbridge* ☎ *020/7201–3833* ⊕ *www.dinnerbyheston.com* Ⓜ *Knightsbridge* ✛ *4:F1.*

$$$ ✗ **Mari Vanna.** All of London's Russian molls, dolls, and porcelain-

RUSSIAN skinned babushkas squeeze into this White Russian fantasy dining salon in Knightsbridge, which overflows with a maximalist decor of vintage chandeliers, Tiffany lamps, tchotchkes , *cheburashkas,* and a Russian *pechka* stove. Snap into character with a horseradish vodka shot, then carb-up on pierogi sea bass savories, Siberian *pelmeni* (dumpling) soup, or smoked salmon blini. **Known for:** fantastically kitsch prerevolution Russian dining room; tasty borscht, blinis, and beef Stroganoff; sweet crepes for dessert. $ *Average main: £28* ✉ *The Wellington Court, 116 Knightsbridge, Knightsbridge* ☎ *020/7225–3122* ⊕ *www.marivanna. ru/london* Ⓜ *Knightsbridge* ✛ *4:F1.*

BELGRAVIA

$$$ ✗ **Pétrus.** A talented Gordon Ramsay team conducts a flawless dining

MODERN FRENCH experience at this Michelin-starred haute cuisine honeypot in Knights-

FAMILY bridge. The dining salon may be a tad beige and dated, but between the impeccable food, assured sommelier, remarkable cheeseboard, and charming service, you've got a full-court gastro press. **Known for:** Gordon Ramsay flagship restaurant; 25-day Casterbridge beef fillet with Barolo sauce; fleet-footed and formidable service. $ *Average main: £32* ✉ *1 Kinnerton St., Belgravia* ☎ *020/7592–1609* ⊕ *www.gordonramsayrestaurants.com/petrus* Ⓜ *Knightsbridge, Hyde Park Corner* ✛ *4:G1.*

14

NOTTING HILL AND BAYSWATER

Ever since Hugh Grant and Julia Roberts starred in *Notting Hill* and put the area on the global map, Notting Hill's had a rep as London's most glamorous neighborhood, with its myriad boutiques, chic cafés, patisseries, restaurants, buzzy bars, and the famous Portobello Road Market's collection of antiques shops, vintage-clothing stands, and food stalls. Portobello is one of London's most popular street markets, so get there early on Saturday morning (the market is open 8–6) to beat the crowds. Peruse the antiques and vintage clothes stalls, and when you want to eat, head to the north end where you'll find fresh fruit-and-veg stalls, artisan bakeries, and rare Spanish olive and French cheese purveyors, plus numerous hot-food stalls peddling savory crepes, gourmet hamburgers, spicy German chicken rolls, paella, Moroccan kebabs, and Malaysian noodles.

NOTTING HILL

$$$$
MODERN FRENCH
FAMILY

✕ **The Ledbury.** Aussie chef Brett Graham wins hearts, minds, and some serious global accolades at this upbeat, no-dairy, no-carb modern French (with Pacific and British hints) dining landmark in deepest Notting Hill. Global gourmands will struggle to find a more inventive vegetable dish than Graham's ash-baked celeriac with hazelnut and wood sorrel, and it's impossible to best his ultra pretty, precise, and complex mains like roasted quail with walnut cream or roe deer with bone marrow. **Known for:** vegetable-centric dishes like roast celeriac with smoked pheasant; excellent game like Berkshire roe buck with wild hops; fantastic desserts like figs with honey and sourdough ice cream. $ *Average main: £40* ⊠ *127 Ledbury Rd., Notting Hill* ☎ *0207/7792–9090* ⊕ *www.theledbury.com* ⊘ *No lunch Mon. and Tues.* Ⓜ *Westbourne Park, Ladbroke Grove* ✛ *1:A4.*

$$
FRENCH
Fodor'sChoice
★

✕ **Six Portland Road.** The ultimate neighborhood restaurant in west London's wealthy Holland Park section draws diners with its brilliant-but-understated French classics, relaxed service, and interesting, largely French Caves de Pyrene–sourced wines. Dive in for plump Cornish mussels with white wine sauce or perfectly matched Atlantic cod with creamed leeks, shrimps, and sea aster. **Known for:** intimate seating; unpretentious but pitch perfect service; winning boutique wine list. $ *Average main: £18* ⊠ *6 Portland Rd., Notting Hill* ☎ *020/7229–3130* ⊕ *www.sixportlandroad.com* ⊘ *Closed Mon. No dinner Sun.* Ⓜ *Holland Park* ✛ *1:B1.*

BAYSWATER

$
MODERN BRITISH
FAMILY

✕ **Hereford Road.** A Bayswater favorite with the well-connected Notting Hill set, Hereford Road is renowned for its pared-down, pomp-free, and ingredient-driven seasonal British fare, with an emphasis on well-sourced regional British produce. Work your way through uncluttered combos like steamed mussels with cider and thyme, lemon sole with sea dulse, or English rice pudding with a dollop of strawberry jam. **Known for:** paragon of pared-back Modern British nose-to-tail dining; deceptively simple-sounding dishes like duck livers with watercress; famously affordable two-course set lunch. $ *Average main: £15* ⊠ *3 Hereford Rd., Bayswater* ☎ *020/7727–1144* ⊕ *www.herefordroad.org* Ⓜ *Bayswater, Queensway* ✛ *1:B4.*

REGENT'S PARK, HAMPSTEAD, AND ISLINGTON

Stucco-fronted Regent's Park and Islington attract a boho-chic media and high-brow artsy crowd who love the slightly rough-and-rowdy neighborhood restaurants like Lemonia or Oldroyd. Meanwhile, farther north in leafy Hampstead, it's all Dick Turpin 17th-century wood-beam coach houses and inns with roaring fires, house ales, and trouser-busting Sunday lunches.

REGENT'S PARK

$ ✕ **Lemonia.** Primrose Hill's favorite Greek Cypriot, the vine-decked and
GREEK late '80s-taverna-style Lemonia is large and light, and always packed
FAMILY with hoards of hungry families and hobo-chic locals. Besides an endless
supply of Hellenic small-dish meze dips, hot breads, and starters, there
are rustic mains like slow-baked *kleftiko* lamb in lemon and moussaka.
Known for: Greek holiday taverna-style atmosphere; popular meze,
moussaka, and grilled sea bass; great weekday set lunches. ⑤ *Average
main: £16* ✉ *89 Regent's Park Rd., Regent's Park* ☎ *020/7586–7454*
⊙ *No lunch Sat., no dinner Sun.* Ⓜ *Chalk Farm* ✢ *1:F1.*

ISLINGTON

$ ✕ **Bellanger.** Part neighborhood hangout and part city dining destina-
FRENCH tion, this stylish 200-seat Belle Époque–style grand café on Islington
FAMILY Green offers everything from a cup of coffee and cake to full meals
of Alsatian choucroute, *baeckeoffe* (casserole), and a tasty array of
wafer-thin *tartes flambées*. Signature warm hearty pots of choucroute
à L'Alsacienne are layered with ham hock, frankfurters, and sauerkraut, and served on elegant monogrammed plates. **Known for:** hearty
deep dishes of coq au Riesling; thin-crust tartes flambées; variety of
French sausages. ⑤ *Average main: £16* ✉ *9 Islington Green, Islington*
☎ *020/7226–2555* ⊕ *www.bellanger.co.uk* Ⓜ *Angel* ✢ *2:F1.*

$ ✕ **Oldroyd.** Islington's finest squeeze into this tiny 40-seat neighborhood
ITALIAN bistro on Upper Street thanks to the groovy Italian food and warm and
friendly service. Well-priced and ingredient-driven, the daily changing
menu of seasonal small plates might wow with creamy Somerset Cardo
cheese and grilled tardivo radicchio risotto, or simple confit duck leg
with porcini and pearl barley. **Known for:** jam-packed space; earthy
Italian fare like osso buco; popular Italian peas with goat cheese. ⑤ *Average main: £13* ✉ *344 Upper St., Islington* ☎ *020/8617–9010* ⊕ *www.
oldroydlondon.com* Ⓜ *Angel* ✢ *2:F1.*

THE THAMES UPSTREAM

These wealthy, leafy suburbs may be under the Heathrow flight path
and follow the meandering course of the River Thames, but there's
nothing sleepy about the neighborhood dining scene here, which
is becoming more and more "West End" in style and substance by
the day. One fanatical locavore maverick stands out: the bearded
Mikael Jonsson, a self-taught Swedish obsessive genius, who knows
his wild scallops from his foraged blueberries, and meals of staggering brilliance.

14

CHISWICK

$$$$
MODERN
EUROPEAN
Fodor's Choice
★

✕ **Hedone.** Only a loony or genius would serve an appetizer of half a Cévennes onion with a few pear shavings and beurre blanc, but luckily Swedish chef Mikael Jonsson falls triumphantly in the latter camp at his 22-seat, no-fixed-menu foodie haven in Chiswick. A former lawyer and food blogger, Jonsson's obsessive approach to the provenance of his largely British-sourced ingredients—often rare, wild, or foraged—means his daily changing dishes are some of the most vivid and distinctive around. **Known for:** rare, wild, or forage-based destination dining; Ise of Mull hand-dived scallops, stonecrop, and sea aster; no menu means the multicourse dishes are left up to the chef. ⑤ *Average main: £38* ✉ *301–303 Chiswick High Rd., Chiswick* ☎ *020/8747–0377* ⊕ *www.hedonerestaurant.com* ☯ *Closed Sun. and Mon.* Ⓜ *Chiswick Park* ✛ *1:A2.*

LONDON
DINING AND
LODGING ATLAS

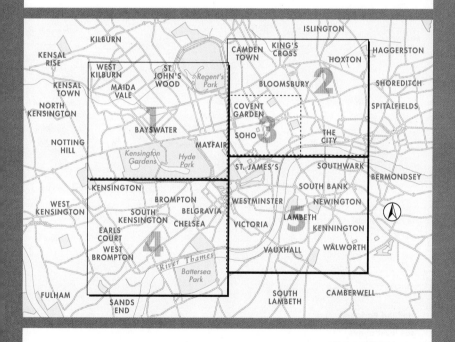

KEY

☐ *Hotels*

▦ *Restaurants*

▦ *Restaurant in Hotel*

Ⓤ WESTMINSTER
Station
London Underground

⇌ *National Rail Connection*

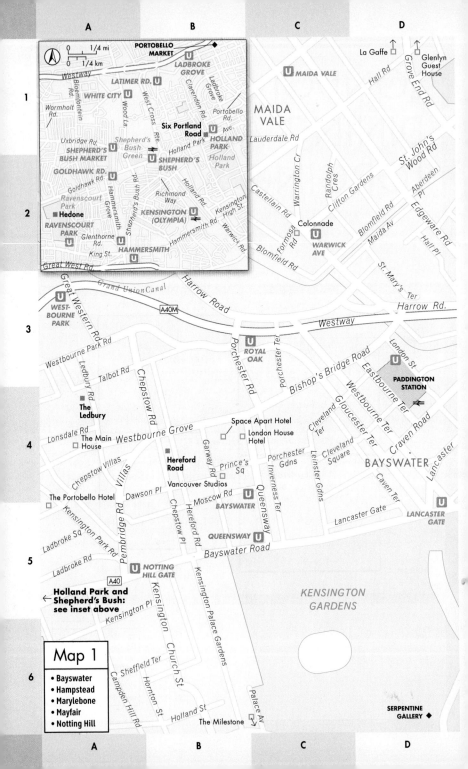

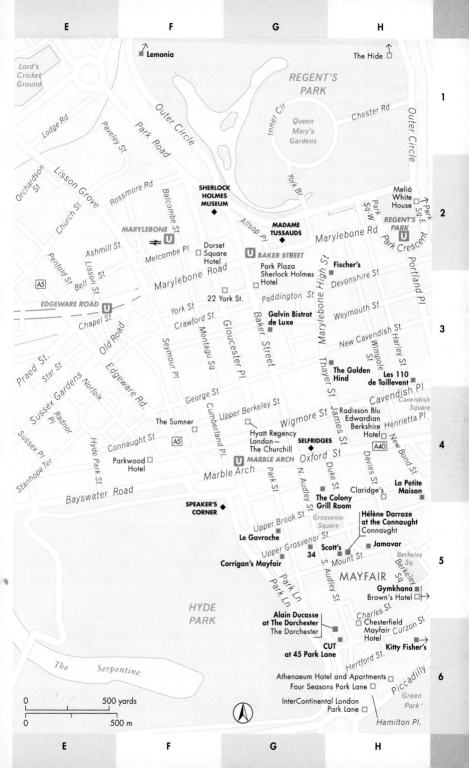

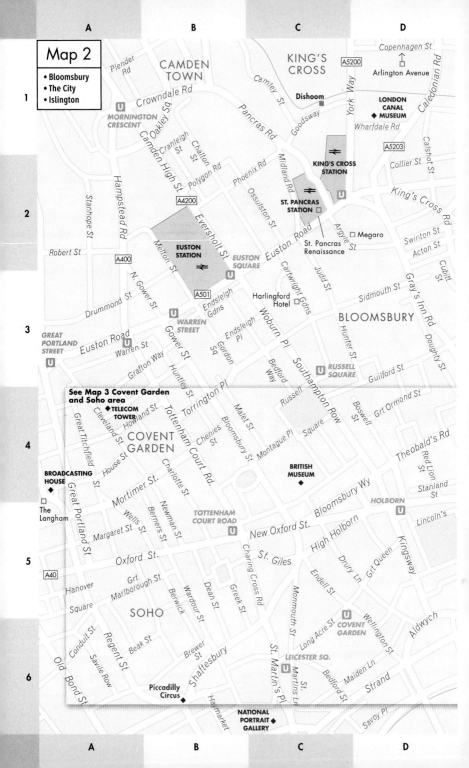

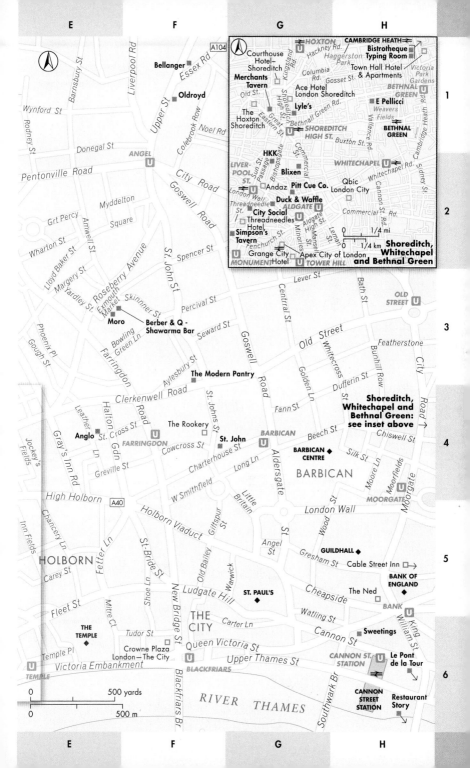

Shoreditch, Whitechapel and Bethnal Green

A104

HOXTON

CAMBRIDGE HEATH

Bistrotheque
Typing Room

Courthouse
Hotel–
Shoreditch

Hackney Rd.

Haggerston
Park

Victoria
Park
Gardens

Merchants
Tavern

Columbia
Rd.

Gosset St.

Town Hall Hotel
& Apartments

Kingsland Rd.

Old St.

Ace Hotel
London Shoreditch

BETHNAL
GREEN

Shoreditch High St.

The
Hoxton
Shoreditch

Lyle's

Bethnal Green Rd.

E Pellicci

Weavers
Fields

Great
Eastern St.

SHOREDITCH
HIGH ST.

Vallance Rd.

BETHNAL
GREEN

Cambridge Heath Rd.

Buxton St.

C St.

WHITECHAPEL

1

HKK

Commercial

LIVER-
POOL
ST.

Sun St.
Passage

Bishopsgate

Blixen

Pitt Cue Co.

Whitechapel Rd.

Sidney St.

London Wall

Andaz

Duck & Waffle

Qbic
London City

Cannon St. Rd.

Threadneedle
St.

ALDGATE

Aldgate
High St.

Commercial St.

City Social

Threadneedles
Hotel

Minories

Leman St.

2

Simpson's
Tavern

Fenchurch St.

Mansell St.

1/4 mi

MONUMENT

Grange City
Hotel

Apex City of London

TOWER HILL

0   1/4 km

**Shoreditch,
Whitechapel
and Bethnal Green**

E

Bellanger

Essex Rd.

Liverpool Rd.

Barnsbury St.

Oldroyd

Upper St.

Noel Rd.

Colebrook Row

Wynford St.

Rodney St.

Donegal St.

City Road

ANGEL

Goswell Road

Pentonville Road

Myddelton
Square

Grt Percy

Amwell St.

Spencer St.

St. John St.

Lever St.

Central St.

Bath St.

OLD
STREET

1

Wharton St.

Lloyd Baker St.

Margery St.

Roseberry Avenue

Skinner St.

Percival St.

Old Street

Whitecross St.

Bunhill Row

Featherstone

City Road

3

Phoenix Pl

Gough St.

Yardley St.

Exmouth
Market

Moro

Berber & Q -
Shawarma Bar

Bowling
Green Ln.

Seward St.

Goswell
Road

Golden Ln.

Dufferin St.

**Shoreditch,
Whitechapel and
Bethnal Green:
see inset above →**

Farringdon Road

Aylesbury St.

The Modern Pantry

St. Johns St.

Fann St.

Beech St.

Silk St.

Moore St.

Chiswell St.

4

Clerkenwell Road

Leather

Halton Cross St.

The Rookery

FARRINGDON

Cowcross St.

St. John

Charterhouse St.

Long Ln.

BARBICAN

Aldersgate St.

BARBICAN
CENTRE

Moorfields

Moorgate

MOORGATE

Gray's Inn Rd.

Anglo

St. Cross St.

Greville St.

BARBICAN

Wood St.

Jockey's
Fields

High Holborn

A40

W Smithfield

Giltspur St.

Little
Britain

London Wall

Chancery Ln.

Holborn Viaduct

Angel
St.

Gresham St.

GUILDHALL

Cable Street Inn

5

HOLBORN

Carey St.

St-Bride St.

Shoe Ln.

Old Bailey

Warwick

Ludgate Hill

ST. PAUL'S

Cheapside

The Ned

BANK OF
ENGLAND

BANK

King William St.

Fleet St.

Mitre Ct.

Fetter Ln.

New Bridge St.

Carter Ln.

THE
CITY

Watling St.

Cannon St.

Sweetings

THE
TEMPLE

Tudor St.

Crowne Plaza
London–The City

Queen Victoria St.

Upper Thames St.

CANNON ST.
STATION

Le Pont
de la Tour

6

Temple Pl

TEMPLE

Victoria Embankment

BLACKFRIARS

Blackfriars Br.

Southwark Br.

CANNON
STREET
STATION

Restaurant
Story

0   500 yards

0   500 m

RIVER   THAMES

E   F   G   H

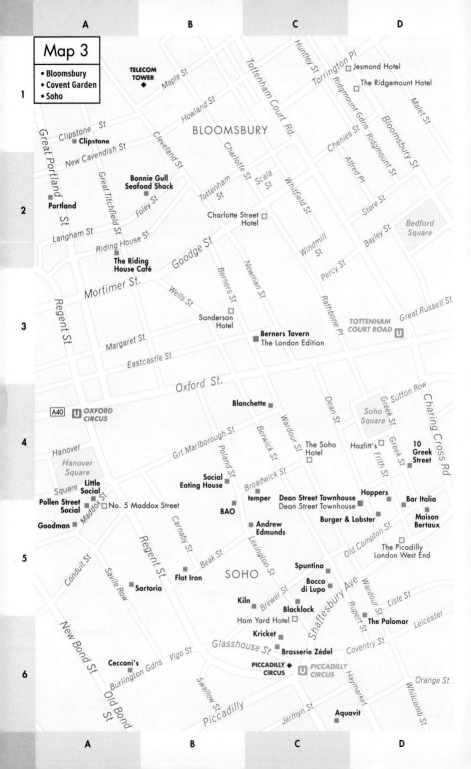

Map 3

- Bloomsbury
- Covent Garden
- Soho

A **B** **C** **D**

1

TELECOM TOWER ◆

Jesmond Hotel □

The Ridgemount Hotel □

Huntley St

Torrington Pl

Maple St

Tottenham Court Rd.

Ridgmount Gdns

Chenies St

Ridgmount St

Bloomsbury St

Malet St

Howland St

BLOOMSBURY

2

Clipstone St

Clipstone ■

New Cavendish St

Great Portland St

Portland ■

Great Titchfield St

Bonnie Gull Seafood Shack ■

Foley St

Cleveland St

Charlotte St

Scala St

Tottenham St

Whitfield St

Alfred Pl

Store St

Bayley St

Bedford Square

Langham St

Riding House St

Charlotte Street Hotel □

Windmill St

Percy St

3

The Riding House Café ■

Goodge St

Berners St

Newman St

Rathbone Pl

TOTTENHAM COURT ROAD U

Great Russell St

Mortimer St.

Wells St

Regent St

Margaret St

Sanderson Hotel

Berners Tavern ■
The London Edition

Eastcastle St

Oxford St.

4

A40 U OXFORD CIRCUS

Blanchette ■

Dean St

Soho Square

Greek St

Sutton Row

Charing Cross Rd

Hanover

Hanover Square

Grt Marlborough St

Poland St

Berwick St

Wardour St

The Soho Hotel

Hazlitt's □

Frith St

Greek St

10 Greek Street

5

Square

Little Social ■

Pollen Street Social ■

Maddox St

□ No. 5 Maddox Street

Social Eating House ■

Broadwick St

temper ■

Dean Street Townhouse
Dean Street Townhouse

Hoppers ■

Bar Italia ■

Goodman ■

BAO ■

Carnaby St

Lexington St

Burger & Lobster ■

Old Compton St

Maison Bertaux ■

Andrew Edmunds ■

The Picadilly London West End □

Conduit St

Saville Row

Regent St

Beak St

SOHO

Flat Iron ■

Spuntino ■

Bocca di Lupo ■

Shaftesbury Ave

Wardour St

Lisle St

Sartoria ■

Kiln ■

Brewer St

Blacklock ■

Rupert St

The Palomar ■

Leicester

Ham Yard Hotel □

6

New Bond St

Old Bond St

Cecconi's ■

Burlington Gdns

Vigo St

Swallow St

Glasshouse St

Kricket ■

Brasserie Zédel ■

PICCADILLY CIRCUS ◆

U PICCADILLY CIRCUS

Coventry St

Haymarket

Whitcomb St

Orange St

Piccadilly

Jermyn St

Aquavit ■

A **B** **C** **D**

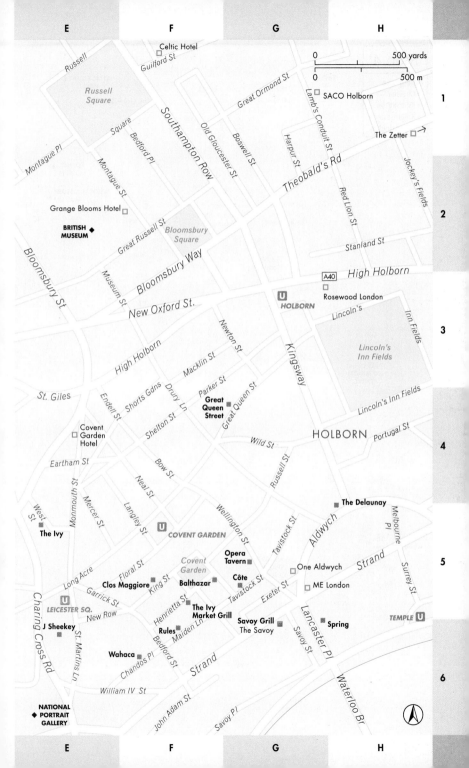

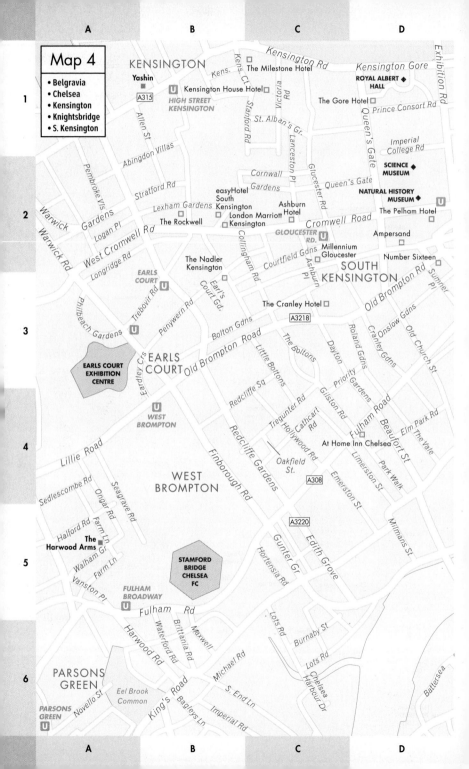

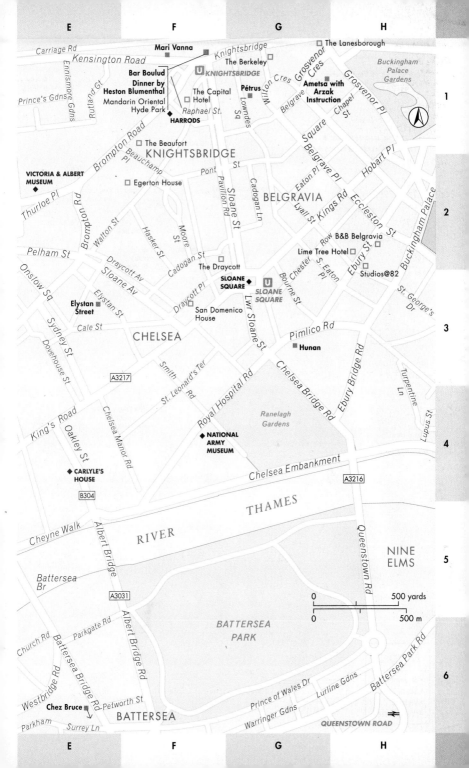

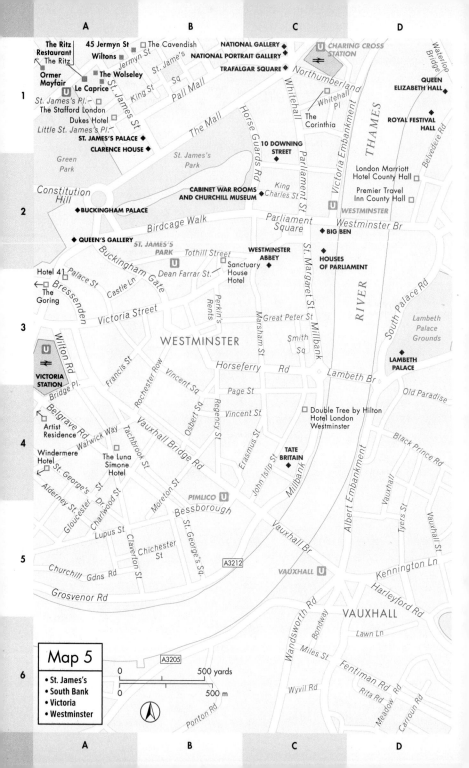

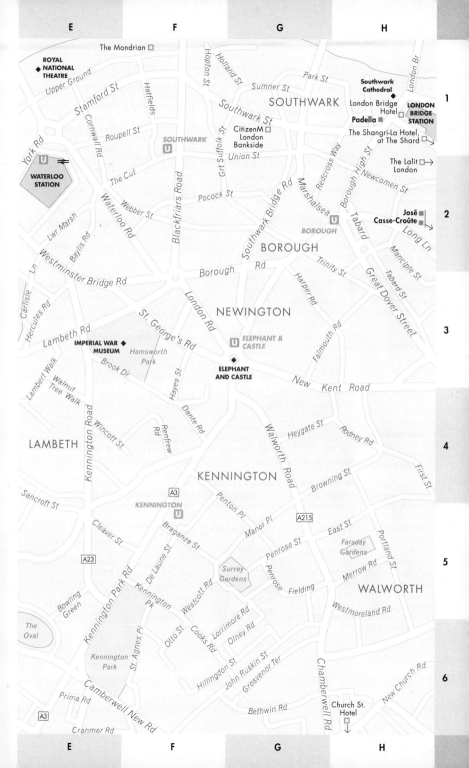

WHERE TO STAY

Updated by
Toby Orton

If your invitation from Queen Elizabeth still hasn't shown up in the mail, no worries—staying at one of London's grande dame hotels is the next best thing to being a guest at the palace—and some say it's even better. Luckily there is no dearth of options where friendliness outdistances luxe; London has plenty of atmospheric places that won't cost a king's ransom.

That noted, until fairly recently it was extremely difficult to find a decent hotel in the center of town for less than £150 per night. Things have improved, thanks to a flurry of new midpriced hotels that have sprung up in recent years. You'll still have to shop around for deals— never assume you'll be able to find somewhere good *and* cheap on short notice.

Of course, it's very different if money is no object. London has some of the very best and most luxurious hotels in the world. Freshly minted billionaires favor the rash of supertrendy hot spots like the Corinthia or ME London, while fashionistas gravitate toward Kit Kemp's superstylish hotels like the Covent Garden and the Charlotte Street. But even these places have deals, and you can sometimes snag a bargain within reach of mere mortals, particularly in the off-season, or just be a spectator to all the glamour by visiting for afternoon tea, the most traditional of high-society treats.

Meanwhile, several midrange hotels have dropped their average prices in response to the choppy waters of the global economy, which has pulled some fantastic places, such as Hazlitt's, the Rookery, and Town Hall, back into the affordable category. There's also a clutch of new, stylish, and supercheap hotels that are a real step forward for the city. The downside is that these places tend to be a little out of the way, but that's often a price worth paying. Another attractive alternative includes hotels in the Premier and Millennium chains, which offer sleek, modern rooms, lots of up-to-date conveniences, and sales that frequently bring room prices well below £100 a night.

At the budget level, London has come a long way in the last couple of years, with a familiar catch: to find a good, reasonably priced B&B, you must be prepared to look outside the very center of town. This means that you have to weigh the city's notoriously high transport costs against any savings—but on the plus side, the Tube can shuttle you out to even some far-flung suburbs in less than 20 minutes. Prepare to be just a little adventurous with your London base and you will be rewarded by a collection of unique and interesting B&Bs and small boutiques, in the kinds of neighborhoods real Londoners live in—places like King Henry's Road, the Cable Street Inn, and the Church Street Hotel. If you're willing to fend for yourself, the city also has some great rental options.

But if you are interested in luxury, London is just the place. Although the image we love to harbor about Olde London Towne may be fast fading in the light of today's glittering city, when it comes time to rest your head, the old-fashioned clichés remain enticing. Choose one of London's heritage-rich hotels—Claridge's supplies perfect parlors; the Savoy has that river view—and you'll find that these fantasies can, and always will, be fulfilled.

15

PLANNING

NEED A RESERVATION?

Yes, hotel reservations are an absolute necessity when planning your trip to London, so book your room as far in advance as possible. The further in advance you can book, the better a deal you're likely to get. Just watch out if you change your mind—cancellation fees can be hefty. On the other hand, it is possible to find some amazing last-minute deals at mid- to high-range places, but this is a real gamble, as you could just as easily end up paying full rate. Fierce competition means properties undergo frequent improvements, so when booking inquire about any ongoing renovations that may interrupt your stay.

CHECKING IN

Typical check-in and checkout times are 2 pm and 11 am, respectively. Many flights from North America arrive early in the morning, but having to wait six hours for a room after arriving jet-lagged at 8 am isn't the ideal way to start a vacation. Alert the hotel of your early arrival; large hotels can often make special early check-in arrangements, and almost all will look after your luggage in the meantime. Be prepared to drop your bags and strike out for a few hours. On the plus side, this can effectively give you a whole extra day for sightseeing.

HOTEL QUALITY

Note that rooms can vary considerably in a single hotel. If you don't like the room you're given, ask to see another. Hotels often renovate room by room—you might find yourself allocated a dark, unrenovated room, whereas bright, newly decorated quarters await just down the hall. Be prepared for the fact that, while smoking is now banned in public areas, this doesn't apply to hotel rooms; be firm and ask to change if you're given a smoking room and didn't request one.

BREAKFAST

Some hotels include breakfast in the price of the room. It ranges from a gourmet spread to what is known as the "full English" (one fried egg, two "bangers," or English-style sausage links, two thick slices of bacon, a grilled tomato, sautéed mushrooms or baked beans, and toast). In many budget hotels and B&Bs, this is the only hot breakfast available. Most expensive hotels (and the most imaginative small ones) may also offer pancakes, French toast, waffles, and omelets. Luckily, virtually all accommodations also offer packaged cereals, muffins, yogurt, and fresh fruit, so when the sausage-and-bacon brigade begins to wear you down, go continental.

FACILITIES

Keep in mind that some facilities come with the room rate while others cost extra. So, when pricing accommodations, always ask what's included. Modern hotels usually have air-conditioning, but B&Bs and hotels in older buildings often do not, and it is generally not the norm in London. Wi-Fi is common, but don't assume it's free (large hotels in particular can charge outrageous fees). If you want a double room, specify whether you want a double bed or a twin (two single beds next to each other). *All hotels listed here have private bathrooms unless otherwise noted.*

PRICES

If you're planning to visit in fall, winter, or early spring, start monitoring bargain rates online a few months before your trip and book whenever you see a good rate. Chains such as Hilton, Premier, and Millennium are known for their low-season sales during which prices can be as little as half the normal rate. And business-oriented hotels frequently have lower rates on weekends.

The exchange rate between the pound and the dollar is also unpredictable, so if it's looking good when you book, an advance-payment deal could end up saving you a decent amount of money. ■ TIP→ The Visit London Accommodation Booking Service (www.visitlondon.com) offers a best-price guarantee. Also try the clearinghouse websites Late Rooms (www.laterooms.com), Booking (www.booking.com), and Last Minute (www.lastminute.com).

WHAT IT COSTS IN POUNDS			
$	$$	$$$	$$$$
Hotels Under £125	£125–£250	£251–£400	Over £400

Prices in the reviews are the lowest cost of a standard double room in high season, including 20% V.A.T.

WHERE SHOULD I STAY?

	Neighborhood Vibe	Pros	Cons
Westminster, St. James's, and Royal London	This historic section is home to major tourist attractions like Buckingham Palace.	Central area near tourist sites; easy Tube access; considered a safe area to stay.	Mostly expensive lodging options; few good restaurants and entertainment venues nearby.
Mayfair and Marylebone	Traditional, old money; a mixture of the business and financial set with fashionable shops.	In the heart of the action; some of London's best hotels are found here.	Pricey part of town; the city-that-never-sleeps buzz makes peace and quiet hard to come by.
Soho and Covent Garden	A tourist hub with endless entertainment—this is party central for young adults.	Buzzing area with plenty to see and do; late-night entertainment abounds; wonderful shopping district.	Perhaps London's busiest (and noisiest) district after dark; few budget hotels.
Bloomsbury and Holborn	Diverse area that is part bustling business center and part tranquil respite with tree-lined streets and parks.	Easy access to Tube, and 15 minutes to city center; major sights, like the British Museum in Bloomsbury.	Holborn has busy and noisy streets; the area around King's Cross can be sketchy—particularly at night.
The City	London's financial district, where most of the city's banks and businesses are headquartered.	Extremely central with easy transportation access and great hotel deals.	The City can be as quiet as a tomb on weekends—even the pubs close.
East London	East of the city center, one of London's trendiest areas, with a great arts scene.	Great for art lovers, shoppers, and business execs with meetings in Canary Wharf.	Still a transitional area; parts of Hoxton can be a bit dodgy at night; 20-minute Tube ride from central London.
South of the Thames	South of the river is a vibrant cultural hub, centered on the South Bank, the Globe, and the Royal National Theatre.	South of the River is London's unofficial cultural quarter, and walking distance from the West End theaters.	You don't have to go very far from the South Bank before you hit some of London's dodgiest neighborhoods.
Kensington, Chelsea, Knightsbridge, and Belgravia	These are some of London's most upscale neighborhoods and a hub of London's tourist universe.	Diverse hotel selection; great area for meandering urban walks; London's capital of high-end shopping.	Depending on where you are, the nearest Tube might be a hike; residential area might be too quiet for some.
Notting Hill and Bayswater	This is an upscale, trendy area favored by locals, with plenty of good hotels.	Hotel deals abound if you know where to look; gorgeous greenery in Hyde Park.	Choose the wrong place and you may end up in a flea pit; residential area may be quiet.
Regent's Park and Hampstead	A mix of arty, fashionable districts with a villagelike feel in other places.	Some of London's most fashionable neighborhoods; easy to fall in love with.	Some distance from center; lack of hotel options.

15

HOTEL REVIEWS

Listed alphabetically by neighborhood. Use the coordinate (⊹ 1:B2) at the end of each listing to locate a site on the corresponding map. To locate the property on a map, turn to the London Dining and Lodging Atlas at the end of the Where to Eat chapter. The first number after the symbol indicates the map number. Following that is the property's coordinate on the map grid.

Hotel reviews have been shortened. For full information, visit Fodors.com.

WESTMINSTER, ST. JAMES'S, AND ROYAL LONDON

WESTMINSTER

$$$$
HOTEL
Fodor's Choice
★
🏨 **The Corinthia.** The London outpost of the exclusive Corinthia chain is design heaven-on-earth, with levels of service that make anyone feel like a VIP. **Pros:** so much luxury and elegance you'll feel like royalty; low rate guarantee means they'll match the price of a cheaper room of the same standard at another hotel; excellent fine dining options. **Cons:** prices jump to the stratosphere once the least expensive rooms sell out; not many special offers; not all room prices include breakfast. ⑤ *Rooms from: £534* ⊠ *Whitehall Pl., Westminster* ☎ *020/7930–8181* ⊕ *www.corinthia.com* ⟳ *294 rooms* ⑪ *Breakfast; No meals* Ⓜ *Embankment* ⊹ *5:C1.*

$$
HOTEL
FAMILY
🏨 **DoubleTree by Hilton Hotel London Westminster.** Spectacular views of the river, Big Ben, and the London Eye fill the floor-to-ceiling windows in this rather stark, steel-and-glass building steps from the Tate Britain, and a plethora of techy perks await inside. **Pros:** amazing views; flat-screen TVs and other high-tech gadgetry; can be surprisingly affordable for the location. **Cons:** small bedrooms; tiny bathrooms; TV has to be operated through a computer (confusing if you're not used to it). ⑤ *Rooms from: £179* ⊠ *30 John Islip St., Westminster* ☎ *020/7630–1000* ⊕ *www.doubletreewestminsterhotel.com* ⟳ *460 rooms* ⑪ *Some meals* Ⓜ *Westminster, Pimlico* ⊹ *5:C4.*

$$$$
HOTEL
🏨 **The Goring.** With Buckingham Palace just around the corner, this hotel, built in 1910 and now run by third-generation Gorings, has always been a favorite among discreet VIPs—including Kate Middleton's family on the night before her marriage to Prince William in 2011. **Pros:** elegant, spacious rooms; overlooks Buckingham Palace; great attention to detail. **Cons:** price is still too high for what you get; interiors a bit fussy; the basic gym is small. ⑤ *Rooms from: £401* ⊠ *15 Beeston Pl., Grosvenor Gardens, Westminster* ☎ *020/7396–9000* ⊕ *www.thegoring.com* ⟳ *69 rooms* ⑪ *Some meals* Ⓜ *Victoria* ⊹ *5:A3.*

$$$
HOTEL
Fodor's Choice
★
🏨 **Hotel 41.** With faultless service, sumptuous designer furnishings, and a sense of fun to boot, this impeccable hotel breathes new life into the cliché "thinks of everything," yet the epithet is really quite apt. **Pros:** impeccable service; beautiful and stylish; Buckingham Palace is on your doorstep. **Cons:** unusual design is not for everyone; expensive; the private bar can feel stuffy. ⑤ *Rooms from: £370* ⊠ *41 Buckingham Palace Rd., Westminster* ☎ *020/7300–0041* ⊕ *www.41hotel.com* ⟳ *30 rooms* ⑪ *Breakfast* Ⓜ *Victoria* ⊹ *5:A3.*

$$ Lime Tree Hotel. In a central neighborhood where hotels veer from
HOTEL wildly overpriced at one extreme to grimy boltholes at the other, the
Lime Tree gets the boutique style just about right—and at a surprisingly
reasonable cost for the neighborhood. **Pros:** lovely and helpful hosts;
great location; rooms are decent size. **Cons:** cheaper rooms are small;
some are up several flights of stairs and there's no elevator; two-night
minimum stay on weekends. $ *Rooms from: £185 ⊠ 135–137 Ebury
St., Westminster ☎ 020/7730–8191 ⊕ www.limetreehotel.co.uk ➠ 25
rooms* ⦿*l Breakfast* Ⓜ *Victoria, Sloane Sq.* ✦ *4:H2.*

$$ Sanctuary House Hotel. This is a classic example of what the Brit-
B&B/INN ish mean when they refer to an "inn"—a pub with bedrooms, albeit
one of better-than-average quality for London. **Pros:** cozy, authentic
London feel; friendly staff; "wow" location right in the heart of Westminster. **Cons:** pub can be noisy (light sleepers should ask for a room
as far from the ground floor as possible); the afterwork crowd keeps
the pub busy; breakfast not included in the room price. $ *Rooms
from: £166 ⊠ 33 Tothill St., Westminster ☎ 020/7799–4044 ⊕ www.
sanctuaryhousehotel.co.uk ➠ 33 rooms* ⦿*l No meals* Ⓜ *St. James's
Park* ✦ *5:B2.*

$$ Windermere Hotel. This sweet and rather elegant old hotel, on the
HOTEL premises of London's first B&B (1881), is a decent, well-situated
FAMILY option. **Pros:** good location close to Victoria Station; free Wi-Fi; good
amenities for an old hotel of this size, including air-conditioning and
an elevator. **Cons:** rooms and bathrooms are tiny; traditional decor
might not suit all tastes; many major attractions are a 20-minute
walk away. $ *Rooms from: £195 ⊠ 142–144 Warwick Way, Westmin-
ster ☎ 020/7834–5163 ⊕ www.windermere-hotel.co.uk ➠ 19 rooms*
⦿*l Breakfast* Ⓜ *Victoria* ✦ *5:A4.*

ST. JAMES'S

$$$ Dukes Hotel. At this small, exclusive hotel in a discreet cul-de-sac,
HOTEL ample natural light brightens contemporary-style rooms. **Pros:** low-
key ambience; peaceful setting in a central location; excellent restaurant. **Cons:** maybe a bit too quiet for some; price is still rather high for
what's available; the price of breakfast is steep. $ *Rooms from: £341
⊠ 35 St. James's Pl., St. James's ☎ 020/7941–4840, 800/381–4702
in U.S. ⊕ www.dukeshotel.com ➠ 90 rooms* ⦿*l Breakfast* Ⓜ *Green
Park* ✦ *5:A1.*

$$$$ The Ritz. If you're wondering if the *Downton Abbey*–style world of
HOTEL the old British upper class still exists, look no further than here; the Ritz
is as synonymous with London's high society and decadence today as
it was when it opened in 1906. **Pros:** historic luxury hotel; service at
every turn; iconic restaurant and bar. **Cons:** snooty service; tediously
old-fashioned dress code; located on a congested road. $ *Rooms from:
£460 ⊠ 150 Piccadilly, St. James's ☎ 020/7493–8181 ⊕ www.therit-
zlondon.com ➠ 136 rooms* ⦿*l Some meals* Ⓜ *Piccadilly Circus* ✦ *5:A1.*

$$$ The Stafford London. This is a rare find: a posh hotel that's equal
HOTEL parts elegance and friendliness, and located in one of the few peace-
Fodor'sChoice ful spots in the area, down a small lane behind Piccadilly. **Pros:** great
★ staff; home to one of London's original "American Bars"; quiet loca-
tion. **Cons:** traditional style is not to all tastes; perks in the more

15

expensive rooms could be more generous (free airport transfer, but one-way only; free clothes pressing, but only one item per day); some rooms can feel small. $ *Rooms from: £372* ✉ *16–18 St. James's Pl., St. James's* ☎ *020/7493–0111* ⊕ *www.thestaffordlondon.com* ↪ *104 rooms* ❖| *Breakfast* Ⓜ *Green Park* ✛ *5:A1.*

MAYFAIR AND MARYLEBONE

MAYFAIR

$$$
HOTEL
Athenaeum Hotel and Apartments. This grand hotel overlooking Green Park offers plenty for the money: rooms are both comfortable and lavishly decorated, with deeply comfortable Hypnos beds, plasma-screen TVs, luxurious fabrics, and original contemporary artworks. **Pros:** peaceful park views; handy for Buckingham Palace and Piccadilly; great value for elegant setting. **Cons:** bathrooms are almost all small; some rooms can feel tiny; only some rooms come with park views. $ *Rooms from: £346* ✉ *116 Piccadilly, Mayfair* ☎ *020/7499–3464* ⊕ *www.athenaeumhotel.com* ↪ *164 rooms* ❖| *Breakfast* Ⓜ *Green Park* ✛ *1:H6.*

$$$$
HOTEL
Brown's Hotel. Founded in 1837 by James Brown, Lord Byron's "gentleman's gentleman," this hotel occupying 11 Georgian townhouses holds a treasured place in London society. **Pros:** elegant spaces; attentive service; good afternoon tea. **Cons:** even the most basic room is very pricey; renovation detracted from the hotel's historic atmosphere; low availability for the most basic rooms. $ *Rooms from: £450* ✉ *33 Albemarle St., Mayfair* ☎ *020/7493–6020, 888/667–9477 in U.S.* ⊕ *www.roccofortehotels.com* ↪ *117 rooms* ❖| *Breakfast* Ⓜ *Green Park* ✛ *1:H5.*

$$$
HOTEL
Fodor's Choice
★
The Cavendish. Located next door to Fortnum and Mason (one of the most luxurious department stores in the world), it seems appropriate that the Cavendish comes with a touch of Gilded Age history, a whiff of historical scandal, and a pleasant air of joie de vivre. **Pros:** sophisticated yet relaxed; great service; unbeatable location. **Cons:** guestrooms are small; some street noise; rooms near the elevator can be particularly noisy. $ *Rooms from: £258* ✉ *81 Jermyn St., Mayfair* ☎ *020/7930–2111* ⊕ *www.thecavendish-london.co.uk* ↪ *230 rooms* ❖| *Breakfast* Ⓜ *Piccadilly* ✛ *5:B1.*

$$$
HOTEL
Chesterfield Mayfair Hotel. Deep in the heart of Mayfair, the former townhouse of the Earl of Chesterfield welcomes guests in wood-and-leather public rooms that match the dark-wood furnishings in the bedrooms—small but like fashion magazine spreads, with bold designer wallpaper or tones of fawn and gray. **Pros:** laid-back atmosphere; attentive service; great afternoon tea. **Cons:** prices rise sharply if you don't get the cheapest rooms; some rooms are tiny; restaurant is very expensive. $ *Rooms from: £295* ✉ *35 Charles St., Mayfair* ☎ *020/7491–2622, 877/955–1515 in U.S.* ⊕ *www.chesterfieldmayfair.com* ↪ *107 rooms* ❖| *Breakfast* Ⓜ *Green Park* ✛ *1:H6.*

$$$$
HOTEL
FAMILY
Fodor's Choice
★
Claridge's. The well-heeled have been meeting—and eating—at Claridge's for generations, and the tradition continues in the original art deco public spaces of this super-glamorous London institution. **Pros:** see-and-be-seen dining and drinking; serious luxury everywhere—this is an old-money hotel; comics, books, and DVDs to help keep kids

amused. **Cons:** better pack your designer wardrobe if you want to fit in with the locals; all that luxury means an expensive price tag; to protect the privacy of guests, photographs are prohibited in some areas. $ *Rooms from: £510* ⊠ *Brook St., Mayfair* ☎ *020/7629–8860, 866/599–6991 in U.S.* ⊕ *www.claridges.co.uk* ⊷ *202 rooms* ❖❘ *Breakfast* Ⓜ *Bond St.* ✛ *1:H4.*

$$$$
HOTEL
FAMILY
Fodor's Choice
★

The Connaught. A huge favorite of the "we wouldn't dream of staying anywhere else" monied set since its opening in 1917, the Connaught has many dazzlingly modern compliments to its famously historic delights. **Pros:** legendary hotel; great for star-spotting; Michelin-starred dining. **Cons:** history comes at a price; bathrooms are small; the superior king room is small for the price. $ *Rooms from: £570* ⊠ *Carlos Pl., Mayfair* ☎ *020/7499–7070, 866/599–6991 in U.S.* ⊕ *www.the-connaught.co.uk* ⊷ *121 rooms* ❖❘ *Breakfast* Ⓜ *Bond St.* ✛ *1:H5.*

$$$$
HOTEL
Fodor's Choice
★

The Dorchester. Few hotels this opulent manage to be as personable as the Dorchester, which opened in 1939 and boasts a prime Park Lane location with unparalleled glamour; gold leaf and marble adorn the public spaces, and guest quarters are awash in English country house meets art deco style. **Pros:** historic luxury in 1930s building; lovely views of Hyde Park; excellent spa. **Cons:** traditional look is not to all tastes; prices are sky-high; some rooms are disappointingly small. $ *Rooms from: £592* ⊠ *53 Park La., Mayfair* ☎ *020/7629–8888* ⊕ *www.thedorchester.com* ⊷ *250 rooms* ❖❘ *Breakfast* Ⓜ *Marble Arch, Hyde Park Corner* ✛ *1:H6.*

$$$$
HOTEL

Four Seasons Park Lane. A racy departure for the Four Seasons, this hotel has an English clubhouse look with a dose of boudoir. **Pros:** highly elegant rooms; excellent spa; lovely location next to Hyde Park. **Cons:** not for strict traditionalists; haute design comes with high prices; breakfast is an additional fee. $ *Rooms from: £730* ⊠ *Hamilton Pl., Park La., Mayfair* ☎ *020/7499–0888* ⊕ *www.fourseasons.com/london* ⊷ *193 rooms* ❖❘ *No meals* Ⓜ *Hyde Park Corner* ✛ *1:H6.*

$$$$
HOTEL

InterContinental London Park Lane. Overlooking busy Hyde Park Corner and the grounds of Buckingham Palace (much to the Queen's chagrin, allegedly), this hotel's luxurious rooms are aimed at high-end business travelers. **Pros:** great location; feel-like-a-million-dollars service; good business facilities. **Cons:** no park views with standard rooms; prices sky-high in midsummer; without the wow factor of some similarly priced Park Lane hotels. $ *Rooms from: £463* ⊠ *1 Hamilton Pl., Park Ln., Mayfair* ☎ *020/7409–3131* ⊕ *parklane.intercontinental.com* ⊷ *447 rooms* ❖❘ *Breakfast* Ⓜ *Hyde Park Corner* ✛ *1:H6.*

$$$
HOTEL
Fodor's Choice
★

The Langham. Hotel pedigrees don't come much greater than this one; built in 1865, the Langham was *the* original luxury hotel in the city, all but inventing the very image of what a great London hotel looked like. **Pros:** beautiful historic building; outstanding service; great restaurant and bar. **Cons:** price rises considerably once cheapest rooms sell out; bathrooms in basic rooms are somewhat utilitarian; some modernized rooms don't share the building's historic charm. $ *Rooms from: £390* ⊠ *1C Portland Pl., Mayfair* ☎ *020/7636–1000* ⊕ *www.langhamhotels.co.uk* ⊷ *380 rooms* ❖❘ *Breakfast* Ⓜ *Oxford Circus* ✛ *2:A4.*

15

$$$
RENTAL
FAMILY

🏠 **No. 5 Maddox Street.** Just five minutes' walk from Oxford Street, this is a great option for those who tire of traditional hotels: 12 luxury suites—some with balconies and working fireplaces—filled with everything you could ever need, including a handy kitchen. **Pros:** cozy and private; room service will deliver meals from local restaurants; guests have access to nearby health club. **Cons:** no elevator; no communal lobby can make you feel isolated; central location can (predictably) be noisy. $ *Rooms from: £311* ✉ *5 Maddox St., Mayfair* ☎ *020/7647–0200* ⊕ *www.living-rooms.co.uk/hotel/no5maddoxstreet* ⬏ *12 suites* ⦿*No meals* Ⓜ *Oxford Circus* ✛ *3:A5.*

$$$
HOTEL

🏨 **The Picadilly London West End.** This hotel couldn't be better situated for theater lovers; it's right in the famed West End district with three such venues within sight of the front door alone. **Pros:** unbeatable location; some thoughtful extras; attentive staff. **Cons:** noise is unavoidable; you're paying for the location rather than the amenities, and it shows; rooms are compact. $ *Rooms from: £260* ✉ *65–73 Shaftesbury Ave., Mayfair* ☎ *020/7871–6000, 877/898–1586 in U.S.* ⊕ *www.piccadillypremierlondon.co.uk* ⬏ *67 rooms* ⦿*Breakfast* Ⓜ *Piccadilly Circus* ✛ *3:D5.*

$$
HOTEL

🏨 **Radisson Blu Edwardian Berkshire Hotel.** In a dangerously good location for shopaholics, with Oxford Street on the doorstep, the pleasant and well-run Radisson Berkshire offers a similar level of service to some of the more established hotels in the neighborhood, at a lower rate. **Pros:** great central location; good restaurant; free Wi-Fi. **Cons:** walk-in rate is still quite expensive; small bedrooms; some rooms suffer from street noise. $ *Rooms from: £229* ✉ *350 Oxford St., Mayfair* ☎ *020/7629–7474, 0800/374–411 toll-free in U.K., 800/333–3333 toll-free in U.S.* ⊕ *www.radissonblu-edwardian.com* ⬏ *149 rooms* ⦿*Breakfast* Ⓜ *Bond St.; Oxford Circus* ✛ *1:H4.*

$$
B&B/INN

🏨 **22 York Street.** This lovely Georgian townhouse has a cozy, family feel, with polished pine floors and fetching antiques decorating the homey, individually furnished guest rooms. **Pros:** live out your London townhouse fantasy; nicely flexible check-in times; good location for shoppers. **Cons:** if you take away the great location, you're paying a lot for a B&B; not everyone enjoys socializing with strangers over breakfast; some guests won't enjoy the lack of anonymity. $ *Rooms from: £150* ✉ *22 York St., Mayfair* ☎ *020/7224–2990* ⊕ *www.22yorkstreet.co.uk* ⬏ *10 rooms* ⦿*Breakfast* Ⓜ *Baker St.* ✛ *1:G3.*

MARYLEBONE

$$
HOTEL
Fodor's Choice
★

🏨 **Dorset Square Hotel.** This fashionable boutique hotel occupies a charming old townhouse in one of London's most upscale neighborhoods. **Pros:** ideal location; lovely design; good afternoon tea. **Cons:** some rooms are small; no bathtub in some rooms; fee for Wi-Fi. $ *Rooms from: £246* ✉ *39 Dorset Sq., Marylebone* ☎ *020/7723–7874* ⊕ *www.firmdalehotels.com* ⬏ *38 rooms* ⦿*Breakfast* Ⓜ *Baker St.* ✛ *1:F2.*

$$$$
HOTEL

🏨 **Hyatt Regency London—The Churchill.** Even though it's one of London's largest hotels, the Churchill is always abuzz with guests smiling at the perfection they find here, including warmly personalized service and calmly alluring guest rooms. **Pros:** comfortable and stylish; efficient service; up to three can stay in one room. **Cons:** feels more geared to business than leisure travelers; lots of renovation; prices are steep.

$ *Rooms from: £409* ✉ *30 Portman Sq., Marylebone* ☎ *020/7486–5800* ⊕ *londonchurchill.regency.hyatt.com* ⤳ *440 rooms* ⊠ *Breakfast* Ⓜ *Marble Arch* ✛ *1:G4.*

$$ 🏨 **Park Plaza Sherlock Holmes Hotel.** Named in honor of the fictional
HOTEL detective who had his home on Baker Street, rooms here have a mas-
culine edge with lots of earth tones and pinstripe sheets (along with
hypermodern bathrooms stocked with fluffy bathrobes). **Pros:** nicely
decorated; international electrical outlets, including those that work
with American equipment; famous literary location. **Cons:** have to
walk through the bar to get to reception; not well soundproofed
from the noisy street; total lack of Benedict Cumberbatch. $ *Rooms
from: £186* ✉ *108 Baker St., Marylebone* ☎ *020/7486–6161* ⊕ *www.
parkplazasherlockholmes.com* ⤳ *119 rooms* ⊠ *Breakfast* Ⓜ *Baker
St.* ✛ *1:G3.*

$$ 🏨 **The Sumner.** You can feel yourself relaxing the minute you enter this
HOTEL elegant Georgian townhouse. **Pros:** excellent location for shopping;
small enough that the staff know your name; attractive conservatory
and garden. **Cons:** services are limited; high prices; most rooms have
small bathrooms. $ *Rooms from: £180* ✉ *54 Upper Berkley St., Marble
Arch, Marylebone* ☎ *020/7723–2244* ⊕ *www.thesumner.com* ⤳ *19
rooms* ⊠ *Breakfast* Ⓜ *Marble Arch* ✛ *1:F4.*

15

SOHO AND COVENT GARDEN

SOHO

$$$ 🏨 **Dean Street Townhouse.** Discreet and unpretentious—and right in the
HOTEL heart of Soho—this oh-so-stylish place has a bohemian vibe and an
Fodor's Choice excellent modern British restaurant, hung with pieces by renowned
★ artists like Peter Blake and Tracy Emin. **Pros:** ultracool vibe; resembles
an upper-class pied-à-terre; great location in the heart of Soho. **Cons:**
some rooms are extremely small; rooms at the front of the building can
be noisy, especially on weekends; the crowd can often feel cooler-than-
thou. $ *Rooms from: £330* ✉ *69–71 Dean St., Soho* ☎ *020/7434–1775*
⊕ *www.deanstreettownhouse.com* ⤳ *39 rooms* ⊠ *Breakfast* Ⓜ *Leices-
ter Sq., Tottenham Court Rd.* ✛ *3:D5.*

$$$ 🏨 **Ham Yard Hotel.** Luxurious, playful, and riotously good fun, the Ham
HOTEL Yard Hotel is the latest addition to the burgeoning hit parade of London
FAMILY hotel designer extraordinaire, Kit Kemp. **Pros:** great design; excellent
Fodor's Choice service; fun facilities, including a bowling alley. **Cons:** rates can get
★ very pricey; some will find the scene at the hotel a little too trendy;
with a cinema, bowling alley and spa on-site, you might not leave the
hotel. $ *Rooms from: £390* ✉ *1 Ham Yard, Soho* ☎ *020/3642–2000*
⊕ *www.firmdalehotels.com/hotels/london/ham-yard-hotel* ⤳ *98 rooms*
⊠ *Some meals* Ⓜ *Piccadilly Circus* ✛ *3:C6.*

$$ 🏨 **Hazlitt's.** This disarmingly friendly place, full of personality, robust
HOTEL antiques, and claw-foot tubs, occupies three connected early 18th-
Fodor's Choice century houses, one of which was the last home of essayist William
★ Hazlitt (1778–1830). **Pros:** great for lovers of art and antiques; historic
atmosphere with lots of small sitting rooms and wooden staircases;
truly beautiful and relaxed. **Cons:** no in-house restaurant; breakfast

is £12 extra; no elevators. $ *Rooms from: £239* ✉ *6 Frith St., Soho* ☎ *020/7434–1771* ⊕ *www.hazlittshotel.com* 🛏 *30 rooms* ⦿*No meals* Ⓜ *Tottenham Court Rd.* ✛ *3:D4.*

$$$
HOTEL

🛏 **The Soho Hotel.** This supertrendy hotel personifies Soho's enduring hipness with its artsy, urban chic vibe. **Pros:** small and sophisticated; excellent service; great restaurant. **Cons:** bar can be crowded and noisy on weeknights; some lower level rooms lack the amenities of pricier rooms; expensive for a boutique hotel. $ *Rooms from: £336* ✉ *4 Richmond Mews, off Dean St., Soho* ☎ *020/7559–3000* ⊕ *www.firmdalehotels.com/hotels/london/the-soho-hotel* 🛏 *95 rooms* ⦿*Breakfast* Ⓜ *Tottenham Court Rd.* ✛ *3:C4.*

COVENT GARDEN

$$$
HOTEL
Fodor'sChoice
★

🛏 **Covent Garden Hotel.** It's little wonder this is now the London home-away-from-home for off-duty celebrities, actors, and style mavens, with its Covent Garden location and guest rooms that are design-magazine stylish, using mix-and-match couture fabrics to stunning effect. **Pros:** great for star-spotting; supertrendy; basement cinema for movie buffs. **Cons:** you can feel you don't matter if you're not famous; location in Covent Garden can be a bit boisterous; only some rooms come with balcony views. $ *Rooms from: £330* ✉ *10 Monmouth St., Covent Garden* ☎ *020/7806–1000, 800/553–6674 in U.S.* ⊕ *www.firmdalehotels.com/hotels/london/covent-garden-hotel* 🛏 *58 rooms* ⦿*Some meals* Ⓜ *Covent Garden* ✛ *3:E4.*

$$$
HOTEL
Fodor'sChoice
★

🛏 **ME London.** A shiny fortress of luxury, the ME brings a splash of modern cool to a rather stuffy patch of the Strand. **Pros:** sleek and fashionable; full of high-tech comforts; stunning views from rooftop bar. **Cons:** design can sometimes verge on form over function; very small closets and in-room storage areas; the rooftop bar can get uncomfortably busy. $ *Rooms from: £323* ✉ *336 The Strand, Covent Garden* ☎ *0808/234–1953* ⊕ *www.melia.com* 🛏 *157 rooms* ⦿*Breakfast* Ⓜ *Covent Garden* ✛ *3:G5.*

$$$
HOTEL

🛏 **One Aldwych.** An Edwardian building, with an artsy lobby and understated blend of contemporary and classic, provides pure, modern luxury in a great location for theaters and shopping. **Pros:** understated luxury; ultracool atmosphere; good deals and special offers, including big advance booking discounts. **Cons:** all this luxury doesn't come cheap; fashionable ambience is not always relaxing; rooms are relatively plain. $ *Rooms from: £340* ✉ *1 Aldwych, Covent Garden* ☎ *020/7300–1000* ⊕ *www.onealdwych.co.uk* 🛏 *105 rooms* ⦿*Breakfast* Ⓜ *Charing Cross, Covent Garden* ✛ *3:G5.*

$$$$
HOTEL
Fodor'sChoice
★

🛏 **The Savoy.** One of London's most iconic hotels maintains its status at the top with winning attributes of impeccable service, stunning decor, and a desirable Covent Garden location. **Pros:** one of the top hotels in Europe; iconic pedigree; Thames-side location. **Cons:** everything comes with a price tag; street noise is surprisingly problematic, particularly on lower floors; right off the superbusy Strand. $ *Rooms from: £504* ✉ *The Strand, Covent Garden* ☎ *020/7836–4343, 800/257–7544 in U.S.* ⊕ *www.fairmont.com/savoy-london* 🛏 *269 rooms* ⦿*Breakfast* Ⓜ *Covent Garden, Charing Cross* ✛ *3:G6.*

BLOOMSBURY, HOLBORN, AND FITZROVIA

BLOOMSBURY

$ 🖼 **Celtic Hotel.** This is a solid, dependable budget choice in an otherwise
HOTEL expensive district (close to the West End and British Museum), where
you'll be hard-pressed to find a better price. **Pros:** free Wi-Fi; good
location; bargain rates. **Cons:** no-frills approach means few extras; no
elevator; not all rooms have private bathrooms. $ *Rooms from: £90*
✉ *61–63 Guilford St., Bloomsbury* ☎ *020/7837–6737* ⊕ *www.stmarga-*
retshotel.co.uk ↩ *35 rooms* ⦿ *Breakfast* Ⓜ *Russell Sq.* ✛ *3:F1.*

$$$ 🖼 **Charlotte Street Hotel.** Tradition and modern flair are fused together in
HOTEL this superstylish retreat, a short walk from Oxford Street. **Pros:** elegant
Fodor's Choice and luxurious; great attention to detail; decent chance at finding a good
★ deal. **Cons:** the popular bar can be noisy; reservations essential for the
restaurant; some rooms are small considering the price. $ *Rooms from:*
£306 ✉ *15–17 Charlotte St., Bloomsbury* ☎ *020/7806–2000, 800/553–*
6674 in U.S. ⊕ *www.firmdalehotels.com* ↩ *52 rooms* ⦿ *Breakfast*
Ⓜ *Goodge St.* ✛ *3:C2.*

$ 🖼 **Grange Blooms Hotel.** In this white Georgian-townhouse hotel, just
HOTEL around the corner from the British Museum, rooms are not too tiny by
London standards, and those in the back look out onto a leafy green
garden. **Pros:** great location; overall good value; excellent rates if you
book early through the website. **Cons:** guests can be bumped to sister
hotel if fully booked; no air-conditioning; street noise in some rooms.
$ *Rooms from: £106* ✉ *7 Montague St., Bloomsbury* ☎ *020/7323–*
1717, 800/2247–2643 ⊕ *www.grangehotels.com* ↩ *27 rooms* ⦿ *Some*
meals Ⓜ *Russell Sq.* ✛ *3:F2.*

$$ 🖼 **Harlingford Hotel.** The most contemporary of the hotels around
HOTEL Bloomsbury's Cartwright Gardens offers sleek, quiet, and comfortable
bedrooms and perfectly appointed public rooms. **Pros:** good location;
friendly staff; private garden. **Cons:** rooms are small; no air-conditioning; no elevator. $ *Rooms from: £128* ✉ *61–63 Cartwright Gardens,*
Bloomsbury ☎ *020/7387–1551* ⊕ *www.harlingfordhotel.com* ↩ *39*
rooms ⦿ *Breakfast* Ⓜ *Russell Sq.* ✛ *2:C3.*

$ 🖼 **Jesmond Hotel.** This friendly little hotel is great value given the loca-
B&B/INN tion: a short walk from the British Museum in one direction, and Soho
and Covent Garden in the other. **Pros:** great location; friendly staff;
free Wi-Fi. **Cons:** some rooms are very small; nearly half have shared
bathrooms; decor is inoffensive but uninspiring. $ *Rooms from: £90*
✉ *63 Gower St., Bloomsbury* ☎ *020/7636–3199* ⊕ *www.jesmondhotel.*
org.uk ↩ *15 rooms* ⦿ *Breakfast* Ⓜ *Goodge St., Euston Sq., Warren*
St., Russell Sq. ✛ *3:C1.*

$$ 🖼 **Megaro.** Directly across the street from St. Pancras International sta-
HOTEL tion, the snazzy, well-designed, modern rooms here surround guests
with startlingly contemporary style and amenities that include powerful
showers and espresso machines. **Pros:** comfortable beds; great location
for Eurostar; short hop on Tube to city center. **Cons:** neighborhood isn't
great; standard rooms are small; interiors may be a bit stark for some.
$ *Rooms from: £190* ✉ *Belgrove St., King's Cross* ☎ *020/7843–2222*
⊕ *www.hotelmegaro.co.uk* ↩ *57 rooms* ⦿ *Breakfast* Ⓜ *King's Cross*
St. Pancras ✛ *2:C2.*

15

$ 🖼 **The Ridgemount Hotel.** Mere blocks away from the British Museum and
B&B/INN London's West End theaters, this handsomely fronted guesthouse has
clean, neat, and plainly decorated rooms at bargain rates. **Pros:** good
location for theaters and museum; helpful staff; family rooms (accommodating up to five) are excellent value. **Cons:** decoration is basic; no
elevator; cheapest rooms have shared bathrooms. ⑤ *Rooms from: £94*
✉ *67 Gower St., Bloomsbury* ☎ *020/7636–1141* ⊕ *www.ridgemoun-*
thotel.co.uk ⤵ *32 rooms* ❮◯❯ *Breakfast* Ⓜ *Goode St.* ✢ *3:D1.*

$$ 🖼 **St. Pancras Renaissance.** This stunningly restored Victorian land-
HOTEL mark—replete with gingerbread turrets and castlelike ornaments—
Fodor's Choice started as a love letter to the golden age of railways, and now it's one of
★ London's most sophisticated places to stay. **Pros:** unique and beautiful;
faultless service; close to the train station. **Cons:** very popular bar and
restaurant; streets outside are busy 24/7; some cheaper rooms don't
include free Wi-Fi. ⑤ *Rooms from: £237* ✉ *Euston Rd., King's Cross*
☎ *020/7841–3540* ⊕ *www.marriott.com/hotels/travel/lonpr-st-pancras-*
renaissance-hotel-london ⤵ *245 rooms* ❮◯❯ *Breakfast* Ⓜ *King's Cross St.*
Pancras. National Rail: Kings Cross, St. Pancras ✢ *2:C2.*

HOLBORN

$$$$ 🖼 **Rosewood London.** So striking it was featured in the movie *Howards*
HOTEL *End,* this landmark structure (built by the Pearl Assurance Company in
1914) now houses a beautiful hotel with a clubby atmosphere, subtly
elegant India Jane fabrics, and huge, comfortable beds. **Pros:** gorgeous,
romantic space; excellent restaurant; great spa. **Cons:** luxury comes at
a price; area is a ghost town at night and on weekends; the rooms can't
quite match the splendor of the public areas. ⑤ *Rooms from: £450*
✉ *252 High Holborn, Holborn* ☎ *020/7781–8888, 888/767–3966 in*
U.S. ⊕ *www.rosewoodhotels.com/en/london* ⤵ *306 rooms* ❮◯❯ *Break-*
fast Ⓜ *Holborn* ✢ *3:G3.*

$$ 🖼 **SACO Holborn.** Down a quiet backstreet, a 10-minute walk from
RENTAL the British Museum, these serviced apartments are spacious, modern,
FAMILY and extremely well-equipped, including a kitchen with dishwasher
and washing machine. **Pros:** more independence than hotels; pleasant and spacious accommodations; on-site parking. **Cons:** exterior is
dated; responsible for your own dining; the area is empty on weekends. ⑤ *Rooms from: £249* ✉ *Spens House, 72–84 Lamb's Conduit*
St., Holborn ☎ *0330/202–0505* ⊕ *www.sacoapartments.co.uk* ⤵ *32*
apartments ❮◯❯ *No meals* Ⓜ *Russell Sq.* ✢ *3:G1.*

FITZROVIA

$$$ 🖼 **The London Edition.** A solidly bohemian air permeates this handsome
HOTEL hotel in the heart of Fitzrovia, the second hotel in Ian Schrager's ven-
Fodor's Choice ture with Marriott. **Pros:** very trendy; great bars; beautifully designed
★ bedrooms. **Cons:** rooms may feel small to some; lobby can get crowded
with trendsetters descending upon the bars and nightclub; can at times
feel more like an events space than a hotel. ⑤ *Rooms from: £325* ✉ *10*
Berners St., Fitzrovia ☎ *020/7781–0000* ⊕ *edition-hotels.marriott.com/*
london ⤵ *173 rooms* ❮◯❯ *Breakfast* Ⓜ *Oxford Circus* ✢ *3:C3.*

$$$ 🖼 **Sanderson Hotel.** At this fashionable and surreal urban spa in a con-
HOTEL verted 1950s textile factory, the lobby looks like a design museum;

bedrooms have sleigh beds and a mix of over-the-top Louis XV and postmodern furnishings. **Pros:** popular with design mavens; your every whim gratified; unique afternoon tea. **Cons:** "designer cool" can be self-consciously hip; bar and restaurant are so exclusive it's hard to get in; you need to book far in advance to get lower rates. ⑤ *Rooms from: £292* ✉ *50 Berners St., Fitzrovia* ☎ *020/7300–1400* ⊕ *www.sanderson-london.com* ⤴ *150 rooms* ⦿| *Breakfast* Ⓜ *Oxford Circus, Tottenham Court Rd.* ✛ *3:B3.*

THE CITY

$$
⬚ Apex City of London. At this sleek, modern branch of the small Apex
HOTEL chain near the Tower of London, bedrooms are reasonably spacious, with contemporary color schemes, 40-inch flat screen TVs, and little sofas. **Pros:** great location; helpful staff; good advance booking discounts. **Cons:** geared more to business than leisure travelers; price can rise sharply during busy times; the neighborhood is hardly the most buzzing on weekends. ⑤ *Rooms from: £179* ✉ *1 Seething La., City of London* ☎ *020/7702–2020* ⊕ *www.apexhotels.co.uk* ⤴ *209 rooms* ⦿| *Breakfast* Ⓜ *Tower Hill* ✛ *2:G2.*

$$
⬚ Crowne Plaza London—The City. Don't let the hotel's all-business
HOTEL appearance put you off: it's a polished operation, with stylish minimalist rooms, just steps from the Blackfriars Tube and train station in one direction and bustling Fleet Street in the other. **Pros:** good rates available with advance booking; great location near the river and transport; two excellent dining options. **Cons:** neighborhood is super busy during the day and empty at night; breakfast not included in the price of rooms; rooms are all uncreatively decorated. ⑤ *Rooms from: £175* ✉ *19 New Bridge St., City of London* ☎ *0871/942–9190* ⊕ *www.cplondoncityhotel.co.uk* ⤴ *204 rooms* ⦿| *No meals* Ⓜ *Blackfriars* ✛ *2:F6.*

$$
⬚ Grange City Hotel. With an eye on business, this sleek City hotel has
HOTEL everything the workaholic needs to feel right at home: chic bedrooms subtly decorated, modern furnishings, and plenty of space (by London standards). **Pros:** good-sized rooms; rates can drop considerably on weekends; female-friendly rooms are great for lone female travelers. **Cons:** a bit off the tourist track; some rooms overlook train platform; prices can soar midweek. ⑤ *Rooms from: £142* ✉ *8–14 Cooper's Row, City of London* ☎ *020/7863–3700* ⊕ *www.grangehotels.com* ⤴ *307 rooms* ⦿| *Breakfast* Ⓜ *Tower Hill, Aldgate, Monument* ✛ *2:G2.*

$$
⬚ The Ned. Bursting with eye-catching art deco design and achingly hip
HOTEL interiors, the Ned is as close to the glamor of the 1920s Jazz Age as
Fodor's Choice you'll find in contemporary London. **Pros:** amazing variety of bars and
★ restaurants, all of high quality; rooftop pool with views of St. Paul's Cathedral; beautiful interiors in all rooms. **Cons:** location in The City means public spaces get very busy after work; neighborhood is deserted on weekends; also doubles as a private members' clubs, so the vibe can get snooty. ⑤ *Rooms from: £150* ✉ *27 Poultry, City of London* ☎ *020/3828–2000* ⊕ *www.thened.com* ⤴ *252 rooms* ⦿| *Breakfast* Ⓜ *Bank* ✛ *2:H5.*

15

$$ **The Rookery.** An absolutely unique and beautiful 1725 townhouse, the
HOTEL Rookery is the kind of place where you want to allow quality time to
Fodor's Choice enjoy and soak up the atmosphere. **Pros:** helpful staff; free Wi-Fi; good
★ deals in the off-season. **Cons:** breakfast costs extra; Tube ride to tourist
sites; no restaurant in the hotel. $ *Rooms from: £189* ✉ *12 Peter's La.,
at Cowcross St., City of London* ☎ *020/7336–0931* ⊕ *www.rookeryho-
tel.com* ⤳ *33 rooms* ⦿| *No meals* Ⓜ *Farringdon* ✛ *2:F4.*

$$ **Threadneedles Hotel.** The elaborate building housing this grand hotel
HOTEL in the financial district is a former bank, and the vast old banking hall—
beautifully adapted as the lobby, with luxurious marble and mahogany
panels—really sets the scene. **Pros:** lap of luxury; excellent service; a
good variety of drinking and dining options. **Cons:** a bit stuffy for some
tastes; can be at least three times more expensive weekdays; neighborhood is quiet at night. $ *Rooms from: £185* ✉ *5 Threadneedle St., City
of London* ☎ *020/7657–8080* ⊕ *www.hotelthreadneedles.co.uk* ⤳ *74
rooms* ⦿| *Breakfast* Ⓜ *Bank* ✛ *2:G2.*

$$ **The Zetter.** The five-story atrium, art deco staircase, and slick Euro-
HOTEL pean restaurant hint at the delights to come in this converted ware-
Fodor's Choice house—a breath of fresh air with its playful color schemes, elegant
★ wallpapers, and wonderful views of The City from the higher floors.
Pros: huge amounts of character; big rooms; free Wi-Fi. **Cons:** rooms
with good views cost more; the contemporary style won't appeal to
everyone; the property's best bar is across the street at the Zetter Town-
house. $ *Rooms from: £221* ✉ *86–88 Clerkenwell Rd., Clerkenwell*
☎ *020/7324–4444* ⊕ *www.thezetter.com* ⤳ *59 rooms* ⦿| *Breakfast*
Ⓜ *Farringdon* ✛ *3:H1.*

EAST LONDON

$$ **Ace Hotel London Shoreditch.** The first European outlet of the super hip
HOTEL Ace hotel chain fits right into the scenery in achingly cool Shoreditch,
surrounded by galleries and on-trend boutiques every bit as style con-
scious as its own creatively minimalist interiors. **Pros:** extremely fashionable; large and comfortable bedrooms; great bar. **Cons:** not everyone
will enjoy being surrounded by hipsters; street noise can be a problem; frustrating online booking system. $ *Rooms from: £149* ✉ *100
Shoreditch High St., Shoreditch* ☎ *020/7613–9800* ⊕ *www.acehotel.
com* ⤳ *258 rooms* ⦿| *Breakfast* Ⓜ *Shoreditch High St.* ✛ *2:G1.*

$$ **Andaz.** Swanky and upscale, this hotel sports a modern, masculine
HOTEL design, and novel check-in procedure—instead of standing at a desk,
guests sit in a lounge while a staff member with a tablet takes their
information. **Pros:** nice attention to detail; no standing in line to check
in; "healthy minibars" are stocked with nuts, fruit, and yogurt. **Cons:**
sparse interior design is not for all; rates rise significantly for midweek
stays; no pool in the hotel. $ *Rooms from: £241* ✉ *40 Liverpool St.,
East End* ☎ *020/7961–1234, 800/492–8804 in U.S.* ⊕ *www.andaz.
hyatt.com* ⤳ *269 rooms* ⦿| *Breakfast* Ⓜ *Liverpool St.* ✛ *2:G2.*

$$ **Cable Street Inn.** Wonderful modern art lines the walls of this former
B&B/INN Victorian pub a mile east of the Tower of London, which has been
Fodor's Choice beautifully restored and converted into a modern B&B. **Pros:** true one-
★ of-a-kind place; beautiful art; wonderful host. **Cons:** 20-minute journey

by DLR then Tube to the center; historic nature of the building makes it unsuitable for those with mobility problems; with only three rooms, availability can be low. ⑤ *Rooms from: £130* ⌧ *232 Cable St., East End* ☎ *020/7790–4019* ⊕ *www.cablestreetinn.co.uk* ↝ *3 rooms* ⑩ *Breakfast* Ⓜ *DLR: Shadwell* ✛ *2:H5.*

$$$
HOTEL

Courthouse Hotel – Shoreditch. Housed within a beautifully restored former courthouse, this hip Shoreditch hotel contributes its own contemporary flair to the grand architectural style of the original building, with chic rooms that provide the perfect base to explore the surrounding trendy neighborhood. **Pros:** great views over neighboring rooftops from the terrace; lively bar; excellent facilities including cinema and bowling alley. **Cons:** not all rooms are located in the historic former courthouse; a 20-minute tube ride into central London; the size and scope of the public spaces can lead to some areas feeling deserted. ⑤ *Rooms from: £260* ⌧ *335–337 Old St., Shoreditch* ☎ *020/3310–5555* ⊕ *www.shoreditch.courthouse-hotel.com* ↝ *128 rooms* ⑩ *Breakfast* Ⓜ *Old Street* ✛ *2:G1.*

$
HOTEL
Fodor's Choice
★

The Hoxton Shoreditch. The design throughout this trendy East London lodging is contemporary—but not so modern as to be absurd—and in keeping with a claim to combine a country-lodge lifestyle with true urban living, a fire crackles in the lobby. **Pros:** cool vibe; neighborhood known for funky galleries and boutiques; huge weekend discounts. **Cons:** price skyrockets during the week; away from major tourist sights; cheapest rooms are called "shoeboxes" for a reason. ⑤ *Rooms from: £119* ⌧ *81 Great Eastern St., East End* ☎ *020/7550–1000* ⊕ *www.thehoxton.com/london/shoreditch/hotels* ↝ *182 rooms* ⑩ *Breakfast* Ⓜ *Shoreditch High St.* ✛ *2:G1.*

$
HOTEL

Qbic London City. A contrast to the super expensive business hotels that proliferate in this part of the East End on the edge of The City, the Qbic is a modern and surprisingly affordable option in a trendy corner of town. **Pros:** quirky, original vibe; great value for money; environmentally friendly. **Cons:** bit out of the way; not everyone will love the style; cheapest rooms have no windows. ⑤ *Rooms from: £83* ⌧ *42 Adler St., East End* ☎ *020/3021–3300* ⊕ *www.qbichotels.com* ↝ *171 rooms* ⑩ *Breakfast* Ⓜ *Aldgate East* ✛ *2:H2.*

$$
HOTEL

Town Hall Hotel and Apartments. An art deco town hall, abandoned in the early 1980s and turned into a chic hotel 30 years later, is now a lively and stylish place, with the best of the building's elegant original features intact. **Pros:** beautifully designed; lovely staff; big discounts on weekends. **Cons:** the area is far from the major sights; a 15-minute Tube ride from Central London; some rooms choose style over function. ⑤ *Rooms from: £185* ⌧ *Patriot Sq., Bethnal Green, East End* ☎ *020/7871–0460* ⊕ *www.townhallhotel.com* ↝ *90 rooms* ⑩ *Breakfast* Ⓜ *Bethnal Green* ✛ *2:H1.*

SOUTH OF THE THAMES

$
HOTEL
Fodor's Choice
★

Church Street Hotel. Like rays of sunshine in gritty South London, these rooms above a popular tapas restaurant are individually decorated in rich, bold tones, and authentic Central American touches like elaborately painted crucifixes, tiles handmade in Guadalajara, and homemade iron bed frames. **Pros:** unique and arty; great breakfasts; closer

15

to central London than it might appear. **Cons:** would suit adventurous young people more than families; a mile from a Tube station (though bus connections are handier); some rooms have shared bathrooms. Ⓢ *Rooms from: £90* ✉ *29–33 Camberwell Church St., Camberwell, South East London* ☎ *020/7703–5984* ⊕ *www.churchstreethotel.com* ⤳ *31 rooms* ⦿ *Breakfast* Ⓜ *Oval St.* ✛ *5:H6.*

$ 🔲 **CitizenM London Bankside.** High-concept, high-tech, and supertrendy,
HOTEL the CitizenM chain has a unique selling point—nearly everything at the hotel is self-service, and that includes check-in and breakfast. **Pros:** great budget concept; stylish and modern; no waiting in line for checkout. **Cons:** only really qualifies as "budget" on certain nights (price is higher midweek); might be too much technology for some; rooms are compact. Ⓢ *Rooms from: £112* ✉ *20 Lavington St., Bankside* ☎ *020/3519–1680* ⊕ *www.citizenm.com/destinations/london/london-bankside-hotel* ⤳ *192 rooms* ⦿ *No meals* Ⓜ *Southwark* ✛ *5:G1.*

$$$ 🔲 **The LaLit London.** A stone's throw from City Hall and just down the road
HOTEL from Tower Bridge, this luxurious hotel plays on the building's former incarnation as a historic grammar school to create a unique boarding experience where rooms are known as "classrooms" and meeting spaces as "laboratories." The first international expansion from the India-based Lalit chain, it is an architectural dream, filled with striking wooden paneling and vaulted ceilings competing for attention. **Pros:** set in a beautiful historic building; close to the Tower of London and the Southbank; complimentary minibar in all rooms. **Cons:** basic rooms are much smaller than their more expensive counterparts; the Rejuve Spa doesn't have a pool; the junction outside can get noisy. Ⓢ *Rooms from: £310* ✉ *181 Tooley St., London Bridge* ☎ *020/3765–0000* ⊕ *www.thelalit.com/the-lalit-london* ⤳ *70 rooms* ⦿ *Breakfast* Ⓜ *London Bridge* ✛ *5:H2.*

$$ 🔲 **London Bridge Hotel.** Steps away from the London Bridge rail and Tube
HOTEL stations, and handy for the South Bank, this thoroughly modern, stylish hotel is popular with business travelers, but leisure travelers find it just as appealing. **Pros:** good location for visiting South Bank attractions; free Wi-Fi; good deals available online in the off-season. **Cons:** small bedrooms; prices rise by £100 or more midweek; the area is filled with crowds on evenings and weekends. Ⓢ *Rooms from: £144* ✉ *8–18 London Bridge St., Southwark* ☎ *020/7855–2200* ⊕ *www.londonbridge-hotel.com* ⤳ *141 rooms* ⦿ *Breakfast* Ⓜ *London Bridge* ✛ *5:H1.*

$$$ 🔲 **London Marriott Hotel County Hall.** This grand hotel on the Thames
HOTEL enjoys perhaps the most iconic view in the city—right next door is the London Eye, and directly across the Thames are the Houses of Parliament and Big Ben. Until the 1980s this building was the seat of London's government, and the public areas are suitably grand, full of pedimented archways, bronze doors, and acres of polished mahogany. **Pros:** handy for South Bank arts scene, London Eye, and Westminster; great gym; good weekend discounts. **Cons:** interior design can be overdone for some tastes; rooms facing the river cost extra; high summer midweek rates are just ridiculous. Ⓢ *Rooms from: £305* ✉ *London County Hall, Westminster Bridge Rd., South Bank* ☎ *020/7928–5200, 888/236–2427 in U.S.* ⊕ *www.marriott.com/hotels/travel/lonch-london-marriott-hotel-county-hall* ⤳ *206 rooms* ⦿ *Breakfast* Ⓜ *Westminster, Waterloo. National Rail: Waterloo* ✛ *5:D2.*

$$ ▦ **The Mondrian.** A quirky yet sophisticated addition to the burgeoning
HOTEL South Bank, the Mondrian is a fun callback to the area's docklands
Fodor's Choice history. Pros: excellent bars and restaurants; beautiful river views; short
★ riverside walk to Tate Modern and Shakespeare's Globe. Cons: river-
view rooms are pricey (of course); public areas, outside the lobby and
bars, are a little bland; standard rooms are small. $⑤ Rooms from: £192$
⊠ *Sea Containers House, 20 Upper Ground, Southwark* ☎ *020/3747–*
1000 ⊕ *www.morganshotelgroup.com/mondrian/mondrian-london*
➥ *359 rooms* ⎮⊙⎮ *Breakfast* Ⓜ *Blackfriars, Southwark* ✛ *5:F1.*

$ ▦ **Premier Travel Inn County Hall.** The small but nicely decorated rooms
HOTEL at this budget choice share the same County Hall complex as the fan-
FAMILY cier London Marriott Hotel County Hall, and though it has none of
the spectacular river views, and facilities are more basic, the selling
point is the same convenient location at a fraction of the price. **Pros:**
fantastic location for the South Bank; bargains to be had if you book
in advance; kids (sharing with adults) stay free. **Cons:** limited services;
cookie-cutter chain-hotel atmosphere; on a busy road. $⑤ Rooms from:$
£102 ⊠ *County Hall, Belvedere Rd., South Bank* ☎ *0871/527–8648*
⊕ *www.premierinn.com* ➥ *318 rooms* ⎮⊙⎮ *Breakfast* Ⓜ *Westminster,*
Waterloo. National Rail: Waterloo ✛ *5:D2.*

$$$$ ▦ **The Shangri-La Hotel, at The Shard.** With its floor-to-ceiling windows, the
HOTEL city's highest cocktail bar and infinity pool, and unrivaled views of the
Fodor's Choice London skyline from 1,016 feet above the South Bank of the Thames,
★ the Shangri-La has become one of London's most chic addresses. **Pros:**
matchless views; excellent service; superb restaurants and cocktail bar.
Cons: a design flaw corners allows some guests to see into their neigh-
bor's rooms at night; decor may feel cold to some; restaurant, bar, and
elevator often overcrowded due to popularity of the view. $⑤ Rooms$
from: £488 ⊠ *32 London Bridge St., South Bank* ☎ *0207/234–8000*
⊕ *www.the-shard.com/shangri-la/* ➥ *200 rooms* ⎮⊙⎮ *No meals* Ⓜ *Lon-*
don Bridge Station ✛ *5:H1.*

KENSINGTON, CHELSEA, KNIGHTSBRIDGE, AND BELGRAVIA

KENSINGTON

$$ ▦ **Ampersand.** A sense of style emanates from every surface of this sump-
HOTEL tuous hotel in the heart of Kensington, and the playful, vintage vibe
Fodor's Choice lends the property a refreshingly down-to-earth feel in a neighborhood
★ that can feel stodgy. **Pros:** flawless design; great service; good restaurant.
Cons: ground-floor rooms can be noisy; breakfast is not included in the
price of a room; the area swarms with tourists visiting the museums
on weekends. $⑤ Rooms from: £216$ ⊠ *10 Harrington Rd., Kensington*
☎ *020/7589–5895* ⊕ *www.ampersandhotel.com* ➥ *111 rooms* ⎮⊙⎮ *No*
meals Ⓜ *Gloucester Rd.* ✛ *4:D2.*

$$ ▦ **Ashburn Hotel.** A short walk from Gloucester Road Tube station and
HOTEL within walking distance of Harrods and the Kensington museums, the
Ashburn is one of the better "boutique" hotels in this part of town.
Pros: friendly atmosphere; free Wi-Fi; turndown gift (different every
night). **Cons:** summer prices sometimes hike the cost; some rooms on
the small side; no full restaurant. $⑤ Rooms from: £153$ ⊠ *111 Cromwell*

15

Rd., Kensington ☎ *020/7244–1999* ⊕ *www.ashburn-hotel.co.uk* ⤵ *38 rooms* ◉ *Breakfast* Ⓜ *Gloucester Rd.* ✛ *4:C2.*

$$ 🏨 **The Cranley Hotel.** Old-fashioned British propriety is the overall feel-
HOTEL   ing at this small, Victorian-townhouse hotel, where high ceilings, huge windows, and a pale, creamy color scheme flood the bedrooms with light. **Pros:** good-size rooms; attractively decorated; free evening treats (and champagne) are a nice touch. **Cons:** steep stairs into lobby; no restaurant; prices rise in midsummer. ⑤ *Rooms from: £204* ✉ *10–12 Bina Gardens, South Kensington* ☎ *020/7373–0123* ⊕ *www.cranleyhotel. com* ⤵ *39 rooms* ◉ *Breakfast* Ⓜ *Gloucester Rd.* ✛ *4:C3.*

$ 🏨 **easyHotel South Kensington.** London's original "pod hotel" has tiny
HOTEL   rooms with a double bed, private shower room, and little else—each brightly decorated in the easyGroup's trademark orange and white (to match their budget airline easyJet). **Pros:** amazing rates; safe and decent enough space; good location. **Cons:** not for the claustrophobic—rooms are truly tiny and most have no windows; six floors and no elevator; basic as basic can be. ⑤ *Rooms from: £39* ✉ *14 Lexham Gardens, Kensington* ⊕ *www.easyhotel.com* ⤵ *34 rooms* ◉ *No meals* Ⓜ *Gloucester Rd.* ✛ *4:B2.*

$$ 🏨 **The Gore Hotel.** Just down the road from the Albert Hall, this gor-
HOTEL   geous, friendly hotel has a luxurious mixture of the comfortable and
Fodor'sChoice the extraordinary. **Pros:** gorgeously designed and spacious rooms;
★   outstanding, attentive service; air-conditioning in all rooms. **Cons:** Wi-Fi is not free; bar can be noisy; a 10-minute walk to the nearest Tube station. ⑤ *Rooms from: £230* ✉ *190 Queen's Gate, Kensington* ☎ *020/7584–6601, 888/757–5587 in U.S* ⊕ *www.gorehotel.com* ⤵ *50 rooms* ◉ *Breakfast* Ⓜ *Gloucester Rd.* ✛ *4:D1.*

$ 🏨 **Kensington House Hotel.** A short stroll from High Street Kensington
HOTEL   and Kensington Gardens, this refurbished 19th-century townhouse has streamlined, contemporary rooms with large windows letting in plenty of light and comfortable beds with luxurious fabrics and soft comfort-ers. **Pros:** attractive design; relaxing setting; free Wi-Fi. **Cons:** rooms are small; bathrooms are minuscule; room decor might feel quite plain to some. ⑤ *Rooms from: £120* ✉ *15–16 Prince of Wales Terr., Kensington* ☎ *020/7937–2345* ⊕ *www.kenhouse.com* ⤵ *41 rooms* ◉ *Breakfast* Ⓜ *High Street Kensington* ✛ *4:C1.*

$$ 🏨 **London Marriott Kensington.** A big favorite for the business crowd,
HOTEL   this pleasant, modern outpost of the Marriott megachain is just one of several big-name hotels on busy Cromwell Road. **Pros:** friendly, effi-cient service; good neighborhood; one-minute Tube ride to Kensington museums. **Cons:** "could be anywhere in the world" business ambience feels impersonal; bedrooms are on the small side; not the most attractive location on busy Cromwell Road. ⑤ *Rooms from: £165* ✉ *147 Crom-well Rd., Kensington* ☎ *020/7973–1000* ⊕ *www.marriott.com/hotels/ travel/lonlm-london-marriott-hotel-kensington* ⤵ *216 rooms* ◉ *Some meals* Ⓜ *Earl's Ct., Gloucester Rd.* ✛ *4:B2.*

$$$$ 🏨 **The Milestone Hotel.** This pair of intricately decorated Victorian
HOTEL   townhouses overlooking Kensington Palace and Gardens is an inti-
Fodor'sChoice mate, luxurious alternative to the city's more famous high-end hotels,
★   offering thoughtful hospitality and sumptuous, distinctive rooms full

of antiques. **Pros:** beautiful and elegant; big rooms, many with park views; excellent location. **Cons:** actual room rate discounts are rare; luxury and elgance comes at a high price; some guests might find the decor a little over-the-top. $ *Rooms from: £408* ✉ *1 Kensington Ct., Kensington* ☎ *020/7917–1000* ⊕ *www.milestonehotel.com* 🛏 *62 rooms* ⚭ *Breakfast* Ⓜ *High Street Kensington* ✛ *4:C1.*

$
HOTEL
🏨 **Millennium Gloucester.** With a Tube station opposite and Kensington's many attractions nearby, this hotel is both convenient and alluring. **Pros:** great location; elegant design; good deals available if you book in advance. **Cons:** lighting in some bedrooms is a bit too subtle; bathrooms are relatively small; the modestly decorated rooms will appeal more to business travelers. $ *Rooms from: £122* ✉ *4–18 Harrington Gardens, Kensington* ☎ *020/7373–6030* ⊕ *www.millenniumhotels.co.uk* 🛏 *610 rooms* ⚭ *Breakfast* Ⓜ *Gloucester Rd.* ✛ *4:C2.*

$$
HOTEL
🏨 **The Nadler Kensington.** Known as an "aparthotel," this creamy white Georgian townhouse offers a useful compromise between full-service hotel and the freedom of self-catering in the form of comfortable rooms with a stylish, modern look and tiny kitchenettes. **Pros:** handy mini-kitchens; free Wi-Fi; 24-hour reception. **Cons:** basic rooms are small; movies in entertainment system are pay-per-view; 15-minute Tube ride to central London. $ *Rooms from: £129* ✉ *25 Courtfield Gardens, South Kensington* ☎ *020/7244–2255* ⊕ *www.nadlerhotels.com* 🛏 *65 rooms* ⚭ *No meals* Ⓜ *Earl's Ct.* ✛ *4:B3.*

$$$
HOTEL
Fodor's Choice
★
🏨 **Number Sixteen.** Rooms at this lovely luxury guesthouse, just around the corner from the Victoria & Albert Museum, look like they come from the pages of *Architectural Digest,* and the delightful garden is an added bonus. **Pros:** just the right level of helpful service; interiors are gorgeous; the afternoon tea is excellent. **Cons:** no restaurant; small elevator; the intimate nature of the small boutique hotel won't appeal to everyone. $ *Rooms from: £282* ✉ *16 Sumner Pl., South Kensington* ☎ *020/7589–5232, 888/559–5508 in U.S.* ⊕ *www.firmdale.com* 🛏 *41 rooms* ⚭ *Breakfast* Ⓜ *South Kensington* ✛ *4:D2.*

$$$
HOTEL
🏨 **The Pelham Hotel.** One of the first and most stylish of London's famed "boutique" hotels, this still-chic choice is but a short stroll away from the Natural History, Science, and Victoria & Albert museums. **Pros:** great location for museum-hopping; elegant interior design; lovely staff. **Cons:** taller guests will find themselves cursing the top-floor rooms with sloping ceilings; some rooms are on the small side given the price; some suites are only accessible via the stairs. $ *Rooms from: £280* ✉ *15 Cromwell Pl., South Kensington* ☎ *020/7589–8288, 888/757–5587 in U.S.* ⊕ *www.pelhamhotel.co.uk* 🛏 *52 rooms* ⚭ *Breakfast* Ⓜ *South Kensington* ✛ *4:D2.*

$
HOTEL
🏨 **The Rockwell.** Despite being on the notoriously traffic-clogged Cromwell Road, this excellent little place is one of the best boutique hotels in this part of London—and windows have good soundproofing. **Pros:** large bedrooms; stylish surroundings; helpful staff. **Cons:** on a busy road; 20-minute Tube ride to central London; street noise is a potential problem. $ *Rooms from: £109* ✉ *181 Cromwell Rd., South Kensington* ☎ *020/7244–2000* ⊕ *www.therockwell.com* 🛏 *40 rooms* ⚭ *Breakfast* Ⓜ *Earl's Ct.* ✛ *4:B2.*

15

CHELSEA

$$
B&B/INN
FAMILY

⊡ **At Home Inn Chelsea.** King's Road and the rest of superrich Chelsea is just a short stroll from this delightfully informal B&B, and you'd be hard pressed to find a better room in this neighborhood for the price. **Pros:** picturesque top floor terrace; short Tube ride to tourist sites; can be booked as a whole apartment. **Cons:** only accessible via the owners' own apartment's main entrance; few extras; only two guest rooms available. ⑤ *Rooms from: £125* ⊠ *5 Park Walk, Chelsea* ☎ *07790/844–008* ⊕ *www.athomeinnchelsea.com* ⬑ *2 rooms* ⦿⦿ *Breakfast* Ⓜ *Fulham Broadway* ✦ *4:D4.*

$$$
HOTEL
FAMILY
Fodor's Choice
★

⊡ **The Draycott.** This elegant yet homey boutique hotel near Sloane Square has become the stuff London dreams are made on—if your dream is to live like a pleasantly old-fashioned, impeccably mannered, effortlessly stylish Chelsea lady or gentleman. **Pros:** lovely traditional town house; great service; discreet and peaceful. **Cons:** no restaurant or bar; single rooms are very small; elevator is tiny. ⑤ *Rooms from: £282* ⊠ *26 Cadogan Gardens, Chelsea* ☎ *020/7730–0236* ⊕ *www.draycotthotel.com* ⬑ *35 rooms* ⦿⦿ *Breakfast* Ⓜ *Sloane Sq.* ✦ *4:F3.*

$$$
HOTEL
Fodor's Choice
★

⊡ **San Domenico House.** Discreet, beautiful, and exceptionally well run, this converted Chelsea town house makes for a restful hideaway. **Pros:** unique and beautiful design; great neighborhood, with the King's Road and Saatchi Gallery a short walk away; exceptional service. **Cons:** no bar or restaurant; not including a basic breakfast for the (pretty expensive) cheapest rates is cheeky; only some rooms have bathtubs. ⑤ *Rooms from: £254* ⊠ *29–31 Draycott Pl., Chelsea* ☎ *020/7581–5757* ⊕ *www.sandomenicohouse.com* ⬑ *19 rooms* ⦿⦿ *Breakfast* Ⓜ *Sloane Sq.* ✦ *4:F3.*

KNIGHTSBRIDGE

$$$
HOTEL

⊡ **The Beaufort.** This gracious boutique hotel is a favorite entry in the little black books of many a visiting high-society fashionista— Harrods is the merest toss of a diamond from the front door. **Pros:** gorgeous interiors; friendly and professional staff; free Wi-Fi. **Cons:** standard doubles are much smaller than the price might indicate; the sights of the West End are a 20-minute Tube ride away; no restaurant on-site. ⑤ *Rooms from: £312* ⊠ *33 Beaufort Gardens, Knightsbridge* ☎ *020/7584–5252* ⊕ *www.thebeaufort.co.uk* ⬑ *22 rooms* ⦿⦿ *Breakfast* Ⓜ *Knightsbridge* ✦ *4:F1.*

$$$
HOTEL
FAMILY
Fodor's Choice
★

⊡ **The Berkeley.** Convenient for Knightsbridge shopping, the very elegant Berkeley is known for its renowned restaurants and luxuries that culminate—literally—in a splendid penthouse swimming pool. **Pros:** lavish and elegant; attentive service; great drinking and dining options. **Cons:** you'll need your best designer clothes to fit in; even the cheapest rooms are expensive; while beautiful, the style is very traditional. ⑤ *Rooms from: £390* ⊠ *Wilton Pl., Knightsbridge* ☎ *020/7235–6000, 800/637–2869 in U.S.* ⊕ *www.the-berkeley.co.uk* ⬑ *190 rooms* ⦿⦿ *Breakfast* Ⓜ *Knightsbridge* ✦ *4:G1.*

$$$
HOTEL

⊡ **The Capital Hotel.** Nothing is ever too much at this elegant hotel that was formerly a private house; mattresses are handmade, sheets are 450-thread count, bathrooms are marble, and everything is done in impeccable taste. **Pros:** beautiful space; handy for shopping at Harrods; excellent restaurant. **Cons:** breakfast is expensive; cheaper rooms are small for the price;

neighborhood can be pricey. $Rooms from: £327 ✉ 22–24 Basil St., Knightsbridge ☎ 020/7589–5171, 800/926–3199 in U.S. ⊕ www.capit-alhotel.co.uk ↝ 49 rooms ⦿ Breakfast Ⓜ Knightsbridge ✦ 4:F1.

$$$
HOTEL
Fodor'sChoice
★

Egerton House. A sensationally soigné and chic space that feels like your own private London home, this hotel has some truly luxuriant design touches, including guest rooms lavishly decorated with rich fabrics and a knockout white-on-gold dining room. **Pros:** lovely staff; magnificent interiors; striking art. **Cons:** some style touches are a little too froufrou; sensory overload from the decor of some rooms; the tradi-tional elegance won't appel to everyone. $Rooms from: £275 ✉ 17–19 Egerton Terr., Knightsbridge ☎ 020/7589–2412, 877/955–1515 in U.S. ⊕ www.redcarnationhotels.com ↝ 28 rooms ⦿ Breakfast Ⓜ Knights-bridge, South Kensington ✦ 4:F2.

$$$$
HOTEL
Fodor'sChoice
★

The Lanesborough. Beautiful, traditional, and luxurious, the Lanes-borough is like a gilded cocoon for the seriously wealthy that exudes a spectacular richness, from the design-magazine perfection of the bed-rooms to the magnificent 19th-century antiques. **Pros:** beautiful and historic; great service; your wish is their command—there's even an in-house butler. **Cons:** prices are extraordinary; might be too fancy for some; Hyde Park Corner is often clogged with heavy traffic. $Rooms from: £587 ✉ Hyde Park Corner, Knightsbridge ☎ 020/7259–5599, 800/999–1828 in U.S. ⊕ www.lanesborough.com ▭ No credit cards ↝ 93 rooms ⦿ Breakfast Ⓜ Hyde Park Corner ✦ 4:G1.

$$$$
HOTEL
Fodor'sChoice
★

Mandarin Oriental Hyde Park. Built in 1880, the Mandarin Oriental welcomes you with one of the most exuberantly Victorian facades in town, then fast-forwards you to high-trend modern London, thanks to striking and luxurious guest rooms filled with high-tech gadgets. **Pros:** great shopping at your doorstep; amazing views of Hyde Park; excellent service. **Cons:** nothing comes cheap; you must dress for din-ner (and lunch and breakfast); located on a traffic clogged stretch of Knightsbridge. $Rooms from: £600 ✉ 66 Knightsbridge, Knights-bridge ☎ 020/7235–2000 ⊕ www.mandarinoriental.com/london ↝ 83 rooms ⦿ Breakfast Ⓜ Knightsbridge ✦ 4:F1.

BELGRAVIA

$$
HOTEL
Fodor'sChoice
★

Artist Residence. As packed with character and charm as they come, this artsy boutique hotel oozes bohemian sophistication. **Pros:** romantic and charming; close to Victoria Station; great staff. **Cons:** the wrong side of Victoria for most attractions; stairs to climb; the rustic chic won't appeal to more traditional tastes. $Rooms from: £230 ✉ 52 Cambridge St., Belgravia ☎ 020/7931–8946 ⊕ www.artistresidence-london.co.uk ↝ 10 rooms ⦿ Breakfast Ⓜ Victoria, Pimlico ✦ 5:A4.

$
B&B/INN

B&B Belgravia. At this modern guesthouse near Victoria Station, a clean, chic white color scheme, simple modern furniture, and a lounge where a fire crackles away in the winter are all geared to homey com-forts. **Pros:** nice extras like free use of a laptop in hotel lounge; coffee and tea always available; superb value for money in a vibrant area. **Cons:** rooms and bathrooms are small; can be noisy, especially on lower floors; great value means no frills. $Rooms from: £116 ✉ 64–66 Ebury St., Belgravia ☎ 020/7259–8570 ⊕ www.bb-belgravia.com ↝ 28 rooms ⦿ Breakfast Ⓜ Sloane Sq., Victoria ✦ 4:H2.

15

$$ **⛭ The Luna Simone Hotel.** This delightful and friendly little family-run
HOTEL   hotel, a short stroll from Buckingham Palace, is a real find for the price
in central London. **Pros:** friendly and well run; family rooms are out-
standing value; superb location. **Cons:** tiny bathrooms; thin walls; no
elevator or air-conditioning. *⑤ Rooms from: £145 ⊠ 47–49 Belgrave
Rd., Belgravia ☎ 020/7834–5897 ⊕ www.lunasimonehotel.com ⤳ 36
rooms ❘⊙❘ Breakfast Ⓜ Pimlico, Victoria ✛ 5:A4.*

$ **⛭ Studios@82.** A great little side operation from B&B Belgravia, these
RENTAL   self-catering apartments present a fantastic value. **Pros:** great rates;
lovely location; all the independence of self-catering. **Cons:** lots of stairs
and no elevator; check-in is at B&B Belgravia, six doors down the street;
can be subject to street noise. *⑤ Rooms from: £116 ⊠ 82 Ebury St.,
Belgravia ☎ 020/7259–8570 ⊕ www.bb-belgravia.com ⤳ 9 apartments
❘⊙❘ Breakfast Ⓜ Knightsbridge ✛ 4:H2.*

NOTTING HILL AND BAYSWATER

NOTTING HILL

$$ **⛭ The Main House.** A stay in this delightfully welcoming B&B feels more
B&B/INN   like sleeping over at a friend's house than a stay in a hotel—albeit
Fodor's Choice   a particularly wealthy and well-connected friend. **Pros:** unique and
★   unusual place; charming and helpful owners; room prices decrease for
longer stays. **Cons:** three-night minimum stay is restrictive; few in-house
services; no single night stays. *⑤ Rooms from: £150 ⊠ 6 Colville Rd.,
Notting Hill ☎ 020/7221–9691 ⊕ www.themainhouse.com ⤳ 4 rooms
❘⊙❘ Breakfast Ⓜ Notting Hill Gate ✛ 1:A4.*

$$ **⛭ The Portobello Hotel.** One of London's quirkiest hotels, the little Por-
HOTEL   tobello (formed from two adjoining Victorian houses) has attracted
scores of celebrities to its small but stylish rooms over the years, and the
decor reflects these hip credentials with joyous abandon. **Pros:** stylish
and unique; celebrity vibe; guests have use of nearby gym and pool.
Cons: all but the priciest rooms are quite small; may be too eccentric for
some; a 25-minute tube ride into central London. *⑤ Rooms from: £195
⊠ 22 Stanley Gardens, Notting Hill ☎ 020/7727–2777 ⊕ www.porto-
bellohotel.com ⤳ 21 rooms ❘⊙❘ Breakfast Ⓜ Notting Hill Gate ✛ 1:A5.*

BAYSWATER

$$ **⛭ Colonnade.** Near a canal filled with colorful "narrowboats" in the
HOTEL   Little Venice neighborhood, this lovely townhouse offers individually
styled rooms, some of which are split-level; others have balconies filled
with rich brocades, velvets, and antiques. **Pros:** beautifully decorated;
unique and little-known part of London, five minutes from Paddington
Station; free Wi-Fi. **Cons:** you have to go through shoddier parts of
town to get here; rooms are small; not the closest location for visiting
major sights. *⑤ Rooms from: £198 ⊠ 2 Warrington Crescent, Bayswater ☎ 020/7286–1052 ⊕ www.colonnadehotel.co.uk ⤳ 43 rooms
❘⊙❘ Breakfast Ⓜ Warwick Ave. ✛ 1:C2.*

$ **⛭ London House Hotel.** Set in a row of white Georgian townhouses, this
HOTEL   excellent budget option in hit-or-miss Bayswater is friendly, well run,
and spotlessly clean. **Pros:** friendly and efficient; emphasis on value;
good location. **Cons:** some public areas feel a bit too clinical; smallest

rooms are tiny; the area isn't quite as vibrant as neighboring Notting Hill. $ *Rooms from: £89* ⊠ *81 Kensington Garden Sq., Bayswater* ☏ *020/7243–1810* ⊕ *www.londonhousehotels.com* ⇕ *103 rooms* ❚❘❘ *Breakfast* Ⓜ *Queensway, Bayswater* ✛ *1:B4.*

$ ᵀ **Parkwood Hotel.** Just seconds from Hyde Park in one of London's
B&B/INN   swankiest enclaves, this sweet little guesthouse is an oasis of value, with warm and helpful hosts and bright guest rooms that are simply furnished with pastel color schemes and reproduction antique beds. **Pros:** lovely hosts; free Wi-Fi; hotel guarantees to match or beat rate of any other hotel of its class in the area. **Cons:** often booked up in advance; no elevator and no ground-floor bedrooms; front-facing rooms can be noisy. $ *Rooms from: £120* ⊠ *4 Stanhope Pl., Bayswater* ☏ *020/7402–2241* ⊕ *www.london-parkwood.com* ⇕ *16 rooms* ❚❘❘ *Breakfast* Ⓜ *Marble Arch* ✛ *1:F4.*

$$ ᵀ **Space Apart Hotel.** These studio apartments near Hyde Park are done in
RENTAL   soothing tones of white and gray, with polished wood floors and attractive modern kitchenettes equipped with all you need to make small meals. **Pros:** especially good value; the larger suites have space for four people; handy location. **Cons:** no in-house restaurant or bar; two-night minimum stay; standard apartments are small. $ *Rooms from: £160* ⊠ *36–37 Kensington Gardens Sq., Bayswater* ☏ *020/7908–1340* ⊕ *www.aparthotel-london.co.uk* ⇕ *30 rooms* ❚❘❘ *No meals* Ⓜ *Bayswater* ✛ *1:B4.*

$$ ᵀ **Vancouver Studios.** This pleasant aparthotel, in a converted Victorian
RENTAL   townhouse, is full of quirky design flourishes, from flock wallpaper in the sitting room to a suit of armor at the top of the stairs. **Pros:** more space than most traditional hotel rooms; unique and pleasantly designed little apartments; everything you need in your own private space. **Cons:** a bit out of the way; no meals included; a good base but the neighborhod isn't lively. $ *Rooms from: £149* ⊠ *30 Prince's Sq., Bayswater* ☏ *020/7243–1270* ⊕ *www.vancouverstudios.co.uk* ⇕ *48 studios* ❚❘❘ *No meals* Ⓜ *Bayswater, Queensway* ✛ *1:B4.*

REGENT'S PARK, HAMPSTEAD, AND ISLINGTON

REGENT'S PARK

$$ ᵀ **Meliá White House.** Converted from a beautiful modernist 1930s
HOTEL   apartment block, this stylish hotel is filled with nods to its prewar ori-
FAMILY   gins. **Pros:** great location near Regent's Park and Oxford Street; good restaurant; families are well treated—kids get a gift on arrival. **Cons:** classic rooms are small; the vast size means a stay lacks the intimacy of smaller hotels; bathrooms are generally tiny. $ *Rooms from: £185* ⊠ *Albany St., Regent's Park* ☏ *020/7391–3000* ⊕ *www.melia.com/en/hotels/united-kingdom/london/melia-white-house* ⇕ *700 rooms* ❚❘❘ *Some meals* Ⓜ *Great Portland St.* ✛ *1:H2.*

HAMPSTEAD

$ ᵀ **Glenlyn Guest House.** An excellent option for travelers who don't mind
B&B/INN   being a long Tube ride away from the action, this converted Victorian townhouse offers a high standard of accommodation a few miles north of Hampstead. **Pros:** comfortable and friendly; you get more for your money than you would in central London; five-minute walk to Tube

15

station. **Cons:** you have to factor in the cost and inconvenience of a half-hour Tube ride to central London; no in-house restaurant; room decor is simple yet uninspiring. $ *Rooms from: £90* ⊠ *6 Woodside Park Rd., Hampstead* ☎ *020/8445–0440* ⊕ *www.glenlynhotel.com* ⤸ *24 rooms* ⦿| *Breakfast* Ⓜ *Woodside Park* ✛ *1:D1.*

$
HOTEL
Fodor's Choice
★

⚏ **The Hide.** This cozy, chic little hideaway is exceptional value for money and exceeds virtually anything you could hope to find in central London for the price; the downside is that the half-hour Tube ride to and from town can be exhausting after a long day of sightseeing. **Pros:** excellent value; great service; free Wi-Fi. **Cons:** far from the center; somewhat dull neighborhood; no restaurant on-site. $ *Rooms from: £105* ⊠ *230 Hendon Way, Hendon, Hampstead* ☎ *020/8203–1670* ⊕ *www.thehidelondon.com* ⤸ *23 rooms* ⦿| *Breakfast* Ⓜ *Hendon Central* ✛ *1:H1.*

$
B&B/INN

⚏ **La Gaffe.** The name of this simple B&B means "the mistake" in Italian, and is also the punchline to the unlikely tale of how the original husband-and-wife proprietors met in the 1950s—but it also rather neatly chimes with the Cockney term "gaff," meaning a simple, cozy residence. **Pros:** unusual place with a cheerful atmosphere; great price; comes with the convenience of a traditional Italian restaurant below. **Cons:** few services; no elevator; outside city center. $ *Rooms from: £105* ⊠ *107–111 Heath St., Hampstead* ☎ *020/7435–8965* ⊕ *www. lagaffe.co.uk* ⤸ *18 rooms* ⦿| *Breakfast* Ⓜ *Hampstead* ✛ *1:D1.*

ISLINGTON

$
B&B/INN

⚏ **Arlington Avenue.** A find like this in London is quite rare: an immaculate, friendly, Georgian-townhouse B&B, full of character, not too far from the city center, *and* at a rock-bottom rate. **Pros:** genuinely stylish and comfortable; friendly hosts; cheap as you'll ever hope to find for a place this nice in London. **Cons:** really more of a private house with guest rooms than a B&B, which isn't to everyone's taste; shared guest bathroom; 20-minute commute into city center (including a long walk). $ *Rooms from: £60* ⊠ *Arlington Ave., Islington* ☎ *07711/265–183* ⊕ *www.arlingtonavenue.co.uk* ⤸ *2 rooms* ⦿| *Breakfast* Ⓜ *Angel, Essex Rd.* ✛ *2:D1.*

NIGHTLIFE

Updated by Alex Wijeratna

There isn't a London nightlife scene—there is a multitude of them. As long as there are crowds for obscure teenage rock bands, Dickensian-style pubs, comedy cabarets, and "bodysonic" dance nights, someone will create clubs and venues for them in London. The result? London has become a veritable utopia for excitement junkies, culture fiends, and those who—simply put—like to party.

Nearly everyone who visits London these days is mesmerized by the city's energy, which reveals itself in layers. Whether you prefer rhythm and blues with fine French food, the gritty guitar-riff music of Camden Town, the boutique beers of East London, a pint and a gourmet pizza at a local gastropub, or swanky cocktails and sushi at London's sexiest lair, London is sure to feed your fancy.

PLANNING

GETTING AROUND

London's nightlife has been given a big boost with five Night Tube lines serving central London (see ⊕ *www.tfl.gov.uk* for details) that run all night on Friday and Saturday, making getting home after a night out cheaper and easier than ever before. The rest of the network stops running around 12:30 am Monday through Saturday and midnight on Sunday. Night buses are largely safe and reliable but far slower than taxis, as you'd expect. The best place to hail a black taxi is at the front door of one of the major hotels; or find a licensed local minicab firm on the Transport for London website. Avoid unlicensed taxis that tout for business around closing time.

PUBS

Pubs are where Londoners go to hang out, see and be seen, act out the drama of life, and, for some, drink themselves into varying degrees of oblivion. The pub is still a vital part of London life, though many of the traditions of the pub experience are evolving. There are few better places to meet Londoners in their local habitat. There are somewhere around 4,000 pubs in London; some are dark and woody, others plain and functional, a few still have original Victorian etched glass, Edwardian panels, and art nouveau carvings.

Not long ago, before the smoking ban, pubs tended to be smoky, male-dominated places with a couple of ubiquitous beers on tap and the only available food a packet of salt-and-vinegar-flavor crisps (potato chips). All that has changed. Gastropub fever swept through London around the turn of the 21st century and at many places, char-grills are installed in the kitchen and inventive pub grub is on the menu. A new wave of enthusiasm for craft beers is now having a similar effect on the liquid offerings.

The big decision is what to drink. The beer of choice among Britons has traditionally been **"bitter,"** lightly fermented, with an amber color, and getting its bitterness from hops. It's usually served at cellar temperature (that is, cooler than room temperature but neither chilled, nor, as common misconception would have it, warm). **Real ales,** served from wooden kegs and made without chilling, filtering, or pasteurization, are flatter than other bitters and are enjoying a renaissance. Many small London breweries have sprung up in recent years, and bottled designer and American beers can be found in most bars across London. **Stouts,** like Guinness, are a meal in themselves and something of an acquired taste—they have a dark, caramel-infused flavor and look like thickened flat Coke with a frothy top. Chilled continental **lagers,** most familiar to American drinkers, are light in color and carbonated. ■TIP➔ The most commonly served lagers in Britain are from continental Europe.

16

Many English pubs are owned by chains such as Mitchells and Butlers, Punch Taverns, or Samuel Smith, and are tenanted, meaning that they are run on a sort of franchise basis. Most are not obviously branded and retain at least some independence. Independently owned pubs, sometimes called "free houses," tend to offer a more extensive selection of beer. Other potations available include apple-based **ciders,** ranging from sweet to dry and from alcoholic to very alcoholic (Irish cider, served over ice, is now also ubiquitous), and **shandies,** a mix of beer and lemonade. Friendly pubs will usually be happy to give you a taste of the brew of your choice before you order.

LIQUOR AND SMOKING LAWS

Laws now allow London drinking establishments to extend their opening hours beyond the traditional 11 pm closing, and smoking is banned. Most pubs and bars still close by midnight or a few short hours later.

CAN I TAKE MY KIDS TO THE PUB?

As pubs increasingly emphasize what's coming out of the kitchen alongside what's flowing from the tap, bringing the kids is more of an option. The law dictates that children ages 14–17 may enter a pub but are not permitted to purchase or drink alcohol, and children under 14 are not permitted in the bar area of a pub unless the pub has a "children's certificate" and the kids are accompanied by an adult. Some pubs have a section set aside for families, especially during the day, but many don't allow children in the evening.

WHAT TO WEAR

As a general rule, you won't see too many people in the upscale London nightspots wearing jeans and sneakers. People are more likely to dress down for an evening in the pub.

FIND OUT WHAT'S PLAYING WHERE

Because today's cool spot is often tomorrow's forgotten or closed venue, check the weekly listings in the *Evening Standard* (⊕ *www.standard. co.uk*) and especially *Time Out* (⊕ *www.timeout.com/london*). Other websites to consult are ⊕ *www.londontown.com* or ⊕ *www.allinlondon.co.uk*. Although most clubs are frequented by those under 30, there are plenty of others that are popular with patrons of all ages and types. One particularly useful website for clubs and club nights is ⊕ *www. residentadvisor.net*.

Door and bar staff are hawkish about underage drinking, so take photo ID with you on a night out.

NIGHTLIFE REVIEWS

WESTMINSTER, ST. JAMES'S, AND ROYAL LONDON

Elegant drinking holes catering to London's political and social elites abound in these central neighborhoods. Streets that are thronged with tourists and workers by day quiet down by evening, leaving the area to its few residents and a handful of sophisticated drinkers and diners.

WESTMINSTER

BARS

FAMILY **Cinnamon Club.** In the ground floor of what was once the Reading Room of the old Westminster Library, the book-lined Library Bar of this contemporary Indian restaurant (the curries are superb) has Indian-theme cocktails (mango mojitos, "Delhi mules"), delicious bar snacks, and a clientele that includes fashionable young politicos and apparatchiks. ⊠ *The Old Westminster Library, 30–32 Great Smith St., Westminster* ☎ *020/7222–2555* ⊕ *www.cinnamonclub.com* Ⓜ *St James's, Westminster.*

Fodor'sChoice **Gordon's Wine Bar.** Nab a rickety candelit table in the atmospheric, low-
★ slung brick vaulted cellar interior of what claims to be the oldest wine bar in London, or fight for standing room in the long pedestrian-only alley garden that runs alongside it. Either way, the mood is always cheery as a diverse crowd sips on more than 60 different wines, ports, and sherries. Tempting cheese and meat plates are great for sharing. ⊠ *47 Villiers St., Westminster* ☎ *020/7930–1408* ⊕ *www.gordonswine-bar.com* Ⓜ *Charing Cross, Embankment.*

ST. JAMES'S

BARS

FAMILY **American Bar.** Festooned with a chin-dropping array of club ties, signed
Fodor'sChoice celebrity photographs, sporting mementos, and baseball caps, this sen-
★ sational hotel cocktail bar has superb martinis and manhattans. The name dates from the 1930s, when hotel bars in London started to cater to growing numbers of Americans crossing the Atlantic in ocean

WHAT'S IN A NAME?

Pictorial signs traditionally helped illiterate customers identify establishments. The practice goes back to Roman times, with tavernas hanging vines outside to advertise the fact that they sold wine. The naming of pub and inns was widespread by the 12th century, and in 1393 King Richard II made it law for all pubs to display a sign, in order to make it easier for the official ale-taster to find the establishments he needed to visit.

The most common pub names offer an illustrated guide to Britain's past, with various monarchs, legends, and eras referenced in the colorful signs swinging above the doors of drinking dens all over the country. The Red Lion, for example, one of the most common pub names in use today, dates to the time when King James VI of Scotland became James I of the united kingdoms of England and Scotland and ordered that the heraldic lion of Scotland be displayed on all important buildings. Other pub names highlight the importance of specific events (the battle of Trafalgar), mythical figures (Robin Hood), and technological advances (the Railway).

In "pub cricket," a game traditionally played on long car journeys in the United Kingdom, players take turns at "bat." For each pub passed, the batter gets a score corresponding to the number of legs possessed by any beings that are part of the pub's name. For instance, passing the Swan gets you two points, because swans have two legs. The batter continues to accrue points until he or she is "batted out" by passing a pub with "head" or "arms" in its name (the Queen's Head, for example). The next player then takes over and the game continues until the end of the journey, when whoever has the highest score is declared the winner.

16

liners, but it wasn't until the 1970s, when a customer left a small carved wooden eagle, that the collection of paraphernalia was started. ⊠ *The Stafford, 16–18 St. James's Pl., St. James's* 🕾 *020/7493–0111* ⊕ *www. thestaffordlondon.com* Ⓜ *Green Park.*

MAYFAIR

Bars in this upscale central neighborhood—many of which can be found within luxury hotels—attract a polished crowd. Cocktails, fine wines, and rare aged spirits are the tipples of choice. Even the pubs tend to be as upscale as the people who frequent them, but you'll also find plenty of informal establishments with a lot of character.

BARS

Fodor's Choice
★

Claridge's Bar. This elegant Mayfair meeting place remains unpretentious even when it brims with beautiful people. The bar has an art deco heritage made hip by the sophisticated touch of designer David Collins. A library of rare champagnes and brandies as well as a delicious choice of traditional and exotic cocktails—try the Flapper or the Black Pearl—will occupy your taste buds. Request a glass of vintage Cristal in the darkly moody leather-walled 36-seat Fumoir. ⊠ *55 Brook St., Mayfair* 🕾 *020/7629–8860* ⊕ *www.claridges.co.uk* Ⓜ *Bond St.*

Fodor's Choice
★

Mr Fogg's Residence. Explorers of all stripes will be captivated by this Jules Verne–inspired townhouse cocktail parlor, which is chock-full of the weathered maps, hunting trophies, taxidermy, suspended Penny-farthings and *Around the World in 80 Days* globetrotting detritus of eccentric fictional Victorian British adventurer, Phileas J Fogg. Expect Victorian tipples and gin-based Afternoon "Tipsy teas" from staff in bow ties and waxed mustaches. ✉ *15 Bruton La., Mayfair* ☎ *020/7036–0608* ⊕ *mr-foggs.com* Ⓜ *Green Park, Oxford Circus.*

JAZZ AND BLUES

Jazz in London is highly eclectic. You can expect anything from danceable, smooth tunes played at a supper club to groovy New Orleans–style blues to exotic world-beat rhythms, which can be heard at some of the less central venues throughout the capital. London hosts the **London Jazz Festival** (⊕ *www.efglondonjazz-festival.org.uk*) in November, which showcases top and emerging artists in experimental jazz.

Fodor's Choice
★

Sketch. One seat never looks like the next at this downright extraordinary collection of esoteric living-room bars off Savile Row. The exclusive Parlour, a patisserie during the day, exudes plenty of rarefied charm; the intimate East Bar at the back is reminiscent of a sci-fi film set; and in the Glade it's permanently sunset in a forest. The space-age dinosaur egg-pod-shape restrooms are surely London's quirkiest. ✉ *9 Conduit St., Mayfair* ☎ *020/7659–4500* ⊕ *www.sketch.london* Ⓜ *Oxford Circus.*

PUBS

FAMILY

The Punch Bowl. In a quiet corner of Mayfair, the cozy little Punch Bowl has a worn wood floor and well-spoken staff. The pub dates to 1750 and the interior remains steadfastly old-fashioned, with a painting of Churchill, candles, polished dark wood, and engraved windows. Try the place's own ale, made specially in Scotland by Caledonian. A dining area at the rear buzzes at lunchtime with locals who come for the upscale English pub food, and there's a fancier restaurant upstairs. ✉ *41 Farm St., Mayfair* ☎ *020/7493–6841* ⊕ *www.punchbowllondon.com* Ⓜ *Green Park, Bond St.*

SOHO AND COVENT GARDEN

The center of town is famous for its vibrant gay scene, atmospheric music, cabaret venues, and acclaimed comedy clubs. Traditional British "boozers" stand side-by-side with informal continental-style drinking dens. Drop in for a late drink and you may find yourself rubbing shoulders with musicians and actors from the West End's many theaters. In Covent Garden, recent bar openings have also brought in some new buzz.

SOHO

BARS

Fodor's Choice
★

Bar Américain. The art deco interior of this underground bar just north of Piccadilly Circus is so opulent and glamorous that you'd be forgiven for thinking it had been here since the 1930s. In fact it's a relatively new arrival and has been a hit since it opened in 2012, along with the

Brasserie Zédel and racy Crazy Coqs Cabaret & Bar that share the premises. The cocktails aren't quite as imaginative or accomplished as they might be, but the beaux arts surroundings make up for what the drinks don't quite deliver. ⊠ *20 Sherwood St., Soho* ☎ *020/7734–4888* ⊕ *www.brasseriezedel.com* Ⓜ *Piccadilly Circus.*

Fodor'sChoice **The Blind Pig.** Chances are you won't have heard of half the ingredients
★ on the cocktail menu at this dark and sultry bar above Jason Atherton's smart casual restaurant, Social Eating House in Soho, but the sense of mystery only adds to the experience. So, too, do the antique mirrored ceilings and copper-topped bar, the delectable small plates (for instance, macaroni and cheese with shaved mushroom, and black pepper prawn crackers), and the knowledge that you've nabbed a seat at one of the coolest spots in Soho. ⊠ *58 Poland St., Soho* ☎ *020/7993–3251* ⊕ *www. socialeatinghouse.com* Ⓜ *Oxford Circus, Tottenham Court Rd.*

Fodor'sChoice **Experimental Cocktail Club.** It's easy to miss the unmarked shabby chic
★ black door with a scuffed wash of red paint on Chinatown's hectic main drag Gerrard Street, but once you finally find it and make your way past the hard-to-please doorman, you'll be in a secret three-floor speakeasy-style cocktail bar that is also one of London's coolest bars. With a lively crowd, creative cocktails, subtle lighting, and a DJ spinning smooth sounds, the vibe is laid back sexy Parisian cool. ⊠ *13A Gerrard St., Chinatown* ✛ *Look for unmarked scuffed black and red door* ☎ *020/7434–3559* ⊕ *www.experimentalcocktailclublondon.com* ▤ *£5 cover charge after 11 pm* Ⓜ *Leicester Sq., Covent Garden.*

Fodor'sChoice **Mark's Bar.** Knock back decidedly British cocktails (from age-old recipes)
★ like the Britz Spritz or a Full English Negroni or stick to the Punch Bowls, perfectly executed classic cocktails, or British ales at bon vivant Mark Hix's relaxed basement Soho haunt tucked below his modern British restaurant, Hix Soho. Clubby with Kilim rugs, suede poufs, a low bar, and large leather Chesterfields, first rate bar snacks include oysters, pork crackling with rhubarb sauce, and Scotch quail eggs. ⊠ *66–70 Brewer St., Soho* ☎ *020/7292–3518* ⊕ *www.hixrestaurants. co.uk* Ⓜ *Piccadilly Circus.*

COMEDY

Amused Moose Comedy. This roving West End comedy night group is often considered the best place to see breaking talent as well as household names doing "secret" shows. Ricky Gervais, Eddie Izzard, and Russell Brand are among those who have graced the Amused Moose stage, and every summer a handful of the Edinburgh Fringe comedians preview here. The bar is open late (and serves food), and there's a DJ and dancing after the show. Tickets are often discounted with a printout from their website, and shows are mainly on Saturday. ⊠ *The Water Rats theatre, 328 Grays Inn Rd., King's Cross* ☎ *020/7287–3727* ⊕ *www.amusedmoose.com* ▤ *£12 and up* Ⓜ *Tottenham Court Rd.*

Fodor'sChoice **The Comedy Store.** Before heading off to prime time, some of the United
★ Kingdom's funniest stand-ups cut their teeth here, at what's considered the birthplace of alternative comedy. Comedy Store Players, a team with six comedians doing improvisation with audience suggestions, entertain on Wednesday and Sunday; the Cutting Edge steps in with a

LONDON'S GAY SCENE

Gay nightlife is as busy as it is in New York or Los Angeles. Soho's the traditional hub, and "Voho," the previously unfashionable Vauxhall, south of the river, is one upstart area for gay London (though the vibe here can be pretty hardcore).

Clubs in London cater to almost every desire, whether that be the suited-up Tommy Hilfiger–look–alike scene, dingy dives for cruising, flamboyant drag shows, lesbian tea dances, or themed fetish nights.

There's also a cornucopia of queer theater and performance art that runs throughout the year. Whatever your tastes, you'll be able to satisfy them with a night on the town in London.

Choices are admittedly much better for men than women; although many of the gay clubs are female-friendly, those catering strictly to lesbians are rare.

The British Film Institute puts on BFI Flare: London LGBT Film Festival (⊕ www.bfi.org.uk/flare) in late March and early April every year.

Pride London in June (an annual event that encompasses a parade, sports, art, comedy, theater, music, cabaret, and dance) welcomes anyone and everyone, and claimed around 1 million participants in 2017. This extravagant 40,000-strong pageant spirals its way through London's streets, with major events taking place in Trafalgar Square and Leicester Square, and culminates in Victoria Embankment with ticketed parties continuing on afterward. See ⊕ www.prideinlondon.org for details.

For up-to-date listings, consult *QX Magazine* (⊕ www.qxmagazine.com) or *Boyz* (⊕ www.boyz.co.uk).

BARS, CAFÉS, AND PUBS
Most bars in London are gay-friendly, though there are a number of cafés and pubs that are particularly known as gay hangouts after-hours. The latest serve drinks until 3 am (11 pm on Sunday).

CLUBS
Many of London's best gay dance clubs can be found on particular nights in mixed clubs like Fabric.

topical take every Tuesday; and Thursday, Friday, and Saturday have the best stand-up acts. There's also a bar with food. You must be over 18 to enter. ⊠ *1A Oxendon St., Soho* ☎ *020/7024–2060 for tickets and booking* ⊕ *www.thecomedystore.co.uk* 🎟 *£15–£23.50* Ⓜ *Piccadilly Circus, Leicester Sq.*

GAY AND LESBIAN

Fodor's Choice **The Friendly Society.** An unremarkable-looking door in a Soho alleyway
★ leads down some dingy steps into one of the most fun LGBTQ joints in the neighborhood. Hopping with activity almost any night of the week, the place is known for its welcoming atmosphere to everyone, gay, trans, or straight. The interior alone—including garden gnome stools and a ceiling covered in Barbie dolls and disco balls—is enough to lift the spirits. ⊠ *79 Wardour St., Soho* ☎ *020/7434–3804* Ⓜ *Leicester Sq.*

The Shadow Lounge. This fabulous little lounge and dance club glitters with twinkling fiber-optics after an extensive makeover. It has a serious A-list celebrity factor, with the glamorous London glitterati camping out in the snug booths around the dance floor. Members are given priority to enter when the place gets full, especially on weekends, so show up early, book onto the guest list online, or prepare to wait in line. ☒ *5–7 Brewer St., Soho* ☎ *020/7317–9270* Ⓜ *Leicester Sq.*

She. This basement club, part of the popular Ku group of gay venues, is a recent arrival on the Soho scene. It welcomes a mostly young lesbian crowd for informal cocktails early in the evening followed by dancing—of the pop and house variety—later on. The vibe is fun and friendly, especially on the last Thursday of each month, when She hosts London's only drag-king open-mic night. ☒ *23A Old Compton St., Soho* ☎ *020/7437–4303* ⊕ *www.she-soho.com* 🎫 *£5 cover Fri. and Sat. after 9 pm* Ⓜ *Leicester Sq., Piccadilly Circus.*

The Yard. A corridor of kitsch leads to a surprisingly laid-back bar and spacious terrace at The Yard. This oasis of calm in the middle of Soho attracts a mixed, friendly crowd. ☒ *57 Rupert St., Soho* ☎ *020/7437–2652* ⊕ *www.yardbar.co.uk* Ⓜ *Piccadilly Circus.*

ECLECTIC MUSIC

100 Club. Since this small club opened in 1942, many of the greats have played here, from Glenn Miller and Louis Armstrong to the Who, the Damned, the Clash, and the Sex Pistols. Saved from closure in 2010 by a campaign led by Sir Paul McCartney, the space now reverberates to jazz, '60s R&B, and northern soul. ☒ *100 Oxford St., Soho* ⊕ *www.the100club.co.uk* 🎫 *£9–£24* Ⓜ *Oxford Circus, Tottenham Court Rd.*

Fodor'sChoice ★ **Phoenix Artist Club.** Nonmembers can gain free entry before 9 pm at this legendary West End open-mike musical theater, cabaret, impromptu arts review, brasserie, and late-night private members' club of boozed-up thespians, critics, Soho habitués, and chorus-line divas. You might catch a raunchy cabaret, see a Theaterland star jump up for the "Gotta Sing" Thursday night open-mike sessions, or be transported by the anecdotes of a fading one-time movie star raconteur. ☒ *1 Phoenix St., Soho* ☎ *020/7836–1077* ⊕ *www.phoenixartistclub.com* Ⓜ *Tottenham Court Rd.*

JAZZ AND BLUES

Ain't Nothin' But... This sweaty, fun place does exactly what its name suggests. Local blues musicians, as well as some notable names, squeeze onto the tiny stage and there's good bar food of the chili-and-gumbo variety. Most weekday nights there's no cover. ☒ *20 Kingly St., Soho* ☎ *020/7287–0514* ⊕ *www.aintnothinbut.co.uk* 🎫 *£7 cover Fri. and Sat. after 8:30 pm* Ⓜ *Oxford Circus.*

Fodor'sChoice ★ **Pizza Express Jazz Club (Soho).** One of the United Kingdom's most ubiquitous pizza chains also runs a leading Soho jazz venue. The dimly lighted restaurant hosts both established and emerging top-quality international jazz acts every night, with food available in the downstairs venue (as opposed to the upstairs restaurant) around 90 minutes before stage time. The Italian-style thin-crust pizzas are about what you'd expect from a major chain. ☒ *10 Dean St., Soho* ☎ *020/7439–4962 for club, 020/7437–9595 for restaurant* ⊕ *www.pizzaexpresslive.com* 🎫 *£16–£36* Ⓜ *Tottenham Court Rd.*

16

FodorśChoice **Ronnie Scott's.** London's best-known jazz club has attracted big names—
★   from Stan Getz to Count Basie and Ella Fitzgerald—since opening in
1959. It's usually crowded and hot, but the food and service are better
than they used to be. The mood can't be beat, even since the sad departure of the eponymous founder and saxophonist. Shows take place every
night, with additional late gigs on Friday and Saturday. Reservations
are recommended. ⊠ *47 Frith St., Soho* ☎ *020/7439–0747* ⊕ *www.ron-
niescotts.co.uk* 🖭 *£24–£46* Ⓜ *Leicester Sq.*

PUBS

FAMILY **The Dog and Duck.** A beautiful example of a late 19th-century London
FodorśChoice pub, the Dog and Duck has a well-preserved Heritage-listed interior
★   furnished with tiles, mirrors, and polished wood, though it's often so
packed that it's hard to get a good look. There's a decent selection of real
ales at the bar and a restaurant serving outstanding ale-battered fish-
and-chips. The cozy upstairs dining room is named for writer George
Orwell who frequented this spot. ⊠ *18 Bateman St., Soho* ☎ *020/7494–
0697* ⊕ *www.nicholsonspubs.co.uk* Ⓜ *Tottenham Court Rd.*

FodorśChoice **The French House.** In the pub where the French Resistance under Charles
★   de Gaulle convened during World War II, Soho hipsters and eccentrics
now rub shoulders with theater people and the literati—more than
shoulders, actually, because this tiny, tricolor-waving, photo-lined pub
is almost always packed. In the French style, beer is served in half-pints
only. If you're around on July 14, come and join in the rapturous Bas-
tille Day celebrations. ⊠ *49 Dean St., Soho* ☎ *020/7437–2477* ⊕ *www.
frenchhousesoho.com* Ⓜ *Leicester Sq., Tottenham Court Rd.*

COVENT GARDEN
BARS

Le Salon Bar. Renowned French chef Joël Robuchon's intimate, relaxed,
and elegant bar with black and red undertones is in the same location
as his restaurants, L'Atelier and La Cuisine. Set on the third floor and
with a hidden all-weather roof terrace, the drink and nibbles menu
changes regularly, with new flavors and textures sure to entice your taste
buds. ⊠ *13–15 West St., Covent Garden* ☎ *020/7010–8600* ⊕ *www.
joel-robuchon.com* Ⓜ *Leicester Sq.*

Terroirs. Specializing in "natural wines" (organic, unfiltered, and sustainably produced with minimal added ingredients), Terroirs has an
unusually careful selection of 220 wines from small French and Italian
artisan winemakers. These are served, along with delicious, relatively
simple dishes—charcuterie, tapas, and more substantial French-inspired
dishes—at a bar and bare oak tables surrounded by whitewashed walls
and wooden floors. Closed Sunday. ⊠ *5 William IV St., Covent Garden*
☎ *020/7036–0660* ⊕ *www.terroirswinebar.com* Ⓜ *Charing Cross.*

GAY AND LESBIAN

FodorśChoice **Heaven.** With the best light show on any London dance floor, Heaven
★   is unpretentious, loud, and huge, with a labyrinth of rooms, bars, and
live-music parlors. Thursday through Saturday nights it's all about the
G-A-Y club and comedy nights. Check in advance about live performances—they can take place any night of the week. If you go to just one
gay club in London, Heaven should be it. ⊠ *Under the Arches, Villiers*

St., Covent Garden ☎ *0844/847–2351 24-hr ticket line* ⊕ *www.heav-ennightclub-london.com* ◨ *£15–£21* Ⓜ *Charing Cross, Embankment.*

PUBS

FAMILY **Harp.** This is the sort of friendly flower-decked local you might find on some out-of-the-way backstreet, except that it's right in the middle of town, between Trafalgar Square and Covent Garden. As a result, the Harp can get crowded, especially because it was recently named British pub of the year by the Campaign for Real Ale, but the squeeze is worth it for the excellent beer and cider (there are usually 10 carefully chosen ales, often including a London microbrew, plus 10 ciders and perries) and a no-frills menu of high-quality British sausages, cooked behind the bar. ✉ *47 Chandos Pl., Covent Garden* ☎ *020/7836–0291* ⊕ *www. harpcoventgarden.com* Ⓜ *Charing Cross.*

Lamb & Flag. This refreshingly ungentrified 17th-century pub was once known as the Bucket of Blood because the upstairs room and front yard were used as a ring for winner-takes-all bare-knuckle boxing contests. Now it's a friendly (and *bloodless*) place, serving food and real ale. It's on the edge of Covent Garden, up a hidden alley off Garrick Street. ✉ *33 Rose St., Covent Garden* ☎ *020/7497–9504* ⊕ *www.lambandflag-coventgarden.co.uk* Ⓜ *Covent Garden.*

16

BLOOMSBURY, FITZROVIA, AND ISLINGTON

The gorgeous pubs of Bloomsbury attract tourists in the daytime and huge crowds of after-work drinkers in the early evening. They tend to quiet down as the night advances, making this a great spot for a relaxing night out. The redevelopment of the area around King's Cross St. Pancras station has especially invigorated the nightlife scene here. Fitzrovia, meanwhile, manages to blend sophistication, informality, and a certain edginess that's not found elsewhere in the center of town.

Exmouth Market and Upper Street are the main nightlife hot spots in Islington, just north and east of central London. The fun, informal bars here make it a reliable choice for going out.

BLOOMSBURY
PUBS

The Lamb. Charles Dickens and his contemporaries drank here, but today's enthusiastic clientele make sure this intimate and eternally popular pub avoids the pitfalls of feeling too old-timey. For private chats at the bar, you can close a delicate etched-glass "snob screen" to the bar staff, opening it only when you fancy another pint. ✉ *94 Lamb's Conduit St., Bloomsbury* ☎ *020/7405–0713* ⊕ *www.youngs. co.uk* Ⓜ *Russell Sq.*

FAMILY **Museum Tavern.** Across the street from the British Museum in Bloomsbury, this friendly and classy Victorian pub makes an ideal resting place after the rigors of the culture trail. Karl Marx unwound here after a hard day in the British Museum Library. He could have spent his *Kapital* on any of around 15 well-kept beers available on tap. ✉ *49 Great Russell St., Bloomsbury* ☎ *020/7242–8987* ⊕ *www.greeneking-pubs. co.uk* Ⓜ *Tottenham Court Rd., Holborn.*

FAMILY **The Queen's Larder.** The royal associated with this tiny pub is Queen Charlotte, who is said to have stored food here for her "mad" husband, George III, when he was being treated nearby. The interior preserves its antique feel, with dark wood and old posters, and in the evenings fills up quickly with office workers and students. In good weather, you might prefer to grab one of the seats outdoors. ✉ *1 Queen's Sq., Bloomsbury* ☎ *020/7837–5627* ⊕ *www.queenslarder.co.uk* Ⓜ *Russell Sq.*

HOLBORN

BARS

Fodor'sChoice **Scarfes Bar.** Settle in with Indian-inspired bar snacks and complimen-
★ tary nightly jazz and other entertainment at the Rosewood's impossibly glamorous Scarfes Bar—a cross between an Edwardian gentleman's library and a Downton Abbey baronial drawing room. Sit on sofas by a roaring log fire or sink into velvet armchairs and explore their collection of over 400 gins and 30 assorted tonics. Be sure to check out London-born artist (and the bar's namesake) Gerald Scarfe's paintings and political cartoons adorning the walls. ✉ *The Rosewood, 252 High Holborn, Holborn* ☎ *020/3747–8670* ⊕ *www.scarfesbar.com* Ⓜ *Holborn.*

PUBS

Fodor'sChoice **Princess Louise.** This fine, popular pub is an exquisite museum piece of
★ a Victorian interior, with glazed tiles and intricately engraved glass screens that divide the bar area into cozy little annexes. It's not all show, either. There's a good selection of excellent-value Yorkshire real ales from Samuel Smith's brewery. ✉ *208 High Holborn, Holborn* ☎ *020/7405–8816* ⊕ *www.princesslouisepub.co.uk* Ⓜ *Holborn.*

FITZROVIA

BARS

Artesian. They don't take reservations at this jewel box of a cocktail bar at the Langham Hotel, but you can order a drink while you wait for a chic mirror-top table surrounded by some of the most beautiful people in London. The cocktails—highly innovative creations involving ingredients like sandalwood, Mexican raicilla, and Japanese salt seasoning—are pricey, but service is top-notch, making this a nightlife experience that's hard to fault. After 6 pm it's for ages 18 and over only. ✉ *1C Portland Pl., Fitzrovia* ☎ *020/7636–1000* ⊕ *www.artesian-bar.co.uk* Ⓜ *Oxford Circus, Goodge St.*

Fodor'sChoice **The London Edition bars.** Visitors to Ian Schrager's London Edition hotel
★ are spoiled for choice when it comes to bars. High ceilings, eclectic artwork, and innovative cocktails can be found at the all-day Berners Tavern and in the Lobby Bar, which opens in the evening. You'll need a reservation to get into the cozy wood-paneled and open-fire Punch Room, but the bar's reinventions of traditional punches (the type favored by pirates and privateers) and the exemplary service are worth the extra effort. On the weekend there's dancing until late in the more informal Basement (guest list only; visit ⊕ *www.basementldn.com* for the current lineup). ✉ *10 Berners St., Fitzrovia* ☎ *020/7781–0000* ⊕ *www.editionhotels.com/london* Ⓜ *Tottenham Court Rd., Oxford Circus.*

ISLINGTON

BARS

69 Colebrooke Row. This elegant faux speakeasy must be London's tiniest cocktail lounge. Book one of the handful of tables or a seat at the diminutive bar to sample perfectly made twists on classic cocktails, like the panettone bellini, which uses a puree of the sweet Italian bread instead of peach. Staff are immaculate but approachable. ☒ *69 Colebrooke Row, Islington* ☎ *07540/528–593* ⊕ *www.69colebrookerow. com* Ⓜ *Angel.*

ECLECTIC MUSIC

Union Chapel. The beauty of this sublime old chapel and its impressive multicultural not-for-profit programming make this spot one of London's best musical venues, especially for acoustic shows. Performers have included Björk, Beck, and Goldfrapp, although now you're more likely to hear lower-key alternative country, world music, and jazz, alongside poetry and literary events, film screenings, and stand-up comedy gigs. ☒ *Union Chapel, Compton Terr., Islington* ☎ *020/7226–1686 for venue (no box office; ticket sales numbers vary with each event)* ⊕ *www.unionchapel.org.uk* ✉ *Free–£35* Ⓜ *Highbury & Islington.*

CLERKENWELL AND THE CITY

Workers from The City's many finance firms pour into the neighborhood's pubs at the end of the day, but by 8 pm the party is pretty much over and you'll have no trouble finding a place to sit. It's always worth ducking down a side street, as this is where some of the area's most interesting drinking establishments can be found.

BARS

Café Kick. This homey Iberian-vibe café and sports bar on Exmouth Market is open all day for meals, snacks, coffee, and cocktails. Decked with vintage football paraphernalia, it's famous for its foosball tables, which give the place a fun, informal environment. Deals are available on "cocktails of the month" and house beers during happy hour (4–7). You can reserve foosball tables in advance. There's a branch in Shoreditch. ☒ *43 Exmouth Market, Clerkenwell* ☎ *020/7837–8077* ⊕ *www.cafe-kick.co.uk* Ⓜ *Angel.*

PUBS

FAMILY

Fodor's Choice

★

The Blackfriar. A step from Blackfriars Tube station, this spectacular pub has an Arts and Crafts interior that is entertainingly, satirically ecclesiastical, with inlaid mother-of-pearl, wood carvings, stained glass, and marble pillars all over the place. Under finely lettered temperance tracts on view just below the reliefs of monks, fairies, and friars, there is a nice group of ales on tap from independent brewers. The 20th-century poet Sir John Betjeman once led a successful campaign to save the pub from demolition. ☒ *174 Queen Victoria St., City of London* ☎ *020/7236–5474* ⊕ *www.nicholsonspubs.co.uk* Ⓜ *Blackfriars.*

Craft Beer Co. With 37 beers on tap and 350 more in bottles (one brewed exclusively for the Craft Beer Company), the main problem here is knowing where to start. Luckily, friendly and knowledgeable staff are happy to advise or give tasters—or why not sign up for a guided tasting

16

session? A huge chandelier and a mirrored ceiling lend antique charm to the interior, and a smattering of tourists and beer pilgrims break up the crowds of Leather Lane workers and locals. ⊠ *82 Leather La., Clerkenwell* ☎ *020/7404–7049* ⊕ *www.thecraftbeerco.com* Ⓜ *Chancery La.*

FAMILY

Fodor's Choice

★

Jerusalem Tavern. Owned by the well-respected St. Peter's Brewery in Suffolk, the Jerusalem Tavern is one-of-a-kind: small, historic, and endearingly eccentric. Ancient Delft-style tiles meld with wood and concrete in a converted watchmaker and jeweler's shop dating back to the 18th century. The beer, both bottled and on tap, is some of the best available anywhere in London. It's loved by Londoners and is often busy, especially after work. ⊠ *55 Britton St., Clerkenwell* ☎ *020/7490–4281* ⊕ *www.stpetersbrewery.co.uk/london-pub* Ⓜ *Farringdon.*

The Viaduct Tavern. Queen Victoria opened the nearby Holborn Viaduct in 1869, and this eponymous pub honored the road bridge by serving its first pint the same year. Much of the Victorian decoration is still extant, with gorgeous paintings (depicting the statues on the viaduct), carved wood, and engraved glass. The tavern has a haunted reputation, which stems from its proximity to the former Newgate Prison and its gallows. What are said to be former debtors' prison cells in the basement can be seen with a free tour when staff aren't busy with customers. There are usually three or four ales on tap; lunch is also served. ⊠ *126 Newgate St., City of London* ☎ *020/7600–1863* ⊕ *www.viaducttavern.co.uk* ⊙ *Closed weekends* Ⓜ *St. Paul's.*

Fodor's Choice

★

Ye Olde Cheshire Cheese. Yes, this extremely historic pub (it dates to 1667, the year after the Great Fire of London) on Fleet Street is full of tourists, but it deserves a visit for its sawdust-covered floors, low wood-beam ceilings, and the 14th-century crypt of Whitefriars' Carmelite monastery under the cellar bar. This was the most regular of Dr. Johnson's and Charles Dickens's many locals. Food is served in the Chop Room— one of London's earliest steak houses. ⊠ *145 Fleet St., City of London* ☎ *020/7353–6170* ⊙ *Closed Sun. from 4* Ⓜ *Blackfriars.*

FAMILY

Fodor's Choice

★

Ye Olde Mitre. Hidden off the side of 8 Hatton Gardens (and notoriously hard to find), this cozy pub's roots go back to 1546, though it was rebuilt around 1782. Originally built for the staff of the Bishop of Ely, whose London residence was next door, it remained officially part of Cambridgeshire until the 20th century. Elizabeth I was once spotted dancing round a cherry tree here with a dashing young beau. Now it's a friendly little labyrinthine place, with a fireplace, well-kept ales, wooden beams, and traditional bar snacks. ⊠ *1 Ely Ct., City of London* ✦ *Off 8 Hatton Gardens* ☎ *020/7405–4751* ⊕ *www.yeoldemitreholburn.co.uk* ⊙ *Closed weekends* Ⓜ *Chancery La.*

Ye Olde Watling. This busy corner pub has been rebuilt at least three times since 1666. One of its incarnations was as the drawing office for Sir Christopher Wren, who used it while building nearby St. Paul's Cathedral. The ground floor is a laid-back pub, while upstairs houses an atmospheric restaurant, complete with wooden beams and trestle tables, with a basic English pub menu. ⊠ *29 Watling St., City of London* ☎ *020/7248–8935* ⊕ *www.nicholsonspubs.co.uk* Ⓜ *Mansion House.*

EAST LONDON

East London's bar scene is ever evolving, with the trendy crowd constantly pushing farther east in search of the next big thing. Shoreditch has bars and clubs to suit nearly all tastes these days, while Dalston, the neighborhood to its north, attracts an edgier, younger clientele. In historic neighborhoods such as Spitalfields and Wapping, there's a cozy old drinking den around practically every corner.

BARS

Birthdays. Dalston is probably London's hippest neighborhood for nightlife right now. This stark, industrial bar near the top of the main drag is as hot as it gets. Join the youngish crowd for craft beers and high-end burgers. There's a club in the basement that hosts DJs and live gigs. ✉ *33–35 Stoke Newington Rd., Dalston* ☎ *020/7923–1680* ⊕ *www.birthdaysdalston.com* 🍴 *Bar free, club £6–£13* Ⓜ *Overground: Dalston Kingsland, Dalston Junction.*

DANCE CLUBS

Cargo. Housed under a series of old railroad arches, this spacious brick-wall bar, restaurant, dance floor, and live-music venue pulls a young, international crowd with its hip vibe and diverse selection of music. Long tables bring people together, as does the food, which draws on global influences and is served tapas-style. Drinks are expensive. There's a Banksy in the garden. ✉ *83 Rivington St., Shoreditch* ☎ *020/7739–3440* ⊕ *www.cargo-london.com* 🍴 *Free–£20* Ⓜ *Old St.*

XOYO. Big international DJs regularly play this cool Shoreditch spot that's on a small side street off the main drag. The interior is industrial chic, with some banquet seating in the relaxed upstairs room and a downstairs that's a bit more hardcore. A youngish crowd dances the night away on the weekend, while weeknight live gigs attract a more diverse bunch. ✉ *32–37 Cowper St., Shoreditch* ☎ *020/7354–9993* ⊕ *www.xoyo.co.uk* 🍴 *Club nights £13–£22; gig ticket prices vary* Ⓜ *Old St.*

ECLECTIC MUSIC

Fodor's Choice ★ **Cafe Oto.** A relaxed café by day, and London's leading venue for experimental music by night, Cafe Oto is a Dalston institution. Its programming of free jazz, avant-garde electronica, and much more is enough of a draw that it regularly sells out, with music fans steaming up the windows and spilling out onto the pavement and road outside to smoke in the breaks. Healthy Japanese food is served in the daytime, before customers are kicked out at 5:30 pm to make way for sound checks. It's open as a bar (no cover) on nights when no concerts are taking place. ✉ *18–22 Ashwin St., Dalston* ⊕ *www.cafeoto.co.uk* 🍴 *Café free, concerts free–£30* Ⓜ *Overground: Dalston Junction.*

PUBS

Fodor's Choice ★ **Callooh Callay.** Cocktails are tasty, well-executed classics and a selection of unique instant-classics at this eccentric Hoxton bar where the bells and whistles are left to the decor. There's a secret hidden bar accessed Narnia-like through a wardrobe and an upstairs rock-themed 'Palace of Humbug' bar where VLPs (Very Lovely People) can hide away. ✉ *65 Rivington St., Hoxton* ☎ *020/7739–4781* ⊕ *www.calloohcallaybar.com* Ⓜ *Old St.*

16

Fodor's Choice   **Nightjar.** The feel is moody, Prohibition-era '20s Chicago at this fabu-
★   lously low-lit tin-tiled ceiling speakeasy and basement jazz cocktail bar
in Shoreditch. Book a table or chance it on the door at this no-standing
venue, where live jazz and wing bands nightly keeps things lively. ☒ *129
City Rd., Hoxton* ☎ *020/7253–4101* ⊕ *www.barnightjar.com* 🖂 *£5–£8
music cover charge* Ⓜ *Old St.*

Fodor's Choice   **Prospect of Whitby.** Named after a ship, this is one of London's oldest river-
★   side pubs, dating to around 1520. Although a regular for Dickens, Pepys,
Samuel Johnson, and the American artist James Whistler, once upon a
time it was called the Devil's Tavern because of the lowlifes—thieves
and smugglers—who congregated here. With a 400-year-old flagstone
floor and ornamented with pewter ware and nautical objects, this much-
loved "boozer" has a terrace with views of the Thames, from where boat
trips often point it out. ☒ *57 Wapping Wall, East End* ☎ *020/7481–1095*
⊕ *www.greeneking-pubs.co.uk* Ⓜ *Wapping. DLR: Shadwell.*

The Ten Bells. Although the number of bells in its name have varied
between 8 and 12, depending on how many bells were used by neighboring Christ Church, Spitalfields, this pub retains it original mid-Vic-
torian interior and original tiles, including a frieze depicting the area's
Huguenot weaving tradition on the north wall and particularly fine
floral tiling on two others. Urban legend has it Jack the Ripper's third
victim, Annie Chapman, had a drink here before meeting her gory end.
The pub is depicted in Alan Moore's acclaimed graphic novel *From
Hell.* ☒ *84 Commerical St., Spitalfields* ☎ *020/7247–7542* ⊕ *www.ten-
bells.com* Ⓜ *Liverpool St.*

Worship Street Whistling Stop. Sip back in time to 19th-century London with craft beers and bitters-loaded "ginaissance" cocktails from
London's young independent distillers in this Dickensian cocktail-
lab-meets-gin-palace in Shoreditch. Descend the narrow staircase to a
charisma-filled Victorian saloon kitted out with glazed wood panelling,
exposed brickwork, various Victoriana, and mismatched 19th-century
furniture. ☒ *63 Worship St., Shoreditch* ☎ *020/7274–0015* ⊕ *www.
whistlingshop.com* Ⓜ *Liverpool St., Old St.*

SOUTH OF THE THAMES

Recent years have seen an explosion in South London nightlife, including the gentrification of Brixton, the artistic colonization of Peckham,
and the continuing popularity of Vauxhall's gay clubs. Head to the area
around Borough Market—one of London's oldest neighborhoods—for
lively historic pubs where locals and tourists jostle for craft ales and
gourmet snacks.

BARS

Fodor's Choice   **Aqua Shard.** This classy bar on level 31 of the Shard, London's new
★   skyscraper and the tallest building in the United Kingdom (fourth in
Europe), is worth a visit for the phenomenal views alone. The cocktail
list is pretty special, too—big on fruit purees and unusual bitters. No
reservations are taken in the bar, so be prepared to wait during busy
periods. ☒ *The Shard, 31 St. Thomas St., Level 31, London Bridge*
☎ *020/3011–1256* ⊕ *www.aquashard.co.uk* Ⓜ *London Bridge.*

Dogstar. This popular South London hangout was here years before Brixton's hipster renaissance and is still going strong today. The vibe is unpretentious, with top-name DJs playing cutting-edge sounds Thursday to Saturday in the main bar, comedy and cabaret upstairs, and pizza available until late. ✉ *389 Coldharbour La., Brixton* ☎ *020/7733–7515* ⊕ *www. dogstarbrixton.com* ✉ *£6 cover Fri. and Sat. after 10 pm* Ⓜ *Brixton.*

Fodor's Choice
★

Three Eight Four. Epitomizing a new breed of Brixton bar, Three Eight Four mixes up inventive cocktails. The menu changes seasonally but always involves boutique spirits and unusual mixing techniques—try the Nightshade, which comes with a pipette that you use to add the final ingredient (crème de cassis) yourself. Bare lightbulbs and brick walls seem to be the style of choice for lots of cool London bars these days, but this place manages it with particular panache. A delectable selection of small dishes is also available. ✉ *384 Coldharbour La., Brixton* ☎ *020/3417–7309* ⊕ *www.threeeightfour.com* Ⓜ *Brixton.*

DANCE CLUBS

Ministry of Sound. This is more of an industry than a club, with its own record label, online radio station, and international DJs. Though it's too much a part of the establishment these days to be at the forefront of cool, the stripped-down warehouse-style club has a super sound system and still pulls in the world's most legendary names in dance. There are chill-out rooms, four bars, four dance floors, and a spacious smoking area with its own snack bar. ✉ *103 Gaunt St., Borough* ☎ *020/7740– 8600* ⊕ *www.ministryofsound.com* ✉ *£16–£25* Ⓜ *Elephant & Castle.*

PUBS

FAMILY
Fodor's Choice
★

The George Inn. Shakespeare drank in what is now London's last remaining galleried inn and Dickens featured the place in *Little Dorrit*. Now owned by the National Trust, the George Inn has a cobblestone courtyard where Shakespeare's plays were regularly performed; inside several small, completely untouched 18th-century low-ceilinged rooms lead to a so-so restaurant and the cozy Parliament Bar. ✉ *77 Borough High St., South Bank* ☎ *020/7407–2056* ⊕ *www.george-southwark.co.uk* Ⓜ *London Bridge.*

FAMILY
Fodor's Choice
★

The Market Porter. Opposite the foodie treasures of Borough Market, this atmospheric pub opens at 6 am (weekdays) for the stallholders, and always seems busy. Remarkably, the place manages to remain relaxed, with helpful staff and happy customers spilling out onto the road right through the year. The wide selection of real ales is lovingly tended (and you'll find an astonishing number of pump badges and beer mats covering the ceiling and walls). The pub was transformed into the set of the "Third Hand Emporium" in *Harry Potter and the Prisoner of Azkaban*. ✉ *9 Stoney St., Borough* ☎ *020/7407–2495* ⊕ *www.market-taverns.co.uk* Ⓜ *London Bridge.*

FAMILY
Fodor's Choice
★

The Mayflower. This deeply atmospheric 17th-century riverside inn (rebuilt in the following century) has exposed beams, model tall masts, and a terrace near the onetime berth of the famous ship on which the Pilgrims sailed in 1620 to what became the American colonies. The pub has a heated jetty where customers can sit outside; alternatively, opt to enjoy the ancient wood-beam interiors, although this can get

16

quite packed with sightseers. Those with family connections are invited to sign "The Mayflower Descendants" book. ⊠ *117 Rotherhithe St., South East London* ☎ *020/7237–4088* ⊕ *www.mayflowerpub.co.uk* Ⓜ *Overground: Rotherhithe.*

Fodor'sChoice **O2 Academy Brixton.** This legendary Brixton music venue has seen it
★   all—mods and rockers, hippies and punks—and it remains one of the city's top indie and rock venues. Despite a capacity for almost 5,000, this refurbished Victorian hall with original art deco fixtures retains a clublike charm; it has plenty of bars and upstairs seating. ⊠ *211 Stockwell Rd., Brixton* ☎ *020/7771–3000 for box office* ⊕ *www.o2academy-brixton.co.uk* ⌕ *£15–£50* Ⓜ *Brixton.*

CHELSEA, KNIGHTSBRIDGE, AND BELGRAVIA

The pages of society magazines are full of photographs of gorgeous young people dancing the night away at clubs—many of which are members only—in these famously swanky neighborhoods. Dress up and be prepared to splurge. Pubs here range from classy modern affairs with impressive wine lists and shared plates to tiny local institutions guaranteed to make you feel like you've stepped back into time.

CHELSEA

JAZZ AND BLUES

FAMILY   **606 Club.** This Chelsea jazz club has been doing things speakeasy-style since long before it became a nightlife trend in London. Buzz the door and you'll find a basement venue showcasing mainstream and contemporary jazz by well-known U.K.-based musicians. You must eat a meal in order to consume alcohol, so allow for an extra £30. Reservations are advisable. Lunchtime jazz takes place on select Sundays; call ahead. ⊠ *90 Lots Rd., Chelsea* ☎ *020/7352–5953* ⊕ *www.606club. co.uk* ⌕ *£10–£12 music charge added to bill* Ⓜ *Fulham Broadway. Overground: Imperial Wharf.*

PUBS

FAMILY   **The Anglesea Arms.** This traditional, family-friendly pub has a large terrace out front that's ideal for resting your weary feet after a shopping spree on the King's Road or a culture-packed afternoon at the museums of South Kensington. A menu of pub-grub classics, plus fancier dishes like fresh fish or shoulder of lamb, is available both in the bar and in the more refined dining room upstairs. You'll find six lovingly tended ales on tap, and a wine list with a largely French focus. ⊠ *15 Selwood Terr., Chelsea* ☎ *020/7373–7960* ⊕ *www.angleseaarms.com* Ⓜ *South Kensington.*

KNIGHTSBRIDGE

BARS

The Blue Bar at the Berkeley Hotel. With low-slung dusty-blue walls and Edwardian plasterwork, this black onyx hotel bar at the Berkeley is ever so slightly sexy. Immaculate service, an excellent seasonal cocktail list and a trendy David Collins design make this an ideal spot for a romantic tête-à-tête, complete with jazzy music in the background. ⊠ *The Berkeley, Wilton Pl., Knightsbridge* ☎ *020/7235–6000* ⊕ *www. the-berkeley.co.uk* Ⓜ *Knightsbridge, Hyde Park Corner.*

BELGRAVIA

PUBS

FAMILY **The Grenadier.** Established in 1720, the building was originally the officers' mess for the First Royal Regiment of Foot Guards whose barracks were next door. Opened as a pub in 1818 and renamed after the Grenadier Guards, now it's adorned with antique Guards cartoons and memorabilia, and *may* be haunted by a subaltern named Cedric. Tricky to find off a majestic stucco square, turn up on the annual Regimental Remembrance Day for a colorful army veterans' gathering. ✉ *18 Wilton Row, Belgravia* ☎ *020/7235–3074* ⊕ *www.greeneking-pubs.co.uk* Ⓜ *Knightsbridge, Hyde Park Corner.*

FAMILY
Fodor's Choice
★

The Nag's Head. The landlord of this idiosyncratic little mews pub in Belgravia runs a tight ship, and no cellphones are allowed. The lovingly collected artifacts (including antique penny arcade games) that decorate every inch of the place, high-quality beer, and old-fashioned pub grub should provide more than enough distraction. ✉ *53 Kinnerton St., Belgravia* ☎ *020/7235–1135* Ⓜ *Knightsbridge, Hyde Park Corner.*

NOTTING HILL

16

The focus is more on bars than clubs in this West London neighborhood, although late-night fun is on offer at a few notable exceptions. In general, you can expect a young, moneyed crowd making this their first stop on a wild night out elsewhere. The line between pub and bar is frequently blurred here, with an emphasis on good—often haute—food, sleek style, and extensive wine lists.

BARS

Beach Blanket Babylon. In a Georgian mansion house close to Portobello Market, this always-packed bar is distinguishable by its eclectic indoor–outdoor spaces with Gaudí-esque curves and snug corner spaces—like a candlelit fairy-tale grotto, folly, or a medieval dungeon. A sister restaurant-bar-gallery offers a slightly more modern take on similar themes in an ex-warehouse in Shoreditch (*19–23 Bethnal Green Rd.; 020/7749–3540*). ✉ *45 Ledbury Rd., Notting Hill* ☎ *020/7229–2907* ⊕ *www.beachblanket.co.uk* Ⓜ *Notting Hill Gate.*

FAMILY **Electric Diner.** A huge selection of bottled beers and quirky twists on classic cocktails (Courvoisier, mint, and champagne anyone?) are the attractions at this bar and diner next to Notting Hill's famed Electric Cinema on Portobello Road. Run by the people behind the members-only Soho House, the place exudes the same effortless mixture of posh and cool, but is open to anyone and everyone. Sit in the window and watch the world go by along Portobello, or opt for one of the luxury takes on classic diner fare at a booth in the moody, vaulted interior. ✉ *191 Portobello Rd., Notting Hill* ☎ *020/7908–9696* ⊕ *www.electric-diner.com* Ⓜ *Ladbroke Grove.*

DANCE CLUBS

Notting Hill Arts Club. Rock stars like Liam Gallagher and Courtney Love have been seen at this small basement late-night club-bar. What the place lacks in looks it makes up for in mood, and an alternative crowd swills beer to eclectic music that spans Asian underground, hip-hop,

Latin-inspired funk, deep house, and jazzy grooves. ✉ *21 Notting Hill Gate, Notting Hill* ☎ *020/7460–4459* ⊕ *www.nottinghillartsclub.com* 🎫 *Free–£8* Ⓜ *Notting Hill Gate.*

PUBS

The Cow. Crowds head to this boho-chic mix of fun, haute food, and friendly, retro style for Guinness and rock oysters, either enjoying them in the unpretentious downstairs saloon bar or the more formal dining rooms upstairs. The pub food is all excellent, though pricey, with lots of fresh seafood platters, pies, and steaks. The atmosphere's always warm, welcoming, and buzzing. ✉ *89 Westbourne Park Rd., Notting Hill* ☎ *020/7221–0021* ⊕ *www.thecowlondon.co.uk* Ⓜ *Westbourne Park, Royal Oak.*

REGENT'S PARK AND HAMPSTEAD

London's villagelike northern neighborhoods all boast fantastic local boozers where you can easily while away an afternoon. Camden Town has more of a buzz and attracts a younger crowd with its dance clubs and music venues. Every genre is covered, from folk and pop to jazz and world music, with interesting gigs taking place every night of the week.

REGENT'S PARK

COMEDY AND CABARET

Canal Café Theatre. Famous comics and cabaret stars perform every night of the week in this intimate, canalside venue. The long-running News-Revue is a topical song-and-sketch show performed Thursday through Sunday. ✉ *Bridge House, Delamere Terr., Little Venice* ☎ *020/7289–6054* ⊕ *www.canalcafetheatre.com* 🎫 *Free–£15* Ⓜ *Warwick Ave., Royal Oak, Paddington.*

DANCE CLUBS

KOKO. Once known as Camden Palace, this legendary Victorian theater venue has seen acts from Charlie Chaplin to Madonna, and genres from punk to acid house rave. Furnished with lush reds that make it not unlike a cockney Moulin Rouge, this is still one of London's most stunning venues. Sounds of live indie rock, cabaret, funky house, and club classics keep the big dance floor moving, even when it's not heaving. ✉ *1A Camden High St., Camden Town* ☎ *020/7388–3222* ⊕ *www.koko.uk.com* 🎫 *£5–£30* Ⓜ *Mornington Crescent.*

ECLECTIC MUSIC

Roundhouse. This 1840s former London and Birmingham Railway terminus and onetime gin warehouse in Chalk Farm now hosts some of the most atmospheric medium-scale rock and pop gigs in the capital, plus a varied program of circus, theater, dance, and the occasional art installation. There's a good restaurant on the first floor, and in the summer the terrace bar is transformed into an "urban beach," complete with sand. ✉ *Chalk Farm Rd., Camden Town* ☎ *0300/6789–222* ⊕ *www.roundhouse.org.uk* 🎫 *£5–£40* Ⓜ *Chalk Farm.*

JAZZ AND BLUES

Fodor's Choice ★ **The Jazz Café.** A palace of cool in bohemian Camden, this remains an essential hangout for fans of both the mainstream end of the jazz repertoire and hip-hop, funk, world music, and Latin fusion. It's also the unlikely venue for "I Love the 80s Vs I Love the 90s" on Saturday night. Book ahead if you want a prime table in the balcony restaurant overlooking the stage. ⌂ *5 Parkway, Camden Town* ☎ *020/7485–6834 for venue info, 0844/847–2514 for tickets (Ticketmaster)* ⊕ *www.the-jazzcafelondon.com* ⌑ *£6–£35* Ⓜ *Camden Town.*

ROCK

The Camden Assembly. At one of the finest small clubs in the capital, punk, indie guitar, and new metal rock attract a nonmainstream crowd. Weekend club nights upstairs host DJs (and live bands) who rock the decks. ⌂ *49 Chalk Farm Rd., Camden Town* ☎ *020/7424–0800 for venue, 0844/847–2424 for tickets* ⊕ *www.camdenassembly.com* ⌑ *Free–£13* Ⓜ *Chalk Farm.*

The Dublin Castle. Run by the same family for nearly three decades, The Dublin Castle has hosted almost every British rock group you care to name, from Madness to Coldplay. With four bands on the bill almost every night, and DJs taking over afterward on Friday and weekends, there's something for most tastes at this legendary venue. ⌂ *94 Parkway, Camden Town* ☎ *07949/575–149* ⊕ *www.thedublincastle.com* ⌑ *£4–£8* Ⓜ *Camden Town.*

The Forum. The best up-and-coming and medium-to-big-name rock performers consistently play at this 2,000-capacity club. It's a converted 1920 art deco movie theater, with a balcony overlooking the grungy dance floor. ⌂ *9–17 Highgate Rd., Kentish Town* ☎ *0844/477–2000 for tickets* ⊕ *www.academymusicgroup.com* ⌑ *£12–£60* Ⓜ *Kentish Town.*

HAMPSTEAD
PUBS

The Holly Bush. A short walk up the hill from Hampstead Tube station, the friendly Holly Bush was a country pub before London spread this far north. It retains something of a rural feel, with stripped wooden floors, tobacco-color walls, and an open fire, and is an intimate place to enjoy great ales and organic and free-range pub food. Try the homemade pork scratchings (crispy rinds) and pickled eggs, and don't miss the hot cider in the wintertime. ⌂ *22 Holly Mount, Hampstead* ☎ *020/7435–2892* ⊕ *www.hollybushhampstead.co.uk* Ⓜ *Hampstead.*

FAMILY
Fodor's Choice ★ **The Spaniards Inn.** Ideal as a refueling point when you're on a hike in Hampstead Heath, this historic, country-style, oak-beam pub has a gorgeous garden—the scene of the tea party in Dickens's *Pickwick Papers*. Dick Turpin, the highwayman, frequented the 1585 inn before Dickens's time, and Shelley, Keats, Blake, and Byron hung out here as well. The place is extremely popular, especially on Sunday, when Londoners roll in. It's canine-friendly, too—there's even a dog wash in the garden. ⌂ *Spaniards Rd., Hampstead* ☎ *020/8731–8406* ⊕ *www.thespaniardshampstead.co.uk* Ⓜ *Hampstead.*

16

THE THAMES UPSTREAM

A pint in a riverside pub is a London must, and the capital's western reaches offer some truly picturesque drinking opportunities. Pick a traditional establishment and you'll feel like you've ventured far from the Big Smoke.

RICHMOND
PUBS

FAMILY **Roebuck.** Perched on top of Richmond Hill, the Roebuck has perhaps the best view of any pub in London. The most sought-after seats are the benches found directly across the road, which look out over the Thames as it winds its way into the countryside below. Friendly and surprisingly unpretentious, given its lofty surrounds, it is well worth the long climb up the hill from the center of Richmond. ⊠ *130 Richmond Hill, Richmond* ☎ *020/8948–2329* ⊕ *www.greeneking-pubs.co.uk* Ⓜ *National Rail: Richmond.*

HAMMERSMITH
PUBS

FAMILY

Fodor's Choice ★

The Dove. Read the list of famous ex-regulars, from Charles II and Nell Gwynn to Ernest Hemingway and Dylan Thomas, as you wait for a beer at this smart, comely, and popular 16th-century riverside pub on the Upper Mall towpath in Hammersmith. If—as is often the case—the Dove is too full, stroll upstream along the bank to the Old Ship or Blue Anchor. ⊠ *19 Upper Mall, Hammersmith* ☎ *020/8748–9474* ⊕ *www.dovehammersmith.co.uk* Ⓜ *Hammersmith.*

PERFORMING ARTS

National Theatre

Updated by Jo Caird

"All the world's a stage," said Shakespeare, immortal words heard for the first time right here in London. And whether you prefer your theater, music, and art classical or modern, or as contemporary twists on time-honored classics, you'll find that London's vibrant cultural scene more than holds its own on the world stage.

Divas sing original-language librettos at the Royal Opera House, Shakespeare's plays are brought to life at the reconstructed Globe Theatre, and challenging new writing is produced at the Royal Court. Whether you feel like basking in the lighthearted extravagance of a West End musical or taking in the next shark-in-formaldehyde at the White Cube gallery, the choice is yours.

There are international theater festivals, innovative music festivals, and critically acclaimed seasons of postmodern dance. Short trip or long, you'll find the cultural scene in London is ever-changing, ever-expanding, and ever-exciting.

No matter where you head, London's art and performing arts scenes have been setting global trends for decades—and when you count Shakespearean theater and Handel oratorios, for centuries. Fringe theater, classical ballet, participatory chorales: you name it, London probably did it first and often does it best.

PLANNING

TOP THEATER TIPS

Behind the pillars. Many theaters and concert halls sell discounted seats with restricted views.

Matinees. Afternoon performances are almost always better value than evening ones.

Previews. Tickets to shows are usually less expensive in the first few weeks of their run, before the critics have had their say.

Monday. Most movie theaters and some theaters, including the Royal Court, have a reduced-price ticketing policy on Monday.

Standing. Shakespeare's Globe Theatre and the BBC Proms are the two most prominent places where remaining upright saves you money.

FIND OUT WHAT'S PLAYING WHERE

To find out what's showing now, the free weekly magazine *Time Out* (issued every Tuesday outside major stations and around the city; also online at ⊕ *www.timeout.com*) is invaluable.

The free *Evening Standard* carries listings, many of which are also available online at ⊕ *www.standard.co.uk*. *Metro*, London's other widely available free newspaper, is also worth checking out, as are many Sunday papers, and the Saturday *Independent, Guardian,* and *Times*.

The website ⊕ *www.whatsonstage.com* is an invaluable resource for theater listings.

There are hundreds of small private galleries all over London with interesting work by famous and emerging artists. The bimonthly free pamphlet "new exhibitions of contemporary art" (⊕ *www.newexhibitions.com*), available at most galleries, lists and maps nearly 200 art spaces in London.

FESTIVALS AND EVENTS

Dance Umbrella. The biggest annual event is Dance Umbrella, a 13-day festival in October that hosts international and British-based artists at venues across the city. ⊠ *London* ☎ *020/7257–9380* ⊕ *www.danceumbrella.co.uk* ⊠ *Free–£28*.

PERFORMING ARTS REVIEWS

ST. JAMES'S AND WESTMINSTER

Wander the streets of this chic central London neighborhood—home to aristocrats in the 17th century—to discover small commercial galleries, fine-art auction houses, and antiques dealers mixed in among the high-end tailors and gentlemen's clubs.

ART GALLERIES

Institute of Contemporary Arts. Housed in an elegant John Nash–designed Regency terrace, the ICA's two galleries have changing exhibitions of contemporary visual art. The ICA also programs performances, underground and vintage movies, talks, and photography, and there's an excellent arts bookstore, a cafeteria, and a funky bar. ⊠ *The Mall, St. James's* ☎ *020/7930–3647* ⊕ *www.ica.org.uk* ⊠ *£1, cinema tickets £6–£11* ⊙ *Closed Mon.* Ⓜ *Charing Cross, Piccadilly Circus*.

White Cube. The English role in the exploding contemporary art scene has been major, thanks in good portion to Jay Joplin's influential gallery, which has regularly moved around London since 1993. This striking modern concrete structure was the first freestanding building to be built in the area for 30 years when it opened in 2006. It is home base for an array of British artists who have won the Turner Prize, including

Damien Hirst, Tracey Emin, and Gary Hume. ✉ *25–26 Mason's Yard, St. James's* ☎ *020/7930–5373* ⊕ *www.whitecube.com* 🎫 *Free* 🕙 *Closed Sun. and Mon.* Ⓜ *Green Park, Piccadilly Circus.*

CLASSICAL MUSIC

St. James's Church. The organ was brought here in 1691 after fire destroyed its former home, the Palace of Whitehall. St. James's holds regular classical music concerts and free lunchtime recitals Monday, Wednesday, and Friday at 1:10 pm (free but donation of £3.50 suggested). ✉ *197 Piccadilly, St. James's* ☎ *020/7381–0441* ⊕ *www.sjp.org.uk* 🎫 *Free, but £3.50 donation suggested* Ⓜ *Piccadilly Circus, Green Park.*

St. John's Smith Square. This baroque church behind Westminster Abbey offers chamber music and organ recitals as well as orchestral concerts. There are three or four lunchtime recitals a month. ✉ *Smith Sq., Westminster* ☎ *020/7222–1061* ⊕ *www.sjss.org.uk* 🎫 *Free–£60* Ⓜ *Westminster.*

St. Martin-in-the-Fields Concerts. Popular free lunchtime concerts are held in this lovely 1726 church, as are regular evening concerts. Stop for a snack at the Café in the Crypt. ✉ *Trafalgar Sq., Westminster* ☎ *020/7766–1100* ⊕ *www.stmartin-in-the-fields.org* 🎫 *£3.50 donation suggested* Ⓜ *Charing Cross.*

MAYFAIR AND MARYLEBONE

The historic center of the London art world, Mayfair has a thriving gallery scene that has undergone a renaissance in recent years. With East End gallerists relocating to central London and a number of top international galleries opening new premises here, there's a real buzz about the place. Directly north of Mayfair, Marylebone has more of a village atmosphere, with a few choice galleries and arts institutions dotted around.

MAYFAIR

ART GALLERIES

Marlborough Fine Art. This veteran of the Mayfair art scene has been presenting exhibitions by masters old and new since it was founded in 1946. In the main first floor space is work by great living artists like Paula Rego and Frank Auerbach, plus exhibitions of graphic works from a whole host of starry names. The contemporary gallery on the second floor shows a younger generation of artists from the U.K. and abroad. ✉ *6 Albermarle St., Mayfair* ☎ *020/7629–5161* ⊕ *www.marlboroughfineart.com* 🎫 *Free* 🕙 *Closed Sun.* Ⓜ *Green Park, Piccadilly Circus.*

MARYLEBONE

ART GALLERIES

Lisson. Owner Nicholas Logsdail represents about 50 blue-chip artists, including the minimalist Sol LeWitt and performance artist Marina Abramović, at one of the most respected galleries in London. The gallery is most associated with New Object sculptors like Anish Kapoor and Richard Deacon, many of whom have won the Turner Prize. A branch down the road at 27 Bell Street features work by up-and-coming artists. ✉ *52 Bell St., Marylebone* ☎ *020/7724–2739* ⊕ *www.lissongallery.com* 🎫 *Free* 🕙 *Closed Sun.* Ⓜ *Edgware Rd., Marylebone.*

CLASSICAL MUSIC

FAMILY **Wigmore Hall.** Hear chamber music and song recitals (including concerts
Fodor'sChoice for toddlers) in this charming hall with near-perfect acoustics. Don't
★ miss the Sunday morning concerts (at 11:30 am). ⊠ *36 Wigmore St.,
Marylebone* ☎ *020/7935–2141* ⊕ *www.wigmore-hall.org.uk* ⊠ *From
£10* Ⓜ *Bond St.*

SOHO AND COVENT GARDEN

London's hip center has it all, from multiplexes playing the biggest blockbuster movies to niche contemporary art galleries tucked away in back
streets, and from world-famous opera houses to sultry cabaret joints.

SOHO

ART GALLERIES

Fodor'sChoice **Photographer's Gallery.** Britain's first and foremost photography gallery
★ programs cutting-edge and provocative exhibitions. The prestigious
Deutsche Börse Photography Prize is exhibited and awarded here annually. The gallery also has a print sales room, a bookstore, and a café-
bar—a great spot to escape the bustle of nearby Oxford Street. ⊠ *16–18
Ramillies St., Soho* ☎ *020/7087–9300* ⊕ *www.thephotographersgallery.
org.uk* ⊠ *Free until noon; £4 thereafter* Ⓜ *Oxford Circus.*

Riflemaker. Inside the oldest public building in the West End (a Georgian-era rifle maker's workshop), this hip but accessible gallery exhibits
ambitious works by emerging artists, as well as shining a light on established figures who haven't gotten the recognition they deserve. Names
on the roster include Judy Chicago, Josephine King, and William S.
Burroughs. ⊠ *79 Beak St., Soho* ☎ *020/7439–0000* ⊕ *www.riflemaker.
org* ⊠ *Free* ⊘ *Closed Sun.* Ⓜ *Piccadilly Circus, Oxford Circus.*

Sadie Coles HQ. Containing the work of important British and international artists such as Sarah Lucas and Wilhelm Sasnal, this light-filled
art space overlooking busy Regent Street marked a major expansion for
respected British gallerist Sadie Coles when it opened in fall 2013. ⊠ *62
Kingly St., Soho* ☎ *020/7493–8611* ⊕ *www.sadiecoles.com* ⊘ *Closed
Sun. and Mon.*

FILM

Curzon Soho. This popular, comfortable movie theater runs a vibrant
and artsy program of mixed repertoire and mainstream films, with a
good calendar of director talks and other events, too. The bar is great
for a quiet drink, even when Soho is crawling with people. There are
further Curzon branches in Mayfair, Bloomsbury, Aldgate, Victoria,
Chelsea, Wimbledon, and Richmond. ⊠ *99 Shaftesbury Ave., Soho*
☎ *0330/500–1331* ⊕ *www.curzoncinemas.com* ⊠ *From: £11* Ⓜ *Piccadilly Circus, Leicester Sq.*

FAMILY **Prince Charles Cinema.** This repertory movie theater right off Leicester
Square offers a chance to catch up with independent features, documen-
taries, and even blockbusters you may have missed. A second screen
upstairs shows newer movies at more usual West End prices. This is
where the "sing-along screening" took off; come in character and war-
ble along to *The Sound of Music, Grease, The Rocky Horror Picture*

17

Show, and others. ⊠ *7 Leicester Pl., Soho* ☎ *020/7494–3654* ⊕ *www. princecharlescinema.com* ⌨ *From: £8; sing-alongs £16* Ⓜ *Leicester Sq., Piccadilly Circus.*

THEATER

Fodor'sChoice   **Soho Theatre.** This sleek theater in the heart of Soho is devoted to foster-
★   ing new work and is a prolific presenter of plays by emerging writers,
comedy performances, cabaret shows, and other entertainment. The
bar is always buzzing. ⊠ *21 Dean St., Soho* ☎ *020/7478–0100* ⊕ *www. sohotheatre.com* Ⓜ *Tottenham Court Rd.*

COVENT GARDEN

PERFORMING ARTS CENTERS

The London Coliseum. A veritable architectural extravaganza of Edwardian exoticism, the baroque-style theater has a magnificent auditorium
and a rooftop glass dome with a bar and great views. As one of the city's
most venerable theaters, the coliseum functions mainly as the home of
the English National Opera, which produces innovative opera, sung
in English, for lower prices than the Royal Opera House. In recent
years the company also has presented musicals, sometimes featuring
star opera singers. During opera's off-season (including summertime
and during winter holidays), the house hosts the English National Ballet
(⊕ *www.ballet.org.uk*) and other troupes. Guided tours offering fascinating insights into the architecture and history of the building take
place on selected dates at 11 am and 2 pm. ⊠ *St. Martin's La., Covent
Garden* ☎ *020/7845–9300* ⊕ *www.eno.org* ⌨ *Opera £12–£125, ballet
£10–£79, tours £10* Ⓜ *Leicester Sq., Charing Cross.*

Fodor'sChoice   **Royal Opera House.** Along with Milan's La Scala, New York's Metro-
★   politan, and the Palais Garnier in Paris, this is one of the world's great
opera houses. The resident troupe has mounted spectacular productions
in the past, though recent productions have tended toward more contemporary operas. Whatever the style of the performance, the extravagant theater delivers a full dose of opulence. The famed Royal Ballet
performs classical and contemporary repertoire here, too, and smaller
scale works of both opera and dance are presented in the Linbury Studio
Theatre and Clore Studio Upstairs. A small allocation of tickets for each
performance of main stage productions for the week ahead—even those
that are sold out—goes on sale online at 1 pm every Friday. ■ **TIP→** *If
you wish to see the hall but are not able to procure a ticket, you can
join a backstage tour or one of the less frequent tours of the auditorium;
they book up several weeks in advance.* Tours are also available of the
ROH's fascinating production workshop and costume center in Essex
(30 minutes by train from Fenchurch Street to Purfleet, twice an hour).
BP Big Screens is the ROH's summer series of live relays of its opera
and ballet productions; screenings are free and take place outdoors in
public spaces all over the country, including Trafalgar Square. ⊠ *Bow
St., Covent Garden* ☎ *020/7304–4000* ⊕ *www.roh.org.uk* ⌨ *Performances £4–£270; tours £8–£12* Ⓜ *Covent Garden.*

THEATER

Donmar Warehouse. Hollywood stars often perform at this not-for-profit theater in diverse and daring new works, bold interpretations of the classics, and small-scale musicals. Nicole Kidman, Gwyneth Paltrow, and Ewan McGregor have all been featured. ⊠ *41 Earlham St., Seven Dials, Covent Garden* ☎ *0844/871–7624* ⊕ *www.donmarwarehouse. com* Ⓜ *Covent Garden.*

BLOOMSBURY AND HOLBORN

Once the heart of fashionable literary London, there's still an air of refinement about this neighborhood. A handful of small theaters with links to the colleges with campuses in the area create a vibrant small-scale performance scene with theater, dance, and stand-up comedy.

CLASSICAL MUSIC

Kings Place. This airy concert venue opened in 2008. The cultural jewel in the huge new developments near the Eurostar terminal in King's Cross, it is the permanent home of the London Sinfonietta and the Orchestra of the Age of Enlightenment. It presents a hugely varied cultural calendar of jazz, comedy, folk, and political and literary lectures, plus two gallery spaces. ⊠ *90 York Way, King's Cross* ☎ *020/7520–1490* ⊕ *www. kingsplace.co.uk* ☞ *From £10* Ⓜ *King's Cross.*

DANCE

Peacock Theatre. Sadler's Wells's West End annex, this modernist theater near the London School of Economics (which uses it as a lecture hall during the day) focuses on younger companies and shows in popular dance genres like flamenco, tango, and hip-hop. ⊠ *Portugal St., Holborn* ☎ *020 /7863–8222* ⊕ *www.peacocktheatre.com* ☞ *From £10* Ⓜ *Holborn.*

The Place. The Robin Howard Dance Theatre at The Place is London's only theater dedicated to contemporary dance, and with tickets often under £20 (performances by student dancers, for example, cost just £10) it's good value, too. The "Resolution" festival in January and February is the United Kingdom's biggest platform event for new choreographers. ⊠ *17 Duke's Rd., Bloomsbury* ☎ *020/7121–1100* ⊕ *www. theplace.org.uk* ☞ *Free–£32* Ⓜ *Euston.*

ISLINGTON

Close to central London, yet with its own unique atmosphere, this neighborhood is home to a handful of renowned theaters and music venues that make the short journey northeast well worth the effort.

ART GALLERIES

Victoria Miro Gallery. This large, important commercial gallery, in a former furniture factory, has exhibited some of the biggest names on the British contemporary art scene: Grayson Perry, the Chapman Brothers, and Peter Doig, to name a few. Some exhibitions spill out into the gallery's garden. It also brings in exciting talent from abroad. There's another branch in Mayfair. ⊠ *16 Wharf Rd., Islington* ☎ *020/7336–8109* ⊕ *www.victoria-miro.com* ☞ *Free* Ⓜ *Old St., Angel.*

17

DANCE

FAMILY

Fodor'sChoice

★

Sadler's Wells. Head to this gleaming building, which opened in 1998 and is the seventh on the site in its 300-year history, to see performances by leading classical and contemporary dance companies. The Random Dance company is in residence, and the little Lilian Baylis Studio hosts avant-garde work. ⊠ *Rosebery Ave., Islington* ☎ *020/7863–8000* ⊕ *www.sadlerswells.com* ✉ *From £12* Ⓜ *Angel.*

THEATER

Almeida Theatre. This Off West End venue, helmed by director Rupert Goold, premiers excellent new plays and exciting twists on the classics, often featuring high-profile actors. There's a good café and a licensed bar that serves "sharing dishes," as well as tasty main courses. ⊠ *Almeida St., Islington* ☎ *020/7359–4404* ⊕ *www.almeida.co.uk* ✉ *From £10* Ⓜ *Angel, Highbury & Islington.*

FAMILY **Little Angel Theatre.** Innovative puppetry performances for children and adults have been taking place in this adorable former temperance hall since 1961. The theater runs a number of festivals a year. ⊠ *14 Dagmar Passage, Islington* ☎ *020/7226–1787* ⊕ *www.littleangeltheatre. com* ✉ *From £5* Ⓜ *Angel, Highbury & Islington.*

THE CITY

It may seem at first glance like the denizens of London's financial center are far too busy to take time out for culture, but look a little closer: arts events are taking place all over, courtesy of a number of acclaimed annual festivals. Art exhibits in empty offices and chamber performances in historic churches are regular occurrences.

PERFORMING ARTS CENTERS

FAMILY **Barbican Centre.** Opened in 1982, the Barbican is an enormous Brutalist concrete maze that Londoners either love or hate—but its importance to the cultural life of the capital is beyond dispute. At the largest performing arts center in Europe, you could listen to Elgar, see 1960s photography, and catch German animation with live accompaniment, all in one day. The main theater, known for its acoustics, is most famous as the home of the London Symphony Orchestra. The Barbican is also a frequent host to the BBC Symphony Orchestra. ⊠ *Silk St., City of London* ☎ *020/7638–8891* ⊕ *www.barbican.org. uk* ✉ *Art exhibits free–£14.50, cinema £6–£12, theater and music £10–£150* Ⓜ *Barbican.*

EAST LONDON

Artists and other creative types, no longer able to afford central London rents, have been making their way eastward for years. It began in Shoreditch, but as rents increased there, too, neighborhoods farther and farther out have taken on these new residents. Go gallery hopping in Vyner Street in Bethnal Green or catch a hip band in action at one of Shoreditch's myriad music venues.

CONTEMPORARY ART: LONDON TODAY

In the 21st century, the focus of the city's art scene has shifted from the past to the future. Helped by the prominence of Tate Modern, London's contemporary art scene has never been so high profile. In publicly funded exhibition spaces like the Barbican Gallery, the Hayward Gallery, the Institute of Contemporary Arts, and the Serpentine Galleries, London now has a modern art environment on par with that of Bilbao and New York. The so-called Young British Artists (YBAs, although no longer that young) Damien Hirst, Tracey Emin, and others are firmly planted in the public imagination. The celebrity status of British artists has a lot to do with the annual Turner Prize, which always stirs up controversy in the media during the display of the work, usually at Tate Britain.

Depending on who you talk to, the Saatchi Gallery is considered to be either the savior of contemporary art or the wardrobe of the emperor's new clothes. After a couple of moves it is now ensconced in the former Duke of York's barracks off Chelsea's King's Road.

The South Bank's Tate Modern may house the giants of modern art, but East London is where the innovative action is. There are dozens of galleries in the fashionable spaces around Old Street, and the truly hip have already moved even farther afield, to areas such as Bethnal Green, to the east, and Peckham, to the south. The Whitechapel Art Gallery and Jay Jopling's influential White Cube, with branches in Bermondsey and St. James's, remain essential parts of the new art establishment and continue to show exciting work by emerging British artists.

On the first Thursday of every month, more than 130 museums and galleries in East London stay open late and host talks, workshops, and other events (more information at ⊕ *www.firstthursdays.co.uk*).

17

PERFORMING ARTS CENTERS

Fodor's Choice ★ **Wilton's.** Arguably London's most atmospheric cultural space, Wilton's has been entertaining the crowds since 1743, first as an alehouse, then as a music hall. It now hosts gigs, talks, theater performances, movie screenings (often with live scores), and swing-dance evenings. The cozy Mahogany Bar, the oldest part of the building, serves a good range of quality local ales, along with snacks and meals that change according to what's playing in the theater. There's a cocktail bar upstairs, in what was once the artists' green room. ⊠ *Graces Alley, East End* ☎ *020/7702–2789* ⊕ *www.wiltons.org.uk* ⊒ *From £10* Ⓜ *Aldgate East, Tower Hill.*

THEATER

FAMILY **Hackney Empire.** The history of this treasure of a theater is drama in its own right. Charlie Chaplin is said to have appeared here during its days as a thriving variety theater and music hall in the early 1900s. It now hosts traditional family entertainment and variety shows, opera, music, musical theater, dance, and drama, often with a multicultural slant. Its annual Christmas pantomime show is legendary. ⊠ *291 Mare St., Hackney* ☎ *020/8985–2424* ⊕ *www.hackneyempire.co.uk* ⊒ *From £10* Ⓜ *Overground: Hackney Central.*

SOUTH OF THE THAMES

The South Bank and its easterly near neighbor Bankside together make up one of the richest areas in London when it comes to arts and entertainment. Whether you want to watch a play, hear a concert, or see an art exhibit, you won't have to wander far to find something top class. Venture a little farther into South London for a sprinkling of fringe theaters that act as incubators for the capital's mainstream theater scene.

FILM

FAMILY   **BFI London IMAX Cinema.** The British Film Institute's glazed drum-shaped IMAX theater (now, confusingly, operated by Odeon) has the largest screen in the United Kingdom (approximately 75 feet wide and the height of five double-decker buses). It shows state-of-the-art 2-D and 3-D films. ⊠ *1 Charlie Chaplin Walk, South Bank* ☎ *0330/333–7878* ⊕ *www.bfi.org.uk/imax* ✉ *From £10* Ⓜ *Waterloo.*

FAMILY   **BFI Southbank.** With the best repertory programming in London, the three movie theaters and studio here are effectively a national film center run by the British Film Institute. More than 1,000 titles are screened each year, with art-house, foreign, silent, overlooked, classic, noir, and short films favored over recent Hollywood blockbusters. The center also has a gallery, bookshop, and "mediatheque" where visitors can watch film and television from the National Archive for free (closed Monday). This is one of the venues for the BFI London Film Festival; throughout the year there are minifestivals, seminars, and guest speakers. ■TIP➔ **The BFI Bar & Kitchen, toward the back of the building, is a great secret spot for a drink.** ⊠ *Belvedere Rd., South Bank* ☎ *020/7928–3232* ⊕ *www.bfi.org.uk* ✉ *From £8* Ⓜ *Waterloo.*

PERFORMING ARTS CENTERS

FAMILY   **The Scoop.** This open air amphitheater next to the Thames at City Hall hosts free theater performances, film screenings (including live relays from the Royal Opera House), live music, circus and dance workshops, and talks every night in June, July, and August. Theater productions are usually family-friendly tellings of classic Greek plays, with post-show chats taking place on select dates. ⊠ *Queens Walk* ☎ *0780/491–3946* ⊕ *www.thelondonriviera.com* ✉ *Free* Ⓜ *London Bridge.*

FAMILY   **Southbank Centre.** The public has never really warmed to the Southbank Fodor's Choice   Centre's hulking concrete buildings (beloved by architecture aficio-
★   nados), products of the Brutalist style popular when the centre was built in the 1950s and '60s—but all the same, the masses flock to the concerts, recitals, festivals, and exhibitions held here, Europe's largest arts center. The **Royal Festival Hall** is truly a People's Palace, with seats for 2,900 and a schedule that ranges from major symphony orchestras to pop stars (catch the annual summer Meltdown Festival, where artists like Patti Smith or David Byrne put together a personal selection of concerts by favorite performers). The smaller **Queen Elizabeth Hall** is more classically oriented. It contains the **Purcell Room,** which hosts lectures and chamber performances. For art, head to the **Hayward Gallery,** which hosts shows on top contemporary artists such as Anthony Gormley and Cy Twombly. (The terrace here has

some restaurants worth a visit.) The center's riverside street level has a terrific assortment of restaurants and bars. The BFI's Benugo bar and the Wahaca restaurant at Queen Elizabeth Hall are particularly attractive. Note that the Hayward Gallery, Purcell Room, and Queen Elizabeth Hall have been closed for renovations but are due to open in early 2018. ⊠ *Belvedere Rd., South Bank* ☎ *020/7960–4200* ⊕ *www.southbankcentre.co.uk* ☒ *Free–£120* Ⓜ *Waterloo, Embankment.*

THEATER

Fodor'sChoice ★ **BAC.** Battersea Arts Centre has a reputation for producing innovative new work as well as hosting top alternative stand-up comics. Performances take place in quirky spaces all over this atmospheric former town hall. Check out Scratch events, low-tech theater where the audience provides feedback on works-in-progress. Entry for Scratch events is pay-what-you-can (minimum £3). There's also a fun bar that serves good food. ⊠ *176 Lavender Hill, Battersea* ☎ *020/7223–2223* ⊕ *www.bac.org.uk* ☒ *Pay what you can (£3 suggested)–£18* Ⓜ *National Rail: Clapham Junction.*

FAMILY Fodor'sChoice ★ **National Theatre.** When this theater designed by Sir Denys Lasdun opened in 1976, Londoners weren't all so keen on the low-slung Brutalist block. Prince Charles described it as "a clever way of building a nuclear power station in the middle of London without anyone objecting." But whatever its merits or demerits, the National Theatre's interior spaces are worth a visit. Interspersed with the three theaters—the 1,150-seat Olivier, the 890-seat Lyttelton, and the 450-seat Dorfman—is a multilayered foyer with exhibitions, bars, restaurants, and free entertainment. Musicals, classics, and plays are performed by top-flight professionals, and they sometimes give talks as well. Backstage, costume, and architecture tours are available. The Clore Learning Centre offers courses and events on all aspects of theater making, and you can watch staff at work in the backstage workshops from the Sherling High-Level Walkway. Each weekend in August, the River Stage Festival presents live music, dance, workshops, and DJ sets in the area in front of the theater. ⊠ *Belvedere Rd., South Bank* ☎ *020/7452–3000* ⊕ *www.nationaltheatre.org.uk* ☒ *£15–£65, tours £10–£12.50* Ⓜ *Waterloo.*

The Old Vic. In 2015 Matthew Warchus, the director behind *Matilda the Musical,* took over as artistic director at this grand old theater, the former haunting grounds of such stage legends as John Gielgud, Vivien Leigh, Peter O'Toole, Richard Burton, and Judi Dench. The venue had suffered decades of financial duress before being brought under the ownership of a dedicated trust headed by its previous artistic director, actor Kevin Spacey. It's now in great shape, secure for the future and producing some of the best theater in London. ⊠ *The Cut, Southwark* ☎ *0844/871–7628* ⊕ *www.oldvictheatre.com* ☒ *From £12* Ⓜ *Waterloo, Southwark.*

Shakespeare's Globe Theatre. *See full listing in Chapter 8: South of the Thames.*

17

Southwark Playhouse. This impressive little theater, in what was once a car showroom, produces award-winning new musicals and gritty drama for a fraction of the cost of the West End. The bar-café is good, too, which is fortunate—the surrounding area is something of a culinary no-man's-land. ⊠ *77–85 Newington Causeway, Borough* ☎ *020/7407–0234* ⊕ *www.southwarkplayhouse.co.uk* ✉ *From £20* Ⓜ *Borough, Elephant & Castle.*

FAMILY   **Unicorn Theatre.** Dedicated to innovative work for young audiences, this
Fodor's Choice   modern theater hosts plays, musicals, and interactive theater for every-
★   one from toddlers on up. Inclusivity is a major focus, with performances for those with visual and hearing and other impairments taking place regularly. ⊠ *147 Tooley St., Borough* ☎ *020/7645–0560* ⊕ *www.unicorntheatre.com* ✉ *From £8* Ⓜ *London Bridge.*

Fodor's Choice   **Young Vic.** At this Waterloo theater, big names perform alongside young
★   talent, often in daring, innovative productions of classic plays that appeal to a more diverse audience than is traditionally found on the London scene. Good food is served all day at the bustling bar. ⊠ *66 The Cut, Waterloo, South Bank* ☎ *020/7922–2922* ⊕ *www.youngvic. org* ✉ *From £10* Ⓜ *Southwark, Waterloo.*

KENSINGTON AND CHELSEA

These refined neighborhoods just west of central London have a wide variety of galleries and performance spaces, with several located within the area's large public green spaces.

KENSINGTON
CLASSICAL MUSIC
Cadogan Hall. Once a church, this spacious venue is home to the Royal Philharmonic Orchestra, and the English Chamber Orchestra performs here regularly. The hall also hosts a wide range of choral and chamber concerts, plus the occasional folk, rock, and world-music gig. ⊠ *5 Sloane Terr., Kensington* ☎ *020/7730–4500* ⊕ *www.cadoganhall.com* ✉ *Free–£100* Ⓜ *Sloane Sq.*

Fodor's Choice   **Royal Albert Hall.** Opened in 1871, this splendid iron-and-glass-domed
★   auditorium hosts everything from pop and classical headliners to Cirque du Soleil, awards ceremonies, and sumo wrestling championships, but it is best known for the annual July–September BBC Promenade Concerts. Bargain-price standing-room (or promenading or sitting-on-the-floor) tickets for "the Proms" are sold on the night of the concert. The circular 5,272-seat auditorium has a terra-cotta exterior surmounted by a mosaic frieze depicting figures engaged in cultural pursuits. The hall is open most days for daytime guided tours and Tuesday through Sunday for afternoon tea. ⊠ *Kensington Gore, Kensington* ☎ *0207/589–8212* ⊕ *www.royalalberthall.com* ✉ *From £6; tours £13* Ⓜ *South Kensington.*

OPERA
FAMILY   **Opera Holland Park.** In summer, well-loved operas and imaginative productions of lesser-known works are presented under a spectacular canopy against the remains of Holland House, one of the first great houses built in Kensington. The company has successfully branched out into

opera for families in recent years, too. There are 1,000 tickets offered free to those ages 7–18 every season. Tickets go on general sale in April (earlier for members). ✉ *Holland Park, Kensington High St., Kensington* ☎ *0300/999–1000 for box office (opens Apr.), 020/3846–6222 for inquiries* ⊕ *www.operahollandpark.com* ✉ *From £15* Ⓜ *High Street Kensington, Holland Park.*

CHELSEA
THEATER
Royal Court Theatre. Britain's undisputed epicenter of new theatrical works, the court continues to produce gritty British and international drama. Don't miss the best deal in town: four 10-pence standing tickets go on sale one hour before each performance, and £12 tickets are available on Monday. Backstage and building tours take place at 11:30 am on the first or second Saturday of the month. ✉ *Sloane Sq., Chelsea* ☎ *020/7565–5000* ⊕ *www.royalcourttheatre.com* ✉ *From £12; tours £9* Ⓜ *Sloane Sq.*

NOTTING HILL

This cosmopolitan West London neighborhood, shown to advantage in the 1999 film of the same name, is best known for the Notting Hill Carnival, a lively music-focused street festival that takes over the wider area on the final weekend of August each year. There's a year-round culture scene, too, catering mainly to the neighborhood's trendy young professionals.

FILM
FAMILY **The Electric Cinema.** This refurbished Portobello Road art house screens mainstream and international movies. The emphasis is on comfort, with leather sofas for two, armchairs, coffee tables for your wine and appetizers, and even double beds in the front row. The Electric also has another movie theater in east London on Redchurch Street, with sofas and wine coolers. ✉ *191 Portobello Rd., Notting Hill* ☎ *020/7908–9696* ⊕ *www.electriccinema.co.uk* ✉ *From £17* Ⓜ *Ladbroke Grove, Notting Hill Gate.*

REGENT'S PARK AND HAMPSTEAD

Leafy north London has long been a stomping ground for the capital's cultural elite—stroll through Primrose Hill and you're practically guaranteed to spot a film star or musician—but there's diversity here, too. Camden Town is justifiably famous for its indie music scene, while respected fringe theaters in Swiss Cottage and Kilburn don't shy away from major topics.

REGENT'S PARK
THEATER
FAMILY **Open Air Theatre.** Works by Shakespeare have been performed here
Fodor's Choice every summer since 1932, with casts including luminaries such as
★ Vivien Leigh, Dame Judi Dench, and Damien Lewis. Today the theater also mounts productions of classic plays, musicals, and shows for family audiences among its four annual productions. *A Midsummer*

Night's Dream is the one to catch, if it's on—never has that enchanted Greek wood been better evoked, especially when enhanced by genuine birdsong and a rising moon. There's a covered restaurant for pretheater dining, an informal café, and, of course, a bar. You can also order picnic hampers in advance. The park can get chilly, so bring a blanket. Performances proceed rain or shine (umbrellas aren't allowed) with refunds only in case of a very heavy downpour. ⊠ *Inner Circle, Regent's Park* ☎ *0844/826–4242* ⊕ *www.openairtheatre.com* 🎟 *From £18* Ⓜ *Baker St., Regent's Park.*

HAMPSTEAD

FILM

FAMILY **Everyman Cinema.** Kick off your shoes, curl up on the large comfy sofas, and have tapas and champagne brought to you in front of classic, foreign, cutting-edge, and Hollywood titles. This venue also screens the Metropolitan Opera live from New York, and is a popular place for Hampstead denizens to bring their kids. Other branches around London also tend to offer a movie experience a cut above average. ⊠ *5 Holly Bush Vale, Hampstead* ☎ *0871/906–9060* ⊕ *www.everymancinema. com* 🎟 *From £16* Ⓜ *Hampstead.*

THEATER

FAMILY **Tricycle Theatre.** Committed to representing the cultural diversity of its community, the Tricycle shows the best in black, Irish, Jewish, Asian, and South African drama, and also promotes new work. There is a movie theater, too: expect top-quality new European and international cinema, including films from the United States, occasionally screened at film festivals the theater organizes. Discounted movie tickets are available on Monday. ⊠ *269 Kilburn High Rd., Kilburn* ☎ *020/7328–1000* ⊕ *www.tricycle.co.uk* 🎟 *Theater £18–£30, movies £6–£9.50* Ⓜ *Kilburn.*

SHOPPING

Updated by
Ellin Stein

The keyword of London shopping has always been "individuality," whether expressed in the superb custom tailoring of Savile Row, the nonconformist punk roots of quintessential British designer Vivienne Westwood, or the unique small stores that purvey their owners' private passions—be they paper theaters, toy soldiers, or buttons. This tradition is under threat from the influx of chains (global luxury, domestic midmarket, and international youth) but the distinctively British mix of quality and originality, tradition, and character remains.

You can try on underwear fit for a queen at Her Majesty's lingerie supplier, track down a leather-bound Brontë classic at an antiquarian bookseller, or find a bargain antique on Portobello Road. Whether you're just browsing—there's nothing like the size, variety, and sheer theater of London's street markets to stimulate the acquisitive instinct—or on a fashion-seeking mission, London shopping offers something for all tastes and budgets.

Although it's impossible to pin down one particular look that defines the city, London style tends to fall into two camps: one is the quirky, individualistic, somewhat romantic look exemplified by homegrown designers like Matthew Williamson, Vivienne Westwood, and Lulu Guinness; the other reflects Britain's celebrated tradition of classic knitwear and suiting, with labels like Jaeger, Pringle, and Brora, while Oswald Boateng, Paul Smith, and Richard James take tradition and give it a very modern twist. Traditional bespoke men's tailoring can be found in the upscale gentlemen's shops of Jermyn Street and Savile Row—there's no better place in the city to buy custom-made shirts and suits—while the handbags at Mulberry, Asprey, and Anya Hindmarch are pure classic quality. If your budget can't stretch that far, no problem; the city's chain stores like Topshop, Zara, and H&M, aimed at the younger end of the market, are excellent places to pick up designs copied straight from the catwalk at a fraction of the price, while mid-market chains like Reiss, Jigsaw, and L.K. Bennett offer smart design and better quality for the more sophisticated shopper.

If there's anything that unites London's designers, it's a commitment to creativity and originality, underpinned by a strong sense of heritage. This combination of posh and rock 'n' roll sensibilities turns up in everyone from Terence Conran, who revolutionized product and houseware design in the '60s (and is still going strong), to Alexander McQueen, who combined the Punk aesthetic with the rigor of couture. You'll see it in fanciful millinery creations by Philip Treacy and Stephen Jones, and in the work of imaginative shoemakers Nicholas Kirkwood, United Nude, and Terry de Havilland—and it keeps going, right through to current hot designers Erdem, Christopher Kane, and Christopher Bailey, the latter responsible for making traditional label Burberry relevant again.

One reason for London's design supremacy is the strength of local fashion college Central St. Martin's, whose graduates include Conran, Kane, McQueen, his successor at his eponymous label—and designer of the Duchess of Cambridge's wedding dress—Sarah Burton, and Stella McCartney's equally acclaimed successor at Céline, Phoebe Philo.

To find the McQueens, McCartneys, and Baileys of tomorrow, head for the independent boutiques of the East End and Bermondsey. If anything, London is even better known for its vibrant street fashion than for its high-end designers. Stock up from the stalls at Portobello, Camden, and Spitalfields markets.

Aside from bankrupting yourself, the only problem you may encounter is exhaustion. London's shopping districts are spread out over the city, so do as savvy locals do: plan your excursion with military precision, taking in only one or two areas in a day, and stopping for lunch with a glass of wine or for a pint at a pub.

18

PLANNING

OPENING HOURS

Most shops are open from about 9:30 or 10 am to 6 or 6:30 pm. Larger department stores generally stay open until 7 or even as late as 9. Because shop hours, particularly for the smaller shops, vary, it's a good idea to phone or check websites ahead. Stores that have late shopping—and not all do—are usually open until 7 or 8 pm on Thursday only. On Sunday, many shops open between 11 am and noon and close at 5 or 6 pm. Most stores are open on Sunday in December for the Christmas season.

WATCH YOUR LANGUAGE

Locals like to say that Brits and Americans are separated by a common language. Here are a few confusing terms to watch for when out and about in the shops:

Pants means underwear. Every other type of long-legged bottoms (except jeans) are called **trousers.** Also in the underwear category is the **vest** (undershirt in the United States); if you are looking for a vest, ask for a **waistcoat.**

Knickers are ladies' underwear. If you want pantyhose, ask for **tights.**

Jumper means sweater—unless it's a cardigan, in which case it may be shortened to **cardie.** If you ask for a **sweater,** you may be offered a sweatshirt.

Men use **braces** to hold up their trousers; in England **suspenders** is another word for garters.

If you want some Adidas- or Nike-type athletic shoes, ask for **trainers,** not sneakers.

Don't ask for a pocketbook or a purse if you mean a **handbag**—the former will be incomprehensible, and the latter will produce a coin purse. If you ask for a fanny pack, it will produce a laugh—"fanny" means something altogether different in the United Kingdom; ask for a **bum-bag.**

Nightgowns are usually abbreviated to **nighties** and bathrobes may be **dressing gowns.**

A WORD ABOUT SERVICE
American standards of customer service are rare in London—you may find attentive customer service at old-school, traditional names and some independent stores, but salespeople elsewhere can seem abrupt or indifferent.

SHOPPING REVIEWS

ST. JAMES'S

ACCESSORIES

Fodor's Choice ★ **Lock & Co. Hatters.** Need a silk top hat, a flat-weave Panama, or a traditional tweed flat cap? Or, for ladies, an occasion hat? James Lock of St. James's has been providing hats from this wood-paneled shop since 1676 for customers ranging from Admiral Lord Nelson, Oscar Wilde, and Frank Sinatra to, more recently, Robert Downey Jr., Guy Ritchie, and Kate Middleton, as well as trendsetting musicians and models. ⊠ 6 St. James's St., St. James's ☎ 020/7930–8874 ⊕ www.lockhatters.co.uk ⊗ Closed Sun. Ⓜ Green Park.

Fodor's Choice ★ **Swaine Adeney Brigg.** Providing practical supplies for country pursuits since 1750, Swaine Adeney Brigg carries beautifully crafted umbrellas, walking sticks, and hip flasks, or ingenious combinations, such as the umbrella with a slim tipple-holding flask secreted inside the stem. The same level of quality and craftsmanship applies to the store's leather goods, which include attaché cases (you can buy the "Q Branch" model that James Bond carried in *From Russia with Love*) and wallets. You'll find scarves, caps, and the Herbert Johnson "Poet Hat," the iconic headgear (stocked since 1890) worn by Harrison Ford in every Indiana Jones film. ⊠ 7 Piccadilly Arcade, St. James's ☎ 020/7409–7277 ⊕ www.swaineadeneybrigg.com ⊗ Closed Sun., except by appointment Ⓜ Green Park.

ANTIQUES AND COLLECTIBLES

The Armoury of St. James's. Besides fine toy soldiers in lead or tin representing conflicts ranging from the Crusades through WW II with prices starting at £15 and going into four figures, the shop has regimental brooches and drums, historic orders and medals, Royal memorabilia, and military antiques. ✉ *17 Piccadilly Arcade, St. James's* ☎ *020/7493–5082* ⊕ *www.armoury.co.uk* ☉ *Closed Sun.* Ⓜ *Piccadilly Circus.*

BEAUTY

Floris. What did Queen Victoria, Mary Shelley, and Marilyn Monroe have in common? They all used products from Floris, one of the most beautiful shops in London, with gleaming glass-and-Spanish-mahogany showcases salvaged from the Great Exhibition of 1851. In addition to scents for both men and women (including the current queen), Floris has been making its own shaving products (plus combs, brushes, and fragrances) since 1739, reflecting its origins as a barbershop. Other gift possibilities include goose-down powder puffs, a famous rose-scented mouthwash, and beautifully packaged soaps and bath essences. There's another branch in Belgravia. ✉ *89 Jermyn St., St. James's* ☎ *020/7747–3612* ⊕ *www.florislondon.com* Ⓜ *Piccadilly Circus, Green Park.*

BOOKS

Fodor's Choice
★

Hatchards. This is the United Kingdom's oldest bookshop, open since 1797 and beloved by writers themselves—customers have included Oscar Wilde, Rudyard Kipling, and Lord Byron. Despite its wood-paneled, "gentleman's library" atmosphere and eclectic selection of books, Hatchards is owned by the large Waterstone's chain. Nevertheless, the shop still retains its period charm, aided by the staff's old-fashioned helpfulness and expertise. Look for the substantial number of books signed by notable contemporary authors on the well-stocked shelves. There's another branch in the St. Pancras International train station. ✉ *187 Piccadilly, St. James's* ☎ *020/7439–9921* ⊕ *www.hatchards. co.uk* Ⓜ *Piccadilly Circus.*

CLOTHING

Dover Street Market. With its creative displays and eclectic, well-chosen mix of merchandise, this four-floor emporium is as much art installation as store. The merchandise and its configuration change every six months, so you never know what you will find, which is half the fun. The creation of Comme des Garçons' Rei Kawakubo, Dover Street Market showcases all of the label's collections for men and women alongside a changing roster of other ultrafashionable designers, including Junya Wantanabe, Gucci, Alaia, Loewe, and Rick Owens, all of whom have their own customized miniboutiques—plus sneaker and denim collaborations, eyeglass frames, and jewelry. An outpost of the Rose Bakery on the top floor makes for a good break. ✉ *18–22 Haymarket, St. James's* ☎ *020/7518–0680* ⊕ *london.doverstreetmarket.com* Ⓜ *Piccadilly Circus.*

Thomas Pink. Originally founded in London more than 200 years ago as a maker of scarlet hunting coats, Pink's is now an international luxury chain best known for its wide range of stylish formal shirts for both men and women, many in fine fabrics such as Sea Island or Egyptian cotton. More casual shirts are for sale as well, along with ties, boxers,

18

pajamas, belts, and other accessories. For women, there are dresses, skirts, jackets, and knitwear. Bespoke shirts for men can be ordered at the Jermyn Street branch. There are other branches in The City, Chelsea, Canary Wharf, Heathrow, the Westfield shopping center, and Waterloo, Paddington, and St. Pancras International train stations. ✉ *85 Jermyn St., St. James's* ☎ *020/7930–6364* 🌐 *www.thomaspink.co.uk* Ⓜ *Green Park, Piccadilly Circus.*

Turnbull & Asser. The Jermyn Street store sells luxurious jackets, cashmere sweaters, suits, ties, pajamas, ready-to-wear shirts, and accessories perfect for the billionaire who has everything. The brand is best known for its superb custom-made shirts—worn by Prince Charles, Woody Allen, and every filmic James Bond, to name a few. These can be ordered at the nearby Bury or Davies Street branch. At least 15 separate measurements are taken, and the cloth, woven to the company's specifications, comes in 1,000 different patterns—the cottons feel as good as silk. The first order must be for a minimum of six shirts, which start at £195 each. ✉ *71–72 Jermyn St., St. James's* ☎ *020/7808–3000* 🌐 *www.turnbullandasser.co.uk* ⏲ *Closed Sun.* Ⓜ *Green Park.*

FOOD

Fodor's Choice ★ **Berry Bros. & Rudd.** Nothing matches Berry Bros. & Rudd for rare offerings and a unique shopping experience. A family-run wine business since 1698 (Lord Byron was a customer), BBR stores more than 4,000 vintage bottles and casks in vaulted cellars that are more than 300 years old. The in-house wine school offers educational tasting sessions, while the dedicated spirits room also has an excellent selection of whiskeys, cognacs, rums, and more. The shop has a quirky charm and the staff are extremely knowledgeable—and not snooty if you're on a budget. ✉ *3 St. James's St., St. James's* ☎ *800/280–2440* 🌐 *www.bbr.com* ⏲ *Closed Sun.* Ⓜ *Green Park.*

Fortnum & Mason. Although F&M is jokingly known as "the Queen's grocer" and the impeccably mannered staff still wear traditional tailcoats, its celebrated food hall stocks gifts for all budgets, including irresistibly packaged luxury foods stamped with the gold "By Appointment" crest for under £5. Try the teas, preserves (including the unusual rose-petal jelly), condiments, or Gentleman's Relish (anchovy paste). The store's famous hampers are always a welcome gift. The gleaming food hall spans two floors and incorporates a sleek wine bar, with the rest of the store devoted to upscale housewares, men's and women's accessories and toiletries, a dedicated candle room, and a jewelry department featuring exclusive designs by breakthrough talent. If you start to flag, take a break in the tea salon, the café offering tastes of the Food Hall, the contemporary 45 Jermyn Street restaurant (the three-course set menu is good value), or an indulgent ice-cream parlor, where you can find decadent treats like a banana split or a less-traditional gin-and-cucumber float. There's another branch at St. Pancras International train station. ✉ *181 Piccadilly, St. James's* ☎ *020/7734–8040* 🌐 *www.fortnumandmason.com* Ⓜ *Green Park, Piccadilly Circus.*

Paxton & Whitfield. In business for more than 200 years, this venerable and aromatic London shop stocks hundreds of the world's greatest artisanal cheeses, particularly British and French varieties (a homesick General de Gaulle shopped here during World War II). The cheeses are laid on straw on refrigerated shelves, with tasting samples set out on a marble-top counter. You can pick up some ham, pâté, condiments, preserves, wine, or port, as well as cheese-related accessories like boards or knives. There's another branch in Chelsea. ✉ *93 Jermyn St., St. James's* ☎ *020/7930–0259* ⊕ *www.paxtonandwhitfield.co.uk* Ⓜ *Piccadilly Circus, Green Park.*

SHOES

Loake Shoemakers. Long established in England's Midlands and a provider of boots to the British armed forces in both world wars, this family-run firm specializes in classic handcrafted men's shoes. Whether you're after brogues, loafers, or deck shoes, the staff will take the time to ensure you have the right fit. In terms of quality and service, Loakes represents real value for money, though they definitely aren't inexpensive. There's another branch on Bow Lane in The City. ✉ *39c Jermyn St., St. James's* ☎ *020/7734–8643* ⊕ *www.loake.co.uk* Ⓜ *Piccadilly.*

SPECIALTY STORES

Geo F. Trumper. If you don't have the time for an old-fashioned hot-towel shave at this "traditional gentlemen's barbers" established in 1875, pick up a razor, a shaving brush, or other mens' grooming accessory to take home for yourself or as a gift. The Extract of Limes Skin Food is a popular, zingy aftershave, and the Coconut Oil Hard Shaving Soap, which comes in a hand-turned wooden bowl, is a classic. There is also a store at 9 Curzon Street in Mayfair. ✉ *1 Duke of York St., St. James's* ☎ *020/7734–6553* ⊕ *www.trumpers.com* ☾ *Closed Sun.* Ⓜ *Piccadilly Circus.*

18

MAYFAIR AND MARYLEBONE

MAYFAIR
ACCESSORIES

Mulberry. Staying true to its rural Somerset roots, this luxury goods company epitomizes *le style anglais,* a sophisticated take on the earth tones and practicality of English country style. Best known for highly desirable luxury handbags—such as the Lily, Chiltern, and Bayswater models—the company also produces gorgeous leather accessories, from wallets to luggage, as well as shoes and clothing for men and women. Aside from the New Bond Street flagship, there are branches in Knightsbridge, Covent Garden, Heathrow, and the Westfield Centres, along with Mulberry concessions in most of the major upscale department stores. The small store on St. Christopher's Place in Marylebone stocks accessories only. ✉ *50 New Bond St., Mayfair* ☎ *020/7491–3900* ⊕ *www.mulberry.com* Ⓜ *Bond St.*

William & Son. William Asprey, scion of a jewelry dynasty, sells his carefully chosen, British-made luxury goods using a friendlier and less formal approach. You'll find all sorts of items here that you didn't know you needed, like Pininfarina brushed aluminum retractable pencils, green crocodile backgammon sets, or a silver champagne bottle stopper. The jewelry is tasteful and subtle rather than knock-your-eyes-out, and the store will also do custom work. ✉ *34–36 Bruton St., Mayfair* ☏ *020/7493–8385* ⊕ *www.williamandson.com* ⊘ *Closed Sun.* Ⓜ *Bond St.*

ANTIQUES

Grays Antique Centre. There are approximately 200 dealers here, specializing in everything from Bakelite items to Mughal art. The majority focus on jewelry, ranging from contemporary to antique. Bargains are not out of the question, and proper pedigrees are guaranteed. Go on a weekday for the most choice; not all stalls are open on Saturday. Also try Grays at 1–7 Davies Mews around the corner: stalls there sell less expensive merchandise, including antique dolls at Glenda's and excellent vintage clothing at Vintage Modes. ✉ *58 Davies St., Mayfair* ☏ *020/7629–7034* ⊕ *www.graysantiques.com* ⊘ *Closed Sun.* Ⓜ *Bond St.*

BOOKS AND STATIONERY

Fodor's Choice ★ **Heywood Hill.** Open since 1936, this is considered by some to be the best small bookstore in the English-speaking world—John Le Carré, who set a scene in *Tinker Tailor Soldier Spy* here, is a long-standing customer. Browse for a leather-bound volume on architecture, gardening, natural history, or topography—just some of the topics in which the antiquarian collection specializes. The contemporary selection emphasizes literature, history, biography, travel, architecture, and children's books, and the knowledgeable staff are happy to provide advice. During World War II, author Nancy Mitford helped keep the bookstore going. Today, the 12th Duke of Devonshire, a descendant of her brother-in-law, the 11th Duke, is the owner. ✉ *10 Curzon St., Mayfair* ☏ *020/7629–0647* ⊕ *www.heywoodhill.com* ⊘ *Closed Sun.* Ⓜ *Green Park.*

Smythson of Bond Street. No hostess of any standing would consider having a leather-bound guest book made by anyone besides this elegant stationer, and the shop's social stationery and distinctive diaries with their pale-blue pages are the epitome of British good taste. These, along with other made-in-Britain leather goods including a small line of handbags, backpacks, and luggage tags, can be personalized. There are branches in Chelsea, Notting Hill, and The City, plus concessions in leading department stores. ✉ *40 New Bond St., Mayfair* ☏ *020/3535–8009* ⊕ *www.smythson.com* Ⓜ *Bond St., Oxford Circus.*

Waterstone's. At this megabookshop (Europe's largest, with more than 8 miles of bookshelves) in a former art deco department store near Piccadilly Circus, browse for your latest purchase or admire the view with a glass of wine or a snack at the 5th View Bar and Food (open until 9). Waterstone's is the country's leading book chain, and it's pulled out all the stops to make its flagship as comfortable and welcoming as a bookstore can be. There are several smaller branches throughout the city. ✉ *203–206 Piccadilly, Mayfair* ☏ *0207/851–2400* ⊕ *www.waterstones.com* Ⓜ *Piccadilly Circus.*

CLOTHING

Alexander McQueen. Since the legendary designer's untimely death in 2010, his right-hand woman, Sarah Burton, has been at the helm, receiving raves for continuing his tradition of theatrical, darkly romantic, and beautifully cut clothes incorporating corsetry, lace, embroidery, and hourglass silhouettes, all of which were exemplified in Burton's celebrated wedding dress for Kate Middleton. Can't afford a gala gown? Go home with a skull-print silk scarf. ⊠ *4–5 Old Bond St., Mayfair* ☎ *020/7355–0088* ⊕ *www.alexandermcqueen.com* Ⓜ *Bond St.*

Belstaff. For years the purveyors of Britain's coolest motorcycle leathers, Belstaff has expanded into dresses, skirts, and handbags, as well as knitwear, boots, tops, and trousers for men, women, and children. Outerwear in general and leather jackets in particular remain a strength. All the items reflect the brand's functional yet unconventional heritage, and now, under new Italian ownership, come with added fashion flair. Previous customers include Lawrence of Arabia, Amelia Earhart, and Che Guevara. There's another branch in Spitalfields. ⊠ *135–137 New Bond St., Mayfair* ☎ *020/7495–5897* ⊕ *www.belstaff.co.uk* Ⓜ *Bond St.*

Browns. This shop occupying interconnecting townhouses was a pioneer designer boutique in the 1970s. Now owned by online luxury retailer Farfetch.com, Brown's focuses on well-established international luxury designers such as Vetements, Valentino, or St. Laurent. The men's store at No. 23 has a similar designer selection, while footwear occupies No. 24. There is a smaller boutique on Sloane Street, too. If you're about to go down the aisle, check out the two bridal boutiques, one at 12 Hinde Street, which stocks various designers, and another at 59 Brook Street, devoted to Vera Wang gowns exclusive to Browns in the United Kingdom. ⊠ *24–27 S. Molton St., Mayfair* ☎ *020/7514–0016* ⊕ *www.brownsfashion.com* ⊙ *Closed Sun.* Ⓜ *Bond St.*

Burberry. Known for its trademark tartan, this company has cultivated an edgy, high-fashion image in recent years, with designs like fetish-y boots and sexy leather jackets perfect for any catwalk. The raincoats are still a classic buy, along with plaid scarves in every color imaginable and handbags. If you're up for a trek, there's a huge factory outlet in Hackney on Chatham Place that has clothes and accessories for men, women, and children at half price or less. There are also branches in Mayfair, Knightsbridge, Covent Garden, and the Westfield shopping center in addition to this spectacular flagship store. ⊠ *121 Regent St., Mayfair* ☎ *020/7806–8904* ⊕ *uk.burberry.com* Ⓜ *Piccadilly Circus.*

Fodor's Choice ★ **Fenwick.** A manageably sized department store, Fenwick is a welcome haven of affordability in a shopping area where stratospheric prices are the norm. The store is particularly strong on accessories (notably lingerie, wraps, and hats), cosmetics, perfumes, and chic, wearable fashion by both big names and more niche designers such as Goat, J Brand, and Victoria Victoria Beckham. There are also three small spas (Chantecaille, Clarins, and a Blink waxing room), various beauty services (including a hair salon, nail bar, and Blink brow bar), and three restaurants plus a men's department in the basement. ⊠ *163 New Bond St., Mayfair* ☎ *020/7629–9161* ⊕ *www.fenwick.co.uk* Ⓜ *Bond St.*

18

Isabel Marant London. The first London store from Marant, a favorite of French fashion editors, this airy skylit space is full of her signature slim-cut pants, slouchy knits, wedge sneakers, and rock-chick miniskirts, all exuding Left Bank boho cool. ✉ *29 Bruton St., Mayfair* ☎ *020/7499–7887* ⊕ *www.isabelmarant.com* ⊙ *Closed Sun.* Ⓜ *Bond St.*

Stella McCartney. It's not easy emerging from the shadow of a Beatle father, but Stella McCartney is a major force in fashion in her own right. Her signature jumpsuits and tuxedo pantsuits embody her design philosophy, combining minimalist tailoring with femininity and sophistication with ease of wear. Her love of functionality and clean lines has led to her branching off into lingerie, accessories, swimwear, and sportswear, designing a line for Adidas. A vegetarian like her parents, she refuses to use fur or leather, making her a favorite with similarly minded fashionistas. There's another boutique in South Kensington. ✉ *30 Bruton St., Mayfair* ☎ *020/7518–3100* ⊕ *www.stellamccartney. com* ⊙ *Closed Sun.* Ⓜ *Bond St.*

Vivienne Westwood. From its beginnings as the most shocking and outré designer around, Westwood (now Dame Vivienne) has become a standard-bearer for high-style British couture. At the Chelsea boutique where she first sold the lavish corseted ball gowns, dandyfied nipped-waist jackets, and tartan-meets-punk daywear that formed the core of her signature look, you can still buy ready-to-wear—mainly items from the more casual Anglomania diffusion line and the exclusive Worlds End label, which draws from her archives. The small Davies Street boutique sells only the more expensive Gold Label and Couture collections (plus bridal), while the flagship Conduit Street store carries all of the above. There's also a Men's collection at 18 Conduit Street. ✉ *44 Conduit St., Mayfair* ☎ *020/7439–1109* ⊕ *www.viviennewestwood.com* Ⓜ *Oxford Circus.*

DEPARTMENT STORES

Thomas Goode. This spacious luxury housewares shop has been at the same smart Mayfair address since 1845. The china, silver, crystal, and linen, whether from the store's own line or from luxury brands like Christofle and Puiforcat, are simply the best that money can buy, a legacy of its original customer base of international royals and heads of state. The store still holds two royal warrants, but anyone who can afford it can commission their own bespoke set of china. If such luxury is beyond you, visit anyway for the shop's small museum of plates, either antique or designed for royalty, including some created for Princess Diana's wedding. ✉ *19 S. Audley St., Mayfair* ☎ *020/7499–2823* ⊕ *www.thomasgoode.co.uk* ⊙ *Closed Sun.* Ⓜ *Green Park.*

FOOD

Charbonnel et Walker. Established in 1875, this master chocolatier's Mayfair shop specializes in traditional handmade chocolates (rose-petal creams and champagne truffles, for example) and has been creating these beautifully packaged, high-quality candies from long before most of today's fashionable brands appeared. Their drinking chocolate—coarsely grated fine chocolate in a tin—is worth carrying home in a suitcase. ✉ *One The Royal Arcade, 28 Old Bond St., Mayfair* ☎ *020/7318–1075* ⊕ *www.charbonnel.co.uk* Ⓜ *Green Park.*

JEWELRY

Asprey. The company's "global flagship" store displays exquisite jewelry—as well as silver and leather goods, watches, china, and crystal—in a discreet, very British setting that oozes quality, expensive good taste, and hushed comfort. If you're in the market for an immaculate 1930s cigarette case, a silver cocktail shaker, a pair of pavé diamond and sapphire earrings, or a ladylike handbag, you won't likely be disappointed. And, for the really well-heeled, there's custom service available as well (Ringo Starr had a chess set made here). This store has occupied the premises since 1847, some 66 years after Asprey was established in 1781. ✉ *167 New Bond St., Mayfair* ☎ *020/7493–6767* ⊕ *www.asprey. com* ⊙ *Closed Sun.* Ⓜ *Green Park.*

Garrard. The oldest jewelry house in the world, Garrard has been in business since 1735. Between 1843 and 2007, the company was responsible for the upkeep of the Crown Jewels in the Tower of London and for creating several royal crowns (you can see some on display in the Tower). Today the focus is on precious gems in simple, classic settings, along with silver accessories. Although some collections are definitely contemporary (with items like minimalist hoop earrings or two-finger rings), many of the designs are traditional and impressive—which will be handy should you be in the market for an old-school diamond tiara. ✉ *24 Albemarle St., Mayfair* ☎ *207/518–1070* ⊕ *www.garrard.com* ⊙ *Closed Sun.* Ⓜ *Green Park.*

MEN'S CLOTHING

Alfred Dunhill. For more than 100 years, Dunhill has been synonymous with the most luxurious and sophisticated men's goods, including accessories, briefcases, and superbly tailored clothes. This Georgian mansion, their flagship, also features a barbershop, men's spa, humidor, cellar bar, courtyard restaurant, and bespoke services, where you can order custom-fitted menswear or unique versions of the brand's celebrated leather goods. The smaller, original St. James's shop has been on Jermyn Street since 1906. ✉ *Bourdon House, 2 Davies St., Mayfair* ☎ *020/3425–7300* ⊕ *www.dunhill.com* ⊙ *Closed Sun.* Ⓜ *Bond St.*

Gieves and Hawkes. One of the grand men's tailoring houses of Savile Row, this company made its name outfitting British royals who served as officers in the armed forces. The company still supplies custom-made military uniforms, as well as beautifully tailored civilian wear. Prices for a bespoke suit start around £3800, but you can find ready-made versions from around £900 (separates from £200), while a new line of casualwear has several items under £200. ✉ *1 Savile Row, Mayfair* ☎ *020/7432–6403* ⊕ *www.gievesandhawkes.com* Ⓜ *Piccadilly Circus.*

Ozwald Boateng. The dapper menswear by Ozwald Boateng (pronounced "Bwa-teng") combines contemporary funky style with traditional Savile Row quality. His made-to-measure suits have been worn by the likes of Jamie Foxx, Mick Jagger, and Laurence Fishburne, who appreciate the sharp cuts, luxurious fabrics, and occasionally vibrant colors (even the more conservative choices have jacket linings in bright silk). ✉ *30 Savile Row, Mayfair* ☎ *020/7437–2030* ⊕ *www.ozwaldboateng.co.uk* ⊙ *Closed Sun.* Ⓜ *Piccadilly Circus.*

18

SHOES

Nicholas Kirkwood. Kirkwood is one of Britain's most fashionable shoe designers, and this is his only retail boutique. You won't be able to hike in his imaginative, elegant, sky-high stilettos (be warned: prices are similarly high), but you will be able to make quite an entrance. There are also more wearable styles that are equally flattering and gorgeous. ⊠ *5 Mount St., Mayfair* ☎ *020/7290–1404* ⊕ *www.nicholaskirkwood. com* ⊘ *Closed Sun.* Ⓜ *Green Park.*

Rupert Sanderson. Designed in London and made in Italy, Sanderson's elegant shoes have been a huge hit in fashion circles with their lavish ornamentation on heels and flats alike. Red-carpet-ready high heels—worn by celebs including Claire Danes, Nicole Kidman, and Sandra Bullock—come in gorgeous colors and prints; peep toes are signature elements. The high prices reflect the impeccable craftsmanship. ⊠ *19 Bruton Pl., Mayfair* ☎ *0207/491–2260* ⊕ *www.rupertsanderson.com* ⊘ *Closed Sun.* Ⓜ *Bond St., Green Park.*

MARYLEBONE

ANTIQUES

Alfie's Antique Market. This four-story, bohemian-chic labyrinth is London's largest indoor antiques market, housing more than 75 dealers specializing in art, lighting, glassware, textiles, jewelry, furniture, and collectibles, with a particular strength in vintage clothing and 20th-century design. Come here to pick up vintage (1900–70) clothing, accessories, and luggage from Tin Tin Collectables, antique and vintage glassware and vases at Robinson Antiques, or a spectacular mid-20th-century Italian lighting fixture at Vincenzo Caffarrella. The atmosphere may be funky but the prices are not. There's also a rooftop café with free Wi-Fi if you need a coffee break. In addition to the market, this end of Church Street is lined with excellent antiques shops. ⊠ *13–25 Church St., Marylebone* ☎ *020/7723–6066* ⊕ *www.alfiesantiques.com* ⊘ *Closed Sun. and Mon.* Ⓜ *Marylebone.*

BEAUTY

Space.NK.apothecary. Aficionados of hard-to-find cult beauty products flock to this upscale chain that now has more than 20 locations throughout London. The minute you step inside, you're surrounded by dozens of luxurious and sought-after cosmetic and skincare brands like Lipstick Queen, Chantecaille, Caudalie, By Terry Perricone MD, and Nars, along with fragrances by the likes of Acqua di Parma and candles by Diptique. The helpful staff is happy to offer knowledgeable advice. The Notting Hill branch also offers spa treatments, while men have a branch of their own in Soho. ⊠ *83A Marylebone High St., Marylebone* ☎ *020/7486–8791* ⊕ *uk.spacenk.com* Ⓜ *Baker St.*

BOOKS

Daunt Books. An independent bookstore chain (there are additional branches in Belsize Park, Chelsea, Hampstead, Holland Park, and Cheapside), Daunt favors a thoughtful selection of contemporary and classic fiction and nonfiction. The striking Marylebone branch is an original Edwardian bookstore, where a dramatic room with a long oak-paneled gallery under lofty skylights houses the noted travel section, which includes not only guidebooks but also related literature and poetry. The Hampstead branch is strong on children's books. ✉ *83 Marylebone High St., Marylebone* ☎ *020/7224–2295* ⊕ *www.daunt-books.co.uk* Ⓜ *Baker St.*

CLOTHING

Matches Fashion. This carefully curated boutique carries fashion from designers both rising and established, including Christopher Kane, Erdem, J.W. Anderson, Proenza Schouler, Vetements, McCartney, McQueen, Balenciaga, Balmain, Valentino, Saint Laurent, Marni, and Chloé. There's also an equally stylish menswear department, plus jewelry, lingerie, footwear, and accessories. Other branches can be found in Notting Hill and southwest London. ✉ *87 Marylebone High St., Marylebone* ☎ *020/7487–5400* ⊕ *www.matchesfashion.com* Ⓜ *Regent's Park, Baker St.*

Reiss. With an in-house design team whose experience includes stints at Gucci and Calvin Klein and customers like Beyoncé and the Duchess of Cambridge, who wore a Reiss dress for her official engagement picture, this reliable chain brings luxury standards of tailoring and details to mass-market women's and menswear. The sleek and contemporary style doesn't come cheap, but does offer value for money. There are branches in Knightsbridge, The City, Covent Garden, Chelsea, Hampstead, Islington, Soho, Kensington, and basically all over London. ✉ *10 Barrett St., Marylebone* ☎ *020/7486–6557* ⊕ *www.reiss.com* Ⓜ *Oxford St.*

DEPARTMENT STORES

Marks & Spencer. You'd be hard-pressed to find a Brit who doesn't have something in the closet from Marks & Spencer (or M&S, as it's popularly known). This major chain is famed for its classic, dependable clothing for men, women, and children—affordable cashmere and lambswool sweaters are particularly good buys—and occasionally scores a fashion hit. The food department at M&S is consistently good, especially for frozen food, and a great place to pick up a sandwich or premade salad on the go (look for M&S Simply Food stores all over town). The flagship branch at Marble Arch and the Pantheon location at 173 Oxford Street have extensive fashion departments. ✉ *458 Oxford St., Marylebone* ☎ *020/7935–7954* ⊕ *www.marksandspencer.com* Ⓜ *Marble Arch.*

Fodor's Choice ★ **Selfridges.** This giant, bustling store (the second largest in the United Kingdom after Harrods) gives Harvey Nichols a run for its money as London's most fashionable department store. Packed to the rafters with clothes ranging from midprice lines to the latest catwalk names, the store continues to break ground with its innovative retail schemes, especially the ground-floor Wonder Room (for extravagant jewelry and luxury gifts, with self-contained Fendi, Dior, and Van Cleef and Arpels boutiques), the self-contained Louis Vuitton "townhouse," a dedicated Denim Studio, an array of pop-up shops, and the Concept Store, used for a rotating series of themed displays. There are so many zones that merge into one another—from youth-oriented Miss Selfridge to audio equipment to the large, comprehensive cosmetics department—that you practically need a map. Don't miss the Shoe Galleries, the world's largest

18

shoe department, which is filled with more than 5,000 pairs from 120 brands, displayed like works of art under spotlights. Take a break with a glass of wine at the rooftop restaurant or pick up some tea in the Food Hall as a gift. At the Everyman movie theater in the basement, you can watch first-run art-house movies. ⊠ *400 Oxford St., Marylebone* ☎ *0800/123400* ⊕ *www.selfridges.com* Ⓜ *Bond St.*

JEWELRY

Kabiri. A carefully curated array of exciting contemporary jewelry by emerging and established designers from around the world is packed into this small shop. There is something to suit most budgets and tastes, though understated, minimalism predominates. You can score an elegant, one-of-a-kind piece here for a very reasonable price. ⊠ *94 Marylebone La., Marylebone* ☎ *020/7317–2150* ⊕ *www.kabiri.co.uk* Ⓜ *Baker St.*

SPECIALTY STORES

Fodor's Choice ★ **The Button Queen.** Extremely specialized shops like this one once helped make London so distinctive, but today they are in danger of disappearing. The Button Queen began life as a market stall in the 1950s, and now it has amassed a vast selection of buttons, from antique to modern, encompassing an array of styles and prices. You can also have a set made using fabric you supply. ⊠ *76 Marylebone La., Marylebone* ☎ *020/7935–1505* ⊕ *www.thebuttonqueen.co.uk* ✆ *Closed Sun.* Ⓜ *Oxford Circus.*

SOHO AND COVENT GARDEN

SOHO

ACCESSORIES

Fodor's Choice ★ **Peckham Rye.** On the small cobblestone streets leading off Carnaby Street, among other little specialty shops, the family-run Peckham Rye sells heritage-style men's accessories: handmade silk and twill ties, bow ties, and scarves, all using traditional patterns drawn from the archives going back to 1799. Embodying the Ralph Lauren aesthetic even more than Ralph Lauren, the socks, striped shirts, and handkerchiefs attract modern-day dandies like Mark Ronson and David Beckham. Bespoke tailoring for men is also offered. ⊠ *11 Newburgh St., Soho* ☎ *0207/734–5181* ⊕ *www. peckhamrye.com* ⊘ *Closed Sun.* Ⓜ *Oxford St.*

BOOKS

Fodor's Choice ★ **Foyles.** Founded in 1903 by the Foyle brothers after they failed the Civil Service exam, this family-owned bookstore is in a 1930s art deco building, once the home of the renowned art college Central Saint Martins. Foyles carries more than 200,000 titles on its 4 miles of bookshelves. One of London's best sources for textbooks and the United Kingdom's largest retailer of foreign language titles, Foyles also stocks everything from popular fiction to military history, sheet music, medical tomes, graphic novels, and handsome illustrated fine arts books. It also offers the store-within-a-store Ray's Jazz (one of London's better outlets for music) and a cool café. Foyles has branches in the Southbank Centre, the Westfield shopping center in Stratford, and the St. Pancras International and Waterloo stations. ⊠ *107 Charing Cross Rd., Soho* ☎ *020/7437–5660* ⊕ *www.foyles.co.uk* Ⓜ *Tottenham Court Rd.*

CLOTHING

Other. Aimed at men and women in search of stylish cool, this independent boutique stocks its own brand of entirely made-in-England clothing, as well as accessories, housewares, books, and clothing from other carefully selected, high-end cult brands such as Christopher Lemaire and Peter Jensen. The look is understated, slightly geeky, and totally contemporary. ⊠ *3 Berwick St., Soho* ☎ *020/7734–6846* ⊕ *other-shop. com* Ⓜ *Oxford Circus.*

Primark. The huge, two-story flagship is fantastic for low-cost, trendy clothing, but keep in mind, you get what you pay for: some of the fabrics and finishes reflect the store's budget prices, and its labor practices have drawn criticism. This is the home of fast, youthful, disposable fashion, so don't expect attentive service or classic styling. There are branches in Hammersmith and Kilburn. ⊠ *499–517 Oxford St., Soho* ☎ *020/7495–0420* ⊕ *www.primark.co.uk* Ⓜ *Marble Arch.*

Wolsey. Specializing in men's knitwear since 1755, this long-established company now sells rugged but stylish outerwear, sweaters, shirts, hats, scarves, socks, T-shirts, sweatshirts, sleepwear, and underwear (the undies of choice for polar explorers Roald Amundsen, Captain Robert Scott, and Ernest Shackleton). The company also supplied woollen garments to British troops in 1914. It's not all heritage, though; Wolsey also makes hoodies, and its padded jackets and vests employ the latest in thermalwear technology. The interior reflects this blend of the traditional and the contemporary, with exposed brick walls, brushed steel beams, and photographs of expeditions the brand has outfitted. There's another branch in Covent Garden. ⊠ *83A Brewer St., Soho* ☎ *020/7434–4257* ⊕ *wolsey.com* Ⓜ *Piccadilly Circus.*

DEPARTMENT STORES

Fodor's Choice ★ **Liberty.** The wonderful black-and-white mock-Tudor facade, created from the timbers of two Royal Navy ships, reflects this store's origins in the late-19th-century Arts and Crafts movement. Leading designers were recruited to create the classic art nouveau Liberty prints that are still a centerpiece of the brand, gracing everything from cushions and silk kimonos to embossed leather bags and photo albums. Inside, Liberty is a labyrinth of nooks and crannies stuffed with thoughtfully chosen merchandise, including niche beauty, perfume, footwear, and housewares lines. Clothes for both men and women focus on high quality and high fashion, with labels like Alexander Wang and Etro. The store regularly commissions new prints from contemporary designers, and sells both these and its classic patterns by the yard. If you're not so handy with a needle, an interior design service will create soft furnishings for you. There's also a florist, a hair salon, a traditional men's barber, beauty treatment rooms, a brow bar, a piercing studio, and a foot spa. ⊠ *Regent St., Soho* ☎ *020/7734–1234* ⊕ *www.liberty. co.uk* Ⓜ *Oxford Circus.*

FOOD

Fodor's Choice ★ **The Vintage House.** If whiskey is more to your taste than wine, visit the Vintage House, which has the country's largest selection of single malts (more than 1,300), including many rare bottles and some exclusive to the shop. You'll also find more than 100 tequilas as well as

18

Cuban cigars. The shop is open until 11 pm (10 pm on Sunday). ✉ *42 Old Compton St., Soho* ☎ *020/7437–2592* ⊕ *www.vintagehouse.london* Ⓜ *Leicester Sq.*

SHOES

Irregular Choice. If you want to blend in with the crowd, these shoes are not for you; but if you like footwear that is fun and flattering (not to mention reasonably priced), head for Irregular Choice. Styles tend toward Louis XIV–like court shoes ornamented with big ribbon ties or silk flowers, but there are also pumps in interesting patterns, bejeweled flats, glittery sneakers, and tropical-print platform sandals, as well as clutch bags and whimsical jewelry. Best of all, many have round toes and supportive heels, proving that comfortable doesn't have to be dull. There's another branch near Camden Market. ✉ *35 Carnaby St., Soho* ☎ *020/7494–4811* ⊕ *www.irregularchoice.com* Ⓜ *Oxford Circus.*

TOYS

FAMILY **Hamleys.** When British children visit London, this institution—the oldest toy store in the world—is at the top of their agenda. Its six floors hold the latest dolls, soft toys, video games, and technological devices; such old-fashioned pleasures as train sets, drum kits, and magic tricks; plus every must-have on the preteen shopping list (some parents may find the offerings to be overly commercialized, as they're heavy on movie and TV tie-ins). Hamleys is a madhouse at Christmastime, but the Santa's grotto is one of the best in town. There's a smaller branch in St. Pancras International train station. ✉ *188–196 Regent St., Soho* ☎ *0371/704–1977* ⊕ *www.hamleys.com* Ⓜ *Oxford Circus, Piccadilly Circus.*

COVENT GARDEN

BOOKS AND PRINTS

Grosvenor Prints. London's largest collection of 17th- to early-20th-century prints emphasizes views of the city and architecture as well as sporting and decorative motifs. The selection is eclectic, with prices ranging from £5 to the thousands. ✉ *19 Shelton St., Covent Garden* ☎ *020/7836–1979* ⊕ *www.grosvenorprints.com* ⊘ *Closed Sun.* Ⓜ *Covent Garden, Leicester Sq.*

Fodor's Choice **Stanfords.** When it comes to encyclopedic coverage, there is simply no
★ better travel shop on the planet. At this location for more than 100 years, Stanfords is packed with a comprehensive selection of travel books and travel accessories, as well as ordinance surveys, cycle route maps, travel adaptors, globes, replicas of antique maps, mosquito nets, and more. Even the floor is decorated with giant maps. Whether you're planning a day trip to Surrey or an adventure to the South Pole, this should be your first stop. ✉ *12–14 Long Acre, Covent Garden* ☎ *020/7836–1321* ⊕ *www.stanfords.co.uk* Ⓜ *Covent Garden.*

CLOTHING

Jack Wills. The heritage and country sports-inspired styles here have a fresh, sexy edge. Crowds of lithe teens don't mind the pumping music while they browse the collection—slim-line Fair Isle sweaters, fitted plaid shirts, little black dresses, and short floral sundresses for the girls, and sweatshirts, blazers, skinny cords, and rugby shirts for the boys. The store also carries backpacks, baseball hats, laptop cases, branded water bottles, and other youthful lifestyle items. Other branches are in Soho and Battersea. ✉ *St. Martin's Courtyard, 136 Long Acre, Covent Garden* ☎ *020/7240–8946* ⊕ *www.jackwills.com* Ⓜ *Leicester Sq., Covent Garden.*

Paul Smith. British classics with an irreverent twist define Paul Smith's collections for women, men, and children. Beautifully tailored suits for men and women take hallmarks of traditional British style and turn them on their heads with humor and color, combining exceptional fabrics with flamboyant linings or unusual detailing. Gift ideas abound—wallets, scarves, diaries, spectacles, even a soccer ball—all in Smith's signature rainbow stripes. There are several branches throughout London, in Notting Hill, Soho, Marylebone, and Canary Wharf, plus a Mayfair shop that includes vintage furniture. ✉ *40–44 Floral St., Covent Garden* ☎ *020/7379–7133* ⊕ *www.paulsmith.co.uk* Ⓜ *Covent Garden.*

Tabio. This Japanese-owned specialty store reflects the country's noted enthusiasm for socks and is the place to find them, as well as leg warmers, tights, and stockings, all in a wide assortment of weights. Styles range from functional to fanciful and patterns from simple and elegant to lively and attention-getting. There's another branch on King's Road in Chelsea. ✉ *66 Neal St., Covent Garden* ☎ *020/7836–3713* ⊕ *www.tabio.com* Ⓜ *Covent Garden.*

HOUSEHOLD

Cath Kidston. Lovers of chintz and colorful patterns adore Cath Kidston's bright feminine signature look. Textiles bearing ginghams, polka dots, and lots of big, blooming roses appear on everything in sight, from ceramics and bed linens to fine china, stationery, and doggie beds. There are clothing and nightwear lines for women and children, along with handbags, totes, knapsacks, and cosmetic bags. Branches can be found throughout the city, including in Marylebone, Chelsea, Notting Hill, St. Pancras International train station, and a flagship store on Piccadilly. ✉ *28–32 Shelton St., Covent Garden* ☎ *020/7240–8324* ⊕ *www.cathkidston.co.uk* Ⓜ *Covent Garden.*

MARKETS

Covent Garden Market. This popular destination includes three separate market areas: the Apple Market, the East Colonnade Market, and the Jubilee Market. In the covered area, originally designed by Inigo Jones and known as the Apple Market, forty stalls sell handcrafted jewelry, clothes, ceramics, antiques, curios, and other unique items. The East Colonnade Market has stalls with mostly handmade specialty items that include handmade soaps and jewelry, as well as housewares, accessories, and magic tricks. The Jubilee Market, in Jubilee Hall toward Southampton Street, tends toward the more pedestrian (kitschy T-shirts, unremarkable household goods, and the like) Tuesday through Friday, but has vintage collectibles on Monday and worthwhile handmade goods on weekends. A "real food" market on Thursday offers artisanal street food. Largely aimed at the tourist trade in the past, Covent Garden Market is now going for a more sophisticated image (and correspondingly high prices) with the opening of upscale restaurants and chains in the surrounding arcades, including the world's largest Apple Store and

18

a Disney store; beauty outlets for Chanel, Bobbi Brown, and Dior; and boutiques for brands like Mulberry and N. Peal. ■TIP➜ Don't miss the magicians, musicians, and escape artists who perform in the open-air piazza, all still free (though contributions are welcome). ⊠ *The Piazza, off Wellington St., Covent Garden* ⊕ *www.coventgarden.london, jubileemarket.co.uk* Ⓜ *Covent Garden.*

SHOES

Fodor'sChoice **United Nude.** Cocreated by famed architect Rem Koolhaas (who also ★ designed this Covent Garden flagship store) and Galahad Clark (of the Clarks shoes dynasty), this brand sells distinctive, futuristic designs that use up-to-the-minute techniques such as carbon-fiber heels and injection-molded soles. The shoes' edginess doesn't stop them from being flattering, affordable, and surprisingly comfortable. ⊠ *13 Floral St., Covent Garden* ☏ *0207/240–7106* ⊕ *www.unitednude.com* Ⓜ *Covent Garden.*

TOYS

FAMILY **Benjamin Pollock's Toyshop.** This landmark shop still carries on the tra-
Fodor'sChoice dition of its founder, who sold miniature theater stages made from
★ richly detailed paper from the late 19th century until his death in 1937. Among his admirers was Robert Louis Stevenson, who wrote, "If you love art, folly, or the bright eyes of children, speed to Pollock's." Today the antique model theaters are expensive, but there are plenty of magical reproductions for less than £10. There's also an extensive selection of new but nostalgic puppets, marionettes, teddy bears, spinning tops, jack-in-the-boxes, and similar traditional children's toys from the days before batteries were required (or toys were even run on them). ⊠ *44 The Market Bldg., Covent Garden* ☏ *020/7379–7866* ⊕ *www.pollockscoventgarden.co.uk* Ⓜ *Covent Garden.*

The Tintin Shop. Before there was Harry Potter, there was Tintin. Created by the Belgian cartoonist Hergé, the story of the fictional boy detective and his intrepid dog Snowy has been a cult favorite for generations. At this namesake shop devotees can find Tintin-related books, posters, T-shirts, metal and resin figurines, die-cast model airplane, alarm clocks, and more. ⊠ *34 Floral St., Covent Garden* ☏ *020/7836–1131* ⊕ *thetintinshop.uk.com* Ⓜ *Covent Garden.*

BLOOMSBURY, HOLBORN, ISLINGTON, AND FITZROVIA

BLOOMSBURY

ACCESSORIES

Fodor'sChoice **James Smith & Sons Ltd.** This has to be the world's ultimate umbrella
★ shop (it is definitely Europe's oldest), and a must for anyone interested in real Victorian London. The family-owned shop has been in this location on a corner of New Oxford Street since 1857 and sells every kind of umbrella, parasol, cane, and walking stick imaginable (including some containing a small flask or a corkscrew). The interior is unchanged since the 19th century; you will feel as if you have stepped back in time. Umbrellas range from about £60 for a folding umbrella to more than £250 for a classic man's umbrella with a carved animal-head handle and thousands for bespoke items. If the umbrella prices

are too steep, James Smith also sells smaller accessories and handmade wooden bowls. ⊠ *Hazelwood House, 53 New Oxford St., Bloomsbury* ☎ *020/7836–4731* ⊕ *www.james-smith.co.uk* ⊘ *Closed Sun.* Ⓜ *Tottenham Court Rd., Holborn.*

BOOKS

Gay's the Word. Open since 1979, this is London's leading gay and lesbian bookshop. Thousands of titles, from literature and thoughtful nonfiction to erotica and prodiversity children's books, fill the shelves. The shop is a well-loved fixture on the scene (it features prominently in the 2014 movie *Pride*) and often hosts discussion groups, readings, and other events. ⊠ *66 Marchmont St., Bloomsbury* ☎ *020/7278–7654* ⊕ *www.gaystheword.co.uk* Ⓜ *Russell Sq.*

Maggs Bros. Ltd. How could any book lover resist a shop with such a Dickensian name? Resembling the library of a bibliophilic gentleman more than a commercial enterprise, Maggs has been selling rare antiquarian books and manuscripts since 1853 and is one of the world's oldest and largest such dealers (it also deals in autographs). The staff—with specialists in Early British and Early European works, Travel, and Japanese photography—are expert enough to advise important collectors, but are friendly and helpful to all interested visitors. Maggs also has a tradition of carrying works on subversion, extremism, punk, the occult, and more. There are occasional themed exhibitions featuring manuscripts and rare editions, and there's an annex shop on Curzon Street in Mayfair. ⊠ *48 Bedford Sq., Bloomsbury* ☎ *020/7493–7160* ⊕ *www.maggs.com* ⊘ *Closed weekends* Ⓜ *Goodge St., Tottenham Court Rd.*

Fodor's Choice ★ **Persephone Books.** A must for all lovers of fiction and nonfiction by women, Persephone is a gem of a bookshop specializing in its own reprints of mostly neglected 20th-century works from predominately female writers. Exquisitely decorated endpapers make these books perfect gifts for your bibliophile friends. ⊠ *59 Lamb's Conduit St., Bloomsbury* ☎ *020/7242–9292* ⊕ *www.persephonebooks.co.uk* ⊘ *Closed Sun.* Ⓜ *Russell Sq., Holborn.*

SPECIALTY STORES

Blade Rubber. This unique shop near the British Museum specializes in rubber stamps, with everything from businesslike "Paid" stamps to *Alice in Wonderland* characters, Egyptian gods, VW Beetles, flying saucers, and more. Get a custom-made personal stamp—a great gift for a young person—or bring back stamps of British icons like a double-decker bus, the Tower of London, or a bust of Shakespeare as souvenirs. It also carries scrapbooking materials and offers scrapbooking classes on Saturday. ⊠ *12 Bury Pl., Bloomsbury* ☎ *020/7831–4123* ⊕ *www.bladerubberstamps.co.uk* Ⓜ *Holborn.*

HOLBORN

ANTIQUES

London Silver Vaults. Originally built in 1876 as Britain's first safe deposit building, with basement strong rooms for storing household valuables like jewelry, silver, and documents, this extraordinary underground space has been converted to more than 30 small units housing silver

18

(plus a few jewelry) dealers, the majority of which are family businesses. Products range from 16th-century items to contemporary pieces (with everything in between), and from the spectacularly over-the-top costing thousands to smaller items—like teaspoons, candlesticks, or a set of Victorian cake forks—at £25. ⊠ *53–64 Chancery La., Holborn* ☎ *020/7242–3844* ⊕ *www.silvervaultslondon.com* ☾ *Closed Sun.* Ⓜ *Chancery La.*

ISLINGTON
HOUSEHOLD

Fodor'sChoice ★ **TwentyTwentyOne.** A must for lovers of modernist design, this shop carries a huge selection of 20th-century classics, including a chaise longue from Le Corbusier as well as pieces from Noguchi, Aalto, Prouvé, Saarinen, and the husband-and-wife team Robin and Lucienne Day, in the form of both originals and licensed reissues. Also among the offerings are contemporary pieces from modern masters like Tom Dixon, Thomas Heatherwick, and Marc Newson. The kids' line is particularly cool, with items like a classic elephant sculpture/toy from another married design team, Charles and Ray Eames. Small accessories like tote bags and cushions will easily fit into your luggage. ⊠ *274–275 Upper St., Islington* ☎ *020/7288–1996* ⊕ *www.twentytwentyone.com* Ⓜ *Highbury & Islington.*

FITZROVIA
CLOTHING

Fodor'sChoice ★ **So Tiny London.** This small store has loads of imaginative gifts for babies and young children, such as distinctive onesies and T-shirts emblazoned with Union Jacks, "Darth Vader Is My Father," "Baby Gaga," and logos of rock bands like Pink Floyd, Motörhead, and the Rolling Stones. You'll also find pretty dresses with an English Rose print, dragon costumes for dress-up, Jellycat plush toys (favorites of royal babies William and Charlotte), and child-friendly joke items like rubber chickens. ⊠ *64 Great Titchfield St., Fitzrovia* ☎ *020/7636–3501* ⊕ *www.sotinylondon. com* Ⓜ *Oxford Circus.*

Topshop. A hot spot for straight-from-the-runway affordable fashion, Topshop is destination shopping for teenagers and fashion editors alike. Clothes, shoes, and accessories are geared to the youthful end of the market, although women who are young at heart and girlish of figure can find plenty of wearable items here—so long as you can tolerate the loud music and busy dressing rooms. The store also features collections designed by a rotating roster of high-end designers and its own premium designer line called Topshop Unique. The amount of stock at this flagship store is vast, but a clear layout helps make it navigable. Keep an eye out for pop-up extras like free minimakeovers, a blow-dry bar, or nail art from Wah Nails. Topman brings the same fast-fashion approach to clothing for men. If the crowds become too much, head to one of the smaller Topshops in Kensington High Street, Knightsbridge, Victoria, Marble Arch, The City, or Holborn. ⊠ *36–38 Great Castle St., Fitzrovia* ☎ *0207/927–7644* ⊕ *www.topshop.com* Ⓜ *Oxford Circus.*

CAMDEN
MARKETS

The Camden Markets. Begun in the early 1970s, when weekend stalls sold the output of nearby craft workshops, Camden Lock Market later expanded to four markets: Camden, Camden Lock, The Stables, and Camden Lock Village, all grouped around two locks on the Regent's Canal. Though much of the merchandise is targeted at young street-fashion aficionados as well as aging hippies, anyone with a taste for alternative culture—Goths are particularly well catered for—will also find plenty that appeals. This shopping experience is best suited to those who don't mind large crowds and a boisterous atmosphere, especially on weekends. For many years, the markets have hosted more than 1,000 stalls offering a wide-ranging array of merchandise—vintage and new clothes, antiques and junk, rare vinyl, ceramics, Indian bedspreads, fetishwear, obscure band memorabilia, and toys.

The outdoor Camden Market on Camden High Street mainly sells cheap jeans, secondhand clothes, and tacky pop-culture paraphernalia; Camden Lock Market is the place to go for crafts; and The Stables Market, which has expanded into the so-called Catacombs (Victorian brick arches), has more than 700 shops and stalls and is where you go for furniture. Camden Lock Village is closed while it's being turned into a mixed-use retail and residential development. All four markets are earmarked for redevelopment, so their focus is likely to change—enjoy the scrappy, bohemian atmosphere while you can. ⊠ *Camden High St. to Chalk Farm Rd., Camden Town* ⊕ *www.camdenmarket.com* Ⓜ *Camden Town, Chalk Farm.*

18

EAST LONDON

ACCESSORIES

Fodor'sChoice ★ **Bernstock Speirs.** Here since 1982, Paul Bernstock and Thelma Speirs have put a quirky, fashionable spin on traditional hats for men and women, with street-smart trilbies, whimsical rabbit-ear baseball caps, and knitted beanies that feature unusual colors and detailing (like veils, for instance). ⊠ *234 Brick La., Spitalfields* ☎ *020/7739–7385* ⊕ *www.bernstockspeirs.com* Ⓜ *Overground: Shoreditch High St.*

Deciem. One of the few brick-and-mortar outlets for beauty editors' favorite Deciem and its cult brands The Ordinary (quality skincare products at very reasonable prices thanks to stripped-down packaging and low margins) and its premium (though still affordable) range, Niod, which stands for "Non-Invasive Options In Dermal Science," epitomizing the brand's function-not-frills approach. In addition, the store stocks the umbrella company's food and health supplements as well as its haircare, hand and body care, and men's grooming products. ⊠ *Old Spitalfields Market, 18 Lamb St., Shoreditch* ☎ *020/3884–1959* ⊕ *deciem.com* Ⓜ *Shoreditch High Street.*

CLOTHING

Absolute Vintage. This is a warehouse of all sorts of handpicked items from the 1930s through the 1980s, but the specialty here is shoes and bags. The shop has the largest collection of vintage shoes in the United

Kingdom—more than 1,000 pairs—and, best of all, prices are reasonable. There's another branch on Commercial Street. ⊠ *15 Hanbury St., Spitalfields* ☎ *020/7274–3883* ⊕ *www.absolutevintage.co.uk* Ⓜ *Overground: Shoreditch High St.*

Beyond Retro. The more than 10,000 vintage items for men and women here—from cowboy boots to bowling shirts to prom dresses—include the largest collection of American retro in the United Kingdom. There's another outpost in Dalston and one in Soho. ⊠ *110–112 Cheshire St., Spitalfields* ☎ *020/7297–9001* ⊕ *www.beyondretro.com* Ⓜ *Whitechapel. Overground: Shoreditch High St.*

Fodor's Choice ★ **Hostem.** Drawing style-conscious customers from nearby tech start-ups, Hostem is for the man who wants to be well dressed without looking like he's trying too hard, with a mixture of casual luxury, street wear, and fashion-forward edge from tastemaker favorites including John Alexander Skelton, Casey Casey, and Geoffrey B. Small. The womenswear area offers pieces by designers like Commes des Garçons and Yohji Yamamoto. There's also a bespoke service for clothing and exquisite men's shoes by cobbler Sebastain Tarek. It's achingly hip (clothes hang from a wooden "monolithic site specific sculpture"), but in superb taste. The store also operates a three-bedroom guesthouse (a converted Georgian townhouse in Whitechapel), where you can buy the crockery, bed linens, glassware, and more at the end of your stay. ⊠ *28 Old Nichol St., Shoreditch* ☎ *020/7739–9733* ⊕ *www.hostem.co.uk* Ⓜ *Overground: Shoreditch High St.*

Rokit. Here's where to find the perfect outfit for a Mad Men party. Magazine and music stylists love these two premises along Brick Lane that carry everything from handbags and ball gowns to jeans, military garb, and Western wear. The ever-changing stock spans the 1920s to the 1990s. There are also branches in Camden and Covent Garden. ⊠ *101 and 107 Brick La., Spitalfields* ☎ *020/7375–3864* ⊕ *www.rokit.co.uk* Ⓜ *Overground: Shoreditch High St.*

Fodor's Choice ★ **Sunspel.** This British firm has been making fine men's underwear since the mid-19th century and it's still its specialty, along with luxury basics such as knitwear, outerwear, and swimwear. Prince Charles is a real-life customer and James Bond, a cinematic one (he wore their shorts in *Thunderball* and polo shirt in *Quantum of Solace*). Sunspel also carries elegant, minimalist T-shirts, sweaters, and sweats for women. There are other branches in Marylebone, Notting Hill, St. James's, and Soho. ⊠ *7 Redchurch St., Shoreditch* ☎ *020/7739–9729* ⊕ *www.sunspel.com* Ⓜ *Overground: Shoreditch High St.*

FOOD

Fodor's Choice ★ **Cundall & Garcia.** All of the traditional or retro foodstuffs here—such as jars of locally produced honey, relish, or even "Mother's Ruin" gin—are British-made and make excellent and portable presents. Also available in this re-creation of a village shop are stylish gift baskets and old-fashioned picnic hampers, as well as freshly made take-out sandwiches (like honey roast ham with cheddar and apple and pear chutney), salads, homemade cakes, and hot daily specials. ⊠ *42 Brushfield St., Spitalfields* ☎ *020/7247–2487* ⊕ *www.agoldshop.com* ☉ *Closed Sun.* Ⓜ *Overground: Shoreditch High St.*

HOUSEHOLD GOODS

Fodor's Choice ★ **Labour & Wait.** Although mundane items like colanders and clothespins may not sound like ideal souvenirs, this shop (something of a hipster heaven selling both new and vintage items) will make you reconsider. The owners are on a mission to revive retro, functional British household goods, such as enamel kitchenware, genuine feather dusters, bread bins, aluminum dustpans, and traditional Welsh blankets. ✉ *85 Redchurch St., Shoreditch* ☎ *020/7729–6253* ⊕ *www.labourandwait.co.uk* ⊗ *Closed Mon.* Ⓜ *Overground: Shoreditch High St.*

MARKETS

Brick Lane. The noisy center of the Bangladeshi community is a hubbub of buying and selling on Sunday. Stalls have food, hardware, household and electrical goods, books, bikes, shoes, clothes, spices, and traditional saris. Some of the CDs and DVDs are pirated, and the bargain iron may not have a plug, so check carefully. Shoppers nevertheless flock to the market to enjoy the buzz, sample curries and Bangladeshi sweets, or indulge in salt beef on a bagel at Beigel Bake—London's 24-hour bagel bakery, a survivor of the neighborhood's Jewish past. Brick Lane's activity spills over into nearby Petticoat Lane Market, where there are similar goods but less atmosphere. ✉ *Shoreditch* ⊕ *www.visitbricklane. org* ⊗ *Closed Mon.–Sat.* Ⓜ *Aldgate E. Overground: Shoreditch High St.*

Fodor's Choice ★ **Broadway Market.** This parade of shops in hipster-centric Hackney (north of Regent's Canal) is worth visiting for the specialty bookshops, independent boutiques, organic cafés, neighborhood restaurants, and even a traditional (but now rare) pie-and-mash shop. But wait for Saturday (9–5), when it really comes into its own with a farmers' market and more than 100 street-food and produce stalls rivaling those of south London's famed Borough Market. Artisanal breads, cheeses, chocolates, organic meats, fruit and vegetables, oysters, smoked salmon, and international food offerings: this is foodie heaven. There are also stalls selling vintage clothes, crafts, jewelry, and more. ✉ *Broadway Market, Hackney* ☎ *0787/246–3409* ⊕ *www. broadwaymarket.co.uk* Ⓜ *London Fields.*

Fodor's Choice ★ **Columbia Road Flower Market.** London's premier flower market is about as pretty and photogenic as they come, with more than 50 stalls selling flowers, shrubs, bulbs, and trees—everything from bedding plants to 10-foot banana trees—as well as garden tools, pots, and accessories at competitive prices. The stallholders' patter is part of the fun. It's on Sunday only, and it's all over by 2 pm. Columbia Road itself is lined with interesting independent shops purveying art, fashion, furnishings, and jewelry, and the local cafés are superb. ✉ *Columbia Rd., Hoxton* ⊕ *www.columbiaroad.info* ⊗ *Closed Mon.–Sat.* Ⓜ *Old St. Overground: Hoxton.*

Old Spitalfields Market. Once the East End's wholesale fruit and vegetable market and now restored to its original architectural splendor, this fine example of a Victorian market hall is at the center of the area's gentrified revival. The original building is largely occupied by shops (including upscale brands like Rag & Bone, Lululemon, and Superga), with traders' stalls in the courtyard. A modern shopping precinct under a Norman Foster–designed glass canopy adjoins the old

18

building and holds many more traders' stalls. You may have to wade through a certain number of stalls selling cheap imports to find the good stuff, which includes crafts, vintage and new clothing, handmade rugs, jewelry, hand-carved toy trains, unique baby clothes, rare vinyl, and cakes. Thursday is particularly good for vintage and antiques; Friday for fashion, art, and a biweekly record fair; Saturday is built around varying themes; and on Sunday, traders offer a little of everything. The food outlets (mostly small, upscale chains but some indies as well) sell Spanish tapas, Thai satays, and many other dishes from all over. ⊠ *16 Horner Sq., Brushfield St., Spitalfields* ☎ *020/7375–2963* ⊕ *www. oldspitalfieldsmarket.com* ⊗ *Stalls closed Mon.–Wed.* Ⓜ *Liverpool St. Overground: Shoreditch High St.*

MUSIC
Rough Trade East. Although many London record stores are struggling, this veteran indie-music specialist in the Old Truman Brewery seems to have gotten the formula right. The spacious surroundings are as much a hangout as a shop, complete with a stage for live gigs, a café, and Internet access. There's another branch on Talbot Road in Notting Hill. ⊠ *Dray Walk, Old Truman Brewery, 91 Brick La., Spitalfields* ☎ *020/7392–7788* ⊕ *www.roughtrade.com* Ⓜ *Liverpool St. Overground: Shoreditch High St.*

SOUTH OF THE THAMES

ART
Oxo Tower Wharf. The artisans creating fashion, jewelry, home accessories, textiles, prints and photographs, furniture, and other design items have to pass rigorous selection procedures to set up in these prime riverside studios, where they make, display, and sell their work. The Oxo Tower Restaurant & Brasserie on the top floor is expensive, but with its fantastic view of London, it's worth popping up for a drink. There's also a public terrace where you can take in the view. ⊠ *Oxo Tower Wharf, Bargehouse St., South Bank* ☎ *020/7021–1686 24-hr info* ⊕ *www.coinstreet.org* ⊗ *Closed Mon.* Ⓜ *Waterloo.*

MARKETS
Bermondsey Square Antiques Market. The early bird catches the worm at this Friday market, so come before dawn (flashlight recommended) to bag a bargain at London's largest antiques market. Dealers also arrive before dawn to snap up the best curios and silver, paintings, objets d'art, and furniture. The early start grew out of wrinkle in the law (dating from when the market began on the site in 1885) under which stolen goods bought here during the hours of darkness when provenance could not be determined. While stolen goods are no longer welcome here, the market has expanded to some 200 stalls, including food, clothing, and crafts. It finishes at 2 pm. ⊠ *Long La. and Bermondsey Sq., Bermondsey* ⊕ *www.bermondseysquare.net* ⊗ *Closed Sat.–Thurs.* Ⓜ *London Bridge.*

Fodor'sChoice **Borough Market.** There's been a market in Borough since Roman times. ★ This latest incarnation, spread under the arches and railroad tracks leading to London Bridge station, is where some of the city's best food sellers set up stalls. Fresh coffees, gorgeous cheeses, olives, and baked goods complement the organically farmed meats, fresh fish, fruits, and vegetables.

Don't make any other lunch plans for the day; this is where celebrity chef Jamie Oliver's scallop man cooks them up fresh at Shell Seekers, and The Ginger Pig's rare-breed sausages sizzle on grills, while for the sweets lover there are chocolates, preserves, and Whirld's artisanal confectionery, as well as 18 restaurants and cafés, most above average. The Market Hall hosts workshops, tastings, and demonstrations, and also acts as a greenhouse. On Monday and Tuesday only stalls for hot food and produce are open.

Originally established by eight breakaway Borough Market traders, a separate, highly regarded market operates on nearby Maltby Street every Saturday morning beginning at 9 am. Stalls include African Volcano, purveyors of Mozambique-style hot sauces and marinades. ⊠ *8 Southwark St., Borough* ☏ *020/7402–1002* ⊕ *www.boroughmarket. org.uk* ⊘ *Closed Sun.* Ⓜ *London Bridge.*

KENSINGTON, CHELSEA, KNIGHTSBRIDGE, AND BELGRAVIA

KENSINGTON

CLOTHING

FAMILY **Marie-Chantal.** If you love beautiful, tasteful, and somewhat formal clothing for babies and children, head to this boutique created by Princess Marie-Chantal of Greece. As you'd imagine, the look is elegant and the prices are high. Materials used include silk, linen, and Liberty prints (plus less fancy T-shirts). There's another branch in Notting Hill. ⊠ *148 Walton St., South Kensington* ☏ *020/7838–1111* ⊕ *www.mariechantal. co.uk* ⊘ *Closed weekends* Ⓜ *South Kensington.*

HOUSEHOLD GOODS

The Conran Shop. This is the brainchild of Sir Terence Conran, who has been a major influence on British taste since he opened Habitat in the 1960s. Although he is no longer associated with Habitat, his Conran Shops remain bastions of similarly clean, unfussy modernist design. Housewares from furniture to lighting, stemware, and textiles—both handmade and mass-produced, by famous names and emerging designers—are housed in a building that is a modernist landmark in its own right. Both the flagship store and the branch on Marylebone High Street are bursting with great gift ideas. ⊠ *Michelin House, 81 Fulham Rd., South Kensington* ☏ *020/7589–7401* ⊕ *www.conranshop.co.uk* Ⓜ *South Kensington.*

Mint. Owner Lina Kanafani has scoured the globe to curate an eclectic mix of conceptual statement furniture, art, ceramics, glassware, and home accessories. Mint also showcases avant-garde works by an international selection of up-and-coming designers and sells plenty of limited edition and one-off pieces. If you don't want to ship a couch home, consider a miniature flower vase or a handmade ceramic pitcher. ⊠ *2 North Terr., at Alexander Sq., South Kensington* ☏ *020/7225–2228* ⊕ *www.mintshop.co.uk* ⊘ *Closed Sun.* Ⓜ *South Kensington.*

18

Skandium. Largely thanks to its TV dramas and *hygge,* Scandinavia is having a moment in Britain. Skandium brings together many of the region's top designers of furniture, lighting, rugs, and housewares under one roof. Designers include giants of Scandinavian Modernism like Artek, Fritz Hansen, and Georg Jensen, as well as non-Scandinavian modernists, such as Knoll. Clean lines and stripped-down, unfussy elegance abound (although the Moomins make an appearance on ceramics). There's another branch in Marylebone. ✉ *245–249 Brompton Rd., South Kensington* ☎ *020/7584–2066* ⊕ *www.skandium.com* Ⓜ *South Kensington.*

JEWELRY

Butler & Wilson. Specialists in bold costume jewelry and affordable glamor, Butler & Wilson have added semiprecious stones to its foundation diamanté, colored rhinestone, and crystal collections. Flamboyant skull brooches or dainty floral earrings make perfect gifts. ✉ *189 Fulham Rd., South Kensington* ☎ *020/7352–3045* ⊕ *www.butlerandwilson.co.uk* ⊙ *Closed Sun.* Ⓜ *South Kensington.*

CHELSEA
ACCESSORIES

Anya Hindmarch. Exquisite leather bags and personalized, printed canvas totes are what made Hindmarch famous, and this store sells her complete collection of bags, several with a whimsical motif. You can also order a custom piece like the "Be A Bag," a washbag imprinted with your chosen photo. There are also branches around the corner on Pont Street, in Mayfair, in Hackney, and in Notting Hill. ✉ *157–158 Sloane St., Chelsea* ☎ *020/7730–0961* ⊕ *www.anyahindmarch.com* Ⓜ *Sloane Sq., Knightsbridge.*

The Shop at Bluebird. The brainchild of the couple behind popular womenswear brand Jigsaw, this 10,000-square-foot space in the old Bluebird garage brings together men's and women's fashion from of-the-moment designers like Tabitha Simmons, Alexander Wang, Isabel Marant, and Victoria Beckham as well as numerous hip denim lines like Acne. There's also furniture, collectibles, designer tech accessories, and music—all chosen for style and originality. It's worth visiting for the displays alone, which change regularly, although the funky ceiling-light installation of more than 1,000 bulbs seems to be a constant feature. After browsing, unwind with a treatment at the small on-site Blink spa or join the ladies who lunch at the restaurant in the same complex. It's a good 20-minute walk from the nearest Tube station at Sloane Square, so catch Bus No. 11 or 22 along King's Road. There are other branches in St. James's and on Duke Street in Mayfair. ✉ *350 King's Rd., Chelsea* ☎ *020/7351–3873* ⊕ *www.theshopatbluebird.com* Ⓜ *Sloane Sq.*

BOOKS

John Sandoe (Books) Ltd. This atmospheric warren that crams some 25,000 titles into an 18th-century building off King's Road is the antithesis of a soulless chain bookstore, so it's no surprise it has attracted equally idiosyncratic customers like Tom Stoppard and Keith Richards. Staff members are wonderfully knowledgeable (don't try to figure out how the stock is organized without their help), and there are a lot of them per customer—if a book isn't in stock, they will try to find it for you, even if it is out of print. ✉ *10 Blacklands Terr., Chelsea* ☎ *020/7589–9473* ⊕ *www.johnsandoe.com* Ⓜ *Sloane Sq.*

CLOTHING

Brora. The knitwear is cozy, but the style is cool in this contemporary Scottish cashmere emporium for men, women, and kids. There are dressed-up camisoles, sweaters and cardigans, and adorable baby ensembles, as well as noncashmere items such as picnic blankets and scarves. Other branches are in Marylebone, Islington, Covent Garden, and farther down King's Road. ✉ *6–8 Symons St., Chelsea* ☎ *020/7730–2665* ⊕ *www.brora.co.uk* Ⓜ *Sloane Sq.*

Hackett. If Ralph Lauren isn't preppy enough for you, try Hackett, with branches in Covent Garden, Spitalfields, St. James's, Soho, Canary Wharf, and The City. Originally a posh thrift shop recycling cricket flannels, hunting pinks, Oxford brogues, and other staples of a British gentleman's wardrobe, Hackett now creates its own line and has become a genuine—and very good—men's outfitter. The look is traditional and classic best buys include polo shirts, corduroys, and striped scarves. There's also a boys' line for the junior man-about-town. ✉ *137–138 Sloane St., Chelsea* ☎ *020/7730–3331* ⊕ *www.hackett.com* Ⓜ *Sloane Sq.*

Jigsaw. The quality of fabrics and detailing belie the reasonable prices here, where clothes are classic yet trendy and elegant without being dull—and where cuts are kind to the womanly figure. The style is epitomized by the Duchess of Cambridge, who, as Kate Middleton before her marriage, was a buyer for the company. Although there are numerous branches across London, no two stores are the same. Preteens have their own line, Jigsaw Junior. ✉ *The Chapel, 6 Duke of York Sq., Chelsea* ☎ *020/730–4404* ⊕ *www.jigsaw-online.com* Ⓜ *Sloane Sq.*

DEPARTMENT STORES

Fodor's Choice
★

Peter Jones. A beloved local institution since it opened in 1937—the poet John Betjeman remarked that come the end of the world he would like to be in the haberdashery department of Peter Jones, "because nothing bad could ever happen there"—this tasteful department store is the traditional default wedding-list option of Kensington & Chelsea brides. The selection of bed and bath linens (many provided by John Lewis, the store's parent company), flatware, ceramics, and glassware is outstanding, with offerings at all price points. There's also an extensive and eclectic beauty department, as well as kitchenware and appliances, tech stuff, a florist, clothing, shoes, and accessories for the whole family, and pretty much everything else you can think of, along with a restaurant and Clarins, Décleor, and Elemis treatment rooms. ✉ *Sloane Sq., Chelsea* ☎ *020/7730–3434* ⊕ *www.johnlewis.com* Ⓜ *Sloane Sq.*

FOOD

L'Artisan du Chocolat. Praised by top chefs Gordon Ramsay and Heston Blumenthal, L'Artisan raises chocolate to an art form. "Couture" chocolates are infused with fruits, nuts, and spices (including such exotic flavorings as Szechuan pepper and tobacco). This is one of the

18

few chocolate shops in the world that makes liquid salted caramels. There's another branch in Notting Hill. ⊠ *89 Lower Sloane St., Chelsea* ☎ *0845/270–6996* ⊕ *www.artisanduchocolat.co.uk* Ⓜ *Sloane Sq.*

HOUSEHOLD GOODS

Designers Guild. Tricia Guild's exuberantly patterned fabrics, wallpapers, paints, furniture, and bed linens have decorated design-conscious British homes for several decades, and her soft-furnishings book has taught many budget-conscious do-it-yourselfers how to reupholster a sofa or make lined draperies. The shop also stocks contemporary furniture, wallpapers, and home accessories by other designers like Christian Lacroix. There's another branch in Marylebone. ⊠ *267–277 King's Rd., Chelsea* ☎ *020/351–5775* ⊕ *www.designersguild.com* ☉ *Closed Sun.* Ⓜ *Sloane Sq.*

SHOES

Fodor's Choice   **Manolo Blahnik.** Blink and you'll miss the discreet sign that marks fash-
★   ionista footwear central. Blahnik, the man who single-handedly managed to revive the sexy stiletto, has been trading out of this small shop on a Chelsea side street since 1973. It's a must for shoe lovers with generous budgets. If you decide to wear your new Manolos, hop on Bus No. 11 or 22 or grab a cab—the nearest Tube station is about a 20-minute totter away. ⊠ *49–51 Old Church St., Chelsea* ☎ *020/7352–8622* ⊕ *www.manoloblahnik.com* ☉ *Closed Sun.* Ⓜ *Sloane Sq., South Kensington.*

SPECIALTY STORES

Green & Stone Art Materials. This fabulous cave of artists' materials, papers, art books, easels, and mannequins is one of the longest-established shops on King's Road. It began life in 1927 as part of the Chenil Gallery, run by a distinguished group that included the artist Augustus John and the playwright George Bernard Shaw. At the current location since 1934, the shop also has a framing service, antique paint boxes, and craft supplies. Francis Bacon and David Hockney have been among its clients. ⊠ *259 King's Rd., Chelsea* ☎ *020/7352–0837* ⊕ *www.green-andstone.com* Ⓜ *Sloane Sq.*

KNIGHTSBRIDGE

CLOTHING

Egg. Tucked away in a residential mews, this spartan shop in a former Victorian dairy is the brainchild of Maureen Doherty, once Issey Miyake's assistant. More than half the minimalist, unstructured styles for men and women—in natural luxury fabrics such as silk, cashmere, and antique cotton—are handmade. Garments may be casually hung on hooks or folded on wooden tables, but the price tags are anything but unassuming. The clientele includes the likes of Donna Karan and British PM Theresa May. One-of-a-kind ceramics and jewelry are also on display. ⊠ *36 Kinnerton St., Knightsbridge* ☎ *020/7235–9315* ⊕ *eg-gtrading.com* ☉ *Closed Sun.* Ⓜ *Knightsbridge.*

FAMILY   **Rachel Riley.** Specializing in traditional English style for boys and girls, Riley's luxurious, vintage-inspired collection includes classics like duffel coats and hand-smocked floral dresses. Mothers who love the Riley look (including the Duchess of Cambridge, who has put her two royal offspring in Riley clothes) can pick up coordinating outfits for themselves here or at the Marylebone High Street location. ✉ *14 Pont St., Knightsbridge* ☎ *020/7259–5969* ⊕ *www.rachelriley.co.uk* ⊗ *Closed Sun.* Ⓜ *Knightsbridge.*

Rigby & Peller. Many of London's most affluent women shop at this luxury lingerie shop, because the quality is excellent and the service impeccably knowledgeable—and perhaps because it's the Queen's favored underwear supplier. R&P also provides maternity wear to the Duchess of Cambridge. Despite its wealthy and royal clientele, it's much friendlier than you might expect. Brands include Primadonna and Aubade as well as R&P's own line, and if the right fit eludes you, there's a made-to-measure service that starts at around £300. There are also branches in Mayfair, Chelsea, St. John's Wood, and The City. ✉ *2 Hans Rd., Knightsbridge* ☎ *020/7225–4760* ⊕ *www.rigbyandpeller. com* Ⓜ *Knightsbridge.*

DEPARTMENT STORES

Harrods. With an encyclopedic assortment of luxury brands, this Knightsbridge institution, now owned by the Qatar Investment Authority, has more than 300 departments and 25 eating and drinking options, all spread over 1 million square feet on a 4½-acre site. Now populated more by window-shopping tourists and superrich visitors from abroad than by the bling-averse natives, Harrods is best approached as the world's largest, most upscale and expensive mall. Focus on the spectacular food halls, the huge ground-floor perfumery and jewelry departments, the excellent Urban Retreat spa, and Shoe Heaven, Europe's biggest shoe department. The new Superbrands area houses haute couture from top international designers such as Dior, Fendi, Prada, Valentino, and Chanel, while the children's department has a mini-me version for the toddler who wouldn't be seen in anything less than the likes of Burberry, Baby Dior, Chloé for Kids, Moncler, and Armani Junior. Be prepared to brave the crowds, especially on weekends. ✉ *87–135 Brompton Rd., Knightsbridge* ☎ *020/7730–1234* ⊕ *www.harrods.com* Ⓜ *Knightsbridge.*

Harvey Nichols. While visiting tourists flock to Harrods, local fashionistas shop at Harvey Nichols, aka "Harvey Nicks." The womenswear and accessories departments are outstanding, featuring top designers like Tom Ford, Elie Saab, Yeezy, Lanvin, Louboutin, and just about every fashionable name you can think of. The furniture and housewares are equally gorgeous (and pricey), although they become somewhat more affordable during the biannual sales in January and July. The Fifth Floor bar is the place to see and be seen, but if you're in search of food, the same floor also has a café, a Wallpaper* Bar and Kitchen, a branch of Burger & Lobster, the carnivore-friendly Zelman Meats, or sushi-to-go from Yo! Sushi. To keep you looking as box-fresh as your purchases, the Beauty Room features a rotating menu of treatments from brands such as Elemis, La Mer, and Dermalogia; for something more intense, the Light Salon offers LED facials. There are also blow-dry, nail, and brow bars. ✉ *109–125 Knightsbridge, Knightsbridge* ☎ *020/7235–5000* ⊕ *www.harveynichols.com* Ⓜ *Knightsbridge.*

18

BELGRAVIA
ACCESSORIES

Fodor's Choice ★ **Philip Treacy.** Magnificent hats by Treacy are annual showstoppers on Ladies Day at the Royal Ascot races and regularly grace the glossy magazines' party pages. Part Mad Hatter, part Cecil Beaton, Treacy's creations always guarantee a grand entrance and are favorites with both Hollywood and actual royalty. In addition to the extravagant, haute couture hats handmade in the atelier, ready-to-wear hats are also for sale, as are some bags. ✉ *69 Elizabeth St., Belgravia* ☎ *020/7730–3992* ⊕ *www.philiptreacy.co.uk* ⊘ *Closed Sun.* Ⓜ *Sloane Sq.*

SPECIALTY STORES

Mungo & Maud. If you don't want to leave London without buying something for your pet, pick up a well-designed coat, leash, harness, bowl, toy, or comfortable bed that will make your dog the snazziest pooch in town (some collars are hand-stitched). Cats are also catered to with baskets, suede collars, and catnip toys. Even owners get a nod with luxurious merino throws (soon to be covered in pet hair) and a leather poop pouch. ✉ *79 Elizabeth St., Belgravia* ☎ *020/7022–1207* ⊕ *www.mungoandmaud.com* ⊘ *Closed Sun.* Ⓜ *Sloane Sq.*

NOTTING HILL
BOOKS

Fodor's Choice ★ **Books for Cooks.** It may seem odd to describe a bookshop as delicious-smelling, but the aromas wafting out of the tiny café in the back of the shop—which serves daily-changing lunch dishes drawn from recipes in the 8,000 cookbooks on the shelves, as well as cakes and culinary experiments—will whet your appetite even before you've opened one of the books. Just about every world cuisine is represented, along with a complete lineup of works by celebrity chefs. Before you come to London, visit the shop's website to sign up for a cooking class in the upstairs test kitchen. ✉ *4 Blenheim Crescent, Notting Hill* ☎ *020/7221–1992* ⊕ *www.booksforcooks.com* ⊘ *Closed Sun. and Mon.* Ⓜ *Notting Hill Gate, Ladbroke Grove.*

CLOTHING

Aimé. French-Cambodian sisters Val and Vanda Heng-Vong launched this shop to showcase the best of French clothing and designer housewares. Expect to find cult French labels like Isabel Marant, A.P.C., and Repetto, along with housewares and a well-chosen collection of ceramics. Petit Aimé, next door, sells children's clothing. There's also a Shoreditch branch. ✉ *32 Ledbury Rd., Notting Hill* ☎ *020/7221–7070* ⊕ *www.aimelondon.com* ⊘ *Closed Sun.* Ⓜ *Notting Hill Gate.*

FAMILY **Caramel Baby & Child.** This is the place for adorable yet unfussy clothes for children six months and up: handcrafted Peruvian alpaca cardigans in sherbet colors, floral cotton dresses for girls; check shirts and earth-tone tees for boys; comfortable pants in twill, corduroy, and cotton for both; and merino cashmere sweaters for extremely fashionable babies, plus shoes and accessories. A new addition is Mom-size lines in a similar vein. Caramel also sells a small selection of children's books and traditional toys, as well as decorative-functional items like mobiles, lamps, and quilts. Prices are no bargain, but the quality is superb. On Monday, Tuesday, and Saturday the shop offers a hair salon for little customers. There are also branches in South Kensington and Soho. ⊠ *77 Ledbury Rd., Notting Hill* ☎ *020/7727–0906* ⊕ *www.caramel-shop. co.uk* Ⓜ *Westbourne Park, Notting Hill Gate.*

The Cross. One of the first "lifestyle boutiques" and still one of the best, this West London favorite carries fashion by in-the-know favorites like Vanessa Bruno, Velvet, Forte Forte, and Chinti & Parker, plus accessories, jewelry, housewares, and kids' clothes. The emphasis is on feminine and quirky boho chic. ⊠ *141 Portland Rd., Notting Hill* ☎ *020/7727–6760* ⊕ *www.thecrossshop.co.uk* ۞ *Closed Sun.* Ⓜ *Holland Park.*

Raey. This affordable in-house offshoot of high-end designer destination ⊕ *matchesfashion.com* has quickly become a fashionista go-to thanks to its minimalist, wearable styles for men and women that use luxurious fabrics and superb cuts far above their price points (T-shirts start at £85 going up to shearling jackets for £1200). This is the brand's first stand-alone store. ⊠ *83 Ledbury Rd., Notting Hill* ☎ *020/7221–1120* ⊕ *www.matchesfashion.com* Ⓜ *Notting Hill Gate.*

Rellik. Now in the modernist landmark known as the Trellick Tower and favored by the likes of Kate Moss, Rellik began as a stall in the Portobello Market. Vintage hunters looking to splurge can find a selection of YSL, Dior, Pierre Cardin, and Ossie Clark as well as items from lesser-known designers. ⊠ *Trellick Tower, 8 Golborne Rd., Notting Hill* ☎ *020/8962–0089* ⊕ *www.relliklondon.co.uk* ۞ *Closed Sun. and Mon.* Ⓜ *Westbourne Park.*

MARKETS

Portobello Road. *See full listing in Chapter 10: Notting Hill and Bayswater.*

MUSIC

Music & Video Exchange. This store is a music collector's treasure trove, with a constantly changing stock refreshed by customers selling and exchanging as well as buying. The ground floor focuses on rock, pop, indie, and punk, both mainstream and obscure, in a variety of formats ranging from vinyl to CD, cassette, and even minidisk. Don't miss the classical music in the basement and the soul, jazz, house, techno, reggae, and more upstairs. Like movies? There's a wide variety of Blu-ray and DVD box sets, as well as bargain classic and cult films. Keep an eye out for rarities—including first pressings and one-offs—in all departments. There are also branches in Soho and Greenwich. A similar comics and books exchange is at Nos. 30 and 32 on nearby Pembridge Road (also a destination for vintage clothing for men [No. 34] and women [No. 20], plus more clothing, accessories, and retro homewares [No. 28]). Note: Stock depends on what customers bring in to exchange, so you'll surely find many more DVDs with European (PAL) formatting than the North American-friendly NTSC format, but the store does get the latter occasionally. ⊠ *38 Notting Hill Gate, Notting Hill* ☎ *020/7243–8573* ⊕ *www.mgeshops.com* Ⓜ *Notting Hill Gate.*

18

SHOES

Emma Hope. The signature look of the footwear here is elegant and feminine, with pointed toes and kitten heels, often ornamented with bows, lace, crystals, or exquisite embroidery (such craftsmanship doesn't come cheap, unfortunately). Ballet flats and sneakers in velvet or animal prints provide glamor without sacrificing comfort. Small but perfectly formed handbags, as well as shoes and accessories for men, are stocked both here and in the Sloane Square branch. ⊠ *207 Westbourne Grove, Notting Hill* ☎ *020/7313–7490* ⊕ *www.emmahope.com* Ⓜ *Notting Hill Gate.*

REGENT'S PARK AND HAMPSTEAD

GIFTS

Susan Wainwright. If you're looking for an alternative to the cheesy and the mass-produced, this eclectic shop packs loads of distinctive, stylish, affordable gifts into a small space. The assortment includes handsome gloves and fake fur accessories, handmade silver jewelry, tweed travel blankets, cashmere shawls, leather handbags, comfortable yet attractive robes and pajamas, natural fiber baby and children's clothes and accessories, retro toys, sophisticated stationery, artisanal creams and lotions, and flasks and leather goods for him. Best of all, prices are reasonable. ⊠ *31 South End Rd., Hampstead* ☎ *020/7431–4337* Ⓜ *Overground: Hampstead Heath.*

HOUSEHOLD GOODS

Graham & Green. Combining style with practicality and a whimsical twist, this delightful interiors shop carries a broad but carefully curated selection of faux fur throws, elegant lamps and lampshades, embroidered cushions, felt animal rugs for children, agate or Venetian glass doorknobs, folding deck chairs (as found in the Royal Parks), shabby-chic sofas, a mug for kids with a small dinosaur lurking within, and more. There are branches in Notting Hill and Bayswater. ⊠ *164 Regent's Park Rd., Primrose Hill* ☎ *020/7586–2960* ⊕ *www.grahamandgreen.co.uk* Ⓜ *Chalk Farm.*

SHOES

Spice. Touring London requires a lot of walking, so if your feet are crying out for mercy, stop in at this long-established boutique that specializes in spiffy but comfortable shoes, sandals, and boots for men and women from brands like Camper, Pretty Ballerina, Chie Mihara, and their own Spice line. There's another branch in Islington. ⊠ *162 Regent's Park Rd., Primrose Hill* ☎ *020/7722–2478* ⊕ *www.spiceshu.co.uk* Ⓜ *Chalk Farm.*

SIDE TRIPS FROM LONDON

Updated by
Kate Hughes

Londoners are undeniably lucky. Few urban populations enjoy such glorious—and easily accessible—options for day-tripping. Even if you have only one day to spare, head out of the city. A train ride past hills dotted with sheep, a stroll through a medieval town, or a visit to one of England's great castles could make you feel as though you've added another week to your vacation.

Not only is England extremely compact, but its train and bus networks, although somewhat inefficient and expensive compared with their European counterparts, are extensive and easily booked (though pricing structures can be confusing), making "a brilliant day out" an easy thing to accomplish.

Although you can do the Warner Bros. Harry Potter Studio Tour in a day, many of the towns near London would make for a frenzied day trip. And in summer, heavy crowds make it difficult to sightsee in a relaxed manner, so consider staying for a day or two instead. You'd then have time to explore a different England—one with quiet country pubs, tree-lined lanes, and neat fields. No matter where you go, lodging reservations are a good idea June through September, when foreign visitors saturate the English countryside.

PLANNING

WHAT IT COSTS				
	$	$$	$$$	$$$$
Restaurants	Under £14	£14–£23	£24–£31	Over £31

Prices in the reviews are the average cost of a main course at dinner or, if dinner is not served, at lunch. Note: If a restaurant offers only prix-fixe (set-price) meals, it has been given the price category that reflects the full prix-fixe price.

TO GET TO ...	TAKE THE TRAIN FROM ...	TAKE THE BUS FROM ...
Cambridge	King's Cross (45–90 minutes, every 10 or 20 minutes); Liverpool St. (80 minutes, every 30 minutes)	Victoria Coach (about 3 hours, every 60–90 minutes)
Oxford	Paddington (55–110 minutes, every 3–20 minutes)	Victoria Coach (100 minutes, every half hour) or Oxford Tube, Buckingham Palace Rd. (100 minutes, every 12–20 minutes)
Stratford-upon-Avon	Marylebone (2–2½ hours, every 2 hours); or Euston (1½ hours, every 20 or 40 minutes or hourly)	Victoria Coach (3 hours 25 minutes, about 3 times daily)
Warner Bros. Harry Potter Studio Tour	Euston Station (20 minutes) to Watford, then shuttle bus to attraction	Watford (15 minutes, every 20 minutes), after taking London train from Euston.
Windsor	Paddington (25–50 minutes, every 5–30 minutes) or Waterloo (1 hour 5 minutes, every half hour)	Green Line Coach, Victoria (1 hour 5 minutes, hourly)

GETTING AROUND

Normally the towns near London are best reached by train. Bus travel costs less, but can take twice as long. Wherever you're going, plan ahead: check the latest timetables before you set off, and try to get an early start. ⇨ *Also see Travel Smart London.*

STATION TIPS

You can reach any of London's main-line train stations by Tube. London's bus stations can be confusing for the uninitiated, so here's a quick breakdown:

Green Line Coach Station is on Bulleid Way, in front of the Colonnades Shopping Centre on Buckingham Palace Road; it's the departure point for most Green Line and Megabus services.

Victoria Bus Station is where many of the local London bus services arrive and depart, and is directly outside the main exits of the train and Tube stations.

Victoria Coach Station is on Buckingham Palace Road: it's a five-minute walk from Victoria Tube station. This is where to go for coach departures; arrivals are at a different location, a short walk from here.

19

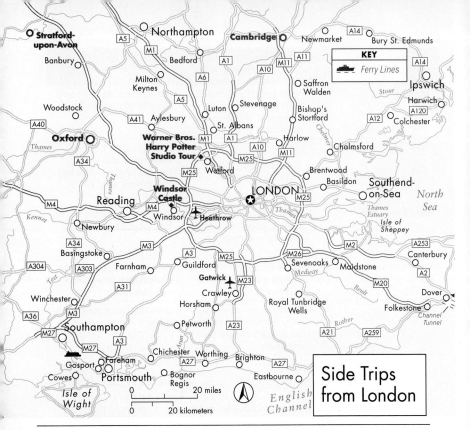

Side Trips
from London

CAMBRIDGE

60 miles northeast of London.

With the spires of its university buildings framed by towering trees and expansive meadows, its medieval streets and passages enhanced by gardens and riverbanks, the city of Cambridge is among the loveliest in England. The city predates the Roman occupation of Britain, but there's confusion over exactly how the university was founded. The most widely accepted story is that it was established in 1209 by a pair of scholars from Oxford, who left their university in protest over the wrongful execution of a colleague for murder.

This university town may be beautiful, but it's no museum. Even when the students are on vacation, there's a cultural and intellectual buzz here. Well-preserved medieval buildings sit cheek-by-jowl with the latest in modern architecture (for example, the William Gates building, which houses Cambridge University's computer laboratory) in this growing city—dominated culturally and architecturally by its famous university, whose students make up around one fifth of the city's 109,000 inhabitants, and beautified by parks, gardens, and the quietly flowing River Cam. One quintessential Cambridge pursuit is punting on the Cam (one occupant propelling the narrow, square-end, flat-bottom boat with a long pole), followed by a stroll along the Backs, the left bank of the river fringed by St. John's, Trinity, Clare, King's, and Queens' colleges, and by Trinity Hall.

VISITING THE COLLEGES

College visits are certainly a highlight of a Cambridge tour, but remember that the colleges are private residences and workplaces, even when school isn't in session. Each is an independent entity within the university; some are closed to the public, but at others you can see the chapels, dining rooms (called halls), and sometimes the libraries, too. Some colleges charge a fee for the privilege of nosing around. All are closed during exams (usually mid-April–late June), and the opening hours often vary. Additionally, all are subject to closure at short notice (especially King's); check the websites in advance. For details about visiting specific colleges not listed here, contact Cambridge University.

TOURS

City Sightseeing. This company operates open-top bus tours of Cambridge, including the Backs, colleges, and Botanic Gardens. Tours can be joined at marked bus stops in the city. Ask the tourist office about additional tours. ⊠ *Cambridge Train Station, Station Rd.* ☎ *01223/433–250* ⊕ *www.city-sightseeing.com* 🎫 *From £16.*

Visit Cambridge. Walking tours are led by official Blue or Green Badge guides. The 1½- or 2-hour tours leave from the tourist information center at Peas Hill. Hours vary according to the tour, with the earliest leaving at 11 am and the latest at 1 or 2 pm. ⊠ *The Guildhall, Peas Hill* ☎ *01223/791–501* ⊕ *www.visitcambridge.org/official-tours* 🎫 *From £18.50.*

ESSENTIALS

Visitor Information Cambridge Visitor Information Centre. ⊠ *The Guildhall, Peas Hill* ☎ *01223/791–500* ⊕ *www.visitcambridge.org.*

EXPLORING

TOP ATTRACTIONS

Fodor's Choice
★

Fitzwilliam Museum. In a classical revival building renowned for its grand Corinthian portico, this museum, founded by the 7th Viscount Fitzwilliam of Merrion in 1816, has one of Britain's most outstanding collections of art and antiquities. Highlights include two large Titians, an extensive collection of French impressionist paintings, and many works by Matisse and Picasso. The opulent interior displays these treasures to marvelous effect, from Egyptian pieces like inch-high figurines and painted coffins to sculptures from the Chinese Han dynasty of the 3rd century BC. Other collections of note here include a fine collection of flower paintings, an assortment of medieval illuminated manuscripts, and a fascinating room full of armor and muskets. ⊠ *Trumpington St.* ☎ *01223/332–900* ⊕ *www.fitzmuseum.cam.ac.uk* 🎫 *Free* ☉ *Closed Mon. except bank holiday Mon.*

King's College. Founded in 1441 by Henry VI, King's College has a magnificent late-15th-century chapel that is its most famous landmark. Other notable architecture includes the neo-Gothic Porters' Lodge, facing King's Parade, which was a comparatively recent addition in the 1830s, and the classical Gibbs building. ■TIP→ Head down to the river, from where the panorama of college and chapel is one of the university's most photographed views. Past students of King's College include the novelist E.M. Forster, the economist John Maynard Keynes, and the World War I poet Rupert Brooke. ⊠ *King's Parade* ☎ *01223/331–212* ⊕ *www.kings. cam.ac.uk* ⊠ *£9, includes chapel* ⊙ *Times vary: check website.*

Fodor's Choice
★
King's College Chapel. Based on Sainte-Chapelle, the 13th-century royal chapel in Paris, this house of worship is perhaps the most glorious flowering of perpendicular

A GIFT FOR SCIENCE

For centuries Cambridge has been among the country's greatest universities, rivaled only by Oxford. Since the time of one of its most famous alumni, Sir Isaac Newton, it's outshone Oxford in the natural sciences. The university has taken advantage of this prestige, sharing its research facilities with high-tech industries. Surrounded by technology companies, Cambridge has been dubbed "Silicon Fen," a comparison to California's Silicon Valley.

Gothic in Britain. Henry VI, the king after whom the college is named, oversaw the work. From the outside, the most prominent features are the massive flying buttresses and the fingerlike spires that line the length of the building. Inside, the most obvious impression is of great space— the chapel was once described as "the noblest barn in Europe"—and of light flooding in from its huge windows. The brilliantly colored bosses (carved panels at the intersections of the roof ribs) are particularly intense although hard to see without binoculars. An exhibition in the chantries, or side chapels, explains more about the chapel's construction. Behind the altar is *The Adoration of the Magi,* an enormous painting by Peter Paul Rubens. ■TIP→ The chapel, unlike the rest of King's College, stays open during exam periods. Every Christmas Eve, a festival of carols is sung by the chapel's famous choir. It's broadcast on national television and considered a quintessential part of the traditional English Christmas. To compete for the small number of tickets available, join the line at the college's main entrance early—doors open at 7 am. ⊠ *King's Parade* ☎ *01223/331–212* ⊕ *www.kings.cam.ac.uk* ⊠ *£9, includes college and grounds* ⊙ *Times vary; sometimes closed for events; check ahead to confirm.*

Fodor's Choice
★
Polar Museum. Beautifully designed, this museum at Cambridge University's Scott Polar Research Institute chronicles the history of polar exploration. There's a particular emphasis on the British expeditions of the 20th century, including the ill-fated attempt by Robert Falcon Scott to be the first to reach the South Pole in 1912. Norwegian explorer Roald Amundsen reached the pole first; Scott and his men perished on the return journey, but their story became legendary. There are also collections devoted to the science of modern polar exploration; the indigenous people of northern Canada, Greenland, and Alaska; and frequently changing art installations. ⊠ *Scott Polar Research Institute, Lensfield Rd.* ☎ *01223/336–540* ⊕ *www.spri.cam.ac.uk/museum* ⊠ *Free* ⊙ *Closed Sun. and Mon. except bank holiday Mon.*

WORTH NOTING

Emmanuel College. The master hand of architect Sir Christopher Wren (1632–1723) is evident throughout much of Cambridge, particularly at Emmanuel, built on the site of a Dominican friary, where he designed the chapel and colonnade. A stained-glass window in the chapel has a likeness of John Harvard, founder of Harvard University, who studied here. The college, founded in 1584, was an early center of Puritan learning; a number of the Pilgrims were Emmanuel alumni, and they remembered their alma mater in naming Cambridge, Massachusetts. ✉ *St. Andrew's St.* ☎ *01223/334200* ⊕ *www.emma.cam.ac.uk* ✆ *Free* ⊙ *Closed during exam periods.*

Queens' College. One of the most eye-catching colleges, with a secluded "cloister court" look, Queens' is named after Margaret, wife of Henry VI, and Elizabeth, wife of Edward IV. Founded in 1448 and completed in the 1540s, the college is tucked away on Queens' Lane, next to the wide lawns that lead down from King's College to the Backs. Queens' masterpiece is the **Mathematical Bridge,** the original version of which is said to have been built without any fastenings. The current bridge (1902) is securely bolted. The college is closed to visitors late May–late June. ✉ *Queens' La.* ☎ *01223/335511* ⊕ *www.quns.cam.ac.uk* ✆ *£3* ⊙ *Closed weekends Jan. and Feb. and during exam periods, certain wks Apr.–July; call to confirm.*

Trinity College. Founded in 1546 by Henry VIII, Trinity replaced a 14th-century educational foundation and is the largest college in either Cambridge or Oxford, with nearly 1,000 undergraduates. In the 17th-century great court, with its massive gatehouse, is **Great Tom,** a giant clock that strikes each hour with high and low notes. The college's greatest masterpiece is Sir Christopher Wren's **library,** colonnaded and seemingly constructed with as much light as stone. Among the things you can see here is A. A. Milne's handwritten manuscript of *The House at Pooh Corner.* Trinity alumni include Sir Isaac Newton, William Thackeray, Lord Byron, Lord Tennyson, and 31 Nobel Prize winners. ✉ *St. John's St.* ☎ *01223/338400* ⊕ *www.trin.cam.ac.uk* ✆ *£3* ⊙ *College and chapel closed exam period and event days; Wren library closed Sun.*

19

WHERE TO EAT

$$
SEAFOOD
✕ **Loch Fyne.** Part of a Scottish chain that harvests its own oysters, this airy, casual place across from the Fitzwilliam Museum is deservedly popular. The seafood is fresh and well prepared, served in a traditional setting with a modern ambience. **Known for:** Bradan Rost smoked salmon; Scottish oysters; great Scotch whisky menu. ⑤ *Average main: £17* ✉ *37 Trumpington St.* ☎ *01223/362433* ⊕ *www.lochfyne-seafoodand grill.co.uk.*

$$$$
FRENCH
Fodor's Choice
★
✕ **Midsummer House.** Beside the River Cam on the edge of Midsummer Common, this gray-brick 19th-century villa holds a two–Michelin star restaurant set in a comfortable conservatory. Fixed-price menus for lunch and dinner (with five to eight courses) present innovative French and Mediterranean-influenced dishes that often include apples from the trees in the garden. **Known for:** great river views; beautiful historic

setting; multicourse set menus with a homegrown flair. ⑤ *Average main: £57* ✉ *Midsummer Common* ☎ *01223/369299* ⊕ *www.midsummerhouse.co.uk* ☉ *Closed Sun. and Mon. No lunch Tues.*

$$$ ╳ **River Bar Steakhouse & Grill.** Across the river from Magdalene College,
MODERN BRITISH this popular waterfront bar and grill serves delicious steak burgers and pies, plus specialties such as lobster mac and cheese, and salmon steak with molasses and spices. Perhaps leave room for a bread and butter pudding with a marmalade glaze. **Known for:** classic British mains; rooftop terrace dining; huge cocktail menu. ⑤ *Average main: £20* ✉ *Quayside, Thompsons La., off Bridge St.* ☎ *01223/307030* ⊕ *www.riverbarsteakhouse.com.*

OXFORD

55 miles northwest of London.

With arguably the most famous university in the world, Oxford has been a center of learning since 1167, with only the Sorbonne preceding it. It doesn't take more than a day or two to explore its winding medieval streets, photograph its ivy-covered stone buildings and ancient churches and libraries, and even take a punt down one of its placid waterways. The town center is compact and walkable, and at its heart is Oxford University. Alumni of this prestigious institution include 48 Nobel Prize winners, 26 British prime ministers (including David Cameron), and 28 foreign presidents (including Bill Clinton), along with poets, authors, and artists such as Percy Bysshe Shelley, Oscar Wilde, and W. H. Auden.

Oxford is northwest of London, at the junction of the rivers Thames and Cherwell. The city is more interesting and more cosmopolitan than Cambridge, and although it's also bigger, its suburbs aren't remotely interesting to visitors. The interest is all at the center, where the old town curls around the grand stone buildings, great restaurants, and historic pubs. Victorian writer Matthew Arnold described Oxford's "dreaming spires," a phrase that has become famous. Students rush past on the way to exams, clad with antiquarian style in their requisite mortar caps, flowing dark gowns, stiff collars, and crisp white bow ties. ■**TIP**➔ Watch your back when crossing roads, as bikes are everywhere.

VISITING THE COLLEGES

You can explore the town's major sights in a day, but it takes more than a day to spend an hour in each of the key museums and absorb the college scene. Some colleges are open only in the afternoons during university terms. When undergraduates are in residence, access is often restricted to the chapels, dining rooms, and libraries, and you're requested to refrain from picnicking in the quadrangles. All are closed certain days during exams, usually mid-April–late June.

TOURS

City Sightseeing. This company runs hop-on, hop-off bus tours with 20 stops around Oxford. Your ticket, purchased from the driver, is good for 24 hours. ☎ *01865/790522* ⊕ *www.citysightseeingoxford.com* ✉ *From £16.*

Radcliffe Camera, an unmissable circular library at Oxford University

Oxford Visitor Information Centre. You can find information here on the many guided walks of the city. The best way of gaining access to the collegiate buildings is to take the two-hour university and city tour, which leaves the Tourist Information Centre at 10:45 and 1 and 2 daily from March through October. You can book in advance online. ✉ *15–16 Broad St.* ☎ *01865/686441* ⊕ *www.experienceoxfordshire.org* ✈ *From £14.*

EXPLORING

TOP ATTRACTIONS

Fodor'sChoice
★
Ashmolean Museum. Britain's oldest public museum displays its rich and varied collections from the Neolithic to the present day over five floors. Innovative and spacious galleries on the theme of "Crossing Cultures, Crossing Time" explore connections between the priceless Greek, Roman, and Indian artifacts, as well as the Egyptian and Chinese objects, all of which are among the best in the country. In regards to the superb art collection, not to be missed are drawings by Raphael, the shell-encrusted mantle of Powhatan (father of Pocahontas), the lantern belonging to Guy Fawkes, and the Alfred Jewel, set in gold, which dates to the reign of King Alfred the Great (ruled 871–899). There's too much to see in one visit, but the free admission makes return trips easy. The rooftop Ashmolean Dining Room is a good spot for refreshments. ✉ *Beaumont St.* ☎ *01865/278000* ⊕ *www.ashmolean. org* ✈ *Free* ☉ *Closed Mon. except bank holiday Mon.*

Fodor'sChoice
★
Magdalen College. Founded in 1458, with a handsome main quadrangle and a supremely monastic air, Magdalen (pronounced "*maud*-lin") is one of the most impressive of Oxford's colleges and attracts its most

artistic students. Alumni include such diverse people as P. G. Wode-house, Oscar Wilde, and John Betjeman. The school's large, square tower is a famous local landmark. ■ TIP➡ To enhance your visit, take a stroll around the Deer Park and along Addison's Walk; then have tea in the Old Kitchen, which overlooks the river. ⊠ *High St.* ☎ *01865/276000* ⊕ *www.magd.ox.ac.uk* ⊠ *£6* ☯ *Closed mornings Oct.–June.*

FAMILY

Fodor'sChoice

★

Pitt Rivers Museum. More than half a million intriguing archaeological and anthropological items from around the globe, based on the collection bequeathed by Lieutenant-General Augustus Henry Lane Fox Pitt Rivers in 1884, are crammed into a multitude of glass cases and drawers. Labels are handwritten, and items are organized thematically rather than geographically, an eccentric approach that's surprisingly thought-provoking. Give yourself plenty of time to wander through the displays of shrunken heads, Hawaiian feather cloaks, and fearsome masks. Children will have a field day, as they use flashlights to explore the farthest corners and spot the world's smallest dolly. ⊠ *S. Parks Rd.* ☎ *01865/270927* ⊕ *www.prm.ox.ac.uk* ⊠ *Free (donations welcome). Flashlights £2 (refundable).*

WORTH NOTING

Christ Church. Built in 1546, the college of Christ Church is referred to by its members as "The House." This is the site of Oxford's largest quadrangle, Tom Quad, named after the huge bell (6¼ tons) that hangs in the Sir Christopher Wren–designed gate tower and rings 101 times at five past nine every evening in honor of the original number of Christ Church scholars. The vaulted, 800-year-old chapel in one corner has been Oxford's cathedral since the time of Henry VIII. The college's medieval dining hall contains portraits of many famous alumni, including 13 of Britain's prime ministers, but you'll recognize it from its recurring role in the Harry Potter movies (although they didn't actually film here, the room was painstakingly re-created in a film studio). ■ TIP➡ Plan carefully, as the dining hall is often closed between noon and 2 during term time. Lewis Carroll, author of *Alice in Wonderland,* was a teacher of mathematics here for many years; a shop opposite the meadows on St. Aldate's sells Alice paraphernalia. ⊠ *St. Aldate's* ☎ *01865/276492* ⊕ *www.chch. ox.ac.uk* ⊠ *£8 (£9 in July and Aug.)* ☯ *Sometimes closed for events; check website to confirm.*

Radcliffe Camera and Bodleian Library. A vast library, the domed Radcliffe Camera is Oxford's most spectacular building, built in 1737–49 by James Gibbs in Italian baroque style. It's usually surrounded by tourists with cameras trained at its golden-stone walls. The Camera contains part of the Bodleian Library's enormous collection, begun in 1602 and one of six "copyright libraries" in the United Kingdom. Like the Library of Congress in the United States, this means it must by law contain a copy of every book printed in Great Britain. The shelves are therefore very crowded—the collection grows by about 5,000 items a week. It also contains valuable treasures such as a Gutenberg Bible and a Shakespeare First Folio. Tours reveal the magnificent Duke Humfrey's Library, which was the original chained library, completed in 1488 (the ancient tomes are dusted once a decade). Guides can show you the spots used for Hogwarts School in the Harry Potter films. For those 11 and older, there are three to six tours daily plus extended tours on Wednesday and Saturday, all of which can be prebooked; audio tours are open to all and do not require reservations. ■TIP➔ **If you haven't prebooked, arrive early to secure tickets for the nonaudio tours.** ✉ *Broad St.* ☎ *01865/287400* ⊕ *www.bodleian.ox.ac.uk* ✉ *From £3* ⊙ *Sometimes closed for events; call to confirm.*

St. John's College. One of Oxford's most attractive campuses, St. John's has seven quiet quadrangles surrounded by elaborately carved buildings. You enter the first through a low wooden door. This college dates to 1555, when Sir Thomas White, a merchant, founded it. His heart is buried in the chapel (it's a tradition for students to curse as they walk over it). The Canterbury Quad represented the first example of Italian Renaissance architecture in Oxford, and the Front Quad includes the buildings of the old St. Bernard's Monastery. ✉ *St. Giles* ☎ *01865/277300* ⊕ *www.sjc.ox.ac.uk* ✉ *Free.*

University Church of St. Mary the Virgin. Seven hundred years' worth of funeral monuments crowd this galleried and spacious church, including the alter-step tombstone of Amy Robsart, the wife of Robert Dudley, who was Elizabeth I's favorite suitor. One pillar marks the site where Thomas Cranmer, author of the *Anglican Book of Common Prayer,* was brought to trial for heresy by Queen Mary I (Cranmer had been a key player in the Protestant reforms). He was later burned at the stake nearby on Broad St. The top of the 14th-century tower has a panoramic view of the city's skyline—it's worth the 127 steps. The Vaults and Garden Café, part of the church accessible from Radcliffe Square, serves breakfasts and cream teas as well as good lunches. ✉ *High St.* ☎ *01865/279111* ⊕ *www.university-church.ox.ac.uk* ✉ *Church free, tower £4.*

WHERE TO EAT

$$ ✗ **Brasserie Blanc.** Raymond Blanc's sophisticated brasserie in the Jericho
FRENCH neighborhood is the more affordable chain restaurant cousin of Le Manoir aux Quat'Saisons in Great Milton. The changing menu always lists a good selection of steaks and innovative adaptations of bourgeois French fare, sometimes with Mediterranean or Asian influences. **Known for:** French classics like bouillabaise; affordable prix-fixe lunch menu; kid-friendly options. ⑤ *Average main: £17* ✉ *71–72 Walton St.* ☎ *01865/510999* ⊕ *www.brasserieblanc.com.*

$ ✗ **Jamie's Italian.** One of chef Jamie Oliver's missions is to re-create
ITALIAN the best rustic Italian fare all over the country, and it's no different at this big and buzzing eatery. There's a diverse range of starters, pastas, and mains like truffle tagliatelle with Parmesan and crab spaghetti with fennel, capers, and garlic. **Known for:** star chef Jamie Oliver's Italian hotspot; young and lively crowds; crab spaghetti. ⑤ *Average main: £14* ✉ *24–26 George St.* ☎ *01865/838383* ⊕ *www.jamieoliver. com/restaurants.*

19

STRATFORD-UPON-AVON

104 miles north of London.

Stratford-upon-Avon has become adept at accommodating the hordes of people who stream in for a glimpse of William Shakespeare's world. Filled with distinctive, Tudor half-timber buildings, this is certainly a handsome town, and the Royal Shakespeare Theatre is a don't-miss for those who want to see Shakespeare performed in England. But the town can feel, at times, like a literary amusement park, so if you're not a fan of the Bard, you may want to explore elsewhere.

TOURS AND TICKETS

City Sightseeing. Hop-on, hop-off guided tours of Stratford are run by City Sightseeing, and you can combine the tour (about 90 minutes with no stops) with entry to either three or five Shakespeare houses. ☎ *01789/412680* ⊕ *www.city-sightseeing.com* ✉ *From £14.*

Shakespeare Birthplace Trust. The main places of Shakespearean interest (Anne Hathaway's Cottage, Hall's Croft, Mary Arden's House, Shakespeare's New Place, and Shakespeare's Birthplace) are run by the Shakespeare Birthplace Trust. Buy a money-saving combination ticket to five properties for £27, or pay separate entry fees if you're visiting only one or two. Family tickets are an option, too. Advance booking online gives you a 10% discount and tickets are valid for a year. ☎ *01789/204016* ⊕ *www.shakespeare.org.uk.*

Stratford Town Walk. This walking tour runs year-round and also offers ghost-themed walks on Saturday nights (booking essential). ☎ *0785/576–0377, 01789/292478* ⊕ *www.stratfordtownwalk.co.uk* ✉ *From £6.*

ESSENTIALS

Visitor Information Stratford-upon-Avon Tourist Information Centre. ✉ *Bridgefoot* ☎ *01789/264293* ⊕ *www.visitstratforduponavon.co.uk.*

EXPLORING

Hall's Croft. One of the finest surviving Jacobean (early 17th century) townhouses, this impressive residence has a delightful walled garden. Hall's Croft was the home of Shakespeare's elder daughter, Susanna, and her husband, Dr. John Hall, a wealthy physician who, by prescribing an herbal cure for scurvy, was well ahead of his time. One room is furnished as a medical dispensary of the period, and throughout the building are fine examples of heavy oak Jacobean furniture, including a child's high chair and some 17th-century portraits. The café serves light lunches and afternoon teas. ✉ *Old Town* ☎ *01789/338533* ⊕ *www. shakespeare.org.uk* ✉ *£18, includes admission to Shakespeare's Birthplace and Shakespeare's New Place.*

Holy Trinity Church. The burial place of William Shakespeare, this 13th-century church sits on the banks of the Avon with a graceful avenue of lime trees framing its entrance. Shakespeare's final resting place is in the chancel, rebuilt in 1465–91 in the late Perpendicular style. He was buried here not because he was a famed poet but because he was a lay rector of Stratford, owning a portion of the township tithes. On the north wall of the sanctuary, over the altar steps, is the famous marble bust created by Gerard Jansen in 1623 and thought to be a true likeness of Shakespeare. The bust offers a more human, even humorous, perspective when viewed from the side. Also in the chancel are the graves of Shakespeare's wife, Anne; his daughter, Susanna; his son-in-law, John Hall; and his granddaughter's husband, Thomas Nash. Nearby, the Parish Register is displayed, containing Shakespeare's baptismal entry (1564) and his burial notice (1616). ⊠ *Trinity St.* ☎ *01789/266316* ⊕ *www.stratford-upon-avon.org* ☒ *£3 for Shakespeare's Grave* ☾ *Closed Sun. morning.*

Fodor'sChoice **Royal Shakespeare Company.** One of the finest repertory troupes in the ★ world and long the backbone of the country's theatrical life, the company performs plays year-round in Stratford and at venues around Britain. The stunning Royal Shakespeare Theatre, home of the RSC, has a thrust stage based on the original Globe Theater in London. The Swan Theatre, part of the theater complex and also built in the style of Shakespeare's Globe, stages plays by Shakespeare and contemporaries such as Christopher Marlowe and Ben Jonson, and contemporary works are staged at The Other Place nearby. Prices run from £5. ■TIP➔ Seats book up fast, but day-of-performance and returned tickets are sometimes available. ⊠ *Waterside* ☎ *01789/403493 for tickets* ⊕ *www.rsc.org.uk.*

Shakespeare's New Place. Originally built in 1483 "of brike and tymber" for a lord mayor of London, **New Place** was Stratford's grandest piece of real estate when Shakespeare bought it in 1597 for £60. It remained his home until his death in 1616. Along with a celebrated mulberry tree, revered for being planted by Shakespeare himself, the house was torn down in 1759 by the Reverend Francis Gastrell, who was angry at the hordes of Shakespeare-related sightseers. This in turn provoked the wrath of the local inhabitants, who drove him out of town. Imaginatively reinterpreted in 2016, it now shows the footprint of the original house and contains specially commissioned sculptures that interpret the essence of Shakepeare and a restored Elizabethan knot garden. Next door is the residence of Thomas Nash, who married Shakespeare's last direct descendant, his granddaughter Elizabeth Hall; the exhibition there explains the story of the house and Shakespeare's family life within it. The colorful Great Garden has a fine display of cloud topiary. ⊠ *Chapel St.* ☎ *01789/338536* ⊕ *www.shakespeare.org.uk* ☒ *£18, includes admission to Shakespeare's Birthplace and Hall's Croft.*

Fodor'sChoice **Shakespeare's Birthplace.** A half-timber house typical of its time, the play- ★ wright's birthplace is a much-visited shrine that has been altered and restored since he lived here. Passing through the modern visitor center, you are immersed in the world of Shakespeare through an exhibition that displays the First Folio, deeds to his properties, what is thought to be his signet ring, busts, and other memorabilia. The house itself is across the garden from the visitor center. Colorful wall decorations and the furnishings reflect comfortable, middle-class Elizabethan domestic life. Shakespeare's father, John, a glove maker and wool dealer, purchased the house; a reconstructed workshop shows the tools of the

19

Stratford-upon-Avon honors Shakespeare's birthday with an annual procession.

glover's trade. Mark Twain and Charles Dickens were both pilgrims here, and you can see the signatures of Thomas Carlyle and Walter Scott scratched into Shakespeare's windowpanes. In the garden, actors present excerpts from the plays. There's also a café and bookshop on the grounds. ⊠ *Henley St.* ☎ *01789/204016* ⊕ *www.shakespeare.org. uk* ⊠ *£18, includes entry to Hall's Croft and Shakespeare's New Place.*

AROUND STRATFORD

Two additional stops on the Shakespeare trail are just outside Stratford; also nearby is spectacular Warwick Castle.

Fodor'sChoice
★
Anne Hathaway's Cottage and Gardens. The most picturesque of the Shakespeare Trust properties, on the western outskirts of Stratford, is the family home of the woman Shakespeare married in 1582. The "cottage," actually a substantial Tudor farmhouse, has latticed windows and a grand thatch roof. Inside is period furniture, including the settle where Shakespeare reputedly conducted his courtship, and a rare carved Elizabethan bed; outside is a garden planted in lush Edwardian style with herbs and flowers. A stroll through the adjacent orchard takes you to willow cabins where you can listen to sonnets and view sculptures with Shakespearean themes, while the nearby arboretum has trees, shrubs, and roses mentioned in Shakespeare's works. ■TIP→ **The best way to get here is on foot, especially in late spring when the apple trees are in blossom.** The signed path runs from Evesham Place (an extension of Grove Road) opposite Chestnut Walk. Pick up a leaflet with a map from the tourist office; the walk takes a good half hour. ⊠ *Cottage La., Shottery* ☎ *01789/338532* ⊕ *www.shakespeare.org.uk* ⊠ *£11; Five House*

Pass £27, includes Hall's Croft, Mary Arden's Farm, Shakespeare's New Place, and Shakespeare's Birthplace.

FAMILY **Mary Arden's Farm.** A working farm, where food is grown using methods common in the 16th century, is the main attraction at Mary Arden's House (the childhood home of Shakespeare's mother) and Palmer's Farm. This bucolic stop is great for kids, who can try their hand at basket weaving and gardening, listen as the farmers explain their work in the fields, and watch the cooks prepare food in the Tudor farmhouse kitchen—it all brings the past to life. There are crafts exhibits, a café, and a garden. The site is 3 miles northwest of Stratford; you need to walk or drive here, or else go with a tour. ✉ *Off A3400, Wilmcote* ☎ *01789/338535* ⊕ *www.shakespeare.org.uk* 🎫 *£14; Five House Pass £27, includes Anne Hathaway's Cottage and Gardens, Hall's Croft, Shakespeare's New Place, and Shakespeare's Birthplace* ⊗ *Closed Nov.–mid-Mar.*

FAMILY **Warwick Castle.** The vast bulk of this medieval castle rests on a cliff
Fodor's Choice overlooking the Avon, "the fairest monument of ancient and chivalrous
★ splendor which yet remains uninjured by time," to use the words of Sir Walter Scott. Today the company that runs the Madame Tussauds wax museums owns the castle, and the exhibits and diversions can occupy a full day. Warwick is a great castle experience for kids, and although it's pricey, there are family rates. Warwick's two soaring towers, bristling with battlements, can be seen for miles: the 147-foot-high Caesar's Tower, built in 1356, and the 128-foot-high Guy's Tower, built in 1380. The castle's most powerful commander was Richard Neville, Earl of Warwick, known during the 15th-century Wars of the Roses as the Kingmaker. Warwick Castle's monumental walls enclose an impressive armory of medieval weapons, as well as state rooms with historic furnishings and paintings by Peter Paul Rubens, Anthony van Dyck, and other old masters. Twelve rooms are devoted to an imaginative wax exhibit, *A Royal Weekend Party—1898.* Other exhibits explore the castle's history through the ages, display the sights and sounds of a great medieval household as it prepares for an important battle, and tell the story of a princess's fairy-tale wedding. At the Mill and Engine House, you can see the turning water mill and the engines used to generate electricity early in the 20th century. Be prepared both to play your part and be spooked in the gruesome dungeon experience (50 minutes and not recommended for under-10s) as you travel through scenes of torture, poisonings, and death sentences. Elsewhere, a working trebuchet (a kind of catapult), falconry displays, and rat-throwing (stuffed, not live) games add to the atmosphere. Below the castle, strutting peacocks patrol the 60 acres of grounds elegantly landscaped by Capability Brown in the 18th century. ■ TIP→ **Arrive early to beat the crowds. If you book online, you save 30% on ticket prices.** Lavish medieval banquets take place throughout the year, and plenty of food stalls serve lunches. For the ultimate castle experience, you can "glamp" (glamorously camp) in a medieval tent, stay in a wooden lodge in the Knight's Village or stay in your own luxury suite in Caesar's Tower. ✉ *Castle La. off Mill St., Warwick* ☎ *01926/495421, 0871/265–2000 for info (24 hrs), 0871/663–1676 for accommodations* ⊕ *www.warwick-castle.com* 🎫 *£32 castle and dungeon, £27 castle only; parking £6.*

19

WHERE TO EAT

$ × **The Black Swan/The Dirty Duck.** The only pub in Britain to be licensed
BRITISH under two names (the more informal one came courtesy of Ameri-
Fodor's Choice can GIs who were stationed here during World War II), this is one
★ of Stratford's most celebrated pubs—it's attracted actors since the
18th-century days of thespian David Garrick. Along with your pint
of bitter, you can choose from the extensive menu of baked pota-
toes, steaks, burgers, and grills; there are also good-value set menus.
Known for: classic English pub atmosphere; reservations only for dinner; veranda overlooking the river. ⑤ *Average main: £12* ⊠ *Waterside*
☎ *01789/297312* ⊕ *www.oldenglishinns.co.uk.*

$ × **Opposition.** Hearty, warming meals are offered at this informal,
MODERN BRITISH family-style restaurant in a 16th-century building on the main dining
street near the theaters. The English and international dishes—chicken
roasted with banana and served with curry sauce and basmati rice, for
instance—win praise from the locals. **Known for:** historical ambience;
plenty of vegetarian and healthy options; summertime crowds. ⑤ *Average main: £14* ⊠ *13 Sheep St.* ☎ *01789/269980* ⊕ *www.theoppo.co.uk*
☉ *Closed Sun.*

WARNER BROS. HARRY POTTER STUDIO TOUR

20 miles northwest of London.

Popular and family-friendly, the Warner Bros. Harry Potter Studio Tour
has sets and props from the successful films, and plenty of engaging
interactive diversions for all ages. The train and a special shuttle bus
from Watford get you here.

EXPLORING

FAMILY **Warner Bros. Harry Potter Studio Tour.** Muggles, take note: this spectacular
Fodor's Choice attraction just outside Watford gives you a good three hours of the
★ magical world of Harry Potter. From the Great Hall of Hogwarts—
faithfully restored—to magical props beautifully displayed in a vast
studio space, each section of this attraction showcases the real sets,
props, and special effects used in the eight movies. Visitors enter the
Great Hall, a fitting stage for costumes from each Hogwarts house.
You can admire the intricacies of the huge Hogwarts Castle model,
ride a broomstick, try butterbeer, explore the Forbidden Forest, and
gaze through the shop windows of Diagon Alley. The Hogwarts
Express section—at a faithfully reproduced Platform 9¾—allows you
to walk through a carriage of the actual steam train and see what it's
like to ride with Harry and the gang. Tickets, pegged to a 30-minute
arrival time slot, must be prebooked online. The studio tour is a
20-minute drive from St. Albans. You can also get here by taking a
20-minute train ride from London's Euston Station to Watford Junction (then a 15-minute shuttle-bus ride). Via car from London, use
M1 and M25—parking is free. ⊠ *Studio Tour Dr., Leavesden Green*
☎ *0345/084–0900* ⊕ *www.wbstudiotour.co.uk* ☞ *£39.*

WINDSOR CASTLE

21 miles west of London.

The tall turrets of Windsor Castle, one of the homes of the Royal Family, can be seen for miles around. The grand stone building is the star attraction in this quiet town with some remaining medieval elements—although Eton College, England's most famous public school, is also just a lovely walk away across the Thames.

ESSENTIALS

Visitor Information Royal Windsor Information Centre. ⊠ *Old Booking Hall, Windsor Royal Station, Thames St.* ☎ *01753/743900, 01753/743907 for accommodations* ⊕ *www.windsor.gov.uk.*

EXPLORING

Fodor's Choice ★ **Eton College.** Signs warn drivers of "Boys Crossing" as you approach the splendid Tudor-style buildings of Eton College, the distinguished boarding school for boys ages 13–18 founded in 1440 by King Henry VI. It's all terrifically photogenic—during the college semester students still dress in pinstripe trousers, swallowtail coats, and stiff collars. Rivaling St. George's at Windsor in terms of size, the Gothic **Chapel** contains superb 15th-century grisaille wall paintings juxtaposed with modern stained glass by John Piper. Beyond the cloisters are the school's playing fields where, according to the Duke of Wellington, the Battle of Waterloo was really won, since so many of his officers had learned discipline and strategy during their school days. Among the country's prime ministers to be educated here is David Cameron. The **Museum of Eton Life** has displays on the school's history and vignettes of school life. The school gives public tours on Friday afternoons between early May and early September, bookable online. ⊠ *Brewhouse Yard, Eton* ☎ *01753/370603* ⊕ *www.etoncollege.com* 🎟 *£10* ☾ *Closed mid-Sept.–early May.*

Fodor's Choice ★ **Windsor Castle.** From William the Conqueror to Queen Victoria, the kings and queens of England added towers and wings to this brooding, imposing castle, the largest inhabited castle in the world and visible for miles. Despite the multiplicity of hands involved in its design, the palace manages to have a unity of style and character. The most impressive view of Windsor Castle is from the A332 road, coming into town from the south. Admission includes an audio guide and, if you wish, a guided tour of the castle precincts. Entrance lines can be long in season, and you're likely to spend at least half a day here, so come early.

William the Conqueror began work on the castle in the 11th century, and Edward III modified and extended it in the mid-1300s. One of Edward's largest contributions was the enormous and distinctive

19

Round Tower. Later, between 1824 and 1837, George IV transformed the still essentially medieval castle into the fortified royal palace you see today. Most of England's kings and queens have demonstrated their undying attachment to the castle, the only royal residence in continuous use by the Royal Family since the Middle Ages.

As you enter the castle, **Henry VIII's gateway** leads uphill into the wide castle precincts, where you're free to wander. Across from the entrance is the exquisite **St. George's Chapel** (closed Sunday). Here lie 10 of the kings of England, including Henry VI, Charles I, and Henry VIII (Jane Seymour is the only one of his six wives buried here). One of the noblest buildings in England, the chapel was built in the Perpendicular style popular in the 15th and 16th centuries, with elegant stained-glass windows; a high, vaulted ceiling; and intricately carved choir stalls. The colorful heraldic banners of the Knights of the Garter—the oldest British Order of Chivalry, founded by Edward III in 1348—hang in the choir. The ceremony in which the knights are installed as members of the order has been held here with much pageantry for more than five centuries. The elaborate **Albert Memorial Chapel** was created by Queen Victoria in memory of her husband.

The **North Terrace** provides especially good views across the Thames to Eton College, perhaps the most famous of Britain's exclusive public schools (confusingly, "public schools" in Britain are highly traditional, top-tier private schools). From the terrace, you enter the **State Apartments,** which are open to the public most days. On display to the left of the entrance to the State Apartments in Windsor Castle, **Queen Mary's Dolls' House** is a perfect miniature Georgian palace-within-a-palace, created in 1923. Electric lights glow, the doors all have tiny keys, and a miniature library holds Lilliputian-size books written especially for the young queen by famous authors of the 1920s. Five cars, including a Daimler and Rolls-Royce, stand at the ready. In the adjacent corridor are exquisite French couturier–designed costumes made for the two Jumeau dolls presented to the Princesses Elizabeth and Margaret by France in 1938.

Although a fire in 1992 gutted some of the State Apartments, hardly any works of art were lost. Phenomenal repair work brought to new life the **Grand Reception Room,** the **Green and Crimson Drawing Rooms,** and the **State and Octagonal Dining Rooms.** A green oak hammer-beam (a short horizontal beam that projects from the tops of walls for support) roof looms magnificently over the 600-year-old **St. George's Hall,** where the Queen gives state banquets. The State Apartments contain priceless furniture, including a magnificent Louis XVI bed and Gobelin tapestries; carvings by Grinling Gibbons; and paintings by Canaletto, Rubens, Van Dyck, Holbein, Dürer, and Bruegel. The tour's high points are the **Throne Room** and the **Waterloo Chamber,** where Sir Thomas Lawrence's portraits of Napoléon's victorious foes line the walls. You can also see arms and armor—look for Henry VIII's ample suit. A visit October to March also includes the Semi-State rooms, the private apartments of George IV, resplendent with gilded ceilings.

To see the castle come magnificently alive, check out the Changing the Guard, which takes place daily at 11 am April to July, and on alternate days at the same time August to March. Confirm the exact schedule before traveling to Windsor. ⊠ *Castle Hill* ☎ *0303/123–7304 for tickets* ⊕ *www.royalcollection.org.uk* 🖃 *£21 for Precincts, State Apartments, Gallery, St. George's Chapel, and Queen Mary's Dolls' House; £12 when State Apartments are closed.*

Fodor's Choice ★ **Windsor Great Park.** The remains of an ancient royal hunting forest, this park stretches for some 5,000 acres south of Windsor Castle. Much of it is open to the public and can be explored by car or on foot. Its chief attractions are clustered around the southeastern section, known (or at least marketed) as the **Royal Landscape.** These include **Virginia Water,** a 2-mile-long lake that forms the park's main geographical focal point. More than anything, however, the Royal Landscape is defined by its two beautiful gardens. **Valley Gardens,** located on the north shore of Virginia Water, is particularly vibrant in April and May, when the dazzling multicolored azaleas are in full bloom.

If you're feeling fit, the romantic **Long Walk** is one of England's most photographed footpaths—the 3-mile-long route, designed by Charles II, starts in the Great Park and leads all the way to Windsor Castle.

Divided from the Great Park by the busy A308 highway, the smaller **Windsor Home Park**, on the eastern side of Windsor Castle, is the private property of the Royal Family. It contains **Frogmore House**, a lavish royal residence. Completed in 1684, Frogmore was bought by George III as a gift for his wife, Queen Charlotte. The sprawling white mansion later became a beloved retreat of Queen Victoria. Today it's mainly used for official functions, but you can visit by guided tour (£10) on a handful of days in June; see ⊕ *www.royalcollection.org. uk,* or call *0303/123–7321* for more information. ⊠ *Entrances on A329, A332, B383, and Wick La.* ☎ *01753/860222* ⊕ *www.windsor-greatpark.co.uk* 🖃 *Free; Savill Garden £11 Mar.–Nov., free Dec.–Feb.*

19

WHERE TO EAT

$$$$
MODERN BRITISH
Fodor's Choice
★
✕ **Fat Duck.** One of the top restaurants in the country, and ranked by many food writers among the best in the world, this extraordinary place packs in fans of hypercreative, hyperexpensive cuisine, who enjoy it for the theater as much as for the food. "Culinary alchemist" Heston Blumenthal is famed for bizarre taste combinations and his laboratory-like kitchen, where this advocate of molecular gastronomy creates his dishes. With an "itinerary," complete with magnifying glass in hand rather than a menu, diners take a five-hour nostalgic journey back to an English childhood seaside holiday, starting with the anticipation felt the night before and ending with sweet dreams in bed. **Known for:** creative and immersive multicourse menu; strict booking process and long waiting list for reservations; dishes that take out on a journey through the English seaside. 💲 *Average main: £265* ⊠ *High St., Bray* ☎ *01628/580333* ⊕ *www.fatduck.co.uk* 🕙 *Closed Sun. and Mon.*

$ ✗ **Two Brewers.** Locals congregate in a pair of low-ceiling rooms at this
BRITISH   tiny 17th-century establishment by the gates of Windsor Great Park.
Those under 18 aren't allowed inside the pub (although they can be
served at a few outdoor tables), but adults will find a suitable collection of wine, espresso, and local beer, plus an excellent menu with
such dishes as liver and bacon with mash and pea gravy, fish cakes,
and a good selection of hot and cold sandwiches. **Known for:** classic, adults-only British pub; traditional lunchtime roast on Sundays;
historic setting. ⑤ *Average main: £14* ✉ *34 Park St.* ☎ *01753/855426*
⊕ *www.twobrewerswindsor.co.uk* ☺ *No dinner Sun.–Fri.*

UNDERSTANDING LONDON

LONDON AT-A-GLANCE

ENGLISH VOCABULARY

LONDON AT-A-GLANCE

FAST FACTS

Type of government: Representative democracy. In 1999 the Greater London Authority Act reestablished a single local governing body for the Greater London area, consisting of an elected mayor and the 25-member London Assembly. Elections, first held in 2000, take place every four years.

Population: Greater London 8.788 million

Population density: 3,900 people per square mile

Median age: 38.4

Language: English. More than 300 languages are spoken in London. All city government documents are translated into Arabic, Bengali, Chinese, Greek, Gujurati, Hindi, Punjabi, Turkish, Urdu, and Vietnamese.

Ethnic and racial groups: White British 70%, White Irish 3%, Other White 9%, Indian 6%, Bangladeshi 2%, Pakistani 2%, other Asian 2%, Black African 6%, Black Caribbean 5%, Chinese 1%, Other 3%.

Religion: Christian 58%, nonaffiliated 15%, Muslim 8%, Hindu 4%, Jewish 2%, Sikh 1%, other religion 1%, Buddhist 0.8%.

When a man is tired of London, he is tired of life; for there is in London all that life can afford.

—Samuel Johnson

GEOGRAPHY AND ENVIRONMENT

Latitude: 51° N (same as Calgary, Canada; Kiev, Ukraine; Prague, Czech Republic)

Longitude: 0° (same as Accra, Ghana). A brass line in the ground in Greenwich marks the prime meridian (0° longitude).

Elevation: 49 feet

Land area: City, 67 square miles; metro area, 625 square miles

Terrain: River plain, rolling hills, and parkland

Natural hazards: Drought in warmer summers, minor localized flooding of the Thames caused by surge tides from the North Atlantic

Environmental issues: The city has been improving its air quality, but up to 1,600 people die each year from health problems related to London's polluted air. Only half of London's rivers and canals received passing grades for water quality from 1999 through 2001. More than £12 million ($22 million) is spent annually to ensure the city's food safety.

I'm leaving because the weather is too good. I hate London when it's not raining.

—Groucho Marx

ENGLISH VOCABULARY

You and a Londoner may speak the same language, but some phrases definitely get lost in translation once they cross the Atlantic.

BRITISH ENGLISH	ENGLISH

BASIC TERMS AND EVERYDAY ITEMS

BRITISH ENGLISH	ENGLISH
bill	check
flat	apartment
holiday	vacation
lift	elevator
nappy	diaper
note	bill (currency)
plaster	Band-Aid
queue	line
row	argument
rubbish	trash
tin	can
toilet/loo/WC	bathroom

CLOTHING

braces	suspenders
bum bag	fanny pack
dressing gown	robe
jumper	sweater
pants/knickers	underpants/briefs
rucksack	backpack
suspender	garter
tights	pantyhose
trainers	sneakers
trousers	pants
vest	undershirt
waistcoat	vest

TRANSPORTATION

bonnet	hood
boot	trunk
coach	bus (long-distance)
pavement	sidewalk

BRITISH ENGLISH	ENGLISH
petrol	gas
pram	baby carriage
puncture	flat
windscreen	windshield

FOOD

aubergine	eggplant
banger	sausage
biscuit	cookie
chips	fries
courgette	zucchini
crisps	potato chips
jam	jelly
main course (or main)	entrée
pudding	dessert
rocket	arugula
starter	appetizer
sweet	candy
tea	early dinner

SLANG

all right	hi there
cheers	thank you
chuffed	pleased
fit	attractive
geezer	dude
guv'nor, gaffer	boss
hard	tough
mate	buddy
sound	good
Ta	thank you

TRAVEL SMART LONDON

GETTING HERE AND AROUND

Central London and its surrounding districts are divided into 32 boroughs (33, counting the City of London). More useful for finding your way around, however, are the subdivisions of London into postal districts. The first one or two letters give the location: N means north, NW means northwest, and so on. Don't expect the numbering to be logical, however. You won't, for example, find W2 next to W3. The general rule is that the lower numbers, such as W1 or SW1, are closest to Buckingham Palace, but it is not consistent—SE17 is closer to the city center than E4, for example.

▌ AIR TRAVEL

Flying time to London is about 6½ hours from New York, 7½ hours from Chicago, 11 hours from San Francisco, and 21½ hours from Sydney.

For flights out of London, the general rule is that you should be at the airport at least one hour before your scheduled departure time for domestic flights and two hours before international flights for off-peak travel.

Airline Security Issues Transportation Security Administration. ☎ 866/289–9673 ⊕ www.tsa.gov.

AIRPORTS

Most international flights to London arrive at either Heathrow Airport (LHR), 15 miles west of London, or at Gatwick Airport (LGW), 27 miles south of the capital. Most flights from the United States go to Heathrow, which is divided into five terminals, with Terminals 3–5 handling transatlantic flights. Gatwick is London's second gateway. It has grown from a European airport into an airport that also serves dozens of U.S. destinations. A third airport, Stansted (STN), is 35 miles northeast of the city; it handles European and domestic traffic. Three smaller airports, Luton (LTN), 30 miles north of town, Southend (SEN), 40 miles

to the east, and business-oriented London City (in East London E16) mainly handle flights to Europe.

Airport Information Gatwick Airport. ☎ 0844/892–0322 ⊕ www.gatwickairport. com. **Heathrow Airport.** ☎ 0844/335–1801 ⊕ www.heathrow.com. **London City Airport.** ☎ 020/7646–0088 ⊕ www.londoncityairport. com. **Luton Airport.** ☎ 01582/405–100 ⊕ www.london-luton.co.uk. **Southend Airport.** ☎ 01702/538–500 ⊕ www.southendairport. com. **Stansted Airport.** ☎ 0800/093–7851 ⊕ www.stanstedairport.com.

GROUND TRANSPORTATION

London has excellent if pricey bus and train connections between its airports and central London. If you're arriving at Heathrow, you can pick up a map and fare schedule at the Transport for London (TfL) Information Centre, in the Underground station serving Terminals 1–3. Train service can be quick, but the downside (for trains from all airports) is that you must get yourself and your luggage to the train via a series of escalators and connecting trams. Airport link buses (generally National Express airport buses) may ease the luggage factor and drop you off closer to central hotels, but they're subject to London traffic, which can be horrendous and make the trip drag on for hours. Taxis can be more convenient than buses, but beware that prices can go through the roof. Airport Travel Line has additional transfer information and takes advance booking for transfers between airports and into London.

Heathrow by Bus: National Express buses take one hour to reach the city center (Victoria) and cost from £5 one-way and £10 round-trip (book online for best prices). The National Express Hotel Hoppa service runs from all airports to 29 hotels near the airport (from £5). SkyShuttle offers a shared minibus service between Heathrow and any London hotel. The N9 night bus runs to Aldwych every 20 minutes midnight–5 am; it takes just over

FROM HEATHROW TO CENTRAL LONDON		
TRAVEL MODE	TIME	COST
Taxi	1 hour-plus	£50–£80 (depending on traffic)
Heathrow Express Train	15 minutes	£22 (£37 round-trip), £32 for first class
Underground	50 minutes	£6 one-way (less with Oyster card)
National Express Bus	1 hour	From £5 one-way

an hour and costs £2 (you need to pay with an Oyster card or a contactless debit/credit card; see explanation later). Please note: the N9 doesn't stop at Terminal 4; take Bus Nos. 490 or 482 to Terminal 5 and catch it there.

Heathrow by Tube and Train: The cheap, direct route into London is via the Piccadilly line of the Underground (London's extensive subway system, or "Tube"). Trains normally run every four to eight minutes from all terminals from early morning until just before midnight. The 50-minute trip into central London costs £6 one-way and connects with other central Tube lines. The Heathrow Express train is comfortable and convenient, if costly, speeding into London's Paddington station in 15 minutes. Standard one-way tickets cost £22 (£37 round-trip) and £32 for first class. Tickets are more expensive to buy on board, so book ahead (online is the cheapest option; at a counter/kiosk, less so). There's daily service 5:10 am (6 am on Sunday)–11:40 pm, with departures usually every 15 minutes. The Heathrow Connect service leaves from Paddington station and makes five local stops before arriving at Terminals 1, 3, and 5. It takes 25 minutes, only a little more time than the Express, although trains are less frequent (two an hour in peak times). One-way tickets are £11.

Heathrow by Taxi: This is an expensive and time-consuming option. The city's congestion charge (£12) may be added to the bill if your hotel is in the charging zone; you run the risk of getting stuck in traffic; and if you take a taxi from the stand, the price will be even more expensive (whereas a minicab booked ahead is a set price). The trip can take more than an hour and can cost in the region of £60, depending on time of day.

Gatwick by Bus: An hourly bus service runs from Gatwick's north and south terminals to London's Victoria station, with stops at Hooley, Coulsdon, Mitcham, Streatham, Stockwell, and Pimlico. The journey takes upward of 90 minutes (depending on time of day) and costs from £5 one-way. The easyBus service runs to West London (Earl's Court) or Waterloo from as little as £2 if booked in advance; the later the ticket is booked online, the higher the price (up to £11 onboard).

Gatwick by Train: The fast, nonstop Gatwick Express leaves for Victoria station every 15 minutes 5:50 am–11:20 pm. The 30-minute trip costs £20 one-way, and £35 round-trip, though cheaper tickets are available online. The Thameslink Great Northern rail company runs nonexpress services that are cheaper; Thameslink trains run regularly throughout the day to St. Pancras International, London Bridge, and Blackfriars stations; departures are every 15 minutes (hourly during the night), and the journey takes 45–55 minutes. Tickets are from £11 one-way to St. Pancras International.

Stansted by Bus: Hourly service on National Express Airport bus A6 (24 hours a day) to Victoria Coach station costs from £12 one-way, £19 round-trip, and takes about 1 hour 45 minutes. Stops include Golders Green, Finchley Road, St. John's Wood, Baker Street, Marble Arch, and Hyde Park Corner. The easyBus service to Victoria via Baker Street costs from £2 one-way, but book early and online for best prices.

Stansted by Train: The Stansted Express to Liverpool Street station (with a stop at Tottenham Hale) runs daily every 15 minutes, 5:30 am–12:30 am. If booked online, the 50-minute trip costs £19 one-way and £32 round-trip; tickets cost more when purchased onboard.

Luton by Bus and Train: An airport shuttle runs from Luton Airport to the nearby Luton Airport Parkway station, from which you can take a train or bus into London (this shuttle is free if you have bought a rail ticket in advance; otherwise it's £2 one-way). From there, the Thameslink Great Northern train service runs to St. Pancras, Farringdon, Blackfriars, and London Bridge. The journey takes about 30 minutes. Trains leave every 10 minutes or so during the day, and hourly during the night. Single tickets cost from £13 one-way, if booked in advance. The Green Line 757 bus service from Luton to Victoria station runs three times an hour, takes about 90 minutes, and costs from £10 one-way, if booked in advance.

TRANSFERS BETWEEN AIRPORTS

Allow at least two to three hours for an interairport transfer. The cheapest option—but most complicated—is public transportation: from Gatwick to Stansted, for instance, you can catch the nonexpress commuter train from Gatwick to Victoria station, take the Tube to Liverpool Street station, then catch the train to Stansted from there. To get from Heathrow to Gatwick by public transportation, take the Tube to King's Cross, then change to the Victoria line, get to Victoria station, and then take the commuter train to Gatwick.

The National Express airport bus is the most direct option. Between Gatwick and Heathrow, buses pick up passengers every 15–20 minutes 5:35 am–midnight from both airports. The trip takes around 75 minutes, and the fare is from £20 one-way, but it's advisable to book tickets in advance. National Express buses between Stansted and Gatwick depart every 30–45 minutes and can

take 3–4½ hours, depending on traffic. The adult one-way fare is from £20. Some airlines may offer shuttle services as well—check with your travel agent in advance of your journey.

Contacts easyBus. ⊕ www.easybus.co.uk. **Gatwick Express.** ☎ 0345/850–1530 ⊕ www.gatwickexpress.com. **Heathrow Express.** ☎ 0345/600–1515 ⊕ www.heathrowexpress.com. **National Express.** ☎ 0871/781–8181 ⊕ www.nationalexpress.com. **SkyShuttle.** ☎ 0845/481–0960 ⊕ www.skyshuttle.co.uk. **Stansted Express.** ☎ 0345/600–7245 ⊕ www.stanstedexpress.com. **Thameslink.** ☎ 0345/026–4700 ⊕ www.thameslinkrailway.com.

Transfer Information Airport Travel Line. ☎ 0871/200–2233 ⊕ www.travelline.co.uk.

FLIGHTS

British Airways is the national flagship carrier and offers mostly nonstop flights from more than 20 U.S. cities to Heathrow and Gatwick airports, along with flights to Manchester, Birmingham, and Glasgow. It also offers flights to New York from London City Airport near Docklands.

Airline Contacts American Airlines. ☎ 207/660–2300, 0844/369–9899 in London ⊕ www.aa.com. **British Airways.** ☎ 800/247–9297 in U.S., 0344/493–0787 in U.K. ⊕ www.britishairways.com. **Delta Airlines.** ☎ 800/241–4141 for international reservations, 020/7660–0767 in U.K. ⊕ www.delta.com. **United Airlines.** ☎ 800/864–8331 for international reservations, 0845/607–6760 in U.K. ⊕ www.united.com. **Virgin Atlantic.** ☎ 800/862–8621 in U.S., 0344/874–7747 in U.K. ⊕ www.virgin-atlantic.com.

▌ BIKE TRAVEL

Nicknamed "Boris bikes" after the former mayor and dedicated cyclist Boris Johnson, a 24-hour bike-rental program called Santander Cycles enables Londoners to pick up a bicycle at one of more than 750 docking stations and return it at another. The first 30 minutes are free, then it's £2 for every 30-minute period thereafter. There is also a £2-per-day access charge. You pay at the docking station, using credit or debit cards only (cash is not accepted)—simply follow the instructions on the touch screen and away you go.

▮ BUS TRAVEL

ARRIVING AND DEPARTING

National Express is the biggest British long-distance bus operator and the nearest equivalent to Greyhound. It's not as fast as traveling by train, but it's comfortable (with bathrooms onboard). Services depart mainly from Victoria Coach station, a well-signposted short walk behind the Victoria mainline train station. The departures point is on the corner of Buckingham Palace Road; this is also the main information point. The arrivals point is opposite, at Elizabeth Bridge. National Express buses travel to all large and midsize cities in southern England and the midlands. Scotland and the north are not as well served. The station is extremely busy around holidays and weekends. Arrive at least 30 minutes before departure so you can find the correct exit gate. Smoking is not permitted onboard.

Another bus company, Megabus, offers cross-country fares for as little as £1 per person. The company's single- and double-decker buses serve an extensive array of cities across Great Britain with a cheerful budget attitude. In London, buses for all destinations depart from the Green Line bus stand at Victoria station. Megabus does not accommodate wheelchairs, and the company strictly limits luggage to one piece per person checked, and one piece of hand luggage.

Green Line serves the counties surrounding London, as well as airports. Bus stops (there's no central bus station) are on Buckingham Palace Road, between the Victoria train station and Victoria Coach station.

Tickets on many long-distance routes are cheaper if purchased in advance, and traveling midweek costs less than over weekends and at holiday periods.

GETTING AROUND LONDON

Private, as opposed to municipal, buses are known as coaches. Although London is famous for its double-decker buses, the old beloved rattletrap Routemasters, with the jump-on, jump-off back platforms, now only serve a single "heritage" route (No. 15)—from Trafalgar Square down Fleet Street and on to St. Paul's Cathedral and the Tower of London. That said, modernized Routemaster buses have taken to the streets on other routes.

Bus stops are clearly indicated; signs at bus stops feature a red TfL symbol on a plain white background. You must flag the bus down at some stops. Each numbered route is listed on the main stop, and buses have a large number on the front with their end destination. Not all buses run the full route at all times; check with the driver to be sure. You can pick up a free bus guide at a TfL Travel Information Centre (at Euston, Liverpool Street, Piccadilly Circus, King's Cross, and Victoria Tube stations; and at Heathrow Airport).

Buses are a good way of seeing the town, particularly if you plan to hop on and off to cover many sights, but don't take a bus if you're in a hurry, as traffic can really slow them down. To get off, press the red "Stop" buttons mounted on poles near the doors. You will usually see a "Bus Stopping" sign light up. Expect to get sardined during rush hour, 8–9:30 am and 4:30–6:30 pm.

Night buses, denoted by an "N" before their route numbers, run midnight–5 am on a more restricted route than day buses. However, some night-bus routes should be approached with caution, and the top deck avoided (the danger is that muggings are most likely to occur there, since it's farthest from both the exit doors and the drivers). All night buses run by request stop, so flag them down if you're waiting, or push the button if you want to alight.

All London buses are now cash-free, which means you must buy your ticket *before* you board the bus. There are a number of ways to do this. One-day paper bus passes are available at underground and rail stations as well as London Transport Visitor Centres and cost £5. An easier, and cheaper, option is to pay by prepaid Oyster card or "contactless" bank card. Visitor Oyster cards must be purchased before you arrive; they cost £3 but a day's bus travel is capped at £5. Normal Oyster cards, which cost £5, are available from ticket desks at all major airports or at any Tube station and are transferable if you have money left over. Contactless cards are the future of London travel: you touch a compatible debit or credit card on a bus or Tube-station's reader, and the fare is automatically debited from your bank account.

One alternative is to buy a one- or seven-day Travelcard, which is good for both Tube and bus travel. Travelcards can be bought at Tube stations, travel information centers, and some newsagents. However, note that seven-day Travelcards bought in London *must be loaded onto an Oyster card*. Although using a Travelcard may save you some money, it might be easier to just add additional money to your Oyster card as needed, since there are machines at all Tube stations and at lots of London newsagents. A seven-day paper Travelcard can only be purchased in advance, online. However you buy your ticket, just make sure you have one: traveling without a valid ticket makes you liable for a significant fine (£80). Buses are supposed to swing by most stops every five or six minutes, but in reality you often end up waiting a bit longer, although those in the city center are quite reliable.

Long-Distance Bus Contacts
easyBus. ⊕ *www.easybus.co.uk.* **Green Line.** ☎ *0344/801–7261* ⊕ *www.green-line.co.uk.* **Megabus.** ☎ *0900/160–0900* ⊕ *www.megabus.com.* **National Express.** ☎ *0871/781–8181* ⊕ *www.nationalexpress.com.*

Bus Information Transport for London. ☎ *0343/222–1234* ⊕ *www.tfl.gov.uk.* **Victoria Coach Station.** ⊠ *164 Buckingham Palace Rd., Victoria* ☎ *0343/222–1234* Ⓜ *Victoria.*

▌CAR TRAVEL

The best advice on driving in London is this: don't. London's streets are a winding mass of chaos, made worse by one-way roads. Parking is also restrictive and expensive, and traffic is tediously slow at most times of the day; during rush hours (8–9:30 am and 4:30–6:30 pm) it often grinds to a standstill, particularly on Friday, when everyone wants to leave town. Avoid city-center shopping areas, including the roads feeding Oxford Street, Kensington, and Knightsbridge. Other main roads into the city center are also busy, such as King's Cross and Euston in the north. Watch out also for cyclists and motorcycle couriers, who weave between cars and pedestrians that seem to come out of nowhere, and you may get a heavy fine for straying into a bus lane during its operating hours—check the signs.

If you are staying in London for the duration of your trip, there's virtually no reason to rent a car, because the city and its suburbs are widely covered by public transportation. However, you may want a car for day trips to castles or stately homes out in the countryside. Consider renting your car in a medium-size town in the area where you'll be traveling, and then journeying there by train and picking up the car once you arrive. Rental rates are generally reasonable, and insurance costs are lower than in comparable U.S. cities. Rates generally begin at £20 per day for a small economy car (such as a subcompact General Motors Vauxhall Corsa, or Renault Clio), usually with manual transmission. Air-conditioning and unlimited mileage generally come with the larger-size automatic cars.

In London your U.S. driver's license is acceptable (as long as you are over 23 years old, with no driving convictions). If you have a driver's license from a country other than the United States, it may not be recognized in the United Kingdom. An International Driver's Permit is a good idea no matter what; it's available from the American or Canadian Automobile Association (AAA and CAA, respectively) and, in the United Kingdom, from the Automobile Association (AA) or Royal Automobile Club (RAC). International permits are universally recognized, and having one may save you a problem with the local authorities.

Remember that Britain drives on the left, and the rest of Europe on the right. Therefore, if you cross the Channel into Britain in a right-side rental, you may want to leave it there and pick up a left-side rental.

CONGESTION CHARGE

Designed to reduce traffic through central London, a congestion charge has been instituted. Vehicles (with some exemptions) entering central London on weekdays 7 am–6 pm (excluding public holidays) have to pay £12 per day; it can be paid up to 90 days in advance, or on the day of travel, or on the following "charging day," when the fee goes up to £14. Day-, month-, and yearlong passes are available on the Congestion Charging page of the Transport for London website, at gas stations, parking lots (car parks), by mail, by phone, and by SMS text message. One day's payment is good for all access into the charging zone on that day. Traffic signs designate the entrance to congestion areas, and cameras read car license plates and send the information to a database. Drivers who don't pay the congestion charge by midnight of the next charging day following the day of driving are penalized £130, which is reduced to £65 if paid within 14 days.

Information Congestion Charge Customer Service. ☎ 0343/222–2222 in U.K. only, 0343/222–2222 ⊕ www.cclondon.com. **Transport for London.** ☎ 0343/222–1234 ⊕ www.tfl.gov.uk.

GASOLINE

Gasoline (petrol) is sold in liters and is expensive (at this writing about £2 per liter—around $7 per gallon). Unleaded petrol, denoted by green pump lines, is predominant. Premium and Super Premium are the two varieties, and most cars run on regular Premium. Supermarket pumps usually offer the best value. You won't find many service stations in the center of town; these are generally on main, multilane trunk roads out of the center. Service is self-serve, except in small villages, where gas stations are likely to be closed on Sunday and late evening. Most stations accept major credit cards.

PARKING

During the day—and probably at all times—it's safest to believe that you can park nowhere except at a meter, in a pay-and-display bay, or in a garage; otherwise, you run the risk of an expensive ticket, plus possibly even more expensive clamping and towing fees (some boroughs are clamp-free). Restrictions are indicated by the "No Waiting" parking signpost on the sidewalk (these restrictions vary from street to street), and restricted areas include single yellow lines or double yellow lines, and Residents' Parking bays. Parking at a bus stop is prohibited; parking in bus lanes, restricted. On Red Routes, indicated by red lines, you are not allowed to park or even stop. It's illegal to park on the sidewalk, across entrances, or on white zigzag lines approaching a pedestrian crossing.

Meters have an insatiable hunger in the inner city—a 20p coin may buy just three minutes—and some will permit only a maximum two-hour stay. Meters take 20p and £1 coins, pay-and-display machines 10p, 20p, 50p, £1, and £2 coins. Some take payment by credit card. In some parts of central London, meters have been almost entirely replaced by pay-and-display machines that require payment by cell phone. You will need to set up an account to do this (⊕ www.westminster.

gov.uk). Meter parking is free after 6:30 or 8:30 in the evening, on Sunday, and on holidays; always check the sign. In the evening, after restrictions end, meter bays are free. After meters are free, you can also park on single yellow lines—but not double yellow lines. In the daytime, take advantage of the many NCP parking lots in the center of town (from about £9 per hour, up to six hours).

Information NCP. ☎ *0345/050 7080* ⊕ *www.ncp.co.uk.*

ROADSIDE EMERGENCIES

If your car is stolen, you're in a car accident, or your car breaks down and there's nobody around to help you, contact the police by dialing 999.

The general procedure for a breakdown is the following: position the red hazard triangle (which should be in the trunk of the car) a few paces away from the rear of the car. Leave the hazard warning lights on. Along highways (motorways), emergency roadside telephone booths are positioned at intervals within walking distance. Contact the car-rental company or an auto club. The main auto clubs in the United Kingdom are the Automobile Association (AA) and the RAC. If you're a member of the American Automobile Association (AAA), check your membership details before you depart for Britain; under a reciprocal agreement, roadside assistance in the United Kingdom should cost you nothing. You can join and receive roadside assistance from the AA on the spot, but the charge is higher (around £95) than a simple membership fee.

Emergency Services American Automobile Association. ☎ *800/564–6222* ⊕ *www. aaa.com.* **Automobile Association.** ☎ *0800/085–2721, 161/333–0004 from outside U.K., 0800/887–766 for emergency roadside assistance from mobile phones* ⊕ *www.theaa.com.* **Royal Automobile Club.** ☎ *0800/828–282 for emergency roadside assistance, 0330/159–1111 for membership inquiries* ⊕ *www.rac.co.uk.*

RULES OF THE ROAD

London is a mass of narrow, one-way roads and narrow, two-way streets no bigger than the one-way roads. The speed limit is either 20 or 30 mph—unless you see the large 40 mph signs found only in the suburbs. Speed bumps are sprinkled about with abandon in case you forget. Speed is strictly controlled and cameras, mounted on occasional lampposts, photograph speeders for ticketing.

Medium-size circular intersections are often designed as "roundabouts" (marked by signs in which three curved arrows form a circle). On these, cars travel left in a circle and incoming cars must yield to those already on their way around from the right. Make sure you're in the correct lane when approaching a roundabout—this will make leaving the roundabout at your desired exit easier. Stay in the left lane if you wish to go left, the middle lane for going straight ahead, and the right-hand lane for turning right. Signal when about to leave the roundabout.

Jaywalking is not illegal in London and everybody does it, despite the fact that striped crossings with blinking yellow lights mounted on poles at either end—called "zebra crossings"—give pedestrians the right-of-way to cross. Cars should treat zebra crossings like stop signs if a pedestrian is waiting to cross or already starting to cross. It's illegal to pass another vehicle at a zebra crossing. At other crossings (including intersections) pedestrians must yield to traffic, but they do have the right-of-way over traffic turning left at controlled crossings.

Traffic lights sometimes have arrows directing left or right turns; try to catch a glimpse of the road markings in time, and don't get into the turn lane if you mean to go straight ahead. Turning on a red light is not permitted. Signs at the beginning and end of designated bus lanes give the time restrictions for use (usually during peak hours); if you're caught driving on bus lanes during restricted hours, you will be fined. By law, seat belts must be worn in the front and back seats. Drink-driving laws are strictly enforced, and it's safest to avoid alcohol altogether if you'll be driving. The legal limit is 80 milligrams of alcohol per 100 milliliters of blood, which roughly translated means two units of alcohol—two small glasses of wine, one pint of beer, or one glass of whiskey.

■ DLR: DOCKLANDS LIGHT RAILWAY

For reaching destinations in East London, the quiet, driverless Docklands Light Railway (DLR) is a good alternative, with interesting views of the area.

The DLR connects with the Tube network at Bank and Tower Hill stations as well as at Canary Wharf. It goes to London City Airport, the Docklands financial district, and Greenwich, running 5:30 am–12:30 am Monday–Saturday, 7 am–11:30 pm Sunday. The DLR takes Oyster cards, contactless bank cards, and Travelcards, and fares are the same as those on the Tube.

Information Transport for London.
☎ 0343/222-1234 ⊕ www.tfl.gov.uk.

■ RIVER BUS

One legacy of the 2012 Olympics was a new push to develop river travel as part of London's overall public transportation system. The service, operated by Thames Clippers, stops at eight piers between London Eye/Waterloo and Greenwich, with peak-time extensions to Putney in the west and Woolwich Arsenal in the east. The Waterloo–Woolwich commuter service runs 7 am–11:40 pm on weekdays, 9:30 am–midnight on weekends (peak-time frequency: every 20 minutes). Tickets are £9, with a one-third discount for Travelcard holders and a 15% discount for Oyster card holders. When there are events at the O2 (North Greenwich Arena), a half-hourly express service runs to and from Waterloo starting three hours before the event. Thames Clippers also operate the special Tate to Tate Boat, a 15-minute trip between Tate Modern and Tate Britain that costs £9. Boats run every 40 minutes, usually 10–4 on weekdays and 9–7 on weekends. A River Roamer ticket (£19 per day) offers unlimited river travel after 9 am.

Contacts Thames Clippers. ⊕ www.thames-clippers.com.

■ TAXI

Universally known as "black cabs" (even though many of them now come in other colors), the traditional big black London taxicabs are as much a part of the city's streetscape as red double-decker buses, and for good reason: the unique, spacious taxis easily hold five people, plus luggage. To earn a taxi license, drivers must undergo intensive training on the history and geography of London. The course, and all that the drivers have learned in it, is known simply as "the Knowledge." There's almost nothing your taxi driver won't know about the city. Partly because of lobbying efforts by the black cab industry, companies such as Uber have yet to make significant inroads into the London market, although the battle is ongoing.

Hotels and main tourist areas have cabstands (just take the first in line), but you can also flag one down from the roadside. If the orange "For Hire" sign on the top is lighted, the taxi is available. Cab drivers sometimes cruise at night with their signs unlighted so that they can choose their passengers and avoid those they think might cause trouble. If you see an unlighted, passengerless cab, hail it: you might be lucky.

Fares start at £3 and charge by the minute—a journey of a mile (which might take 6–13 minutes) will cost £6–£9 (the fare goes up 10 pm–5 am—a system designed to persuade more taxi drivers to work at night). A surcharge of £2 is applied to a telephone booking. At Christmas and New Year, there is an additional surcharge of £4. You may, but do not have to, tip taxi drivers 10% of the tab. Usually passengers round up to the nearest pound.

Minicabs, which operate out of small, curbside offices throughout the city, are generally cheaper than black cabs, but are less reliable and less trustworthy. These are usually unmarked passenger cars, and their drivers are often not native Londoners, and do not have to take or pass "the Knowledge" test. Still, Londoners use them in droves because they are plentiful and cheap. If you choose to use them, do not ever take an unlicensed cab: anyone who curb-crawls looking for customers is likely to be unlicensed. Unlicensed cabs have been associated with many crimes and can be dangerous. All cab companies with proper dispatch offices are likely to be licensed. Look for a small purple version of the Underground logo on the front or rear window with "private hire" written across it.

There are plenty of trustworthy and licensed minicab firms. For London-wide service try Lady's and Gent's Mini Cabs, or Addison Lee, which uses comfortable minivans but requires that you know the full postal code for both your pickup location and your destination. When using a minicab, always ask the price in advance when you phone for the car, then verify with the driver before the journey begins.

Black Cabs Dial-a-Cab. ☎ *020/7253–5000 for cash bookings, 020/7426–3420 for credit/ debit card bookings* ⊕ *www.dialacab.co.uk.*

Minicabs Addison Lee. ☎ *020/7407–9000* ⊕ *www.addisonlee.com.* **Lady's and Gent's MiniCabs.** ☎ *020/8888–9999* ⊕ *www.ladys- andgentsminicabs.com.*

■ TRAIN TRAVEL

The National Rail Enquiries website is the clearinghouse for information on train times and fares as well as the main place for booking rail journeys around Britain—and the earlier the better. Tickets bought two to three weeks in advance can cost a quarter of the price of tickets bought on the day of travel. However, journeys within commuting distance of city centers are sold at unvarying set prices, and those can be purchased on the day you expect to make your journey without any financial penalty. You may also be able to purchase a PlusBus ticket, which adds unlimited bus travel at your destination. Note that, in busy city centers such as London, all travel costs more during morning rush hour. You can purchase tickets online, by phone, or at any train station in the United Kingdom. Check the website or call the National Rail Enquiries line to get details of the train company responsible for your journey and have them give you a breakdown of available ticket prices. Regardless of which train company is involved, many discount passes are available, such as the 16–25 Railcard (for which you must be under 26 and provide a passport-size photo), the Senior Railcard, and the Family & Friends Travelcard, which can be bought from most mainline stations. But if you intend to make several long-distance rail journeys, it can be a good idea to invest in a BritRail Pass, available to non-U.K. residents (which you must buy before you leave home).

You can get a BritRail Pass valid for London and the surrounding counties, for England, for Scotland, or for all of Britain. Discounts (usually 20%–25%) are offered if you're between 16 and 25, over 60, traveling as a family or a group, or accompanied by a British citizen. The pass includes discounts on the Heathrow Express and Eurostar. BritRail Passes come in two basic varieties. The Consecutive Pass allows travel on consecutive days, and the FlexiPass allows a number of travel days within a set period of time. The cost (in U.S. dollars) of a BritRail Consecutive Pass adult ticket for 8 days is $340 standard and $506 first-class; for 15 days, $506 and $748; and for 22 days, $634 and $950. The cost of a BritRail FlexiPass adult ticket for 4 days' travel within one month is $302 standard and $437 first-class; for 8 days' travel within one month, $432 and $642; and for 15 days' travel within one month, $649 and $1959. Prices drop by about 20% for off-peak travel passes November–February.

Most long-distance trains have refreshment carriages, called buffet cars. Most trains these days also have "quiet cars," where the use of cell phones and music devices is banned. Smoking is forbidden in all railcars.

Generally speaking, rail travel in the United Kingdom is expensive and the ticketing system unnecessarily convoluted: for instance, a round-trip ticket to Bath from London can cost more than £150 per person at peak times, although for an off-peak ticket purchased far enough in advance, that price can drop to £20 or even less. It's best to avoid the frantic business commuter rush (before 9:30 am and 4:30–7 pm). Credit cards are accepted for train fares paid in person, by phone, and online.

Delays are not uncommon, but they're rarely long. You almost always have to go to the station to find out if there's going to be one (because delays tend to happen at the last minute). Luckily, most stations have coffee shops, restaurants, and pubs where you can cool your heels while you wait for the train to get rolling. National Rail Enquiries provides an up-to-date state-of-the-railroads schedule.

Most of the time, first-class train travel in England isn't particularly first class. Some train companies don't offer at-seat service, so you still have to get up and go to the buffet car for food or drinks. First class is generally booked by business travelers on expense accounts because crying babies and noisy families are quite rare in first class and quite common in standard class.

Short of flying, taking the Eurostar train through the Channel Tunnel is the fastest way to reach the continent: it's 2 hours 15 minutes from London's St. Pancras International station to Paris's Gare du Nord. You can also go from St. Pancras to Midi station in Brussels in around two hours. If purchased in advance, round-trip tickets from London to Belgium or France cost from as little as £59, especially if you travel in the very early or very late hours of the day. If you want to bring your car over to France (ask the rental company if this is permitted), you can use the Eurotunnel Shuttle, which takes 35 minutes from Folkestone to Calais, plus at least 30 minutes to check in. The Belgian border is just a short drive northeast of Calais.

Information BritRail Travel. ☎ 866/938–7245 in U.S. and Canada ⊕ www.britrail.com. **Eurostar.** ☎ 03432/186–186, 1233/617–575 outside U.K. ⊕ www.eurostar.com. **National Rail Enquiries.** ☎ 0345/748–4950 ⊕ www. nationalrail.co.uk.

Channel Tunnel Car Transport Eurotunnel. ☎ 0844/335–3535 in U.K., +33/3–21–00–20–61 from outside Europe ⊕ www.eurotunnel. com.

▌ UNDERGROUND TRAVEL: THE TUBE

London's extensive Underground train system (Tube) has color-coded routes, clear signage, and many connections. Trains run out into the suburbs, and all stations are marked with the London Underground circular symbol. (Do not be confused by similar-looking signs reading "subway," which is British for "pedestrian underpass.") Trains are all one class; smoking isn't allowed onboard or in the stations. There is also an Overground network serving the farther reaches of Inner London. These now accept Oyster cards.

Some lines have multiple branches (Central, District, Northern, Metropolitan, and Piccadilly), so be sure to note which branch is needed for your particular destination. Do this by noting the end destination on the lighted sign on the platform, which also tells you how long you'll have to wait until the train arrives. Compare that with the end destination of the branch you want. When the two match, that's your train.

London is divided into six concentric zones (ask at Underground ticket booths for a map and booklet, which give details of the ticket options), so be sure to buy a ticket for the correct zone or you may be liable for an on-the-spot fine of £80. Don't panic if you do forget to buy a ticket for the right zone: just tell a station attendant that you need to buy an "extension" to your ticket. Although you're meant to do that in advance, if you're an out-of-towner, they generally don't give you a hard time.

Oyster cards are "smart cards" that can be charged with a cash value and then used for discounted travel throughout the city. A Visitor Oyster card, which you must buy before arriving in the United Kingdom, costs £3. Normal Oyster cards cost £5 and you can open an Oyster account online or pick up an Oyster card at any London Underground Station, and then prepay any amount you wish for your expected travel while in the city. Each time you take the Tube or bus, you place the blue card on the yellow readers at the entrance and the amount of your fare is deducted.

Passengers using Oyster cards pay lower rates. For one-way Tube fares paid in cash, a flat £5 price per journey now applies across all central zones (1–2), whether you're traveling one stop or twelve. However, the corresponding Oyster card fare is £3. One-day Travelcards used to be good value for money but now, costing from £13 per card, they're a much less attractive option. If you're planning several trips in one day, it's much cheaper to buy an Oyster card: because of the system's daily "cap," you can make as many journeys as you want in Zones 1–2 for just £7 (or, in Zones 1–3 for £8). If you're going to be in town for several days, a seven-day Travelcard gives you the same value as an Oyster card (£33 for Zones 1–2, £61 for Zones 1–6). Children aged between 11–15 can travel at discounted rates on the Tube and travel free on buses and trams with an Oyster photocard (order at least four weeks before date of travel), while those under 11 travel free on all buses, and on the Tube if accompanied by an adult or

with an Oyster photocard. Young people aged 16–18 and students over 18 get discounted Tube fares with an Oyster photocard. Oyster card Tube fares start at £2 and go up depending on the number of zones you're covering, the time of day, and whether you're traveling into Zone 1. Most fares have been frozen until 2020.

However, although Oyster cards sound like the way of the future, they will soon be a thing of the past. Moves are underway to gradually phase out Oyster cards and to encourage passengers to move to a system of direct payments using their bank debit or credit cards instead. In practice, this means swiping a "contactless" bank card instead of your Oyster card at ticket barriers. The cheaper fares available to Oyster card holders are the same as those who pay by contactless cards.

Tube trains now run for 24 hours a day on weekends on five major lines: Piccadilly, Victoria, Northern, Central, and Jubilee. On all other lines the usual timetable still applies, with trains running from just after 5 am Monday to Saturday, and with the last services leaving central London between midnight and 12:30 am. On Sunday, trains start an hour later and finish about an hour earlier. The frequency of trains depends on the route and the time of day, but normally you should not have to wait more than 10 minutes in central areas.

There are TfL Travel Information Centres at the following Tube stations and travel locations: Liverpool Street (9 am–5 pm); Piccadilly Circus (9:30 am–4 pm); King's Cross, Paddington, and Euston (Mon.–Sat. 8 am–6 pm, Sun. 8:30 am–6 pm); Victoria (8 am–6 pm); Gatwick Airport, North & South Terminals (9:15 am–4 pm); and at Heathrow Airport, Terminals 2 and 3 and Underground stations (7:30 am–8:30 pm).

Important note: You need to have your ticket (Oyster card, Travelcard, or regular ticket) handy in order to exit the turnstiles of the Tube system, not just to enter them.

Information Transport for London.
☎ *0343/222–1234* ⊕ *www.tfl.gov.uk.*

▌ NAVIGATING LONDON

London is a confusing city to navigate, even for people who've visited it a few times. Its streets are arranged in medieval patterns that no longer make much sense, meaning that you can't always use logic to find your way around. A good map is essential, and public transportation can be a lifesaver: buses will take you magically from point A to point B, and the Tube is often the quickest way to reach your destination. Here are some basic tips to help you find your way around.

■ Although free tourist maps can be handy, they're usually quite basic and include only major streets. If you're going to be doing lots of wandering around, buy the pocket-size map book *London A–Z*, which is sold in bookstores and Tube and train stations throughout the city. Its detailed maps are invaluable.

■ To find your way, look for tall landmarks near where you are headed: the London Eye, for example, or the cross atop St. Paul's Cathedral—or the most obvious of all, Big Ben.

■ If you get properly lost, the best people to ask are the Londoners hustling by you, who know the area like nobody else. The worst people to ask are the people working in souvenir kiosks, and street vendors handing out the local *Evening Standard* newspaper; they're famously rude and unhelpful to lost tourists.

■ The tourist hubs of Soho, Covent Garden, Leicester Square, and Trafalgar Square are separated from one another by only a few blocks. Taking the Tube from one to another actually takes longer than walking.

■ On the other hand, when you're lost, the Tube is often the shortest distance between two points. Don't hesitate to use it.

ESSENTIALS

▌ BUSINESS SERVICES AND FACILITIES

There are several Color Company outlets and Mail Boxes Etc. locations in London to handle your photocopying, next-day mail, and packaging needs. Check their websites for more locations.

Contacts The Color Company (*FedEx Office*). ✉ *1 Curzon St., Mayfair* ☎ *0800/939–493* ⊕ *www.color.co.uk* Ⓜ *Green Park.* **Mail Boxes Etc.** ✉ *19–21 Crawford St., Marylebone* ☎ *020/7224–2666* ⊕ *www.mailboxes-etc.co.uk* Ⓜ *Marylebone.*

▌ COMMUNICATIONS

INTERNET

If you're traveling with a laptop, carry a spare battery and adapter: new batteries and replacement adapters are expensive. If you do need to replace them, head to Tottenham Court Road (W1), which is lined with computer specialists. For Apple computers, there's the Apple Stores on Regent Street off Oxford Street, and in the Covent Garden Piazza. John Lewis department store and Selfridges, on Oxford Street (W1), also carry a limited range of computer supplies.

In London, free Wi-Fi is increasingly available in hotels, pubs, coffee shops—even certain branches of McDonald's—and broadband coverage is widespread; generally speaking, the pricier the hotel, the more likely you are to find Wi-Fi there, though it is not usually included in rates.

Contacts Cybercafes. ⊕ *www.cybercafes.com.*

PHONES

The good news is that you can now make a direct-dial telephone call from virtually any point on Earth. The bad news? You can't always do so cheaply. Calling from a hotel is almost always the most expensive option; hotels usually add huge surcharges to all calls, particularly international ones. Calling cards usually keep costs to a minimum, but only if you purchase them locally. And then there are cell phones, which are also likely to be cheaper than calling from your hotel.

The minimum charge from a public phone is upwards of 60p for a two-minute call. To make cheap calls it's a good idea to pick up an international phone card, available from newsstands, which can be used from residential, hotel, and public pay phones. With these, you can call the United States for as little as 5p per minute.

To dial from the United States or Canada, first dial 011, then Great Britain's country code, 44. Continue with the local area code, dropping the initial "0." The code for London is 020 (so from abroad you'd dial 20), followed by a 7 for numbers in central London, or an 8 for numbers in the Greater London area. Freephone (toll-free) numbers start with 0800 or 0808; low-cost national information numbers start with 0345, 0343, or 0844.

A word of warning: 0900 numbers are *not* toll-free numbers; in fact, numbers beginning with this prefix are "premium rate" numbers, and it costs extra to call them. The amount varies and is usually relatively small when dialed from within the country, but it can be excessive when dialed from outside the United Kingdom.

CALLING WITHIN BRITAIN

There are three types of phones: those that accept (1) only coins, (2) only British Telecom (BT) phone cards, or (3) BT phone cards and credit cards, although with the advent of cell phones, it's increasingly difficult to find any type of public phone, especially in London.

The coin-operated phones are of the push-button variety; the workings of coin-operated telephones vary, but there are usually instructions on each unit.

Most take 10p, 20p, 50p, £1, and £2 coins. Insert the coins *before* dialing (the minimum charge is 60p). If you hear a repeated single tone after dialing, the line is busy; a continual tone means the number is unobtainable (or that you have not dialed the prefix—or not the correct prefix). The indicator panel shows you how much money is left; add more whenever you like. If there is no answer, replace the receiver and your money will be returned.

There are several different directory-assistance providers. For information anywhere in Britain, try dialing 118–365 (55p per call, then 55p per minute); you'll need to know the town and the street (or at least the neighborhood) of the person or organization for which you're requesting information. For the operator, dial 100.

You don't have to dial London's central area code (020) if you are calling inside London itself—just the eight-digit telephone number. However, you do need to use it if you're dialing a 0207 (Inner London) number from a 0208 (Outer London) number, and vice versa.

For long-distance calls within Britain, dial the area code (which begins with 01), followed by the number. The area-code prefix is used only when you are dialing from outside the destination. In provincial areas, the dialing codes for nearby towns are often posted in the booth.

CALLING OUTSIDE BRITAIN

For assistance with international calls, dial 155.

To make an international call from London, dial 00, followed by the country code and the local number.

The United States country code is 1.

Access Codes AT&T Direct. ☎ *0800/890–011 in U.K.* **MCI.** ☎ *0800/279–5088 in U.K., 800/888–8000 for U.S. and other areas.* **Sprint International Access.** ☎ *0808/234–6616 in U.K.*

CALLING CARDS

Public card phones operate either with cash or with special cards that you can buy from post offices or newsstands. Ideal for longer calls, they are composed of units of 10p, and come in values of £5, £10, and more. To use a card phone, lift the receiver, insert your card, and dial the number. An indicator panel shows the number of units used. At the end of your call, the card will be returned. Where credit cards are taken, slide the card through, as indicated.

CELL PHONES

If you have a multiband phone (Britain uses different frequencies from those used in the United States) and your service provider uses the world-standard GSM network (as do T-Mobile, AT&T, and Verizon), you can probably use your phone abroad. Roaming fees can be steep, however: 99¢ per minute is considered reasonable. And overseas you normally pay the toll charges for incoming calls. It's almost always cheaper to send a text message than to make a call, since text messages have a very low set fee (often less than 5¢).

If you just want to make local calls, consider buying a new SIM card (note that your provider may have to unlock your phone for you to use a different SIM card) and a prepaid service plan in London. You'll then have a local number and can make local calls at local rates. If your trip is extensive, you could also simply buy a new cell phone in your destination, as the initial cost will be offset over time.

■TIP➔ **If you travel internationally frequently, save one of your old cell phones or buy a cheap one online; ask your cell phone company to unlock it for you, and take it with you as a travel phone, buying a new SIM card with pay-as-you-go service in each destination.**

Any cell phone can be used in Britain if it's tri-band/GSM. Travelers should ask their cell phone company if their phone is tri-band and what network it uses, and make sure it is activated for international calling before leaving their home country.

You can rent a cell phone from most car-rental agencies in London. Some upscale hotels now provide loaner cell phones to their guests. Beware, however, of the per-minute rates charged, as these can be shockingly high.

Contacts Cellular Abroad. ☎ 800/287–5072 in U.S., 310/862–7100 international, 800/3623–3333 in U.K. ⊕ www.cellular-abroad.com. **Mobal.** ☎ 888/888–9162 in U.S., 01543/426–999 in U.K. ⊕ www.mobal.com. **Planet Fone.** ☎ 888/988–4777 ⊕ www.planetfone.com.

∎ CUSTOMS AND DUTIES

You're always allowed to bring goods of a certain value back home without having to pay any duty or import tax. But there's a limit on the amount of tobacco and liquor you can bring back duty-free, and some countries have separate limits for perfumes; for exact figures, check with your customs department. The values of so-called "duty-free" goods are included in these amounts. When you shop abroad, save all your receipts, as customs inspectors may ask to see them as well as the items you purchased. If the total value of your goods is more than the duty-free limit, you'll have to pay a tax (most often a flat percentage) on the value of everything beyond that limit.

There are currently two levels of duty-free allowance for entering Britain: one for goods bought outside the European Union (EU) and the other for goods bought within the EU.

Of goods bought outside the EU you may import the following duty-free: 200 cigarettes or 100 cigarillos or 50 cigars or 250 grams of tobacco; 4 liters of still wine and 16 liters of beer and, in addition, either 1 liter of alcohol over 22% by volume (most spirits), or 2 liters of alcohol under 22% by volume (fortified or sparkling wine or liqueurs).

Of goods bought within the EU, you should not exceed the following (unless you can prove they are for personal use): 800 cigarettes, 400 cigarillos, 200 cigars, or 1 kilo of tobacco, plus 10 liters of spirits, 20 liters of fortified wine such as port or sherry, 90 liters of wine, or 110 liters of beer.

Pets (dogs and cats) can be brought into the United Kingdom from the United States without six months' quarantine, provided that the animal meets all the PETS (Pet Travel Scheme) requirements, including microchipping and vaccination. Other pets have to undergo a lengthy quarantine, and penalties for breaking this law are severe and strictly enforced.

Fresh meats, vegetables, plants, and dairy products may be imported from within the EU. Controlled drugs, switchblades (aka flick knives), obscene material, counterfeit or pirated goods, and self-defense sprays may not be brought into the United Kingdom; firearms (both real and imitation) and ammunition, as well as souvenirs made from endangered plants or animals, are barred except with relevant permits.

Information HM Revenue and Customs. ☎ 0300/200–3700 ⊕ www.hmrc.gov.uk. **U.S. Customs and Border Protection.** ⊕ www.cbp.gov.

∎ ELECTRICITY

The electrical current in London is 220–240 volts (coming into line with the rest of Europe at 230 volts), 50 cycles alternating current (AC); wall outlets take three-pin plugs, and shaver sockets take two round, oversize prongs. For converters, adapters, and advice, stop in one of the many STA Travel shops around London or at Nomad Travel.

Consider making a small investment in a universal adapter, which has several types of plugs in one lightweight, compact unit. Most laptops and cell phone chargers are dual voltage (i.e., they operate equally well on 110 and 220 volts), and thus require only an adapter. These days the same is true of small appliances such as hair dryers. Always check labels and manufacturer instructions to be sure. Don't use 110-volt outlets marked "For Shavers Only" for high-wattage appliances such as hair dryers.

Contacts Nomad Travel. ⊠ *11 S. Moulton St., Mayfair* ☎ *0134/155–5061* ⊕ *www. nomadtravel.co.uk.* **Walkabout Travel Gear.** ⊕ *www.walkabouttravelgear.com.*

▍EMERGENCIES

London is a relatively safe city, though crime does happen (more so than in New York City), especially in tourist meccas. If you need to report a theft or an attack, head to the nearest police station or dial 999 for police, fire, or ambulance (be prepared to give the telephone number you're calling from). National Health Service hospitals give free round-the-clock treatment in Accident and Emergency sections, where waits can be up to four hours, depending on the severity of your ailment or injury. If you are admitted to a hospital for treatment, or referred to a hospital by a General Practitioner, as a non-EU foreign visitor you will be expected to pay for any treatment you receive before you leave the country. Prescriptions are valid only if made out by doctors registered in the United Kingdom. All branches of Boots are dispensing pharmacies.

Doctors and Dentists Dental Emergency Care Service. ☎ *020/8748–9365* ⊕ *www.24hour-emergencydentist.co.uk.* **Medical Express Clinic.** ⊠ *117A Harley St., Marylebone* ☎ *020/7499–1991* ⊕ *www. medicalexpressclinic.co.uk* Ⓜ *Regent's Park.* **UCL Eastman Dental Hospital.** ⊠ *256 Gray's Inn Rd., King's Cross* ☎ *020/3456–7899* ⊕ *www.uclh.nhs.uk* Ⓜ *Russell Sq., King's Cross St. Pancras.*

Foreign Embassies U.S. Embassy. ⊠ *Riverside Court, 20 Nine Elms La., Battersea* ☎ *020/7499–9000* ⊕ *uk.usembassy.gov* Ⓜ *Vauxhall.*

General Emergency Contacts Ambulance, fire, police. ☎ *999 in U.K. only, 112 pan-European.*

Hospitals and Clinics Charing Cross Hospital. ⊠ *Fulham Palace Rd., Fulham* ☎ *020/3311–1234* ⊕ *www.imperial.nhs. uk/charingcross* Ⓜ *Hammersmith.* **Royal Free Hospital.** ⊠ *Pond St., Hampstead* ☎ *020/7794–0500* ⊕ *www.royalfree.nhs. uk* Ⓜ *Belsize Park.* **St. Thomas's Hospital.** ⊠ *Westminster Bridge Rd., Lambeth* ☎ *020/7188–7188* ⊕ *www.guysandstthomas. nhs.uk* Ⓜ *Westminster.* **University College Hospital.** ⊠ *235 Euston Rd., Bloomsbury* ☎ *020/3456-7014* ⊕ *www.uclh.nhs.uk* Ⓜ *Euston Sq., Warren St.*

Hotlines Samaritans. ☎ *116–123 Freephone* ⊕ *www.samaritans.org.*

Pharmacies Boots. ⊠ *44–46 Regent St., Piccadilly Circus* ☎ *020/7734–6126* ⊕ *www. boots.com* Ⓜ *Piccadilly Circus.*

▍HOLIDAYS

Standard holidays are New Year's Day, Good Friday, Easter Monday, May Day (first Monday in May), spring and summer bank holidays (last Monday in May and August, respectively), Christmas, and Boxing Day (December 26). On Christmas Eve and New Year's Eve, some shops, restaurants, and businesses close early. Some museums and tourist attractions may close for at least a week around Christmas, or operate on restricted hours—call to verify.

▍MAIL

Stamps can be bought from post offices (generally open weekdays 9–5:30, Saturday 9–noon), from stamp machines outside post offices, and from some newsagents and newsstands. Mailboxes are known as post or letter boxes and are painted bright red; large tubular ones are set on the edge of sidewalks, whereas smaller boxes are set into post-office walls. Allow seven days for a letter to reach the

United States. Check the Yellow Pages for a complete list of branches, though you cannot reach individual offices by phone.

Airmail letters up to 10 grams (0.35 ounce) to North America, Australia, and New Zealand cost £1.17. Letters under 9.4 inches by 6.4 inches within Britain are from 65p for first class, 56p for second class. Large letters (larger than 9.4 inches by 6.4 inches, smaller than 13.8 inches by 9.8 inches) cost from 98p first class, 76p second class within the United Kingdom, depending on weight. Airmail is assessed by weight alone.

If you're uncertain where you'll be staying, you can have mail sent to you at the London Main Post Office, c/o poste restante. The post office will hold international mail for one month.

Contact **Post Office.** ☎ *0345/722–3355* ⊕ *www.postoffice.co.uk.*

Main Branch **London Main Post Office.** ✉ *24–28 William IV St., Charing Cross* ⊕ *www. postoffice.co.uk* Ⓜ *Charing Cross.*

SHIPPING PACKAGES
Most department stores and retail outlets can ship your goods home. You should check your insurance for coverage of possible damage. Private delivery companies such as DHL, FedEx, and Parcelforce offer two-day delivery service to the United States, but you'll pay a considerable amount for the privilege.

Express Services **DHL.** ☎ *0844/248–0844* ⊕ *www.dhl.com.* **FedEx.** ☎ *0345/600–0068* ⊕ *www.fedex.com.* **Parcelforce.** ☎ *0344/800–4466* ⊕ *www.parcelforce.com.*

■ MONEY

London is one of the most expensive cities in the world: getting around is expensive, eating can be pricey, travel costs are steep, and hotels aren't cheap. However, for every yin there's a yang, and travelers do get a break in other places: most museums are free, for example, and Oyster cards help cut the price of travel.

ATMS AND BANKS
Your own bank will probably charge a fee for using ATMs abroad; the foreign bank you use may also charge a fee. Nevertheless, you'll usually get a better rate of exchange at an ATM than you will at a currency-exchange office or even when changing money in a bank. And extracting funds as you need them is a safer option than carrying around a large amount of cash.

■TIP➔ PINs with more than four digits are not recognized at ATMs in many countries. If yours has five or more, remember to change it before you leave.

Credit cards or debit cards (also known as check cards) will get you cash advances at ATMs, which are widely available in London. To make sure that your Cirrus or Plus card (to cite just two of the leading names) works in European ATMs, have your bank reset it to use a four-digit PIN before your departure.

CREDIT CARDS
■TIP➔ Remember to inform your credit-card company before you travel, especially if you're going abroad and don't travel internationally very often. Otherwise, the credit-card company might put a hold on your card owing to unusual activity—not a good thing halfway through your trip. Record all your credit-card numbers—as well as the phone numbers to call if your cards are lost or stolen—in a safe place, so you're prepared should something go wrong. MasterCard and Visa have general numbers you can call (collect if you're abroad) if your card is lost, but you're better off calling the number of your issuing bank, because MasterCard and Visa usually just transfer you to your bank; your bank's number is usually printed on your card.

If you plan to use your credit card for cash advances, you'll need to apply for a PIN at least two weeks before your trip. Although it's usually cheaper (and safer) to use a credit card abroad for large purchases (so you can cancel payments or be reimbursed if there's a problem), note that some credit-card companies *and* the banks that issue them add substantial percentages to all foreign transactions, whether they're in a foreign currency or not. Check on these fees before leaving home, so there won't be any surprises when you get the bill.

■ TIP→ Before you charge something, ask the merchant whether he or she plans to do a dynamic currency conversion (DCC). In such a transaction the credit-card processor (the shop, restaurant or hotel, not Visa or MasterCard) converts the currency and charges you in dollars. In most cases, you'll pay the merchant a 3% fee for this service in addition to any credit-card company and issuing-bank foreign-transaction surcharges.

Dynamic currency conversion programs are becoming increasingly widespread. Merchants who participate in them are supposed to ask whether you want to be charged in dollars or the local currency, but they don't always do so. And even if they do offer you a choice, they may well avoid mentioning the additional surcharges. The good news is that you *do* have a choice. And if this practice really gets your goat, you can avoid it entirely thanks to American Express; with its cards, DCC simply isn't an option.

Credit cards are accepted virtually everywhere in London.

Reporting Lost Cards American Express. ☎ 800/528–4800 in U.S., 0800/917–8047 in U.K. ⊕ www.americanexpress.com. **Diners Club.** ☎ 800/234–6377 in U.S., 514/881-3735 collect from abroad ⊕ www.dinersclub.com. **MasterCard.** ☎ 800/627–8372 in U.S., 0800/964–767 in U.K. ⊕ www.mastercard.com. **Visa.** ☎ 800/847–2911 in U.S., 020/7795–5777 in U.K. ⊕ www.visa.com.

CURRENCY AND EXCHANGE

The unit of currency in Great Britain is the pound sterling (£), divided into 100 pence (p). Bills (called notes) come in denominations of £50, £20, £10, and £5; coins are for £2, £1 (100p), 50p, 20p, 10p, 5p, 2p, and 1p.

Even if a currency-exchange booth has a sign promising no commission, rest assured that there's some kind of huge, hidden fee. And as for rates, you're almost always better off getting foreign currency at an ATM or exchanging money at a bank or post office.

■ TIP→ Banks never have every foreign currency on hand, and it may take as long as a week to order. If you're planning to exchange funds before leaving home, don't wait until the last minute.

▌PACKING

London's weather is unpredictable. It can be cool, damp, and overcast, even in summer, but the odd summer day can be uncomfortably hot, as not many public venues, theaters, or the Tube are air-conditioned. In general, you'll need a heavy coat for winter and light clothes for summer, along with a lightweight coat or jacket. Always pack a small umbrella that you can easily carry around with you. Pack as you would for any American city: jackets and ties for expensive restaurants and nightspots, casual clothes elsewhere. Jeans are popular in London and are perfectly acceptable for sightseeing and informal dining. Sports jackets are popular with men. In five-star hotels, men can expect to be asked to wear a jacket and tie in the restaurant and bar, and women might feel out of place unless they're in nice clothes. Otherwise, for women, ordinary dress is acceptable just about everywhere.

▌PASSPORTS AND VISAS

U.S. citizens need only a valid passport to enter Great Britain for stays of up to six months. If you're within six months of your passport's expiration date, renew it before you leave—nearly extinct passports are not strictly banned, but they make immigration officials anxious and may cause you problems.

PASSPORTS

It's always surprising how few Americans have passports—only 35% at this writing. This number is expected to grow now that it is impossible to reenter the United States from trips to neighboring Canada or Mexico without one. Remember this: a passport verifies both your identity and nationality—a great reason to have one.

U.S. passports are valid for 10 years. You must apply in person if you're getting a passport for the first time; if your previous passport was lost, stolen, or damaged; or if your previous passport has expired and was issued more than 15 years ago or when you were under 16. All children under 18 must appear in person to apply for or renew a passport. Both parents must accompany any child under 14 (or send a notarized statement with their permission) and provide proof of their relationship to the child.

There are 24 regional passport offices, as well as 7,000 passport acceptance facilities in post offices, public libraries, and other governmental offices. If you're renewing a passport, you can do so by mail. Forms are available at passport acceptance facilities and online.

The cost to apply for a new passport is $140 for adults, $95 for children under 16; renewals are $140. There is an additional "execution fee" of $25. Allow six weeks for processing, both for first-time passports and renewals. For an expediting fee of $60 you can reduce this time to about two weeks. If your trip is less than two weeks away, you can get a passport even more rapidly by going to a passport office with the necessary documentation. Private expediters can get things done in as little as 48 hours, but charge hefty fees for their services.

■TIP➜ Before your trip, make two copies of your passport's data page (one for someone at home and another for you to carry separately). Or scan the page and email it to someone at home and/or yourself.

VISAS

A visa is essentially formal permission to enter a country. Visas allow countries to keep track of you and other visitors—and generate revenue (from application fees). You *always* need a visa to enter a foreign country; however, many countries routinely issue tourist visas on arrival, particularly to U.S. citizens. When your passport is stamped or scanned in the immigration line, you're actually being issued a visa. Sometimes you have to stand in a separate line and pay a small fee to get your stamp before going through immigration, but you can still do this at the airport on arrival. Getting a visa isn't always that easy. Some countries require that you arrange for one in advance of your trip. There's usually—but not always—a fee involved, and said fee may be nominal ($10 or less) or substantial ($100 or more).

If you must apply for a visa in advance, you can usually do it in person or by mail. When you apply by mail, you send your passport to a designated consulate, where your passport will be examined and the visa issued. Expediters—usually the same ones who handle expedited passport applications—can do all the work of obtaining your visa for you; however, there's always an additional cost (often more than $50 per visa).

Most visas limit you to a single trip—basically during the actual dates of your planned vacation. Other visas allow you to visit as many times as you wish for a specific period of time. Remember that requirements change, sometimes at the drop of a hat, and the burden is on you to make sure that you have the appropriate visas. Otherwise, you'll be turned away at the airport or, worse, deported after you arrive in the country. No company or travel insurer gives refunds if your travel plans are disrupted because you didn't have the correct visa.

U.S. Passport Information U.S. Department of State. ☎ 877/487–2778 ⊕ travel.state.gov/passport.

U.S. Passport and Visa Expediters **A. Briggs Passport & Visa Expeditors.** ☎ *800/806–0581* ⊕ *www.abriggs.com.* **American Passport Express.** ☎ *800/455–5166* ⊕ *www.american-passport.com.* **Travel Document Systems.** ☎ *800/874–5100, 202/638–3800* ⊕ *www.traveldocs.com.* **Travel the World Visas.** ☎ *866/886–8472* ⊕ *www.world-visa.com.*

▌ SAFETY

The rules for safety in London are the same as in New York City or any big metropolis. If you're carrying a considerable amount of cash and do not have a safe in your hotel room, it's a good idea to keep it in something like a money belt, but don't get cash out of it in public. Keep a small amount of cash for immediate purchases in your pocket or purse.

Beyond that, use common sense. In central London, nobody will raise an eyebrow at tourists studying maps on street corners, and don't hesitate to ask for directions. However, outside of the center, exercise general caution about the neighborhoods you walk in: if they don't look safe, take a cab. After midnight, outside of the center, take cabs rather than wait for a night bus. Although London has plenty of so-called minicabs—normal cars driven by self-employed drivers in a cab service—don't ever get into an unmarked car that pulls up offering you "cab service." Take a licensed minicab only from a cab office, or, preferably, a normal London "black cab," which you flag down on the street.

If you carry a purse, keep a firm grip on it (or even disguise it in a local shopping bag). Store only enough money in the purse to cover casual spending. Distribute the rest of your cash and any valuables among deep front pockets, inside jacket or vest pockets, and a concealed money pouch. Never leave your bag beside your chair or hanging from the back of your chair. Be careful with backpacks, as pickpockets can unzip them on the Tube, or even as you're traveling up an escalator.

Advisories U.S. Department of State. ⊕ *travel.state.gov.*

▌ TAXES

Departure taxes are divided into two bands. The Band A tax on a per-person Economy fare for flights of under 2,000 miles is £13; Band B, for everything over, is £78. The fee is subject to government tax increases.

The British sales tax (V.A.T., value-added tax) is 20%. The tax is almost always included in quoted prices in shops, hotels, and restaurants.

Most travelers can get a V.A.T. refund (no minimum amount is required) by either the Retail Export or the more cumbersome Direct Export method. Many, but not all, large stores provide these services, but only if you request them; they will handle the paperwork. For the Retail Export method, you must ask the store for Form VAT 407 when making a purchase (you must have identification—passports are best). Some retailers will refund the amount on the spot, but others will use a refund company or the refund booth at the point when you leave the country. For the latter, have the form stamped like any customs form by U.K. customs officials when you leave the country, or, if you're visiting several European Union countries, when you leave the EU. After you're through passport control, take the form to a refund-service counter for an on-the-spot refund (which is usually the quickest and easiest option), or mail it to the address on the form (or the envelope with it) after you arrive home. You receive the total refund stated on the form (the retailer or refund company may deduct a handling fee), but the processing time can be long, especially if you request a credit-card adjustment. This may be preferable to a check, however, as U.S. banks will charge a fee for depositing a check in a foreign currency.

With the Direct Export method, the goods are shipped directly to your home. You must have a Form VAT 407 certified by customs, the police, or a notary public when you get home and then send it back to the store, which will refund your money. For inquiries, contact Her Majesty's Revenue & Customs office.

Global Blue (formerly, Global Refund) is a worldwide service with 270,000 affiliated stores and more than 200 Refund Offices. Its refund form, called a Tax Free Check, is the most common across the European continent. The service issues refunds in the form of cash, check, or credit-card adjustment.

V.A.T. Refunds Global Blue. ☎ 866/706–6090 in U.S., 800/32–111–111 in U.K. ⊕ www.globalblue.com. **Her Majesty's Revenue & Customs.** ☎ 0300/200–3700 within U.K., 292/050–1261 from outside U.K. ⊕ www.hmrc.gov.uk/vat.

▌ TIME

London is five hours ahead of New York City at most times of the year. In other words, when it's 3 pm in New York (or noon in Los Angeles), it's 8 pm in London. Note that Great Britain and most European countries also move their clocks ahead for the one-hour differential when daylight saving time goes into effect (although they make the changeover several weeks after the United States).

Time Zones Timeanddate.com. ⊕ www.timeanddate.com/worldclock.

▌ TIPPING

Tipping is done in Britain just as in the United States, but at a lower level. Tipping less than you would back home in restaurants—and not tipping at all in pubs—is not only accepted, but standard. Do not tip movie or theater ushers, elevator operators, or bar staff in pubs—although you can always offer to buy the latter a drink.

TIPPING GUIDELINES FOR LONDON	
Bartender	In cocktail bars, if you see a tip plate, it's fine to leave £1–£2. For table service, tip 10% of the cost of the bill. However, the gratuity is often included in the check at more expensive bars.
Bellhop	£1 per bag, depending on the level of the hotel.
Hotel Concierge	£5 or more, if a service is performed for you.
Hotel Doorman	£1 for hailing taxis or for carrying bags to check-in desk.
Hotel Maid	It's extremely rare for hotel maids to be tipped; £1–£2 would be generous.
Porter at Airport or Train Station	£1 per bag
Skycap at Airport	£1–£3 per bag
Taxi Driver	Optional 10%–12%, perhaps a little more for a short ride.
Tour Guide	Tipping optional; £1–£2 would be generous.
Waiter	10%–15%, with 15% being the norm at high-end restaurants; nothing additional if a service charge is added to the bill.
Other	Restroom attendants in expensive restaurants expect some small change (50p or so). Tip coat-check personnel £1 unless there is a fee (then nothing). Hairdressers and barbers get 10%–15%.

▌ TOURS

BIKE TOURS

Whether you join the Santander Cycles hire scheme or just, per usual, get one from a rental shop, remember that London is still a busy metropolis: unless you're familiar with riding in London traffic, the best way to see it on two wheels is probably to contact one of the excellent cycle-tour companies.

Santander Cycles. ☎ *0343/222–6666* ⊕ *www.tfl.gov.uk/modes/cycling/santander-cycles.*

Tour Operators Cycle Tours of London. ☎ *07788/994430* ⊕ *www.biketoursoflondon.com.* **Fat Tire Bike Tours.** ☎ *07882/338779* ⊕ *www.fattirebiketours.com.* **London Bicycle Tour Company.** ☎ *020/7928–6838* ⊕ *www.londonbicycle.com.*

BOAT TOURS

Year-round, but more frequently April–October, boats cruise the Thames, offering a different view of the London skyline. Most leave from Westminster Pier, Charing Cross Pier, and Tower Pier. Downstream routes go to the Tower of London, Greenwich, and the Thames Barrier via Canary Wharf. Upstream destinations include Kew, Richmond, and Hampton Court (mainly in summer). Most of the launches seat between 100 and 250 passengers, have a public-address system, and provide a running commentary on passing points of interest. Some include musical entertainment. Depending on the destination, river trips may last from one to four hours.

Details on all other operators are available as a PDF from Transport for London's River Services page ⊕ *www.tfl.gov.uk.*

River Cruise Operators Bateaux London. ☎ *020/3504–8522* ⊕ *www.bateauxlondon.com.* **London Duck Tours.** ☎ *020/7928–3132* ⊕ *www.londonducktours.co.uk.* **Thames Cruises.** ☎ *020/7928–9009* ⊕ *www.thamescruises.com.* **Thames River Boats.** ☎ *020/7930–2062* ⊕ *www.wpsa.co.uk.* **Thames River Services.** ☎ *020/7930–4097* ⊕ *www.thamesriverservices.co.uk.*

BUS, COACH, AND TAXI TOURS

Guided sightseeing tours from the top of double-decker buses, which are open-top in summer, are a good introduction to the city, as they cover all the main central sights. A number of companies run daily bus tours that depart (usually 8:30–9 am)

from central points. In hop-on, hop-off fashion, you may board or alight at any of the numerous stops to view the sights and reboard on the next bus. Most companies offer this hop-on, hop-off feature, but others, such as Best Value, remain guided tours in traditional coach buses. Tickets can be bought from the driver and are good all day. Prices vary according to the type of tour. For that more personal touch, try out a guided tour in a taxi.

Bus Tour Operators Best Value Tours. ☎ *0870/803–1316* ⊕ *www.bestvaluetours.co.uk.* **Big Bus Tours.** ☎ *020/7808–6753* ⊕ *www.bigbustours.com.* **Black Taxi Tour of London.** ☎ *020/7935–9363* ⊕ *www.blacktaxitours.co.uk.* **Golden Tours.** ☎ *020/7630–2028 in U.K., 800/509–2507 in U.S.* ⊕ *www.goldentours.co.uk.* **Original London Sightseeing Tour.** ☎ *020/8877–1722* ⊕ *www.theoriginaltour.com.* **Premium Tours.** ☎ *020/7713–1311, 800/815–4003 in U.S.* ⊕ *www.premiumtours.co.uk.*

CANAL TOURS

The tranquil side of London can be found on narrow boats that cruise the city's two canals, the Grand Union and Regent's Canal; most vessels operate on the latter, which runs between Little Venice in the west (nearest Tube: Warwick Avenue on the Bakerloo line) and Camden Lock (about 200 yards north of Camden Town Tube station). Fares start at about £14 for 1½-hour round-trip cruises.

Canal Tour Operators Jason's Trip. ⊕ *www.jasons.co.uk.* **London Waterbus Company.** ☎ *020/7482–2550* ⊕ *www.londonwaterbus.com.*

EXCURSIONS

Evan Evans, Green Line, and National Express all offer day excursions by bus to places within easy reach of London, such as Hampton Court, Oxford, Stratford-upon-Avon, and Bath.

Tour Operators Evan Evans. ☎ *020/7950–1777, 866/382–6868 in U.S.* ⊕ *www.evanevanstours.co.uk.*

WALKING TOURS

One of the best ways to get to know London is on foot, and there are many guided and themed walking tours available. For more options, pick up a copy of *Time Out* magazine and check the weekly listings for upcoming one-off tours.

Walking Tour Operators Blood and Tears Walk. ☎ 07905/746–733 ⊕ www.shocking-london.com. **Blue Badge.** ☎ 020/7403–1115 ⊕ www.britainsbestguides.org. **Context London.** ☎ 020/3514–1780, 800/691–6036 in U.S. ⊕ www.contexttravel.com/city/london. **London Walks.** ☎ 020/7624–3978 ⊕ www.walks.com. **Richard Jones's London Walking Tours.** ☎ 020/8530–8443 ⊕ www.londondiscoverytours.co.uk. **Shakespeare City Walk.** ☎ 07905/746–733 ⊕ www.shakespeareguide.com.

▌ VISITOR INFORMATION

You can get good information at the Travel Information Centre near the Eurostar arrivals area at St. Pancras International train station and at Victoria and Liverpool Street stations. These are helpful if you're looking for brochures for London sights, or if something's gone horribly wrong with your hotel reservation—if, for example, you don't have one—as they have a useful reservations service. The Victoria station center, opposite Platform 8, is open daily 8 am–6 pm; the King's Cross/St. Pancras center, the Euston station center (opposite Platform 10), and the center at Paddington Station (opposite Platform 1) are open Monday–Saturday 8 am–6 pm and Sunday 8:30 am–6 pm. The center at Liverpool Street is open daily 9 am–5 pm, while the one at Piccadilly Circus Tube station is open daily 9:30 am–4 pm. The Travel Information Centre at Heathrow is open daily 7:30 am–8:30 pm, and at Gatwick Airport (North and South Terminals) daily 9:15 am–4 pm. There are also London Tourist Information Centres in Greenwich and some other Outer London locations.

Official Websites: ⊕ *www.visitbritain.com* ⊕ *www.visitlondon.com*

Other Websites: ⊕ *www.londontown.com* ⊕ *www.standard.co.uk* ⊕ *www.bbc.co.uk*

Entertainment Information: ⊕ *www.timeout.com/london* ⊕ *www.officiallondontheatre.co.uk*

INDEX

PHOTO CREDITS

Front cover: Prochasson Frederic/Shutterstock [Description: Red phone box with Big Ben in background, London, England]. 1, Sylvain Grandadam / age fotostock. 2-3, Heeb Christian/age fotostock. 4, VisitEngland/Diana Jarvis. 5 (top), Robertharding / Alamy. 5 (bottom), Danbreckwoldt I Dreamstime.com. 6 (top left), Alexeyfedoren I Dreamstime.com. 6 (top right), PA Images / Alamy. 6 (bottom right), Mariagroth I Dreamstime.com. 6 (bottom left), Mirohasch I Dreamstime.com. 7 (top), Ml12nan I Dreamstime.com. 7 (bottom), Matt Child / Alamy. 8 (top left), Lucidwaters I Dreamstime. com. 8 (top right), Tony French / Alamy. 8 (bottom right), Gavin Bates I Dreamstime.com. 8 (bottom left), Peter D Noyce / Alamy. 9 (top), Dan Breckwoldt / Shutterstock. 9 (bottom), Tupungato / Shutterstock. 10 (top left), Lowerkase I Dreamstime.com. 10 (top right), Peter Phipp/Travelshots.com / Alamy. 10 (botttom), Ross Brinkerhoff / Fodor's Travel. 11 (top), Tim Gartside london / Alamy. 11 (bottom), Swisshippo I Dreamstime.com. 13, Jarno Gonzalez Zarraonandia/Shutterstock. **Chapter 1: Experience London:** 16-17, Jeff Gilbert / Alamy. **Chapter 2: Westminster, St. James's, and Royal London:** 35, Peter Phipp/Travelshots.com / Alamy. 37, Songquan Deng / Shutterstock. 38, Peter Adams/ age fotostock. 44-45, Doug Pearson/age fotostock. 46, John Sturrock/Alamy. 48, Chlodvig I Dreamstime.com. 52, ktylerconk/Flickr. **Chapter 3: Mayfair & Marylebone:** 57, Derek Croucher/Alamy. 59, Cath Harries / Alamy. 60, David Noton Photography/Alamy. 61, Benedict Johnson. 62, Pawel Libera/ Alamy. 64, PCL/Alamy. **Chapter 4: Soho & Covent Garden:** 67, Courtesy of Courtauld Gallery. 69, Bikeworldtravel / Shutterstock. 70, Dean Street Townhouse. 73, Ann Steer/iStockphoto. 75, British Tourist Authority. **Chapter 5: Bloomsbury & Holborn:** 77, Michael Jenner/Alamy. 79, antb / Shutterstock. 80, Londonstills.com / Alamy. 82, Jarno Gonzalez Zarraonandia/Shutterstock. 83 and 84 (top), British Museum. 84 (bottom), Grant Rooney/Alamy. 86, British Museum. 87, James McCormick/britainonview.com. 88, Eric Nathan/Alamy. **Chapter 6: The City:** 95, PSL Images/Alamy. 97, Ryan Fox/ age fotostock. 98, Jerry Millevoi/age fotostock. 100-01, Jason Hawkes. 103, Tomas1111 I Dreamstime.com. 105, iStockphoto. 107 (left), Walter Bibikow/ viestiphoto.com. 107 (right), Tom Hanley/ Alamy. 108 (top), Natasha Marie Brown/HRP/newsteam.co.uk. 109, Peter Phipp/age fotostock. 110 (left), Mary Evans Picture Library/Alamy. 110 (center), Reflex Picture Library/Alamy. 110 (right), Classic Image/Alamy. 111, Jan Kranendonk/iStockphoto. **Chapter 7: East London:** 115, MAISANT Ludovic hem / age fotostock. 117, Neil Setchfield/Alamy. 118, Brians101 I Dreamstime.com. 119, Jon Arnold/age fotostock. 123, Elly Godfroy/Alamy. **Chapter 8: South of the Thames:** 127, Mike Peel/ wikipedia/org. 129, Ron Ellis / Shutterstock. 130, PCL/Alamy. 131, Melba / age fotostock. 133, Lance Bellers / Shutterstock. 138, piotreknik / Shutterstock. **Chapter 9: Kensington, Chelsea, Knightsbridge & Belgravia:** 141, Cahir Davitt/age fotostock. 143, British Tourist Authority. 144, Robert Harding Picture Library Ltd/Alamy. 147, Londonstills.com/Alamy. 151, Kiev.Victor / Shutterstock. **Chapter 10: Notting Hill & Bayswater:** 153, Roger Cracknell 01/classic / Alamy. 155, Doug Scott/age fotostock. 156, David H. Wells/age fotostock. 157, Andreykr I Dreamstime.com. **Chapter 11: Regent's Park and Hampstead:** 161, VisitEngland Images. 163, Chris Seddon / Shutterstock. 164, Bildarchiv Monheim GmbH/Alamy. 172, Pictorial Press Ltd/Alamy. **Chapter 12: Greenwich:** 175, Michael Booth/ Alamy. 177, Visit London. 178, one-image photography/Alamy. 180, Jon Arnold Images Ltd/Alamy. 182, Alicephotography I Dreamstime.com. 184, Mcginnly/wikipedia.org. **Chapter 13: The Thames Upstream:** 187, Mark6138 I Dreamstime.com. 189 and 190, Danilo Donadoni/Marka/age fotostock. 191, Terry Harris / Alamy. 195, Emotionart I Dreamstime.com. **Chapter 14: Where to Eat:** 199, Les 110 de Taillevent. 200, Patronestaff I Dreamstime.com. 201 (top), Ross Brinkerhoff / Fodor's Travel. 201 (bottom), Tntightlines I Dreamstime.com. 202, Atlantide S.N.C./age fotostock. **Chapter 15: Where to Stay:** 243, Danita Delimont/Alamy. 244, Araraadt I Dreamstime.com. **Chapter 16: Nightlife:** 269, Peter Phipp/Travelshots.com / Alamy. 270, Anizza I Dreamstime.com. **Chapter 17: Performing Arts:** 291, David Jensen. 292, Claudiodivizia I Dreamstime.com. **Chapter 18: Shopping:** 305, Anizza I Dreamstime.com. 306, Edonalds I Dreamstime.com. **Chapter 19: Side Trips from London:** 337, Andrew Holt/Alamy. 338, Mark Sunderland/Alamy. 345, British Tourist Authority/Tourism South East. 350, John Martin/Alamy. **Back cover, from left to right:** Victor10947 I Dreamstime.com; Gbphoto27 I Dreamstime.com; Paul B. Moore/Shutterstock. **Spine:** Tomas1111 I Dreamstime.com. **About Our Writers:** All photos are courtesy of the writers except for the following: Kate Hughes, courtesy of Ellen Hughes; Ellin Stein, courtesy of Paul Rider; Alex Wijeratna, courtesy of Heathcliff O'Malley.

NOTES

NOTES

NOTES

NOTES

NOTES

NOTES

ABOUT OUR WRITERS

 Jo Caird is a travel and arts journalist who writes on theater, visual arts, film, literature, and food and drink, as well as cycling and scuba diving. Her travel stories, city guides, and arts features appear regularly in the *Guardian,* the *Independent,* the *Sunday Telegraph,* the *Economist, Condé Nast Traveler,* and *World of Interiors.* Born and raised in London, Caird has an endless fascination for the city, and is delighted to write about it whenever the opportunity arises. For this edition, she updated the Westminster and St. James; Soho and Covent Garden; East London; Greenwich; Thames Upstream; and the Performing Arts chapters. Follow her on Twitter (⊕ *www.twitter.com/jocaird*) or visit her website (⊕ *www.jocaird.com*).

 Writer and editor **Kate Hughes** studied classical literature in Liverpool and also has a master's degree in garden history, so she feels qualified to pass judgment on matters both urban and rural. She updated the Side Trips From London chapter and also updates parts of *Fodor's England.*

 James O'Neill loves London and—as his work updating our chapters on Mayfair and Marylebone; Bloomsbury and Holborn; Notting Hill and Bayswater; and Travel Smart for this edition proves—loves rediscovering it, too. Although originally from Ireland, he's lived in London for almost 20 years—and still loves it just as much now as he did back then. He has written extensively for TV (BBC and Channel 4), the stage, and the page. He is currently finishing his debut novel, which is set in—where else?—London.

 Having studied in London and never left—aside from a brief sojourn in Madrid— **Toby Orton** has experienced everything in the capital from Hackney to Notting Hill, Highgate to Peckham, and still finds it the most inspiring city in the world. He credits the bookshops, bars, galleries, clubs, and streets of London with making him the person he is today. He has written about travel, cycling, food, and drink for a range of websites and publications. He updated the Where to Stay chapter this edition.

 Ellin Stein has written for publications on both sides of the Atlantic, including the *New York Times,* the *Times* (London), the *Guardian,* the *Telegraph,* and *InStyle,* for whom she was European correspondent. Her book *That's Not Funny, That's Sick: The National Lampoon and the Comedy Insurgents Who Captured the Mainstream,* was published by W. W. Norton & Co. in 2013. Originally from Manhattan, she has lived in London for two decades. For this edition, she updated our chapters on The City; Kensington, Chelsea, Knightsbridge, and Belgravia; South of the Thames; Regent's Park and Hampstead; and Shopping.

 London restaurant maven **Alex Wijeratna** is permanently blown away by the capital's rocket-fueled restaurant scene. From locavore heroes and street-food gourmet democrats, to global gastro-panjandrums, Alex tickles out the best joints that restaurant-mad London has to offer. Alex has also written for the *Times* (London), the *Guardian,* the *Independent,* the *Daily Mail,* the *Daily Express,* and the *Face.* For this edition, he updated the Where to Eat, Nightlife, and Experience London chapters.

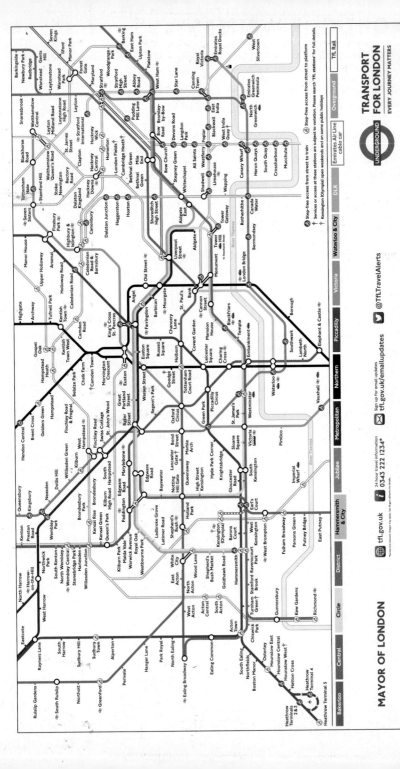